Routledge Handbook of Social Futures

Featuring chapters from an international range of leading and emerging scholars, this *Handbook* provides a collection of cutting-edge, interdisciplinary research that sheds new light on contemporary futures studies. Engaging with key defining questions of the early twenty-first century such as climate change, big data, AI, the future of economics, education, mental health, cities and more, the *Handbook* provides a review and synthesis of futures scholarship, highlighting the role that societies can and should play in their making. While the various chapters demonstrate how futures emerge and take shape in particular places at particular times, the distinctive insight provided by the volume overall is that futures thinking today must be social and contextual.

By presenting a range of futures work from contexts around the globe, the *Handbook* contextualizes techniques – forecasting, backcasting, scenario planning, collaboration and co-production – to ask how different dimensions of the social are created and circulated in the process. Through its thirty chapters, the volume explores and interrogates narratives, anticipations, enactments, ecologies, collaborations, prospections and so on to highlight which versions of the social are legitimized and which are encouraged and foreclosed.

This *Handbook* opens an important conversation about the centrality of the social in futures thinking. By bringing arts, humanities and social sciences scholars and practitioners into conversation with biologists and environmental, climate and computer scientists, this volume seeks to encourage new pathways across, between and within multiple disciplines to interrogate the futures we need and want. The social must be our starting point if we are to steer our planet in a direction that supports good lives for the many, everywhere.

Carlos López Galviz, PhD, is Senior Lecturer in the Theories and Methods of Social Futures at Lancaster University, UK. His books include *Global Undergrounds* (2016) and *Cities, Railways, Modernities: London, Paris and the Nineteenth Century* (2019).

Emily Spiers, PhD, is Senior Lecturer in Creative Futures at Lancaster University, UK. They are the author of *Pop-Feminist Narratives: The Female Subject under Neoliberalism in North America, Britain and Germany* (2018) and the co-editor, with Tobias Boes and Rebecca Braun, of *World Authorship* (2020).

"Thinking intelligently about the future has never been more important. Too often, however, it is dominated by the failed futurisms of prediction and probability. This book brings together in one place a host of new insights into how social futures are being made today – from the relationship between pasts and futures and conflicting temporalities, to the role of narratives, new technologies, migration and planetary change. It is essential reading for anyone interested in the study of social futures and, in particular, for all of those interested in creating better futures. The book has the potential to set out a new, practice based, contextual and situated approach to the study of futures that locates 'the social' at the heart of futures studies, creating a new interdisciplinary dialogue that will enrich the field."
— *Keri Facer, Professor of Educational and Social Futures, University of Bristol, Editor in Chief Futures*

"We are experiencing the end of a certain type of epoch. And with that end comes a broad range of alternative options. This *Handbook* makes an important contribution to the need for re-assessing diverse aspects of our social, built and natural environments and of the logics we use to understand what needs to be done. With this collection, the editors Carlos López Galviz and Emily Spiers give us one of the most distinctive analytics for an alternative set of options. The originality and the daring set of issues here proposed make this *Handbook* a must read".
— *Saskia Sassen, the Robert S. Lynd Professor of Sociology, Columbia University*

Routledge Handbook of Social Futures

Edited by Carlos López Galviz and Emily Spiers

WITH MONIKA BÜSCHER AND ASTRID NORDIN

LONDON AND NEW YORK

First published 2022
by Routledge
2 Park Square, Milton Park, Abingdon, Oxon OX14 4RN

and by Routledge
605 Third Avenue, New York, NY 10158

Routledge is an imprint of the Taylor & Francis Group, an informa business

© 2022 selection and editorial matter, Carlos López Galviz and
Emily Spiers; individual chapters, the contributors

The right of Carlos López Galviz and Emily Spiers to be identified as the
author of the editorial material, and of the authors for their individual
chapters, has been asserted in accordance with sections 77 and 78 of the
Copyright, Designs and Patents Act 1988.

All rights reserved. No part of this book may be reprinted or reproduced
or utilised in any form or by any electronic, mechanical, or other
means, now known or hereafter invented, including photocopying and
recording, or in any information storage or retrieval system, without
permission in writing from the publishers.

Trademark notice: Product or corporate names may be trademarks
or registered trademarks, and are used only for identification and
explanation without intent to infringe.

British Library Cataloguing-in-Publication Data
A catalogue record for this book is available from the British Library

Library of Congress Cataloging-in-Publication Data
A catalog record has been requested for this book

ISBN: 978-1-138-34033-6 (hbk)
ISBN: 978-1-032-12954-9 (pbk)
ISBN: 978-0-429-44071-7 (ebk)

DOI: 10.4324/9780429440717

Typeset in Bembo
by codeMantra

Printed in the United Kingdom
by Henry Ling Limited

Contents

List of tables and figures	*x*
Editors	*xii*
List of contributors	*xiii*
Acknowledgements	*xxi*

	Introduction: Why social futures? *Carlos López Galviz and Emily Spiers*	1
1	A beginning: A critical history of scenarios *Andrew Curry*	19
2	Agency: Futures literacy and Generation Z *Emily Spiers*	38
3	AI: The social future of intelligence *Richard H.R. Harper*	52
4	Anticipation: Flourishing for the future *Christopher Groves*	59
5	BioFutures: Where futurists and biologists meet *Derek Gatherer*	69
6	Borders: Retravelling Nickelsdorf *Michael Hieslmair and Michael Zinganel*	79
7	Climate change: Transformational adaptation in Bangladesh *Riadadh Hossain, Shababa Haque and Saleemul Huq*	93
8	Collaboration: Collaborative future-making *Kristina Lindström, Per-Anders Hillgren, Ann Light, Michael Strange and Li Jönsson*	104

Contents

9 Data: The futures of personal data   117
   Deborah Lupton

10 Ecology: Thinking futures ecologically   126
   Lauren Rickards

11 Economics: Catalysing large-scale system change   136
   Stewart Wallis

12 Family: Homeland connections and family futures   148
   Earvin Charles Cabalquinto

13 Higher education: The future university   157
   Carl Gombrich and Ashley Jay Brockwell

14 Inquiries: Healthcare futures   169
   Dawn Goodwin and Richard Tutton

15 Lines: Material cultures of future mobility   180
   Nicola Spurling

16 Literary futures: How fiction can help policy makers   189
   Rebecca Braun

17 Mental health: What can social futures teach us?   198
   Liz Brewster

18 Mobility justice: Sustainable mobility futures   206
   Mimi Sheller

19 Multi-planetary worlds: Mobilities of the space age   216
   Katarina Damjanov

20 Narrative: Telling social futures   224
   Genevieve Liveley

21 Postcolonial futures: Urban eventualities   233
   AbdouMaliq Simone

22 Prospection: Producing social futures   242
   Barbara Bok and Ted Fuller

23 Publics: Infrastructuring proto-futures   252
   Georgia Newmarch

| 24 | Queering: Liberation futures with Afrofuturism
Lonny J Avi Brooks, Jason Tester, Eli Kosminsky and Anthony D. Weeks | 260 |
|---|---|---|
| 25 | Smart cities: Policy without polity
Paul Graham Raven | 275 |
| 26 | Urbanism: Creating urban futures
Cecilia Dinardi | 284 |
| 27 | Utopia: Futurity, realism and the social
Lisa Garforth | 292 |
| 28 | Visible cities: Envisioning social futures
Nick Dunn | 304 |
| 29 | Walking futures: Following in the footsteps of mobility pioneers
Farzaneh Bahrami | 314 |

Index   *325*

Tables and Figures

Tables

4.1 Nussbaum's list of core capabilities (from Nussbaum, 2003)   62

Figures

1.1 Making the future visible   29
2.1 A table listing (1) Things I take for granted, (2) Things I fear happening in the future and (3) Things I hope for   42
2.2 The journal entry of Macy Hawkins   45
2.3 The smart-house surveillance box   45
2.4 The turtle poem as an acrostic   46
6.1 Hieslmair and Zinganel, 2016. Vienna at the centre of a network of international bus connections. Most notable are the many stops in east- and south-east Europe. The map is redrawn from the timetable data on bus connections and estimated passenger numbers provided by the management of Vienna International Bus Terminal. However, many smaller bus lines depart from, and arrive at, other often quite informal coach stops around the city   81
6.2 Hieslmair and Zinganel, 2016. Cross-sectional diagram of a tour coach operated by the Bulgarian company Air Kona connecting Vienna and Sofia: For many, buses are the preferred means of transport, not only because of the reasonable ticket prices but moreover because a bus can take them much closer to their source and target destinations. Buses are also able to transport goods of significant size – which is important for small suitcase traders and those wishing to send gifts to family and friends   83
6.3 Hieslmair and Zinganel, 2016. Reactivation of border infrastructure: From July to October 2015, thousands of refugees assembled at the Austria-Hungary border checkpoint of Nickelsdorf every day. Within a few hours, auxiliary structures had been provided by emergency aid NGOs and event industries for first aid and onward transport coordination   84
6.4 Hieslmair and Zinganel, Gerhard Zapfl, 2016. This drawing is a preliminary stage to Figure 6.3 and is based on conversations with Gerhard Zapfl, mayor of the border village of Nickelsdorf, who was in charge of managing the flows of forced migration and first aid for migrants arriving at the station. In fact, the map was revised in several stages, each time the mayor found important elements missing   86

6.5	Hieslmair and Zinganel, Bus Stop Nickelsdorf, 2016. Video stills from an animated graphic novel, 12 min., describing passengers' experiences of the Nickelsdorf border station on the Austria-Hungary border plus fragments about the management of the enormous bottleneck of refugees in 2015 from the point of view of three bus drivers: The first drove Austrian tourists across the open border station before the event, the second drove Bulgarian labour migrants to Vienna and got held up in the reactivated border checkpoint and the last was hired by the emergency aid organizer to drive refugees from the Hungary-Austria border to improvised accommodation units in Vienna or directly to the Austria-Germany border. To watch the animation, please follow this link: https://tracingspaces.net/bus-stop/	87
8.1	Local government aids formation of communities focussed on trade policy where interests are not pre-political but form via ongoing dialogue	108
8.2	Repurposed glass jar for composting plastics	109
8.3	Instructions for making a world machine	110
8.4	Holding the world in your hand	111
8.5	Counterfactual Worlds Generator (credit and build: Deborah Mason)	111
8.6	Table with thickening ingredients where the label describes one specific hope or concern in regard to the future for pollinators	113
10.1	A Short History of America, cartoon by Robert Crumb (1979). Coloured by Peter Poplaski. Published in Coevolution Quarterly. Copyright © Robert Crumb, 1979. Used with permission	127
11.1	The five needs identified by WEAll's 150 organizational members	139
11.2	A diagram from the New Economics Foundation in 2013 showing how neoliberalism is sustained in the United Kingdom	142
11.3	Strategies for system change	143
18.1	Contingency table of four future urban mobility scenarios	211
24.1	Jason Tester's Mars Booth at Creating Change (2019)	267
24.2	The United Queerdom Game Board	271
24.3	Envisioning a Queer California with its Pride flag at Creating Change (2019)	272
24.4	UQ Tension cards ©2019	273
24.5	UQ Object cards ©2019	273
24.6	UQ Inspiration cards ©2019	274
28.1	Taxonomy for visualization of future cities 2014. Nick Dunn, Paul Cureton and Serena Pollastri	306
28.2	Timeline of the 6 principal paradigms and 28 future city categories between 1900 and 2014. Nick Dunn, Paul Cureton and Serena Pollastri	307
28.3	Timeline of principal paradigms 2020. Nick Dunn, Paul Cureton and Serena Pollastri	310

Editors

Carlos López Galviz is a Senior Lecturer and founding Associate Director of the Institute for Social Futures at Lancaster University, UK. His work focusses on the historic relationship of cities and infrastructure, particularly urban mobility and transport, and how we can connect our understanding of that relationship in the past to its future today. He has published widely on nineteenth-century London and Paris, deploying a 'past futures' perspective. His recent publications include *Global undergrounds* (Reaktion, 2016) and the monograph *Cities, railways, modernities: London, Paris and the nineteenth century* (Routledge, 2019). In 2020, he was elected President of T2M, the International Association for the History of Transport, Traffic and Mobility.

Emily Spiers is a Senior Lecturer in Creative Futures and Associate Director of the Institute for Social Futures at Lancaster University, UK. Their work focusses on future-oriented, innovative trends in communicative, socio-digital and literary practices. They explore how futures are being envisaged, anticipated and made through art and literature – and how creative narratives can help articulate multiple futures in fields as diverse as defence, education and climate science. They are the author of *Pop-feminist narratives: The Female Subject under Neoliberalism in North America, Britain and Germany* (OUP, 2018) and the co-editor, with Tobias Boes and Rebecca Braun, of *World authorship* (OUP, 2020). They contribute regularly to the journal *Futures* as author and reviewer; their most recent article explores narrative as a tool for futures literacy (2021).

Contributors

Farzaneh Bahrami is an Assistant Professor in Urban Design and Mobility at the Faculty of Spatial Sciences at the University of Groningen, the Netherlands. She holds a PhD from the Swiss Federal Institute of Technology, Lausanne (EPFL), Laboratory of Urbanism. She was a Visiting Fellow from the Swiss National Science Foundation at the Bartlett Centre for Advanced Spatial Analysis, UCL, in 2019. Her research on the interplay between mobility systems and urban forms focusses on sustainability transitions and futures of mobility.

Barbara Bok is a researcher at Swinburne University of Technology at the Centre for Urban Transitions and the Faculty of Business and Law, Melbourne, Australia. Her most recent work involves collaborating in teams on projects related to low-carbon urban living, healthy cities and smart cities. Barbara's research interests are in advancing futures and foresight at collective levels. Her research has explored this interest from postgraduate education and futures methodology perspectives. Barbara has been involved in a Sustainable Built Environment National Research Centre project (Project 2.7) using morphological scenarios and technology roadmaps to develop research priorities for the Australian construction industry. Prior to her academic career, she worked in engineering and technology roles in process manufacturing and minerals processing industries.

Rebecca Braun is Executive Dean of the College of Arts, Social Sciences and Celtic Studies at the National University of Ireland, Galway. A founding Associate Director and Co-Director of the Institute for Social Futures from 2017 to 2020 at Lancaster University, UK, she led the Institute's development of a distinctive Creative Futures methodology with partners across government and academe in the UK, Europe, South Africa and North America. Her futures work builds on a deep understanding of the power of people and stories, which she has traced in numerous books on authorship, world literature, transnationalism and cultural value. These include *World authorship*, co-edited with Tobias Boes and Emily Spiers (Oxford: OUP, 2020), and *Transnational German Studies*, co-edited with Benedict Schofield (Liverpool: LUP, 2020).

Liz Brewster is a Senior Lecturer in Medical Education at Lancaster Medical School at Lancaster University, UK, and she is a Fellow of the Institute for Social Futures. Her research focusses on interventions for mental health and well-being in diverse settings including libraries, higher education and medical education. In 2018, she contributed to and co-edited the book *Bibliotherapy* (Facet publishing). She has previously worked at the University of Sheffield and University of Leicester, undertaking research on topics ranging from telehealth to facilitating quality improvement in healthcare.

Contributors

Ashley Jay (Ash) Brockwell is an Associate Professor at the London Interdisciplinary School, UK, with inter- and transdisciplinary expertise in a variety of areas including qualitative and mixed methods, sustainability, well-being, participation, design theory and values-centred evaluation. He holds an MBiochem (Hons) in Molecular and Cellular Biochemistry from the University of Oxford, an MSc in Environmental Anthropology and a PhD in Interdisciplinary Social Sciences with a focus on evaluating education for sustainability. Ash is an author or co-author of more than 30 publications in diverse disciplines and interdisciplinary areas of study, and was awarded the inaugural Community Activation and Social Innovation Centre (CASIC) International Working Paper Prize from Keele University in 2015 for a paper integrating visual art and poetry alongside conventional academic prose.

Lonny J Avi Brooks is an Associate Professor in the Department of Communication at California State University, East Bay, where he has piloted the integration of futures thinking into the communication curriculum for the last 15 years. A leading voice of Afrofuturism 2.0, Brooks contributes to journals, conferences and anthologies, and is co-executive producer, with Ahmed Best, of *The Afrofuturist Podcast*; co-editor of the special issue 'When is Wakanda? Afrofuturism & dark speculative futurity' (*Journal of Futures Studies*); lead co-organizer in Oakland for the Black Speculative Arts Movement; and Co-Creative Director with Ahmed Best of the *Afro-Rithms Futures Group*, using gaming for imaginative, action-oriented thinking to democratize the future. Brooks creates games envisioning social justice futures for Black, Indigenous and Queer liberation with the game *Afro-Rithms from the Future*. Brooks is the Co-Director of the Community Futures School, Museum of Children's Arts (Oakland); Research Affiliate for the Institute for the Future; and a Long Now Foundation Research Fellow. Brooks is co-editor of the book series *Afrofuturist studies & the speculative arts* (Lexington Press) and is on the editorial board for the *Handbook of universal foresight* (forthcoming).

Earvin Charles Cabalquinto is a Lecturer in Communication in the School of Communication and Creative Arts (SCCA) at Deakin University, Australia. He is also a member of the Alfred Deakin Institute for Citizenship and Globalisation. In 2019, he was a Visiting Scholar in the Centre for Mobilities Research (Cemore) at Lancaster University, UK. His expertise lies in the intersections of digital media, mobilities and migration. His book entitled *(Im)mobile homes: Family life at a distance in the age of mobile media* is forthcoming as part of the Studies in Mobile Communication series of Oxford University Press.

Andrew Curry is a practising futurist based in London, UK, where he is the Director of Futures for SOIF at the School of International Futures. Since the turn of the century, he has run hundreds of futures projects for clients across the public, non-profit and commercial sector, using a wide range of methods. He has written widely on futures techniques. His 2008 paper with Anthony Hodgson on Three Horizons introduced the approach to the futures community. He also edited the Association of Professional Futurists' tenth anniversary collection *The future of futures* (2012).

Katarina Damjanov is a Senior Lecturer in Digital Media and Communication Design at the University of Western Australia. Her research interests revolve around considerations of the changing relationships between humans, technologies and environments. Some of her recent work situates these inquiries in outer space.

Cecilia Dinardi is a sociologist working as a Senior Lecturer and Director of Research at ICCE in the Institute for Creative and Cultural Entrepreneurship at Goldsmiths at University of London, UK. Before joining Goldsmiths, she worked in research and education at City, University of London, and the London School of Economics and Political Sciences (LSE), and in public policy for the Government of the City of Buenos Aires. With a background in urban and cultural sociology (PhD and MSc from the LSE and BSc from the University of Buenos Aires), her work focusses on three main areas: Cultural policies, the creative industries and culture-led urban regeneration. She acts as an expert reviewer for various UK research funding bodies and international academic journals.

Nick Dunn is a Professor of Urban Design and Executive Director of Imagination, the design and architecture research lab at Lancaster University, UK. He is a Senior Fellow at the Institute for Social Futures, examining the insights that the arts and humanities can bring to the ways we think, envision and analyse the futures of people, places and planet. Nick has authored numerous books, journal articles and commissioned reports. His expertise on cities, darkness, futures and health has led to curated exhibitions and keynotes around the world.

Ted Fuller holds the UNESCO Chair on Responsible Foresight for Sustainable Development at the University of Lincoln, UK. The Chair involves a team of colleagues working together with international partners in the Global South to develop sustainable futures. His research has been largely about the ways that futures are created, both in terms of enterprising and innovative practices and as futures studies. His current research, relating to the UNESCO Chair, is on the meaning of responsible foresight and ways in which it can be enacted. Ted is Editor in Chief of the journal *Futures*, a leading academic journal in futures studies. He has been involved in futures studies since the 1990s and was Chair of the European COST Action (22) on Foresight Methodologies. His career has included the founding of new enterprises and university research centres as well as holding leadership positions in the universities of Durham, Teesside and Lincoln, UK.

Lisa Garforth is a Senior Lecturer in Sociology at Newcastle University, UK. Her work focusses on environmental and Anthropocene futures and on the relationship between utopia and the social. Her 2017 monograph *Green utopias* (Polity) explores environmental hope before and after nature. Her recent research has focussed on empirical studies of science fiction reading and readers as part of the AHRC project Unsettling Scientific Stories. She is currently working on a new book showing how speculative fictional imaginaries might help sociology face the challenges of the Anthropocene.

Derek Gatherer learned his trade as a molecular biologist in Glasgow, London, Quito, Warwick and Cambridge, after which he was a Lecturer at Liverpool John Moores University, UK, from 1996 to 1999. He has been a Lecturer in the Division of Biomedical and Life Sciences at Lancaster University since 2013. During the intervening period, he worked as a capitalist running dog in the pharmaceutical industry and then as a faceless bureaucrat for the UK Medical Research Council. Since his first undergraduate paper in the journal *Human Genetics* in 1986, he has published over 120 articles, 14 of which have been cited more than 100 times each, with an overall h-index of 34 by mid-2020. Since 2014, he has also taken to the airwaves, giving over 300 TV and radio interviews.

Contributors

Carl Gombrich is Academic Lead at the London Interdisciplinary School and was a Professorial Teaching Fellow of Interdisciplinary Education at UCL. From 2010 to 2019, he was the Programme Director of the vanguard interdisciplinary Arts and Sciences BASc degree, which he led from its design phase to graduating more than 500 students. He has degrees in Maths, Physics and Philosophy and is also a graduate of the National Opera Studio where he was the Royal Opera House scholar. Carl regularly publishes and speaks on themes related to interdisciplinarity and liberal arts and sciences education. His interests include the future of work and changing notions of expertise. He was a member of the British Academy Working Group on Interdisciplinarity and is a Principal Fellow of the Higher Education Academy.

Dawn Goodwin is a Senior Lecturer at Lancaster Medical School at Lancaster University, UK, where she teaches on aspects of sociology of health and illness. Drawing primarily on science and technology studies, medical sociology and anthropology, her research interests have focussed on public inquiries into the safety of healthcare, medical decision-making and accountability, human–machine relations and diagnostic work. Dawn Goodwin is the author of *Acting in anaesthesia: Ethnographic encounters with patients, practitioners and medical technologies* (Cambridge University Press) and editor of *Ethnographies of diagnostic work: Dimensions of transformative practice* (Palgrave MacMillan).

Christopher Groves' work focusses on how people and institutions negotiate and deal with an intrinsically uncertain future – one increasingly imagined against the backdrop of global environmental change and accelerating technological innovation. Along with the ethical and political implications of a range of future-oriented discourses and practices (e.g. risk management, precautionary regulation, building resilience, responsible innovation), he examines how our ideas about what it means for individuals and whole societies to take responsibility for their futures are being changed by technological innovation – from nano- and biotechnology to the decarbonization of energy systems. The monograph *Future matters: Action, knowledge, ethics* (Brill, 2007), co-authored with Barbara Adam, followed by *Care, uncertainty and intergenerational ethics* (Palgrave, 2014), examines these themes in depth. He is currently co-writing a monograph on uncertainty and social injury for PCCS Books, provisionally entitled *How we suffer* and due to be published in 2023.

Shababa Haque is an environmental researcher, working in the field of climate change and development. Her research area includes gender and livelihood, climate change in the Sundarbans and transformative adaptation in Bangladesh. Shababa is currently a PhD candidate at Durham University's Geography Department, UK, and is working on opportunities for sustainable social entrepreneurship for women in the Bangladesh Sundarbans region.

Richard Harper became the UK's first Professor of Socio-Digital Systems in 1999 and is currently Co-Director of the Institute for Social Futures at Lancaster University. His research focusses on the design and role of new computer systems and devices, and explorations of their philosophical and social consequences. He has published or edited 18 books, the most recent of which is *Skyping the family: Interpersonal video communication and domestic life* (Harper et al., 2020).

Michael Hieslmair studied Architecture at the Graz University of Technology, Austria, and Delft University of Technology, the Netherlands. He was a Fellow at Künstlerhaus Büchsenhausen Innsbruck and architect in residence at the MAK Centre for Art and Architecture

Los Angeles and taught at various universities such as the University for Art and Design Burg Giebichenstein Halle an der Saale, Innsbruck University and Graz and Vienna Technical Universities. He collaborated on the research project 'Crossing Munich, Places, Representations and Debates on Migration in Munich' (with Sabine Hess) which culminated in an exhibition at the Rathausgalerie. In 2012, he co-founded the independent research institute Tracing Spaces, also producing and curating the art in public space project City on the Move – a Farewell to a Logistic Area (with Michael Zinganel). From 2014 to 2016, he was research associate at the Academy of Fine Arts Vienna and co-head of research of 'Stop and Go: Nodes of Transformation and Transition' investigating the production of space along Pan-European traffic corridors in East Europe (tracingspaces.net).

Per-Anders Hillgren is a Professor in Interaction Design at the School of Arts and Communication at Malmö University, Sweden, and has been active in the research field of participatory design for a number of years. He is interested in how we can embrace diverse understandings of the worlds we live in and how this can go hand in hand with opportunities to change these worlds in more sustainable directions. At present, he coordinates the research platform Collaborative Future-Making at Malmö University.

Riadadh Hossain is an international development practitioner with an emphasis on climate change adaptation, climate policy, finance and governance. He is currently a Programme Coordinator at the International Centre for Climate Change and Development (ICCCAD) based in Dhaka, Bangladesh, where he oversees a number of projects in varying capacities.

Saleemul Huq is the Director of the International Centre for Climate Change and Development (ICCCAD) at Independent University, Bangladesh. Saleemul's recent activities have focussed on building negotiating capacity and supporting the engagement of the least developed countries (LDCs) in the United Nations Framework Convention on Climate Change, including negotiator training workshops for LDCs and policy, as well as research into vulnerability and adaptation to climate change in the LDCs.

Li Jönsson is an Associate Senior Lecturer in Design Theory and Practice at Malmö University, Sweden. She works in the field of STS, participatory design and speculative design. She has broad experience in making and engages in questions related to how design can open up alternative ways of understanding, intervening and expanding issues that focus on contributions to the publics' experience and engagement with nature and the more-than-human.

Eli Kosminsky is an educational game designer and developer from Osmo, where he creates applications to teach first graders math and empathy. He was the Director of Boston's largest group of tabletop game designers and New England's largest independent games festival. In collaboration with Lonny Avi Brooks, Eli has organized Afrofuturist game jams and developed physical games for forecasting Queer and Afrofuturist stories.

Ann Light is a Professor of Design and Creative Technology at the University of Sussex, UK, and Professor of Interaction Design, Social Change and Sustainability at Malmö University, Sweden. Her work addresses themes of social and ecological justice, the co-making of futures and the politics of design. She has specialized in participatory practice and the social impact of technology, bringing a background in arts, humanities, AI and human–computer

Contributors

interaction to bear on innovation in social process, culture and well-being. She is currently investigating how creative practices can promote transformations to sustainability.

Kristina Lindström is a designer and Senior Lecturer at the School of Arts and Communication at Malmö University, Sweden. She works at the intersection of participatory design, speculative design and feminist technoscience, with a focus on public engagement. She is currently researching the topic of (un)making, as a way of exploring alternatives to progressivist imaginaries within design. Prior to her position at Malmö University, she was a Postdoctoral Fellow at Umeå Institute of Design, Sweden.

Genevieve Liveley is a Professor of Classics, RISCS Fellow and Turing Fellow at the University of Bristol. She is a narratologist with particular research interests in narratives and narrative theories (both ancient and modern), and their impact on futures thinking. She is the author of *Narratology* (OUP, 2019) and has published a number of books and articles examining the stories that programme cultural and sociotechnical narratives about human interactions with new technology.

Deborah Lupton is a SHARP Professor in the Faculty of Arts and Social Sciences at UNSW Sydney, Australia, working in the Centre for Social Research in Health and the Social Policy Research Centre and leading the Vitalities Lab. Professor Lupton is a Chief Investigator and leader of the UNSW Node of the Australian Research Council Centre of Excellence in Automated Decision-Making and Society (2020–2026). She is a Fellow of the Academy of the Social Sciences in Australia and holds an Honorary Doctor of Social Science degree awarded by the University of Copenhagen.

Georgia Newmarch is a design strategist. Having completed a PhD with the Institute of Social Futures at Lancaster University, UK, and exploring the relationships between complexity, design thinking and everyday practices, she has since worked on several futures thinking projects. She has exhibited at international design weeks; her design practice is interdisciplinary and experimental, creating 'translation tools' to increase futures literacy. Currently, she is working on digital transformation projects within both the public and private sector.

Paul Graham Raven researches the narrative rhetorics of sociotechnical and climate imaginaries for Lund University, Sweden. His doctoral thesis proposed a novel model of sociotechnical change based on social practice theory, and a narrative prototyping methodology for infrastructure foresight. He is also a writer and critic of science fiction, an occasional journalist and essayist, a collaborator with designers and artists and a (gratefully) lapsed consulting critical futurist. He currently lives in Malmö with a cat, some guitars and sufficient books to constitute an insurance-invalidating fire hazard.

Lauren Rickards is a Professor at RMIT University, Australia, where she leads a cross-university initiative, the Urban Futures Enabling Capability Platform and the Climate Change Transformations research programme. With a background in ecology and human geography, Lauren's research focusses on the social and cultural dimensions of climate change, particularly agriculture and food futures. She is a Lead Author with the Intergovernmental Panel on Climate Change and co-lead of the Institute of Australian Geographer's study group on Nature, Risk and Resilience.

Mimi Sheller is a Professor of Sociology, Head of the Sociology Department and founding Director of the Center for Mobilities Research and Policy at Drexel University, Philadelphia, USA. She is founding co-editor of the journal *Mobilities* and past President of the International Association for the History of Transport, Traffic and Mobility. She helped to establish the 'new mobilities paradigm', has published more than 125 articles and book chapters and is the author or co-editor of 15 books, including, most recently, *Advanced introduction to mobilities* (Edward Elgar, 2021); *Island futures: Caribbean survival in the Anthropocene* (Duke University Press, 2020) and *Mobility justice: The politics of movement in an age of extremes* (Verso, 2018).

AbdouMaliq Simone is a Senior Professorial Fellow at the Urban Institute at the University of Sheffield, UK, and Visiting Professor of Urban Studies at the African Centre for Cities at the University of Cape Town, South Africa. His key publications include *For the city yet to come: Urban change in four African cities* (Duke University Press, 2004); *City life from Jakarta to Dakar: Movements at the crossroads* (Routledge, 2009); *Jakarta: Drawing the city near* (University of Minnesota Press, 2014); *New urban worlds: Inhabiting dissonant times* (with Edgar Pieterse, Polity, 2017); *Improvised lives: Rhythms of endurance for an urban South* (Polity, 2018) and *The surrounds: Urban life within and beyond capture* (Duke University Press, forthcoming).

Nicola Spurling is the Director of the Centre for Mobilities Research at Lancaster University, UK, and a Senior Lecturer in Sociology. She was an Associate Director of Lancaster's Institute for Social Futures from 2016 to 2020. Her background is in Anthropology and Sociology, and she is interested in theories of practice, the mobilities paradigm and futures thinking. Her work encounters and addresses a range of contemporary issues and problems associated with climate change. Nicola has extensive experience researching the social embeddedness of high-carbon mobilities, and how decarbonized mobilities could and should be achieved. Recent publications include 'Parking futures: The relationship between parking space, everyday life and travel demand in the UK', *Land Use Policy*, v.91 (2020); and 'Matters of timing: Materiality and the changing temporal organization of everyday energy consumption', in the *Journal of Consumer Culture*, Online First (2018).

Michael Strange is Reader in International Relations at the Department of Global Political Studies at Malmö University, Sweden. His research looks at the emergence of political subjectivities and everyday forms of democracy, with an empirical focus that includes healthcare, trade politics and migration. He has published widely within international peer-reviewed journals and advised legislative bodies. He currently co-directs the externally funded project 'Precision Health and Everyday Democracy'.

Jason Tester is a strategic foresight researcher, facilitator and speculative designer with specialties in emerging technologies, their cultural impacts and social justice futures. He was a Research Affiliate with the Institute for the Future (IFTF) for ten years, where he is now Research Director. Currently, Jason is launching a collaborative research project at QueerTheFuture.org to understand and map the many intersections of LGBTQ people and disruptive long-term future forces.

Richard Tutton is a Senior Lecturer in the Department of Sociology and Co-Director of the Science and Technology Studies Unit (SATSU) at the University of York, UK. His research interests are in science, technology and social futures. He is the author of

Contributors

Genomics and the reimagining of personalized medicine (Ashgate, 2014) and the editor of *New genetics and society*.

Stewart Wallis is an advocate for a new economic system. He worked for Oxfam from 1992 to 2002, for which he was awarded an OBE. From 2003 to 2016, he was an Executive Director of the New Economics Foundation. Currently, Wallis is the Chair for the Wellbeing Economy Alliance (WEAll), which is a new major initiative to create a global new economy movement. In 2016, he was awarded an Honorary Doctorate by Lancaster University.

Anthony D. Weeks is an illustrator, visual storyteller and public listener based in San Francisco, CA. He has more than 20 years of experience working with senior-level product and strategy development teams to think visually and turn data into stories. In the role of public listener and illustrator, Anthony collaborates with project teams to create visually rich chronicles and murals of conversations in real time. Anthony's documentary films have been screened at numerous venues nationally and internationally. He was a 2009 grant recipient from the Princess Grace Foundation in New York/Monaco. He was honoured with an Emmy and a student Academy Award for his 2010 documentary short entitled *Imaginary circumstances*. In 2011, Anthony was one of several American film directors selected by the US State Department to travel to embassies and consulates abroad as part of the American Documentary Showcase, a cultural exchange programme. In addition to directing documentary media, Anthony has illustrated a number of books.

Michael Zinganel graduated from the Faculty of Architecture at Graz University of Technology and obtained a PhD in contemporary history from the University of Vienna, Austria. He was a Research Fellow at the IFK (International Centre for Cultural Studies) in Vienna and taught at various universities and academies, such as the postgraduate academy of Bauhaus Dessau Foundation, AAU Klagenfurt and TU Graz and Vienna. In 2012, he co-founded the independent research institute Tracing Spaces, also producing and co-editing *Holiday after the fall: Seaside architecture and urbanism in Bulgaria and Croatia* (with Elke Beyer and Anke Hagemann, Jovis Verlag, 2013). From 2014 to 2016, he was research associate at the Academy of Fine Arts Vienna and head of research for 'Stop and Go: Nodes of Transformation and Transition' investigating the production of space along Pan-European traffic corridors in East Europe (tracingspaces.net).

Acknowledgements

We would like to thank the Directors and Fellows of the Institute for Social Futures at Lancaster University, past and present, for their support in the creation of this Handbook. Debate, critique and discussion at several conferences including Anticipation in London (2017) and Constructing Social Futures in Turku, Finland (2019), provided a fitting forum from which many valuable insights were gained and relationships forged. The Handbook is the result of an iterative process and sustained exchange between authors, reviewers and editors. Our sincere thanks to reviewers and, especially, authors who believed in this project and helped shape it as their chapters progressed.

Carlos López Galviz would like to thank colleagues and friends of the European network Cultural Politics of Sustainable Urban Mobility and partners of the UKRI-GCRF-funded project Gridding Equitable Urban Futures in Areas of Transition (GREAT) in Cali, Colombia, and Havana, Cuba.

Emily Spiers would like to thank fellow members of FLNT (Futures Literacy through Narrative), Genevieve Liveley and Will Slocombe, as well as the leaders of the futures communities of practice at Dstl and DEFRA for supporting the development of their research.

In memoriam John Urry

Introduction
Why social futures?

Carlos López Galviz and Emily Spiers

Social futures: A manifesto

What does it mean for futures to be social? How does social-futures thinking complement the dominant paradigm of futures thinking prevailing in the west, especially in the Anglo-American tradition, since the end of the Second World War? In the arena of corporate futures, involved with 'future-proofing' businesses, markets and governments, economic and technological trends constitute the main drivers of futures, and they are often viewed as both the singular guide for and the telos of 'the future'. While economics and technology are important, social futures makes the case for attending to a wider range of social considerations necessary for humanity, other species and the planet to flourish, and adopting a broader, more creative, set of approaches and methods in order to do so.

Foregrounding social futures reveals a shift to the embodied and embedded ways that humans anticipate, imagine and live futures in their messy, socially imbricated lives. We encourage, in this way, a resistance to the deracinated macro impetus of much futures work today and a shift in gaze to matters of difference, to specific *times, places and people*, from which intersections futures emerge. This is futures thinking as localized and lived, not putatively generalized (indeed, generalizable) and abstract.[1] Futures, like identities, emerge out of repetitive, lived practices, which themselves arise from a complex nexus of conditions, and are performed in a pluralistic, incoherent process within a regulatory social system (Spiers, 2018). As this analogy shows, insights from feminist and gender studies, among other fields, can serve to develop our critical thinking vis-à-vis the future. Just as the concept of a pre-discursive, coherent and *predictable* selfhood sustains essentialist notions of a 'natural' or 'universal' gender identity (Spiers, 2018, p. 25), contemporary modes of prediction, forecasting, extrapolation and 'future-proofing' run the risk of naturalizing or universalizing some futures, while foreclosing others. The futures we shape are neither 'natural' nor 'universal', nor are they pre-ordained. Futures, we argue, are contextual.

Futures have histories and geographies that differ according to where we position ourselves across space and over time. Charting the different modes, means, capabilities, approaches and practices involved in the localized act of entertaining the question of what the future holds is a challenge this Handbook tackles head on. By assembling a range of futures, each with its own geography and history, we give context to techniques – forecasting, backcasting, scenario planning, co-production and more – with which specific versions and trajectories of the social are made.

In the third decade of the twenty-first century, futures studies have turned a weather eye to the conditions of the past and present that inform the capacities of individuals and societies to access their futures (see Sand, 2019; Groves, in this volume; Spiers, in this volume). Whether one adopts a 'capabilities' or 'futures literacy' approach (see Sen, 1985; Nussbaum, 2011; Miller, 2006a, 2015), or a focus on the intricate processes of human anticipation (Poli, 2017, 2018), the distinctive insight of this volume is that futures thinking today must be social.

Taken together, the chapters included in this Handbook interrogate the different versions of the social that futures methods create as well as those that they foreclose, related to which is the reality of growing social inequalities facing governments, societies and families in the climate emergency. The question is no longer one of 'how the other half lives', but in what meaningful ways we can comprehend what connects the wealth of the 1% to the worries of the remaining 99%, as highlighted, among others, by the Occupy Movement in the early years of the twenty-first century.

Values are central to thinking the future from the social, that is, the values we wish the societies and social worlds of which we are part to hold. Equality, closing the gap between rich and poor, is one such value, so are fairness, individual freedom, self-development, conservation and ecological restoration. The values and the methods that shape the future do not always match. Put differently, certain techniques – projecting trends by extrapolating from observed patterns in the past – have implicit values underpinning them: Markets should be free; growth is good; and more is better. Futures defined by other values – equality, fairness, justice and inclusivity – require techniques that differ from those used in crafting the futures we learn about through newspapers, newsrooms and reports by think tanks and governments. Those tend to be limited to short-term political cycles and the trends that the next year will bring, the ever-newer gadgets, new variations on the theme of the smart phone, tablet, clean energy, or the driverless car. More importantly, highlighting values invites us to devise new ways of thinking the social in a manner that enables us to articulate those values in the future tense.

In 2016, for example, residents of Lancaster in the United Kingdom responded to a question about life in 2051 by stating how important it was for nature, parks and greenery to be part of their future lives (see also Spiers, this volume).[2] Responses varied across generations, ranging from the over-70s, who could not imagine themselves playing a part 35 years into the future, through to the schoolchildren, whose drawings captured the wildest visions of what life in their forties might mean. The narratives underpinning how they made the future present in their everyday lives determined the kind of futures they considered possible and, by extension, the futures that appeared foreclosed.

Ways of understanding and developing techniques to envision and shape the future are contingent upon where and when these emerge and evolve. Visions, stories, enactments of the future differ in the qualities that frame each projection, themselves subject to conditions determining, for example, the possible, probable and preferable futures (Amara, 1978; Urry 2016) that we wish to bring to life. This Handbook is an invitation to open an important conversation about the futures we wish to shape and the extent to which they can and should be social. It springs from a particular place and a particular time, namely, Lancaster, in particular the Institute for Social Futures (ISF), founded in 2015 at Lancaster University. In their original manifesto, founding directors Linda Woodhead and John Urry placed the future at the centre of research in the social sciences and urged us to consider what theories and methods might aid us in interrogating and better understanding the future (see Urry, 2016). Grounded in an ongoing interdisciplinary conversation spanning across the arts, humanities and the social, environmental, materials, health and computational sciences, the ISF encourages future-forming research collaborations across disciplines with the aim of helping understand and better shape futures where the social is key

After six years of engaging in this work at the ISF, we have assembled a collection of contributions to this Handbook that capture three important ways in which futures thinking can be made social: (1) Sustaining an open and critical understanding of the relationship between the past and the future, enabling, among other things, a move beyond probabilistic techniques such as forecasts; (2) Entertaining a range of timescales, human and otherwise, in the process of shaping the futures we want and need; and (3) Paying attention to the narrative impulse at the heart of all futures thinking and the links between questions of voice and agency. In what follows we turn to each in order to delineate our social futures manifesto.

The past into the future and back

The possibility, probability or preferability of certain futures relates directly to the kinds of claims made about how we can know, anticipate and shape the future. Implicit in these claims is a very specific, often instrumental, understanding of the relationship between the past, the present and the future. By the 1970s, Wendell Bell would state that 'there are no past possibilities and no future facts' (quoted in Adam, 2011, p. 591). This is closely related to whether or not we assign to different temporalities the status of being real and the status of things or phenomena we can sense as actual, recognize as tangible and qualify as factual. The debate around future facts is both varied and extensive (see, for example, Adam and Groves, 2007; Appadurai, 2013; Poli, 2017) and one there is no need to rehearse here. More closely aligned with the aims of our discussion is the question of what past possibilities mean. There have been and there are at any time in history competing visions of the future, which means possibilities in the past abound; things could have been different, and agencies and structures might have interacted in other ways to produce outcomes that differ significantly from what we may call our present (López Galviz, 2019). A present, we should add, that shifts constantly over time. Stating that there are no possibilities in the past is closing it, giving it a definite status neither the past nor the present has. It creates an artificial narrative shaping the versions of history we learn from and the manner of learning. Importantly, it shapes imaginaries of the past by delineating the options of what can be remembered (Hurlbut, 2015; Jasanoff, 2015; see also Jedlowski, 2017).

Denying the past, its possibilities, also fixes events to positions from which we can extrapolate safely, if inaccurately, in the form of, for example, trends. One important tradition to which trends are key is forecasting. By the early twenty-first century, as Jens Beckert has shown, 'macroeconomic forecasting has become a veritable industry', connected to national governments; central and regional banks; institutions such as the Organisation for Economic Co-operation and Development, the International Monetary Fund and the European Commission; and 'private banks, rating agencies and investments funds' (2016, p. 219). This ubiquity continues despite the fact that forecasts are well known for their failure to predict, for example, financial crises. The Harvard Economic Society in 1929, the US Federal Reserve in December 2007 and the German forecast institutes in the prelude to the financial crash of 2008, all had a different future linked to the horizons their models showed. An important part of what forecasts do is to establish the authority with which fictions can be turned into policy:

> Forecasting should be considered as an instrument for the construction of fictional expectations. Forecasts are imaginaries of a future state of the world [that] do not need to be correct to set actors' minds at ease or to help them make decisions – they merely need to be convincing. The credible claim for correctness is a substitute for actual accuracy.
> *(Beckert, 2016, p. 231)*

The very significant resources, including money, spent by governments, companies and institutions in inaccurate predictions of what the economic and technological future will bring should give us pause for thought. 'A century of econometric forecasting of macroeconomic indicators and the development of many quantitative and qualitative techniques to predict technological progress', Beckert goes on to argue, 'has not brought us any closer to predicting the future' (2016, pp. 241–242). Yet 'the failure of prediction is rarely taken as an opportunity to reflect upon whether or not it is actually possible [to predict the future], but instead as a justification for building even more sophisticated models' (2016, p. 244).

Much of the thinking underpinning forecasting and similar probabilistic techniques is based on a key fictive character, *homo economicus*, a 'solitary, calculating, competing and insatiable' individual, almost always male, moving in an unrealistic world where the main vehicle resembles a plane in which we, society, take off. Never to land. This is the compelling way in which Kate Raworth (2018) characterizes the main actors, plots and storylines central to the doctrines of twentieth-century economics. Her alternative is for an embedded economy, regenerative by design, supporting flourishing lives and interlocking the earth, society and the economy, one that pays equal attention to the state, the market, the commons and the household. Context, values and purpose are central to imagining the kind of economies we need in the early part of the twenty-first century:

> Rethinking economics is not about finding the correct one (because it doesn't exist), it's about choosing or creating one that best serves our purpose – reflecting the context we face, the values we hold, and the aims we have. As humanity's context, values, and aims continually evolve, so too should the way that we envision the economy.
> *(Raworth, 2018, pp. 22–23)*

The encouraging news is that alternatives are already in the making. As Stewart Wallis outlines in his chapter ('Economics', this volume), the Wellbeing Economy Alliance (WEAll), founded in 2017, has gathered (by the end of 2020) 160 movements, alliances and organizations as well as the willingness of governments in Scotland, New Zealand, Wales, Iceland, Canada and California to test multi-sector, multilevel hubs where new economies can be brought into existence. One of WEAll's aims is to reverse the concentration of wealth (concerning income and lobbying power) and the social inequalities that it engenders. As Wallis reminds us, 'the world's 2,153 billionaires [had in 2020] more wealth than the 4.6 billion people who make up 60% of the planet's population'. Dignity, living within our natural planetary limits, a sense of belonging, fairness and participation are the five key needs, or 'non-negotiables', on the basis of which WEAll seeks to create a different social future.

Sound alternatives like Raworth's and WEAll, placing the social at their core, are both timely and urgent. They remind us of the multiple past ways of thinking about time across different cultures and religions, which see things, for example, in a cyclical way – we progress and regress, we can repeat and re-enact in meaningful ways, returning to the wealth of what has come before, in imitation of the natural world and even the cosmos itself. Thinking of social futures with the tools of a distinctively modern belief in endless progress and growth and twentieth-century economics runs into the risks of cognitive bias.[3] It also reproduces the kind of doctrinal thinking that with similar insistence and tone places faith in free markets, or in particular readings of the nature of God's presence in the world (Guyer, 2007). Engaging with the process of understanding and helping shape the social futures we seek to create requires a bigger, richer and more varied set of approaches than that which has become dominant since at least the second half of the twentieth century. One way of enhancing the repertoire of techniques is by considering a range of timescales.

The scales, scapes and spans of time

Considering the interdependence of different timescales is central to devising how we can resist overly parsimonious understandings of how individuals and societies envision, shape and enact their futures. In every rendering and rendition of the future, we can find overlapping timescales, timelines and time frames being reproduced. Barbara Adam (2021, pp. 120–121) cites at least five 'irreducible features of time', namely, timeframes, temporality, tempo, timing and 'the temporal modalities of past, present and future', that is, the multiple ways in which the three modes of time familiar to most of us interact with and shape one another. The openness of these interactions is key. By contrast, one way of characterizing our contemporaneous consumer and services society, as Marc Augé (2015, pp. 63–64) has remarked, is as a 'society that would still care about its immediate future, but would no longer need to look further ahead'. This is a stark reminder of the risks of an overriding presentism.

The relationship between immediate needs and how far into the future we place ourselves is contingent upon time and place and is determined in large part by the politics of the aspirations foregrounded on our behalf by governments, companies, institutions and individuals. Foregrounding aspirations implies, by extension, ignoring and side-lining those aspirations that do not match the picture that is celebrated. Ideas such as progress and innovation underpin the immediacy and framing of our needs in relation to consumption rather than, say, citizenship or the environment. Building on the work of Bertrand de Jouvenel, Adam and Groves (2007, p. 33) argue that

> our knowledge of the future is inversely proportional to the rate of progress […] in contexts of accelerating innovation, knowledge of the future is moved progressively closer to the present and knowledgeable extension into the long-term future recedes ever further out of reach.

Is this inverse relation between immediate progress and distant futures an inevitable conundrum? What does it take for our imaginations to span decades, centuries and millennia; to delve into the past with those timelines so that we position ourselves to help shape better social futures? How long is long ago? How soon is the here and now?

In the mid-nineteenth century, William Thomson, later Lord Kelvin, estimated that the age of the earth was finite and close to 20 million years. Over 150 years later, geologists posit that the earth is around 4.5 billion years old (England, Monar and Richter, 2007). Between four and five billion years from now, the sun will begin to cease being the supporting bright star holding together the solar system of which the earth is part. The cluster of islands that make up Tuvalu in Polynesia has been submerging as sea levels in the Pacific continue to rise.

Recent estimates predict that most of the archipelago will have disappeared by 2050, a trend also affecting large cities such as Shanghai, Jakarta, Bangkok, Kolkata and Dhaka (Kulp and Strauss, 2019). Global warming has intensified since the 1960s with a rapidity the existing historical and geological record suggests is unprecedented. Since 1960, the trend of increasing greenhouse emissions dating back to the beginnings of the industrial revolution (circa 1750) has been called the Great Acceleration (Steffen et al., 2015). That acceleration is the speeding up of a human-made process centuries in the making, prompting reactions from the earth and its ecosystems that have taken over millennia, millions of years to be what they are in the early part of the twenty-first century.

The longevity of the earth, the life expectancy of the solar system, the immediacy of flash floods and islands or coastlines gradually submerged by rising sea levels, as well as the relatively new yet significant rise in global temperatures, might at first seem unrelated to our capacity to envision different worlds. They all operate at different timescales. Each, in turn, has a model, including the assumptions on which that model is based, allowing scientists, experts and others to calculate if the consequences to humans, societies and the environment are observable and by what point the crossing of a certain threshold becomes irreversible.[4]

What the contrast between different timescales suggests is twofold. It highlights the significant dissonance between timescales and measurements that we struggle to grasp and which, frankly, play little or no part in the everyday decision-making concerning our future, however distant or near that future might be. This, of course, is not the case for the 11,000 or so inhabitants of Tuvalu for whom favourite spots in their homeland have disappeared in recent years (Roy, 2019). The contrast is also a means of recovering what deep time, time measured in millions or billions of years, has to offer to the human imagination. This is an exercise in unthinking the thinkable, in other words, relearning the process of what times and which timescales we consider when imagining new social futures, which complements calls by Herman Kahn, Amitav Ghosh and others to think the unthinkable and, in the process, reconfigure the rules of how we normally think the future. Moreover, the contrast of timescales allows us to explore the extent to which our ideas and visions of a collective future might connect the immediacy of urgent change (relocating one's home) to timescales beyond the human (the earth drifting out of the solar system). The contrast is also a means 'to accompany our actions to their eventual destinations', a way of inserting responsibility, ethics and care into the making and unmaking of the worlds around us. As Adam says, 'we could take responsibility not only for actions that extend over space—our footprints—but also for actions that extend over time', actions that Adam calls 'timeprints' (2021, p. 128).

Storytelling and storyknowing

From the times of oracles and prophets (which are always and now), futures thinking has revolved around the attempt to mitigate against uncertainty, and it has manifested in the human attempt to build jetties of knowledge, predictions and forecasts across a sea of intrinsic uncertainty about the future. Scrying, divination (Woodhead, 2021), palm-reading, tarot, seeing, forecasting, prediction (Andersson, 2021), scenarios (Curry, 2012, this volume), foresight (Slaughter, 1995), horizon scanning, prospection (Fuller, 2017; Bok and Fuller, this volume), anticipation (Poli, 2017, 2018; Groves, this volume), futures literacy (Miller, 2006a, 2015; Spiers, this volume), visioning (Schultz, 1995, 1996), alternative futures and the Manoa method (Dator, 2009), 'futuring' (Smith and Ashby, 2020) and 'defuturing' (Fry, 2020): The list of terms could continue, but serves here to gesture towards the plethora of methods that have been developed over time to do the fundamentally impossible.

The variety of methods attests to the pressing need for imagination when it comes to futures thinking. To think the unthinkable, *qua* 'future presents' (Adam and Groves, 2007), requires our brains, hardwired for storytelling as they are (see Turner, 1998; Wolf, 2008; Zak, 2015), and our intersubjective cultural practices. As Miller (2006a) points out: 'it is crucial to recognize that the elaboration of exploratory situations (for human society) is largely a storytelling task' (p. 7). Indeed, as Genevieve Liveley et al. (2021) observe: 'When we speculate about the probabilities, possibilities, and desirabilities of any futures, we are dealing with present imaginaries of future possible worlds – that is, with fictional *story* worlds' (p. 1). Narrative and storytelling have a long tradition of playing with and bringing to life new worlds where the relationship between, for example, past, present and future remains open. The catalogue is extensive, from the mythical Cassandra, who carried the gendered burden of not being believed, to Dante's exchange with the shadows in the Tenth Canto of the *Divine Comedy*, to the White Queen who remembers future events in *Through the Looking Glass* and Victor Hugo's understanding of history as 'an echo of the past' reverberating 'in the future (*l'avenir*) as well as 'a reflection of the future over the past' in *L'Homme Qui Rit*.

However, the value of narrative to social-futures thinking is not merely as a representational repository of futures imaginaries. Certainly, engaging with literature like speculative fiction, or SF, can help us understand that 'speculation always occurs *from* somewhere and someone' (Liveley et al., 2021, p. 7). As such, SF narratives can provide 'new perspectives on how we set about dealing with the challenge of contextual bias when imagining possible futures' (p. 7). Yet, as Liveley et al. (2021) observe, narrative is vital in '(1) framing, (2) shaping and (3) critiquing the world-building techniques that form the foundation of futures thinking' (p. 1). From this, we can see that an understanding of narratology helps us, first, to explore the heuristics that inform the ways in which we think about possible futures, including moments when we remain stuck in our own cognitive biases, contexts or jump to conclusions. Second, engaging in collaborative storytelling as a practice of futures thinking can 'activate an agentic relationship with an uncertain and complex future on the part of those participating in performative anticipatory practice' like storytelling. (p. 7) Finally,

> embodied and situated modes of 'storyknowing' can provide possible futures that illuminate messy but important ontological perspectives, and reveal [] how narrative identification or dis-identification not only echoes the difficulty of encountering the future's alterity but also provides a tool for overcoming that challenge.
>
> *(p. 7)*

Engaging with the narrative impulse at the heart of futures thinking allows us, therefore, to understand futures in and as part of their context; to illuminate the ways in which narrative frames open or foreclose particular futures; and to rehearse, through the creation of storyworlds, encounters with alterity, ranging from fictional characters and their worlds to the otherness of the future itself.

Outline of chapters

The second part of this Introduction is organized around six thematic clusters. This constitutes an invitation to reflect on common themes emerging out of the chapters, which appear in alphabetical order according to their keyword. The commissioning, development and curating of the volume, in collaboration with the authors, thus resonate with the contrasts that Andersson and Kemp (2021, p. 7) advocate, namely, 'ways of knowing the past and the present, often straddling the scientific and the religious, the verifiable and the imagined, the objective and the emotional'. To these phenomena, we add agency and worlding, the means and purposes of knowledge and learning, futures that are social and material, urban and rural, on the move and at a standstill.

Methods, or ways of worlding futures

This group of chapters explores the landscape of contemporary methods for thinking and shaping futures, including their advantages and limitations, beginning with a pivotal period in the mid-twentieth century. Andrew Curry's opening chapter unfolds the ways in which 'modern' futures thinking, embedded as it was, in the west, in the post-Second World War context, emerged as part of the military-industrial complex in North America, seeking out methods for futures thinking that drew on a positivist tradition of trends analysis and extrapolation. Pitted against the promises of positivism lies the insight, explored by these chapters, that every forecast or prediction is only, ultimately, a guess – however educated – at what will unfold in the future.[5] As our contributors show, the human desire to mitigate against uncertainty is so great that we invest deeply, on a cognitive and emotional level, in the plausible futures we construct. However, this often means that, when a chain of events unfolds in an unpredictable or unanticipated way, we are not prepared for the experience of disorientation, or estrangement, from our expectations. Rebecca Braun's chapter on 'Literary Futures' posits that 'literature can itself be seen as a tool with practical application for work in social futures' precisely because 'narrative plots routinely upend any straightforward chronological understanding of causality'. Braun thus makes the case for literature as a resilience-building tool in tackling our over-reliance on causal extrapolation and in coming to terms with ontological uncertainty.

Barbara Bok and Ted Fuller's chapter on 'Prospection' performs a synthesis of current social science methodologies for futures thinking that explores the status of claims to knowledge about the future as a methodological issue. The chapter thus goes to the heart of the divergent trends, noted above, that inaugurated futures thinking in the contemporary era: How can we legitimize any claims about the future? How can we evidence that knowledge? Alternatively, are these the right questions to be asking? As Bok and Fuller argue, central to these questions about prospection is the distinction between the 'phenomena being predicted' and the 'prospection enterprise itself'.

In contrast, and as Genevieve Liveley and Rebecca Braun explore in their chapters on 'Narrative' and 'Literary futures', we should consider all claims about the future as components of a narrative, a performative act of storytelling. Are futures, in fact, shaped by the stories that we tell about them? Moreover, if this is so, then the question of who speaks, who has a voice to tell a story, becomes a more pressing issue than the legitimacy of any one claim to knowledge. As Spiers notes in their chapter on 'Agency',

> for the field of social futures research to be truly social, it must ask difficult questions about how [...] diverse and multiple forms of everyday, embodied agency intersect with the seemingly invisible ways in which broader material-discursive and institutional technologies become licensed to exert power over how futures unfold.

In 'Anticipation' (this volume), Groves, in turn, avers that anticipation should be treated as a kind of 'meta-capability, essential to any notion of a flourishing life'. Access to or prevention from the means of anticipation illuminates the question of ethics and politics that lies at the heart of social-futures thinking.

For Kristina Lindström, Per-Anders Hillgren, Ann Light, Michael Strange and Li Jönsson ('Collaboration', this volume), the dual methods of critical imagination and collaborative future making represent an 'ethos of democratizing processes of change, that is, to acknowledge people's skills and rights to influence their everyday environments'. What matters for Lindström et al., indeed for the many contributors of this Handbook, is the 'shift from engaging with the future through forecasting to a concern with how critical imagination can challenge basic assumptions, norms and structures to widen the perspectives on what constitutes socially, culturally, ecologically and economically sustainable futures'.

Data, learning, intelligence: Different claims to knowledge

What is intelligence? How do we 'know' what we 'know'? Moreover, to what uses should we put our knowledge? These are the fundamental questions asked by this group of chapters. The ways in which humans have historically sought to understand their own epistemological claims about the past and the present extend into territory that is still more fraught when the future is concerned. Many of the chapters in this Handbook tackle the issues at the heart of our current modes of learning and knowing – whether that be in the accrual of knowledge for education and training, or in the process of seeking to 'avoid the mistakes of the past' – and how these issues prove problematic for the ways in which futures unfold.

Ashley Jay Brockwell and Carl Gombrich explore the future of the university in terms of our current and potential understandings of the uses of higher education. Their chapter considers whether, if we shift our thinking in terms of how universities respond to or inform the social, we can imagine future universities that 'remain radically open to, informed by and integrated with wider society, whilst offering visions of and practical steps towards a better future'. Dawn Goodwin and Richard Tutton's chapter on 'Inquiries' explores how the use that is made of the work of public inquiries in the National Health Service in the United Kingdom is limited by the ways in which the future is conceptualized. Goodwin and Tutton show how inquiries, through the painstaking process of pinning down events of the past, tend to characterize futures as 'identifiable', controllable and avertable. Thus, all too often mistakes are repeated as the future unfolds in slightly but significantly different contexts.

Richard Harper's chapter on artificial intelligence demonstrates the ways in which dominant narratives surrounding artificial intelligence as a mechanism fail to do justice to the variety of forms and uses of (human) intelligence and so, in turn, are limiting the futures of AI in the process. Deborah Lupton's chapter on the futures of personal data illuminates the relationships that individuals have with their own data. Lupton's empirical research reveals the ways in which individuals may resist future imaginaries that rest upon the two dominant, normative, if opposing, narratives of data futures: Those of a utopian vision of ubiquitous datafication, on the one hand, and their dystopian counterparts, on the other. Lupton shows how, in practice, individuals retain a sense of their own agency vis-à-vis their future imaginaries of personal data and their uses. In a similar vein, Earvin Charles Cabalquinto provides a case study of migrant Filipino workers in Australia who, by engaging with digital news media from and about the Philippines, use their digital connective practices to imagine and navigate a potential possible future for themselves and their families.

Social and material futures: Accessing the future

This group of chapters asks important questions about the relationship between the social and the material. How does biology intersect with social structures to impact upon people's lived experiences and, in turn, their futures? How can the histories and lived experiences of marginalization and oppression transform our understandings of the future? How can normative and exclusionary futures practices be productively queered in order to galvanize new modes of thinking, anticipation and liberation? How can infrastructural disruptions be harnessed to produce different futures through the development of new social practices? These chapters show us how existing social inequalities impact upon how people approach the future, but also how the experiences of marginalization, if we attend carefully to them, may reveal new forms of resilience and imaginaries for the future.

Derek Gatherer's chapter performs a retrospective of past biological thought that can be re-evaluated as protean futures thinking. Combing through biology's past, Gatherer discerns both utopian and dystopian futures and asks whether biology – reconceptualized as BioFutures – might have a larger role to play in current debates about social futures. Liz Brewster also casts an eye back over mental-health provision of the past and present in the United Kingdom. She explores the paradigm shift away from a biomedical model of health to a biopsychosocial one, which assesses not only biological factors, such as chemical imbalances and genetics, in mental health, but also the role of trauma, distress and structural inequalities.

Lonny Avi Brooks et al. examine the traumatic roots of queer and Afrofutures in order to move towards a radical rethinking of contemporary Western, Eurocentric futures thinking. The chapter makes the case for the potential of queer and Afrofutures perspectives to shatter complacent and normative hierarchies that have historically entitled some communities to 'have a future', while excluding others from the right to look ahead with dignity and agency. 'Radical empathy and visions of justice', Brooks et al. relate, 'often reside in a place of discomfort and vulnerability'. This uncomfortable place, indeed encounters with difference *per se*, requires from us the recognition of damaging legacies, as seen in the growing protests against institutional racism, and its murderous consequences, as well as the iconoclastic contestation of the many statues of slave owners and colonialists across the world, since 2020.

Georgia Newmarch, in turn, explores the ways in which communities in the UK have been re-forming in resilient new ways at moments of social and structural disruption to create what Newmarch calls 'proto-futures'. These proto-futures are moments when, in the face of local crises, such as power outages, new practices first emerge in a 'temporal choreography of participation' to prove themselves as possible new departure points, as the linchpins of new infrastructures, of new social futures.

Of submerged lives, drifting planets and future ecologies

To what extent should societies flourish to the detriment of the environments with which they interact? What timescales should we consider when judging the effects of lifestyles on the places we live in and those we leave behind both immediate and remote? Does it matter that the timescales of the earth and the timescales of human life and other species are different? Do these timescales converge and, if so, how?

The chapters on 'Climate Change', 'Ecology', 'Multi-Planetary Futures' and 'Utopia' engage in their own ways with these questions less to resolve them than to show the value of different approaches. Climate vulnerability, as Riadadh Hossain, Shababa Haque and Saleemul Huq discuss in their chapter ('Climate Change'), involves 'a crisis of survival for the poorest and most vulnerable', especially in low-lying delta areas, of which Bangladesh provides but one example. Different timescales are already at work for communities to adapt effectively, equip themselves with the right tools and develop sufficient responses to the latent risks and hazards of environmental change. In Bangladesh, this includes technology-based solutions such as hydroponic farming at household level; understanding and weighing the importance of intersectionality, more specifically, empowering women by securing their access through mobile phones to real-time meteorological data of value for tending their crops and farms; and taking the long view as per the development, policies and actions related to the Bangladesh Delta Plan 2100.

Reading ecological thinking through the lens of utopian modes of narrative ('if this continues then', 'what if' and 'if only') allows Lauren Rickards to highlight the kinds of relationships made in the forging of different ecologies both real and imagined. Rather than advocating specific kinds of relationships within closed systems, Rickards invites us to 'cultivate different orientations to and assumptions about the future'. Thinking ecologically, Rickards argues, involves reflecting on our 'uneasy and ever-shifting position within the world – a world that we are intentionally and unintentionally co-creating with highly uncertain results' ('Ecology', this volume). Orientation and relationships are also key aspects of utopias, as Lisa Garforth argues, in turn ('Utopia', this volume). The future is not a realm of 'telos, endpoints or blueprints', but the never-ending and never-final process of crafting an orientation to our everyday lives in ways that are better suited to dealing with the consequences of our actions, inactions, patterns of living and our insistence on retaining certain lifestyles. A key challenge is for that orientation to be equitable and just across generations, social and spatial units (the family, school, workplace, neighbourhood, country and world). One of the many insights that literary utopias provide is precisely the capacity to 'interrogate and expose the limits of what is imaginable' (Garforth, this volume). She observes that such limits prevent us from 'imagining changes in our own society and world', except, as Fredric Jameson adds, 'in the direction of dystopia and catastrophe' (Jameson, 2010, p. 23).

The common corollary of dystopia and catastrophe is escapism, leaving the island of utopia, or planet earth. Such is the thinking of a select few promoters of and players in the new space age, led not by nation states and cold war rivalries but instigated and funded in large part by private companies, with billionaires at their helm. As Katarina Damjanov shows, outer space has now, in the early twenty-first century, a presence in our lives in various guises that, nevertheless, reproduce tropes of the frontier and economies of colonization and extraction. Besides the alleged shared feeling of outer space as commons, through the dissemination of striking images, reports and memorabilia involving, for example, Mars rovers, there is also the realm where the security of nation states continues to be at stake and the firm interest of private companies making clear strides in securing returns for their investment. 'Assembling human societies around the bounty of [outer] space', Damjanov remarks, 'perpetuates and augments patterns of uneven access and unequal participation in shared resources'. To what extent is access to these resources distributed fairly, by whom and in whose interest, are questions we can both recognize in the past and temporalize into the future. We may all end up being colonizers, if we were to follow the Bransons, Musks and Bezoses of the new space age, or colonize the different times 'of an empty future ready to be occupied' (Adam and Groves, 2007, p. 140).

Social futures in an urbanizing world

What does it mean for futures to be social in a world that, according to counts and estimates by the United Nations and others, appears to be urbanizing rapidly? Urbanization has long been linked to other processes such as industrialization and development. In its most hopeful incarnation, urbanization is seen as a means of raising the standards of living of a population, of 'lifting' people out of poverty. The first principle, out of four, of a recent UN-Habitat

III report, stated that: 'In an urbanized world, in which global urban population will reach 70 per cent in 2050, urbanization becomes the key element of global development' (UN-Habitat III, 2017, p. 42). Despite their limitations, and the instrumentalism that accompanies them (Kaika, 2017), institutions and governments see the UN Sustainable Development Goals as a force for good. To supplement and critique the kind of thinking that normalizes urbanization as a global trend, we must think of qualities like creativity; deploy critique to counter the onset of companies that see cities as the most profitable of markets; interrogate taxonomies of visual cities so that invisible yet important aspects of what makes a city are made apparent; and recognize the eventualities that are part of the different temporalities constantly unfolding in informal cities. This is, of course, only a start.

The chapters by Cecilia Dinardi, Paul Graham Raven, AbdouMaliq Simone and Nick Dunn invite us to reflect on what qualifying urbanization means and involves, particularly in the context of cities. Dinardi explores what artistic, cultural and creative interventions do in cities, including how they differ from policies based on the creative class as advocated by Richard Florida and others. Central to creative urbanism, Dinardi writes, is 'the importance of culture, creativity and the arts for place-making, urban revitalization and social cohesion'. By contrast, policies encouraging creative clusters and hubs tend to reduce structural problems such as growing social inequalities and unaffordable housing to the solutionism of attracting investment and funding innovation, often ignoring the specific conditions of the contexts and communities where these new clusters are planned. These are also policies running the risks of reproducing what Saskia Sassen (2014) has called 'geographies of extraction' whereby shell companies seek, successfully, to maximize profits on their investments by sinking their capital into the ever more unaffordable and increasingly privatized centres of cities like London, Paris, New York, Tokyo or Hong Kong. The trend is also part of what Lees et al. call 'planetary gentrification', namely, the process through which cities in Europe, Asia, Latin America and beyond have grown if only to accommodate investment, often by policy and choice. Investment, by and large, targets the upper classes and a transnational elite while, at the same time, limiting the options and ignoring the needs of all other residents (Lees et al., 2016).

A distinct variant of the solutionist approach to urban change is encapsulated in the discourses and visions of the smart city, with which both Raven and Dunn engage with critically. The smart city, Raven argues, is a 'solutionist utopia of policy without polity', in other words, a city lacking friction; a city where problems are solvable through computing power; and a city consisting of data points rather than citizens and civic institutions. As Raven shows, the 'smart' of the cities by IBM, Cisco, Intel and others betrays a genre that can be deconstructed by recourse to the toolbox of the critical utopias of science fiction. Doing so reveals the smart city for what it is: 'A city of (and for) cyphers, a rigid and over-quantified simulacrum, a hyperreal dystopia for all but those sat safely within its "nerve centres" and control rooms'. Importantly, this is a question of the power of data entangled with the erosion of the democratic spaces that cities have long accommodated and protected.

In his chapter, Dunn explores the value of creating taxonomies of cities envisioned since 1900 and assessing the extent to which, during specific periods, architects, planners, designers and others have contributed to the emergence of 'echo chambers for novel visualization techniques', on which, we must add, much of the training of future generations is based. Cities made visual have different temporalities in them: From the conservation of the distant past, say, the archaeology and 'brecciation' of a city like Rome (Bartolini, 2013) to the 'now and next' advocated by the smart-city promoters. What counts, Dunn argues, are the social, global and technological dimensions of the futures envisioned as well as recognizing who engages with what kinds of future, what agendas these futures advocate and when, and which motivations we can reveal in them. Casting a net wide enough so that futures beyond the technological make it into the archive of visions that policymakers can see is a means of highlighting other important issues such as ecological concerns, nomadic lifestyles and the integration of urban and rural spaces.

A similar kind of visibility to which academic work can contribute is that of the plurality of eventualities and actors who make the informal cities of the so-called Global South. The futures that the residents of informal settlements can envision are significantly different from the visions filling the catalogues and books recording the work of well-known architects. The qualities their futures offer us are different. Theirs is an orientation towards the future that is unsettled, informal, provisional, riddled with dispossessions, evictions and precarity. Residents of places like Tanah Tinggi in Jakarta, Indonesia, Simone tells us, have 'little conviction in any linear progression toward a better a future' and have instead a cornucopia of 'bluffing, coaxing, luring, and blustering' that may or may not translate into the money, resources and opportunities to make their lives more liveable. Recognizing that, through the distinctiveness of their lives residents of informal settlements weave and make unique forms of infrastructure (Simone, 2015) is also a means of capturing the human labour, including the values underpinning it, that goes into shaping the lives and livelihoods of one in every four urban residents worldwide, or one billion people as recorded in 2016 (UN, 2020, pp. 119–120).

The rhythms and crossings of social futures

The relationship between societies and their futures can be characterized as one of movement (Urry, 2000; Büscher et al., 2010; Sheller and Urry, 2016). This is so through both everyday acts by individuals moving along in life and constantly shifting iterations of the imagination. In de Jouvenel's evocative image, these movements are 'jetties' into the uncertain worlds ahead:

> As a consequence, the future is known not through the guesswork of the mind, but through social efforts, more or less conscious, to cast 'jetties' out from an established order and into the uncertainty ahead. The network of reciprocal commitments traps the future and moderates its mobility. All this tends to reduce the uncertainty.
> *(de Jouvenel, cited in Adam and Groves, 2007, p. 8)*

Uncertainty is a deterrent of movement to some but not all. Whether and how movement enters our everyday lives is determined by a variety of conditions, some external (the money and resources to travel, the existence of a pavement or not) and other internal (the limitations that we might experience through our own bodies). What do movement and stasis do to the rendering of certain futures desirable and other futures unthinkable? Do the questions of who moves where, why, how and under which circumstances help us reveal aspects of social futures that otherwise would go unnoticed? In what ways is the embodied experience of moving necessary to thinking different social futures?

The contributions by Michael Hieslmair and Michael Zinganel, Mimi Sheller, Nicola Spurling and Farzaneh Bahrami all engage with these questions in various ways. Nickelsdorf, a town in the border between Austria and Hungary, has witnessed migrations, forced and otherwise, dating back to at least the wars related to the breakup of former Yugoslavia (1991–2001). In 2015, border crossings at Nickelsdorf were by refugees, the majority fleeing conflict in Syria, Afghanistan or Iraq. Through their use of a range of creative methods including maps and the making of a graphic novel, Hieslmair and Zinganel capture the significance of cultural memory in shaping the kinds of social futures open and foreclosed in moments of crisis. This includes the memory of residents who have witnessed similar crises before and recognize the value of human readiness to help those most in need. The population of forcibly displaced people worldwide doubled between 1990 and 2019 from circa 40 million to nearly 80 million as recorded by the UN Refugee Agency. Around 40% of them were children (UNHCR, 2019). As Büscher (2018, p. 189) has remarked data and its absence are a reminder of 'how the privileges of the few [can be found] on the same map as the suffering of the many'.

The fragility, uncertainty, unpredictability and precarity of the futures that can be envisioned in moments of crisis are not limited to the large number of people forced to be on the move. As Sheller reminds us, these are also qualities that people can observe in the mobility systems available, for example, in cities. The uneven distribution of privileges concerning the means, frequency and conditions of mobility and transport is directly related to social inequalities, accessibility and the extent to which movement is a choice. The future of cities is often seen through the lens of future transport technologies, in a process that, Sheller argues, is political whether through favouring state regulation or by giving free rein to the market. Our very democracies are at stake in the making and unmaking of these techno-futures, including ambitious plans such as the Green New Deal in the United States: 'We need to pay greater attention to the injustice of digital systems and the ways in which the concentration of digital power is in tension with democratic determination of mobility transitions' (Sheller, this volume).

An important part of the restrictions to how and by which means people move is a function of legislation, the practices it encourages and prevents. Lines on pavements, roads and car parks may seem innocuous, serving a purpose we care not to question. Inspired by Tim Ingold's 'anthropology of the line', Spurling invites us to think twice and ask whether the way our everyday practices are directed by, for example, traffic and other related lines provides any insights for envisioning decarbonized mobility futures. Her rendition of painted lines and the practices they make possible as the weft and the warp (the intersecting threads of fabric in cloth-making) of mobility practice is one way in which we may envision mobility futures differently, not least futures beyond the car. Equally central to Spurling's argument is the recognition of the role that new fabrics and new patterns can and should play in shaping decarbonized cities and places. One potential illustration of the latter is, in turn, the focus of Bahrami's chapter, namely, long-distance walking in London, Lausanne and Tehran. The irony, we might say, is that there is nothing new to walking; it is something of an old yet useful weft. Yet, some cities and the places where people live and work have been designed with the car, not the pedestrian, as the main character of the narratives instigating their change. The fact that CAVs, or connected autonomous vehicles, gather the interest of industry, authorities and citizens alike, and foster debate in the terms they do, is a clear sign of the specific directions along which cities should change. That is, change according to companies like IBM, Intel, Cisco or Google telling us that the future of mobility is already here (for critical treatments of this see the chapters 'Smart Cities' and 'Visible Cities') and all that is left for us pedestrians is to adapt or be left behind. Bahrami argues instead that the pedestrian should be seen as the transcalar character, that is, the character who moves across different scales, as the driver of the mobility futures where the social is key. COVID-19 restrictions on movements across the world have shown a different future, one where the suspension of past daily routines can engender alternatives many people did not consider possible let alone feasible before.

Coda futura

Like the real, the social is produced in 'dense and extended sets of relations' (Law and Urry, 2004, pp. 395–396), as the chapters in this volume demonstrate. These relations have a history and change according to the specific places where they unfold. An important part of reflecting upon what social futures we want concerns recognizing emergent futures where the social matters in ways beyond the idea of what that social might be, as defined by governments, businesses, individuals and, indeed, academic disciplines. Our goal in making the social central to whatever futures we dare to think echoes Guyer's 'ethnography of the near future of the twenty-first century', one that privileges 'emergent socialities rather than ideational forms' (2007, p. 410). True, the future requires ideas, which we ought to locate in time and space. Thinking about socialities, or the making of the social, allows us to resist the many and powerful attempts to turn the future into a closed domain, emptied of values, filled with versions of the social that serve only exclusionary interests. The social, coupled with futures in the plural, provides us with a heuristic with which we can nourish future worlds that are inclusive, fair, equitable, just and resilient.

Our Handbook makes the case for the social lying at the heart, not only of the arts, humanities and social sciences, but also at the core of all of our academic endeavours. Our call is for futures to be seen, heard and performed through the social. While individual chapters illuminate important corners of knowledge on their own, together, the performative impact of a collected volume like this one extends beyond their solitary insights. By bringing arts, humanities and social scientists into conversation with biologists, environmental, climate and computer scientists, this Handbook seeks to open new pathways across, between and with multiple disciplines that have something to say about the futures we need and want. The future, our futures, is too important to reside in one field or discipline alone (Urry, 2016). Indeed, they are too important to restrict the conversation to academia alone. As our contributors show, the conversation must thrive across disciplines, but also across the social, economic, cultural and political sectors that actively shape how futures unfold. The social must be our starting point if we are to steer our planet in a direction that supports good lives for the many, everywhere.

Notes

1 On this point, readers will note that the subject pronoun 'we' is used throughout the Introduction. This mode of address does not assume a taken-for-granted, consistent and 'generalizable' experience applicable to all humans everywhere. Rather, we use it, first, in a direct manner, to refer to concrete choices we made as Editors. However, we also deploy it performatively, in order to implicate the authors (us) directly in the values, beliefs and endeavours of which we write. This decision underscores a belief that academic discourse, which often seeks to evidence objectivity with passive constructions and the avoidance of personal pronouns, nonetheless always stems from the values held by the authors. Our choice here is to speak as part of those communities seeking to forge social futures, not separate from them.
2 This was funded in part by a small AHRC grant towards Lancaster University's contribution to the Utopia Fair in Somerset House, London, 24-26 June 2016, entitled 'Mobile Utopias 1851-2051'. See López Galviz et al., 2020.
3 As expressed by, among others, Abraham Maslow (1966) and the well-known expression: 'If all you have is a hammer everything looks like a nail'. One recent iteration occurs in the film *Arrival* (2016) when the main character Louise, a linguist, tries to explain to her military colleagues the meaning of 'tool' as drawn by the alien heptapods.
4 One variant of this is the theory of 'eight thresholds' and the extent to which macro-historical models, as articulated by advocates of Big History, can help inform global foresight (Voros, 2017).

5 Critiques of forecasting date back to the emergence of futures studies, in particular critiques by key authors such as Robert Jungk, Johan Galtung, Ossip Flechtheim and Bertrand de Jouvenel, for whom forecasts and related probabilistic techniques represented an approach that was 'belligerent, imperialist, and directly involved in reproducing the military and industrial interests of the US' (Andersson, 2012, p. 1426). As Curry (this volume) remarks: 'A second approach emerged in Europe [post World War II] as a way to reconstruct societies rather than to win wars'.

References

Adam, B. (2011). 'Wendell Bell and the sociology of the future: Challenges past, present and future', *Futures*, 43(6), pp. 590–95.
Adam, B. (2021). 'Futures honed'. In Kemp, S. and Andersson, J. (eds.). *Futures*. Oxford: Oxford University Press, pp. 119–34.
Adam, B. and Groves, C. (2007). *Future matters. Action, knowledge, ethics*. Leiden and Boston, MA: Brill.
Amara, R. (1978). 'Probing the future'. In Fowles, J. (ed.). *Handbook of futures research*. Westport, CT: Greenwood Press, pp. 41–51.
Andersson, J. (2012). 'The great future debate and the struggle for the world', *The American Historical Review*, 117(5), pp. 1411–1430.
Andersson, J. (2021). 'The future boardgame: Prediction as power over time'. In Kemp, S. and Andersson, J. (eds.). *Futures*. Oxford: Oxford University Press, pp. 20–34.
Andersson, J. and Kemp, S. (2021). 'Introduction'. In Kemp, S. and Andersson, J. (eds.). *Futures*. Oxford: Oxford University Press, pp. 1–15.
Appadurai, A. (2013). *The future as cultural fact: Essays on the global condition*. London: Verso.
Augé, M. (2015). *The future*, translated by John Howe. London: Verso.
Bartolini, N. (2013). 'Rome's pasts and the creation of new urban spaces: Brecciation, matter, and the play of surfaces and depths', *Environment and Planning. D, Society and Space*, 31(6), pp. 1041–1061.
Beckert, J. (2016). *Imagined futures fictional expectations and capitalist dynamics*. Cambridge, MA and London: Harvard University Press.
Büscher, M. (2018). 'Social futures'. In Jensen, O.B., Kesselring, S. and Sheller, M. (eds.). *Mobilities and Complexities*. London: Routledge, pp. 185–196.
Büscher, M., Urry, J. and Witchger, K. (2010). 'Introduction'. In Büscher, M, Urry, J. and Witchger, K. (eds.). *Mobile methods*. London: Routledge, pp. 1–19.
Curry, A. (2012). 'The scenarios question'. In Curry, A. (ed.). *The future of futures*. Houston, Texas: The Association of Professional Futurists, pp. 11–15.
Dator, J. (2009). 'Alternative futures at the Manoa school', *Journal of Futures Studies*, 14(2), pp. 1–18.
Fry, T. (2020). *Defuturing: A new design philosophy*. London and New York: Bloomsbury Publishing.
Fuller, T. (2017). 'Anxious relationships: The unmarked futures for post-normal scenarios in anticipatory systems', *Technological Forecasting and Social Change*, 124, pp. 41–50.
Guyer, J.I. (2007). 'Prophecy and the near future: Thoughts on macroeconomic, evangelical and punctuated time', *American Ethnologist*, 34(3), pp. 409–421.
Hurlbut, J.B. (2015). 'Remembering the future: Science, law, and the legacy of Asilomar'. In Jasanoff, S. and Kim, S.-H. (eds.). *Dreamscapes of modernity: Sociotechnical imaginaries and the fabrication of power*. Chicago, IL and London: The University of Chicago Press, pp. 126–151.
Inayatullah, S. (1998). 'Causal layered analysis: Poststructuralism as method', *Futures*, 30(8), pp. 815–829.
Inayatullah, S. (2015). *What works: Case studies in the practice of foresight*. New Taipei: Tamkang University Press.
Jameson, F. (2010). 'Utopia as method, or the uses of the future'. In Gordin, M.D., Tilley, H. and Prakash, G. (eds.). *Utopia/dystopia conditions of historical possibility*. Princeton, NJ and Oxford: Princeton University Press, pp. 21–44.
Jasanoff, S. (2015). 'Future imperfect: Science, technology, and the imaginations of modernity'. In Jasanoff, S. and Kim, S.-H. (eds.). *Dreamscapes of modernity: Sociotechnical imaginaries and the fabrication of power*. Chicago, IL and London: The University of Chicago Press, pp. 1–33.
Jedlowski, P. (2017). *Memorie del futuro. Un percorso tra sociologia e studi culturali*. Rome: Carocci.
Kaika, M. (2017). '"Don't call me resilient again!": The New Urban Agenda as immunology, or, what happens when communities refuse to be vaccinated with "smart cities" and indicators', *Environment and Urbanization*, 299(1), pp. 89–102.

Law, J. and Urry, J. (2004). 'Enacting the social', *Economy and Society*, 33(3), pp. 390–410.

Lees, L., Shin, H.B. and López Morales, E. (2016). *Planetary gentrification*. Malden, MA: Polity Press.

Liveley, G., Slocombe, W. and Spiers, E. (2021). 'Futures literacy through narrative', *Futures*, 125, p. 102663, ISSN 0016-3287, https://doi.org/10.1016/j.futures.2020.102663. (https://www.sciencedirect.com/science/article/pii/S0016328720301531).

López-Galviz, C. (2019). *Cities, railways, modernities. London, Paris and the nineteenth century*. New York and London: Routledge.

López-Galviz, C., Büscher, M. and Freudendal-Pedersen, M. (2020). 'Mobilities and utopias: A critical reorientation', *Mobilities*, 15(1): 1–10.

Miller, R. (2006a). 'From trends to futures literacy. Reclaiming the future'. Centre for Strategic Education. Seminar Series Paper (No. 160). CSE Publications, Victoria.

Miller, R. (2006b). *Futures studies, scenarios, and the "possibility-space" approach*. Paris: Organization for Economic Co-Operation and Development (OECD). doi: 10.1787/9789264023642-7-en.

Miller, R. (2015). 'Learning, the future, and complexity. An essay on the emergence of futures literacy', *European Journal of Education*, 50(4), pp. 513–523.

Nussbaum, M.C. (2011). *Creating capabilities: The human development approach*. Cambridge, MA: Harvard University Press.

Poli, R. (2017). *Introduction to anticipation studies* (Vol. 1). Abingdon: Routledge.

Poli, R. (2018). 'Introducing anticipation'. In Poli, R. (ed.). *Handbook of anticipation: Theoretical and applied aspects of the use of future in decision making* (pp. 1–14). Abingdon: Routledge.

Raworth, K. (2018). *Doughnut economics: Seven ways to think like a 21st-century economist*. London: Penguin Random House.

Roy, E.A. (2019). '"One day we'll disappear": Tuvalu's sinking islands', *The Guardian*, 19 May 2019.

Sand, M. (2019). 'On "not having a future"', *Futures*, 107, pp. 98–106.

Sassen, S. (2014). *Expulsions: Brutality and complexity in the global economy*. Cambridge, MA: The Belknap Press of Harvard University Press.

Schultz, W. (1995). *Futures fluency: Explorations in leadership, vision, and creativity*. PhD Thesis. Retrieved from: https://www.researchgate.net/publication/297424.70_Futures_fluency_explorations_in_leadership_vision_and_creativity/link/54b285ac0cf28ebe92e2c265/download

Schultz, W. (1996). 'Essential visioning: Overview and comparative analysis of visioning techniques'. Retrieved from: http://www.infinitefutures.com/essays/fs11.shtml

Sen, A. (1985). 'Well-being, agency and freedom: The Dewey Lectures 1984', *The Journal of Philosophy*, 82(4), pp. 169–221.

Sheller, M. and Urry, J. (2016). 'Mobilizing the mobilities paradigm', *Applied Mobilities*, 1(1), pp. 10–25.

Simone, A.M. (2015). 'Relational infrastructures in postcolonial urban worlds'. In Graham, S. and McFarlane, C. (eds.). *Infrastructural lives urban infrastructure in context* (pp. 17–38). London and New York: Routledge.

Slaughter, R.A. (1995). *The foresight principle: Cultural recovery in the 21st century*. Westport, CT: Praeger.

Slaughter, R.A. (2013). *Futures beyond dystopia: Creating social foresight*. Abingdon: Routledge.

Smith, S. and Ashby, M. (2020). *How to future: Leading and sense-making in an age of hyperchange*. New York and London: Kogan Page.

Spiers, E. (2018). *Pop-feminist narratives: The female subject under neoliberalism in North America, Britain and Germany*. Oxford: Oxford University Press.

Steffen, W., Broadgate, W., Deutsch, L., Gaffney, O. and Ludwig, C. (2015). 'The trajectory of the Anthropocene: The Great Acceleration', *The Anthropocene Review*, 2(1), pp. 81–98.

Turner, M. (1998). *The literary mind: The origins of thought and language*. Oxford: Oxford University Press.

UN Department of Economic and Social Affairs (2020). *World social report 2020 inequality in a rapidly changing world*. New York: United Nations Publication.

UN-Habitat III (2017). *A conference of 30,000 voices*. Habitat III UN conference on housing and sustainable urban development, Quito, Ecuador, 17–20 October 2016 (United Nations).

UNHCR (2019). 'Global trends forced displacement in 2019'. Retrieved from: https://www.unhcr.org/globaltrends2019/, accessed 15 March 2021.

Urry, J. (2000). *Sociology beyond societies. Mobilities for the twenty-first century*. London and New York: Routledge.

Urry, J. (2016). *What is the future?* Cambridge: Polity.

Voros, J. (2017). 'Big history and anticipation'. In Poli, R. (ed.). *Handbook of anticipation*. Cham: Springer. Doi: 10.1007/978-3-319-31737-3_95-1.

Wolf, M. (2008). *Proust and the squid: The story and science of the reading brain*. London: Icon Books.

Woodhead, L. (2021). 'Apocalyptic, world-repair, divination: Persistent modes of future-knowing and their continuing relevance'. In Kemp, S. and Andersson, J. (eds.). *Futures*. Oxford: Oxford University Press, pp. 214–229.

Zak, P.J. (2015). 'Why inspiring stories make us react: The neuroscience of narrative', *Cerebrum: The Dana Forum on Brain Science*, 2015, p. 2. Retrieved from: https://www.ncbi.nlm.nih.gov/pmc/articles/PMC4445577/.

1
A beginning
A critical history of scenarios

Andrew Curry

Part 1

A woman is newly arrived in heaven, and St. Peter gives her the induction tour. Over here, in an outdoor cafe, Hindus and Muslims are studying chess problems. Over there, Buddhists and Confucians are vying to out-zen each other. To her left, in the woods, Protestants and Unitarians are involved in good-natured theological debate. To her right, in the endless warm sunshine, Jews and Rastafarians are playing table-tennis.

Then abruptly, the little train pulls up sharply against a vast wall. It is nine or ten metres tall, and it stretches in both directions as far as the eye can see.

'What's on the other side of the wall?', she asks.

'Oh', says St. Peter. 'That's the Catholics. They like to imagine that they're the only people here'.[1]

Introduction

The history of scenarios and scenario planning is a myopic one. As written, it often detaches itself from the wider body of futures practice and futures thinking. Further, several of the more influential accounts exclude significant bodies of *scenarios* practice, focussing narrowly on methods devised largely in North America and used mostly by the commercial sector and to a lesser extent by the military.

At the same time, scenario planning has also become a dominant practice within futures. Other futures approaches, such as visioning, have been eclipsed as the body of scenarios work and commentary has waxed. Even within the area of scenarios practice, which includes a wide range of methods, a narrow set of approaches has become prevalent. The so-called 'intuitive logics' school, which is often a shorthand for the 2×2 scenario matrix method promoted by Global Business Network (GBN) from the late 1980s onwards, has become a dominant method.[2]

In this chapter, I will sketch a social history of scenarios practice that explains how and why this happened, what has been lost in the process and the nature of the response to this scenarios monoculture. There are some relevant geographical strands. There is also a deeper

DOI: 10.4324/9780429440717-0

story, for although much writing on futures is all but oblivious to epistemology, some of the differences traced in this chapter are embedded in assumptions about our knowledge of the future that are rarely challenged. I am a practitioner, and this should be thought of as a practitioner's account, even if it is one that is informed by a broad reading of the literature.

There is a puzzle within this story. Futures remain a young practice, largely dating from the 1950s. Its methods can be traced to the Second World War and its aftermath (Bell, 2003, pp. 27–30, 60). One approach to futures practice emerged from American wartime operational planning (Seefried, 2014, pp. 2–3). The dominant strand of scenarios work seen in business and military use today can be traced back to this work. A second approach emerged in Europe as a way to reconstruct societies rather than to win wars. This strand was associated with ideas about visioning and desirable futures.

As scenarios practice emerged into the futures mainstream in the 1970s and after, this second strand – which had much stronger ideas within it about agency and the ability to change the future – all but disappeared for a generation from the literature and from practice. It started to be reclaimed by theorists and practitioners in the late 1990s and early 2000s. In writing this chapter, I am also interested in the social processes at play in this process of loss and re-emergence. Part of my purpose is to reattach a discussion of scenarios practice and theory to the wider body of foresight and futures of which it is part. For this reason, my discussion here ranges beyond the narrow scenarios literature.

What is a scenario?

It is often asserted that futures work in general, and scenarios in particular, suffers from 'methodological confusion' (for example, Bishop, Hines and Collins, 2007, p. 6; Millett, 2003, p. 16, 2011, p. 186; Wilkinson, 2009, p. 107). The claim was made by Khakee in 1991 (Spaniol and Rowland, 2018, p. 2) and has been widely repeated. To support this case, writers point to the relative youth of futures practice. They note that it has been more influenced by practitioners than by academics (Amer, 2012, p. 25; Bradfield, Derbyshire and Wright, 2016, p. 6; van der Heijden, 1996, p. 133) and that the academic base remains slight, in terms of the number of departments or institutes worldwide specializing in futures. Futures is not yet a discipline (Miller, 2012, p. 40), in the sense that when a subject becomes a discipline, 'the terms and institutions that define and limit the practice become familiar and obvious'.

It is also true that the taxonomies that have been produced of scenarios approaches convey the impression of more noise and less signal. For example, Bishop, Hines and Collins (2007) listed eight general categories of scenario technique, and 21 subcategories, in their review of the field (there are also some gaps). The taxonomy by van Notten et al. (2003) identified 14 characteristics of scenario-building components. Chermack's (2011, p. 18) incomplete list describes ten different types of methods. The range appears to reflect Bell's (2003, p. 316) argument that 'scenarios can be produced by any and all of the specific methods used by futurists'. However, these claims of 'confusion' are overstated.

Rowland and Spaniol's (2018) extensive and structured review of the literature demonstrates that there is in practice broad agreement on what constitutes a scenario. They list six characteristics of scenarios that are repeated across the literature. Scenarios (a) are future oriented; (b) are about the external environment; (c) have a narrative description; (d) are plausibly possible; (e) are a systematized set and (f) are comparatively different. While the claim of 'plausibility' is contested (Schultz, 2015b, p. 2; van Notten, 2004, p. 20), this list is broadly one that most practitioners would concur with. van Notten's (2004, p. 20) definition, based on a critical review of the literature, comes to a similar conclusion: 'Scenarios are coherent descriptions of alternative hypothetical futures that reflect different perspectives on past, present and future developments, which can serve as a basis for action'. These broadly comparable descriptions of the characteristics of scenarios also enable us better to trace their emergence as a form of dominant practice within the futures field: What problem did the scenarios approach resolve for the field?

Bodies of practice

As noted above, two divergent approaches emerged after the Second World War. The first is a set of operational techniques developed by the American policy think tank Research and Development (RAND), initially created in late 1945 to work on the future of military technology as Project RAND within the Douglas Aircraft Corporation, and to a lesser extent Stanford Research Institute, now SRI. Much of this work was funded by the US Department of Defense. This was part of a wider trend: In the US in the post-war period, 'research institutes proliferated […] on the basis that the production of new scientific knowledge could be used to create wealth, achieve national goals, improve human life and solve social problems' (Schon, 1983, p. 38). RAND's roots in military planning and analysis led it to a 'scientific' approach to futures, using techniques that drew on data and probability. RAND alumnus Herman Kahn evolved an early and distinctive scenarios practice that modelled the outcomes of nuclear war (Bell, 2003, pp. 30–32, Bradfield, 2004, p. 4). We owe the word 'scenarios' to Kahn's later work, *The Year 2000*, a term borrowed from the days of silent movies (Bradfield, 2004, pp. 4–5; Kleiner, 1996, p. 150).

The second approach emerged in the 1950s in Europe as part of the process of post-war reconstruction. In the Netherlands, Fred Polak argued in *The Image of the Future* (1973), published in Dutch in 1955, that our shared cultural images of the future shape our view of it and in turn our ability to shape it. In France, Gaston Berger set up in 1957 the Centre International de la Prospective – likely the world's first futures research centre – with a similar ambition. As he wrote, 'To turn toward the future, instead of looking at the past… is to pass from "seeing" to "doing"' (Berger, cited in Cornish, 1977, p. 81). The future is a basis for action that should be informed by possible and desirable futures (Godet, 2008, pp. 12–14). His French contemporary Bertrand de Jouvenel, an influential figure in the development of futures concepts, set up the consultancy Futuribles with a similar ambition. The social base of this work was more associated with public organizations and civil society. The use of images of the future was adopted by visioning practitioners in the peace movement and by community activists. The peace campaigner Elise Boulding, for example, taught herself Dutch to produce an English-language version of Polak's book.

Much of the American work in the 1950s and beyond concerned itself with increasingly sophisticated forms of trends analysis. Kahn's early work was based in game theory. It was largely positivist in tone, perhaps in keeping with American traditions in academic disciplines such as economics and sociology. In contrast, the work of Polak, Berger and de Jouvenel would be recognized today as being associated with 'desired' or 'preferred' futures. To (over)simplify, if the American approach tended to be driven by forecast models, game theory and probabilistic approaches, the European approach was framed by images and narratives.

In practice, it took time for conceptual ideas about different types of futures to emerge in the futures field. Roy Amara's famous distinction between probable, possible and preferable futures, which covers the range of futures described here, was not published until 1981 (Masini, 2000, p. 492). Bertrand de Jouvenel (1967) used the French term '*futuribles*' in the 1960s to frame the idea of multiple possible futures, although French innovation in the field has received less attention in the literature (Bradfield, 2004, p. 9). John McHale writes of 'necessary, allowable and ultimately desirable' futures in an essay published after the Mankind 2000 conference in Oslo in 1967 (McHale, 1969, p. 256). Indeed, in her introduction to the futures field, Gidley (2017, pp. 54–56) suggests – partly following the work of Seefried – that the notion of 'plural futures' first gained common currency among futures researchers as a result of Mankind 2000[3]: 'Mankind 2000 and subsequent events that spun from it marked the post-positivist turn in future studies: The how, when and why of "the future" became "a multitude of futures"' (p. 56).

Mankind 2000

Mankind 2000 was convened by Johan Galtung and Robert Jungk in a spirit of critical futures.[4] The two men consistently attempted to problematize futures around questions of power and authority. 'Future research was in the early autumn of 1967 no longer brand new', wrote Jungk (1969, pp. 9–10) in the preface to the published collection of papers. 'It had grown, especially in the United States, from its first haphazard beginnings in 1944 to a large "think industry" [...]. But almost all this work had so far been financed mainly directly or indirectly by the armament effort'.

In a short postscript co-written with Johan Galtung (1969, p. 368), they returned to the theme:

> There is indeed—and we are very much aware of it—the danger that a better, a more complex and more informed grasp of things to come might become the monopoly of power groups served by experts in the new branch of 'futurism'. Such a dangerous development is already well under way. At least four-fifths of the work done in the field has been ordered and financed either by governmental departments, military establishments, or large corporations.

Mankind 2000 was the first significant international gathering in the nascent field and had the effect of making futures visible to a range of new audiences. Their warnings went largely unheard.

The late 1960s and early 1970s instead saw corporations decide that scenario planning might be the solution to an emerging crisis in planning processes, notably General Electric (GE) and Shell (Bradfield et al., 2005, p. 800; Jefferson, 2012, p. 187; Millett, 2011, pp. 187–188). There is little discussion in the literature of *why* companies might have experienced a planning crisis at this time, and it is usually presented as a social fact (Bradfield, 2004, pp. 5–6; Kleiner, 1996, p. 144). However, it seems reasonable to attribute it to signs of the coming end of the long post-war boom in 1973 (Levinson, 2016, p. 6) and increasing awareness of the dimensions of an impending environmental crisis (Meadows et al., 1972; The Ecologist, 1972). Ansoff, writing at the end of the 1960s, notes 'a marked acceleration in the rate of change in the environment of the firm and particularly in its product-process technology' (1969, p. 7). Strategic planning had 'not proven its ability to inform organization leaders about massive political, environmental, economic and/or societal changes' (Chermack, Lyhman and Runa, 2001, p. 7).

Conceptually, ideas about the contextual environment of organizations (Emery and Trist, 1965), open systems and the notion of 'wicked problems' (Lang and Allen, 2010, pp. 49–50) started to inflect management thinking. Rosenzweig also notes that steady growth is harder when the business environment is unstable (2008, pp. 147–148). There is almost no public record of GE's scenarios programme, beyond the fact of it.[5] Ian Wilson, who ran it, moved to SRI. In sharp contrast, Shell's scenario programme is both over-documented in the literature and not properly understood (Jefferson, 2012), as discussed below.

By the early 1970s, the notion of possible futures or 'alternate futures' made conceptual sense, but they were hard to create in practice. Herman Kahn's methods were so personally identified with him that they are characterized as 'genius forecasting' (Bishop, Hines and Collins, 2007, p. 11). The futurist Joseph Coates (1996) notes, 'There are no Kahnian disciples, there is no Kahnian school, there is no conceptual methodological framework he developed that others follow through with'.

At Shell, in a sympathetic and well-funded environment, it took Ted Newlands and Pierre Wack several attempts to develop a scenarios approach that produced credible results (Kleiner 1996, pp. 158–159, 161), even though Wack had visited the United States to attend events at Kahn's Hudson Institute (Williams, 2016, p. 524). Fortunately for them, Shell had a patient business culture. The method that did emerge owed much to Shell's existing corporate culture, and something to Wack's gift for storytelling, a characteristic that he shared with Kahn.

The next section of this paper will contextualize these methods. For the moment, it is worth noting four elements of Shell's work that led to its wider influence in the scenarios field. The first is that they worked; Shell came out of the 1973 oil crisis more effectively than its competitors, at least partly because of actions taken as a result of the scenarios work (Kleiner, 1996, p. 173; van der Heijden, 1996, p. 128). Second, they operated at scale and over time, creating a considerable body of practice and theory about the Shell approach (Wilkinson and Kupers, 2013). Third, this practice and the principles that informed it were published (Jaworski, 1998; Kahane, 2004; Schwartz, 1996; van der Heijden, 1996; Wack, 1985a, 1985b). The fourth is that many of those who worked on Shell's scenarios moved on to other roles as futurists in and around the corporate sector and elsewhere.

One of these was Peter Schwartz, Pierre Wack's successor in the Shell scenarios group. In 1987, he returned to the United States to set up a futures consultancy, GBN, with, among others, his Shell scenarios colleague Napier Collyns. Schwartz had worked at SRI before joining Shell, and a former SRI colleague, Jay Ogilvy, also came to the new business.

GBN was perfectly positioned for the 1990s, based in San Francisco just as Silicon Valley took off, with a close relationship with the decade's hottest magazine, *Wired*, and associates that included the counter-culturalist Stewart Brand and the electronic musician Brian Eno. From this base, Schwartz published the first mainstream book on scenarios, *The Art of the Long View* ([1991]/1996). At Ogilvy's suggestion, he included in an appendix (Schwartz, 1996, pp. 241–246) the process for developing 2×2 'double uncertainty' matrices, based on a method used by SRI (Curry, 2012). For the first time, a scenarios method was made accessible and, apparently, simple (List, 2007, p. 78).[6]

GBN went from strength to strength. The consultancy earned its own section in Fred Turner's (2006, pp. 181–194) book on the cultural roots of Silicon Valley. It blended the techno-cultural and the counter-cultural. Wack's practice at Shell had combined data, models and his learnings from Gurdjieff and from Indian and Japanese mystics. SRI, once the Stanford Research Institute, had been 'the first university-based research institute to offer consulting services for business, the military and scientific organizations' (Turner, 2006, p. 188) but was also plugged into the Bay Area's alternative culture. But, while some of the excitement about GBN was about its connections to the rapidly emerging digital culture, that was not where the money was.

The founders quickly extended GBN's network to include the former leaders of the cold war military-industrial complex. Over the next ten years, GBN listed as clients both multinational corporations, such as Xerox, IBM, BellSouth, AT&T, Arco and Texaco and also the Joint Chief of Staff and the Defense Department (Turner, 2006, p. 188).

It was as if Mankind 2000 had never happened.

Part 2

Typologies

The arguments around scenarios *methods* that populate the literature can descend into the narcissism of tiny differences. However, embedded in some of the distinctions between *typologies* are real epistemological differences – and real differences in practice – that are sometimes concealed by the overdone focus on methods.

Slaughter's (2002) critique of the different types of approaches in the field is a useful starting point. Slaughter used the four layers of Causal Layered Analysis (CLA) – the litany layer; the problem or system layer; and the worldview and metaphor layers – in a process he called 'structural mapping'. This was a strategy to get beyond the dominant empirical tradition within futures. CLA, which will be referenced later in this paper, was designed by Sohail Inayatullah to open up 'the present and the past to create alternative futures' (2004, p. 2).

Slaughter's structural mapping identified three approaches to futures: 'Pop futurism', which corresponds to the litany layer of CLA; 'problem-oriented futures', which correspond to the systems layer; and 'critical and epistemological futures studies', which correspond to the worldview and metaphor layers.

For our present purposes, we can follow Slaughter in discounting 'pop futures'. This is the realm of the megatrend and the conference keynote speaker and 'tends to be acultural and ahistorical' (p. 496). Problem-oriented futures work represents, as Slaughter observes, 'the central area of mainstream futures activity'. There are, he argues, 'strong assumptions of continuity in existing social institutions and the rules', while a 'great deal of emphasis is paid to the tools of rational analysis' (p. 498).

In terms of the histories represented in this chapter, problem-oriented futures represent the world of RAND, the Hudson Institute, SRI, Shell and GBN and a slew of methods associated with them. These include intuitive logics, critical uncertainties, FAR/morphological scenarios[7] and methods such as probabilistic trends analysis and cross-impact analysis.

Slaughter's third group references critical and epistemological futures work, which draws on 'the tools of post-modern analysis and "peel away" the layers of received opinion and discern the foundations of social life'. Through these tools and processes, 'many of the options for renewal and recovery' are revealed (pp. 503–504). We can guess where his sympathies lie.

This more radical view of the purpose of futures is seen in the tradition that connects Polak to Jungk and Galtung and the work of Elise Boulding. This dissenting strand never went away, but perhaps disappeared from mainstream view in the 1980s and 1990s. In these decades, it is associated with the work on values and on theories of social change seen in the Hawai'i school under the leadership of James Dator (from 1971 to 2014) and in methods such as alternative futures (Bezold, 2009; Dator, 2009), CLA (Inayatullah, 2004), images of the future, the Manoa method (Schultz, 2015), Schultz's (1995) visioning methods, integral futures (Slaughter, 1998) and, more recently, post-normal futures (Sardar, 2017; see also 'Prospection' in this volume). Anticipation studies (Poli, 2010, 2011) draws on some of the philosophical roots of futures (represented by Gaston Berger, Ossip Flechtheim and others) to construct a different relationship between 'present' and 'future'.

There are three observations worth making here. The first is the role of Hawai'i in providing a centre for some of this thinking (Schultz and Inayatullah are Hawai'i alumni). The second is that much of this innovation took place in the Pacific region, well removed from the dominant North American or European centres of practice. The third is the role of the World Futures Studies Federation [WFSF] in protecting and developing these views of the future, for the WFSF emerged from discussions initiated by Jungk, Galtung and others at Mankind 2000 (Gidley, 2017, p. 56; Schultz, 2012, p. 5).

Indeed, Elenora Masini, who succeeded Dator as WFSF president, characterized different futures approaches as having different ontological approaches, in a way that prefigures Slaughter's later formulation. Empirical futures, embedded in the philosophical tradition of John Locke, are associated with probable futures and can be summarized as 'something *is* changing'. Visionary and utopian futures, connected to the critical and post-modern tradition and associated with preferred futures, can be summarized as 'something *must* be changed'. In a third layer, possible and probable futures mesh with desirable futures to create agency: 'Something *can* be changed' (Gidley, 2017, pp. 75–76, emphasis in original; Masini, 1993, pp. 45–46).

Fuller and Loogma (2009) observe the role of social constructionist ideas in much of this recent critical futures work, notably that of Slaughter and Inayatullah, and also in the work of Masini.[8] Foresight

> is a social process and its purpose is to construct meaning. [...] The constructivist epistemology and associated theories of knowledge and action are important for foresight. Foresight is intended as a precursor to action and is concerned with generating knowledge about the anticipated consequences of different actions, including historical actions.
> *(Fuller and Loogma, 2009, p. 73)*

These distinctions go to the heart of the futures history represented here, for they allow us to connect methodological differences in futures work with conceptual issues. While the fit is not exact, there is a sufficient correspondence.

One of the recurring distinctions in the literature on practice is whether scenarios have been developed through inductive or deductive means.[9] This distinction is at the heart of the competing perspectives on futures that run through its history. The deductive method effectively relies on forward inference and therefore on notions of causality from the present to the futures; the inductive method deploys backward inferences or diagnostic reasoning (Bradfield, 2007, pp. 270–271).

In one of the few published accounts of a corporate scenarios process based on an inductive scenarios process, Farrington, Henson and Crews (2012, p. 30) explain the difference in this way:

> Inductive scenarios are generated from the bottom up and use systems thinking to explore different ways many trends will interact to create alternative futures. This is in contrast to the more generally used deductive scenarios, which are top down in nature. Deductive scenarios begin with the top two or three critical uncertainties and then fill in different scenarios based on how those uncertainties may unfold. They are more appropriate for corporate strategy environments where the chief goal is to delimit the risk space and aid executive decision making.

As practice, '[t]he inductive method is less structured and relies largely on the patience of a group to continue its discussions until a consensus is reached', write Schwarz and Ogilvy

(1998, pp. 61–62). 'In contrast, the deductive approach uses simple techniques of prioritization to construct a 2×2 scenarios matrix of critical uncertainties'.[10] Methods such as probabilistic trend analysis and cross-impact analysis are also deductive methods.

Research by Jungermann (Bradfield, 2007, p. 270) demonstrated that deductive approaches resulted 'in very different scenarios than would have been generated by anticipatory or inductive developmental models that relay on backward inferences and diagnostic effectuality'. People make causal inferences with a greater degree of confidence than they bring to diagnostic inferences and similarly accord more weight to causal judgements than diagnostic ones. (This is one of the issues that is disputed in discussions over the value of 'plausibility' as a criterion for scenarios.)

In exploratory research with shared data from a prior scenarios project, Curry and Schultz (2009, p. 53) used a range of different methods – inductive and deductive – to build sets of scenarios and found widely varying results.

> The scenario stories generated by different methods were very different. In the process we also learned that different methods also produce substantively different types of futures conversations, in terms of the range and type of discussion, and the energy level in the room.

Yet one finds few signs of these distinctions in the scenarios literature. It is dominated by the deductive approach of the 'intuitive logics' school to the point where the neophyte futures researcher conducting a literature review can simply miss other methods. There are striking examples. In their otherwise excellent collection of futures research methods, Glenn and Gordon (2009) offer an introductory paper on scenarios that lists deductive methods in their review of approaches and then focusses on the 2×2 as an example of practice. Chermack (2011) proposes both a theory of practice and an organizational guide on the basis of reviewing a narrow range of methods largely from the intuitive logics school and lacks a critical review of why he has chosen these methods.[11]

Along the way, in this conflation of a practice driven by corporate futures and scenarios theory, some important assumptions have become reified into recommended or best practice. For reasons of space, three examples will suffice here. The first is the notion that the scenarios should describe a set of 'plausible' future worlds, but that the purpose of so doing is to allow the organization to *respond* better to change when it happens. This was popularized by Shell practitioners, although it has its origins earlier. The Shell approach, historically, made a clear distinction between the contextual environment, beyond the boundaries of the business and the transactional environment (van der Heijden, 1996, pp. 155, 108).[12]

Careful reading of accounts of Shell's practice suggests that this was a strategy to gain acceptance within the business for the use of scenarios. But, nonetheless, it became reified along the way. Even Shell insiders eventually concluded that the distinction could not be defended. As Adam Kahane (2004, p. 17) noted, 'Shell […] was in general a beneficiary of the way the world's rules had been written, and actively lobbied for its specific interests'.

The second element, seen repeatedly in descriptions of practice by GBN and SRI practitioners, is that scenarios need to start with a 'decision focus' (Schwartz, 1996, p. 241; Wilson, 1998, pp. 84–85) or a 'focal issue' (Chermack, 2011, p. 19). Mandel and Wilson say of the scenarios process 'that its starting point […] is not the macroenvironment, but rather clarification of the strategic decision the scenarios aim to address and of key decision factors' (Mandel and Wilson, 1993, p. 10). This emphasis derives from Kahn (Rowland and Spaniol,

2017, p. 7), who saw scenario development as being focussed on identifying and charting forthcoming decisions.

The third area: Deductive scenarios start from a surfacing of drivers of change, and, in this process, structural or macro-environmental drivers of change are privileged. In their description of SRI's methodology, Mandel and Wilson (1993, p. 10) are again instructive.

> Analysis of these environmental forces usually focusses on two categories—those at the industry and market (micro) level that most directly affect the key decision factors, and those at the broad social, economic, political and technological (macro) level that set the overall (often global) context for the business environment.

Shell's practice was often blind to the role of values as a source of significant social change.[13] Yet values can and do shift on a generational timescale, sometimes from apparently unpromising beginnings (Solnit, 2005, pp. 33–46). These practices are not ever-present in deductive scenario methods, but they remain common.

Incremental change

These dominant characteristics of deductive scenarios practice affect the way such scenarios work portrays and projects the future. Bruun, Hukkinen and Ekland (2001) argue, 'The problem with the culture of conventional scenario-making is that its analysis of the future is restricted—it can only register the events or trends that its approach allows it to see'. A European Environment Agency study (Greeuw et al., 2000, p. 8) concurred: 'Many scenarios have a "business as usual" character, assuming that current conditions will continue to exist for decades'. '[T]he "axes of uncertainty" method', says Schultz (2009, p. 14), 'can too easily create scenarios that are minor variants of "business as usual", rather than explorations of potentially transformative or disruptive future change driven by emerging paradigms and challenging worldviews'. Slaughter (1998, p. 529), similarly, observes that:

> current ideologies such as: Economic growth, globalization, the pre-eminence accorded to science and technology, and 'man's conquest of nature'—were insufficiently problematized. […] In this view, the future is less open than it might be because it is seen merely as an extension of the present.

Wright (2004b, p. 7) connects these criticisms more broadly to corporate strategy-making processes:

> Deductive strategy making at the corporate centre is largely a mechanistic activity that is industry focused with an emphasis on current knowledge structures. […] It is this context that most scenario planning activities have attempted to influence through establishing 'fit' with corporate perspectives of strategy making.

The discourse is very different among those discussing or recommending the intuitive logics scenarios methods, notably the double uncertainty matrix. Bishop, Hines and Collins (2007, p. 20) commend the 2×2 for having 'the right mix of technical sophistication and ease of use for a professional audience', while cautioning that it is 'almost impossible to fully characterize the uncertainties of the future with just two dimensions'. Schoemaker (1995, p. 27) says the use of scenarios 'is most beneficial' when used 'in corporate-wide strategic planning and vision-building'. Millett (2011, p. 190) notes (blurring the lines between Shell, GBN and SRI practice) that 'The intuitive scenarios approach has many attractive features', among them being that it is 'non-proprietary', is 'highly adaptable', 'can be applied to virtually any topic' and so on. It is clear that there are two different conversations going on here.

Part 3

Embodied futures

In this chapter, so far, I have characterized scenarios and foresight – taking a broad view – as being informed by two competing perspectives. On the one hand, there is a 'positivist' school, which also tends to gravitate towards deductive methods. On the other, a 'critical' futures school tends to gravitate towards inductive methods. These two schools, and their different perspectives, also have different views on the role of agency in futures work.

The 'positivist' approach has its roots in what Donald Schon (1983, pp. 31–33) calls 'Technical Rationality', with its origins in the rise of scientific and technological ideas about society in the nineteenth century (seen, for example, in the thinking of Auguste Comte). Schon argues that Technical Rationality is the expression in practice of positivist philosophy. The second, 'critical', approach might also be called 'relativist', or, perhaps, following Urry (2003, pp. 122–123), 'relational'.[14] It emerged from the intellectual world that opened up in the wake of Einstein's Theory of Relativity. Its roots are in general systems theory, cybernetics and notions of autopoiesis.[15] It sees the world as being characterized by emergence, feedback and non-linearity, which are characteristics of complexity. It is understood through processes of social construction.

These two approaches are structurally different ways of thinking about the world. From a futures perspective, one way to understand this difference is to look at the underlying view of the future embodied within each. Adam and Groves (2007a) offer a way to do this. In *Future Matters*, they characterize two different views of time, which broadly map onto the competing accounts that have been at play in this history of both futures studies and scenarios. In the first version, 'The future is represented as an empty space into which we move unhindered' (p. 57). As a result, it is understood 'as a territory belonging essentially to no-one and hence one that is open to seizure by anyone in the present' (p. 122). This can be connected to a 'fan' model of time, which List (2004, p. 24) says is adopted implicitly by most scenario planning approaches. While assuming multiple possible futures, they also presume a single shared past and present. In turn, this relates to the critique by Bruun et al. (2001, pp. 1, 10), who describe the 'methodological limits of scenarios construction' as a form of 'epistemic closure'. They suggest that this epistemic closure is paralleled by normative closure. However, they continue, this normative aspect remains unidentified because the scenarios that are generated are 'rarely' subjected to critical scrutiny.

The second version (Adam and Groves, 2007a, p. 123) draws on the work of Heidegger and argues that humans understand the past and present by projecting themselves into their potential futures: 'To be human is to be ceaselessly becoming'. The implications are that the future is not 'out there' but 'in us'. Adam and Groves argue (pp. 126–127),

> Our past and present are therefore both products of former futures, and processes of still-latent ones. [...] No-one can ever be outside of the active interweaving of the past, present and future of a collectivity within which the significance of the world is experienced.[16]

In a similar vein, Poli (2011) develops the thinking of Wendell Bell about 'dispositions', or 'situations that may become active if properly activated'. They are

> those features of reality embedded in it beneath its surface. Latents are real forces and structures that work below the threshold of visibility... facts with an anchor in the future; they are facts that can happen if the relevant circumstances are triggered.
>
> *(Poli, 2011, pp. 68, 70)*

There are obvious contrasts here between the models of futures that are implied by these two approaches. This is true both at the level of analysis – Poli specifically references Slaughter's integral futures model and Inayatullah's CLA – and also at the level of expectations. Specifically, dispositions construct a different relation between futures work and agency.

The lens of practice

In the literature, these two schools barely interact. Instead, they tend to be treated as separate discourses, and there are few contributions that seek to integrate them. One exception is a valuable but neglected contribution by Hardin Tibbs (1999). In the context of a broader analysis, Tibbs proposes a layered model of the future as a strategic landscape (see Figure 1.1). 'The Star' represents our enduring role or purpose; 'The Mountain' is a goal that we hope – and plan – to achieve; 'The Chessboard' represents issues, challenges and implementation; and 'The Self' represents our knowledge, awareness, abilities and values as an individual or an organization.[17] The value of this approach is that it allows us to look at futures practice in the context of organizational purpose and practice.

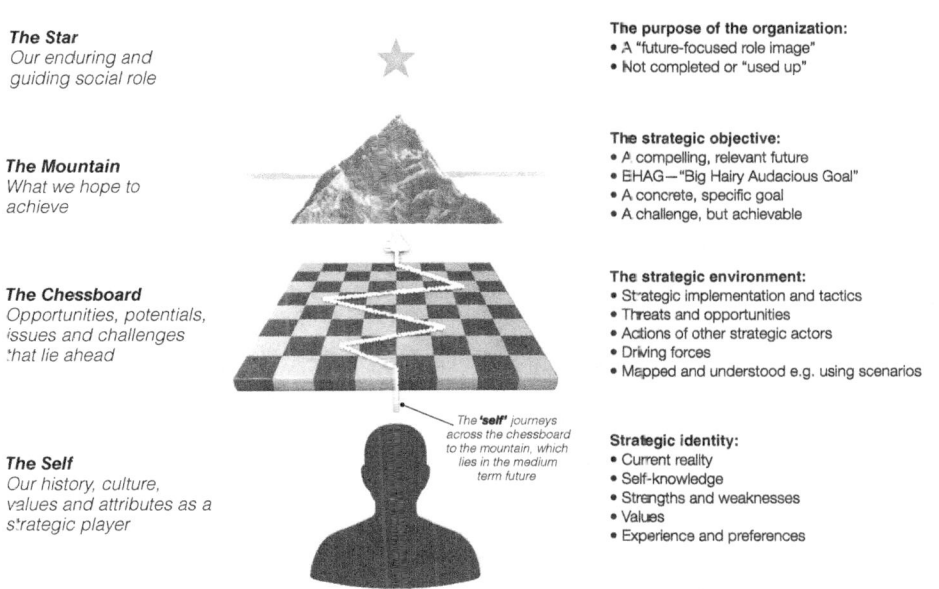

Figure 1.1 Making the future visible
Source: Hardin Tibbs (2021). With thanks to Hardin Tibbs.

Within this schematic, strategic planning and scenarios work sit on The Chessboard, which Tibbs connects to the work of management academics such as Porter, Hamel and Prahalad, and 'Peter Schwartz's scenario planning' (p. 4). They are building blocks on the way to identifying our goals and our visions. Broader perspectives, he suggests, are required to build a perspective of the future that includes both 'aspiration and anticipation'.

If this is indeed the role of scenario planning, one can argue that the conventional criticisms of scenario planning have less force, given the relatively shorter timescales for which it is typically deployed. If a set of scenarios is intended to address, say, a seven- to ten-year timeframe, across a couple of innovation cycles, epistemic and narrative closure may be a feature, not a bug.

Revisiting social construction

Looking at practice within organizations also helps us to understand the nature of the work actually done by them to develop scenarios. It appears, in short, that there is a gap between the discourse about scenario planning and the practices that are deployed to develop scenarios and to use them. The material production of scenarios in organizational settings, even in the driest accounts, includes workshops in which organizational members participate, sometimes with stakeholders (Chermack, 2011; Ringland, 2006; van der Heijden, 1996). Schoemaker (1995) references the role of organizational participants throughout his account of the scenarios process. Millett (2011, p. 191) adds that the intuitive logics method 'places a heavy emphasis on the intuitive qualities of the participants'.

In a pioneering paper, Alex Wright (2004a) used a social constructionist lens to read the accounts of Shell's scenarios practice by Schoemaker (1995) and van der Heijden (1996): 'The scenarios content does not exist independently of the scenario team to be explored, but is created through its collective acts, as such the scenario content is a construction'. Pierre Wack's (1985b, p. 140) language about influencing the 'microcosms' of managers, which in turn 'leads them to change and reorganize their inner models of reality', is, effectively, a social constructionist model of scenario building. It is widely repeated in accounts of Shell's practice (see, for example, de Geus, 1997, p. 59; Kleiner, 1996, pp. 178–179; van der Heijden, 1996, pp. 116–118). Similarly, in their insiders' account of the Shell scenarios history, Wilkinson and Kupers (2013) say, 'Corporations, like human beings, act on the basis of an agreed-upon reality—which is, in essence, a story'.

Social construction, in other words, does happen in business-based scenario and decision processes. If this element of social construction is not usually foregrounded in books and articles that are designed to introduce scenarios to a business audience, this can be understood as a rhetorical strategy designed to align scenarios with the *discourse* of strategy-making, rather than its practice. Li (2014) concludes that social construction also functions at a broader rhetorical level within organizations. Compressing his argument somewhat, 'scenarios can be understood as narratives composed to reflect different power configurations and claims that persuade and legitimate on behalf of particular, competing accounts of reality' (p. 78). Beckert's (2013) work on the relationship between business strategy and 'fictional expectations' takes this one step further. Fictions, he says, 'provide orientation in decision-making'. These 'do not have to be true but must be convincing'.

At the same time, the scenario planning approach is in competition within the organization with other methods of analysis and interpretation, drawn from the wider repertoire of management and strategic practice. On this reading, accounts in the scenarios literature that emphasize more 'scientific' and instrumental aspects of practice are a function of this competition with 'rival, more positivist and quantitatively driven organizational processes' (Li, 2014, p. 85).

Power and purpose

So let us assume that mainstream scenario planning processes draw on forms of constructionism that suggest, in practice, that they are more relativist and more concerned with agency than conventional discourse suggests. Even allowing for this, there is still a gap here between the competing 'positivist' and 'critical' perspectives. This gap is about questions of power relations and purpose. This challenge is made explicitly by Inayatullah (2004, p. 10) in his development of CLA.

> The goal of critical research is thus to disturb present power relations [...]. For an actor who is deriving intellectual, financial or epistemic benefits from the current system a method such as CLA will be uncomfortable, since it reveals his or her interests, including challenging the position that he or she is interest free!

If scenarios do – at a macro level – convey 'an organization's view of the future' (Li, 2014, p. 87), there is a question about how much controversy an organization can bear, or its willingness to reflect self-critically on the nature of the systems it enacts. For all his skills as a scenarios practitioner, and his belief that scenarios should lead to 'reperceiving' (Wack, 1985b) for example, all of Pierre Wack's work was done for extractive industries ('Scenarios 2018', 2018).

Nor does controversy lead necessarily to better social outcomes, or more sustainable ones. Shell broke with its own assumptions in 2005 when it publicly espoused its 'Blueprints' scenario over 'Scramble' (Shell, 2008).[18] But Shell's *behaviour* was far more informed by 'Scramble'. By 2008, it had disposed of most of its investments in renewables and bid heavily for drilling licences in Alaska. Funk observes that Shell's multiple futures allowed it both to imagine global warming and to take advantage of it as a potential market opportunity (Williams, 2016, p. 537).

Such pressures become more intense in turbulent business environments. The combination of the long-run decline in economic growth rates, the business costs of global warming and a financialized investment sector, taken together, produces a toxic cocktail in which short-run returns to shareholders are just as likely to be prioritized as long-run benefits or the creation of shared value (Porter and Kramer, 2011).

Reflections

One conventional way to conclude a piece on the history of scenarios work can be summarized as 'one last push' – a set of 'if only' statements that review a familiar set of gaps and suggest that, if only they were filled, scenarios practice might be able to move on from its current state: If only they were better theorized; if only the discourse on scenarios were less dominated by practitioners; if only there were less methodological fragmentation; if only there were more science and less art; if only there were better proof of effectiveness and if only scenarios work engaged more fully with critical futures perspectives. This hypothesis, in short, positions the scenarios problem as being that not enough work has yet been done at the level of theory and practice. And, if only, what then? Scenarios practice might emerge from the confines of government and business practice and become more widely used.

And yet: It is striking that the intellectual energy in the futures sector has shifted away from scenarios in the last 20 years. In the 1990s, all of the innovation, even excitement, in the world of futures practice and studies was around scenarios. Schwartz ([1991]1996) and van der Heijden (1996) both published their books; Kleiner's *The Age of Heretics* (1996) located the development of Shell's scenarios practice in a counter-cultural history of management.

But since the turn of the century, this has not been true. Successive innovations – with the partial exception of CLA – have barely touched on the scenarios method, from anticipation studies (Poli, 2017) to Three Horizons (Sharpe, 2013) to post-normal futures (Sardar, 2017), to design and experiential futures (Candy and Potter, 2019). One of the largest practice-based projects, Seeds of Hope, combined visioning with weak signals and three horizons to create preferred futures (Pereira et al., 2018). It was funded by SIDA, the Swedish International Development Agency.

In contrast, recent work in scenarios practice has largely involved tidying up the earlier work. A series of papers by Rowland and Spaniol (2015, 2017; Spaniol and Rowland, 2017, 2018) capably tied various loose ends in the literature. The Shell approach has been codified as the Oxford scenario planning approach, largely for corporate clients, by Shell alumni and others at the University of Oxford (Ramírez et al., 2016). It has also been positioned more clearly as a response to 'turbulent environments' (Ramirez, Selsky and van der Heijden, 2010). But a second, rather different, hypothesis about scenario planning also emerges through re-reading the literature and the history. This hypothesis is that scenario planning emerged in the business community when it did, in the early 1970s, and in the form that it did, as the *minimal possible response* to disrupted business conditions. In this version, scenario planning is not an alternative to the business and strategic planning processes that became less fit for purpose at that time. Instead, it is a modification to them that allowed the assumptions and models of the world that informed the processes of strategic planning to continue.

One of the most important assumptions was about rationality. 'In our day', wrote the McKinsey strategist Kenichi Ohmae in the early 1980s, 'the culture of the large corporation exalts logic and rationality. […] It is not unreasonable to say that many large US corporations are run like the Soviet economy' (Ohmae, 1983, p. 3). Corporations are the late-twentieth-century expressions of Technical Rationality. In this world, says Ohmae, 'Analysts rather than innovators tend to get ahead' (p. 3). A basic principle of systems 'is *the preservation of the character of the system*' (Katz and Kahn, [1966]/1969, p. 97, emphasis in original). In behavioural terms, 'systems will attempt to cope with external forces by ingesting them or acquiring control over them' (p. 98). 'Social systems', says Schon (1973, p. 31), 'are self-reinforcing systems which strive to remain in something like equilibrium'. As a result, organizations seek to maintain themselves as a system (Vickers, [1965]/1995).

Schon (1973, pp. 46–47) concluded that this led organizations to behave in a way that he called 'dynamic conservatism'. There are complex organizational strategies at play here, but their purpose is to maintain the social structure of the organization in the face of external change. 'When processes embodying threat cannot be repelled, ignored, contained or transformed, social systems tend to respond by change—but by the *least change* capable of meeting or neutralizing the intrusive process' (emphasis in original).

In strategic terms, then, the approach has moved from a 'planning' model, combining a rationalist view of internal processes and a perspective that the external world is controllable (Mintzberg, Ahlstrand and Lampel, 1998, pp. 49–66), to an 'environmental' strategy approach, where the internal processes are still rationalist but the external perspective is of an 'unpredictable' and 'confusing' world (pp. 288–291).

On this account, scenario planning is still a useful tool when applied intelligently in the right settings. These settings, however, represent a limited range of futures practice. The reason that this range has come to dominate the literature so comprehensively is because these settings are also those which are hegemonic – in corporations, governments and defence.

It also follows that expecting conventional scenarios practice – and notably, the intuitive logics school – to evolve beyond its current range, or to address issues of power or meaning, is a category error. It can do this, in the hands of capable practitioners, but usually only by applying other futures techniques designed to open up such questions.

Scenario planning, in this view, becomes something that works precisely because it is embedded in a rationalist corporate culture. This is a conclusion that Jimenez (2010) reaches, perhaps reluctantly, at the end of an article comparing Future Search conferences with scenario planning. '[S]cenario building—having been used primarily in the context of large corporations, government departments and the military, where hierarchies are dominant—may have evolved to suit this type of organization best' (p. 44). It is hard not to conclude, as environmental conditions become increasingly turbulent, social values become more informal and organizations continue to experiment with being less hierarchical, that scenario planning will be displaced by more critical futures techniques.

Thanks to Sahar Hadidimoud for editorial comments.

Notes

1 Versions of this joke were told by the Irish Catholic comedian Dave Allen. See also Sloterdijk (2016, p. 213).
2 The 2×2 scenarios method identifies two critical uncertainties from the system under scrutiny through researching drivers of change and their relationships. It then uses these as axes to construct four distinctive scenarios. See Curry and Schultz (2009, pp. 42–44).
3 The idea of multiple futures also appears during the 1960s in the cybernetic analysis of Stafford Beer and the work of Buckminster Fuller (J.R. Williams, 2016, p. 497, pp. 506–507).
4 The idea for the Mankind 2000 conference was first conceived by Robert Jungk and James Wellesley-Wesley in London in 1964 at the first conference of the Confederation for Disarmament and Peace (Andersson, 2012, p. 1422).
5 Millett (2011, pp. 187–188) has a brief comparison of similarities and differences between the approaches used by Shell and GE. The similarities are greater than the differences.
6 The scenarios literature repeatedly, and incorrectly, conflates GBN's 2×2 double uncertainty method and the Shell scenarios approach (see Bishop, Hines and Collins, 2005, p. 5; Chermack, 2011, p. 19; Fahey and Randall, p. 17; Millett, 2011, pp. 189–190). This is a misreading. As Wilkinson and Kupers (2013) say,

> Deductive methods for generating scenarios—for example, a 2×2 matrix with axes for public/private and more expensive/less expensive—were never core to the Shell practice, although they are often identified with it because Peter Schwartz, who ran the scenario team in the early 1980s, subsequently promoted their use at the strategy consulting group Global Business Network.

Thomas Chermack told a conference in 2018 ('Scenarios 2018', Warwick Business School) that in reading the papers in the Pierre Wack archive, he found only two 2×2 diagrams, one of which was not a scenarios diagram.
7 FAR, or 'field anomaly relaxation' is a morphologically based scenarios method that identifies the 'fields' of interaction in a given system and then develops potential outcomes for each field. The scenarios are developed by combining different outcomes. The method is most associated, at least in English-language practice, with Geoff Coyle (2004, pp. 62–81) and Tom Ritchey.
8 The concept of the social construction of reality was developed by the sociologists Berger and Luckman (1966).

9 I am aware of discussions of 'abductivist' scenarios construction (Wilkinson, 2009, p. 111), which seeks to bridge these. However, the literature on this remains under-developed.
10 The 2×2 can also be thought of as the minimum condition of a morphological scenario, with two fields and two uncertainties (Bishop, Hines and Collins, 2007, p. 15).
11 Chermack also conflates the Shell approach and the GBN 2×2 (pp. 18–19).
12 Even on its own terms, the practice is contentious. Mason and Herman (2003, pp. 24–25) argue in a paper about their corporate scenarios work that 'co-evolution is more common than independence. [...] Many of our clients were determined to try to create the conditions for their success rather than just waiting to see what happens around them'.
13 In Shell's case, this may be because the company felt it had made errors in its scenario analysis in the late 1970s by assuming that counter-cultural or less materialist values would arrive in the mainstream more quickly than they did (Jefferson, 2012, pp. 191–192).
14 'The linear metaphor of scales, such as that stretching from the micro level to the macro level, or from the life world system world, which has plagued social theory from its inception, should thus be replaced by the metaphor of connections' (Urry, p. 122).
15 The notion of autopoiesis, developed by Humberto Maturana and Francisco Varela, describes a system that is capable of reproducing and maintaining itself; in other words, a living system.
16 In an earlier draft of the manuscript, Adam and Groves (2007b, p. 84) write that 'futures are imagined, pasts are recalled, but only the present is observed and inhabited here and now. From this point of view, the future is nothing but a resource that awaits exploitation'.
17 If this model seems familiar, an adapted version of it is used but not sourced in Sohail Inayatullah's (2008) paper, 'Six Pillars: Futures thinking for transforming'.
18 In Shell's (2008) account:

> In the first scenario – called Scramble – policymakers pay little attention to more efficient energy use until supplies are tight. Likewise, greenhouse gas emissions are not seriously addressed until there are major climate shocks. In the second scenario – Blueprints – growing local actions begin to address the challenges of economic development, energy security and environmental pollution.

Bibliography

Adam, B. and Groves, C. (2007a). *Future matters: action, knowledge, ethics.* Leiden: Brill.
Adam, B. and Groves, C. (2007b). *Future matters: marking, making and minding futures for the 21st century.* Pre-publication manuscript. https://dokumen.tips/documents/future-matters-singlespc-manuscript-120107.html Accessed 11 January 2019.
Andersson, J. (2012). 'The great future debate and the struggle for the world'. *American Historical Review*, 5(117), pp. 1411–1430.
Andersson, J. (2018). *The future of the world: futurology, futurists and the struggle for the post-cold war imagination.* Oxford: Oxford University Press.
Ansoff, H. (ed.). (1969). *Business strategy.* Harmondsworth: Penguin.
Beckert, J. (2013). 'Imagined futures: Fictional expectations in the economy'. *Theory and Society*, 42(3), pp. 219–240.
Bell, W. (2003). *Foundations of futures studies, Volume 1.* Piscataway, NJ: Transaction Publishers (revised edition).
Berger, P. and Luckman, T. (1966). *The social construction of reality.* Harmondsworth: Penguin.
Bezold, C. (2009). 'Jim Dator's alternative futures and the path to IAF's aspirational futures'. *Journal of Futures Studies*, 14(2), pp. 123–134.
Bishop, P., Hines, A. and Collins, T. (2007). 'The current state of scenario development: An overview of techniques'. *Foresight*, 9(1), pp. 5–25.
Bradfield, R. (2004). 'Origin and evolution of scenario techniques in the context of business'. *University of Strathclyde Working Paper Series*, 2004, p. 10.
Bradfield, R. (2007). 'Facilitating scenario development'. In van der Heijden, K. and Sharpe, B. (eds.), *Scenarios for Success.* Chichester: John Wiley and Sons, pp. 259–277.
Bradfield, R., Derbyshire, J. and Wright, G. (2016) 'The critical role of history in scenario thinking: Augmenting causal analysis within the intuitive logics scenario development methodology'. *Futures*, 77, pp. 56–66.

Bradfield, R., Wright, G., Burt, G., Cairns, G. and van Der Heijden, K. (2005). 'The origins and evolution of scenario techniques in long range business planning'. *Futures*, 37, pp. 795–812.

Bruun, H., Hukkinen, J. and Eklund, E. (2001). 'Scenarios as radical alternatives: The case of aquaculture in the Finnish archipelago sea'. https://www.researchgate.net/publication/253903831

Candy, S. and Potter, C. (eds.). (2019). 'Design and futures (Vol 1)'. *Journal of Futures Studies*, Special issue, 23(3), pp. 1–2.

Chermack, T. (2011). *Scenario planning in organizations*. San Francisco, CA: Berrett-Koehler.

Chermack, T., Lynham, S. and Ruena, W. (2001). 'A review of scenario planning literature'. *Futures Research Quarterly*, Summer 2001, pp. 7–31.

Coates, J. (1996). 'Herman Kahn: An appreciation'. *Futures*, 28(8), pp. 787–789.

Cornish, E. (1977). *The study of the future: An introduction to the art and science of understanding and shaping tomorrow's world*. Washington, DC: World Future Society.

Coyle, G. (2004). *Practical strategy: Structured tools and techniques*. Harlow: Pearson Education.

Curry, A. (2012), 'The scenarios question'. In Curry, A. (ed.), *The Future of Futures*. Houston, TX: Association of Professional Futures, pp. 11–15.

Curry, A. and Schultz, W. (2009). 'Roads less travelled: Different methods, different futures'. *Journal of Futures Studies*, 13(4), pp. 35–60.

Dator, J. (2009). 'Alternative futures at the Manoa school'. *Journal of Futures Studies*, 14(2), pp. 1–18.

De Geus, A. (1997). *The living company*. London: Nicholas Brealey.

De Jouvenal, B. (1967). *The art of conjecture*. London: Weidenfeld and Nicholson.

Ecologist, The (1972). *A blueprint for survival*. Harmondsworth: Penguin.

Emery, F. and Trist, J. (1965). 'The causal texture of organisational environments'. *Human Relations*, 18, pp. 21–32.

Farrington, T., Henson, K. and Crews, C. (2012). 'The use of strategic foresight methods for ideation and portfolio management'. *Research-Technology Management*, March–April 2012, pp. 26–33.

Fuller, T. and Loogma, K. (2009). 'Constructing futures: A social constructionist perspective on foresight methodology'. *Futures*, 41(2), pp. 71–79.

Galtung, J. and Jungk, R. (1969). 'Postscript: A warning and a hope'. In Jungk, R. and Galtung, J. (eds.), *Mankind 2000*. London: Allen and Unwin, p. 368.

Gidley, J. (2017). *The future: A very short introduction*. Oxford: Oxford University Press.

Glenn, J. and Gordon, T. (2009). 'Scenarios'. In Glenn, J. and Gordon, T. (eds.), *Futures research methodology version 3.0*. Washington, DC, Millennium Project. http://www.millennium-project.org/publications-2/futures-research-methodology-version-3-0/

Godet, M. (2008). *Strategic foresight: La prospective*. Working Paper #10. Paris: LIPSOR.

Greeuw, S., van Asselt, M., Grosskurth, J., Storms, C., Rijkens-Klomp, N., Rothman, D. and Rotmans, J. (2000). *Cloudy crystal balls*. Copenhagen: European Environment Agency.

Inayatullah, S. (2004). 'Causal layered analysis: Theory, historical context, and case studies'. In Inayatullah, S. (ed.), *The causal layered analysis (CLA) reader*. Taipei: Tamkang University Press.

Jaworski, J. (1998). *Synchronicity: The inner path of leadership*. San Francisco: Berrett-Koehler.

Jefferson, M. (2012). 'Shell scenarios: What really happened in the 1970s and what may be learned for current world prospects'. *Technological Forecasting & Social Change*, 79, pp. 186–197.

Jimenez, J. (2010). 'How do scenarios practices and search conferences complement each other?'. In Ramirez, R., Selsky, J. and van der Heijden, K. (eds.), *Business planning for turbulent times*, 2nd edn. London: Earthscan, pp. 31–46.

Kahane, A. (1999). 'Scenarios for changing the world'. In Senge, P., Ross, R., Kleiner, A., Roberts, C., Roth, G. and Smith, B. (eds.), *The dance of change*. London: Nicholas Brealey, pp. 238–239.

Kahane, A. (2004). *Solving tough problems*. San Francisco: Berrett-Koehler.

Katz, D. and Kahn, R. ([1966]/1969). 'Common characteristics of open systems'. In Emery, F. (ed.), *Systems thinking*. Harmondsworth: Penguin, pp. 86–104.

Kleiner, A. (1996). *The age of heretics*. London: Nicholas Brealey.

Lang, T. and Allen, L. (2010). 'Reflecting on scenario practice: The contribution of a soft system perspective'. In Ramirez, R., Selsky, J. and van der Heijden, K. (eds.), *Business planning for turbulent times*, 2nd edn. London: Earthscan, pp. 47–64.

Levinson, M. (2016). *An extraordinary time*. London: Random House.

Li, Z. (2014). 'Narrative rhetorics in scenario work: Sensemaking and translation'. *Journal of Futures Studies*, 18(3), pp. 77–94.

List, D. (2004). 'Multiple pasts, converging presents, and alternative futures'. *Futures*, 36, pp. 23–43.

List, D. (2007). 'Scenario network mapping'. *Journal of Futures Studies*, 11(4), pp. 77–96.

Masini, E. (1993). *Why futures studies?* London: Grey Seal Books.

Mason, D. and Herman, J. (2003). 'Scenarios and strategy: Making the scenario about the business'. *Strategy and Leadership*, 31(1), p. 23.

McHale, J. (1969). 'Futures research: Some integrative and communicative aspects'. In Jungk, R. and Galtung, J. (eds.), *Mankind 2000*. London: Allen and Unwin, pp. 256–263

Meadows, D.H., Meadows, D.L., Randers, J. and Behrens, W. (1972). *The limits to growth*. New York: Universe Books.

Miller, R. (2012). 'Anticipation: The discipline of uncertainty'. In Curry, A. (ed.), *The future of futures*. Houston, TX: Association of Professional Futurists, pp. 39–43.

Millett, S. (2003). 'The future of scenarios: Challenges and opportunities'. *Strategy & Leadership*, 31(2), pp. 16–24.

Millett, S. (2011). *Managing the future: A guide to forecasting and strategic planning in the 21st century*. Axminster: Triarchy Press.

Mintzberg, H., Ahlstrand, B. and Lampel, J. (1998). *Strategy safari*. Harlow: FT Prentice Hall.

Ohmae, K. (1983). *The mind of the strategist: Business planning for competitive advantage*. New York: Viking Penguin.

Pereira, L., Hichert, T., Hamann, M., Preiser, R. and Biggs, R. (2018). 'Using futures methods to create transformative spaces: visions of a good anthropocene in southern Africa'. *Ecology and Society*, 23(1), p. 19

Polak, F. (1973). *The image of the future*. Translated and abridged by Elise Boulding. Amsterdam: Elsevier.

Poli, R. (2010). 'An introduction to the ontology of anticipation'. *Futures*, 42(7), pp. 769–776. https://doi.org/10.1016/j.futures.2010.04.028

Poli, R. (2011). 'Steps towards an explicit ontology of the future'. *Journal of Futures Studies*, 16(1), pp. 67–78.

Poli, R. (2017). *Introduction to anticipation studies*. Berlin: Springer.

Porter, M. and Kramer, A. (2011). 'Creating shared value'. *Harvard Business Review*, January–February 2011.

Ramírez, R., Churchhouse, S., Palermo, A. and Hoffmann, J. (2017). 'Using scenario planning to reshape strategy'. *MIT Sloan Management Review*, 58(4), pp. 31–37.

Ramírez, R., Selsky, J. and van der Heijden, K. (eds.) (2010). *Business planning for turbulent times*, 2nd edn. London: Earthscan.

Ringland, G. (2006). *Scenario planning*, 2nd edn. Chichester: John Wiley.

Rosenzweig, P. (2008). *The halo effect*. London: Pocket Books.

Rowland, N. and Spaniol, M. (2015). 'The future multiple'. *Foresight*, 17(6), pp. 556–573.

Rowland, N. and Spaniol, M. (2017). 'Social foundation of scenario planning'. *Technological Forecasting and Social Change*, 124, pp. 6–15.

Sardar, Z. (ed.) (2017). *The post-normal times reader*. London: CFPPS.

'Scenarios 2018' (2018). *The Compass Podcast #1*. Houston, TX: Association of Professional Futurists. https://apf.org/2018/12/scenarios-2018-the-compass-podcast/. Accessed 10 February 2019.

Schoemaker, P. (2005). 'Scenario planning: A tool for strategic thinking'. *MIT Sloan Management Review*, 36(2), pp. 25–40.

Schon, D. (1973). *Beyond the stable state*. Harmondsworth: Penguin.

Schon, D. (1983). *The reflective practitioner*. New York: Basic Books.

Schultz, W. (1995). *Futures fluency: Explorations in leadership, vision, and creativity*. PhD thesis. https://www.researchgate.net/publication/29742470_Futures_fluency_explorations_in_leadership_vision_and_creativity. Accessed 4 November 2019.

Schultz, W. (2009). *Scenarios compendium*. Natural England, NECR031

Schultz, W. (2012). 'The history of futures'. In Curry, A. (ed.), *The Future of Futures*. Houston, TX: Association of Professional Futurists, pp. 3–7.

Schultz, W. (2015a). 'Manoa: The future is not binary'. In Curry, A. (ed.), *Compass*. Association of Professional Futurists, pp. 4–8.

Schultz, W. (2015b). 'Crazy futures: Why plausibility is maladaptive'. In Curry, A. (ed.), *Compass*. Association of Professional Futurists, pp. 2–7.

Schwartz, P. (1996). *The art of the long view*. New York: Doubleday.

Schwartz, P. and Ogilvy, J. (1998), 'Plotting your scenarios'. In Fahey, L. and Randall, R., *Learning from the future*. New York: John Wiley and Sons, pp. 57–80.

Seefried, E. (2014). 'Steering the future: The emergence of "Western" futures research and its production of expertise, 1950s to early 1970s'. *European Journal of Futures Research*, 15(29). https://doi.org/10.1007/s40309-013-0029-y

Sharpe, B. (2013). *Three horizons: The patterning of hope*. Charmouth: Triarchy.

Shell (2008). *The Shell global scenarios to 2050*. The Hague: Shell International BV.

Slaughter, R. (1998). 'Transcending flatland'. *Futures*, 30(6), pp. 519–533.

Slaughter, R. (2002). 'Beyond the mundane: reconciling breadth and depth in futures enquiry'. *Futures*, 34, pp. 493–507.

Sloterdijk, P. (2016). *Selected exaggerations: Conversations and interviews, 1993–2012*. Cambridge: Polity.

Solnit, R. (2005). *Hope in the dark*. Edinburgh: Canongate.

Spaniol, M. and Rowland, N. (2017). 'The scenario planning paradox'. *Futures*, 95(January), pp. 33–43.

Spaniol, M. and Rowland, N. (2018). 'Defining scenario'. *Futures and Foresight Science*, 1(1), p. e3.

Tibbs, H. (1999). Making the future visible: Psychology, scenarios, and strategy'. https://static1.squarespace.com/static/570ce46bd51cd428a1ef3190/t/570fe9ac8a65e26c89b61d63/1460660656884/Making+the+Future+Visible.pdf. Accessed 28 January 2019.

Turner, F. (2006). *From counterculture to cyberculture*. Chicago, IL: University of Chicago.

Urry, J. (2003). *Global complexity*. Cambridge: Polity.

Van der Heijden, K. (1996). *Scenarios: The art of strategic conversation*. Chichester: John Wiley and Sons.

Van Notten, P. (2004). *Writing on the wall: Scenario development in times of discontinuity*. Boca Raton, FL: Dissertation.com.

Van Notten, P., Rotmans, J., van Asselt, M. and Rothman, D. (2003). 'An updated scenario typology'. *Futures*, 35, pp. 423–443.

Vickers, G. ([1965]/1995). *The art of judgment*. Thousand Oaks CA: Sage.

Wack, P. (1985a). 'Scenarios: Uncharted waters ahead'. *Harvard Business Review*, September 1985, pp. 73–89.

Wack, P. (1985b). 'Scenarios: Shooting the rapids', *Harvard Business Review*, November 1985, pp. 139–150.

Wilkinson, A. (2009). 'Scenarios practices: In search of theory'. *Journal of Futures Studies*, 13(3), pp. 107–114.

Wilkinson, A. and Kupers, R. (2013). 'Living in the futures'. *Harvard Business Review*, May 2013.

Williams, R.J. (2016). 'World futures'. *Critical Inquiry*, 42, pp. 473–546.

Wilson, I. (1998). 'Mental maps of the future: An intuitive logics approach to scenarios'. In Fahey, L. and Randall, R. (eds.), *Learning from the future*. New York: John Wiley and Sons, pp. 81–108.

Wright, A. (2004a). 'A social constructionist's deconstruction of Royal Dutch Shell's scenario planning process'. *Working paper Series 2004*. Wolverhampton: University of Wolverhampton.

Wright, A. (2004b). 'The use of scenarios in social construction of sense'. *Working paper Series 2004*. Wolverhampton: University of Wolverhampton.

2
Agency
Futures literacy and Generation Z

Emily Spiers

Introduction

At the heart of social futures research lies the thorny issue of agency. Let us assume there are at least as many possible futures as there are humans – approximately 7.8 billion at the time of writing. Each individual will grapple with their own sense of agency at the very least a few times in their lives; each will gain a sense of the degree to which their capacity for reflection, assessment, interaction and action may enhance or diminish their chances, their well-being and their futures, in concert or discord with the myriad discursive and material circumstances of their lived existence. Yet, for the field of social futures research to be truly social, it must ask difficult questions about how such diverse and multiple forms of everyday, embodied agency intersect with the seemingly invisible ways in which broader material-discursive and institutional technologies become licensed to exert power over how futures unfold. My work intersects with that of a wider community of futures thinkers who are using various futures methods to explore just that.[1]

Agency is broadly understood to be the capacity for action. David Weissman (2020) characterizes agency as the signifier of 'purpose, cause, and appraisal in agents who control circumstances and themselves to some degree' (p. 11). For Martha C. Nussbaum (2011), building on Amartya Sen (1984), agency is construed as a 'functioning' or 'capability', rather than necessarily a capacity for action, and is profoundly linked to an individual's values and well-being. This means for an action or inaction to be agentic, it must align with an individual's values, and this successful alignment, along with the unconstrained potential to undertake said action or inaction, remains key to an individual's sense of well-being.

It is here that we begin to see the links between the question of agency and the field of futures literacy (FL), a cornerstone of social futures research. Like the conceptualization of agency above, FL is framed as a 'capability':

> Futures Literacy is a capability that offers insights into both the reasons and the methods humans deploy when they anticipate. Being 'futures literate' enables people, together, to appreciate the world more fully, to use the future to innovate the present.
>
> *(Miller, 2015; Miller, 'Futures Literacy: A Skill for the 21st Century')*

For Miller, FL is vital because how we think about and imagine the future impacts directly on our sense of well-being. In his model of FL, Miller draws on the influential work of Fred Polak, Jim Dator and the Manoa School more broadly, whose research practice revolves around the collating and envisioning of 'images of the future' (Polak, 1973; Jones, 1992; Dator, 2009). As Miller puts it: 'Imagining the future is what generates hope and fear, sense-making and meaning'. Furthermore, the futures we imagine, which 'drive our expectations, disappointments and willingness to invest or to change', necessarily align with, rub up against or diverge from our core values (Miller, 'Futures Literacy: A Skill for the 21st Century').

As an ontological functioning, agency, too, is steeped in futurity. Agency is both anticipatory and realized at the moment of action or inaction; it exists latently, imaginatively, as an anticipation of a future state action or inaction, grounded in and informed by past and present experience and emotion as well as an assessment of the circumstances in which action is to be taken and the likelihood of success. Weissman (2020) calls this 'reality-testing in the near-world' (p. 1). As Christopher Groves observes:

> Having a future is, at one level, inextricably part of all human experience. Phenomenological traditions in philosophy and sociology represent the anticipatory projection of potential futures from within the present through embodied emotion, imagination and conceptual thought *as essential for the organization of belief and action*, and meaning-making more generally.
>
> *(Groves, 2021, n.p.)*

Anticipating a future here becomes an 'essential' aspect of agency, a prerequisite for organizing one's values, beliefs and imagining potential actions. But, for human beings embedded in complex social systems, agency must always emerge from the point of intersection between individual and, to name only a few, social, economic or political contexts. Lois McNay (2000) observes that much post-structuralist writing about subjectivity and agency places an emphasis upon 'discursive construction', i.e. the contingency of the subject, which in turn then becomes a 'form of determinism because of the frequent assumption, albeit implicit, of the essential passivity of the subject' (p. 3). Many post-structuralists, she contends, 'highlight the retentive dimension of the sedimented effects of power on the body' (pp. 4–5). Martin Sand follows this line of argument in relation to an individual's relationship to the future:

> […] it should be pointed out how existing misbalances in power and social standing, which have so often been emphasized (Callaghan, 2018), reappear in the ways in which people approach the future, what they envision and whether they will be able to express these narratives in a manner that increases their momentum in the process of negotiating the future.
>
> *(Sand, 2019, p. 101)*

In his discussion of who does or does not 'have a future' in a climate dominated by a 'vanguard' (2019, p. 98) of elitist visionaries promulgating techno-scientific futures, Sand observes how an individual might be understood to be constrained in four different ways: (1) they lack the capability (Nussbaum, 2011) or skill of FL (Miller, 2015); (2) their circumstances may have wrought the diminishment of hope or aspiration in relation to the future (Appadurai, 2013); (3) they may have aspirations, but these remain latent as they have no faith in being 'heard'[2] and (4) their future vision contrasts so starkly with the dominant future narrative that it gains no purchase in either discursive or political arenas.

However, the focus on what we might call the 'deficit model' (Groves, 2021, n.p.) or the 'negative paradigm' (McNay, 2000, p. 27), i.e. individuals 'lack' a skill, a capability, an emotion or an aspiration, may hide the genuine power imbalance at play by foisting the lack or insufficiency onto the individual:

> I want to suggest that the 'lack' here is not so much a deficit on the part of those who 'do not have a future', but instead stems from a failure of recognition that can be considered as unjust and oppressive, one which also helps to produce particular knowledge practices as reliable means of constructing actionable futures for and by other actors, and in this way helps to create conduits of power.
>
> *(Groves, 2021, n.p.)*

This critique of the individualization of the future-deficit model, a critique which could be levied at FL if it is undertaken carelessly, resonates with Polak's concern, expressed in *The Image of the Future* (1973), that the images we prioritize should be 'shared public ones [...] because we are primarily concerned with the larger social and cultural processes' (p. 14). Dator (2009), too, shares this understanding of images of the future being a broader cultural and social practice, i.e. 'understanding the varieties and sources of different images of the future' (p. 6).

Furthermore, it is vital to be careful with such a deficit model as it also elides the more configurative and creative aspects of human agency. As McNay contends, it is 'crucial to conceptualize [the] creative or productive aspects immanent to agency in order to explain how, when faced with complexity and difference, individuals may respond in unanticipated and innovative ways which may hinder, reinforce or catalyse social change' (2000, p. 5). In McNay's model of agency:

> [t]he coherence of the self is not conceived as an exogenously imposed effect, but as the result of an active process of configuration whereby individuals attempt to make sense of the temporality of existence. Narrative is the privileged medium of this process of self-formation. The process of active appropriation immanent in the construction of narrative identity suggests a more autonomous model of agency than is offered in the negative paradigm.
>
> *(2000, p. 27)*

Like McNay, I understand identity to be a largely narrative-based undertaking and this means that agency is also freed up to be conceptualized as something more configurative and creative (Reason and Heinemeyer, 2016). This links my conception of agency to FL because, as Miller (2006a) points out: 'It is crucial to recognize that the elaboration of exploratory situations (for human society) is largely a storytelling task' (p. 7). As such, the imagination is a key part of developing FL as '[a] futures literate person has acquired the skills needed to decide why and how to use their imagination to introduce the non-existent future into the present' (Miller, 2018, p. 15). In this chapter, I am interested in exploring the relationship between imagining the future and agency.

Due to the importance of imagination, the methods I use draw on a long tradition of socially engaged practice and participatory arts in order to engage people directly with the possibility of shaping alternative futures. By alternative, I mean futures that (are licensed to) deviate from the normative, seemingly locked-in pathways of either one's individual future, or the technologically driven futures that dominate public and institutional imaginations.

This is because the purpose of FL is 'to identify and distinguish different forms of the "potential of the present"; to use the future in the same way that an accomplished reader can distinguish and invent (co-create) many meanings from a given text' (Miller, 2006a, p. 27).

Engaging our narrative selves therefore constitutes a key component of developing FL, precisely because the active 'making' involved in narrative-based creative practice is profoundly connected to agency (Reason and Heinemeyer, 2016). This means that narrative-driven creative practice can engage people critically with both the concept of the 'present future' and that of the 'future present'. For Barbara Adam and Christopher Groves (2007), building on Niklas Luhmann and Reinhart Koselleck, these two terms represent distinct ways in which to position the future modally in relation to the present. Present futures tend to characterize extrapolative trends and the desires and aspirations that cling to them. For Adam and Groves, these present futures represent a narrowing, rather than a dilation of Riel Miller's 'possibility space cone' (a method for constructing scenarios that evoke a wide set of possible futures; Miller, 2006b). Future presents, on the other hand, denote futures borne of imaginative leaps, often driven by an affective impulse, attachment or identification with others. These leaps reveal a multitude of previously unconceptualized possible futures that open up, rather than narrow, the possibility space. I have argued elsewhere (Spiers, 2019; Liveley, Slocombe and Spiers, 2021) that engagement with narrative can enhance one's capacity for thinking in terms of futures presents. This is because the 'worldmaking' (Goodman, 1978) and relationality inherent in narrative-based creative practice have the power to transform patterns of thinking and behaving, overcoming 'locked-in' (*qua* hegemonic) future narratives, or 'used futures' (*qua* a second-hand future imported from another culture/discourse, Inayatullah, 2015, p. 11) and revealing diverse and unanticipated possible futures (Milojević and Izgarjan, 2014; Palmer, 2014). However, this chapter allows space for the voices of those who I have involved in such research practice to express, themselves, how they experienced the work. This is because, as Julia Cook (2017) observes: 'Although the future is necessarily at the forefront of the popular consciousness, the ways in which individuals relate to it remain ambiguous in scholarly work' (p. 2).

Defining the methods

This chapter draws on three years of experimental 'creative futures' practice and research, which took place under the auspices of the Institute for Social Futures at Lancaster University, UK, with representatives of Generation Z (those born between 1997 and 2012/2015). The participants were young adults (university undergraduates and postgraduates) and schoolchildren (two intakes of Key Stage 2 English pupils). The data I draw on below has been taken from a body of feedback accrued from ten workshops over two years carried out with different groupings of university students (participant pool approx. 100 people) and two terms of weekly lessons over a period of two years with approx. 40 schoolchildren. Apart from the schoolchildren's iterative work, and one group of postgraduate students who attended up to three workshops using slightly different methods, most participants attended only one workshop.

The workshops with the university students were framed as an introduction to futures thinking. In the first part of the workshops, I took them through the basics of assembling a 2×2 scenario matrix, beginning with mapping drivers of change and arranging them into quadrants of importance and certainty. At each step, I talked through the problems of the scenario mapping method: The lack of cultural, geopolitical and linguistic context from which to begin, which often entails that the future that emerges is too abstract, or too implicitly Western; the limitations of PESTLE for mapping drivers of change, which often result in a technologically driven future (i.e. a 'present future'); and the cognitive biases of the participants that will, unchecked, naturalize the type of futures produced. I showed how this method, while seeming to be embedded in the positivist tradition of scientific enquiry, was still, in fact, a type of storytelling due to the privileged position and viewpoint of the subject creating the scenario matrix and the fundamental unknowability of the future. Thus, the steps towards building a scenario matrix are always a selective process of world-building, as much as in any type of fictional narrative. In their work, I then supported the students to address and seek ways to overcome these limitations by embedding their futures in a specific cultural and social context; by thinking about the socio-cultural and affective factors that PESTLE often overlooks and by reflecting on their own cognitive biases as they worked. The students were then tasked with writing the scenarios in their groups, the more adventurous created characters from whose perspective the scenarios were related, while others created a more standard genre of scenario script.

The work with the school pupils took place at The Academy School, Hampstead, London, and was framed as a 'futures project' facilitated by their English teacher, Linda Marland, over the summer term. The pupils received special exercise books and were guided through readings of speculative fiction suitable for their age. They were then asked to respond creatively to their readings, either by drawing a visual response, say an advert from the future, or the house of the future, or by creating a narrative of their own. The pupils were also guided through an age-appropriate exercise in uncovering their own anticipatory assumptions about the future (see Figure 2.1).

In this chapter, I do not seek to unpack the methods or processes themselves, as these are being explored elsewhere (see Liveley, Slocombe and Spiers, 2021); I also do not focus too much on the outputs, with the exception of the school pupils' work, which I expose to a 'close reading' in order to uncover concerns about agency. Instead, I will predominantly explore the question of agency in FL through focussing on participants' perceptions of the experience

Figure 2.1 A table listing (1) Things I take for granted, (2) Things I fear happening in the future and (3) Things I hope for

of undertaking creative futures work. In particular, I will explore their felt relationship with the future before and after the workshops and their affective response to the work.

Analysis of feedback from university students and pupils

Feedback from the young adults and schoolchildren clustered around four themes: (1) reflections on participants' sense of personal agency in relation to the future, before and after the workshops; (2) reflections on the intersections between their own perspectives and those of others, either of the other participants they were working with or larger, more macro forces, such as politics, economics, technology and climate change; (3) reflections on their affective or felt experiences of doing the work; and (4) reflections on the collaborative aspect of the work they undertook.

Reflections on agency

Two clear strands of feedback emerged around the question of how the workshops had made participants feel about their own relationship to the future. One strand showed that many had found the experience empowering and that it had resulted in the augmentation of the capability to think and act in an enhanced agentic manner vis-à-vis the future. This evidence builds on earlier findings from futures projects we would do well to revisit, those run by, for example, Robert Jungk in the 1970s across several different countries, whose participants would often say they were 'returning home conscious of having contributed to a better future – one that they felt like actively sponsoring' (Jungk and Müllert, 1987, p. 10).

In my study, one KS 2 schoolchild wrote:

> My class has learned about a number of topics in this project: Animal poem, a smart house, what we think about time travel, our own manifestos, […] and a day in my life on 3rd July 2035. […] I think all schools should teach how to do a project like this. […] I feel personally changed by how many animals are becoming extinct.

Another pupil wrote that the project had made her more aware of the environmental impact of flying, leading her to persuade her family not to use air flight for their summer holiday that year. One university student stated: The workshop 'empowered me to believe that I am also capable of and entitled to think and talk about the future'. Another commented: 'I feel more capable of changing the course of the future, by engaging in things more proactively in the present'. The university student's comment above nods to the importance of feeling 'entitled' to think and talk about the future. This fits with Sand's notion that individuals may often feel disenfranchised from the future, in that they do not expect their voices to count, let alone be heard. For another participant, the workshop opened up a broader sense of agency, echoing Sen's early distinction between an individual's personal 'well-being freedom' and the broader external-facing 'agency freedom': [The workshop] made me realize my direct effect on the wider picture of the future rather than just my own future'.

Nevertheless, a few participants clearly felt a continued sense of distance and disempowerment from the future after the workshop. One commented: 'In my opinion the future is untouchable and always at arm's length', resulting for that participant in a 'continued sense of futility and powerlessness!' For another, it was less about the temporal-ontological conundrum that is one's relationship to the future and more about the material circumstances of early twenty-first-century existence: 'The future seems predetermined to be negative through the prominence of climate change'.

The next cluster of comments demonstrated an acknowledgement of the participants' own agency in relation to the future, but also an awareness of the limitations of their own values, beliefs, actions and anticipatory capabilities when faced with broader power structures shaping certain types of future. One materials scientist PhD student commented:

> I try to do my part in the future, however, you should consider this important fact that the main people who play the most significant role in the future of the world are not scientists, because they do not have enough money.

Another observed:

> I often think about what I can personally do to affect the future, however I don't often consider the actions of those in power as I feel so disillusioned by politics. Although I consider myself as a cautious optimist, I often question whether anything will change in reality. Despite this, I am becoming more conscious about my own personal impacts on global issues.

These two participants identify two obstacles to shaping the kind of future they might like to see: Politics and money. In the first participant's comment about lacking money as a scientist, they imply a belief (underscored by Sand, 2019) that futures are currently made by a wealthy elite and that, without money, one's voice is not heard. Politics preoccupies the second participant here, whose modest conscientiousness vis-à-vis the future seems beaten down by their disillusionment in the current political climate. This diminishment if not complete lack of the 'capacity to aspire' (Appadurai, 2004) has led to her questioning 'whether anything will change in reality'.

The schoolchildren's work also demonstrated a fascination with questions of autonomy, constraint and the possibility of change. They were given Jeffrey McDaniel's poem 'The Quiet World' to read (*The Forgiveness Parade*, 1998), in which the 'government has decided / to allot each person exactly one hundred / and sixty-seven words, per day' in order to 'get people to look / into each other's eyes more'. One pupil took this premise and built a fictional world in the mode of a journal entry by a girl called Macy Hawkins. In this world, children have their voice boxes replaced at birth with an artificial one that only allows people to speak 167 words a day in a robotic voice. In the journal entry, the girl has just been diagnosed with depression by a psychiatrist who has to stop talking to the girl about it mid-sentence, as she runs out of words. The girl, whose 'world is pain', sneaks away to write about this diagnosis in her journal accruing up to 264 words illegally. But she hears footsteps coming and the journal breaks off suddenly and we see red crayon at the bottom of the page, evoking blood splatters (see Figure 2.2). The writerly fascination with the question of (literally) having a voice or not resonates powerfully with the key objectives of the futures project.

In a piece of work designed to get pupils to think about the home of the future, one pupil devised a green box for smart-house surveillance. The box, which is in every home, is 'always watching and listening to EVERYTHING' (see Figure 2.3) and sends all that data to the government every two weeks. Another pupil wrote a story about enforced biochemical changes made to humans at birth that render them incapable of lying because their skin changes colour when they do lie thus alerting the interlocutor to the deceit; this was intended to lead to an end to all wars. Initially welcoming the demise of lying, the pupil's story centres on how she

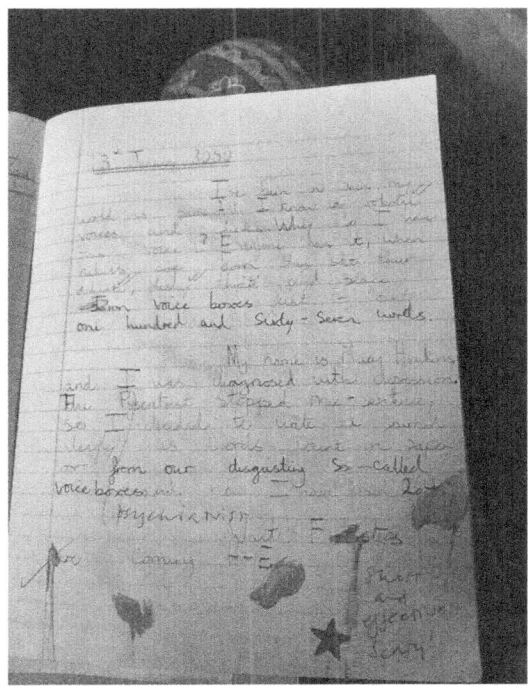

Figure 2.2 The journal entry of Macy Hawkins

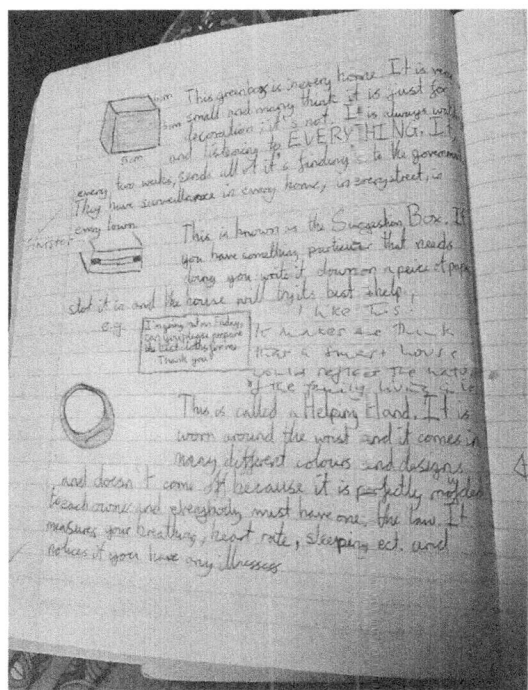

Figure 2.3 The smart-house surveillance box

Emily Spiers

Figure 2.4 The turtle poem as an acrostic

begins to feel when people are caught in lies about her looking nice or it being nice to see her. The enforced brutal honesty takes its toll on her self-esteem causing her to get into more trouble at school. When the pupils were asked to write from the perspective of endangered animals (see Figure 2.4), the pupils' lyrical voice was often emphatic: 'Turtles like me beg you / Infinite changes <u>can</u> be made / Countless lives <u>can</u> be saved'. Time and again, the schoolchildren returned to questions of autonomy, constraint and the possibility of change.

Agency and multiplicity

Of relevance to FL is the common observation made by many participants that the workshops had enabled them to view the future in a more pluralistic manner, moving from conceptions of 'the future' to multiple and 'alternative' possible futures. For some, this multiplicity was a welcome opening up of a phenomenon they had previously understood to be singular: 'The workshop enabled me to envision multiple futures, as opposed to just the one I had imagined myself'. One schoolchild wrote that the part of the future project she enjoyed most was reading the dystopian fiction. She realized that she could also write the kind of narratives she loved to read: 'I find it fascinating thinking up different possible futures and turning them into exciting stories'.

For others, the multiplicity equated with uncertainty: 'Made me think about how truly uncertain of everything about the future we really are'. For one participant, in particular, this uncertainty entailed an increased sense of individual responsibility vis-à-vis the future: 'It made me feel that the future is very uncertain and if we want to improve society it is our own responsibility'.

Another participant made a connection between the pluralizing of future visions and the pluralizing of futures work, specifically in relation to who is entitled to join the conversation about the future:

> Future [sic] is not only black or white, two different things on the spectrum that we can head to. The lines between different worlds that we can create are quite blurred and it's important to think about it. What's even more important is to engage in the conversation and work with people from different backgrounds, different understanding [sic] of the world and with different goals, rather than giving one person or one institution [sic] right not only to decide on the future but also to think about the future.

For another participant, the workshop had encouraged them to think in more detail about the future and had also challenged their anticipatory assumptions (Miller, 2018, p. 15):

> It did make me feel differently about my relationship with the future in the sense that it made me consider what *kind* of future we are going to have. My view is fairly pessimistic and the workshop made me consider alternative possibilities.

Every workshop I run is collaborative. This means that participants always work in small groups to do their thinking and narrative building. This is because I understand subjectivity and agency as inherently relational and humans as 'beings who are formed in relations of dependency' (Butler, 2005, p. 20). As Groves observes, this also relates to how we encounter futurity:

> The future, as a dimension of experience, is for human beings primarily lived through relationships – with significant others, places, institutions and ideals which can be considered objects of emotional attachment that support individual identities, and also sometimes collective ones (Christopher Groves, 2014; Honig, 2012). This lived future (Adam and Groves, 2007) is one worked on through the construction of narratives in which attachments provide structure, connecting the persisting past through a passing present to an insisting future.
>
> *(Groves, 2021, n.p.)*

In feedback gathered from the students, in particular, it became clear that this was the aspect they had enjoyed most about the workshops. They seemed to enjoy the exercise of encountering others' values, beliefs and assumptions about the future, but had become aware that this was probably one of the most challenging aspects of futures thinking on a grand scale. This is because, by placing them in groups, I had deliberately put them in a position of having to reflect on and experience the edges of their own agency in an encounter with another's. Indeed, one student noted that the 'most challenging factor is to unite the way people with different expertise think'. While another observed that it was 'very interesting to explore what may be coming with peers, those who thought the same and those who thought different'.

Some students were confronted early on with their own cognitive biases and with the immense undertaking trying to articulate what are incredibly complex systems:

> I found it difficult to critically analyse drivers for change. Specifically those relating to human, cultural and social aspects are difficult to consider because of my own personal bias and experience. For example, it is challenging to consider global change and the actions of different nations, cultures and ways of life.

But for most, the group work constituted the best mode for enhancing the multiplicity of futures and allowed them to understand the highly subjective and pluralistic epistemology of futures: 'I enjoyed the group contribution aspect where people shared their fears/visions for the future; it made me consider the future from different perspectives'.

Futures literacy and affect

It is one of the premises of FL and my own work with narrative futures that engaging with these kind of workshops can help people become better at 'using the future' (Miller, 2018, p. 15). Implied in that formulation is the question of enhanced anticipatory agency and enhanced agentic manifestations in terms of action. While this seems indeed to be the case, in terms of the feedback analysed here, it is important to note that amongst the participants who were undergraduates at the time of the workshops (approx. 20 years of age), the affective impact was quite negative for many. When I asked the students what the first thing that came into their heads was when they thought about the future two participants said 'fear' to a murmur of agreement from the rest of the group. Here are just some of these negative affective responses:

> [The workshop] made me feel slightly more negative about the present as it made me realize how dangerous some situations can be.
> It was difficult imagining positive outcomes for the future due to the unpleasant way in which it is represented.
> My knowledge of the future has expanded more, which does add a bit more concern.
> I am more concerned/anxious and engaged with our potential future
> [The workshop] made me realize how scary it [the future] is.
> It made me think more about our actions now and how they impact and how they have an impact on the future…perhaps made me nervous…what is possible…
> Even more inclined to prepare for it → nervous.

Other participants had experienced a more optimistic response to thinking more about the future: 'It helped me be more optimistic about the future, as I now understand that many institutions are thinking critically about it, and exploring the ways it might happen'. For this participant, their optimism seems to stem from being reassured that people and institutions are engaged in critical futures thinking. For others, their increased optimism related to having their anticipatory assumptions challenged: '[The workshop] forced me to re-evaluate previously pessimistic view of the future. Negative perceptions about where we are heading with environment/health have been challenged'.

Conclusion

What is powerful about this work is that it begins by unpacking participants' anticipatory assumptions (Miller, 2018, p. 15), bringing individuals and groups face-to-face with what they did and sometimes did not think they thought and felt about the future. As Miller (2018) notes, 'these assumptions are necessary for all "uses-of-the-future" because "imagination" can only be elaborated on the basis of the underlying assumptions' (p. 4). Participants begin with an engagement with the 'present future' and, through the process of narrative world-building, are supported to take the imaginative leap into a vision of a 'future present', a realm in which more possibilities exist. Only one of the (undergraduate) participants felt their relationship with the future remained unchanged after the workshops. The rest were thrust into a different space, in which futures were collaborative and pluralized, and they had begun to re-examine their agentic relationship with possible futures anew. For the school pupils, multiplicity was also key, allowing them 'to envision multiple futures, as opposed to just the one I had imagined myself'. This meant that their creative work often took unexpected turns, subverting the source texts their teacher had used to engage them initially: Utopic premises became sinisterly dystopian and vice versa, but they were all supported in creating fictional avatars, through whose stories they were able to explore the boundaries of (their and their characters') agency, hope, fear, desire and (quite literally) voice vis-à-vis the future.

This all demonstrates the importance of FL work with children and young adults, but also cautions us as researchers and practitioners not to be cavalier about the potent affective response this work may elicit in participants. This early work made clear to me the need for any large-scale project of this kind to have inbuilt pastoral and mental-health support. This is because statistics from the UK government (ONS, 2018) and the *British Medical Journal* (Gunnell et al., 2018) suggest that life today for Generation Z 'appears to be more challenging' than for older generations: 16- to 24-year-olds in the UK are 'more likely to report symptoms of mental ill health', and 'affective disorders in young people are rising substantially, particularly among girls and young women' (ONS, 2018). Across Europe, mental health provision varies significantly. Children in the lowest income quintile are 4.5 times more likely to experience severe mental health problems than those in the highest, suggesting that the income gradient in young people's mental health has worsened considerably over the past decade (Millennium Cohort Study, 2012). The coronavirus pandemic of 2019–2020 has only exacerbated all of these elements.

While alerting us to the need for caution and care in our research in this area, those factors also attest to the urgent need for more FL work with children and young adults. I have demonstrated that anticipating a future can be understood as an essential aspect of agency, a prerequisite for organizing one's values, beliefs and imagining potential actions. For this reason, actively engaging young people and children with futures thinking through as broad an array of channels as possible could become an important method of engaging with them about the challenges they face in the present, to allow them to feel their agentic capacity for imagination and creation, and, in doing so, come to understand the 'creative or productive aspects immanent to agency' (McNay, 2000, p. 5) when faced with complexity, difference and difficulty. At the same time, we must acknowledge and work to expand the currently constrained knowledge practices and limited body of actors that are licensed to action certain legitimized futures, to understand them not as a given but as an accretion of 'authorized practices' (Groves, 2021, n.p.) that can, by virtue of this very social construction, change.

With thanks to Linda Marland, at The Academy School, for her inspired collaboration.

Notes

1 I refer here to the work of Andrew Curry, Wendy Schultz, Riel Miller, the Future Matters Collective, the Seeds of Good Anthropocenes Project and the Manoa School, to name but a few.
2 Director of the School of International Futures (SOIF) Andrew Curry related to me in 2020 that they had

> found an interesting example of this is a recent project on food environments with poorer households in London. They could articulate the future they wanted, but they couldn't imagine how it would come to pass, because their experience of the actors in the system was wholly negative.

Bibliography

Adam, B. and Groves, C. (2007). *Future matters: Action, knowledge, ethics*. Leiden and Boston, MA: Brill.
Appadurai, A. (2004). 'The capacity to aspire: Culture and the terms of recognition', In Rao, V. and Walton, M. (eds.). *Culture and public action*. Palo Alto, CA: Stanford University Press, pp. 59–84.
Appadurai, A. (2013). *The future as cultural fact: Essays on the global condition*. London and New York: Verso.
Cook, J. (2017). *Imagined futures: Hope, risk and uncertainty*. London: Palgrave Macmillan.
Dator, J. (2009). 'Alternative futures at the Manoa school', *Journal of Futures Studies*, 14(2), pp. 1–18.
Groves, C. (2021). 'On profane futures and profane futures literacy', In Sand, M., Nordmann, A. and Grunwald, M. (eds.). *The call of the future – hermeneutics, history, and technology*. Routledge. A draft version is available here: DOI: 10.13140/RG.2.2.23336.19207
Gunnell, D. et al. (2018). 'Adolescent mental health in crisis', *BMJ*, 361. Available at DOI: https://doi.org/10.1136/bmj.k2608 (Accessed 1 September 2020).
Inayatullah, S. (2015). *What works: Case studies in the practice of foresight*. Taipei: Tamkang University Press.
Jones, C.B. (1992). 'The Manoa school of futures studies', *Futures Research Quarterly*, 8(4), pp. 19–25.
Jungk, R. and Müllert, N. (1987). *Future workshops: How to create desirable futures*. London: Institute for Social Inventions (now out of print).
Liveley, G., Slocombe, W. and Spiers, E. (2021). 'Futures literacy through narrative', *Futures*, 125, p. 102663, special issue on 'Futures literacy: character, capabilities and significance', Poli, R. et al. (eds.).
McNay, L. (2000). *Gender and agency: Reconfiguring the subject in gender and social theory*. Cambridge: Polity Press.
'Measuring National Well-being: Quality of Life in the UK' (2018). Office for National Statistics. Available at: https://www.ons.gov.uk/peoplepopulationandcommunity/wellbeing/articles/measuringnationalwellbeing/qualityoflifeintheuk2018
Millennium Cohort Study (2012). Available at: https://cls.ucl.ac.uk/cls-studies/millennium-cohort-study/ (Accessed 1 September 2020).
Miller, R. (2006a). 'From trends to futures literacy. Reclaiming the future', *Centre for strategic education. Seminar series paper* (No. 160). CSE Publications, Victoria.
Miller, R. (2006b). *Futures studies, scenarios, and the "possibility-space" approach*. Paris: Organisation for Economic Co-Operation and Development (OECD). DOI: 10.1787/9789264023642-7-en.
Miller, R. (2015). 'Learning, the future, and complexity. An essay on the emergence of futures literacy', *European Journal of Education*, 50(4), pp. 513–523.
Miller, R. (2018). *Transforming the future: anticipation in the 21st century*. UNESCO Publishing. Available at: http://library.oapen.org/handle/20.500.12657/30271 (Accessed 1 September 2020).
Miller, R. (n.d.). 'Futures literacy: A skill for the 21st century'. Available at: https://en.unesco.org/themes/futures-literacy#:~:text=Futures%20Literacy%20is%20a%20capability, humans%20deploy%20when%20they%20anticipate.&text=In%20this%20way%20Futures%20Literacy, it%20means%20to%20be%20human. (Accessed 1 September 2020).
Milojević, I. and Izgarjan, A. (2014). 'Creating alternative futures through storytelling: A case study from Serbia', *Futures*, 57, pp. 51–61.
Nussbaum, M.C. (2011). *Creating capabilities: The human development approach*. Cambridge, MA: Harvard University Press.

Palmer, J. (2014). 'Past remarkable: Using life stories to trace alternative futures', *Futures*, 64, pp. 29–37.
Polak, F. (1973). *The image of the future*. Trans. by E. Boulding. London and New York: Elsevier.
Reason, M. and Heinemeyer, C. (2016). 'Storytelling, story-retelling, storyknowing: Towards a participatory practice of storytelling', *Research in Drama Education: The Journal of Applied Theatre and Performance*, 21(4), pp. 558–573.
Sand, M. (2019). 'On "not having a future"', *Futures*, 107, pp. 98–106.
Sen, A. (1985). 'Well-being, agency and freedom: The Dewey lectures 1984', *The Journal of Philosophy*, 82(4), pp. 169–221.
Spiers, E. (2019). 'Kate Tempest: A "brand new Homer" for a creative future'. In Cox, F. and Theodorakopoulos, E. (eds.). *Homer's daughters: Women's responses to Homer in the twentieth century and beyond*. Oxford: Oxford University Press, pp. 105–123.
Weissman, D. (2020). *Agency: Moral identity and free will*. Cambridge: Open Book Publishers.

3
AI
The social future of intelligence

Richard H.R. Harper

Introduction

The past few years have shown a society-wide interest in the remarkable developments within machine learning and associated techniques that are enabling what has come to be called the *New AI*. This technology is not just altering our present but many say will alter our futures too. In this view, AI will come to supplement and even substitute human reasoning, with its powers being amply demonstrated in the capacity of AI machines to beat humans at even the most complex rule-based activities, such as the game of *Go*. AI will also come to be at the heart of self-driving cars and will populate human-less factories, and the 'face' of service industries will be artificial assistants.[1]

The benefits that are seen in these prospects are, of course, immense. But so are the concerns. If AI can do more work, will that mean unemployment for the humans who used to be required to do that work, for instance (Carr, 2015)? In the long run, what will be the effect on human dignity if work is no longer the central currency of identity (Markoff, 2015)? If AI is more efficient, what will be the measures used to judge investment? Will AI itself choose where money should go (Kaplan, 2015)? More philosophically, if AI is able to reason more effectively than people, what will be the future of learning and further education? Why should society invest in people if AI is a better learner? Ultimately, will it be AI that does science and wins Nobel Prizes for doing so (Kitano, 2016)?

Much of these claims are hyperbole, and some are simply overexcited. The result of all this is that the true role of AI in the future is unclear, the hyperbole surrounding it is making careful analysis of its potential hard and the full range of consequences that follow on from what the technology might provide remain, in many respects, unexamined. The future of AI, how it affects not only how computers function, but also what those computers can do, and how, in turn, this alters their role in society more generally, is largely muddled territory.[2]

In this chapter, I want to explore what this future might be from a particular view: From a concern with the future itself, and with the ways one might construct a vision of that future that might tell us how we might alter our *current practices* to make a future we want more likely to happen. This is part and parcel of what has come to be called *Futures Thinking*, of course, and hence this book. There are various techniques in *Futures Thinking*, needless to say, but the one I will emphasize entails examining the assumptions that lie hidden in our thinking about the future, and seeing if such an examination may alter them in some way that enables the assembly of a more realistic path to the future we want. In this case, I will want to see if we can unfold a *social future* for intelligence, and not a future that we tend to assume will unfold with standard accounts of AI. These, I will say, emphasize a technological or computational view of intelligence and, as they do, narrow what intelligence might be in the future. I will seek a broader view, a social view, pointing to how intelligence is at once diverse in the way the concept (or label) is used to describe and account for phenomena, and, similarly, when a variant of the concept is used to define and explore the 'method' of it. The AI view, if I can call it thus, is narrower in its scope, constraining what is thought of as intelligent and constraining, as a result, how we imagine ourselves, our endeavours and our tools, intelligent or otherwise. The AI view traps the concept, killing the diverse life it might have and making it singular.

In the first section, I will explore what is said to be intelligence from the 'standard' point of view in AI, the one that is most often marshalled in relevant discourses.[3] This construal points towards how intelligence is 'done', its mechanics if you like, but this comes at the price of occluding larger questions about the purposes that intelligence can be put to. In this view, one is tacitly encouraged to look at similar *mechanisms*, not at *dissimilar purposes*. As a result, we tend to make the future more narrowly than it could be, and indeed ought to be, since we come to be obsessed with means and not purposes.[4] Means and mechanism come to matter more than purposes.

In the next section, I will tease this out by focussing on how one understands a game, a game of football. Here, I will draw a distinction between the mechanics of the human body (crucial to playing the game) which are the *means of football* from the purposes of the game, which are, as any reader will know, to score goals. Winning is the goal in football, one might say in delight at the tautology. My point will be that seeking this purpose intelligently is an altogether different thing from any intelligence 'in the body' used to play the game. I will not argue that one usage is better than another. They do different things. There is, if you like, a social dimension to the use of the concept of intelligence, letting people do various kinds of work when they use it – sometimes to describe ends, sometimes means, sometimes both. This will let me conclude with the claim that we do not want to be constrained in our understanding by the machineries that enable 'intelligence' when intelligence can be delivered in all sorts of ways, for all sorts of ends. For the ends can define intelligence too, and indeed in some cases, it is those that matter – as they do in football. I shall go on to say that such ends can be many; one doesn't only need to think of football. In short, intelligence can and does have many forms; it is a rich, multivalent feature of our lives, and accordingly, its use as a concept is equally so.[5] Given this, we need to ensure that our future will not be made smaller by the machineries with which we enable intelligence; our use of the concept intelligence should not be made less through being limited to reference to them (i.e., the machineries). Our conceptual élan should not be constrained by technological types – such as the ones 'inside' AI. We can avoid this by looking at the assumptions we make about AI at the current time, ones which deliver that narrowness almost without thinking by constraining us to how AI is itself done. Being alert to that we can defend our thinking, and so help create the future we want where this narrowness does not confine us. We want to socialize the use of the concept, intelligence, and thereby let us do more things with intelligence. Thus, *Futures Thinking*.

Richard H.R. Harper

From Norfolk to Silicon Valley

Most commentaries on the meaning of intelligence, when used in combination with the word artificial, point towards ways of calculating. They do not mean, for want of an everyday analogy, the kinds of calculations that an abacus can do (a kind of computer), though, as they are thinking of the kinds of calculating that is entailed when people play *tightly ruled games* – *Go*, as mentioned. In *Go*, players calculate different outcomes given different choices to determine ways forward; they weigh strategies and choose the 'heaviest' (so to say) to succeed in the game. AI machineries, at least the ones that go under the name the *New AI*, entail various forms of machine and deep learning, but all function in a similar way. Elaborate statistical techniques, most often *Bayesian* (after the Norfolk vicar who invented them in the eighteenth century), are combined with new computer architectures in such a fashion that AI computers can win at games, even at *Go*.

That AI systems can do this, beat the human in these games, has led some commentators to the conclusion that this is what intelligence 'is' – beating humans at a game means passing the so-called Turing test, the measure of whether a machine is as intelligent as a person. Whatever one thinks about such measures or tests, in this view, anything that has rule-like, game-like behaviours can be seen as a form of intelligence. From this starting place, commentators have argued that many activities can not only be thought of as game-like but *are* game like. And the proof of this is to be found in the apparent success of AI systems to 'win' in these other activities.

For example, AI can 'see' things in the visual field and does so in a game-like manner. The AI uses probabilistic techniques to interrogate data it gets from its digital cameras to distinguish shapes and labels those shapes (or objects) in terms of classes. The classes can be many things, including persons. However clever these techniques and however startling the power of the computers to label one shape over another (and hence one person from another), all they are doing, in effect, is treating that task of identification as one that can be *calculated in the manner of game-play*. The game entails subtracting, subdividing and combining shapes in data sets in ways determined by elaborate, game-like rules related to the task of recognition; success occurs when the classes match a known shape, a class in the register. This architecture presupposes what machines are to look for (i.e., classes), how they might do this and how they might know when they have seen the things (classes) their calculations are designed to recognize – adequate distinctions between John, Fred, Harry, Sandra and Carolina who are queuing up at the passport gates and being seen by the computer system at the same time. One might note that to see, in this view, is not to *know* that it is Harry or Sandra or whoever; recognition is not familiarity, a cue to say 'Hello!'; on the contrary, it is to behave like a *Go* player making one play rather than another; there is no interest in what is seen or why it is seen. The goal is to win, when in this case, to win is to *recognize the right face*.

As I say, many commentators have started to argue that this is what intelligence is *tout court*. Just as AI machines work this way, so must other 'machines', they think, even biological ones. Some have argued, for example, that mechanisms inside the human body are to be thought of as behaving in this sort of way, calculatively, probabilistically, with rules guiding their decision-making as in a game. When a cell confronts another, in this view, its reaction is determined by probability and game-like rules – the cell plays stratagems, so to say. This vision is used to explain how 'communication' between and across cells occurs, and ultimately within any system of cells. From this, these commentators come to assert that the human 'mind', consciousness in particular, similarly emerges; it is the outcome of a vast, intricate system of probabilistically calculated stratagems.

In the body and the mind (the latter used interchangeably with the word brain), these calculations are undertaken by enzymes and chemical processes, whereas with an AI machine these calculations are done by logical gates carved in silicon by light. But those who hold this view think of both as more or less the same – the machine and the body/mind. The material of the 'machine' in question is irrelevant; 'doing' intelligent activities in this way is common to one and all; these doings *are* intelligence. In essence, this is the argument that gets called *singularity*.[6] Intelligence, consciousness, choice-making – all these have common roots or rather similar machineries. If there is a measure of intelligence, it relates to this. In sum, we are no different from AI machines, they no different from us, or soon won't be.[7]

From Silicon Valley to Wembley Stadium: A case of conceptual analysis

Those on the outside of this particular view, those not taken with the AI perspective, dispute this. Their dispute is not about whether, say, cells react probabilistically in a rule-governed way. It is whether one can say the same about a person calculating in rule-governed ways; in their view, one might say that both are doing intelligent things, but what is meant in each is different. Those who don't hold with the singularity argument would say that what is meant in each case is *not the same*. To explain that a body and/or machine behaves this way is to account for the *outcomes* of the functioning of the body and/or machine, it is not to say that either do, in and of themselves, *choose* (if one can summarize this view with one word). It is to say that their functioning *can be thought* of as being like that. Whether they choose or not is largely irrelevant, but, in contrast, *that a person* chooses is the mark of whether they are intelligent or not.[8] In short, they choose to; one cannot say the same of cells or the systems they are part of. They choose nothing.[9]

This might seem merely a question of words, of conceptual distinctions that seem minor. But there are important issues here to do with what is meant by intelligence and its nested use as a concept with other concepts like choice, and what we mean by the choices that people and machines might make and hence what we mean in turn by intelligence. They might not mean the same thing in each case There might be a distinct form of use for each, a social life for the concepts in question that is variable.

At the current time, the accounts of intelligence that seem to dominate are of one particular kind, emphasizing a particular view about intelligence. This view comes to be assumed, as if it is the only way one might think of it. Are we narrowing our notions to just one view? I think we are.

A simple example can help us here. One might say that there are two ways of looking at the game of soccer. One looks at the way the muscles of a player function when they play. Another looks at the game itself, at the strategies and skills used to win. In my view, those who hold with the singularity argument, the view from Silicon Valley if you like, are looking at intelligence in the former view, that is to say like those who might look at soccer and see muscles acting. To be sure, the mechanisms of the muscles can be explained as being a function of choice, of the physiology of the body operating like an intelligent machine, optimizing this movement to achieve this speed of flex, altering the posture to ensure this kind of poise and balance. Though it is true that muscles need to flex and are controlled inside the body in a way that can be thought of as calculative and hence intelligent, to understand soccer it is better, in my view, to *look at the game*, not at the muscle movements of any of the players, however much one might say that those movements articulate intelligence in the body itself. It is *in* the game, so to speak, that intelligence is to be found – in how people play it, *not in the muscles*. Looking at the game is the preferred view from inside Wembley Stadium, if you like, the perspective that will concern the crowd and the 'bench'. To see it this way, in the Wembley way, AI notions about intelligence simply don't help. Indeed, they can make it hard to see – they can take you away from what you need to look at. Instead of letting one see *play*, the AI perspective encourages one to look at *muscles*.[10]

This does not mean that the assumption that leads one to see intelligence in the machine (so to say) is always wrong; on the contrary, what I propose is a bigger picture of what intelligence might be that includes both *intelligent muscles* and *intelligent play*, both the skills of the game and the processing of well-trained muscles. But by that I am not proposing to bring them together in some über definition. On the contrary, their value is in their conceptual distinctiveness, and the different work they do.

The forms of intelligence

My thesis is deceptively simple: It is that 'intelligence' can have many forms and that, given this, we need to be alert to the places and purposes in which those differences can be found so that we can ensure that our future will be made bigger by the impact of AI rather than smaller. We can achieve this by looking at the assumptions we make about AI at the current time, ones which can deliver that narrowness almost without thinking. Being alert to that we can alter our thinking, and so help create the future we want.

In particular, I have argued that narratives about AI can displace sensible discussion about what we want those applications to do. We end up thinking about how AI works (and to how explain *that*) instead of exploring what AI might help *us do*. We are offered *muscles* and explanations about how they work, I suggested in metaphor, and not games and their various *purposes*. As a result, we lose sight of why we might want to play games, of the purposes that would make doing so worthwhile.

Games are of course only one of the many things we can do, and, as I alluded to above, games are in many ways the opposite of intelligent. We can play them to get away from our minds; we play them since we don't have to think. And yet, to say again, we can sometimes play a game intelligently: Thus, the complexity of conceptual tools – of our language, our ways of organizing ourselves in and through words.[11]

I want to end, though, with a different set of concerns. It has to do with how the development of AI is itself constrained by this predilection for games. That this might be so is being noticed by futures thinking researchers. In '*The future of human-artificial intelligence*', Spelda and Stritecky (2020) argue that the social organization of how AI engineers are developing their technologies, one that focusses research effort on particular commonly agreed game-like tests (identifying this animal or that syntactical structure in a dialogue), has the advantage of allowing researchers to compare each other (and makes giving awards easier too), but is resulting in the AI community narrowing the cognitive scope of the machineries it is developing. In contrast to *Turing theoretic* machines,[12] the model that has underscored the PC revolution and the one which emphasizes generalizability of processing and hence also the general properties of cognition enabled with or through such machines, the AI machines being developed are providing ever more narrowly defined cognitive solutions. This is reflected in their architectures, their algorithms and their outputs. As it happens, Spelda and Stritecky are concerned that the value of these narrow solutions is disproportionate to the environmental impact of using the technology, the energy cost of deep learning being especially high indeed. That may well be right and is certainly something I am researching even now (see also Yeung et al., 2020). But here I take their paper as confirming my thesis: That AI narrows what we want our 'intelligences' to be applied to.

If we want an intelligent future, we need to allow intelligence to have what I have called a social life, one where its use as a concept is rich, nuanced and enabling, a network of (social) possibilities. If we look at the future from the view of AI, that is not a future we shall see or will end up making. Accordingly, to see the future we want and to help make that future with it in mind, one must not look from that perspective. That has been my contention. One must look from a bigger vantage point, I have said, one that sees the complexity of intelligence in all its forms: From being 'in' muscles to being 'in' stories; from being a 'feature of' games and a 'property of' intentions; and in being at once a way of doing things (a machinery) and a label for a thing well done.

Notes

1. The literature on this is immense and enormously varied. I do not seek to offer a literature review of it all but will point towards what seem to be representative contemporary examples at appropriate stages of my argument. But for a good introduction to the many points of view that is not partisan see, Kaplan (2015, 2016); also Boden (1977, 2016). In relation to games like *Go*, see Sadler and Regan (2019).
2. This has been a persistent problem. For example, Stanford University sought to bring clarity to this space with its *AI and Life in 2030* report written in 2015 (published the next year). The muddles it cites are very similar to those I list here, some years later.
3. One could digress and define the range or boundaries of such discourses, but for the purposes here they are simply those that focus on AI as the primary concern and treat AI as a given.
4. That this is so affects all sorts of attempts to explore what AI can do. Some of the better studies from, for example, the social perspective work their way around these mystifications before they can find out what the technology does in the real world and its consequences when seen from the social view. See Neyland (2019).
5. This is a point I take from Wittgenstein (1953).
6. This was originally formulated by John Van Neumann but has been popularized by Kurzweil (2005). But see Stanislaw (1958).
7. So, from this view, while we might think of ourselves as singular – that is to say you and I might like to think of ourselves as such, that our minds are ours and ours alone – in fact, if one believes this view, our consciousness is the outcome of millions of little acts, little calculations and stratagems at the cellular (and system) level that produces this sense of self. Our sense of that self is now seen to be egregious. This is the view that Dennett argued for in his *Consciousness Explained* (1991).
8. This is the rub of Kant, of course: personal accountability. In Kant, the self is a transcendental, a premise that cannot be avoided in understanding human nature. Kant is difficult to read, and often obscure, but the best introduction to this fundamental concept is in Scruton (2001).
9. This is most eloquently expressed by the physicist, R. Jones, in his (2004) *Soft Machines* – a much better book than Dennett's in my view, since it explores the consequence of this important distinction – the one between description of activities and action that is governed by self-awareness. For those interested in exploring this line of argument, they should go back to Anscombe's *Intention* (1957) which explains how motives distinguish human action. In this view, a machine cannot have a motive, though it might have 'reasons for doing what it does' – such as probabilistic reasons. But for an introduction see Harper et al., *Choice* (2018).
10. This is of course an argument that derives from the ordinary language philosophers, Wittgenstein (*op cit*) being the most regarded, if not the easiest to read.
11. Of course, this is brutally expressed this being the conclusion. It is, needless to say, the substance of Wittgenstein's later inquiries (*op cit*, 1953): viz, not that we are *only* to be understood in words, but the relationship between our doings and ways of accounting is subtle and fundamental to how we understand.
12. A Turing Machine is a computer that has been designed to support generalized functions rather than specific, unique ones. A PC is a perfect example – a computer for general purposes. The reason why this is an important concept is because it has turns out that algorithms can be developed that allow generalized hardware to solve particular problems, and algorithms are much easier to make than hardware.

Bibliography

Anscombe, G.E.M. (1957). *Intention*. Cambridge, MA: Harvard University Press.
Boden, M.A. (1977). *Artificial intelligence and natural man*. New York: Basic Books.
———.(2016). *AI: Its nature and future*. Oxford: Oxford University Press.
Carr, N. (2015). *The glass cage: Who needs humans anyway?* London: Vintage Books.
Dennett, D. (1991). *Consciousness explained*. London: The Penguin Press.
Harper, R., Randall, D. and Sharrock, W. (2016). *Choice*. Cambridge: Polity Press.
Kaplan, J. (2015). *Humans need not apply: A guide to health and work in the age of artificial intelligence*. New Haven, CT: Yale University Press.
———. (2016). *Artificial intelligence: What everyone needs to know*. Oxford: Oxford University Press.
Jones, R. (2004). *Soft machines: Nanotechnology and life*. Oxford: Oxford University Press.
Kitano, H. (2016). 'Artificial intelligence to win the Nobel prize', *AI Magazine*, Spring, pp. 39–49.
Kurzweil, R. (2005). *The singularity is near*. London: Penguin.
Markoff, J. (2015). *Machines of loving grace*. New York: Harper Collins.
Neyland, D. (2019). *The everyday life of an algorithm*. London: Palgrave Macmillan.
Sadler, M. and Regan, N. (2019). 'Game changer: AlphaZero's ground-breaking chess strategies and the promise of AI', *New Chess*, The Netherlands.
Sartre, J.P. (1956). *Being and nothingness: An essay on phenomenological ontology*, tr. H. Barnes. New York: Routledge Classics.
Scruton, R. (2001). *Kant: A very short introduction*. Oxford: OUP.
———. (2006). *Sexual desire: A philosophical investigation*. London and New York: Continuum.
Shanker, S. (1998). *Wittgenstein's remarks on the foundations of AI*. London: Taylor and Francis.
Stanford University (2016). *Artificial intelligence and life in 2030*. Stanford University, https://ai100.Stanford.edu
Spelda, P. and Stritecky, V. (2020). 'The future of human-artificial intelligence nexus and its environment costs', *Futures*, https://doi.org/10.1016/j.futures.2020.102531
Stanislaw, U. (1958). 'Tribute to John Van Neumann', *Bulletin of the American Mathematical Society*, 64 (3), part 2: 5.
Wittgenstein, L. (1953/2009). *Philosophical investigations*, 4th edition, tr. G.E.M. Anscombe, P.M.S. Hacker and J. Schulte. Oxford: Wiley-Blackwell.
Yeung, G., Borowiec, D, Friday, A., Harper, R. and Garraghan, P. (2020). 'Towards GPU utilization prediction for cloud deep learning', in *HotCloud20: 12th USENIX workshop on Hot Topics in Cloud Computing*. Boston, MA: ACM Press. Available at: https://eprints.lancs.ac.uk/id/eprint/144290/1/HotCloud20_GPU_Prediction.pdf

4
Anticipation
Flourishing for the future

Christopher Groves

Introduction

> *To most ordinary people, and certainly to those who lead lives in conditions of poverty, exclusion, displacement, violence and repression – the future often presents itself as a luxury, a nightmare, a doubt, or a shrinking possibility.*
>
> (Appadurai, 2013, p. 299)

Arjun Appadurai identifies here a particular kind of negative experience, with both individual and collective aspects, one associated with what we might call a loss of future. What has not been lost is a *specific* future, in the sense of a specific hoped-for outcome or aspired-to state. What has been lost is the possibility of experiencing the capability to aspire to something better. The future *as such* shrinks around the present, shadowing it with a narrowed and generally disturbing set of meanings. What is lost therefore is a particular way of relating to the future, a capability for imagining it as different and better. This capability has often been associated with ideals of cultural and political modernity, connected to the possibility of planning rationally for individual improvement and collective progress, the spread of free education and so on. Appadurai, however, identifies a characteristic form of global inequality constituted by the denial of such a capability to the impoverished and/or oppressed in societies across the world, and particularly in the global South.

> The Ojibwa people have been counting on their native culture for hundreds of years to tune their moral and conceptual reflexes, to organize and give rhythm to their everyday lives, to give shape to things. That old mould was simply broken, and the result was a kind of bewilderment and disorientation that the usual sociological concepts – anomie, estrangement, alienation – are not rich enough to capture or reflect.
>
> (Erikson, 1995)

Is another kind of experience – and perhaps injustice – being identified here by Kai Erikson, recounting the aftermath of a toxic contamination incident which affected the lands of some members of the Asubpeeschoseewagong Ojibwa band of First Nations people in Ontario?

At an apparent distance from cultural modernity, what might in some anthropological literature be referred to as a 'traditional' society is represented here as having undergone the loss of its link to its past, with devastating consequences. There is no mention here of aspiration at all, but instead Erikson mentions the Asubpeeschoseewagong losing the 'old mould' of tradition, and with it, their sense of orientation within the world.

In this chapter, what I want to suggest is going on in each of these cases is actually quite similar. The experience that Erikson suggests is not fully captured by traditional sociological concepts is comparable in one vital aspect to that of the global poor and displaced denied the capacity to aspire. What is lost in each case is a capability, the capability to navigate the future, understood as the horizon of the present. The future is never truly present. Yet as Niklas Luhmann puts it, 'the essential characteristic of an horizon is that we can never touch it, never get at it, never surpass it, but that in spite of that, it contributes to the definition of the situation' (Luhmann, 1976, p. 140). The future, in this sense, is always projected beyond the present, experienced as contributing to our understanding of what is latent in the present. As is underlined by the phenomena of hope or anticipatory fear, our sense of what is to come can change our understanding of what the world is like now and what we should or can do in response.

Human cultures are constantly constructing, through the work of meaning-making, jetties of certainty and security out into an intrinsically unknowable future. Human cultures in this sense are anticipatory endeavours, composed of practices that seek to respond to possible futures but also to actively shape them. Such practices, however, also create specific kinds of vulnerability. When these vulnerabilities are shaken by events, the accompanying experience of loss can erode, not just particular desired futures, but the sense of being able to navigate the future at all. In this, the losses of capability identified by Appadurai and Erikson have, I want to suggest, a similar root. That lies in the erosion of collective as well as individual anticipatory capability. In this chapter, I explore how we can understand the anticipatory character of human society (in its cultural but also material aspects) by using the kinds of concepts developed in recent years within the new interdisciplinary field of anticipation studies. I show how these concepts enable us to understand more precisely the ways in which an erosion of anticipatory capability can be considered the source of particular kinds of harm, and therefore of injustice. In particular, because anticipation should, I argue, be considered a kind of *meta*capability, undermining it can have significant cascade effects upon other vital capabilities.

The capabilities approach

Before we turn to examine the concept of anticipation in the technical sense developed within anticipation studies, we need to explore the idea of capability itself, in the technical sense developed within the work of Amartya Sen, Martha Nussbaum and others. The capabilities approach to justice proposes that understanding the nature of injustice means more than just focussing on how resources are distributed (Nussbaum, 2003; Sen, 1993). Resources, material or otherwise, and how they are distributed are important, but their availability is not the end of the story. Two other concepts, Sen and Nussbaum independently argue, are necessary. *Functionings* are the things we strive for, ends or purposes that provide reasons for action, and which are socially valued as constitutive of some vision or other of a good life. *Capabilities*, on the other hand, are opportunities to act in ways that can realize functionings. Capabilities are thus constitutive of freedom, providing the real possibility of acting towards socially valued ends. They may or may not be present when material and other resources also are, and mark whether or not people 'are able to translate those protections and goods into actual achievements that characterize a life that is worthy of the dignity of human beings' (Holland, 2008, p. 321). Capabilities are thus possibilities for achieving functionings through the exercise of agency. Being healthy for example, is a capability, while being a medal-winning athlete is a functioning. Being politically active in the community is a functioning, while effective freedom of association is a capability. Capabilities and functionings are thus distinct from resources (such as food to support both health and athletic excellence). A lack of such capabilities can therefore be taken to define deprivation and used to help spot inequality and define injustice.

Capabilities are also *relational*, as Robeyns (2005) explains. Whether one has access to capabilities or not is dependent on interactions between a range of distinct conditions. In particular, it is dependent on relationships between characteristics of individuals and characteristics of their environment (conversion factors). People's own individual circumstances (say, if they have a disability) can mean that it is harder for them to convert resources into capability in a particular environment that subjects them to specific constraints (Nussbaum 2006). Wheelchair users, for example, encounter historical biases in the engineering of the public environment. Stairs and narrow doorways present obstacles to them that then require additional resources to be available in order to re-engineer access.

The capabilities approach therefore identifies injustice as a lack of equitable access to vital capabilities. The conditions necessary for such capabilities to exist are a combination of individual and social elements. In this sense, the capabilities approach is ethically individualist – it is access to capabilities for individuals (like the wheelchair user) that is the currency of justice. At the same time, it is arguably not methodologically individualist and definitely not ontologically individualist (Robeyns, 2005). Social conditions – norms, institutional structures, shared practices and so on – are important in determining whether individuals have capabilities (as in the case of the wheelchair user negotiating a world of stairs and narrow doors). It is individuals who suffer detriment through loss of access to capabilities, but such detriment can arise along a variety of pathways that are structural in nature (e.g. discrimination through a caste system, racism, the ways polluting industries cluster in materially deprived or ethnically diverse communities, etc.).

Given this general approach to understanding the significance of capabilities, can we say more about what counts as one? Some theorists such as Sen are less concerned about stipulating what might do so without further empirical research. Nussbaum, however, identifies a list of specific candidates for the status of capabilities, which she views as universally necessary conditions of any form of good life that is composed of any specific set of functionings (see Table 4.1). These include elements that are basic and necessary for physical and psychological survival, but are also in her view, requirements for any form of life that could be called a flourishing or thriving one.

Nussbaum also makes an important point regarding the role of certain capabilities in relation to other ones. Some capabilities, such as practical reason in her table, may play a structuring role in relation to other ones. That is to say, they are *architectonic*, in practice, for the whole set of capabilities, as access to a capability like practical reason enables people to identify other capabilities and prioritize them in the pursuit of particular functionings and with them specific visions of the good life.

This role has been attributed by other theorists more emphatically to some capabilities that they identify as metacapabilities, which must be present in order that other

Table 4.1 Nussbaum's list of core capabilities (from Nussbaum, 2003)

1. Life	Able to live to the end of a normal length human life, and to not have one's life reduced to not worth living.
2. Bodily health	Able to have a good life which includes (but is not limited to) reproductive health, nourishment and shelter.
3. Bodily integrity	Able to change locations freely, in addition to, having sovereignty over one's body which includes being secure against assault (for example, sexual assault, child sexual abuse, domestic violence and the opportunity for sexual satisfaction).
4. Senses, imagination and thought	Able to use one's senses to imagine, think and reason in a 'truly human way' – informed by an adequate education. Furthermore, the ability to produce self-expressive works and engage in religious rituals without fear of political ramifications. The ability to have pleasurable experiences and avoid unnecessary pain. Finally, the ability to seek the meaning of life.
5. Emotions	Able to have attachments to things outside of ourselves; this includes being able to love others, grieve at the loss of loved ones and be angry when it is justified.
6. Practical reason	Able to form a conception of the good and critically reflect on it.
7. Affiliation	A. Able to live with and show concern for others, empathize with (and show compassion for) others and the capability of justice and friendship. Institutions help develop and protect forms of affiliation.
	B. Able to have self-respect and not be humiliated by others, that is, being treated with dignity and equal worth. This entails (at the very least) protections of being discriminated on the basis of race, sex, sexuality, religion, caste, ethnicity and nationality. In work, this means entering relationships of mutual recognition.
8. Other species	Able to have concern for and live with other animals, plants and the environment at large.
9. Play	Able to laugh, play and enjoy recreational activities.
10. Control over one's environment	A. Political – Able to effectively participate in the political life, which includes having the right to free speech and association.
	B. Material – Able to own property, not just formally, but materially (that is, as a real opportunity). Furthermore, having the ability to seek employment on an equal basis as others, and the freedom from unwarranted search and seizure.

capabilities can be exercised at all. Sridhar Venkatapuram, for example, drawing on Judith Jarvis Thompson's concept of a 'cluster right' and Sen's own concept of a 'meta-right', defines a metacapability (such as health, in his view) as 'an overarching capability to achieve a cluster of basic capabilities to be and do things that make up a minimally good human life in the contemporary world' (Venkatapuram, 2013). Two candidates that have been advanced for the status of metacapability are Appadurai's 'meta-capacity' of aspiration, which we encountered earlier, and Breena Holland's concept of a sustainable ecological capacity (SEC) (Holland, 2008).

Aspiration, like Nussbaum' practical reason, is necessary to imagine how to achieve valued functionings, Appadurai argues. If one has access to it, then one is able to marshal clear conceptions of the capabilities that need to be in place to attain those functionings, and also of how one can come to possess them. This capacity to hope for a different future is 'not evenly distributed in any society', as material wealth, power and dignity through recognition grant individuals more opportunities to plan and achieve a future by attaining the stepping stones to goals that form part of some version of the good life. Breena Holland, by contrast, argues that we should 'treat certain ecological conditions as a metacapability necessary for all the capabilities on [Nussbaum's] list of "central human functional capabilities"' (Holland, 2008, p. 321). Rather like the existence of private property (see Nussbaum's capability 10B), SEC is a transindividual capability that is directly instrumentally necessary (Holland, 2008, p. 324) to support human health and life (Nussbaum's 1 and 2) as well as other capabilities like emotional attachments (Nussbaum's 5) and relations with other species more widely (Nussbaum's 8) (Holland, 2008, p. 323).

In either case, lack of access to a metacapability can create harms that cascade through the erosion of other capabilities that themselves depend on the metacapability. Just as with Nussbaum's capabilities, access depends on the interaction between individual attributes and wider conditions. Appadurai notes that people can be denied the opportunity to plan and strive for a different future by social norms, income inequalities, denial of access to education and so on. Holland sees pollution, land-use decisions, environmental racism and so on as having potentially significant impacts on SEC and people's access to it. Lack of access to the metacapability then has knock-on effects on access to other capabilities. Through stunted aspirations, people are less able to seek out other opportunities to flourish. In polluted or degraded environments, lifespans, health, relationships to others and possibly additional opportunities are also degraded.

Anticipation as metacapability

We now have three sets of ideas in view: Relational capabilities, metacapabilities (which are also relational) and the harms and injustices that arise from lack of access to capabilities and metacapabilities. In this section, I discuss anticipation – like capabilities, used in a technical sense – as a candidate for a metacapability and what relational conditions support it, before going on in the next section to discuss the nature of harms and injustice that issue from its degradation. Finally, I connect the discussion back to the two quotations from which we began, to show what the experiences documented by Appadurai and Erikson have in common.

Anticipation, in common usage, has both passive and active aspects. One can await something one is expecting to happen (foreseeing). One can also take action to pre-empt a coming possible future, either to avoid it or to make sure it happens (foreshadowing). The more technical sense of anticipation developed within anticipation studies draws on both these aspects. At the same time, however, it takes us away from any association between anticipation and, say, aspiration as Appadurai uses it. Aspiration involves imagination, emotion and cognition – but at the same time, is still a consciously exercised achievement. Anticipation, as understood within anticipation studies, is an orientation towards the future that is more an achievement of systems or assemblages than it is of individuals. Like the candidates for metacapability status discussed above, it remains dependent on a variety of enabling conditions.

Think of how a keenly present conscious sense of (even relatively passive) anticipation is more like the tip of an iceberg. One's conscious sense of actively awaiting something is the narrowed point of a complex bodily state of tension and poise, of which it is always possible to become more – but perhaps not fully – conscious. As Roberto Poli points out, there are explicit forms of anticipation, which rely on conscious modelling of future states and representational knowledge of potential futures, and more implicit forms, which may be called 'non-representational' as they do not involve explicit cognitive models of the future (Poli, 2010, pp. 772–773).

Anticipation studies examine both living and social systems through this lens, to trace how the pull of the future as well as the push from the past shapes organic and social activity. For example, researchers in systems biology, from Jakob von Uexküll to Francisco Varela (Weber and Varela, 2002) and Kalevi Kull (1999), have insisted that the behaviour of living systems cannot be properly explained or predicted without attending to the anticipatory capacity of living systems. Changing environments demand that organisms respond to them in creative ways. Hesitating between alternatives and improvising unpredictable actions are ways in which living beings express this capacity. More or less complex organisms possess different degrees of freedom affecting the latitude they have for anticipation. Higher degrees of freedom go hand in hand, however, with an increase in the amount of energy an organism has to expend in anticipating potential futures and in responding to them. Humans and other living beings, from relatively simple to complex, can all therefore be located on a continuum of anticipatory capability. At the same time, as Hans Jonas (1982) put it, living beings are also located somewhere on a continuum of degrees of 'needful freedom'. The more sensitivity they have to potential futures, and the more they are able to internally model different outcomes, the more they are vulnerable to uncertainty. There is no freedom to actively anticipate alternative futures without a need for some armature of stability with which one can face these possible alternatives. The alternative is paralysis.

Talking of active and passive anticipation to get at the relationship between alternative futures and stability is therefore not really appropriate either, once we have a more penetrating analysis of the concept. Anticipation implies 'living forward' in response to some felt demand, the pull of the future, the unresolved not-yet that *in*sists in the present (complementing the way the past *per*sists in it). Living entities strive to 'keep themselves together', maintaining a dynamic but stable boundary between themselves and their environment. They have to be able to model or simulate possible future states of themselves and their environment but also to act in a way that prefigures and strives to realize future states. Their functional organization as a set of nested or interlinked systems makes this possible. For example, in living creatures with a central nervous system, the autonomic system, shaped by genetic inheritance and governed by the hypothalamus and limbic systems within the brain, regulates respiration and cardiac function from moment to moment. This provides a base level of anticipation – shaping immediate future states of the organism moment to moment in cyclical rhythms, through contraction and relaxation of the heart muscles and so on.

Further up the scale of complexity, acquired habits form more complex levels of anticipation, shaping the future states of the organism moment to moment. They structure bodily, emotional and cognitive functioning alike, from early developmental stages on. Habits are acquired by individuals, but in social animals they are generally developed in a social context (e.g. meerkats, wolves and chimpanzees). Humans are no different in this and take the process of social acquisition to still higher levels of complexity. Layered upon other forms of habit, emotional regulation is a vital capability for infants, for example, which develops into the ability to self-soothe when fearful or excited. But this individual capacity is itself dependent on attachment behaviours which arise from the interactions between infants and their caregivers. At this level, expectations about the world are built: The caregiver who leaves will (hopefully) return. The world is experienced as something trustworthy or untrustworthy, depending on whether such expectations are met or not. And on top of this level is built the capacity to imagine other outcomes. What happens if the caregiver does not return?

In living beings, the armature of stability I mentioned is therefore primarily manifested as self-regulation, or 'keeping oneself together'. The organism unconsciously or with degrees of awareness aims to keep its systems functioning within an acceptable range of possible states. This includes everything from being able to find food and thus avoid starvation to being able to respond appropriately to social cues and thus avoid violence or ostracism. In each case, the ability to implicitly or with fuller consciousness imagine possible outcomes and act to forestall or actualize them enables a living entity to realize valued states and thus to keep itself together, to persist in its own being, as Spinoza put it.

Flexibility and the ability to pause, hesitate and improvise are thus the hallmarks of higher degrees of freedom in a living system. But as Jonas identified in the concept of needful freedom, the ability to shape the future with more freedom, with more sensitivity and also reach is costly. Where living forward is bound up with complex emotional states of fear, trepidation, hope or yearning, for example, the armature of stability needs to be correspondingly complex. As well as encompassing the material conditions of social reproduction, cultural conditions of social meaning-making are required. For example, the social conditions that sustain emotional regulation through stable attachment to others, for example, encompass networks of interpersonal relationships, but also shared practices and normative ideals (Marris, 1996).

These shared practices and ideals have the broader function of structuring time, creating rhythms of return and thus patterning time, enabling reliable expectations to be formed. Rites of passage (like the traditional Christian trajectory of baptism, confirmation, wedding, funeral) ensure that the path of individuals through the culturally imprinted universe tracks recognizable coordinates. Deeply embedded expectations give shape to the future and are written into the norms and other structures that give shape to social life. The cycles of natural rhythms are bent into cultural circles in which the expectation of the same ritually inscribed moment returns (Adam and Groves, 2007). Such moments are, moreover, generally embedded in places. Culture is enacted in specific places through which humans move with more or less regularity. Places – meaningful, significant locations – can be understood as accumulations of interactions between human and non-human forces, as Tim Ingold (2011) describes them, where humans 'write' on the landscape and the landscape reciprocally exerts a moulding power upon them. Human anticipation can therefore be understood as being more than just human, incorporating material elements including the temporal character of places, bodies living forward in myriad ways moment to moment to keep themselves together and societies organizing their means of production in order to reproduce themselves. Further, it also incorporates meaning-making, conducted through the maintenance of attachment relationships that help to reassure that a trustworthy, reliable world exists, and collective norms which establish a meaningful social 'cosmos'.

Why is anticipation, understood in this complex sense, a metacapability? First, anticipation is necessary for other capabilities to be exercised. From health to emotional attachment to practical reason and political participation, the capacity not only to foresee what may be coming but also to foreshadow what might happen through action is a condition of being able to plan and act. Anticipation identifies a level of systemic functional organization of capabilities at the social level or at the level of the individual that is necessary for any capabilities such as those identified by Nussbaum. Moreover, it is more fundamental than the capability to aspire, as defined by Appadurai. Aspiration itself depends on a sense of a reliable future, which is bound up with both material reproduction and sense-making. At the same time, diverse anticipatory systems are more than just enabling conditions. They involve the participation of the individual and indeed of collectives (when place and culture come under consideration) – in the zone of interactions between environment and agency identified by Robeyns (2005).

A capability (or metacapability) requires the agency of the individual benefiting from it. This means that SEC as defined by Holland may not be a metacapability or capability – it is more like a resource required by capabilities. Anticipation, on the other hand, is an organized form of activity in which the environment and those agents who act within it are implicated together. At the different levels where we can identify anticipation, the past *per*sists in some way – in learnt habit, in personal memory of attachment relationships, in cultural memories of past events and in the paths marked through places. Conversely, the future *in*sists, opening up and demanding a response to uncertainty from within a more or less stable situation. As long as the world can be trusted, such responses may often turn out to be, as it were, variations on accustomed themes. But sometimes more improvisation is required.

Undermining anticipation

If we accept, then, that anticipation is a metacapability that is dependent on both agency and socio-environmental conditions, we then have to ask whether and how it can be undermined, and if so, what effects this can have? This brings us back to the quotation from Erikson with which we began. His case study focusses on the contamination through a mercury spill caused by a paper mill upstream of the ancestral lands of the Asubpeeschoseewagong Ojibwa, and particularly of the river flowing through them. What it shows is how harm visited on one or more capabilities can undermine a metacapability in ways that then erode still other capabilities.

Unable to fish or hunt effectively thanks to the pollution incident, the community was unable to participate in what were culturally vital practices, which affirmed the meaning of their relationship with the lands and which they felt to be constitutive of their individual and group identities. The connections between culture and place 'give rhythm to their everyday lives', as Erikson puts it. They make possible the foresight and foreshadowing which constitute anticipation. The loss of meaningful, identity-constituting practices breaks the band's collective and individual participation in a reliable world. Cultural memory is shaken as access to collectively remembered places is lost.

The community's future becomes lost, not in the sense in which a particular aspiration or hope might be lost, but in the sense that the future as horizon begins to lose the consistency it had always had. Alcoholism and domestic abuse became significant problems within the band as time went on. The 'bewilderment and disorientation' beyond anomie, estrangement and alienation identified by Erikson stems from a sense that the community cannot keep itself together, and nor can the individuals who comprise it keep themselves and their closest relationships together, once the links between culture and place are broken. From this breaking of attachment to culture and place comes degradation of physical and mental health, and of the capacity for association, as the shape of the future is lost.

Attachment to place, affiliation with others and participation in shared practices serve as the 'means of anticipation'. These are not individual attributes or possessions. Instead, they are more like a commons on which individuals draw by virtue of their membership of a collective that shares to some extent in cultural resources or co-inhabits a place. This points beyond the ethical individualism of dominant positions in the capabilities tradition, given that the metacapability of anticipation is dependent on capabilities that are collective in nature (Schlosberg and Carruthers, 2010), and that the trauma stemming from the loss of such capabilities is also shared. This trauma also has to be addressed in ways that involve a whole community trying to re-establish a relationship with its past and its future, a collective work of mourning (Moglen, 2005).

The means of anticipation build jetties of relative certainty out into an intrinsically uncertain future. The loss of them, accompanied by a loss of anticipation as metacapability, followed by further knock-on effects on still other capabilities is an experience widely documented in literature on environmental justice, and experiences of urban planning. It can add up to the loss of a whole, meaningful world; of a diverse set of valued functionings; and of a coherent sense of what a good life might look like. I discuss similar phenomena mentioned in more than three decades of scholarship in Groves (2015), along with my own comparable case study from contemporary south Wales. Peter Marris (1986) in his studies of urban renewal from London and Nigeria and Mindy Fullilove (2004) in her studies of relocation of African American neighbourhoods in the United States both show how the loss of the persistence of the past in the form of place, practice and affiliation is also a loss of future. Just as the capabilities approach identifies ethically significant harm in the loss of access to specific capabilities, I want to suggest that the specific loss that accompanies the erosion of the means of anticipation is a loss of the 'shape of the future', of a reliable world. If this line of ethical argument is accepted then there still remains the question of how access to the means of anticipation becomes unequally distributed. I have already alluded to how this may be dependent on political processes like land-use planning, phenomena like environmental racism and other mechanisms. Groves (2015) gives a treatment of these issues, in relation to the concept of the 'colonization of attachment'. For now, however, they lie outwith the scope of this chapter.

Bibliography

Adam, B. and Groves, C. (2007). *Future matters: Action, knowledge, ethics*. Leiden: Brill.
Appadurai, A. (2013). *The future as cultural fact: Essays on the global condition*. London: Verso.
Erikson, K. (1995). *A new species of trouble: The human experience of modern disasters*. New York W.W. Norton and Co.
Fullilove, M.T. (2004). *Root shock*. New York: Ballantine.
Groves, C. (2015). 'The bomb in my backyard, the serpent in my house: Environmental justice, risk and the colonization of attachment', *Environmental Politics*, 24(6), pp. 853–873.
Holland, B. (2008). 'Justice and the environment in Nussbaum's "capabilities approach": Why sustainable ecological capacity is a meta-capability', *Political Research Quarterly*, 61, pp. 319–332.
Ingold, T. (2011). *Being alive: Essays on movement, knowledge and description*. London and New York, Routledge.
Jonas, H. (1982). *The phenomenon of life*. Chicago, IL and London: University of Chicago Press.
Kull, K. (1999). 'Biosemiotics in the twentieth century: A view from biology', *Semiotica*, 127(1–4), pp. 385–414.
Luhmann, N. (1976). 'The future cannot begin: Temporal structures in modern society', *Journal of Social Research*, 43(1), pp 130–152
Marris, P. (1986). *Loss and change*. London: Routledge and Kegan Paul.
Moglen, S. (2005). 'On mourning social injury', *Psychoanalysis, Culture & Society*, 10, pp. 151–167.
Nussbaum, M.C. (2003). *Women and human development: The capabilities approach*. Cambridge: Cambridge University Press.
Nussbaum, M.C. (2006). *Frontiers of justice: Disability, nationality species membership*. Cambridge, MA: The Belknap Press.
Robeyns, I. (2005). 'The capability approach: A theoretical survey', *Journal of Human Development*, 6(1), pp. 93–117.

Schlosberg, D., and Carruthers, D. (2010). 'Indigenous struggles, environmental justice, and community capabilities', *Global Environmental Politics*, *10*, pp. 12–35.

Sen, A. (1993). 'Capability and well-being'. In Nussbaum, M.C. and Sen, A. (eds.), *The quality of life* (pp. 30–53). Oxford: Clarendon Press.

Venkatapuram, S. (2013). *Health justice: An argument from the capabilities approach.* Cambridge: Polity Press.

Weber, A., and Varela, F.J. (2002). 'Life after Kant: Natural purposes and the autopoietic foundations of biological individuality', *Phenomenology and the Cognitive Sciences*, *1*, pp. 97–125.

5
BioFutures
Where futurists and biologists meet

Derek Gatherer

Introduction

Doing futures frequently involves the conceptualization and visualization of future worlds, tentatively feeling our way through the mights, maybes, coulds and shoulds of the 'not-yet' – Ernst Bloch's *noch nicht* (see Garforth, this volume; Bloch, 2000). These scenarios, these visions, of other worlds may be broadly divided into utopias and dystopias, the preferred and unpreferred extremes of our spectrum of future possibilities. Of course, we more often find ourselves, in the fullness of time, in some intermediate condition, but the unfulfilled utopian and dystopian visions of past generations and soon-to-be unfulfilled ones of the present, serve as beacons illuminating our navigation into the inevitably somewhat different future. I begin with just one such brightly shining beacon, a dystopia from over 200 years ago that still directly engages our attention today.

In 1798, Thomas Robert Malthus published *An Essay on the Principle of Population*. Malthus's deeply dystopian vision of an overpopulated planet ravaged by famine, war and plague was a major influence on Charles Darwin's theory of natural selection and continues to inspire modern neo-Malthusians (e.g. Ehrlich, 2013). Recently, dystopian thought within biology has widened its focus from humans to the entire planet. For instance, Louis Leakey and Roger Lewin's *The Sixth Extinction* (1996) provides some of the theoretical background to activist groups such as Extinction Rebellion, who may be broadly described as eco-dystopian. Juxtaposed to this dystopian strand in biology, a more optimistic outlook has been fostered by the discovery of antibiotics, the implementation of mass vaccination programmes, organ transplantation, *in vitro* fertilization, regenerative medicine and genetic modification, among other technologies. This viewpoint, of which a representative example may be found in Aubrey de Grey and Michael Rae's *Ending Aging* (2007), can be broadly described as techno-utopian. Such biological techno-utopianism has been deeply influential on techno-utopian thought outside of biology, for instance Ray Kurzweil's *The Singularity Is Near* (2005), which envisages the integration of living things into, and their ultimate subsumption within, computer systems.

This chapter proposes that such futures-oriented thought within biology and biological themes within futures thinking (of which more in a later section) may usefully be collated

DOI: 10.4324/9780429440717-6

under the rubric of BioFutures – a retrospective hashtagging of numerous contributions to the area, whether consciously futurological or not, from wherever they sit on the utopian-dystopian spectrum. BioFutures is a discipline that does not yet formally exist, but which I hope to show has existed *avant la lettre* since Thomas More's original *Utopia* of 1516. My purpose in this chapter is to persuade biologists to do futures, to persuade futurists to think about the biological implications of their future visions and to bring both together under the BioFutures umbrella. The first step is to investigate just why Malthus's dystopia was so influential.

The fevers of evolution

In February 1858, naturalist Alfred Russel Wallace lay gravely ill with a fever on the island of Ternate in the Moluccas (now North Maluku Province, Indonesia). In the throes of his delirium, strange dreams began pulsing through his semi-consciousness, dreams of a dystopian world where all living things were engaged in a fight to the death over diminishing natural resources. As Wallace's fever subsided and clarity returned to his mind, he began writing urgently. Wallace realized that the source of his nightmares had been the writings of Malthus, which predicted that humanity would eventually expand beyond the capacity of the planet to support it, triggering terrible famines, wars and pestilences (Malthus, 2004). A common enough nightmare, but Wallace's delirium had also thrown up another idea. Supposing many species are in a state of permanent Malthusian crisis, with population sizes at the ceiling of what the natural environment permits – the 'carrying capacity' as modern ecologists describe it – what would the consequences be? Suppose that one or two individuals were naturally equipped with some physical, constitutional or behavioural advantage that allowed them to survive where their fellow conspecifics died. And suppose that this advantage was heritable through the generations. Wallace pondered what to do with his manuscript, then decided that there was only one possible course of action – to send it to Charles Darwin (Wallace, 1905, pp. 361–363).

'On The Tendency of Varieties to Depart Indefinitely from the Original Type' (Wallace, 1858), more usually referred to as *The Ternate Essay*, was read at a meeting of the Linnean Society in London on the 1st July 1858, along with a hurriedly prepared summary by Darwin of his own thoughts along the same lines. Darwin was unable to attend, having just lost his youngest son, one of six children that died in an outbreak of scarlet fever in the village of Downe in Sussex that summer. The theory of evolution by natural selection was conceived and born in the midst of terrible fevers.

Darwin was already well acquainted with the Malthus family, both intellectually, having read *An Essay on the Principle of Population*, 'for amusement' he claimed, in October 1838 (Darwin and Huxley, 1974, p. 71), and socially – Malthus's daughter had been a bridesmaid at the wedding of Darwin's cousin (Wilson, 2017, p. 156). However, there is little indication that either Darwin or Wallace was much persuaded by Malthus's argument concerning the *future*. The theory of natural selection was about how the natural world had evolved over *past* aeons of time. Darwin's great work, appearing in the following year of 1859, was entitled *On the Origin of Species* (Darwin, 1964), not *On the Future of Species*. Malthus's theory had become a powerful tool to understand the past of all species, but his dystopian vision of the future of humans was quietly brushed off by Victorian optimists.

To modern biologists, 'nothing in biology makes sense except in the light of evolution' (Dobzhansky, 1973). Malthus is thus a pivotal figure in the creation of modern biology, but his dystopian vision sits quietly, even anonymously, at the heart of a theory he did not himself envisage. However, taken on his own terms, Malthus also represents the first example of thinking in a dystopian futures vein written from a biological standpoint. Biologists since Malthus have occasionally also turned their attention to what their discipline can say about the future, and futurists have sometimes added a biological dimension to their predictions and scenarios (see section 'I had a family....'). These activities are usually carried on independently with little interaction between the two perspectives. The construction of an interface between biologists thinking about the future and futurists thinking about biology is what I propose to name BioFutures, a discipline that can be retrospectively reconstructed from both strands of thought. This chapter both attempts this reconstruction and urges its use as a starting point for further work.

Although prediction of the future has been a perennial human interest, thinking about the future has never been just about forecasting. Indeed, futures thinking is just as often a wrangling over the present – as much about what is desirable as it is about what is possible or likely (Amara, 1978). The utopias and dystopias of our dreams and nightmares are devices to shake us out of TINA ('there is no alternative'; see Garforth, this volume) attitudes to the present, a process that Immanuel Wallerstein (1998) has termed 'utopistics'. Modern readings of Malthus often emphasize just such controversialist elements in his work, pointing out that his ideas should be interpreted in the context of his long-running polemical interchange with William Godwin over state welfare policy (Malthus, 2004). Similarly, many of the BioFutures arguments I shall consider come with prescriptive implications, whether explicit or more disguised.

The ghost of Malthus

Exactly 160 years after the publication of *On the Origin of Species* in London, the streets of that city, and to a lesser extent many others across the world, were filled with protestors calling for co-ordinated global action on climate change. Environmental protest is, of course, nothing new. Its intellectual roots can be traced back to Fairfield Osborn's *Our Plundered Planet* (1948) and its leap into the public conscious to Rachael Carson's *Silent Spring* (1965). However, what distinguishes the new generation of protestors is their emphasis on the likelihood of global catastrophe, including a mass extinction event that would wipe out the natural world as we know it. This idea has its origins in Louis Leakey and Roger Lewin's *The Sixth Extinction* (1996) – although modern extinction activists are more likely to have read Elizabeth Kolbert's identically titled work (2014). What Malthus predicted for humans is now predicted for all species according to modern eco-dystopians – a warming, polluted, deforested planet with greatly diminished carrying capacity. Although rarely explicitly mentioned in the climate activism debate, Malthus is back to haunt us.

But the biology that Darwin and Wallace created by co-opting Malthus has other descendants. Two centuries of scientific advances have engendered a spirit of immense optimism about the power of biotechnology to improve our future. The discovery of antibiotics, the implementation of mass vaccination programmes, organ transplantation, *in vitro* fertilization, hormonal contraception, regenerative medicine, genome projects, genetic modification and synthetic biology among other technologies have all made, or are widely predicted to make, massive changes to human life. Ecologists may see planetary degradation, but laboratory scientists more often see a glowing future. This tension between eco-dystopianism and techno-utopianism, both of which are often packaged with their own political agendas, is a central issue in BioFutures. The argument is not just about the biological future we might have, but the future we ought to have.

The singularity is (almost, maybe or perhaps not) near

Biologists have no monopoly on techno-utopias. Ray Kurzweil's *The Singularity is Near* (2005) envisages a point, the singularity, where Moore's Law – the exponential improvement in computer processing power – produces computers that can calculate anything, and therefore solve any problem. Furthermore, having calculated how the human brain and consciousness work, it will then be possible to devise a method of uploading our personal conscious selves onto computers, where we can live immortally *in silico* long after our corporeal bodies have withered and died. Frank Tipler sees such a singularity as the state of perfection that religions have dimly perceived over the millennia in the form of heaven (Tipler, 1995). In Tipler's work, computer science and physics meet Teilhardian theology (Teilhard de Chardin, 1959) in techno-utopian apotheosis.

Kurzweil's silicon-embodied human consciousness has its conceptual roots in transhumanism. Originally another facet of Teilhardian eschatology, transhumanism later took a more materialist form in the thought of Fereidoun M. Esfandiary – for the last years of his life known by his chosen transhuman moniker of FM-2030 – who predicted that by 2030 (his own centenary), biologists would know enough about the ageing process to design medical treatments to halt it. Since 2000, FM-2030 has been in a deep freeze at Alcor, the cryonics repository, his 'deep nostalgia for the future' (Nichols, 2005) provoking him to take a long-odds bet on being resurrected to see it. Transhumanism rapidly entered the popular mainstream, appearing in various forms beginning with Martin Caidin's *Cyborg* (1972) right up to Russell T. Davies' near-future themed television drama series *Years and Years* (2019).

In the transhuman movement today, there are both cyborgisers who wish to replace the fragile flesh of biological components with longer lasting hardware, and those that see synthetic biology as the way forward, a transhumanism which grows replacement parts in the laboratory rather than manufactures them on the assembly line. But not all biotechno-utopians go as far as transhumanism – Aubrey de Grey and Michael Rae's *Ending Aging* (2007) advocates a more conventionally pharmaceutical solution to human life extension. If the process of ageing can be understood at the molecular and cellular level, then it ought to be possible to design drugs that modify or preserve the functions of the relevant subcellular parts. De Grey believes that the first humans who will live forever, or at least for timespans far greater than our current upper limit of 120 years or so, are currently alive.

The plausibility of such techno-utopias depends on the validity of various assumptions they make about exactly how well we understand biology. Nobody doubts that we now understand far more than we did at the time of Darwin, or even at the turn of the present millennium, but, whether we know enough really to engineer life in the way that is proposed, is debatable. Kurzweil's singularity, in particular, makes very large assumptions about both the validity of Moore's Law and how close neuroscience is to understanding conscious awareness. Nevertheless, even if transhumanity and the singularity are still unachievable dreams, the cumulative impact of multiple technological advances on many fronts, which Damien Broderick and Colin Mason have described as 'The Spike' is undeniable (Broderick, 1997; Mason, 2003). For techno-utopians in biology, the spike in computing and telecommunications technology that began in the mid-1990s after many decades in gestation is a sure sign of the coming spike in biotechnology. There is also no doubt that they regard this as a desirable future.

'Might not we unleash horrors... a biological Hiroshima?'

Those looking at biotechnology from the outside have often been less utopian. The protagonist of Mary Shelley's *Frankenstein* (1818) gets into terrible trouble because he irresponsibly experiments, not on explosives, poisons or other weapons, but on life. Exactly 150 years after Shelley, the title of Gordon Rattray Taylor's *The Biological Time Bomb* (1968) speaks for itself. The above quote is not from Taylor's jeremiad, but from a work at the centre of the futures canon, Alvin Toffler's highly influential *Future Shock* (1970, p. 177). Toffler's short-term predictions in the biomedical field for the 1970s were largely accurate, if unambitious – organ transplantation, *in vitro* fertilization, an increase in the proportion of dementia sufferers due to an ageing population and the biotechnology industry were all Toffler prophecies that did indeed come to pass. Toffler only overreached himself on the artificial uterus, which still has not been realized some half a century later. Among these, it was the biotech industry that worried Toffler most. His concerns continued in his sequel *The Third Wave* (1981, p. 158). Again, BioFutures is not just about prediction of the form of future human life, but about influencing its governance.

Similar disquiet can be found in Anthony Giddens' *Runaway World* (1999, pp. 32–33). Giddens offers a more explicit policy recipe than Toffler, leaning towards the 'precautionary principle', which dictates that the implementation of new technologies should only be permitted after extensive investigation into their likely, or perhaps unintended, consequences – taking futures into the realms of regulatory and marketing approval. Giddens in particular discusses genetically modified organisms (GMOs) in this light, but ends by admitting that we may need to have GMOs simply to feed the growing population, a conclusion that Toffler had also slightly reluctantly reached in 1981. Nevertheless, these forebodings have continued to be voiced in more recent work by Francis Fukuyama (2002). On the other hand, one of the godfathers of modern environmental activism, Al Gore, in *The Future* (2013), synthesizes a viewpoint that is broadly techno-utopian while also eco-dystopian. For Gore, biotech is part of the solution to the climate crisis, not another crisis in its own right.

Toffler's 'biological Hiroshima' 1970 quote above was apparently paraphrased from a discussion with 'many of the world's leading scientists' (unnamed) and within a few years discomfort at the potential dangers of biotechnology culminated in a moratorium on genetic engineering research in the United States in 1974. The Asilomar Conference of the following year (Berg and Singer, 1995) formulated safety guidelines that continue to be the basis for academic and industrial biotech research around the world to this day, and from which regulatory frameworks such as the UK Genetically Modified Organisms (Contained Use) Regulations 2014 are descended. Debate about the safety of biotech is now virtually unknown within biology, but the heritage of techno-dystopianism can still be found in reference to 'Franken-foods' in discussions of GMOs in the popular media. European Union Directive 2001/18/EC allowed regional or national EU governments to ban GMOs without the requirement to provide scientific evidence to the European Food Safety Authority (EFSA). Wales and Scotland are among the regions that have implemented 2001/18/EC. Beyond politics, modern biotechno-dystopianism refers back to its Shelleyian roots in H.K. Gruber's opera *Frankenstein* (1977) which contains the aria 'Frankenstein is dancing with the test-tube lady' (official English language translation, although 'baby' might be more idiomatic than 'lady' in this context). Biologists still have some convincing to do to bring large sections of the general public on board.

'I had a family...it got to be a drag, I like it much better here'

Beyond, and prior to, these current debates, futurists have often turned their attention, not so much like Malthus, to the quantity of human procreation, but rather to the variety of its potential future forms. The above quote is from an interviewee in the film version (1972, section beginning 26:08) of Toffler's *Future Shock*, part of which is devoted to what many at the time saw as the inevitable disappearance of the nuclear family and its replacement by more communal forms of living. A strong hint is given that polyandry and polygyny would be prominent components of this new lifestyle.

More radically, Shulamith Firestone's *The Dialectic of Sex*, written in the same year as Toffler's *Future Shock*, looks to a future where reproduction could somehow be de-biologized, echoing Toffler's speculation about artificial uteri, thus liberating women not just from the social tyranny of family life, but from the biological tyranny of pregnancy and childbirth with all their concomitant dangers (Firestone, 1971, pp. 222, 233, 263). Here, we see a further use of futures, not merely predictive, nor even simply normative, but positively performative. A future that is currently implausible is offered as a device to loosen the constraints of the collective imagination. Such performative futures are common in literature. Mary Shelley offers *Frankenstein* as a 'what if' scenario rather than providing scientific details, leaving her more literally minded modern film interpreters to compensate with added scenes involving lightning bolts. Firestone's vision is prefigured in Aldous Huxley's *Brave New World* (1932) where rows of artificial uteri gestate away in baby farms, and contraception is readily available to all women – who carry it in 'Malthusian belts', a nod by Huxley to the father of all bio-dystopias. The slightly less technologically advanced dystopia – One State – of Yevgeny Zamyatin's *We* (1924) has children conceived by sexual appointments. The hero, I-330, finds himself in trouble with the authorities for flirting with D-503 rather than getting down to business. In One State, pregnancy and childbirth are natural, but all resulting children are turned over to the state for a communal education. Further back still, Thomas More's original *Utopia* (1516) has a patrilocal family structure, with distribution of surplus children to childless families, thus maintaining a steady family average size. Utopia's inhabitants risk penalties for 'forbidden embraces before marriage', but should this fail to control societal overpopulation, a colonial policy prevails, sending surpluses to begin new Utopias elsewhere.

The speculations of More, Zamyatin and Huxley are mostly with how future societies might police sexual activity and deal with any resulting children. Other authors have gone beyond this to grasp the potential evolutionary consequences of such controls. H.G. Wells, in *Anticipations* (1902) and *A Modern Utopia* (1903), advocated temporary marriages – although not quite so fleeting as those of Zamyatin – for which generous state subsidies would be available. Access to these arrangements, however, is positively means-tested so only those who have been economically successful may then reproduce. Fertility testing must also be carried out to ensure that the state's aid is spent (re)-productively. Lurking behind this, of course, is the approaching shadow of the eugenics movement. It is very difficult in hindsight to see something that ended in the 'Doctors' Trial' at Nuremberg in 1947 as an exercise in utopianism, but there is no doubt that it began with such intent. Others needed no hindsight – as early as 1913, G.K. Chesterton was campaigning successfully against inclusion of eugenic clauses in the 1913 Mental Deficiency Act, publishing the pamphlet *Eugenics and Other Evils* (Chesterton, 1922). In the United States, Franz Boas was engaged in a similar campaign (Boas, 1916). This is a perilous subject for modern biologists to write about. While we may be convinced that modern biotechnology is a force for good, we have to acknowledge that, as biologists, our track record on eugenics is entirely to our shame. Being sure of our positive contribution as a discipline to the future becomes difficult and uncomfortable when we pause to remember that our very fallible predecessors were usually equally sure of theirs. Part of my intention in advocating the BioFutures approach is to help biologists see our current views, on what is possible/likely/desirable, in the context of the decisions our predecessors made when faced with their own choices.

After Darwin's *Origin of Species*, the second most important book in evolutionary theory is R.A. Fisher's 1930 *The Genetical Theory of Natural Selection* (Fisher, 1999). The first seven chapters are a *tour de force* of scientific brilliance and the remaining five a standard exposition of inter-war eugenics. This dichotomy means that Fisher needs to be taught to modern undergraduates without actually encouraging them to read him. Fisher, a eugenic utopian, has therefore come to sit anonymously at the heart of modern evolutionary theory in the same way that Malthus, a population dystopian, sits anonymously at the heart of its nineteenth-century equivalent. Equally, advocating G.K. Chesterton as a shining opponent of eugenics becomes a little problematic once it is realized that his definition of the practice was wide enough to include birth control and that one of the main targets of his polemics over the years was Marie Stopes. And again, those who wish to highlight Stopes' valiant fight for women's reproductive rights cannot deny that she was, like Fisher, Wells and many others, a eugenicist.

Even to claim, as I did in a previous paragraph, that Nuremberg finally disposed of eugenics, is wishful thinking. There is no doubt that the full realization of the horrors that its practice implied was laid so bare that most remaining advocates turned away in disgust. Nevertheless, compulsory sterilization of those deemed unfit to breed continued in Sweden until 1976, while voluntary sterilization of those deemed fit was restricted. The Canadian provinces of Alberta and British Columbia, among several other jurisdictions around the world, also pursued a compulsory sterilization policy into the 1970s. Lee Kuan Yew's Singapore introduced the Graduate Mothers Scheme in 1984, encouraging Wellsian marriages of economically successful youth, although perhaps without Wells' enthusiasm for their temporariness. Even within futures circles, similar ideas occasionally resurfaced. Writing in Jungk and Galtung's compendium *Mankind 2000*, Werner Hirsch proposed increasing life expectancy and intelligence by administering growth hormones to the foetus during the period of neuronal development (fortunately not seriously contemplated either then or now), and the same Wellsian eugenic pairing of high IQ individuals that Lee Kuan Yew later advocated in Singapore (Hirsch, 1969).

The inescapability of our biological being-in-the-world

Biology is the most morally and socially corrosive of the sciences. Astronomers may gaze at the stars, but we biologists are down in the mud with the cannibal snails and the parasitic wasps. It is no accident that Richard Dawkins, the main modern popularizer of atheism (Dawkins, 2007), is an evolutionary biologist. In the words of the wife of one nineteenth-century bishop, 'I pray that Mr Darwin is wrong, but if he is right, I pray that it may not become widely known'.[1] Ironically, Biblical metaphors of our creation from, and dissolution into, dust seem to capture the biological world view perfectly. Human beings are not separate from the natural world around us, but merely one manifestation of it. This inevitably brings biology into potential conflict with other disciplines, especially sociology. Biology may appear to be making a perpetual 'appeal to nature' argument, imposing a normativity on human existence, insisting that we are prisoners of one or other aspect of our genetic heritage. Exactly which aspects depends on one's disciplinary stance within biology. Evolutionary psychologists (EP), for instance, postulate an Environment of Evolutionary Adaptation (EEA) generally taken to be the central/southern African savannah in the period 350,000–75,000 years before the present (exact boundaries varying according to author). It was in that environment, claim EP practitioners, that modern humans and their immediate ancestors underwent natural selective processes that brought them to a state of almost perfect adaptation. Our current morphology, physical abilities, psychological dispositions, our social organization and even our politics (Rubin, 2002) must be seen against that background. We do not have a 'caveman' mentality (they came later, in Ice Age Europe) but a more 'tribal long-range stamina hunting' mentality. We may look rather like our ape ancestors, but evolution in the EEA has made us more like a voracious pack of bipedal hyaenas. There is little room here for any belief that humans can be whatever we wish and that human society can be what we want it to be, if only we have the will. Firestone's biological tyranny seems to be extendible beyond reproduction, to all of life.

On the other hand, the appeal to nature argument is simply stood on its head by other biologists. We may know our nature and we may not like it – so let's set about working on how we can transcend it. This is part of the motivation for both mainstream biotechnology and its speculative transhumanist futures. Attempts to create utopias of perfect justice, peace and equality, from Robert Owen to the 1960s commune movement, may have foundered because their creators did not know, or had forgotten, that the material with which they were working – genus *Homo*, species *sapiens*, subspecies *sapiens* – is tied to the rest of the natural world through four billion years of evolutionary adaptation, and has been honed in an EEA from which we need to de-adapt now we are no longer in it. Perhaps we *are* prisoners of our biology, but the first step in escaping from any prison is to know its layout, and the routine by which it operates. Only then can planning begin.

The future of BioFutures

In the preceding paragraphs, I have retrospectively constructed a discipline of BioFutures co-opting More, Malthus, Shelley, Wells, Chesterton, Fisher, Huxley, Firestone and Toffler together with contemporary thinkers such as Fukuyama, Giddens, Kurzweil, Leakey, de Grey and Gore. Only from Toffler onwards would the label of futures be recognized, and only Fisher, Leakey and de Grey can be considered as primarily biologists. Even Malthus, whose work was so important to biology, regarded himself as an economist. Nevertheless, all have taken intense interest in what the future holds for us as biological beings, as living, eating, breathing, breeding, chattering, fighting and occasionally thinking animals, and in the power our increasing technological prowess gives us over that future. BioFutures has been alternately, or concurrently, utopian and dystopian; it has been predictive, speculative, normative and performative. Firestone, Kurzweil and de Grey have shocked readers with their insistence on counter-intuitive future possibilities; Fukuyama, Giddens and Leakey have issued dire warnings about human responsibility; and Shelley, Wells and Huxley created classic fictions around BioFutures issues with which we are still grappling today. Biological themes run through futures from More to Gore, and conversely today, in an age dominated by visions of eco-dystopias and techno-utopias, futures have become impossible for biologists to ignore.

Futures thinking, as has been stated, is concerned with what is possible, probable or desirable. Biologists have rather a lot to say about all three. Evolutionary psychologists of the EEA school place great limits on positive possibilities; ecologists of the Malthusian tradition fear the negative possibilities; synthetic biologists push the implausible towards the possible and onward to the probable; and transhumanists propose to solve the possibilities issue by ditching biology entirely. However, despite this explosion of intellectual activity, few of these conversations occur within earshot of the others. BioFutures seeks to create a disciplinary tent within which this can happen and to show that this space has, since the time of Thomas More, always been inhabited by the most interesting interlocutors.

One final BioFuture: The next variety will be departing shortly

It is the year 802,701. A square-jawed late-Victorian scientist arrives in the Garden of Eden in a time machine resembling a steampunk sports car. He is the actor Rod Taylor, in George Pal's 1960 version of H.G. Wells' *The Time Machine* (1895). The apparent paradise turns out, to his disappointment, to be nothing more than an elaborate agribusiness, where the gentle but clueless Eloi, co-incidentally (or not?) in the film portrayed as universally blond and Nordic enough to satisfy any eugenicist, are farmed as a protein supply by the hideous subterranean Morlocks. The twist is that both Eloi and Morlocks are our descendants. Humanity has not gone extinct, as Malthus and modern climate activists fear, but has speciated. *Homo sapiens* has given way to *Homo eloi* and *Homo morlockensis*. In the long run, these are the only two BioFutures, extinction or speciation, oblivion or reincarnation, transformed by natural selection into something rather different.

Although the film does not venture beyond the 803rd millennium, in the novel the time traveller turns the dial several million years forward, to a landscape filled with creatures resembling crabs and butterflies. As in Wallace's fevered dream on Ternate, 'Varieties…Depart Indefinitely from the Original Type'. Our BioFuture has become their distant evolutionary past.

Note

1 The quote is probably apocryphal, but has been circulating since the 1890s.

Bibliography

Amara, R. (1978). 'Probing the future'. In Fowles, J. (ed.) *Handbook of futures research*. Westport, CT: Greenwood Press, pp. 41–51.
Berg, P. and Singer, M.F. (1995). 'The recombinant DNA controversy: Twenty years later'. *Proceedings of the National Academic Science USA*, 92(September), pp. 9011–9013.
Bloch, E. (2000). *The spirit of utopia*. Stanford, CA: Stanford University Press.
Boas, F. (1916). *Eugenics* [Online]. Wikisource. Available at: https://en.wikisource.org/wiki/Eugenics [Accessed 3rd December 2019].
Broderick, D. (1997). *The spike. How our lives are being transformed by rapidly advancing technologies*. New York: Tor Books.
Carson, R. (1965). *Silent spring*. Harmondsworth: Penguin Books.
Chesterton, G.K. (1922). *Eugenics and other evils* [Online]. Wikisource. Available at: https://en.wikisource.org/wiki/Eugenics_and_other_Evils [Accessed 3rd December 2019].
Darwin, C. (1964). *On the origin of species*. Facsimile of 1st ed. Cambridge, MA: Harvard University Press.
Darwin, C. and Huxley, T.H. (1974). *Autobiographies*. New York: Oxford University Press.
Dawkins, R. (2007). *The God delusion*. London: Black Swan.
De Grey, A. and Rae, M. (2007). *Ending aging: The rejuvenation breakthroughs that could reverse human aging in our lifetime*. New York: St. Martin's Press.
Dobzhansky, T. (1973). 'Nothing in biology makes sense except in the light of evolution'. *The American Biology Teacher*, 35(March 1973), pp. 125–129.
Ehrlich, P. (2013). 'The population bomb'. In Robin, L., Sorlin, S. and Warde, P. (eds.) *The future of nature. Documents of global change*. New Haven, CT: Yale University Press, pp. 54-62.
Firestone, S. (1971). *The dialectic of sex. The case for feminist revolution*. London: Jonathan Cape.
Fisher, R.A. (1999). *The genetical theory of natural selection. A complete variorum edition*. Oxford: Oxford University Press.
Fukuyama, F. (2002). *Our posthuman future. Consequences of the biotechnology revolution*. New York: Farra, Straus and Giroux.
Giddens, A. (1999). *Runaway world. How globalisation is reshaping our lives*. London: Profile Books.

Gore, A. (2013). *The future.* New York: WH Allen.
Grasshoff, A. (1972). *Future shock* [Online]. McGraw Hill Films, via YouTube (Jamie Clay). Available at: https://www.youtube.com/watch?v=fkUwXenBokU [Accessed 3rd December 2019].
Gruber, H. (1977). *Frankenstein. A pan-demonium for baritone chansonnier and orchestra after children's rhymes* [Online]. Boosey and Hawkes. Available at: https://www.boosey.com/audiovisual/sample_detail.cshtml?sampleid=24 [Accessed 3rd December 2019].
Hirsch, W.Z. (1969). 'Education and the Future'. In Jungk, R. and Galtung, J. (eds.) *Mankind 2000.* Oslo and London: Universitetsforlaget and Allen and Unwin.
Kolbert, E. (2014). *The sixth extinction. An unnatural history.* New York: Henry Holt and Co.
Kurzweil, R. (2005). *The singularity is near. When humans transcend biology.* London: Gerald Duckworth and Co.
Leakey, R. and Lewin, R. (1996). *The sixth extinction. Biodiversity and its survival.* London: Phoenix.
Malthus, T.R. (2004). *An essay on the principle of population.* 2nd ed. New York: W.W. Norton and Co.
Mason, C. (2003). *The 2030 spike. Countdown to global catastrophe.* London: Earthscan Publications.
More, T. (1516). *Utopia* [Online]. Project Gutenberg. Available at: https://www.gutenberg.org/files/2130/2130-h/2130-h.htm [Accessed 3rd December 2019].
Nichols, J. (2005). *The futurist: FM-2030—F.M. Esfandiary* [Online]. Greenwich Village Gazette. Available at: https://web.archive.org/web/20110714215926/http://www.nycny.com/columns/nichols/nichols09-15-00.html [Accessed 3rd December 2019].
Osborn, H.F. (1948). *Our plundered planet.* 1st ed. London: Faber and Faber.
Rubin, P.H. (2002). *Darwinian politics. The evolutionary origin of freedom.* New Brunswick, NJ: Rutgers University Press.
Taylor, G.R. (1968). *The biological time bomb.* London: Thamas and Hudson.
Teilhard De Chardin, P. (1959). *The phenomenon of man.* London: Collins.
Tipler, F.J. (1995). *The physics of immortality. Modern cosmology, god and the resurrection of the dead.* New York: Anchor Books.
Toffler, A. (1970). *Future shock.* London: The Bodley Head.
Toffler, A. (1981). *The third wave.* Paperback ed. London: Pan Books.
Wallace, A.R. (1858). *On the tendency of varieties to depart indefinitely from the original type* [Online]. Available at: http://rpdata.caltech.edu/courses/Evolution_GIST_2013/files_2013/articles/Ternate_1858_Wallace.pdf [Accessed 3rd December 2019].
Wallace, A.R. (1905). *My life. A record of events and opinions.* London: Chapman and Hall.
Wallerstein, I. (1998). *Utopistics. Or, historical choices of the 21st century.* New York: The New Press.
Wilson, A.N. (2017). *Charles Darwin. Victorian mythmaker.* London: John Murray.

6
Borders
Retravelling Nickelsdorf

Michael Hieslmair and Michael Zinganel

Introduction

This chapter tells the story of Nickelsdorf, a small Austrian municipality at the Hungarian border. It draws on fieldwork conducted there immediately after the refugee crisis of 2015. Due to the 'wave of refugees' in the autumn of 2015, the Nickelsdorf border station was re-activated and assumed a role as a key site for the management of the massive migratory flows. Using arts-based research methods, we show the value of capturing the experiences of border crossing during a period of a crisis bracketed by something like 'normality'. The project engages with the scholarship on borders, infrastructure and mobilities and, in particular, with mapping methods. We also reflect on the social futures and aspirations to a more stable life that the migrants envisage as they cross the border at Nickelsdorf.

Our research and the artistic means of dissemination demonstrate how infrastructures are not only normative systems of control and architectures for the handling of goods and passenger traffic, but are also working and living spaces for mobile subjects who, as they set up temporarily at stops along transnational routes, create informal places of social interaction which can also be understood as 'contact zones' (Horsti, 2019, p. 3). We show that, in transit spaces of this nature, ephemeral 'publics' comprising normal travellers, migrants and refugees may emerge from the exchange of shared experiences or from the pragmatic solution of everyday problems only to dissolve the following day (Collier et al., 2017, p. 7).[1] The artistic translation of our research resulted in an animated graphic novel, Bus Stop Nickelsdorf and added new alternative interpretations of the past to the cumulative processes of memory politics.

The transformation and decline of a border town

Prior to embarking on the Bus Stop Nickelsdorf project, we regarded the border crossings along the Austrian A4 eastern highway, which leads to Hungary, either in the direction of Romania or via Serbia and on to Bosnia and Bulgaria, as nothing more than thresholds in the mobility landscape.

Our views changed as soon as our interactions with local stakeholders on-site began. At first, we overlooked how important the border town of Nickelsdorf had been in recent history both during the Cold War and, subsequently, as the external border of the European Union (EU) until 2004. Soon after the beginning of our fieldwork, we realized how close our views were to the public debate about refugees and European border crossings, a debate which tends to be ahistorical and flattens temporality (Horsti, 2019). This chapter explores how our positioning and understanding of that debate changed.

During the Iron Curtain era, the freight and customs station on the important Vienna-Budapest railway line was situated at Hegyeshalom, on Hungarian territory. Numerous railway workers from Nickelsdorf worked there in shunting yards and conducted customs clearances, crossing the Iron Curtain daily by railbus on their way to and from work.[2] The current transnational road network was developed and improved gradually, the border checkpoint being relocated and extended. Originally, the old main road ran through the village, past small old imperial customs houses and a tollgate to become a street with pubs and stores bustling with activity. However, in the 1980s, the increase in transit cargo traffic that occurred even before the fall of the Iron Curtain resulted in a modern border crossing constructed some distance from the village. In 1994, the road network was upgraded by the A4 motorway, which took most of the high-volume, non-local traffic. Traffic structures are duplicated: Close to the border, the old national road and the motorway run parallel to each other, with border checkpoints on both sides. These control facilities expanded even more between Hungary's accession to the EU in 2004 and the implementation of Schengen Agreement in 2007.

While the former border village went silent, the new border crossing with its motorway entrance and exit ramps and its modern control facilities evolved into an arbitrarily densifying agglomeration of streets and building complexes – a post-urban archipelago (Bittner et al., 2006; Hauser, 2010) typical of the modern mobility landscape often characterized as 'junk space' in architectural discourse (Koolhaas, 2001). Several petrol stations, hotels, motels, restaurants, markets – some partly designed and branded as theme parks (Paprika Csarda) – night clubs, brothels, betting shops, kiosks and truck parks settled along the new route, fighting for the best location and subjecting themselves – especially on the Hungarian side – to tough predatory competition. If, in architectural discourse, it is these physical and spatial aesthetics of the border that are the focus, 'critical border studies' emphasize the connection between place, modes of perception and the sensory experience of borders (Papastergiadis, 2010, p. 11; Schimanski and Wolfe, 2017).

As with any other border in the past, the more strictly it was controlled the more it came to drive the local economy: Restrictions and regulations meant expertise could be sold about evading controls and the differences in availability and prices of goods and services on each side of the border thereby generating booming border economies. This attracted mobile actors and use by those in transit (Konstantinov, 1996; Schlögel, 2005). Initially, we were unaware of the importance of customs agents and border police in border regions. Almost every family in the border villages had at least one member who had worked for them or still did. A smuggler who does not know at least one border officer personally, their work roster and the toleration levels for smuggled goods (or the cost) is considered incompetent. Hence, the reliability of these social networks influences the choice of smuggling routes to allow as many people as possible to have their share of the added value.

This does not only apply to smuggling goods but also to people. In late summer 2015, the majority of the refugees and migrants did not take the regular, low-priced bus connections from Turkey to Bulgaria, as one might expect, and then, within the EU, travel via Vienna to Germany. Many were led along the much more dangerous route across the Mediterranean to Greece and from there, overland, to Macedonia and Serbia. But most of those who reached Bulgaria were again smuggled out of the EU into Serbia and then back into the

Borders

EU via Hungary. This seemingly unnecessary crossing of two EU external borders cannot just be explained by the fact that the border between the two neighbouring EU states, Bulgaria and Romania, is exceptionally well-controlled. Any explanation must take into account the networks that had been growing for many years along the Serbian-Bulgarian and Serbian-Hungarian borders and were of key significance during the wars in Yugoslavia (1991–2001).[3]

After the relocation of the Schengen border to the south-east of Europe in 2007, borders to the west were essentially open (see Figure 6.1). Controls were exceptional and randomized. Accordingly, the personnel for border controls had been gradually minimized and the vast parking lots for trucks became wastelands or were adapted as 'dormitories' for resting truck drivers.

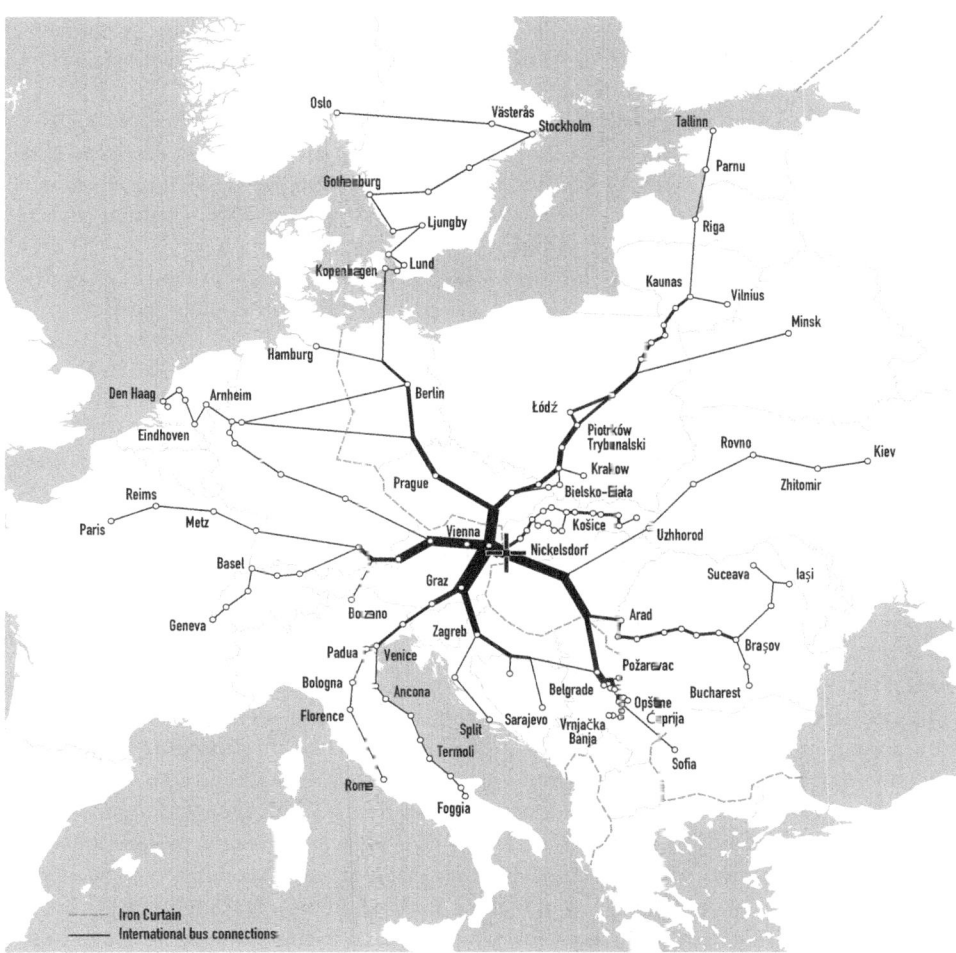

Figure 6.1   Hieslmair and Zinganel, 2016. Vienna at the centre of a network of international bus connections. Most notable are the many stops in east- and south-east Europe. The map is redrawn from the timetable data on bus connections and estimated passenger numbers provided by the management of Vienna International Bus Terminal. However, many smaller bus lines depart from, and arrive at, other often quite informal coach stops around the city

Many other former EU border infrastructures had been dismantled long ago. However, in Nickelsdorf, the customs office, with its large flying roof and loading ramps, was in 2015, as is now in early 2021, staffed by a handful of officials and used for spot checks or to inspect sealed TIR trucks. Freight forwarders had taken up residence in vacated offices. The so-called veterinary station was closed but was still in standby mode.

Mobile methods and artistic research: From cartography to animation

We planned to investigate how the border infrastructure could be reactivated within a very short period of time and then, for a few weeks, become a hot spot for the care of such a large number of refugees. To do this, we organized public bus tours that followed the exact route of the refugees. During the tours themselves, but also in preparation for them, we held discussions with experts and people who had helped with the initial reception and had been involved in refugee management. As a visual guide and trigger for the conversations, we used drawings and maps that we had created.

This mobile and arts-based method derived from our own previous practice and grew out of a cluster of trans-disciplinary fields. It is situated between art, arts-based research, urban and cultural studies and enjoys a significant input from the ethnographic turn in arts (Foster, 1995; Rutten et al., 2013) that occurred within our own work but also through multiple collaborations with activists, historians, anthropologists and ethnographers.

During our research, we largely followed calls for the development of mobile methods and visual representations (Sheller, 2011). We also acknowledged the recent rediscovery of 'Drawing as an Ethnographic Method' (2012–2015), which was influenced, inter alia, by Tim Ingold whose book *Lines* (2007) inspired exhibitions at Tate Modern in 2010 (Schneider and Wright, 2010) and the Centre Pompidou Metz in 2013. At the end of 2013, almost synchronous with our own project, Brett Neilson and Ned Rossiter started the research project, 'Logistic Worlds: Infrastructure. Software. Labour' (2014) which mimetically deployed cartography and infographics.[4] Nick Sousanis published his highly acclaimed non-fiction graphic novel, 'Unflattening' (2015). Finally, the notion of deep mapping, recently introduced in the 'undisciplined', interdisciplinary domain of spatial humanities (Roberts, 2016), proposes a multilayered multimedia and formal practice of mapping, related to the strategy we aimed for.

We are, of course, aware of the reservations of the use of maps in the context of Marxist, post-structuralist and postcolonial critique (Harvey, 1989). As Denis Wood has persuasively argued, the power of maps lies in the interests they represent. In this light, mapping always has a political purpose, and the 'interest' often leads to people being pushed 'off the map' (Wood, 1992). Similar arguments have also informed the strategy of counter-mapping – in critical geography, arts, political and urban activism – whose aim is to make visible who and what has been under-represented or entirely excluded from representation. This approach also reveals the networks of established power structures and shows how the world has been increasingly redefined in terms of dynamic and complex networks of mobilized and demobilized people, objects and capital: 'Mapping has become a way of making sense' (Abrams and Hall, 2006, p. 12).

Following Gilles Deleuze and Felix Guattari (1987) and Bruno Latour (2005), and their interest in the capacities of mapping, we argue that maps are not only an appropriate device for representing mobility patterns but also that live mapping is a great relational tool for stimulating interaction with mobile actors *en route* as well as a tool for evaluating research findings (Zinganel and Hieslmair, 2017).

Our first one-day public bus excursion on December 2015 included a workshop. The tour started at Vienna International Bus Terminal (see Figure 6.2) and visited other urban

Borders

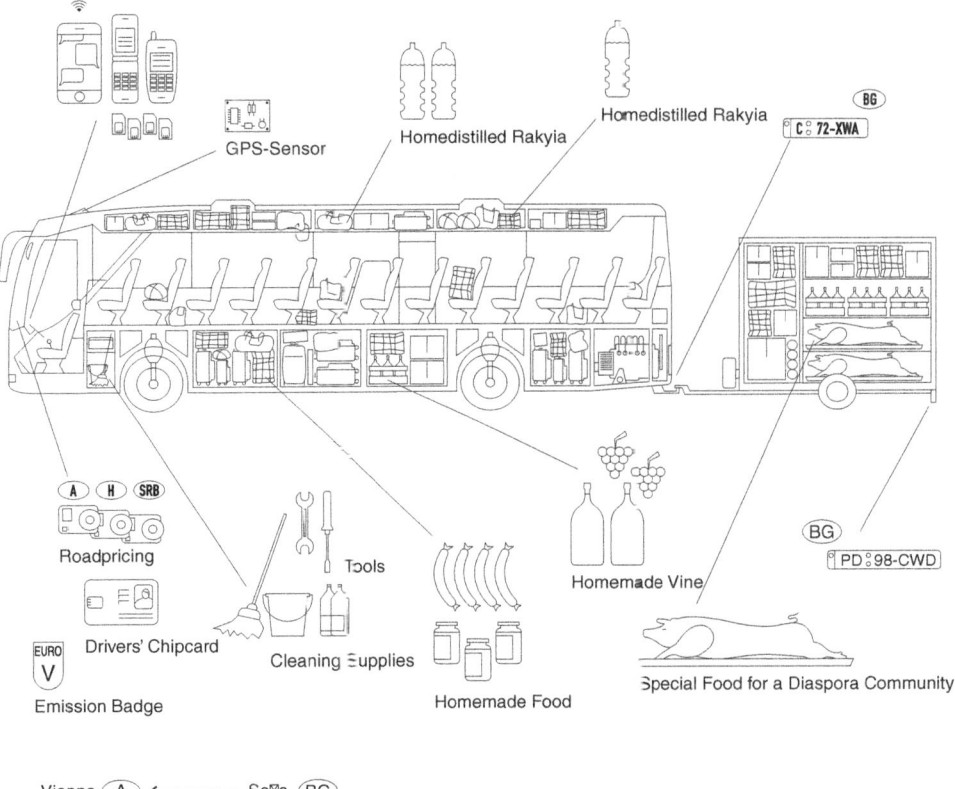

Figure 6.2 Hieslmair and Zinganel, 2016. Cross-sectional diagram of a tour coach operated by the Bulgarian company Air Kona connecting Vienna and Sofia: For many, buses are the preferred means of transport, not only because of the reasonable ticket prices but moreover because a bus can take them much closer to their source and target destinations. Buses are also able to transport goods of significant size – which is important for small suitcase traders and those wishing to send gifts to family and friends

archipelagos and hubs of mobility and migration along the A4 eastern motorway before arriving at the border. To escape accusations of social voyeurism – gazing at masses of refugees and migrants at the border – we consciously chose a time when the wave was over, the station entirely vacant and only remnants of control and initial reception infrastructure remained. Hans-Paul Limbeck, a retired railway worker, amateur historian and head of a local cultural association, had curated two exhibitions in a vacant local pub about waves of refugees during the Hungarian Revolution (1956) and at the end of the Cold War (marked by the collapse of the German Democratic Republic in 1989). Limbeck introduced us to Gerhard Zapfl, the Mayor of Nickelsdorf, who made a notable contribution to the on-site coordination of the recent refugee crisis in 2015. Both guided us to the places in and around Nickelsdorf where just two months previously a tremendous influx of people had to be handled without prior preparation.

The initial meeting point with the local experts was on Hungarian territory, at the border station of Hegyeshalom – depicted bottom right in the picture (see Figure 6.3). During the Iron Curtain era, the extensive rail yards were the workplace of many Nickelsdorf residents who took part in processing the trains crossing the border. On 5 September 2015, refugees arrived here in special trains and buses *en route* from Hungary. From this point, our tour was to follow their route as accurately as possible. During the trip, the mayor recounted his view of events at the time as it related to the locations we saw:

At the beginning of the 'crisis', a crowd of people slowly moved along the four-kilometre stretch of road in clusters, heading for the motorway border terminal on the Austrian side.

On the way, we passed, as they did then, the old, small border checkpoint where they had been supplied with food and drink by volunteers from Austria, Hungary and Slovakia. Later, on the Austrian side of the border, volunteers from Nickelsdorf and a few police officers awaited them at the highway border terminal – depicted in the middle of the drawing. Preparing for a potentially dramatic increase in numbers, representatives of the municipality and engaged citizens coordinated with the local police department and began organizing aid measures on their own. It soon became obvious that the initial reception of a large number of

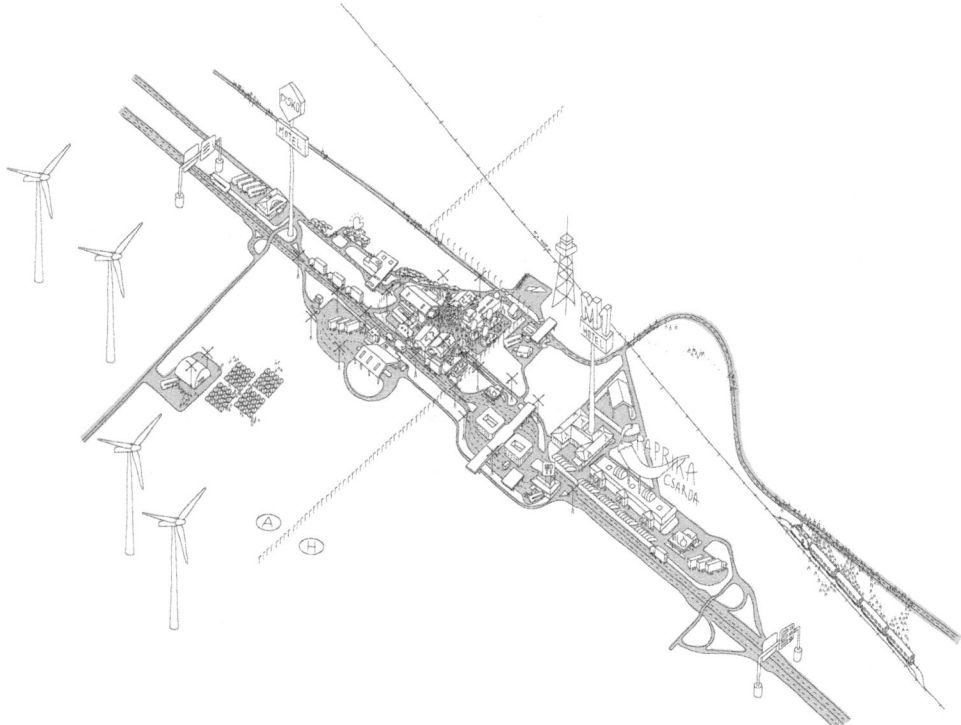

Figure 6.3 Hieslmair and Zinganel, 2016. Reactivation of border infrastructure: From July to October 2015, thousands of refugees assembled at the Austria-Hungary border checkpoint of Nickelsdorf every day. Within a few hours, auxiliary structures had been provided by emergency aid NGOs and event industries for first aid and onward transport coordination

people and delivering emergency provisions to them would require a substantial area of solid terrain. The defunct border terminal on Austrian territory proved ideal for this purpose. Its large-scale infrastructure and spacious asphalt lots situated on both sides of the A4 eastern motorway, for the most part covered by large flying roofs, represented an optimal structure for the quick set-up of temporary facilities for first aid measures. These included ephemeral architectures from the realms of crisis intervention and leisure events, such as tents of different sizes, mobile kitchens, toilets and sanitary facilities.

'At the beginning there was chaos', said Mayor Gerhard Zapfl.[5] The first volunteers from Nickelsdorf organized themselves until the arrival of the Red Cross followed by large crowds of helpers flocking to the border crossing from Vienna, Hungary and Slovakia. Together, under the 'flying roof north' banner, they provided the refugees and migrants with vital supplies – food, clothes and blankets. Besides journalists – the first ones had already come on buses from Budapest's Keleti train station – the momentous event attracted more and more media representatives and also curious spectators. Zapfl, one of the very few authorities that were present, gave one interview after another and said in retrospect: 'The press was everywhere'. Today, the area is completely empty.

We passed the spot on the old main road – located near the centre of the drawing – where, at the time, taxis and private cars collected and, on their own initiative, picked up refugees to take them further 'westwards'. We arrived at the large unpaved car park of the former Grenzland [Borderland] discotheque – in the drawing, slightly closer to the top and located between the main road and the motorway. A collection point for buses was set up here very quickly, and they were dispatched to wherever they were needed to pick up refugees. Initially, these were taken to Nickelsdorf railway station and there waiting for special trains or simply set off towards the Austrian-German border.[6]

From the disco car park, our bus crossed the motorway to visit the Novarock site, two kilometre away from the village centre. The hall situated there is normally used as a backstage zone for one of Austria's largest open air rock festivals and has sanitary facilities. The festivals' operating company has made available the site for use by those in the emergency housing sector in the form of a tent village erected round it. On the return journey, we made a slight diversion to Nickelsdorf station where refugees boarded the special trains but also where the great majority of the mobile toilets used during the rock festival were stored. Back in the centre of Nickelsdorf, the impression was that of a ghost town.

We invited mayor Zapfl to fact-check the drawing we had made to document the many narratives we heard since the beginning of our journey. He willingly took out his own pen and corrected key events during the critical initial phases of providing emergency aid for the refugees (see Figure 6.4). He immediately noticed one of the many things we had overlooked, which, from his point of view, was particularly important. It concerned the role of media, which, to him, was extremely important. In the drawing, he marked exactly where a cluster of outside broadcasting vans quickly formed. He himself gave one interview after another, especially at the beginning of the event, when the official Austrian representatives still kept away from the events. Later on, we consulted with a number of other experts who were involved in refugee management. These included Gerald Tatzgern,[7] Head of the Central Office for Human Smuggling and Trafficking Countermeasures at the Federal Ministry of the Interior, Federal Criminal Police responsible for random controls and Colonel Wolfgang Mayerhofer,[8] Operational Support, Head of Traffic Logistics and Transport, Austrian Army, responsible for the coordination of the buses transporting the refugees. Their input was also included in an updated version of the drawing that thus underwent successive iterations (see Figure 6.3).

Michael Hieslmair and Michael Zinganel

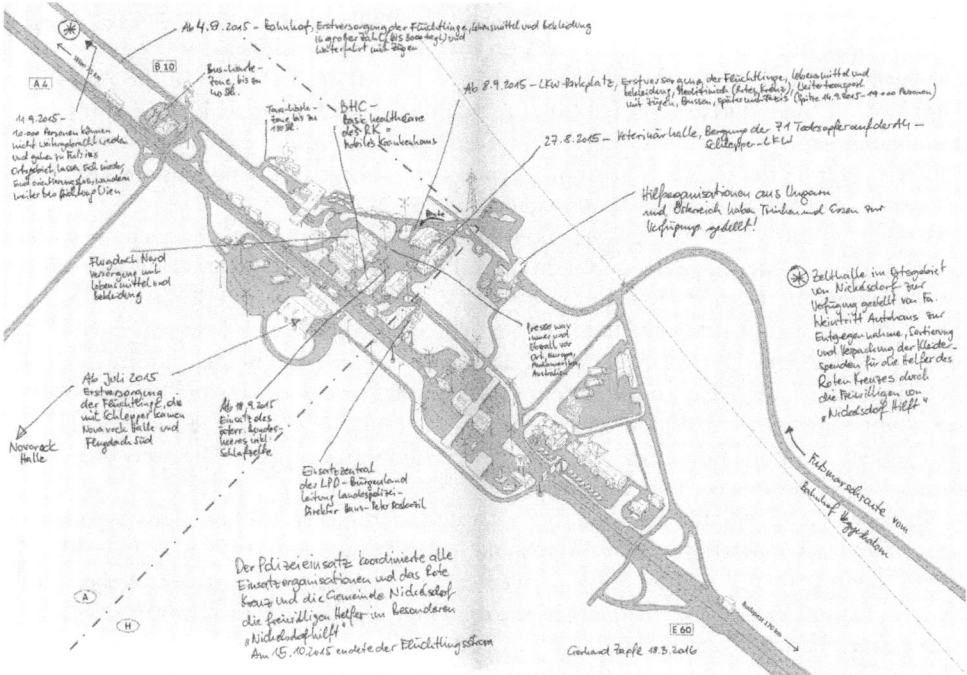

Figure 6.4 Hieslmair and Zinganel, Gerhard Zapfl, 2016. This drawing is a preliminary stage to Figure 6.3 and is based on conversations with Gerhard Zapfl, mayor of the border village of Nickelsdorf, who was in charge of managing the flows of forced migration and first aid for migrants arriving at the station. In fact, the map was revised in several stages, each time the mayor found important elements missing

These sketches are drawn isometrically, a depictive form common in architecture which, with its angled view from above, is intended to give us an overview. However, in our drawings the individual buildings and scenes are not drawn to scale but are intentionally exaggerated as in a comic. We intuitively applied Kevin Lynch's (1960) approach, which seeks to uncover how people navigate the different spatial contexts of city and landscapes, using physical, symbolic and semiotic features including edges, perceived boundaries, sections of the city with a distinct character, nodes, focal points, intersections and landmarks.

These drawings – also used in our previous projects – worked very well as triggers to access tacit knowledge and as relational tools for stimulating interaction in the conversations with our interview partners. They were productive as a research method and served very well as a means of dissemination (Zinganel and Hieslmair, 2013, 2017, 2019). However, this medium turned out to be unsatisfactory for our more specific requirements, because a drawing has enormous imaginative impact but has also limits to its representational ability. In an isometric drawing like this, only a distanced view is possible and there is no way to switch between macro- and micro-views, or even to shift scales. Moreover, for the description of successive events, which is crucial in this case, the possibility of representing temporal changes and rhythms is missing. In response to these shortcomings, we looked to the field of 'mobilities studies' for a technique of 'mobilized' representation that was entirely new to us: We began to create our first animated graphic novel (Figure 6.5).

Borders

Figure 6.5   Hieslmair and Zinganel, Bus Stop Nickelsdorf, 2016. Video stills from an animated graphic novel, 12 min., describing passengers' experiences of the Nickelsdorf border station on the Austria-Hungary border plus fragments about the management of the enormous bottleneck of refugees in 2015 from the point of view of three bus drivers: The first drove Austrian tourists across the open border station before the event, the second drove Bulgarian labour migrants to Vienna and got held up in the reactivated border checkpoint and the last was hired by the emergency aid organizer to drive refugees from the Hungary-Austria border to improvised accommodation units in Vienna or directly to the Austria-Germany border. To watch the animation, please follow this link: https://tracingspaces.net/bus-stop/

The animation is based on the above-mentioned drawings. The content of interviews conducted with various parties was condensed into storylines relating to a few fictional characters in narratives from a micro-political viewpoint. They reflect the real-life experiences of the people interviewed for this project. The comic-like style was also used here because it retains the narrative character of storytelling and yet helps maintain a critical distance in key scenes by compressing the time frames and geographical scope of research findings in a consciously overstated form close to caricature.

In contrast to frozen images such as photos, maps and drawings, animation is perfectly suited to the representation of dynamic movement in time and space, rhythms within a flow, the stops and starts of movement, acceleration and deceleration. It also enables zooming in and out, fluidly scaling up and down between a macro- and micro-political perceptions of routes and nodes, switching from abstract maps to bird's-eye views, from road landscapes to inside vehicles, and close-ups of people. At the same time, the extensive use of drawings and the grade of abstraction defuse several legal-ethical issues related to the photographic or video (mis)representation of people. Furthermore, in the 12-min. animation we produced, the combination of the simultaneity of the filmic images with a soundtrack offered space for narrative elements to unfold.[9]

The animation shows a succession of 'border experiences' – not from the mayor's point of view, or that of refugees, but from the perspective of three bus drivers in a temporally and spatially condensed representation. We let the bus drivers have their say because they have a direct experience of mobility and migration resulting from their regular journeys spanning a longer period of time. This allows us to describe changes at the border that do not just cover the brief period of the 'crisis'. The first is the driver of a tourist bus that passes through the border while it is still open. On its return journey, near Parndorf, the bus passes a refrigerated lorry at the side of the road in which, on 27 August 2015, the bodies of 71 dead refugees were discovered. The second driver is behind the wheel of a bus with migrant labourers. It gets caught in the traffic jam caused by the flow of refugees. The Bulgarian driver feels compelled to allow his passengers to exit the bus temporarily in the border zone. The third is a driver explicitly commissioned to transport refugees from the border crossing to the emergency shelters in Vienna, the train stations and later to the German border. He himself is a second-generation immigrant whose parents fled from the wars in ex-Yugoslavia by bus in the 1990s.[10]

Commemorative action: Rhythms of de- and reactivation

Retravelling sections of the refugee routes and visiting the associated sites on bus tours open to the public and translating that into isometric drawings and an animated video prompted spontaneous responses from our dialogue partners: Complete amateurs felt free to speak their mind on the issue, to question details or to talk about their own experiences. Their responses and our research exemplify what border infrastructures are capable of delivering in normal and emergency situations and that event-specific 'publics' can form and subsequently dissolve as a result.

In contrast to Chouliaraki and Georgiou (2017), who examined the formation and implications of the communicative architecture of humanitarian securitization of the EU border through fieldwork on the Greek island of Chios during the peak of the 'migration crisis' in 2015–2016, we are starting out from a state of normality in which there are as good as no controls. Our animated video shows how, in a matter of hours, a large and seemingly inflexible infrastructural facility such as the former border station could be reactivated.

Soon, it was augmented by auxiliary structures provided by emergency aid NGOs and the event industry and able to accommodate an average of 4,500 (peak: 17,000) refugees per day in a 1,200 people village. However, the justified criticism of a border as 'a site of identification, classification and control of mobile populations' (Chouliaraki and Georgiou, 2017, p. 8) does not apply here. Right from the beginning of the 'crisis', Austrian authorities were eager to transport the refugees and migrants on to Germany as quickly as possible. To avoid anyone being sent back to Austria pursuant of the Dublin II Regulations, refugees in transit were never registered and the identification system of Eurodac (the EU fingerprint database for refugee applications) was not consulted. This meant, according to the policy of non-registration, that Austria was simply a transit country and not the asylum-seekers 'first safe country'.

Buses normally used for commuters and tourists transported refugees to the train station or to emergency shelters located near Vienna's bus terminals, where the local and/or federal government had the authority to immediately appropriate and adapt public buildings for their accommodation. In order to reduce pressure in tense situations, the frequency of the buses varied proportional to the numbers crossing into Austria. The aim was to control the number of refugees staying in the zone designated as first aid point at the border and to keep the refugees on the move in order to avoid unrest by giving the impression of continuous flow.[11]

After Hungary decided to close and control the Schengen border with Serbia and then with Croatia, the routes for refugees were redirected. The border station was once again defunct and life in the village as uneventful as before. This demonstrates just how quickly long-distance decisions can alter refugee routes within a few days. However, a year after the influx of refugees a more permanent infrastructure was installed on the lorry park at Nickelsdorf. The facility comprises containers with booths to check the personal data of those crossing the border, a de facto detention centre for those without the requisite entry permits and prefabricated barrier elements that could be erected in a few hours and turned into a solid fence topped with razor wire.

For the small border village of Nickelsdorf, the experience of the refugee crisis was challenging but not altogether new. Events brought the world press and, according to the proud mayor, the concerted efforts and the 'spectacle of bordering' (Horsti, 2019, p. 6) had had a noticeably positive effect on the village's sense of community.[12] The autumn of 2015 will certainly play an important role in the collective memory of the village.

The mayor emphasized that the state of emergency caused by the mass flight of refugees was not unique in the history of the village: During the Hungarian crisis in November 1956, 180,000 refugees passed through Nickelsdorf, and, in 1989, after the fall of the Iron Curtain, 40,000 exhausted GDR citizens had to be taken care of.[13] These already historical experiences with refugees had become part of the cultural memory (Horsti, 2019) of the border community long before the last 'wave of refugees', at least among the history-conscious inhabitants. Documentation materials of the historical events – as a more vernacular form of memory politics – were already on display in Nickelsdorf in exhibitions by amateur historian Hans-Paul Limbeck. It will not be long before the experiences of 2015 will also be presented as an exhibition and inscribed in the collective memory of the inhabitants too.

Furthermore, the escape routes after October 2015 were not new either: They stretch from Serbia via Croatia and Slovenia to Austria, crossing at Spielfeld, which was the route for guest workers and thus an integral part of mobility and migration history since the 1960s. Many of the bus drivers, who, in the autumn 2015, transported the most recent refugees across Austria, once entered the country through these very roads.

Michael Hieslmair and Michael Zinganel

Postscript

In 2020 when the coronavirus disease (COVID-19) crisis began, the Nickelsdorf border crossing, along with other border checkpoints and control facilities throughout Europe, was reactivated to carry out border controls and health checks. This was facilitated by the extensive asphalted areas and the scale of the supply and distribution networks which raises the question as to whether, as a paradox within 'Europe without border', it makes sense to keep areas such as this on standby, ready for emergencies. Infrastructures like Nickelsdorf's, conceptualized as a 'compensatory vessel', would enable the implementation of emergency measures based on humanitarian principles and controls if needed. They would not necessarily have to be on the border but since they are there anyway, they might be of value and use as emergencies develop.

There are other supplementary infrastructures, those related to what the exhibitions by Limbeck and our graphic novel, Bus Stop Nickelsdorf, emphasize, namely, the culture of remembrance, the tales of individual fates that trigger empathy. Crises like that of 2015 are likely to occur again. The way border towns and villages like Nickelsdorf remember and are themselves remembered should be central to shaping better possible responses to future crises. It is human to remember as is contributing to making an inclusive social future for those facing and experiencing forced displacement.

Notes

1 Joint transient communities of mobile subjects are formed, which – in reference to John Dewey – are 'linked by a "vast current" of circulation and complex interconnection. And it is not formal political organization but these "vast currents"—flowing along what would later be called infrastructures—that are the most important force shaping publics' (Collier et al., 2017, p. 7).
2 According to Hans-Paul Limbeck, retired railroad worker, amateur historian and chairman of Kulturverein Kugel, interviewed by the authors, June 3, 2015 and Gerhard Zapfl, Mayor of Nickelsdorf, interviewed by the authors, March 18, 2016.
3 According to Gerald Tatzgern, interviewed by the authors, September 8, 2016.
4 A first demo of the computer game *Cargonauts* was presented 2015 at the media festival transmediale in Berlin: http://cargonauts.net. For the entire project, please visit: http://logisticalworlds.org/ [both accessed on December 22, 2020].
5 According to observations of Mayor Zapfl.
6 According to Wolfgang Mayerhofer, Operational Support, Head of Traffic Logistics and Transport, Austrian Army, responsible for the coordination of the buses transporting the refugees, interviewed by the authors September 8, 2016.
7 Gerald, Tatzgern, interviewed by the authors, September 8, 2016.
8 Wolfgang Mayerhofer, interviewed by the authors, September 8, 2016.
9 This animation was shown along with, inter alia, the isometric drawings and a safety jacket with the words 'Nickelsdorf hilft' [Nickelsdorf helps] as an original artefact in the exhibition 'Unschärfen und weiße Flecken: Kartografische Annäherung an urbane Räume', [Undefined and Black Spaces: A Cartographic Approach to Urban Space] kunsthaus muerz, Mürzzuschlag/Austria, April 4–June 11, 2017; at the conference 'Mobile Utopia: Pasts, presents, futures' at the Centre for Mobilities Research at Lancaster University, November 2–5, 2017; and at EASA 2018: Staying, Moving, Settling at Stockholm University, August 14–17, 2018; at the 10th SAR International Conference on Artistic Research at Zurich University of the Arts, March 21–23, 2019. The English language version is accessible online: https://tracingspaces.net/bus-stop/ [accessed on February 19, 2021]
  Since 2020, the original drawing together with the animation has been part of the holding of the art collection of the City of Vienna.
10 During the Yugoslav wars between 1991 and 2001, far more people were admitted to Austria than in 2015 and integrated without a great deal of notice or comment.
11 According to Wolfgang Mayerhofer interviewed by the authors September 8, 2016.

12 But, with our research and artistic translation into animation, even we do not escape the 'spectacle of bordering'.
13 According to Gerhard Zapfl, interviewed by the authors, March 18, 2016.

Bibliography

Abrams, J. and Hall, P. (eds.) (2006). *Else/where: Mapping. New cartographies of networks and territories*. Minneapolis: University of Minnesota Press.

Bittner, R., Hackenbroich, W. and Vöckler, K. (eds.) (2006). *Transiträume: Transit spaces* (Edition Bauhaus Vol. 19). Berlin: Jovis.

Chouliaraki, L. and Georgiou, M. (2017). 'Hospitability: The communicative architecture of humanitarian securitization at Europe's borders'. *Journal of Communication*, 67(2), pp. 159–180. DOI: 10.1111/jcom.12291

Collier, S., Mizes, J.C. and von Schnitzler, A. (eds.) (2017). Public infrastructures Infrastructural publics, *Limn* 7. Published as needed. Also available at: http://limn.it/

Deleuze, G. and Guattari, F. (1987). *A thousand plateaus: Capitalism and schizophrenia*. Minneapolis University of Minnesota Press.

Foster, H. (1995). 'The artist as ethnographer?' In: Marcus, G. and Myers, F. (eds.) *The traffic in culture. Refiguring art and anthropology*. Berkeley, LA and London: University of California Press, pp. 302–309.

Harvey, D. (1989). *The condition of postmodernity*. London: Blackwell.

Hauser, S. (2010). 'Die Ästhetik der Agglomeration'. In MAP Markus Ambach Projekte und Urbane Künste Ruhr (eds.) *B1/A40: The beauty of the grand road*. Berlin: Jovis, pp. 202–213.

Horsti, K. (2017). *Solidarities in the Arctic border*. Available at: https://www.law.ox.ac.uk/research-subject-groups/centre-criminology/centreborder-criminologies/blog/2017/06/solidarities (accessed December 22, 2020).

Horsti, K. (ed.) (2019). *The politics of public memories of forced migration and bordering in Europe*. London: Palgrave Macmillan.

Ingold, T. (2007). *Lines: A brief history*. New York: Routledge.

Ingold, T. (2011). *Redrawing anthropology: Materials, movements, lines*. Aldershot: Ashgate.

Konstantinov, Y. (1996). 'Patterns of reinterpretation: Trader-tourism in the Balkans (Bulgaria) as a picaresque metaphorical enactment of post-totalitarianism', *American Ethnologist* 23(4), pp. 762–782.

Koolhaas, R. (2001). 'Junkspace'. In Chung, C.J. et al. (eds.) *Harvard design school guide to shopping*. Köln: Taschen, pp. 408–421.

Latour, B. (2005). *Reassembling the social: An introduction to actor-network-theory*. Oxford: Oxford University Press.

Lippart, L. (2010). 'Farther afield'. In: Schneider, A. and Wright, C. (eds.) *In between art and anthropology: Contemporary ethnographic practice*. Oxford and New York: Berg, pp. 23–34.

Lynch, K. (1960). *The Image of the City*. Cambridge, MA and London: MIT Press.

Neilson, B. and Rossiter, N. (eds.) (2014). *Logistical worlds*, 1 November.

Papastergiadis, N. (2010). *Spatial aesthetics, art, place, and the everyday*. Amsterdam: Institute of Network Cultures.

Roberts, L. (ed.) (2016). 'Deep mapping and spatial anthropology', *Humanities* 16(5), p. 5. DOI: 10.3390/h5010005

Rutten, K., van Dienderen, C. and Soetaert, R. (2013). 'Special issue: Revisiting the ethnographic turn in contemporary art critical arts', *Critical Arts-South-North Cultural and Media Studies*, 27(5), pp. 459–473.

Schimanski, J. and Wolfe, S. (eds.) (2017). *Border aesthetics: Concepts and intersections*. New York: Berghahn Books.

Schlögel, K. (2005). *Marjampole oder Europas Wiederkehr aus dem Geist der Städte*. Munich: Hanser.

Schneider, A. and Wright, C. (2010) *Between art and anthropology: Contemporary ethnographic practice*. Oxford and New York: Berg.

Sheller, M. (2011). 'Mobility', *Sociopedia.isa*, DOI: 10.1177/205684601163

Simone, A.M. (2004). 'People as infrastructure: Intersecting fragments in Johannesburg', *Public Culture* 16(3), pp. 407–29.

Sousanis, N. (2015). *Unflattening*. Cambridge, MA: Harvard University Press.

Tsing, A. (2009). 'Supply chains and the human condition', *Rethinking Marxism* 21(2), pp. 148–176.

Wood, D. (1992). *The power of maps*. New York: Guilford Press.

Zinganel, M. and Hieslmair, M. (2013). 'Stopover: An excerpt from the network of actor-oriented mobility movements'. In: Kesselring, S., Vogl, G. and Witzgall, S. (eds.) *New mobilities regimes in art and social sciences*, Aldershot: Ashgate, pp. 115–134.

Zinganel, M. and Hieslmair, M. (2017a). 'Stop and go. Investigating nodes of transformation and transition'. In: Hannam, K., Kjaerulff, A., Kesselring, S. and Peters, P. (eds.) *Envisioning networked urban mobilities*, Vol. 3. London: Routledge, pp. 96–108.

Zinganel, M. and Hieslmair, M. (2017b). 'Stop and go'. *JAR Journal of Artistic Research*, 14, https://www.researchcatalogue.net/view/330596/330597 (accessed December 22, 2020).

Zinganel, M. and Hieslmair, M. (eds.) (2019). *Stop and go – nodes of transformation and transition* (Publication Series of the Academy of Fine Arts Vienna, Vol. 23). Berlin: Sternberg Press.

7

Climate change

Transformational adaptation in Bangladesh

Riadadh Hossain, Shababa Haque and Saleemul Huq

Climate change: The hallmark crisis for our planet

Climate change is undeniably the most defining crisis of our times. Following the advent of industrial revolution over a century and a half ago, human activities such as rapid industrialization, widespread deforestation and large-scale agriculture have resulted in copious amounts of greenhouse gases being released into the Earth's atmosphere, triggering an unprecedented warming of the globe within a short span of time (Houghton, 2001). In 2017, global average temperatures were estimated to have risen by approximately 1 °C since pre-industrial times, and as we move ahead, a likely increase between 0.1 °C and 0.3 °C is expected per decade (Allen et al., 2018).

This rapid warming has already activated substantial changes in the global climate system, with rising sea levels, shifting weather patterns and increasing frequency and magnitude of extreme weather events (e.g. droughts, cyclones and floods) already being observed all over the world. These have far-reaching impacts on the global economy, infrastructure, human health, ecosystems, biodiversity and the broader society in general (IPCC, 2014). As per the Special Report produced by the Intergovernmental Panel on Climate Change (IPCC) in 2018, it is vital to limit global warming to 1.5 °C, to ensure that devastating and irrecoverable outcomes on natural and human systems can be averted (IPCC, 2018).

At the same time, it is now widely acknowledged that in order to combat the global climate change crisis, reducing greenhouse gas emissions only constitutes half the battle. With the impacts of climate change growing in prominence over the past decade or so, it has become apparent that there is a concurrent need for responses that help individuals, communities, organizations and ecosystems adjust to the changing climate and deal with its inevitable consequences. This, in the global climate change discourse, is known as 'adaptation'.

Evolution of adaptation approaches

The IPCC defines adaptation as 'an adjustment in natural or human systems in response to actual or expected climatic stimuli or their effects, which moderates harm or exploits beneficial opportunities' (IPCC, 2007). While there are several definitions of the term, with subtle differences between them, the central aim of adaptation is usually the same, namely, to reduce vulnerability of a system to the adverse impacts of climate change, both now and in the future. According to the IPCC, this entails diminishing the exposure and sensitivity of a system to climatic risks and hazards and enhancing its adaptive capacity to cope with their consequences. Any action or set of actions that attempts to do so can thus be viewed as adaptation (Houghton et al., 2001).

Researchers, practitioners and decision-makers have long debated the many definitions of adaptation, the actions it entails and how we should distinguish them from 'business-as-usual' development activities. It is important to understand the interrelationship between adaptation and development, considering the implications it has on project design, on policy decisions and most importantly on resource allocation. However, drawing a clear distinction between the two is not only fraught with challenges, but it may potentially lead to adverse outcomes. Rather, adaptation and development can be seen to exist on a continuum, wherein overlap between the two is essentially inevitable. This means that not only activities undertaken to accomplish development objectives will often result in outcomes that support adaptation, but also that certain adaptation actions can be aligned with and contribute towards development goals such as poverty alleviation and equitable growth (McGray et al., 2007). There is also a growing focus on integrating adaptation efforts within development processes, with the core intention of minimizing climate risks, while ensuring socio-economic development is not hindered (Agrawal et al., 2015)

Adaptation can thus take on many shapes and forms, and there is a myriad of interpretations of what an adaptation response could look like. Adaptation solutions could include management strategies for efficient use of water resources, construction of flood defence structures, setting up early warning systems for cyclones, development of drought-tolerant crop varieties and the formulation of policies and strategic plans of action to address challenges posed by climate change (Noble et al., 2014). Adaptation strategies also tend to vary across spatial scales (household, local, national, regional, global) and temporal scales (short-term, long-term, current impacts, future impacts) and their application is largely contingent upon the specific social, economic, political and ecological context of the system in question.

Over time, the global community of research and practice on climate change have devised a variety of means for classifying adaptation approaches, by applying different, sometimes overlapping, characteristics as parameters. For instance, the IPCC distinguishes adaptation responses on the basis of their timing into three types: Autonomous, anticipatory and planned. Autonomous adaptation typically constitutes spontaneous, reactive responses to certain changes in climatic conditions, whereas anticipatory and planned adaptation, often complementary and used as substitutes, are usually marked by proactive measures taken in advance, prior to observing actual impacts (Noble et al., 2014). Adaptation options can also be seen as 'soft' and 'hard'. Typical hard measures include, but are not limited to, climate proofing infrastructure (e.g. embankments and flood walls) and adoption of climate resistant technologies (e.g. saline-tolerant rice varieties). Soft options on the other hand refer to policy, legal, social, management and financial measures for managing climate risks and impacts and could entail building human and institutional capacity through knowledge and skills training, improving governance structures and developing sector-specific strategies to address associated challenges.

One of the ways for categorizing adaptation approaches, which has become increasingly pervasive in recent years, is through the use of a hierarchical framing, wherein they can be classified into three broad types. These are (i) coping adaptation, (ii) incremental adaptation and (iii) transformational adaptation. These approaches can be perceived to have nested pathways with interconnections and have the propensity to build on one another (Chhetri et al., 2019).

Coping vs incremental

Throughout the course of human history, people dependent on natural resource-based livelihoods, and located in ecologically fragile and disaster-prone areas, have devised a myriad of ways to deal with environmental hazards and unpredictable weather conditions (Adger et al., 2003). These approaches have largely been reactive and entail short-term solutions for managing risks and threats from various climatic stimuli. In climate change literature, this is termed as coping adaptation.

Generally independent of external intervention, coping adaptation is characterized by an endogenous adjustment to a system in question and typically constitutes traditional practices employed by households and communities to respond to different climatic shocks and stressors. For instance, farmers changing sowing times for crops in response to a particularly climate-adverse season could be seen as a coping strategy (Adger et al., 2003). Such coping mechanisms are however constrained by the capacity and resources available to individuals, households and communities, and for these mechanisms to be effective, they would need to be equipped with the right skills, knowledge and technology. Therefore, while these strategies tend to provide benefits under the current climate, they are likely to prove insufficient in the face of rapidly accelerating changes in climatic conditions and associated socio-economic and political parameters (Chhetri et al., 2019).

This insufficiency led to conceptualizing the term incremental adaptation, with the majority of adaptation literature to date devoted to this (Kates et al., 2012). Incremental adaptation can be viewed as an extension to coping and is characterized by targeted enhancements made to an existing system, while ensuring its fundamental attributes are maintained. It attempts to improve the efficiency of a system and build adaptive capacity and resilience by leveraging existing resources, technology and institutional capacity present within the system (Kates et al., 2012).

Incremental adaptation can be seen as doing slightly more than what is already being done, and as such, coping and incremental strategies are not necessarily mutually exclusive. However, the key distinction lies in the scale of interventions and the actors involved in the process. Incremental adaptation tends to be relatively larger in both temporal and spatial scopes and often entails the engagement of multiple actors and external agents. It is also more resource intensive and serves to provide longer-term benefits (Chhetri et al., 2019). Most of the adaptation work undertaken to date by multilateral and bilateral agencies as well as national actors has been largely incremental in nature.

Transformation as an emerging concept

In recent years however, the adaptation research community has begun to realize that for certain geographies, and certain systems, vulnerability and risks might be so substantial that incremental approaches are not enough. As the impacts of climate change continue to grow in terms of complexity and uncertainty, threatening to surpass the limits of certain systems to maintain their ability to function, there is a need to think bigger and act at a much a larger scale. This has led to the emergence of transformational adaptation as a concept (Kates et al., 2012).

Transformational adaptation calls for creating substantial changes to fundamental attributes within a system in order to address current and future impacts of climate change and entails responses that are much greater in magnitude and scope. It is distinct from the other two types of adaptation due to its novelty, innovation, scale, intensity and mainly its intended transformative effect on the system in question. It seeks to bring about dynamic shifts in the legal, regulatory, governance and sociocultural structures existent within a system, to catalyse long-term positive outcomes (Kates et al., 2012).

Transformational adaptation generally requires engaging a multitude of exogenous actors, where they play collaborative roles alongside local communities, in the planning, designing and implementation of on-the-ground adaptation actions. It can also entail a combination of proactive and reactive responses taken simultaneously, and for it to be effective, it may need to occur at several scales (Lonsdale, 2015).

The manifold impacts of climate change are already well felt across the globe, and there continues to be growing uncertainty around how these effects will manifest themselves. Several countries and regions across the globe are also about to reach their tipping points, beyond which losses and damages would be irreversible. Climatically volatile, developing economies are particularly under threat. In light of this, transformational adaptation offers a promising solution pathway for ensuring the survival of humanity and society against the most pressing crisis facing the planet today, that is climate change.

Bangladesh and its climate vulnerability

Low-lying deltas of the world have always been more impacted by the effects of a changing climate, and Bangladesh proves to be no exception to this norm. Located in South Asia, the majority of the country lies in the Ganges-Brahmaputra-Meghna delta (GBM delta), which is considered as the largest and most populated deltaic region in the continent (Ericson et al., 2005). Among the Asian Deltas, the GBM delta is known to be the most vulnerable to salinization. Since the 1970s, natural hazards and reductions in upstream river flows have been causing increases in soil and water salinity in this region (Salehin et al., 2018). Attributing to its natural geography and topography, Bangladesh has always been highly susceptible to an array of environmental shocks and stressors. The country is frequently hit by tropical cyclones and experiences incidences of severe cyclones at least every three years (MOEF, 2009). In addition, the country also suffers from regular incidences of heavy coastal and river flooding, tidal surges and riverbank erosion.

Under the current climate change scenario, the average temperature of the region has seen notable increase, leading to erratic rainfall patterns and degradation of the ecosystems. In addition, it is expected that climate change will trigger the occurrences of more intense and frequent extreme events in Bangladesh, while contributing to slow-onset changes such as sea-level rise and increase in salinity levels (Thomas et al., 2013). These changes will have significant impacts on the existing ecosystem services and the livelihoods of those dependent on them, creating a crisis of survival for the poorest and most vulnerable.

Considering the impact of climate change on Bangladesh's ecology and ecosystem, it is well understood that under the current scenario, agriculture and food production in the country is under severe threat. For example, research shows that the production of rice, a staple crop for the country, will be measurably affected as increased temperatures are already reaching critical levels during the susceptible stages of the rice plants (Wassmann et al., 2009). Rising salinity levels in coastal lands will render the soil unsuitable for traditional agriculture and affect deltaic rice production. Salinity issues will also lead to shortage of fresh water supplies, causing detrimental effects on the aquatic ecosystems in the southwest coastal areas of Bangladesh (Dasgupta et al., 2017).

In terms of economic losses, a World Bank report (Yu et al., 2010) suggests that climate change will cost long-term rice production at least 7.4% each year for the period of 2005–2050. Aligned with this projection, it is also estimated that Bangladesh will lose a total of US$121 billion, or 5% of the national GDP, during this period. The majority of the population in Bangladesh still relies on agriculture-based livelihoods, and so lower crop yields due to climate change could potentially cause 15% net increase in poverty levels (Wright et al., 2015), making marginal groups even more vulnerable in the process.

Climate-induced calamities impacting livelihoods tend to be one of the key underlying reasons for internal migration in Bangladesh (Black, 2010). Within climatic hotspots, it is often the poorest and the most marginalized who are forced to migrate in search of economic opportunities. As rural-to-urban migration becomes more common, it is likely to bear additional stresses on the urban poor living in informal settlements (Alam and Rabbani, 2007). Approximately 55% of the urban population in Bangladesh consists of slum dwellers who are already vulnerable to the impacts of climate change (Uddin, 2018). Climate-induced migration then adds to this process of rapid, unplanned urbanization and creates concerns for human security and environmental degradation (Huq, 2001). There is a lack of necessary infrastructure, secure employment opportunities and suitable environmental and health facilities, which makes the urban poor increasingly exposed to the adverse effects of climate-induced disasters. In addition, as most migrants struggle to find suitable employment opportunities in these already crammed urban spaces, they are likely to end up trapped in a cycle of poverty.

For Bangladesh, the combination of biophysical and socio-economic factors within the country creates a unique state of vulnerability to climate change. As the country continues on its trajectory towards economic growth, striving to become a developed nation by 2041, it is imperative that collective and concerted action is taken to tackle the climate crisis. Adaptation efforts will need to be scaled up substantially, supplemented by long-term planning, technological innovations and sustainable capacity building.

Potential seeds of transformational adaptation in Bangladesh

In the past decade, Bangladesh has made remarkable efforts to combat climate change issues. The country has been a forerunner when it comes to adaptation actions and significant steps have been taken by the Government of Bangladesh to incorporate climate action within the frameworks of national plans and policies. Most notably, in 2009, the Bangladesh Climate Change Strategy and Action Plan (BCCSAP) was formulated to serve as the primary strategic framework document for guiding climate action in the country (MoEF, 2009), and subsequently, the Bangladesh Climate Change Trust Fund (BCCTF) was established to implement actions laid out in the BCCSAP. Set up as a block budgetary allocation from the government's revenue, nearly USD 385 million have been allocated to the fund between 2009 and 2016 (Anderson et al., 2017).

In addition, a vast array of small-, medium- and large-scale adaptation interventions has been implemented by the government, development partners, NGOs and the private sector, to help the most vulnerable communities deal with both slow-onset and extreme consequences of a changing climate. Some of the most prominent interventions are infrastructural measures such as construction of coastal embankments, sluice gates and cyclone shelters. These have shown tremendous success when it comes to protecting people against extreme events. For example, when cyclone Aila hit the coasts of Bangladesh in 2009, it created absolute havoc. Countless people lost their homes and livelihoods, and many were forced to migrate to cities (Saha, 2015). Following Aila, the government took drastic measures for increasing the number of cyclone shelters across the country. The effects of this were witnessed as cyclone Amphan swept across the country in 2020. The impacts of Amphan were not nearly as bad as Aila (2009) or its predecessor Sidr (2007). Compared to the thousands killed by Sidr, and hundreds by Aila, the number of deaths caused by Amphan could be limited to a dozen or two. The government took timely measures and prepared at least three times more shelters than in previous years, making these facilities far more accessible for people on the frontline (Eli, 2020).

While these interventions have rendered desirable outcomes under the current climate, it must be noted that they have been largely incremental in nature. In many cases, these measures run the risk of being unsuitable in the long run. For instance, enhancement of coastal embankments has long been one of the most common means of protecting the coast and its people against floods and cyclones in Bangladesh. Accordingly, several large-scale embankment projects have been, and continue to be, put in place by both donors and government. However, complex long-term environmental and economic consequences of these infrastructures have often been ignored in planning processes. For example, as embankments tend to prevent silt from depositing in the land, it ends up reducing the overall fertility of agricultural land in the region. In addition, rainwater is often confined within the embankment walls increasing the chances of waterlogging and drainage congestion. Expansion of embankments without good planning also causes siltation, blocking rivers and canals and causing them to dry out altogether (Dewan, 2020). These are likely to have severe negative consequences in the long run.

It is therefore evident that certain incremental adaptation measures remain susceptible to the growing uncertainties associated with climate change. For vulnerable communities in particular, climate-induced shifts in the ecosystem are further complicated by other drivers of change, creating more scope for uncertainty when planning for adaptation practices (Mehta et al., 2019). These conditions instigate the need to explore sustainable adaptation solutions that go beyond incremental approaches and tap into measures that can lead to societal transformation.

Considering that transformation is something that can only be verified far into the future, in order to fully understand the transformative potential of various adaptation initiatives it is perhaps more suitable to consider them as seeds of transformation. A seed can therefore be defined as an action or initiative that possesses building blocks that can create fundamental changes within the existing system and thereby pave the pathway for transformation over the long run (Chatterjee et al., 2020). A number of initiatives are already in place in Bangladesh that bear substantial promise.

Case study 1 hydroponic agriculture for adapting to rising salinity levels

The ongoing TAPESTRY project, being implemented in the southwestern coastal region of Bangladesh, aims to understand shifts in livelihood patterns in the face of growing uncertainties related to climate change, and how transformations may arise from the bottom-up as a consequence (T2Sresearch, 2020). Some of the research under the project has been looking into the transformative potential of hydroponic farming in salinity-prone coastal areas. Hydroponic farming uses a soilless method to grow plants and vegetables in mineral nutrient solutions, thereby enabling vegetable growth in saline conditions. A common hydroponic system combines traditional aquaculture with hydroponics within a symbiotic environment. The waste products from the fish farmed in the pond serve as nutrients for the vegetables grown within the system (Bethe, 2014). The initiative is relatively low cost and allows farming to take place within a small space, usually within the periphery of a household.

This community-based, low-cost adaptation technique has the potential to be transformational because it helps farmers adapt to the growing issue of salinity by shifting from conventional agriculture, which was not effective under these circumstances, to a new style of agriculture that requires less land space and less fresh water and incorporates multiple staple food groups (fisheries, rice and vegetables) into one complete system to ensure food security for the family all year round. Considering that the impacts of climate change will continue to increase salinity levels in the soil, technological innovations such as this could build livelihood resilience for marginalized farmers and poorer households, enabling them to be the agents of change pioneering the shift towards more sustainable farming practices.

The approach demonstrates true innovation, and it allows for climate-resilient livelihood practices to flourish. This can potentially stir long-term changes within the agriculture system of coastal areas, showcasing the potential to be transformational for the region.

Case study 2 empowering women to cause shift in power dynamics

In Bangladesh, gender inequality, in terms of rights and access to resources, is deeply embedded in the culture and social structures. Women and girls tend to be among the most vulnerable groups to climate change within a community. OXFAM's PROTIC programme is a participatory initiative that has been working to empower women and build their resilience through access to technology. The programme provided training to 300 women farmers, living in climate hotspots, on the use of mobile technology for accessing and utilizing relevant climate knowledge and information (Protic, 2020). Access to agro-meteorological information and customized knowledge regarding climate-resilient farming techniques enhanced women farmer's preparedness to deal with climate-induced risks and hazards. In addition, using mobile phones and digital services enabled women to develop better connections with the market, widening their scope for income generation. For example, in some cases women beneficiaries from the project learned to use mobile phones to start their own business ventures. The project went on to empower women and strengthened their agency within the community, allowing them to actively participate in various decision-making platforms where they were previously under-represented. As a result of these changes, these women's adaptive capacity significantly increased over time.

(Continued)

As such, initiatives like PROTIC have the potential to catalyse transformational change in climate hotspots by effectively reducing the gender gap, giving women access to resources and economic opportunities. This in turn can influence necessary shifts in the restricting power dynamics that exist between different gender groups within a community. By channelling knowledge and employing a learning-oriented approach to adaptation, the project allowed women to avail a diverse range of alternative livelihood options, which is critical for tackling high levels of uncertainty associated with a changing climate (Van Buren et al., 2009). The project addressed deep-rooted vulnerabilities of women by giving them the tools to develop as future change-makers, and thereby demonstrated transformative potential as it enabled system-wide change to occur within the existing socio-economic structures that have historically perpetuated gender inequality in the country.

Case study 3 designing strategies for long-term climate resilience

Mainstreaming adaptation into long-term development planning is considered vital for enacting transformational changes necessary to ensure sustained climate resilience in a country. As such, transformational adaptation can also be induced by the formulation of long-term policies and plans on climate action. The development of the recent Bangladesh Delta Plan 2100 (BDP2100) constitutes a remarkable initiative in this regard. Going up the year 2100, the BDP2100 delineates robust, adaptive and integrated strategies and subsequent interventions for ensuring long-term water and food security, economic growth and environmental sustainability in Bangladesh while effectively reducing vulnerability to natural disasters and building resilience to climate change impacts (GED, 2018). The plan employs a multisectoral, multidisciplinary and system-wide approach, which calls upon a vast range of stakeholders starting from government officials, NGOs, private sector and the civil society members to act as agents of change in the face of the looming threats of climate change.

The BDP2100 covers climate-adaptive measures and strategies across six major climatic hotspots, each with its unique set of risks and hazards. District-wise, hazard ranking has been conducted for all 64 districts. An Investment Plan (2017–2030) has also been developed, which entails 65 infrastructure projects and 15 institutional knowledge development projects in the 6 hotspots identified.

The development of the Delta Plan 2100 was guided by a series of scenario building exercises that outlined some of the anticipated risks, allowing for planning and preparation to tackle uncertainties associated with climatic threats in the future. In addition, the plan has been designed in alignment with national policies and plans, thereby ensuring better coherence and integration with the country's overall governance and political processes. The Delta Plan 2100 promises both long-term and large-scale, social, economic and environmental changes to take place in Bangladesh, which deems it to be transformative in nature.

The three brief case studies above demonstrate the potential to be transformative as they, in different manners, aim to create systemic changes within the country and address some of the root causes of vulnerability in Bangladesh in order to make the country and its people more resilient to the impacts of climate change.

Paving the pathway towards transformational change

This chapter has discussed the uncertainty related to climate change to highlight some of the drawbacks associated with incremental adaptation approaches and encourage a move towards more transformative pathways. Transformative adaptation considers future socio-economic scenarios and acknowledges the need for fundamental shifts that can transcend into long-term benefits.

Considering that the concept of transformation is relatively novel, this chapter has focussed on evaluating its functionality and success through assessing what can be identified as potential seeds of transformation. Adaptation is highly context specific, which means that we ought to reframe our understanding of transformational adaptation, based on existing practices and past lessons. While seeming like the all-encompassing solution, transformational adaptation cannot be seen as a silver bullet against the impacts and uncertainties of a changing climate. If climate action plans are designed without in-depth research and long-term forecasting, seemingly transformative seeds can prove to be unsustainable, for example when they interact with changing social, economic and environmental variables. If issues of intersectionality are not considered, in many instances adaptation measures can benefit one group more than the other, increase the communities' power and class divides and create more vulnerability in the long run. In coastal Bangladesh, for example, shifting from agro-economy to shrimp aquaculture for adapting to the rising salinity in the region has created more vulnerability for the poorest communities. The shift benefitted wealthier businessmen who stood to profit while it proved to be an unfavourable choice for the marginal groups as well as the overall ecosystem, making it ultimately 'maladaptive' (Paprocki and Cons, 2014).

In order to ensure successful transformations, it is essential to establish mechanisms and processes for systemic inquiry with feedback loops that enable continuous learning and allows for better planning and design of future initiatives. This has to be supplemented by robust governance structures that ensure transparency and accountability of adaptation actions. It is also important to invest in long-term capacity building of individuals, organizations and systems as a whole for enhancing their understating of climate change adaptation practices, and conducting better monitoring, evaluation and learning of adaptation actions. Nurturing the culture of learning will not only instigate the development of better designed adaptation practices but will also allow agents the ability to design more flexible adaptation measures that can tackle inevitable uncertainties and stir transformational changes.

Innovation and experimentation have long been considered integral elements for building resilience and adaptive capacity to climate change. So it is without doubt that steering climate action towards transformational pathways would be crucial for catalysing systemic shifts that can ensure enhanced adaptive capacity.

The impacts of climate change cut across all sectors and domains in different ways and in varying degrees. To build sustainable social futures, it is therefore important to understand the issue through a plethora of lenses, including science, politics, gender, culture and heritage. Transformational adaptation proposes an interdisciplinary, society-wide approach for ensuring climate resilience, thereby offering a holistic, and perhaps more lasting, solution to the issue of climate change for future generations.

Bibliography

Adger, W.N., Huq, S., Brown, K., Conway, D. and Hulme, M. (2003). 'Adaptation to climate change in the developing world', *Progress in Development Studies*, 3(3), pp. 179–195.

Agrawal, A. and Lemos, M.C. (2015). 'Adaptive development', *Nature Climate Change*, Vol 5, March 2015.

Alam, M. and Rabbani, M.D.G. (2007). 'Vulnerabilities and responses to climate change for Dhaka', *Environment and Urbanization*, 19(1), pp. 81–97.

Allen, M.R., Dube, O.P., Solecki, W., Aragon-Durand, F., Cramer, W., Humphreys, S. and Zickfeld, K. (2018). 'Framing and context'. In Masson-Delmotte, V. et al. (eds.), *Global Warming of 1.5 C: An IPCC special report on the impacts of global warming of 1.5 C above pre-industrial levels and related global greenhouse gas emission pathways, in the context of strengthening the global response to the threat of climate change, sustainable development, and efforts to eradicate poverty*. Available from: https://www.ipcc.ch/sr15/, accessed 2 August 2021

Anderson, G., Mack, C., Khan, Z.K., Khondker, R. and Hyman, E. (2017). 'Climate finance in Bangladesh: Situation analysis'. *Washington, DC: Climate Economic Analysis for Development, Investment, and Resilience (CEADIR) Activity*. Crown Agents USA and Abt Associates. Prepared for the United States Agency for International Development.

Bangladesh Planning Commission. (2018). 'Bangladesh climate change strategy and action plan'. Ministry of Environment and Forests, Government of the People's Republic of Bangladesh. http://cmsdata.iucn.org/downloads/bangladesh_climate_change_strategy_and_ action_plan_2009.pdf

Bethe, L.A. (2014). *Effect of foliar spray of compost tea on water spinach (Ipomoea aquatica) in Aquaponic System*. MS Thesis, Department of Aquaculture, Bangladesh Agricultural University, Mymensingh.

Black, R. (2010). 'Environmental refugees: Myth or reality? New issues in refugee research'. UNHCR Evaluation and Policy Analysis Unit, Geneva. Working Paper No. 34. http://www.unhcr.org/research/RESEARCH/3ae6a0d00.pdf

Chatterjee, R., Ohte, N., Joshi, P., Bhatt, M., Parthasarathy, D., Movik, S. and Mehta, L. (2020). Introducing TAPESTRY: A transdisciplinary project exploring seeds of transformation to reduce disaster and climate change induced uncertainties in marginal environments. http://gadri.net/4gsridrr/4thGlobalSummit_presentations/19gadri_p53.pdf

Chhetri, N., Stuhlmacher, M. and Ishtiaque, A. (2019). 'Nested pathways to adaptation', *Environmental Research Communications*, 1(1), 015001.

Dasgupta, S., Huq, M., Mustafa, M.G., Sobhan, M.I. and Wheeler, D. (2017). 'The impact of aquatic salinization on fish habitats and poor communities in a changing climate: Evidence from southwest coastal Bangladesh', *Ecological Economics*, 139, pp. 128–139.

Dewan, C. (2020). 'Climate change as a spice': Brokering environmental knowledge in Bangladesh's development industry', *Ethnos*, pp. 1–22. DOI: 10.1080/00141844.2020.1788109

Elli, J. (2020). 'Cyclone Amphan: In Bangladesh, preparedness paid off - Bangladesh'. *ReliefWeb*. https://reliefweb.int/report/bangladesh/cyclone-amphan-bangladesh-preparedness-paid

Ericson, J.P., Vorosmarty, C.J., Dingman, S.L., Ward, L.G. and Meybeck, M. (2005). 'Effective sea-level rise and deltas: Causes of change and human dimension implications', *Global Planetary Change*, 50, pp. 63–82.

General Economics Division. (2018). 'Bangladesh Delta Plan 2100', Bangladesh Planning Commission, Ministry of Planning, Government of the People's Republic of Bangladesh. http://plancomm.portal.gov.bd/sites/default/files/files/plancomm.portal.gov.bd/files/dc5b06a1_3a45_4ec7_951e_a9feac1ef783/BDP%202100%20Abridged%20Version%20English.pdf

Houghton, J.T. (2001). *Climate change 2001: The scientific basis*. https://www.ipcc.ch/site/assets/uploads/2018/07/WG1_TAR_FM.pdf

Huq, S. (2001). 'Climate change and Bangladesh', *Science*, 294(5547), pp. 1617–1618.

Intergovernmental Panel on Climate Change (IPCC). (2007). 'Climate change 2007: Synthesis report'. In Pachauri, R.K. and Reisinger, A. (eds.), *Contribution of working groups I, II and III to the fourth assessment report of the intergovernmental panel on climate change*. Geneva, Switzerland: IPCC, 104 pp.

Intergovernmental Panel on Climate Change (IPCC). (2014). 'AR5 synthesis report: Climate change 2014'.

Intergovernmental Panel on Climate Change (IPCC). (2018). 'Impacts of 1.5 C global warming on natural and human systems'. *Global warming of 1.5° C. An IPCC Special Report*.

Kates, R.W., Travis, W.R. and Wilbanks, T.J. (2012). 'Transformational adaptation when incremental adaptations to climate change are insufficient', *Proceedings of the National Academy of Sciences*, 109(19), pp. 7156–7161.

Lonsdale, K., Pringle, P. and Turner, B. (2015). 'Transformative adaptation: What it is, why it matters and what is needed'. UK Climate Impacts Programme, University of Oxford, Oxford, UK ISBN: 978-1-906360-11-5

Noble, I.R., Huq, S., Anokhin, Y.A., Carmin, J., Goudou, D., Lansigan, F.P. and Villamizar, A. (2014). 'Adaptation needs and options'. In Field, C.B. et al. (eds.), *Climate Change 2014: Impacts, Adaptation, and Vulnerability. Part A: Global and Sectoral Aspects. Contribution of Working Group II to the Fifth Assessment Report of the Intergovernmental Panel on Climate Change*. Cambridge, United Kingdom and New York, USA: Cambridge University Press, pp. 833–868.

Paprocki, K. and Cons, J. (2014). 'Life in a shrimp zone: Aqua- and other cultures of Bangladesh's coastal landscape', *The Journal of Peasant Studies*, 41(6), pp. 1109–1130.

Protic. (2020). 'PROTIC – Participatory action research with the help of ICT'. *Proticbd*. http://proticbd.info/

Saha, C.K. (2015). 'Dynamics of disaster-induced risk in southwestern coastal Bangladesh: An analysis on tropical Cyclone Aila 2009', *Natural Hazards*, 75(1), pp. 727–754.

Salehin, M., Chowdhury, M.M.A., Clarke, D., Mondal, S., Nowreen, S., Jahiruddin, M. and Haque, A. (2018). 'Mechanisms and drivers of soil salinity in coastal Bangladesh'. In Nicholls, R., Hutton, C., Adger, W., Hanson, S., Rahman, M. and Salehin, M. (eds.), *Ecosystem services for well-being in deltas*. Cham: Palgrave Macmillan, pp. 333–347.

T2SResearch. (2020). 'TAPESTRY: Pathways to sustainability in marginal environments'. *T2S*. https://t2sresearch.org/project/tapestry/

Thomas, T.S., Mainuddin, K., Chiang, C., Rahman, A., Haque, A., Islam, N. and Sun, Y. (2013) *Agriculture and adaptation in Bangladesh: Current and projected impacts of climate change*. IFPRI discussion papers 1281 (Vol. 1281). The International Food Policy Research Institute.

Uddin, N. (2018). 'Assessing urban sustainability of slum settlements in Bangladesh: Evidence from Chittagong city', *Journal of Urban Management*, 7(1), pp. 32–42.

Van Buuren, A., Driessen, P., Teisman, G. and van Rijswick, M. (2014). 'Toward legitimate governance strategies for climate adaptation in the Netherlands: Combining insights from a legal, planning, and network perspective', *Regional Environmental Change*, 14(3), pp. 1021–1033.

Wassmann, R., Jagadish, S.V.K., Sumfleth, K., Pathak, H., Howell, G., Ismail, A., Serraj, R., Redona, E., Singh, R.K. and Heuer, S. (2009). 'Regional vulnerability of climate change impacts on Asian rice production and scope for adaptation'. In Sparks, D.L. (ed.), *Advances in agronomy*. London: Academic Press, Vol. 102, pp. 91–133.

Wright, H., Huq, S. and Reeves, J. (2015). 'Impact of climate change on least developed countries: Are the SDGs possible?' IIED Briefing, May 2015. http://pubs.iied.org/pdfs/17298IIED.pdf

Yu, W.M., Alam, M., Hassan, A., Khan, A.S., Ruane, A.C., Rosenzweig, C., Major, D., and Thurlow, J. (2010). *Climate change risks and food security in Bangladesh*. London and Washington, DC: World Bank. http://documents.worldbank.org/curated/en/419531467998254867/pdf/690860ESW0P1050Climate0Change0Risks.pdf.

8
Collaboration
Collaborative future-making

*Kristina Lindström, Per-Anders Hillgren,
Ann Light, Michael Strange and Li Jönsson*

Introduction

The articulation of collaborative future-making (CFM) builds on a long legacy of working with collaborative processes. The authors of this chapter are all situated at Malmö University where participatory design and various forms of democratic design experiments have been central to research and teaching. Along with the wider domain of participatory design, early work at Malmö involved democratizing the workplace and later work has moved into contexts such as social innovation, city planning, cultural production and public engagement. As part of this expansion of the field, scholars at Malmö have had a strong commitment to developing and exploring formats, gatherings and processes, manifesting as design things, infrastructuring, commoning, publics-in-the-making and so on (Ehn et al., 2014).

These projects have been partly successful in demonstrating alternative futures, providing working examples of how things can be different. However, the need to address issues at the level of system change, as sustainable futures require, has also pointed to an increased need for cultivating imagination. In line with arguments within futures studies (see, for example, Vervoort et al., 2015; Angheloiu et al., 2020), the CFM platform thereby sets out to cultivate critical imagination that allows for shifts in values and worldviews.

As a response to this, we, as a group of researchers, have formalized these interests into a faculty platform. With a small amount of funding and a focus for our discussions, the platform acts as a discernible clustering of interests and ambitions among colleagues and collaborators. The authors of this chapter are all signed up to the platform. We see our work as a manifestation of a particular ethos – a desire to create better worlds (or 'reworlding'), through linking theories of transformation with the practices of change. All the authors draw on critical perspectives from the humanities and social sciences, combined with the constructive and collaborative aspects of making and prototyping in design research. Each author has then interpreted the mix of theory and practice in their own fashion, and we have honoured these differences, here, by allowing people to describe their work in their own voices. This too is a political choice and aligns with our ambition to pluralize futures.

Two overarching questions guide and make up the core strands of the research:

1. How can we, through critical imagination, challenge basic assumptions, worldviews, institutions and structures to widen the perspectives of what can constitute socially, culturally, ecologically and economically sustainable futures?
2. How can we set up more inclusive collaborations to prototype and discuss alternative futures, where we not only engage professionals and policymakers, but also citizens and civil society?

These two strands offer a framework that can encompass the multidisciplinary research within the research group. They offer agency to participants as an antidote to forecasting and, while not claiming that the future is wide open, they begin to provide tools for the remaking of structures and systems in line with sustainable and restorative lifestyles.

The two strands of collaborative future-making

In this section, we articulate the two thematic strands that are central to CFM, calling them 'Critical Imagination' and 'Collaborative Engagements'. We do this through a theoretical framing. We follow this with a series of cases from our own research that highlights opportunities and challenges with CFM. Through these cases, we also hope to trouble a strict division between practice and theory and instead highlight the entanglements between concrete matters, issues and practices, as well as underlying imaginaries and worldviews.

Critical imagination

Many scholars have suggested that our capacity to imagine alternative societies is in crisis (Unger, 1987; Harvey, 2000; Kiersy, 2013). Anthropologist David Graeber (2011, pp. 393–394) has articulated this as a collapse of imagination, and Fredric Jameson (2003, p. 76) has suggested that it is easier to imagine the end of the world than the end of capitalism. Partly responding to this collapse or lack of imagination, there are multiple calls to cultivate our imagination and to determine how things could be otherwise (Harvey, 2000; Yusoff and Gabrys, 2011; Dunne and Raby, 2013; Haraway, 2016). While imagination has always had a central role in design research, especially within areas such as speculative and critical design (Dunne and Raby, 2013), political scientists have also started to direct their interest towards literary and media studies to rethink the present (e.g. Kirsey, 2013). As Light says,

> In imagining difference, something changes in our potential for action and the directions it might take. In conceiving new ways of being, we are already performing a part of the work of designing, even if we never pursue imagined difference into the discernible world of materials and tools. [...] We start the confrontation between the fluidity of the mind, where anything imaginable is possible, and the cultural and material choices that already shape possible futures, where (infra)structural commitment is profound.
> *(Light, 2015, p. 86)*

Using critical imagination to break out of (imagined) political and scholarly deadlocks is an important theme within CFM. However, in our work, as we demonstrate through examples, this is directly linked to collaborative and tangible practices of making, rather than abstract exercises.

Collaborative engagements

Coupled with a turn to cultivating critical imagination, we bring a strong interest in participatory design (Schuler and Namioka, 1993; Simonsen and Robertson, 2012) and a tradition in applying it. This field, long associated with the development of effective software, might also be seen as a series of studies in how we can work together. At the centre is an ethos that acknowledges people's skills and rights to influence their everyday environments. Drawing inspiration from science and technology studies (STS) and feminist technoscience, we respect the degree to which both material and social aspects influence agency and processes of change. In our collaborative engagements, we carefully and practically weave actors and processes together, aiming to nurture a plurality of voices and pay special attention to marginalized actors (Hillgren et al., 2016). This brings forward questions such as: What is possible to change (or not) and why? Who can change what and how? How can socio-material networks be opened up to be more inclusive?

Five illustrations of our work

In the next passages, we provide examples of our work, using critical imagination and collaborative engagement as a lens.

The examples that we present differ in their context and the issues that are addressed. The first two examples are taken from older projects and exemplify some of the difficulties of working with collaborative processes, and the need for further developing skills and practices for cultivating critical imagination. The last three are more recent and give an account of projects that make use of collective engagement to cultivate critical imagination. They share commitment and attention to practices of making. Rather than approaching making as an instrumental, productivist or solutionist practice, our accounts bring nuance to these practices of making. We hope to show how different forms of making make it possible to engage with, and negotiate, the future in different ways.

Working worldviews together

Per-Anders Hillgren

Working together to make futures is intricate and the skills involved are not trivial, as this example will reveal. In 2008, I started to collaborate with a multi-ethnic women's NGO with the aim of understanding how self-organized citizen groups could create value in local neighbourhoods. The process started in a very open-ended way with the purpose of getting to know each other better. Quite soon, several opportunities emerged that both participants from the NGO and the university regarded as exciting; these were developed into successful prototypes. This might have been the end of the collaboration but we wanted to see this through to the point of actual success for these would-be innovators. So, to take these ideas further, we made contact with a Swedish business-women's network that was eager to collaborate. Initially, this partnership seemed very promising and many more ideas were discussed. The city of Malmö was also willing to fund further development. However, quite quickly, the whole process came to a stop because the business women requested that the members of the NGO free themselves from the collective spirit of the NGO and step forward as individuals. This was something the NGO members did not feel comfortable doing.

The breakdown occurred because two very different worldviews clashed, reflecting different priorities: Here, women who saw themselves as emancipated individual business entrepreneurs could not see the value provided by the collective to a group of recent newcomers to Swedish culture. The strong emphasis on individuality typically found in Western cultures has recently been criticized as incapable of handling present societal and ecological problems (Haraway, 2016; Bauman, 2017), and the NGO could have been seen as a promising example of collective power. Still, for the business women, independence, rather than interdependence, was the foundation for their activities – they had struggled a long time to become emancipated individual business entrepreneurs.

As this example demonstrates, collaborative engagements in processes of future-making will occasionally be demanding and have to go hand in hand with critical imagination. Not only does one have to cope with a multitude of unfamiliar actors, practices and values, but one also needs critical imagination to articulate and question one's own taken-for-granted assumptions and worldviews and be able to embrace radically different ones. To truly democratize the future, we have to work knowledges together at the most basic level (Verran, 1998). This means acknowledging and supporting diverse ontologies, epistemologies and worldviews. This requires practical design work, but also theoretical exercises and reflexive discussions about power and values.

Democratic policymaking is not the same as interest aggregation

Michael Strange

In this account, I argue against treating democracy as the aggregation of pre-existing interests, instead making the point that for democracy to function we need to foster spaces in which individuals can collaboratively engage with one another to first develop those political interests. In November 2018, I was invited to give oral evidence to the UK Parliamentary Committee on International Trade (UK House of Commons, 2019). The question steering the committee's inquiry was: What should be the role of local government in future UK trade policy? As became clear at the hearing, trade policy is understood as being made through a process of 'interest aggregation'. In that process, the role of local government is to act as an upwards-pointing funnel, channelling local-level trade interests – spoken of mostly in terms of small and medium enterprises – towards the national level, whose job it is to somehow weigh those aggregated interests towards identifying the UK national interest.

Trade politics provides a good example of why assuming policymaking is democratic as long as it aggregates interests is insufficient. To represent one's interests effectively (i.e. to speak the right technical language, as well as to know what is in one's interests (i.e. to identify growth areas and potential threats to one's economy and society) requires a certain level of expertise. That expertise includes knowledge of both economics and trade law, but also understanding of environmental impacts, societal costs and many other potentially relevant fields of knowledge that are not always readily available to actors at the local level (Siles-Brügge, 2019). Applying that knowledge to the question set by the parliamentary committee, the role of local government cannot only be to collect interests since they do not pre-exist the political process. Rather, political processes require *making* interests, including education and awareness-raising.

This is mapped out in Figure 8.1, where the familiar funnel-like structure of interest aggregation is joined by a series of local processes in which local government is active in building the communities capable of expressing interests. Political interests do not exist as

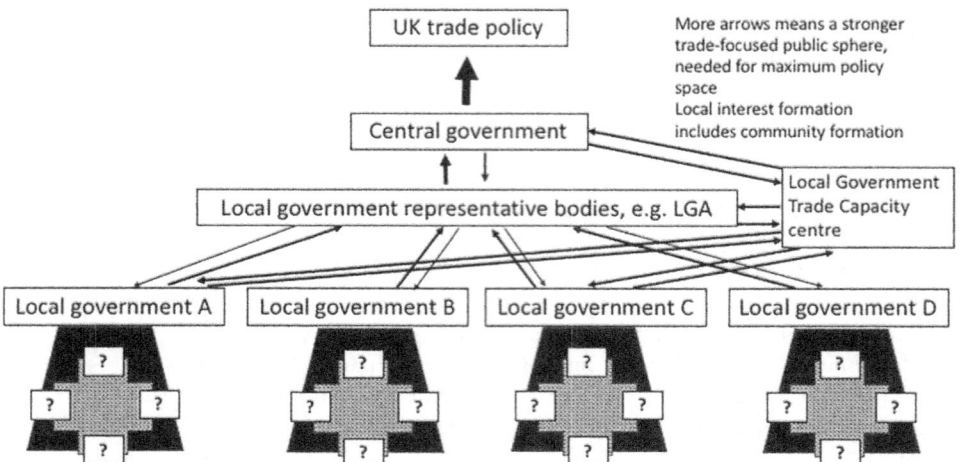

Figure 8.1 Local government aids formation of communities focussed on trade policy where interests are not pre-political but form via ongoing dialogue

crops passively waiting to be harvested; rather, the role of local government is to provide the resources and infrastructure by which individuals may engage in how this particular field of policymaking relates to their lives and so form interest groups that express 'local interests'.

In democratic policymaking, the 'making' involved can never be a simple aggregation of interests since that assumes that they pre-exist the political process, that they are known before the 'making'. Instead, policymaking that connects to all potential actors must include processes of making publics and interests. This underlines the importance of finding ways to encourage collaboration while treating political interests as dynamic social constructs that require an active public sphere, as opposed to treating them as fixed positions just waiting to be acknowledged by the policymakers. The concept of 'interests' needs to be critically re-imagined, in other words, seeing such interests as emergent and changing but, also, fundamentally social rather than intransigent qualities held by individuals. Treating democracy as pure interest aggregation enables disingenuous political leaders to claim a democratic mandate on the simple basis of controlling a majority. However, if we see interests as not pre-existing but part of an ongoing collaborative engagement, we can critically imagine a more accountable form of governance in which political leaders are judged not on a single vote but, rather, their ability and willingness to support a society in which individuals are intellectually equipped to contest policies.

Un/making

Kristina Lindström

My work explores the politics involved in making, in future-making. More specifically, my research, undertaken in collaboration with Åsa Ståhl, is concerned with future-making through the practice of un/making, suggesting a double movement of making and unmaking (Lindström and Ståhl, 2020). Through a combination of conceptual work and hands-on explorations, our work invites hesitation regarding the assumption that all kinds of problems require the application of more design, more things, more making (McNamara et al., 2019). Instead, we contend that this progressivist imaginary has been part of generating the kinds of problems we are facing today, suggesting a need for reworking and rethinking how we understand and practice making.

To foster critical imagination, and to explore how things could be otherwise, we have set up a series of projects that invite people to care for and un/make harmful matters that have emerged in the aftermath of previous makings (Lindström and Ståhl, 2020). In practice, this has involved experiments in how to un/make your own plastic waste through composting in a domestic setting (2016), and how to un/make soil that has been formerly polluted by the glass industry through the use of plants (2019). On the one hand, both experiments have involved concrete attempts to un/make specific matters such as plastics waste and heavy metals in the soil. But, on the other (and, perhaps, more importantly), these engagements have also participated in the un/making, or at least troubling, of the imaginaries that these matters relate to.

Plastics, for example, have participated in the making of modernist imaginaries of human mastery over nature. Through the use of cheap and disposable products, plastics have also enabled a kind of carefree living. In contrast, the practice of composting plastics with the help of common mealworms opened up an understanding of plastic as a matter full of uncertainties and ethical implications, requiring ongoing, more-than-human work and care (Lindström and Ståhl, 2016). This shows how matters, practices and imaginaries are closely entangled, and in constant becoming (see Figure 8.2).

The collaborative engagement, which included not only humans but also more than human actors such as plastic take-away containers, glass jars, common mealworms and their gut enzymes, was not meant to produce knowledge to be fed into the next iteration on a design process, in order to 'solve' the urgent issue of plastic waste once and for all. Rather it aimed to foster critical imagination in how we relate to plastics. Critical imagination, in this case, did not just emerge as a matter of imagining something new, but also as a practice of letting go of, or un/making, practices and imaginaries that have been part of generating the problems we face today.

Figure 8.2 Repurposed glass jar for composting plastics

Commitments of ecological citizenship

Ann Light

I am concerned with how futures become accessible to all. I have three *Worlds* workshops in circulation to consider change in our cultures and expectations. These work quite differently from the workshops described in the previous section, yet my commitment to unpicking material matters is the same and relates to the themes of CFM. I am on a mission to reveal how *designable* the world is (Light, 2019) by making process tools designed to help people come together and understand themselves as agents in collaborative change as we face uncertain, even unwelcome, futures. I ponder on what we can make safely to offer an outlet for design energies. In other words, these collaborative events exist as much to provide a provocation as to how we might refocus our design skills in a post-profligate world as to produce artefacts for use.

The *Worlds* series was conceived to highlight three dimensions of ecological citizenship.

World machines

Revealing the power of the digital to connect, sense and aggregate and exploring how the world could be joined up for greater information, understanding and feedback, people come together to discuss utopias, resistance and tools of change and to make manuals for coordinating local and global resources (Light et al., 2015a, b; see Figure 8.3).

On some other world

Demonstrating how the world has come about by looking at an alternative present with different path dependencies and outcomes, our imaginings show how life could have been different and therefore still could be (Korsmeyer and Light, 2019). The workshop emphasizes the designed-therefore-designable nature of our living and plays with history to problematize the choices dominating our socio-technical systems (see Figures 8.4 and 8.5).

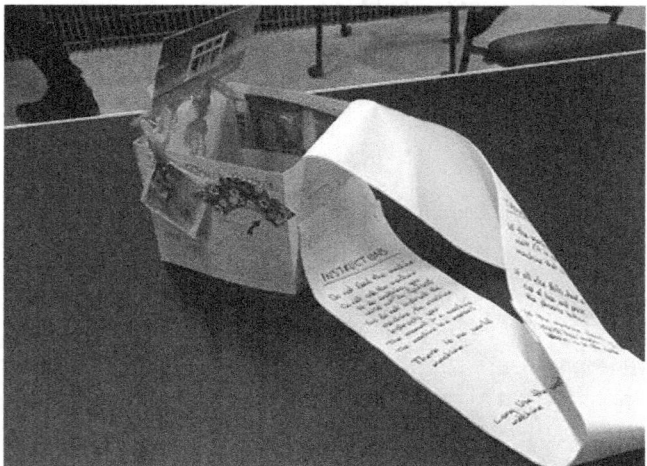

Figure 8.3 Instructions for making a world machine

Collaboration

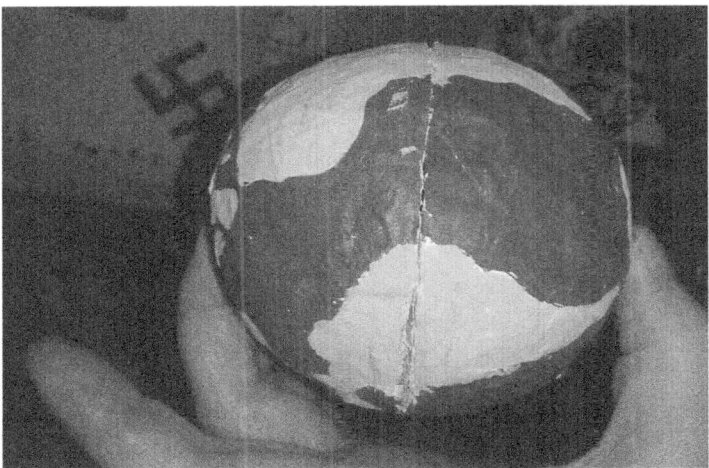

Figure 8.4 Holding the world in your hand

Figure 8.5 Counterfactual Worlds Generator (credit and build: Deborah Mason)

Worlds of/that matter

Working with the affective, this workshop explores what we most care about, how we come to care for the things we value and how we might include more that is fragile in our care. It asks how we make and sustain meaning in uncertain times.

None of the events are didactic; rather each allows people new experiences, posing questions about resource use, directions of travel and care. This ethic is captured in the Craftivist Collective attitude to action for change: 'If we want a world that is beautiful, kind and fair… shouldn't our activism be beautiful, kind and fair?' (Corbett, 2017). The workshops have three purposes: To offer an example of low-consumption alternatives to designing products and services to people who love to design; to demonstrate how such artefacts might reflect the values of the regenerative changes we wish to embrace and to help people encounter their ecological citizenship possibilities in constructive and supportive ways. The work is collaborative by nature, but this reflects an insight that reflection together is the fastest way to transformation: Invoking critical imagination with others brings both more willingness to act on speculations and more types of speculation.

The thickening of futures

Li Jönsson

This section addresses the futures we want to make and how we might imagine worlds otherwise. Not only, as Graeber (2011) points out, is human imagination running the risk of becoming extinct, but, as a series of recent reports clarify so too are many of our current plants and species. Such reports, observations, predictions and speculations can be understood as rather limiting and thin when imagining the future. What we might call a 'thin future' is typically characterized by clear predictions and technological innovation inadvertently becoming statements of one singular future (Yusoff and Gabrys, 2011), which offers a stark contrast to the rich welcoming and 'thick' presents that Haraway (2016) argues for.

In a series of design events (Jönsson, 2014) called *appetizers for futures,* I worked with Åsa Ståhl and Kristina Lindström to ask people to engage with one predicted future concerned with the alarming loss of pollinators (Sánchez-Bayo and Wyckhuys, 2019).

This predicted thin future is one where we have lost pollinators – and, along with them, the plenty of the present: Such as fruits, vegetables, berries and more. To set the scene, appetizers made from corn, a plant that can cross- or self-pollinate is served to the participants on arrival. While digesting these appetizers and thereby literally tasting a predicted future without pollinators, the participants are asked to respond in different ways to the issue, either by producing new alternative recipes or simply by suggesting and bringing new ingredients and information to the table. Attached to each ingredient there is a label that describes one specific hope or concern with regard to the future for pollinators (Figure 8.6). Some labels suggest quick tech and biotech fixes, such as tech-drone pollinators and self-fertile almonds from genetic modification programmes. Others suggest the reviving of past practices, such as rewilding the threatened European dark bees, and some suggest final game-overs. In other words, the ingredients that make up the appetizers do not necessarily solve the issue of pollination, but rather they generate frictions and offer a plurality of ideas and possibilities that allow us to imagine what is to come. They somehow thicken the present by retelling rich pasts (Haraway, 2016), but also through disrupting and staging futures of naive optimism and gritty hopes (Head, 2016).

Collaboration

Figure 8.6 Table with thickening ingredients where the label describes one specific hope or concern in regard to the future for pollinators

These examples show that dwelling on concerns about the failure of imagination (Unger 1987; Harvey, 2000; Graeber, 2011; Kiersy, 2013) need not be alarming or depressing. Rather, they suggest that disruption might be needed in order to open up imaginative acts that support spaces and practices for dealing with uncertain futures by deconstructing some of the current hegemonic environmental imaginaries and narratives. Critical imagination that affords a certain rupture and even notions of deconstruction, as in this case, might even spark more gritty, liveable and fragile stories into being.

Conclusion

We have used two organizing concepts to think through the commitments of collaborative future-making as theory and practice combined: *Critical imagination* and *collaborative engagement*. They represent the performative elements of engaging with anticipatory issues, not to be reduced to words, but capturing the relational qualities of ideas in enactment. In that sense, we hope to trouble the idea of practice as primarily being concerned with solving immediate problems and of theory as just being concerned with critique. Rather than reinforcing this divide, we have shared examples of collaborative future-making that highlight the entanglements between concrete issues and practices, as well as underlying imaginaries and worldviews.

The examples that we have presented in this chapter differ in terms of scale, topic and approach. In line with the organization of the collaborative future-making platform, these examples draw on and make use of perspectives that cut across disciplinary boundaries. Our aim has not been to provide a comprehensive map of this area of research. Instead, we hope that these diverse, situated and partial exemplars of collaborative future-making can draw attention to what Light has articulated as the designable future. It is, however, not enough to recognize that the future is in the making, rather than predetermined. As we show through our examples, to engage in collaborative future-making also involves continuously exploring questions of how futures can be made, what they might be and

113

who gets to participate. How can issues, concerns and alternatives be made tangible and negotiable among heterogeneous actors, including communities, publics, policymakers and more?

Recognizing the extensiveness of the change needed, we argue for future-making practices to move beyond the development of ready-to-be-used toolkits. The presented cases have shown how critical and theoretical concepts such as 'un/making' or the 'thickening of futures' can be instantiated as embodied practices that help us to elaborate on what we have to give up or preserve. As these examples show, collaborative future-making is not just aiming to solve immediate urgent problems, but aims to adopt a systemic approach informed by radical theories of worlding, such as Haraway's (2016). In other words, we argue that in parallel to addressing concrete issues such as plastic pollution or a declining population of pollinators, there is a need to seriously rethink and rework underlying imaginaries guiding politics and society. To do this is to acknowledge the agency of culture in making the problems we face today. Such a reworking might, as we have described, require practices of generative disruption (and unlearning the taken-for-granted) in addition to cultivating capacities to work multiple worldviews together.

This work also reveals that collaboration in making futures is much more than only a matter of practicalities. Collaborating is not, here, the means of putting an acceptable face on neoliberalism by providing a sense of inclusion, nor, indeed, just a preoccupation of Scandinavian participatory designers whose cultural predisposition is to look for collectivities. Collaboration is part of what reconstitutes the world and, in being enacted with critical imagination, provides the prefigurative politics enabling new realities to be born. To that end, concepts from critical theory, for instance, postcolonial studies, can be helpful to ensure that such work does not slide into unreflective consensus, platitudes or participation-for-the-sake-of-it. And, at a more pragmatic level, enacting these political safeguards also works in the moment to support participants in respecting each other's worldviews and allowing greater opportunities for balanced participation. It also means acknowledging that political interests and demands do not exist outside of politics, as if on a shelf awaiting the attention of the powerful, but require an ongoing generative process of dialogue. As such, we see politics as inherently discursive. Ignoring questions of participation and inclusion therefore means not only excluding voices, but also narrowing down the possibility for politics to function productively for the public good.

In conclusion, we five authors have identified the ideas and practices that unite us in collaborative future-making. While demonstrably diverse, two common threads run through them as both theoretical and practical shared ground: Critical imagination and collaborative engagements. Working at the intersection of these, and showing how conceptual space may be actively linked to practice, we propose a designerly understanding of futures, where we acknowledge our potential for collective agency and work with it as profoundly as we can to attend to rapidly changing and unequally distributed opportunities and threats. For us, the future is material to work with – in terms of inclusion, reshaping and pluralizing imaginaries and exchanging the structures we have for the structures we want and need.

Bibliography

Bauman, Z. (2017). *Retrotopia*. Cambridge: Polity Press.
Bleecker, J. (2009). 'Design fiction: A short essay on design, science, fact and fiction'. *Near Future Laboratory*, 29. https://blog.nearfuturelaboratory.com/2009/03/17/design-fiction-a-short-essay-on-design-science-fact-and-fiction/

Corbett, S. (2017). *How to be a craftivist*. London: Unbound Publishing.
Dunne, A. and Raby, F. (2013). *Speculative everything. Design, fiction and social dreaming*. Cambridge MA: MIT Press.
Ehn, P., Nilsson, E.M. and Topgaard, R. (eds.). (2014). *Making futures: Marginal notes on innovation, design, and democracy*. Cambridge MA: MIT Press.
Graeber, D. (2011). *Debt: The first 5000 Years*. Brooklyn, NY: Melville House.
Haraway, D.J. (2016). *Staying with the trouble: Making kin in the Chthulucene*. Durham, NC: Duke University Press.
Harvey, D. (2000). *Spaces of hope*. Berkeley: University of California Press.
Head, L. (2016). *Hope and grief in the Anthropocene: Re-conceptualizing human–nature relations*. London: Routledge.
Hillgren, P.A., Seravalli, A. and Eriksen, M.A. (2016). 'Counter-hegemonic practices: Dynamic interplay between agonism, commoning and strategic design'. *Strategic Design Research Journal*, 9(2), p. 89.
Jameson, F. (2003). 'Future city', *New Left Review*, 21, pp. 65–79.
Jönsson, L. (2015). *Design events: On explorations of a non-anthropocentric framework in design*. København: The Royal Danish Academy of Fine Arts, Schools of Architecture, Design and Conservation.
Kiersey, N.J. (2013). '"The future of humanity begins with a choice": Narrating techno-rational subsumption and micropolitics in international relations and Battlestar Galactica'. In Kiersey, N.J. and Neumann, I.B. (eds.) *Battlestar Galactica and international relations* (pp. 71–91). London: Routledge
Korsmeyer, H. and Light, A. (2019). 'Learning to anticipate worlds through participatory speculative design'. Anticipation 2019, Oslo, October 2019.
Light, A. (2015). 'Troubling futures: can participatory design research provide a constitutive anthropology for the 21st century?' *Interaction Design and Architecture(s) Journal - IxDandA*, 26, pp. 81–94.
Light, A. (2019). 'Redesigning design for culture change: theory in the Anthropocene'. Design research for change. Design Museum, London, Dec 1–12th, 2019.
Light, A., Bardzell, J., Bardzell, S., Cox, G., Fritsch, J. and Hansen, L.K. (2015). 'Making "World Machines": Discourse, design and global technologies for greater-than-self issues'. *Aarhus Series on Human Centered Computing*, 1(1), p. 3.
Light, A., Brereton, M. and Roe, P. (2015, December). 'Some notes on the design of world machines'. In Ploderer, B., Carter, M., Gibbs, M., Smith, W. and Vetere, F. (eds.) *Proceedings of the annual meeting of the Australian special interest group for computer human interaction* (pp. 289–293). New York: Association for Computing Machinery.
Lindström, K. and Ståhl, Å. (2016, August). 'Becoming response-able stakeholders: participatory design in times of uncertainties' In Bossen, C. and Smith, R.C. (eds.) *Proceedings of the 14th participatory design conference: Short papers, interactive exhibitions, workshops-Volume 2* (pp. 41–44). New York: Association for Computing Machinery.
Lindström, K. and Ståhl, Å. (2019). 'Caring design experiments in the aftermath'. *Nordes*, 8, pp. 1–9.
Lindström, K. and Ståhl, Å. (2020). 'Un/making in the aftermath of design'. In del Gaudio, C. and Parra-Agudelo, L. (eds.) *Proceedings of the 16th participatory design conference*. New York: Association for Computing Machinery, pp. 12–21.
McNamara, A., Coombs, G. and Sade, G. (2019). 'Introduction'. In Coombs, G., McNamara, A. and Sade, G. (eds.) *Undesign: A critical practice at the intersection of art and design*. Abingdon, Oxon; and New York: Routledge.
Pigott, A. (2018). 'Imagining socioecological transformation: An analysis of the Welsh Government's policy innovations and orientations to the future'. *Science of the Anthropocen*, 6(1), pp. 60–78.
Sánchez-Bayo, F. and Wyckhuys. K.A. (2019). 'Worldwide decline of the entomofauna: A review of its drivers'. *Biological Conservation* 232, pp. 8–27.
Schuler, D. and Namioka, A. (eds.). (1993). *Participatory design: Principles and practices*. Boca Raton, FL: CRC Press.
Siles-Brügge, G. (2019). 'Bound by gravity or living in a 'post geography trading world'? Expert knowledge and affective spatial imaginaries in the construction of the UK's post-Brexit trade policy'. *New Political Economy*, 24(3), pp. 422–439.
Simonsen, J., and Robertson, T (eds.). (2012). *Routledge international handbook of participatory design*. London: Routledge.
UK House of Commons. (2019) 'UK trade policy transparency and scrutiny'. *International Trade Committee Sixth Report of Session 2017–19*. Available online: https://publications.parliament.uk/pa/cm201719/cmselect/cmintrade/1043/1043.pdf (Last accessed: January 2020).

Unger, R. (1987). *False necessity: Anti-necessitarian social theory in the service of radical democracy.* Cambridge: Cambridge University Press.

Verran, H. (1998). 'Re-imagining land ownership in Australia'. *Postcolonial Studies: Culture, Politics, Economy,* 1(2), pp. 237–254.

Yusoff, K., and Gabrys, J. (2011). 'Climate change and the imagination'. *Wiley Interdisciplinary Reviews: Climate Change,* 2(4), pp. 516–534.

9
Data
The futures of personal data

Deborah Lupton

Introduction

An increasing array of technologies have emerged that are able to generate, archive and process digitized information about people and their everyday lives. These processes, using data from people's online interactions, app use and embedded sensors in mobile and wearable devices and physical environments, have been referred to as the 'datafication' of humans (van Dijck, 2014). The possibilities of using these personal digital data to enhance people's health, well-being and productivity, develop the economy and improve policing, security, planning and welfare provision, among other benefits, have been outlined in promotional accounts by tech developers, policymakers and government agencies (Lupton, 2019). However, both popular media and scholarly analyses now often present a dystopian vision of the social futures of personal data. Numerous writers in media and surveillance studies have expressed concerns about the intensified surveillance of citizens that can be made possible by accessing the digital traces left behind by people's encounters with digital technologies. The term 'dataveillance' is frequently employed to describe these forms of digitized watching (Best, 2010; van Dijck, 2014).

Many hyperbolic popular media accounts of the risks posed to citizens by intensified datafication and dataveillance have been published since Edward Snowden's initial revelations in 2013 about the ways in which nations use digital data to conduct surveillance on their unsuspecting citizens. Several other highly publicized scandals about personal data breaches and exploitation have received attention in the media since then, including the Cambridge Analytica scandal in 2018, in which Facebook was implicated in a data profiling company using information from the platform to seek to influence voting and other behaviours (Isaak and Hanna, 2018). In response, statements claiming the 'death of privacy' and that 'the internet knows everything about you' have been repeatedly made in the popular media (Lupton, 2019) and in some high-profile academic publications (for example, Zuboff, 2019). As such, these accounts outline visions of 'wicked' social futures (Tutton, 2017), rather than promissory narratives of progress related to personal data futures.

Thus far, most critical analyses of datafication and dataveillance have tended to adopt a macropolitical approach, focussing on the social structural aspects and highlighting the power differentials and 'data divide' between government agencies and major internet corporations on the one hand and citizens on the other (for example, Andrejevic, 2014; Sadowski, 2019; Zuboff, 2019). This perspective tends to neglect consideration of the complexities and affects of people's lived experiences of datafication and dataveillance and the emergent and dynamic enactments of humans and non-humans that are part of these experiences. People's views and feelings about the future of personal data have not been investigated to any great extent (Kennedy, 2018; Lupton, 2019; Michael and Lupton, 2016). Yet, these approaches can highlight the micropolitical social dimensions of personal data futures, including how people imagine potential affective and relational connections between humans and non-humans; the agential capacities opened or closed when human data assemblages are formed; and what the implications might be for their identities, embodiment and social lives: In other words, how people live and become with personal data (Lupton, 2018a).

To address this lacuna, in this chapter, I discuss some findings from my Data Personas study. The methods adopted for this study brought together the cultural probe of the 'data persona' with a customized online forum for engaging the responses of the participants. Before discussing the findings of the study, I begin with an overview of its theoretical and conceptual underpinnings, bringing together the concept of sociotechnical imaginaries with recent scholarship in the sociology of futures.

Background

The analytic concept of the sociotechnical imaginary has been used in science and technology studies (STS) research on how organizations conceptualize novel technologies. Jasanoff and colleagues (for example, Jasanoff, 2015; Jasanoff and Kim, 2009) have led this work. Jasanoff defines sociotechnical imaginaries as collectively held visions of how novel technologies might operate in the future and the effects they will have on society, reflected in the design and fulfilment of scientific and technological projects. These imaginaries are 'assemblages of materiality, meaning and morality' (Jasanoff, 2015, p. 4). Multiple imaginaries can be generated and circulated about novel technologies which may be in tension with each other. Jasanoff argues that these imaginaries 'encode not only visions of what is attainable through science and technology but also of how life ought, or ought not, to be lived; in this respect, they express a society's shared understandings of good and evil' (Jasanoff, 2015, p. 4).

For Jasanoff and other researchers who have engaged with the concept of the sociotechnical imaginary, it is important to highlight the material as well as the discursive elements of imaginaries: How imaginaries are performed and what these performances do. As Jasanoff (2015, p. 11) puts it, this approach is interested in 'the imaginative work of varied social actors', including how imaginaries are used for political purposes.

> By turning to sociotechnical imaginaries, we can engage directly with the ways in which people's hopes and desires for the future – their sense of self and their passion for how things ought to be – get bound up with the hard stuff of past achievements.
>
> *(Jasanoff, 2015, p. 22)*

However, most research on sociotechnical imaginaries has focussed on how public institutions, policymakers and other elite groups discursively engage with visions of novel technologies, rather than investigate the lived understandings and experiences of publics and how these public imaginaries are translated into everyday lives (Smith and Tidwell, 2016). In bringing together the concept of the sociotechnical imaginary with anthropological fieldwork, Smith and Tidwell (2016) emphasize that publics draw on the material dimensions of their everyday lived experiences as well as the discursive expressions of futures when configuring their own imaginaries.

Scholars in the sociology of futures (Coleman, 2017; Michael, 2017; Tutton, 2017) similarly draw attention to the importance of considering publics' understandings and experiences. Michael (2017) draws a distinction between the enactments of what he calls 'Big Futures' and 'Little Futures'. Big Futures refer to imaginaries about developments that are positioned as widespread, far-reaching and large-scale. Imaginaries about Big Futures are often expressed in public forums such as media, government and corporate accounts, many of which actors have a vested interest in promoting new technologies. Michael argues that Little Futures, as the title suggests, are smaller-scale, more mundane and less revolutionary. These are the imaginaries enacted and mobilized by publics, as they come to terms with where new technologies may be heading and what implications these developments have for their everyday lives. Little Futures can generate new directions for Big Futures, just as Big Futures can circumscribe how Little Futures are imagined and enacted. Underpinning Michael's analysis is the assumption that futures of any kind are performed, achieving certain rhetorical and governmental ends, such as enrolling actors in the cause of enacting the practices that are required to achieve futures imaginaries. As Michael points out, however, Big Futures are often contested, and publics are called upon to make sense of how best to respond.

Building on this scholarship, my approach in the Data Personas project was to expand the concept of sociotechnical imaginaries to include publics' privately held visions as a way of contributing to a more micropolitical social approach to futures-based research. These imaginaries may not be about the 'desirable futures' referred to by Jasanoff (2015). Indeed, they may be more akin to the dystopian visions of technological developments that are equally as potent as positive imaginaries and which have received high levels of media attention over the past few years as scandal after scandal has erupted concerning the exploitation, breaches and misuse of people's personal data.

Details of the study

Sensory and affective sociological research, including art- or design-based methods that invite creative and imaginative responses, can be one way of eliciting intangible or difficult-to-articulate responses to futures. These approaches can work not only to document imaginaries about the future but to stimulate new ways of thinking about it that go beyond normative assumptions and discourses, generating alternative or resistant imaginaries that encourage thinking otherwise (Coleman, 2017; Lupton, 2018b; Lupton and Michael, 2017; Michael and Lupton, 2016). Bringing this approach to analysing futures acknowledges the interplay between discourse and practice and the importance of both in generating meaning and action in people's lives.

The Data Personas study was intended to stimulate participants to express their understandings and practices related to their personal data and consider the possibilities as well as the drawbacks of datafication and dataveillance. The participants were asked to respond to a cultural probe I devised for the purposes of the project – that of the 'data persona'. A definition of the data persona was provided to the participants as follows:

> A version of you made by finding personal information about you from when you move around in spaces embedded with sensors or use digital devices like smartphones, wearable technologies, tablet computers, laptops and desktop computers.

The terms 'persona' and 'version of you' were deliberately chosen to bestow a sense of selfhood and humanness on the concept. As my theoretical position is to view data personas as human–non-human assemblages, I thought that this terminology would help the participants to envisage their data profiles in a similar way. My data persona concept is an imaginary formulation that draws on a sociotechnical phenomenon: The personalized data profile that is configured by agencies such as government and business to use in targeting advertising and special offers to consumers and algorithmic decision-making concerning whether people are provided with goods and services such as credit, social security support, housing, insurance and employment opportunities (Mittelstadt et al., 2016; Sadowski, 2019).

A customized online platform developed by a market research company was used that is tailored towards qualitative research. Participants were recruited from the company's panel of research volunteers. Questions were uploaded onto the platform, and participants were asked to type in their answers once they had reviewed the project information and agreed to participate in the study. The University of Canberra Human Research Ethics Committee (I was affiliated with this university at the time the study was carried out) approved the study and all participants were given pseudonyms to protect their identities.

A total of 40 participants were involved, from all states in Australia, including 22 women and 18 men. The participant group was on the younger side: 28 were aged 18–39, while 12 were aged over 40 (only two were aged 60 or over). In terms of educational background, 18 participants had high school or technical college training; the remainder (22) had university-level education. The participant group was quite diverse in terms of ethnicity/racial background: 27 reported Anglo-Celtic ancestry while the remaining 13 participants reported other ethnic/racial heritages.

As part of their engagement, the participants were prompted to make future-oriented speculations concerning their data personas. The thinking required of the participants included asking them to consider how their data persona might be configured and used by themselves and others in the contemporary moment. They were also asked to project their imaginations into the future (10 and 20 years hence), responding to questions about what details would be collected about them in future data profiling, how this information would be generated and to what extent their future data personas may be similar or different from them. In the next section of this chapter, I focus on the participants' responses to the questions about the futures of their data personas.

Findings

The participants were readily able to generate ideas about future developments in datafication and dataveillance when they engaged with the data persona questions. Some of the future modes of dataveillance and other forms of digital technologies that they could imagine included the expansion of cryptocurrencies, better algorithmic prediction models and greater connection of different datasets about people. People speculated that increasingly greater amounts of personal data would be collected via new technologies such as advanced AI, facial recognition, fingerprint scanning, retina scanning, DNA profiling, RFID chips in bodies, more home automation, self-driving cars and the invention of more wearable devices. They suggested that there would be more details of preferences and shopping habits, including such technologies as the use of sensors to follow people's movements in stores and more scraping of social media content. Government services and information about people who used these services would be linked to a greater extent. The participants speculated that these future modes of datafication and dataveillance would be able to anticipate humans' needs and desires, better identify and therefore manage health risks and provide more detailed geo-location surveillance of people's movements.

Most participants speculated that their data profiles would be even more detailed in the future, as modes of dataveillance expanded ever further into people's everyday lives. At their most extreme, these imaginaries portrayed a future world in which digitized monitoring of people was pervasive. In outlining his imagined future, for example, Michael evoked the imaginary of a Big Brother society from the novel *1984*.

> 1984 – everyone chipped for identity, tracking and lifestyle choices. Voting, purchasing, health, desires, likes and dislikes up and downloaded from within your body … I can see a stage in the future where you are continually tracked and monitored from birth to death. Further, you could be designed before conception and life and death outcomes predetermined.

For several people, this future of ever-increasing and more detailed datafication and dataveillance of humans would mean very little privacy, as people's personal details would be readily available to a range of third parties:

> [In ten years] I believe it would just be out there for all to see, I can [see] nobody having any privacy at all in 10 years, you will not be able to do anything without it being recorded in same way, shape or form. (Peter)

In terms of future benefits of data personas, some people drew attention to the potential of receiving better targeted and personalized information and offers:

> Hopefully with more data points and more technology our world will be more customized. Google Maps already knows to give me information about traffic to get to work. Things like that should be helpful. (Annemarie)

For Carolyn, a more personalized and customized data persona could help her fulfil her everyday family caring responsibilities, saving her time and effort:

> In 20 years, my data persona would be primarily family focused. I could log into a certain online system, greeted by a virtual version of myself. It would know what groceries I buy regularly, when I'm due for my next health check-up, dental appointment, haircut, etc., when I need to re-fuel my car, do an oil check, book a service, etc. My persona would be more family-focused featuring details about my children and spouse to manage responsibilities, like the above, seamlessly.

Michael envisaged a future where ever-greater details collected and processed about him could both benefit and harm him:

> As time goes on it will control my life with the belief that it will make things better, easier, more fulfilling, be in my best interest and improve my lifestyle. The above can be seen as a disadvantage, being controlled and manipulated in all aspects of life.

It is notable that while a dominant view was maintained by participants that datafication and dataveillance of humans would be ever-more pervasive, only a minority ascribed to an imaginary that considered their future data personas as total representations of their 'real' selves. When they were asked in previous questions how different from or similar their current data personas were to them, the majority view was that the personas could only ever be a partial portrayal of an individual. The rationales the participants gave for this position rested on the idea that there were many aspects of their lives that were not recorded by online technologies, sensors or apps. These included many aspects of people's life histories, personal relationships, secrets, spirituality and private thoughts.

This position was maintained when the participants were asked to consider what their data personas would be like 10 or 20 years hence and what aspects of their lives data profilers would not be able to access. Here again, people evoked imaginaries in which future data personas would still be only incomplete and therefore very superficial versions of themselves, with their inner-most thoughts and feelings remaining private and locked inside, safe from datafication and dataveillance systems. When discussing what data profilers would not know about them, they expressed the following ideas:

> I don't think they would have access to everyday living details – e.g. what goes on behind closed doors, as well as thoughts and feelings. (Emma)

> My data persona will still lack the qualities that make me 'human': i.e. irrational/illogical behaviours that cannot always be predicted, moods and feelings I have in that moment. (Corina)

Most participants imagined a future data persona that would be very different from their current data persona. This was due not only to a proliferation of technologies able to record their personal details but also to changes in their lives as they became older. Their data personas would age with them, taking on new characteristics as people's everyday habits, family arrangements and bodies changed as they grew older. Thus, for example, Gary speculated that:

> My data persona in 20 years would show my interests and lifestyle. Am I nearing retirement? Do I have children? Have my interests from my 20s and 30s shifted majorly or am I now a middle-aged hippy looking to still enjoy life to the fullest and travel and socialize with both younger and older people learning new cultures and cuisines? Have I become introverted? – in which case my profile might suggest I do more solo activities like reading and writing. Have I experienced any hardship in the preceding 20 years that has changed my perspective and ultimately my happiness in life? It would include my achievements and records and my despairs and weaknesses. I think it would ultimately show an extension of my 20 and 30 year old information but perhaps more developed.

There was an acknowledgement in these kinds of speculations that data profiles are dynamic rather than static, changing in response to individuals' changed life circumstances. Another imaginary on future data personas offered by several participants involved a future in which people had better learnt to control and potentially limit the flow of information that could be accessed by data profilers. They suggested that there would be greater transparency about how personal data would be used and that there would be limitations on which third parties could access people's information:

> I would like to think that in the future that we have better security protecting our information and that only the agencies that 'need' to access said information are the only

ones that can see it. I also hope that the agencies that can see this info only have access to the information that is relevant to their needs. (Ella)

Alternative perspectives envisaged a future in which people were taking more control over what data were being made available to third parties. According to David:

My data persona in 20 years will be of a much younger man and will contain data that is way out of date. I'm embarking on a mission to strictly control the amount of information out there about me and this means that in 20 years there should only be a skeleton picture of myself and my data.

Some participants imagined a future in which personal data would be made more available to the people who had generated them:

In 10 years, this data will probably be more accessible than it is now and anybody will be able to access it and use the information as they see fit. (Annemarie)

David's response also highlights a common imaginary articulated by other participants. That their personal data profiles were historical rather than future oriented. As they suggest, data profilers can only access details from the past, as data generation is continual and therefore constantly changing data profiles. Particularly if people take steps to control their data flows, then their data persona will become much more partial and inaccurate versions of themselves destined always to lag behind the changes people experience as they move through their lives.

Discussion

Using the cultural probe of the data persona surfaced a range of intriguing insights into the sociotechnical imaginaries held by the participants in relation to future modes of datafication and dataveillance. The affective forces emerging in the participants' accounts included, for several people, concern about heightened surveillance and lack of privacy. This was expressed at low levels of intensity for most people, however, and as vague anxiety, rather than specified in more concrete terms. More commonly, people imagined a future in which more detailed data profiles would help them navigate their lives. For these participants, future data personas would facilitate useful affective and relational connections between themselves and other people in their lives.

Several people envisaged scenarios in which the generation of capacities to better restrict or control their data flows would provide more personal data privacy and security. It was imagined that in the future, greater access to personal data could be offered to the public themselves, while tighter controls over third-party use could ensure that only those agencies who people wanted to access their details could do so. Such agencies were typically identified as healthcare providers, prospective employers, tax agencies and financial institutions with which people had direct and specific relationships and where they could readily imagine the possibilities that could emerge from using their personal data to establish stronger connections.

There were limits to these imaginaries, however. While some of the participants imagined a personal data future in which virtually everything would be known about them as recorded in data assemblages, most people were convinced that datafication and dataveillance technologies would never be able to access or know their authentic and private body/selves. While many acknowledged the existence of a digitally distributed body/self, as represented in the figure of the data persona they were asked to respond to in their answers, they were reluctant to relinquish the idea of the inherent, closed off, non-mediated body/self that they believed resided in the non-datafied spaces of their lives, particularly inside their individuated bodies.

In these participants' accounts, therefore, was evidence both of their engagement with publicly circulating sociotechnical imaginaries about the futures of personal data and their resistance to accepting these imaginaries unquestioningly, drawing on their personal experiences of being data subjects. The affective forces of suspicion and unease with becoming datafied expressed by these participants were accompanied by feelings of reassurance and confidence that the apparatuses of datafication and dataveillance could never fully access and thereby exploit their 'real' or 'secret' selves. There was little suggestion in the sociotechnical imaginaries of these participants that future datafication and dataveillance systems would be overly invasive or coercive. Their responses to the concept of the data persona for the most part demonstrated an optimistic outlook.

In formulating their accounts, the participants drew on their lived experiences of becoming data subjects and their understandings of how personal data are generated and circulated. Few of these participants professed to have personally experienced negative experiences of datafication and dataveillance beyond intrusive advertising or awareness that internet companies were able to collect many details about them from their online interactions. These Australians' imaginaries of personal data futures, therefore, reflect their relative socioeconomic privilege and their geographical location in a nation in which state governance systems using personal data profiling have not progressed as far as it has in countries like the United States (O'Neil, 2016; Petty et al., 2018), parts of the global South (Arora, 2019) and particularly, China, with its nationalized Social Credit System (Engelmann et al., 2019). While disadvantaged and marginalized social groups in the United States report dealing with loss of opportunities and the entrenchment of disadvantage due to algorithmic processing of their data by government and commercial agencies (Madden et al., 2017; Petty et al., 2018), the participants in my study did not report being confronted with similar experiences.

Implicit in these Australians' accounts of personal data futures, therefore, were their relatively privileged standpoints and limited experiences of being the victims of datafication and dataveillance. Rather than imagining intensified dataveillance as imposing greater threats into the future, these people speculated on new and better ways of benefiting from their data personas or controlling their privacy. Identifying these elements of futures imaginaries can go a long way to introduce the micropolitical, the affective and the social dimensions into futures thinking and research. It is in these enactments and performances that the 'Little Futures' of everyday experience work to mediate the 'Big Futures' (Michael, 2017) of personal data.

Bibliography

Andrejevic, M. (2014). 'The big data divide', *International Journal of Communication*, 8, pp. 1673–1689.
Arora, P. (2019). 'Decolonizing privacy studies', *Television & New Media*, 20, pp. 366–378.
Best, K. (2010). 'Living in the control society: Surveillance, users and digital screen technologies', *International Journal of Cultural Studies*, 13, pp. 5–24.
Coleman, R. (2017). 'A sensory sociology of the future: Affect, hope and inventive methodologies', *The Sociological Review*, 65, pp. 525–543.

Engelmann, S., Chen, M., Fischer, F., et al. (2019). 'Clear sanctions, vague rewards: How China's Social Credit system currently defines "good" and "bad" behavior', *Proceedings of the conference on fairness, accountability, and transparency*. Atlanta, GA: ACM, pp. 59–78.

Isaak, J. and Hanna, M. (2018). 'User data privacy: Facebook, Cambridge Analytica, and privacy protection', *Computer*, 51 pp. 56–59.

Jasanoff, S. (2015). 'Future imperfect: Science, technology, and the imaginations of modernity'. In Jasanoff, S. and Kim, S.-H. (eds), *Dreamscapes of modernity: Sociotechnical imaginaries and the fabrication of power*. Chicago, IL: University of Chicago Press, pp. 1–33.

Jasanoff, S. and Kim, S.-H. (2009). 'Containing the atom: Sociotechnical imaginaries and nuclear power in the United States and South Korea', *Minerva*, 47, pp. 119–146.

Kennedy, H. (2018). 'Living with data: Aligning data studies and data activism through a focus on everyday experiences of datafication', *Krisis: Journal for Contemporary Philosophy*. Available at http://krisis.eu/living-with-data/.

Lupton, D. (2018a). 'How do data come to matter? Living and becoming with personal data', *Big Data & Society*, 5. Available at https://doi.org/10.1177/2053951718786314.

Lupton, D. (2018b). 'Towards design sociology', *Sociology Compass*, 12. Available at https://doi.org/10.1111/soc4.12546.

Lupton, D. (2019). *Data selves: More-than-human perspectives*. Cambridge: Polity Press.

Lupton, D. and Michael, M. (2017) '"Depends on who's got the data": Public understandings of personal digital dataveillance', *Surveillance & Society*, 15, pp. 254–268.

Madden, M., Gilman, M., Levy, K., et al. (2017). 'Privacy, poverty, and big data: A matrix of vulnerabilities for poor Americans', *Washington University Law Review*, 95, pp. 53–125.

Michael, M. (2017). 'Enacting big futures, little futures: Toward an ecology of futures', *The Sociological Review*, 65, pp. 509–524.

Michael, M. and Lupton, D. (2016). 'Toward a manifesto for the public understanding of big data', *Public Understanding of Science*, 25, pp. 104–116.

Mittelstadt, B.D., Allo, P., Taddeo, M., et al. (2016). 'The ethics of algorithms: Mapping the debate', *Big Data & Society*, 3. Available at https://journals.sagepub.com/doi/full/10.1177/2053951716679679.

O'Neil, C. (2016). *Weapons of math destruction: How big data increases inequality and threatens democracy*. London: Penguin Books.

Petty, T., Saba, M., Lewis, T., et al. (2018). *Reclaiming our data* Available at https://www.odbproject.org/wp-content/uploads/2016/12/ODB.InterimReport.FINAL_.7.16.2018.pdf.

Sadowski, J. (2019). 'When data is capital: Datafication, accumulation, and extraction', *Big Data & Society*, 6. Available at https://doi.org/10.1177/2053951718820549.

Smith, J.M. and Tidwell, A.S.D. (2016). 'The everyday lives of energy transitions: Contested sociotechnical imaginaries in the American West', *Social Studies of Science*, 46, pp. 327–350.

Tutton, R. (2017). 'Wicked futures: Meaning, matter and the sociology of the future', *The Sociological Review*, 65, pp. 478–492.

van Dijck, J. (2014). 'Datafication, dataism and dataveillance: Big data between scientific paradigm and ideology', *Surveillance & Society*, 12, pp. 197–208.

Zuboff, S. (2019). *The age of surveillance capitalism: The fight for the future at the new frontier of power*. London: Profile Books.

10
Ecology
Thinking futures ecologically

Lauren Rickards

Introduction

The future is entwined with ecology. Whether in the form of ecological science, physical natures or a social movement, the ambiguous figure of ecology is implicated in multiple Western imaginaries of the future in the form of different modes of ecological thinking. In this chapter, I outline some of these modes, the questions they help pose and the aspects of the world they help illuminate.

A useful starting point for exploring the diverse modes of ecology in Western visions of the future is the deceptively simple but archetypical depiction of the future as a choice between three options – a triptych that Bridgit Schneider (2017) traces to eschatological depictions of the future within Christianity. Schneider argues that a similar triptych features in the Intergovernmental Panel on Climate Change's depictions of possible futures under their Representative Concentration Pathways. Jumping genres, she also suggests that they feature in a 1979/1982 cartoon *A Short History of America* by Robert Crumb. The cartoon depicts the gradual replacement of 'natural landscapes' with urban sprawl, ending in three potential futures: The Ecological Disaster; the Fun Future and the Ecotopian Solution (Figure 10.1). If these depictions of the future sound vaguely familiar, it is because they build on classic narrative forms. In particular, they resonate strongly with a triad of utopian narratives[1] characterized respectively by the phrases 'If this continues then…', 'What if…?' and 'If only…'. In this chapter, I discuss these three different stances on the future and the different meanings that are implicitly given to ecology within each. Although the narratives overlap, this three-part framework usefully highlights some of the different ways ecology is interpreted and enrolled as a resource in arguments about the future.

The following sections present the three distinct ways of 'thinking ecologically' that I argue are associated with the orientations on the future captured by 'If this continues then…', 'What if…?' and 'If only…'. In the concluding section, I then highlight the implicit politics of each framing of ecology and their implications for how we imagine the future.

Ecology

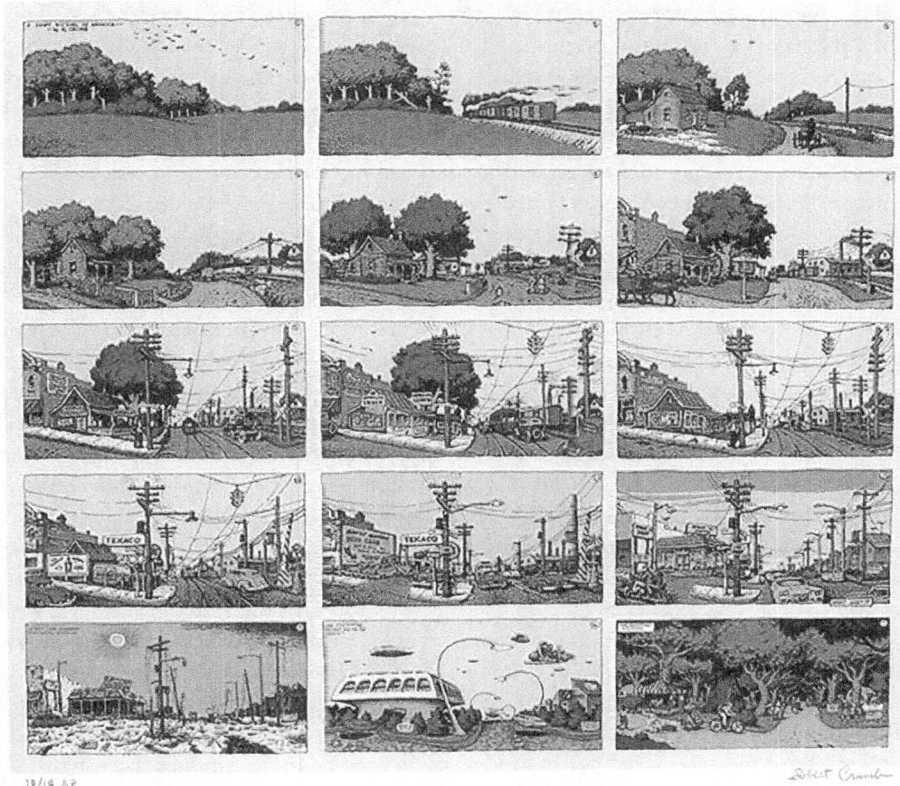

Figure 10.1 A Short History of America, cartoon by Robert Crumb (1979). Coloured by Peter Poplaski. Published in *Coevolution Quarterly*. Copyright © Robert Crumb 1979. Used with permission

Thinking ecologically 1: If this continues then...

The first and foremost interpretation of ecology is as a science. This Ecology (distinguished in this chapter by a capitalized E) provides a window onto the (neglected) real world and, in particular, onto a threatened aspect of the world. In this sense, Ecology operates as a prophet drawing on its understandings of how the world works to provide warnings that 'If this continues, then...'.

More specifically, Ecology warns about threats to Nature. As a scientific discipline focussed on plants, animals and 'the natural environment', Ecology is often presumed to be uniquely placed to adjudicate on the part of the world that Western culture delineates as 'Nature'.[2] Not only is Ecology's object of study a particularly expansive notion of Nature (Castree, 2014) relative to other science's focus on one subcomponent of the natural world, Ecology implicitly helps patrol the border between what is understood as Natural as opposed to Unnatural or Artificial. Such patrolling is key to ecological science's role in identifying threats to Nature.

127

Even when the Nature studied by Ecology is defined as encompassing human beings, or when those humans are imagined as having a 'natural' (animal) core, and even when the impacts of humans upon the rest of Nature are the primary focus, as a science Ecology is predicated on a Natural world imagined as separate from, and discernible by, the human scientist. Like other sciences, its objective is to identify the principles by which this Nature works. Uniquely, it also speaks to what 'Nature' *is* and *means* – a focus that then gives it a distinctive capacity to articulate what humans are in the midst of, rely on, are affecting and should do.

Some of the core concepts underpinning ecological science are diversity, connectedness and adaptation. The first of these – (bio)diversity – speaks to Ecology's roots in eighteenth- and nineteenth-century natural history, which ranged, from detailed, often loving studies of places as integrated wholes, as epitomized by Gilbert White, to Imperial scientific expeditions, as epitomized by Charles Darwin (Worster, 1994). Such painstaking research draws attention to the uniqueness of organisms and their assemblages in different localities. Responses to these assemblages have varied. Imperial science was predominantly used by governing parties to identify potential natural resources and foster extractive and exploitative colonial projects. However, natural history underpinned nature conservation arguments about the intrinsic value of Nature and the need to protect particular organisms and areas, especially as they rapidly became rarer (Glacken, 1967; MacKenzie, 1990).

Early ecological studies also provided an inkling of the intimate relations that exist between different organisms, types and conditions. Darwin's popularization of the ideas of species and natural selection (Darwin, 2004 [1859]) is an enduring outcome of such work. This line of work helped develop a now characteristic feature of Ecology: A focus on connectedness. While in the contemporary, more-than-scientific 'ecological lens on the world' this connectedness is often glossed as 'everything is connected to everything else', actual ecological science has a far more textured perspective. For it, the question is what is connected to what, when, how and why. This desire to identify precise relationships and their spatial and temporal patterns means that it is underpinned less by a simple holism than by a fundamental commitment to understanding the principles of organic coexistence.

One of the principles of coexistence that Ecology has powerfully articulated is that organisms are situated within, and continually adapt to, a dynamic environment. Adaptation, as the third core concept of Ecology, underpins the Darwinian idea of evolutionary fitness and associated, often tautological, assessments of how well something should fit a given context. This ecological principle is not only about where things happen to coexist but about 'what belongs' where and why. In many settler colonial contexts, for example, ecological science has been used to identify pre-European ecologies to establish the 'baseline' for nature conservation efforts. While most ecologists in such contexts now acknowledge that such pre-European ecologies are inherently dynamic and are the outcome of long-standing, intentional cultivation by Indigenous peoples, the immense devastation wrought by European invasions means there is a persistent (and legitimate) sense that some places are characterized by authentic and valuable ecologies, while more recently created ones are often degraded and 'out of whack' with prevailing environmental conditions. Modern interventions in landscapes – from the mind-bogglingly ambitious, to smaller scale and mundane – have tried to engineer conditions significantly different to those that previously existed, often with limited success and far-reaching implications, given the complex interconnections that such interventions are inescapably entangled with.

A key task for Ecology has thus become revealing human *mal*adaptation (see also Climate Change, this volume). Counter to many other knowledges that perceive 'the environment' as merely a stage for human endeavour, in Ecology the environment is understood as the basic conditions needed to enable life In this way, Ecology underlines the value of Nature for humans not only by providing information used to exploit natural resources, but by illuminating that humans themselves exist in a certain niche; are dependent on particular conditions, 'ecological services' and goods; and thus face environmental limits.

Efforts to escape such environmental limits and create new custom-made environments for certain human groups is a key characteristic of Western modernity. These efforts have often physically and conceptually relegated waste products and problems out of sight and mind. But thanks to Ecology and related sciences, as well as the long history of citizen warnings (Bonneuil and Fressoz, 2015), and the rise of citizen science and digital activism such environments and problems have been increasingly made visible. Evidenced by the growing assertion of more reflexive, risk-attuned forms of modernization, there is increasing awareness that past and ongoing efforts to deny environmental limits are triggering physical feedbacks including anthropogenic climate change. These feedbacks radically undermine the liveability of contemporary environments, at least for those without the power to escape the imposition of costs. Indeed, these feedbacks are of such a magnitude that the future of the entire human species – and many others – is now under threat (Refsgaard et al., 2007). Some ecologists are among the scientists now asserting that at a planetary scale human impacts (driven by a subset of humans) have pushed the Earth out of the Holocene epoch into a new, less stable, less habitable Anthropocene epoch (Steffen et al., 2018).

The Anthropocene is arguably an archetypical representation of an 'If this continues then…' narrative. It is a stylized warning to humanity as much as it is a solid scientific hypothesis (Rickards, 2015). Presenting the Holocene as a safe temporal niche for all species, the Anthropocene narrative offers what Aldo Leopold (1949, p. 205) called 'an ecological interpretation of human history'. Some Anthropocene scientists point to two scenarios: The Earth is restabilized or it crosses a threshold and flips into a Hothouse Earth state (Steffen et al., 2018).

Ecologists have long been among those prophets issuing grave warnings about the future of the Earth. Fairfield Osborn's *Our Plundered Planet* and William Vogt's *Road to Survival*, both published in 1948, predicted that unchecked consumption and human population would lead to disaster, with Vogt calling instead for an 'ecological approach' (Robertson, 2012). By the 1970s, when Crumb produced his cartoon (featured above), Ecology was, like the emerging field of climate change science, a key 'impact science' calling into question the un-reflexive character of the 'production sciences' (e.g. geology, chemical engineering) and the aggressive application of them in the name of economic development (Schnaiberg, 1980). Paul Sears (1964) suggested that, if taken seriously, Ecology was in fact a 'subversive science', challenging assumptions and practices of modern societies.

Despite such endorsements, ecological science has long struggled to gain institutional legitimacy. The complexity and political character of its topics, the diversity of its studies, the ambiguities of its theories and its reliance on outdoor observations more than highly controlled laboratory-based experiments means that Ecology has never easily complied with the reductionist, experimental benchmark of 'real science' perpetuated by dominant disciplines like chemistry, and has never accurately mirrored the purportedly disinterested theorizing of disciplines like economics. Indeed, Ecology has been frequently devalued in academic fora as an 'immature' discipline and dismissed in policy as nice but not necessary (Hagen, 1989). Such devaluation has amplified in recent years as Ecology's character as a 'slow science' (Lane, 2017) (focussed on long-term, slow-moving, complex issues) has collided with demands for rapid, economics-based research impact, with resultant cuts to long-term ecological monitoring programs and related ecological science (e.g. Phillips, 2017). Combined with assertions from some social science quarters that Ecology's traditional object of study – Nature – 'no longer exists' or never did so (see 'Thinking ecologically 3: If only...' below), Ecology's future as a cohesive science has itself been questioned – ironically just as the field becomes more important than ever.

Thinking ecologically 2: What if?

In the words of a leading ecologist, the ambiguous status of Ecology as a scientific discipline is driven by the fact that Ecology 'like beauty... is in the eyes of the beholder' (McIntosh, 1985). Today, much of the world is referred to in ecological terms but what is beholden would be unrecognizable as Ecology to most ecological scientists. So-called 'Innovation *ecosystems*', for example, are celebrated as a route to impactful research (e.g. Oh et al., 2016). Yet they have nothing but a stylistic association with actual, physical ecosystems. Furthermore, the concept of innovation itself is more than incidentally related to Ecology. This is obvious in the case of 'ecological innovation' or 'eco-innovation' that seeks environmentally-friendly outcomes and often tries to mimic nature by using it as a muse or design guide (Blok and Gremmen, 2016). Beyond the 'eco' prefix, the concept of innovation shares with Ecology an apparent celebration of life's diversity, novelty and dynamism. In this thematic resonance, ecology as a concept is valued not as a science, context or set of rules, but simply as evidence of the vitality, intelligence and creativity of life itself. As such, ecology is transformed from a limit on the possible, to a stimulus for 'What if...?' imaginings. As discussed below, this has implications for how Ecology sees the world and the sort of guide it provides for nature conservation.

When funnelled into techno-innovation, the 'exuberant ecology' aesthetic can generate the kind of Fun Future vision represented by Crumb's cartoon. This future is made even more fun by its irreverence for the Ecological Disaster future more commonly presented by scientific ecologists. Exemplifying such irreverence is green techno-utopian Stewart Brand. His 2009 book *Whole Earth Discipline* offers a 'fresh perspective' that, according to one reviewer, 'ultimately convinces the reader that the future is not an abyss to be feared but an opportunity for innovative problem solvers to embrace enthusiastically'.[3] Thinking ecologically here is about thriving not surviving, growing not groaning. Survival of the fittest applies, but to organizations not organisms, at least of the non-humankind. Lauded to win are future-makers, or more specifically, *environment*-makers – those who create ecologies of a physical not just metaphorical form to try to enhance performance or at least escape environmental hazards with the ease of computer game heroes.

Further distortions of ecology feature in the related fields of economics and innovation studies. Austrian economist Joseph Schumpeter's idea that 'creative destruction', alongside periods of routinization, is a natural function of capitalism and a source of innovation has strong resonance with a scientific ecological study of lifecycles, ecological cycles and evolutionary dynamics. Specially attuned to the role of cycles of growth, stasis and destruction in the natural world is the now dominant paradigm in ecological science – Disturbance Ecology or New Ecology – which arose, along with the related idea of resilience and adaptation, in the 1970s as neoliberalism escalated. Indeed, Jeremy Walker (2020) argues that these strands of Ecology and neoliberal economics emerged tightly hand in hand.

In the present day, what is clear is that 'What if...?' narratives lead not only to Fun Futures but to potentially very dark ones. In contrast to the neat boxes of the cartoon above – drawn when perhaps the world seemed simpler – this means in practice that there is a strong overlap between the Ecological Disaster and Fun Future visions. But whereas the Ecological Disaster is often focussed on threats, the more generalist ecological thinking outlined in this section is focussed on risk and contingency. The difference, as Aradau et al. (2008, p. 148) explain, is that

> [T]hreat-based interpretations rely on intelligence in an attempt to eliminate danger, while risk relies on actuarial-like data, modelling and speculations that do not simply call for the elimination of risk but *develop strategies to embrace it* (italics added).

Increasingly, not just populations and things but whole 'vital systems' are seen to be at risk. In contrast to earlier assumptions that such risk is manageable with a distributed, 'ecological' approach to governance (Collier and Lakoff, 2015), recent approaches reflect the migration of New or Disturbance Ecology – notably its foundational idea of resilience – into public discourse. As a result, in some quarters, risk management and elimination are evolving into efforts to negotiate profound uncertainty, instability and emergent events (Chandler, 2014). Rather than models rooted in historical data, the future is explored using scenarios, including participatory scenario processes where participants are encouraged to imagine 'what if…?' and 'prepare for the unexpected' (Anderson, 2010).

In other quarters, Ecology as a science has helped orient the question 'what if?' onto humans and their actions and has been used to reinforce the idea that humans should be future and environment makers, not takers. Following the merger of Ecology and systems science into a variant of ecological science known as Systems Ecology in the 1960s – where the concept of the ecosystem began to resemble a machine more than an organism – the normative devaluation of the Artificial has become challenged. As a result, the once-heretical idea of redesigning and reengineering whole ecosystems by manipulating ecosystemic functions has become increasingly mainstream. Defiantly interventionist and a deliberate effort to shape rather than retreat from the future, such efforts are not about denying Nature's agency. Rather, they attempt to work with rather than against the vitality of Nature, doing so in a way that diversifies ecology, harnesses life's inherent creativity and resilience and generates more positive futures (at least for some).

Today, functionalist Ecology informs work on novel ecosystems and their role in (responding to) the Anthropocene (e.g. Clement and Standish, 2018). In contrast to dark visions of futures dominated by disasters and the neat boxing of futures in the cartoon above, such action-oriented, optimistic approaches are more akin to Fun Futures. However, this shift in goal and theoretical basis remains fiercely debated within Ecology. While few ecologists would be aware of the resemblance between New Ecology and neoliberalism mentioned above, some reject 'the new ecological order' as dangerously neglectful of the needs of increasingly threatened species and ecosystems that, they argue, do not need to be remade or inaccurately valourized as resilient, but recognized as inherently valuable and highly vulnerable to the violently destructive forces of the extractive industries and other profit-seeking beneficiaries of neoliberalism (Damiens et al., 2017; Lindenmayer et al., 2008; Miller and Bestelmeyer, 2016). The debate is replayed in a different guise in the third narrative to which we now turn, 'if only…'.

Thinking ecologically 3: If only…

The third narrative associated with ecology takes it in different political, social and ontological directions. In contrast to the narrowly realist and rationalist approaches that can characterize Ecology as a science and form of management, these interpretations of ecology expand its scope and significance, raising challenges for the science that shares its name.

There are two main, interconnected variants to note here. In the first, ecology is adopted as a politicoethical guide. Whereas in the 'What If' narrative, the notion of ecology is celebrated as an expression of the vitality of life in a way that sometimes leads to a *laissez faire* management approach, the 'If Only' narrative is impressed by, but worried about, Nature. The delicate ecological character of the world was an integral idea in the emergence of environmentalism and Green politics from the 1970s, much to the bemusement and frustration of some ecological scientists, especially given Ecology's struggle to be taken seriously as an objective, academic science (discussed above). This reworking of the notion of ecology as the centrepiece of a social and political movement reflects not only growing social concern about protecting diverse non-humans made visible by ecological science but an intellectual and ethical reframing of human society in ecological terms. What this actually means, though, has been highly controversial.

Deep Ecologists such as Arne Naess emphasize a holistic perspective and call for a strong interpretation of sustainability as system integrity (not just resource conservation). They generally reject anthropocentrism and call for ecocentrism or radical equality between Human and Nature (Naess, 1984). While the Deep Ecology movement is often unfairly caricatured, serious criticisms include a perceived tendency to privilege system-level outcomes over (some people's) individual rights, which can begin to slip into eco-facism. One proffered alternative is the Social Ecology theory and vision of Murray Bookchin (1982), who argues that relations of domination between humans and nature cannot be tackled without tackling multiscale relations of domination between humans. As such, Social Ecology, along with eco-feminism, is a more radical agenda than one aimed simply at human harmony with Nature.

Social Ecology exemplifies the way ecology is enrolled in 'If only…' utopian narratives. Proffering a version of the Ecotopian Solution illustrated above, it (like Deep Ecology) takes a holistic, global view that underlines the need to ensure that local 'green havens' of the sort depicted by Crumb are equitably distributed. Today, such social and ecological egalitarianism remains an acute challenge. Yet, it has served as an inspiration and practical guide for progressive initiatives around the world, including those that take a 'pre-figurative' approach in which utopianism and hope are practices, not ideas or emotions (e.g. Levitas, 2013). Widely diverse, some manifestations of practical utopianism are defiantly anarchist in character, and some are regenerative, seeking to remake lost ecologies and 'rewild' landscapes, albeit in speculative, novel ways (e.g. Lorimer and Driessen, 2016).

A second, related variant of ecology as an 'If only…' narrative is an interpretation of ecology in more ontological and spiritual terms. Evident in and beyond the Humanities and Social Sciences, this approach encompasses a diverse array of engagements with systems thinking, complexity science, quantum mechanics and, in some cases, intellectual antecedents in feminist scholarship and Indigenous ontologies (Todd, 2016). Varied in their reading of biotic/abiotic and organic/inorganic boundaries, these perspectives emphasize the relational–material character of the world and the agency of 'non-human things' (e.g. Hollin et al., 2017; Bennett, 2010; Hassard and Law, 1999). Crucially, such non-human things are not always limited to those typically labelled 'Nature' or 'natural', but can include technologies and other human artefacts. The upshot is that the human/non-human distinction tends to dissolve, challenging the classic Human/Nature dualism of Enlightenment thought by not only flattening it into a non-hierarchical binary but also eliminating the duality altogether.

The resultant 'ecology without nature' (Morton, 2007) poses a profound challenge to ecological science, given science's fundamental reliance on Descartes' Human/Nature dualism and its other dualistic derivatives (Plumwood, 1993). Yet, Ecology arguably emerges from this challenge intact, even advantaged compared to more reductionist and productivist sciences.

There is growing public awareness that the world is not only messy, relational and material but is in the midst of an unprecedented disaster that ultimately blurs the Human/Nature dualism. Increasingly codified as the Anthropocene, this disaster is forcing a radical rethink of established hierarchies of knowledge and categories of thought. As Timothy Morton (2007, p. 15) puts it:

> The current ecological disaster… has torn a giant hole in the fabric of our understanding… The ecological thought is as much about opening our mind as it is about knowing something or other in particular.

In contrast to postmodern or techno-optimist notions of openness, this ecological understanding of openness addresses the darkness of the real losses underway. Whether expressed as Deep Ecology, Dark Ecology or something else, these 'If only…' narratives of ecology are characterized by thoughtfulness, concern and a yearning for broad, deep change in the world, over and above preserving non-humans or using eco-designs. Yet, they are entwined with the narratives of 'If this continues, then…' and 'What if…?' outlined above, infecting nature conservation and ecological restoration efforts with uncertainty.

Conclusion

Sitting at the heart of various debates and world-making efforts, the notion of ecology pushes us to appreciate an array of things about the world: Specific non-human ecologies, the reality of the accelerating ecological disaster, the limitations of human understanding, the creativity of life, the capacity to generate new environments, the inequities that characterize capitalist society. Associated with a particular branch of science, ecology has been and is utilized in highly diverse ways in society. These variants reflect and have helped evolve ecological science's understanding of what ecology and Nature are, which in turn has had far-reaching if unorthodox, influences on other professions and agendas. This chapter has outlined the key role of different modes of ecological thinking in helping cultivate different orientations to and assumptions about the future. As outlined in the sections above, variants of ecology have been used, and continue to be used, to help ask 'If this continues then…', 'What if…?' and 'If only…' about an array of feared and longed for outcomes. In this way, ecological thinking, broadly defined, points to the distinct but interconnected images of the future that are nestled within the past and present, from Robert Crumb's three cartoons to the IPCC's depictions of different greenhouse gas trajectories. Simultaneously offering a warning, guide and inspiration about the future ecological thinking implicitly illuminates our uneasy and ever-shifting position within the world we are co-creating, intentionally or not.

Notes

1 This typology is discussed by the late science fiction writer Octavia Butler, who attributes its origin to Robert A. Heinlein, who in his own science fiction writing famously anticipated the scenario played out by the Manhattan Project at the end of Second World War. See Butler, Octavia. '"Devil Girl From Mars": Why I Write Science Fiction'. Lecture, MIT, February 19, 1998. http://web.mit.edu/m-i-t/articles/butler_talk_index.html. Thank you to Mathias Thaler for pointing me to Octavia's lecture.
2 In keeping with academic convention, I am capitalizing nature here to indicate that I am referring to the whole socially constructed, Western notion of nature as the non-human world (see Castree, 2014).
3 See https://www.publishersweekly.com/9780670021215.

Bibliography

Anderson, B. (2010). 'Preemption, precaution, preparedness: Anticipatory action and future geographies', *Progress in Human Geography*, 34, pp. 777–798.
Aradau, C., Lobo-Guerrero, L. and Van Munster, R. (2008). 'Security, technologies of risk, and the political: Guest Editors' Introduction', *Security Dialogue*, 39, pp. 147–154.
Bennett, J. (2010). *Vital materiality: the political life of things*. Durham, NC: Duke University Press.
Blok, V. and Gremmen, B. (2016). 'Ecological innovation: Biomimicry as a new way of thinking and acting ecologically', *Journal of Agricultural and Environmental Ethics*, 29, pp. 203–217.
Bonneuil, C. and Fressoz, J.-B. (2015). *The shock of the Anthropocene: The earth, history and us*. London: Verso.
Bookchin, M. (1982). *The ecology of freedom*. New York: Cheshire Books.
Castree, N. (2014). *Making sense of nature: Representation, politics and democracy*. London: Routledge.
Chandler, D. (2014). *Resilience: The governance of complexity*. London: Routledge.
Clement, S. and Standish, R.J. (2018). 'Novel ecosystems: Governance and conservation in the age of the Anthropocene', *Journal of Environmental Management*, 208, pp. 36–45.
Collier, S.J. and Lakoff, A. (2015). 'Vital systems security: Reflexive biopolitics and the government of emergency', *Theory, Culture & Society*, 32, pp. 19–51.
Damiens, F.L.P., Mumaw, L., Backstrom, A., Bekessy, S.A., Coffey, B., Faulkner, R., Garrard, G.E., Hardy, M.J., Kusmanoff, A.M., Mata, L., Rickards, L., Selinske, M.J., Torabi, N. and Gordon, A. (2017). 'Why politics and context matter in conservation policy', *Global Policy*, 8, pp. 253–256.
Darwin, C. (2004) [1859]. *On the origin of species*. London: Routledge.
Glacken, C.J. (1967). *Traces on the Rhodian shore: Nature and culture in Western thought from ancient times to the end of the eighteenth century*. Los Angeles: University of California Press.
Hagen, J.B. (1989). 'Research perspectives and the anomalous status of modern ecology', *Biology and Philosophy*, 4, pp. 433–455.
Hassard, J. and Law, J. (eds.) (1999). *Actor-network theory and after*. Oxford: Blackwell Publishers.
Hollin, G., Forsyth, I., Giraud, E. and Potts, T. (2017). '(Dis)entangling Barad: Materialisms and ethics', *Social Studies of Science*, 47, pp. 918–941.
Lane, S.N. (2017). 'Slow science, the geographical expedition, and critical physical geography', *The Canadian Geographer/Le Géographe canadien*, 61, pp. 84–101.
Levitas, R. (2013). *Utopia as method: The imaginary reconstitution of society*. London: Palgrave Macmillan.
Lindenmayer, D.B., Fischer, J., Felton, A., Crane, M., Michael, D., Macgregor, C., Montague-Drake, R., Manning, A. and Hobbs, R.J. (2008). 'Novel ecosystems resulting from landscape transformation create dilemmas for modern conservation practice', *Conservation Letters*, 1, pp. 129–135.
Lorimer, J. and Driessen, C. (2016). 'From "Nazi cows" to cosmopolitan "ecological engineers": Specifying rewilding through a history of heck cattle', *Annals of the American Association of Geographers*, 106, pp. 631–652.
Mackenzie, J.M. (ed.) (1990). *Imperialism and the Natural World*. Manchester: Manchester University Press.
Mcintosh, R.P. (1985). *The background of ecology: Concept and theory*. Cambridge: Cambridge University Press.
Miller, J.R. and Bestelmeyer, B.T. (2016). 'What's wrong with novel ecosystems, really?' *Restoration Ecology*, 24, pp. 577–582.
Morton, T. (2007). *Ecology without nature: Rethinking environmental aesthetics*. Cambridge, MA: Harvard University Press.
Naess, A. (1984). 'A defence of the deep ecology movement', *Environmental Ethics*, 6, pp. 265–270.
Oh, D.-S., Phillips, F., Park, S. and Lee, E. (2016). 'Innovation ecosystems: A critical examination', *Technovation*, 54, pp. 1–6.
Phillips, N. (2017). 'Ecologists protest Australia's plans to cut funding for environment-monitoring network', *Nature*, 548, pp. 381–382.
Plumwood, V. (1993). *Feminism and the mastery of nature*. London: Routledge.
Refsgaard, J.C., Van Der Sluijs, J.P., Højberg, A.L. and Vanrolleghem, P.A. (2007). 'Uncertainty in the environmental modelling process—A framework and guidance', *Environmental Modelling & Software*, 22, pp. 1543–1556.
Rickards, L. (2015). 'Metaphor and the anthropocene: Presenting humans as a geological force', *Geographical Research*, 52(3), pp. 280–287.

Robertson, T. (2012). 'Total war and the total environment: Fairfield Osborn, William Vogt, and the birth of global ecology', *Environmental History*, 17, pp. 336–364.

Schnaiberg, A. (1980). *The environment: From surplus to scarcity*. New York: Oxford University Press.

Schneider, B. (2017). 'The future face of the Earth: The visual semantics of the future in climate change imagery of the IPCC'. In Heymann, M., Gramelsberger, G. and Mahony, M. (eds.) *Cultures of prediction in atmospheric and climate science: Epistemic and cultural shifts in computer-based modelling and simulation*. London: Routledge, pp. 231–251.

Sears, P.B. (1964). 'Ecology—a subversive subject', *Bioscience*, 14, pp. 11–13.

Steffen, W., Rockström, J., Richardson, K., Lenton, T.M., Folke, C., Liverman, D., Summerhayes, C.P., Barnosky, A.D., Cornell, S.E., Crucifix, M., Donges, J.F., Fetzer, I., Lade, S.J., Scheffer, M., Winkelmann, R. and Schellnhuber, H.J. (2018). 'Trajectories of the Earth system in the anthropocene', *Proceedings of the National Academy of Sciences*, 115, pp. 8252–8259.

Todd, Z. (2016). 'An Indigenous feminist's take on the ontological turn: "Ontology" is just another word for colonialism', *Journal of Historical Sociology*, 29, pp. 4–22.

Walker, J. (2020). *More heat than life: The tangled roots of ecology, energy, and economics*. Cham: Springer Books.

Worster, D. (1994). *Nature's economy: A history of ecological ideas*. Cambridge: University of Cambridge Press.

11
Economics
Catalysing large-scale system change

Stewart Wallis

Introduction

This chapter provides a manifesto for catalysing large-scale economic system change. The idea behind it came into being in late 2017 but has roots that go back much farther. I am referring here to the creation of the Wellbeing Economy Alliance (WEAll), a new global collaboration of organizations, alliances, movements and individuals working together to change the economic system to create a well-being economy – an economy that delivers human and ecological well-being.

The need for a different economic system

People have changed and are still changing the Earth so much, warming and polluting it, that many scientists have turned to a new way to describe the time we live in: The Anthropocene – the age of humans (Borenstein, 2014). The Anthropocene is a proposed new geological epoch dating from the commencement of significant human impact on the Earth's geology and ecosystems. This in turn has profound implications for the political economy.[1] The economic model that has become so dominant today has various names: 'Neoliberal', 'market fundamentalist', 'overly financialized', 'extractive' or 'toxic'. What it is called does not matter so much as how our imaginations and our sense of possibility have been constrained: The current economy is often seen as the only kind of economy that we can have and to resist it is futile.

While delivering improvements to many, the current economic system is now jeopardizing progress achieved to date. For those whose lives it has improved, it has done so by creating major inequality and social instability elsewhere and by working against the planet, pushing it to the edge of catastrophic climate change and major biodiversity loss. It has four major systemic and interlinked flaws: It is unsustainable, unfair, unstable and making far too many people unhappy.

Not only is there a serious risk of runaway climate change with dire consequences for humans and other creatures (IPCC, 2018), but biodiversity on the planet is also being destroyed at an unprecedented rate – the population sizes of mammals, birds, fish, amphibians and reptiles have seen an alarming average drop of 68% since 1970 (WWF Living Planet Report 2020). The crucial point is not that we are *risking* environmental breakdown, we are already *in* an environmental breakdown.

The societal effects of serious inequalities in wealth, income and power are well documented, as is the fact that in many countries such inequalities have been worsening in the last few years. To give just one example, the world's 2,153 billionaires now have more wealth than the 4.6 billion people who make up 60% of the planet's population (Oxfam Press Release, 2020).

There is widespread agreement in the richer countries of the world that the social contract is broken – especially the link between hard work, reward and security. Many people fear the loss of their jobs and insecurity in old age. Globally, population increases and demographics mean that 50 million new jobs or livelihoods need to be created every year between now and 2050 (UN, 2015) – at the same time, artificial intelligence experts are forecasting 25% of global unemployment by 2050 unless the economic system is changed (Glenn and Florescu, 2016). Our current economic system cannot provide full-time jobs for everybody (even if this was desirable) and the quest to do so conventionally would cause irreparable harm to the planet. We are in a situation where neither the brake nor the accelerator works anymore in our economic system. If we try to put our foot harder on the accelerator, we burn up the planet even faster; if we put our foot on the brake, we cause greater inequality, underemployment and unemployment. People intuitively know that the system is broken even if they do not articulate it in such terms, and this is a major cause of societal instability.

In January 2020, the Edelman Trust Barometer Report, which draws data from 34,000 people in 34 countries, found that less than 20% of people believed their economic systems were working for them anymore. By contrast, 56% believed that the existing capitalist system is doing more harm than good and 83% of employees feared losing their jobs. There are increased levels of insecurity, despair and loneliness in many countries; and in desperate searches for ways to cope, many people turn inwards or against each other as trust in society and in institutions withers away.

Systemic interaction and forces keeping the current economic system in place

In 2020, these interlinked environmental, social and economic crises have been joined by a global health crisis in the form of the coronavirus pandemic. On top of the increased suffering (physical and mental) and death this has already caused, the global economic system has suffered its biggest downturn in living memory. Health services have been overwhelmed, there is widespread hunger in the poorest countries on the planet and the International Labour Organization says half the global workforce might become unemployed or lose their livelihoods (ILO Monitor, April 2020). Given how these crises are interacting, it is unsurprising that populism and social instability are on the rise. Fundamentally, the economic system is not working anymore both for the majority of people and for the planet.

The root cause of this is how the economy is currently configured: It does not account for nature; it is almost blind to the distribution of resources; it prioritizes efficiency over resilience; it does not reward the best attributes of people and it puts measures of progress such as short-term profit and GDP to the fore. However, the economy is a structure that has been designed by humans – and hence can be designed differently, with a different purpose. Nevertheless, the forces maintaining the current system are strong. They include:

1   The power of entrenched groups who benefit from the current system and have the resources to influence politics, policies and institutions and their change over time;
2   Myths and half-truths about economics that have significant influence over policymaking at all levels;
3   Fundamental flaws in economic theory as currently taught and practised;
4   Strong social modelling influences around fame, money, success and pursuing self-interest;
5   Despair and feelings of powerlessness as systemic problems and threats seem overwhelming and feel too big for any one individual to make a difference;
6   Democratic political systems which are currently very short term and often dysfunctional;
7   Populist voices which are able to divert the blame for harm onto immigration and other factors.

Following the 2009 financial crash, there was brief hope that such a catastrophic failure of the prevailing economic system would be the catalyst for a transformation to an economic system that better served both people and the planet. That this did not happen is testament both to the strength of the forces maintaining the current system and to the failure of the groups arguing for a systemic change to work together effectively and to articulate a positive alternative. It was to address these two failures that a number of individuals and organizations came together in late 2017 to create the Wellbeing Economy Alliance (WEAll).

The story of WEAll

WEAll is a global collaboration of organizations, alliances, movements and individuals working together to change the economic system to create a well-being economy – one that delivers human and ecological well-being. It has a small Amp (amplification) team of ten spread across North America, mainland Europe and the United Kingdom. Its primary focus is the creation of a new power base to exert pressure for change at all levels of the economic system, to influence societal habits and norms and to support the formation of an effective and dynamic global movement. This mission is supported by the formulation and dissemination of positive new narratives and is underpinned by a strong and coherent knowledge and evidence base.

WEAll has many 'mothers' or roots (Costanza et al., 2020). One of the roots was the merger in May 2017 of the Alliance for Sustainability and Prosperity, formed by a number of academics and scientists who had been advising the King and Government of Bhutan, and a US-based group, Leading for Wellbeing, with strong business and faith connections. This took place at a conference in Boulder, Colorado, where the author of this chapter was persuaded to come out of retirement to help coordinate this new venture and the audience pledged over $50,000 towards it. Another root was a gathering in Spain in April 2017 of over 700 people and 40 organizations and movements, many with strong Latin American and European connections, organized by the New Economy and Social Innovation Forum. A third root was the work over many years by an Oxfam researcher (who now works for WEAll) and an academic based at the University of Pretoria (who went on to be Italy's Education Minister for a period) to catalyse a group of governments to work together on well-being economy policies. This culminated in October 2017 in a gathering in Adam Smith's original home in Edinburgh of representatives of the governments of Scotland, Costa Rica, Slovenia and New Zealand hosted by Nicola Sturgeon, the First Minister of Scotland. Following this gathering, leaders of each of these three different roots met together in a house

Economics

on the shores of Loch Fyne and agreed to merge their efforts and resources. WEAll was born.

In 2020, speaking at WEAll's Wealth of Nations 2.0 conference, Sturgeon expressed her continued support for WEAll:

> It's why I do believe that the work of [WEAll] is so important. Because by building the case for change – and we shouldn't yet assume that that case for change has been won – being evangelists for that case is very important. Also, in demonstrating the benefits, you are making a hugely positive difference. As today shows you're helping more and more people to learn about the idea of the wellbeing economy and what it means in practice, and you're helping to inspire ideas and action, which will make it a reality.[2]

WEAll's vision is a well-being economy – one that delivers both human and ecological well-being. Put simply, a well-being economy foregrounds quality of life, flourishing for all people, sustainability and regeneration of the planet. In 2019, WEAll asked its 150 organizational members, many of whom, in turn, represent many thousands of individuals, what they believed to be the key elements of a well-being economy. There was a remarkable consensus on the goals and values of such an economy. The five key needs or non-negotiables that emerged were (see Figure 11.1):

1 Dignity: Everyone has enough to live in comfort, safety and happiness. This means an economy that prioritizes meeting fundamental human needs for all over satisfying the wants of the economically powerful few. Such needs include health, education, economic security, food and housing as well as a sense of dignity and purpose, value and respect and self-determination;

Figure 11.1 The five needs identified by WEAll's 150 organizational members

139

2   Nature: A restored and safe natural world for all life. This means an economy that operates within local and global planetary limits and where the focus is on regenerating the natural world;
3   Connection: A sense of belonging and institutions that serve the common good. This means an economy where all institutions, including businesses, pursue social and environmental goals, and where profit, when relevant, is a means to achieve such goals not an end in itself;
4   Fairness: Justice in all its dimensions is at the heart of economic systems, and the gap between the richest and poorest is greatly reduced. This means an economy where power, wealth, income, time and esteem are fairly distributed rather than relying on redistribution;
5   Participation: Citizens are actively engaged in their communities and locally rooted economies. This means a much greater focus on both decentralization and economic democracy.

Clearly, different contexts and cultures will require very different policies to achieve a well-being economy, but there is a remarkable level of agreement across cultures and contexts about the type of economic system most people want. This shared vision for a better way of doing things can also be found across a surprising range of texts and backgrounds (Trebeck and Williams, 2019). It is embedded in the scripts of many religions. It is contained in world views of First Nations communities. It can be read in the scholarship of development experts and in research findings of what makes people flourish. This vision emerges in evidence from psychology about human needs (Pirson, 2017), from neuroscience about what makes our brains react and, perhaps most importantly, can be heard loud and clear in deliberative policy conversations with people all over the world about what really matters to them in their lives (see, for example, Costanza et al., 2015).

Similarly, in September 2020, the All-Party Parliamentary Group on the Green New Deal in the United Kingdom published a report (Reset Report) on their findings from engagement with over 55,000 people, including two nationally representative polls of 2,000 people; in-depth workshops with 108 people; and interviews with people who are digitally excluded. They found that 66% of UK adults want the government to prioritize the health and well-being of citizens over GDP growth, and only one in five think the government should continue to prioritize GDP as its main economic goal. Furthermore, 57% support some form of universal basic income, 63% support a job guarantee and 50% support a shorter working week.

A theory of change

I worked for 13 years, up to early 2016, for the New Economics Foundation (NEF), one of the world's leading think-and-do tanks working for economic system change. NEF's theory of change involved carrying out rigorous ground-breaking research, communicating this in creative ways, lobbying and campaigning and working with communities and businesses to test ideas in practice. NEF was very successful in achieving individual policy changes, but, together with its allies, it clearly did not achieve its wider goal of system change. We therefore carried out research into successful system changes both in the economic and social spheres, and this showed that, while all of our existing strategies were indeed necessary, on their own they were not sufficient.

In addition, three other key strategies were found to be pivotal (Gill and Cadman, 2015):

1   Discrediting the existing story or narrative and creation of a compelling new story or narrative based on a coherent body of theory and practice;
2   Weakening existing power bases and construction of new power bases;
3   Seizing opportunities provided by current events.

These three strategies were crucial in the achievement of successful system change in non-economic spheres such as civil rights and anti-slavery. But, they were also vital in the achievement of the two major economic transformations in advanced Western economies of the twentieth-century. From the 1940s to 1960s, Western economies shifted to a Keynesian model, with its emphasis on the management of markets and the provision of health, education and social safety nets. And, from the late 1970s to the 2000s, neoliberalism ascended with a focus on individual freedom and market freedom. In the case of Keynesianism, the vision was of solidarity, the right of all to education and health and the need for government to intervene to ensure full employment. Government needed to enhance its authority, while Wall Street and business needed to be weakened. The Great Depression hastened its introduction, as did the Second World War.

In the case of neoliberalism, its proponents' vision was, and is, focussed on freedom (Mirowski and Plehwe, 2009; Stedman Jones, 2012). They created a compelling, positive story based on the view that government was too big; markets would serve everyone if allowed to be truly free; and freedom of the individual was a fundamental right. These principles and the ideas flowing from them now permeate all arenas of human life. As William Allen (1993), a former Chancellor of the Delaware Court of Chancery put it, 'One of the marks of a true dominant intellectual paradigm is the difficulty people have in even imagining an alternative point of view'.

The proponents of neoliberalism set up think-tanks such as Heritage, Cato and the Institute of Economic Affairs. They 'captured' some of the most important economic departments of the world and became prominent on editorial boards of key economic publications. They created a new power base which, helped by the oil price shocks in the 1970s, lifted Margaret Thatcher and Ronald Reagan into power at the end of that decade and put neoliberal economic theory into practice around the world (see Figure 11.2).

WEAll's theory of change was informed by our analysis that, while the neoliberal narrative had become widely discredited, a positive alternative based on a coherent body of theory and practice was still lacking. Furthermore, in seeking to help catalyse a new power base, we were clear that the detailed tactics of the neoliberals could not be simply copied. The neoliberals were extremely well funded by a small group of billionaires and the power base they created was fundamentally an elite one seeking to strengthen the power of an elite group. WEAll is seeking to catalyse a power base that will have the power of millions of hearts and hands rather than billions of dollars.

Global strategy

WEAll's strategy is summarized as follows (see also Figure 11.3):

1   Galvanize new power bases across sectors, geographies and levels (both bottom-up and top-down) through place-based hubs and a global network of individuals, organizations and movements working together;
2   Synthesize and disseminate knowledge and evidence about what a well-being economy looks like and how we get there;

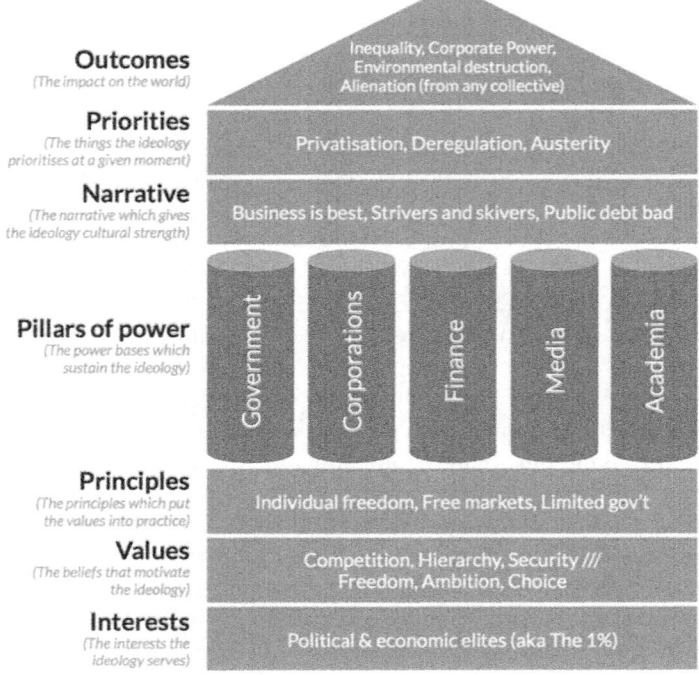

Figure 11.2 A diagram from the New Economics Foundation in 2013 showing how neoliberalism is sustained in the United Kingdom

3   Shift popular narratives around the purpose of the economy;
4   Leverage key events such as the current global health pandemic.

We have found that successful system change necessitates a combination of all of the above approaches simultaneously. What is vital is a critical mass of people and organizations coming together to form a new dynamic movement to influence and inspire. This way, the collective impact is substantially multiplied. WEAll's role is to help catalyse this multiplication process. As Pedro Tarak, cofounder of Sistema B in Argentina observes:

> WEALL offers Sistema B a wonderful feeling… humbleness…. Nobody can change the world alone, nobody knows enough, everybody is part of an infinite diversity of experiences, of perspectives and unique complementary solutions seeking the evolution of an economy which could be good for Life. Being part of WEALL has granted more legitimacy to Sistema B as part of its strategy of global alliances.

In the 24 months since it was first established, WEAll has instigated the Wellbeing Economy Governments (WEGo) partnership (Trebeck, 2019). This is the only living laboratory at scale that is testing this alternative economic paradigm. The partnership currently consists of New Zealand, Iceland, Scotland and Wales with several other nations interested in joining. New Zealand implemented the world's first well-being budget last year, Iceland has done so in 2020, Scotland has passed climate change legislation with the world's most ambitious targets and Wales has established a Future Generations Act.

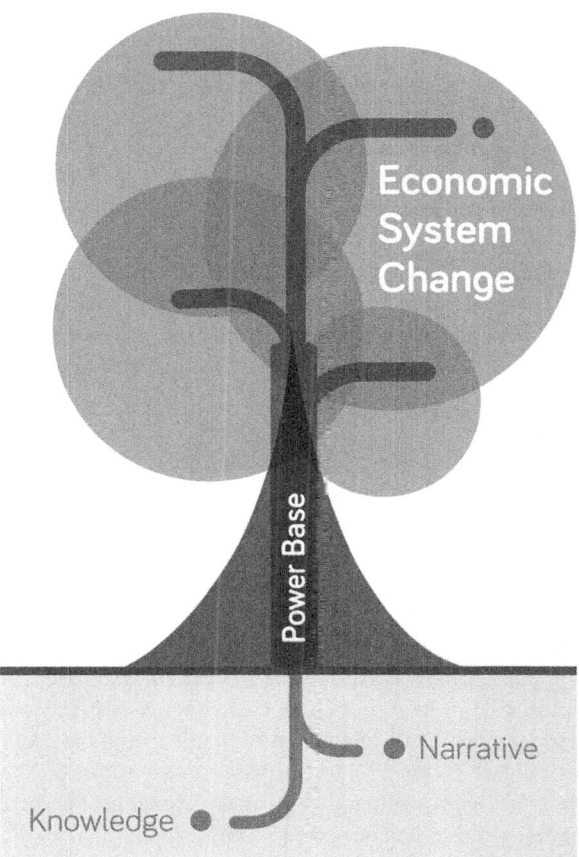

Figure 11.3 Strategies for system change

We have also grown to an organizational membership of over 160 movements, alliances and organizations. Organizations include leading think-tanks (Club of Rome, Democracy Collaborative, New Economics Foundation and the Institute for Ecological Civilization); environmental groups (Earth Charter, IUCN and the David Suzuki Foundation); movements and coalitions (Economy for the Common Good, WE Africa, Green Economy Coalition and the New Economy Network Australia); business–systems experts (Sistema B, B Corps, Lift Economy and Future Fit); new finance associations (Global Alliance for Banking on Values, Positive Money and Finance Watch) and community regeneration networks (Regenerative Network and Local Futures).

Over the last two years, WEAll has also supported the creation of multi-sector, multilevel hubs, which are place-based groups that facilitate collaboration and action towards building a well-being economy. WEAll has invested significantly in supporting the efforts of its first place-based hub, WEAll Scotland, which is now an independent charity with involvement from all sectors of Scottish life (Community Groups, businesses, environmental groups, civil servants, NGOs, universities, faith groups, student groups, finance houses and banks and unaffiliated citizens). Its achievements in two years have been amazing (see WEAll Scotland Briefing Document, 2020).

We have seed-funded WEAll hubs in New Zealand, Costa Rica, Canada and California to support their development and to provide case studies for a well-being-economy policy design guide. Glo Gonzales, of the Omina Foundation in Costa Rica, has remarked: 'Our admiration and gratitude for you and the WEAll team are beyond measure. We strongly believe in WEAll and want to be as involved as possible in its growing process'.

The Canadian and Californian hubs had their launch events in fall 2020. In addition, we have launched an online global citizen platform where over 2,000 individual change-makers are connecting and collaborating across the world's continents, and we have supported WEAll Youth groups, which are now active in three continents – Europe, Australia and Africa. WEAll Youth was selected by the United Nations out of over 4,000 applicants as one of the world's top 50 most-impressive youth initiatives helping the implementation of the Sustainable Development Goals. Linda Gessner, from the Centre for the Understanding of Sustainable Prosperity, the United Kingdom, observes that she is:

> Very proud to be a member of the wonderfully bold, engaged and generous community that WEAll is. Working with comms colleagues from all over the world is a huge enrichment not only in terms of knowledge (and tech hacks) exchange but seeing these young eloquent people from the Youth hub, so organized and well-spoken in a foreign language is also something else!

There are four young women leading the WEAll Youth initiative. We asked them about their motivations for investing their time and energy in WEAll. Helene Schnelle commented: 'I believe that young people play a powerful role in bringing change to systems, institutions, etc. as they are the managers, leaders and professionals of tomorrow. I want to make more young people realize and act upon this power'. Esther Snijder mentions the enthusiasm she feels when she sees 'youth all over the world coming together to make a change for their future. For a real change to be made people need to be connected'. Mara Tippmann sees the work on new economies as an 'essential part for our generation to take matters into our own hands and make a difference!'. She continues:

> A stable economic system is the base for a prosperous society, but with our current systems, we seem to hinder any work done for a more equal, clean and healthy planet. […] If we young people work together as the WEAll Youth movement, we gain the exposure and means to take action and start to make a change.

Finally, Pien Gerards considers sustainability and education to be two of the most 'crucial topics if you think about changing the world'. Gerards brings her passion to 'involving young people and creating more awareness', hoping to 'create a positive change in this world'. She warns against forgetting about the youth, because 'young people are our future'.

Over the last 24 months, we have also delivered or contributed to mainstream media coverage in at least 15 countries, promoting the need for economic system change.[3] We are currently working to expand and deepen the WEGo partnership, co-create with members and others just transition policies in existing and potential WEGo countries/territories and showcase these policies at COP26 in Glasgow in 2021.

We have also partnered with WEAll members, other networks and creative partners to start to identify key well-being economy narratives in different regions of the world. In the United Kingdom, this will see the publication in 2020 of a narrative's playbook with guiding principles for telling the new economy story, providing visual stimulus, hooks, framing and language. In the United States and Australia, analysis of surveys undertaken will produce a report analysing well-being economy stories that resonate in these regions. In Africa, WEAll co-created with leading WEAll African members an economic leapfrogging narrative proposal for connecting the general public with the African Union's 2063 Agenda.

We have also begun amplifying the economic solutions of our members in agenda promotion work and via curated coherent guides. For example, the 'Business of Wellbeing' guide and the 'Wellbeing Economy Policy Guide' (see wellbeingeconomy.org) launched in 2020, while the work of over 150 globally renowned academics has resulted in, amongst other things, the publication of six briefing papers with many more forthcoming. Working on the fiscal benefits of a well-being economy and planning detailed work on so-called litmus test policies are our two current priorities. This is because transformation requires policies that can simultaneously achieve a variety of well-being goals, such as the creation of decent jobs while simultaneously reducing inequality, poverty and carbon emissions, or policies that can regenerate biodiversity and ecosystems, improve human well-being and yield positive impact on public finances. In short, policymakers need an approach to developing policies that simultaneously deliver human and ecological well-being.

In response to the coronavirus pandemic, WEAll is working very actively with a wide coalition of other groups and movements and with all its members under the theme Build Back Better (Büchs et al., 2020). A paper has already been published on the key principles and actions needed by individual governments; papers on the global economy and the US economy are in preparation.

WEAll's ambition

Over the period 2021–2025, WEAll plans to facilitate the deepening of connections between government, business and civil society within the WEGo countries. It also plans an expansion of hubs stretching into the global South, expanding WEAll's reach to over 20 territories. COP26 (assuming it is held in 2021) should provide an early showcase for the WEGo partnership and further expand interest in a well-being economy through cultural events delivered by WEAll and its members. WEAll also plans to work strategically with other global movements and coalitions in areas such as climate change, biodiversity, interfaith collaboration, financial reform, new business models and social justice.

This period will also see an escalation of efforts to synthesize well-being economy knowledge and solutions (guides and briefings), as well as offer training and support for decision-makers (policymakers, business and civil society) to utilize these resources, which are housed in an interactive and searchable Wellbeing Economy (WE) Portal. User Robert Wanalo from Kenya calls the experience of using the portal 'like Christmas!! I just might spend the entire day there'. New stories about an economy in service of life begin to be created by a dedicated storytelling unit comprised of multiple members and disseminated in different parts of the world.

Between 2025 and 2028, the goal is for the WEGo partnership to have become a dominant grouping in international arenas with over 20 governments signed up. The idea of replacing GDP with well-being as the primary goal of the economy is being pursued among the members of WEGo. The WE Portal has become a resource widely used in education from the primary level through to economics in higher education. Stories of how economies can be based on connection, participation, fairness, dignity and nature are taking hold at all levels of society. Businesses are aligning their purposes with this new goal, and a growing movement of WEAll citizens is actively participating through WEAll hubs in local policy formulation, rewriting the rules of the game.

If WEAll is successful, it will be as just one element catalysing a broader global well-being economy movement. This movement will be far bigger than WEAll and not controlled by any grouping or collaboration. To the extent that such a movement emerges and comes increasingly to master the three key strategies for successful system change, there is every reason to expect it could prove as successful as Keynesianism and neoliberalism before it in bringing about a new economic paradigm – and, this time, as never before, avoid a major global system collapse.

Notes

1 Here we understand 'political economy' to refer to interdisciplinary research drawing upon economics, sociology and political science that explains how political institutions, the political environment and the economic system influence each other (Weingast and Wittman, 2008).
2 All quotations from WEAll members and collaborators are taken from personal correspondence with the WEAll team, and permission was granted for these comments to be shared in the public domain.
3 See the website for information about WEAll's achievements: https://wellbeingeconomy.org

Bibliography

Allen, W.T. (1993). 'Contracts and communities in corporation law', *Washington and Lee Law Review*, 50(4), pp. 1395–1407.
Borenstein, S. (14 October 2014). 'With their mark on Earth, humans may name era, too'. Associated Press. https://apnews.com/article/c999a20fb7114f818c0398c0e40720ab
Büchs, M., Baltruszewicz, M. et al. (2020), 'Wellbeing economics for the COVID-19 recovery. Ten principles to build back better'. https://wellbeingeconomy.org/wp-content/uploads/2020/05/Wellbeing_Economics_for_the_COVID-19_recovery_10Principles.pdf [Accessed 9 November 2020].
Costanza, R. et al. (2015). 'Scenarios for Australia in 2050: A synthesis and proposed survey', *Journal of Futures Studies*, 19, pp. 49–76.
Costanza, R., Erickson, J.D. et al. (eds.) (2020). *Sustainable wellbeing futures*. Cheltenham: Edward Elgar Publishing.
Edelman Trust Barometer Report (2020). https://www.edelman.com/trustbarometer [Accessed 9 November 2020].
Gill, S. and Cadman, D. (eds.) (2015). *Why love matters: Values in governance*. Bern: Peter Lang.
Glenn, J.C. and Florescu, E. (2016). 'Future work/technology 2050 real-time Delphi study'. 2015–2016 State of the Future, Millennium Project. https://www.researchgate.net/publication/312922945_Future_WorkTechnology_2050_Real-Time_Delphi_Study_Excerpt_from_the_2015-16_State_of_the_Future_Report [Accessed 9 November 2020].
ILO Monitor (April 2020). https://www.ilo.org/global/about-the-ilo/newsroom/news/WCMS_743036/lang--en/index.htm [Accessed 9 November 2020].
IPCC (2018). Global warming of 1.5°C. An IPCC Special Report on the impacts of global warming of 1.5°C above pre-industrial levels and related global greenhouse gas emission pathways. https://www.ipcc.ch/sr15/ [Accessed 9 November 2020].
Mirowski, P. and Plehwe, D. (eds.) (2009). *The road from Mont Pelerin: The making of the neoliberal thought collective*. Cambridge, MA: Harvard University Press.
Oxfam Press Release (2020, January 20). https://www.oxfam.org/en/press-releases/worlds-billionaires-have-more-wealth-46-billion-people [Accessed 9 November 2020].
Pirson, M. (2017). *Humanistic management: Protecting dignity and promoting well -being*. Cambridge: Cambridge University Press.
Reset Report (2020). https://reset-uk.org/static/TimeToReset-3a6ee92ce4fff64d024c62404f53fe5c.pdf [Accessed 9 November 2020].
Stedman Jones, D. (2012). *Masters of the universe: Hayek, Friedman, and the birth of neoliberal politics*. Princeton, NJ: Princeton University Press.

Trebeck, K. (2019), 'Here we go'. https://wellbeingeconomy.org/here-we-go-first-wellbeing-economy-governments-policy-lab-underway-katherine-trebeck [Accessed 9 November 2020].

Trebeck, K. and Williams, J. (2019). *The economics of arrival*. Bristol: Policy Press.

WEAll Brochure (2020). https://wellbeingeconomy.org/wp-content/uploads/2019/12/WEAll-brochure_Jan20_HiRes.pdf [Accessed 9 November 2020].

WEAll Scotland Briefing Document (2020). https://wellbeingeconomy.org/wp-content/uploads/2020/09/WEAll-Scotlands-achievements-briefing.pdf [Accessed 9 November 2020].

Weingast, B.R. and Wittman, D. (eds.) (2008). *The Oxford handbook of political economy*. Oxford: Oxford University Press.

World Population Prospects, Key findings and advanced tables, UN (2015). https://esa.un.org/unpd/wpp/publications/files/key_findings_wpp_2015.pdf [Accessed 9 November 2020].

WWF Living Planet Report (2020). https://www.wwf.org.uk/press-release/living-planet-report-2020 [Accessed 9 November 2020].

12
Family
Homeland connections and family futures

Earvin Charles Cabalquinto

Introduction

Several studies of Philippine migration have unravelled how providing a better and stable future for oneself and one's family members has been one of the driving forces behind transnational migration among Filipinos (Asis, 2005; McKay, 2007, 2012; Parreñas, 2001b). Given the limited access, or lack thereof, to various social welfare systems, public services and job opportunities in the Philippines (San Juan, 2011), overseas migration is considered as a survival strategy for the entire family (Asis, 1994). To ensure the maintenance of ties despite family separation, Filipino migrants and their left-behind family members use digital communication technologies. Surrounded by various mobile devices and networked online platforms in a polymedia environment (Madianou and Miller, 2012), transnational linkages are fostered via the circulation of information, remittances and care packages. While there have already been many studies that uncover how the production and distribution of digital information and material goods contribute to navigating a pathway towards achieving a good life (Madianou and Miller, 2012; Mckay, 2016; Parreñas, 2001a, 2005, 2008), there remains a notable gap in understanding how imaginaries of family futures are tied both to sustaining homeland connections and to the broader social systems that create division and marginalizing conditions for Filipino migrants, as well as their left-behind family members.

The findings presented in this chapter are part of a broader project that examined the role of mobile communication technologies in sustaining ties among Filipino migrants in Melbourne, Australia, and their left-behind family members in the Philippines. I specifically examined how 12 Overseas Filipino Workers (OFWs) in Melbourne, Australia, used mobile devices and online channels in accessing homeland information. I analysed how diverse digital practices present ways of imagining family futures, paying close attention to how digital media practices become a site for imagining settlement and reunification. The OFWs in Melbourne were Subclass Visa 457 holders or Temporary Work (Skilled) Visa holders.[1]

The duration of migrants' stay in Australia depends on their long- or short-term contracts, which are provided by their employers (Larsen, 2013). They typically have to pay for other expenses if they wish to bring their family members to Australia. Moreover, their visa status limits their access to various benefits provided by the national government to permanent residents and citizens (Larsen, 2013). As such, they often aim to apply for a permanent residency or even citizenship when they meet the requirements of a point-based system (Papademetriou and Sumption, 2011). With a successful application, they become entitled to a dual citizenship (Rodriguez, 2010), as well as having access to Australia's social welfare services for their family members. Given this transnational arrangement, they invest in and use mobile devices and online channels to communicate, settle everyday familial needs and imagine and work on their plans for the family's future

Upon uncovering the communicative affordances and challenges of digital media use, I conducted a mapping out of how ideals of advancement and stability for migrants and their left-behind family members are constructed by the Philippine state. This approach was significant in relation to comparing the different 'futures' that are imagined and aspired to by different individuals or institutions (Urry, 2016). Ultimately, the methods helped in problematizing notions of transnational family futures by drawing the connections between mobile practices, affective narratives and the imaginaries of futures by several key and interconnected social actors.

According to Urry (2016), referring to the imaginaries of the future is critical in inquiring about, reflecting on, contesting and changing present practices. For him, ideal futures are often imagined and constructed by various social actors who are embedded and interact in various complex systems, such as government, migration and so forth (Urry, 2016). Significantly, Urry (2016) also places emphasis on how unequal power relations might impact the construction and articulation of futures for certain individuals and groups. For instance, anticipating the work of Büscher (2018), Urry (2016) pinpoints how dominant, exclusionary and capitalist frames by certain groups, business enterprises or institutions tend to shape imagined futures for individuals. As such, for mobilities scholars, zooming into the future allows for a critical examination of present everyday practices, which is crucial for the development of inclusive and participatory planning and techniques (Büscher, 2018; Urry, 2016). Significantly, in the context of migration, notions of futures can be linked to the imagination (Appadurai, 2005) and the ways in which imagined worlds and selves are facilitated by media contents. Building on these propositions, this chapter illuminates and problematizes the imaginaries of family futures among migrants.

This chapter addresses four objectives. First, it seeks to unpack how migrants aspire to and work towards a better future through transnational migration. Second, it aims to examine the role of mobile device use in sustaining homeland linkages, facilitating the continuities needed for enabling a better life in the future. Third, it unpacks the diverse experiences of accessing and digesting diverse information, which are instrumental in the work of imagination towards activating a plausible future (Amara, 1981). Lastly, it problematizes how many mobile practices and ambivalent experiences are tied to the hierarchical imagined futures of the Philippine government. Such an approach opens conversations about how broader power structures in contemporary society influence the planning and envisioning of the future through everyday mobile practices. Nevertheless, interrogating the imagined family futures of migrants reveals the intertwining of personal, affective, familial and national imaginaries that govern mobility, settlement and inclusion.

Discursive imaginaries in the homeland and overseas

To analyse the mobile practices and affective experiences of the Filipino migrants, it is important to engage with the conception of the homeland in the Philippine context. This approach foregrounds the politics of imagined futures that is governed by economic, political and even socio-historical conditions. According to Filipino scholar San Juan (2001), the conception of a Philippine homeland should be approached by looking at the socio-historical, socio-political and socio-economic transformations in Philippine society. In the first instance, the formation of a homeland is moulded by the country's colonial past (San Juan, 2001). Particularly, the allegiance between the colonizers and the elite Filipinos, as well as the rise of oligarchic and political systems in a post-colonial Philippines, has resulted in the birth of a symbolic homeland that is indexed by kinship and particular traditions that are reconstituted in diverse and dispersed localities (San Juan, 2001). Here, political dynasties, the privileging of transnational and multinational business, the prevalent corruption, as well as the escalating poverty, underemployment and unemployment in the nation state have made those affected ordinary Filipinos perceive the homeland as run by a few elites and manipulative politicians (San Juan, 2001). As a result, Filipinos see, experience and negotiate the homeland as facilitated by strong linkages among family members, friends and acquaintances in various regional areas, and not as deeply connected to the nation state. The homeland is then performed and embodied through family- and community-based connections (Mckay, 2012; San Juan, 2001). Notably, for Filipino migrants, the homeland is accessed, experienced and imagined through the consumption of a diverse range of media channels and contents (Anderson, 1998), as well as physical commodities such as indigenous food, dance and music (San Juan, 2000). These practices, as pinpointed by Anderson (1998), manifest as forms of long-distance nationalism.

To date, according to the data produced by the Philippine Overseas Employment Agency (POEA) between 2015 and 2016, approximately 2.5 million Filipinos worked abroad, including two million land-based workers and 501 thousand sea-based workers (POEA, 2019). Mass media channels play a huge role in reconstructing settlement among migrants, as well as in the homeland (cf. Aksoy and Robins, 2000; Cunningham and Sinclair, 2001; Gillespie, 1995; Karim, 2003; Naficy, 1993, 2003; Madianou, 2005). Ethnic and transnational media forms afford the production of media content that targets specific audiences according to their varying relationships to the homeland and host land (Naficy, 1993, 2003). Media use can be driven by nostalgia, fetishization of the homeland, a burning desire for return (Naficy, 2003) or a reassurance of connections (Aksoy and Robins, 2000; Naficy, 1993). Significantly, Appadurai (1996) argues that diverse media channels and content comprise 'mediascapes' and enable homeland connections (Appadurai, 1996). Here, 'scapes' serve as building blocks of imagined worlds among migrants (Appadurai, 1996). In the age of electronic media, circulating digital information is considered as an 'archive' that affords the work of imagination (Appadurai, 2003). Archives are often considered as 'maps' or a 'guide to the uncertainties of identity building under adverse conditions' (Appadurai, 2003, p. 23). Paradoxically, mass media content can serve as a push-and-pull factor in migration. As Appadurai (1996) states: 'For migrants, both the politics of adaptation to new environments and the stimulus to move or return are deeply affected by a mass-mediated imaginary that frequently transcends national space' (p. 6).

In this chapter, I highlight how the imaginaries of family futures among Filipino migrants are tied to political systems and nationalist discourse. For instance, Philippine scholar Neferti Tadiar (2004) has critiqued the imaginaries of the Philippine government in outlining an advanced and stable future for the Filipinos. She contends that the visions of the Philippine government preserve colonial domination and increase capital accumulation. She particularly uses the case studies of Filipino migrant workers, articulating how ordinary Filipinos often bear the burden of the nation state's foray into global partnerships and neoliberal policies (Tadiar, 2004). Through a privilege bestowed to the few elites and global corporations, advancement in the Philippines produces disadvantageous outcomes for those who lack diverse capital. This is reflected in the prostitution of women and children (Tadiar, 2004), as well as the exportation of cheap and often feminized human labour (see Parreñas, 2001b; Rodriguez, 2010).

Rodriguez (2010) and Guevarra (2010) build on the scholarship of Tadiar (2004) by demonstrating the various techniques used by the Philippine government to achieve its economically driven and politically charged visions for the nation. Here, the government's imaginaries for a promising Philippine future are developed and reflected in the brokering of surplus labour. The government develops training programmes with certifications and disseminates campaign materials to construct a submissive, hardworking and entrepreneurial migrant – one who supports the needs of family members and helps the nation (Guevarra, 2010; Rodriguez, 2010). Remittance and courier companies that promote their services to Filipino migrants have also capitalized on this nationalist discourse for profit accumulation (Cabalquinto and Wood-Bradley, 2020). Notably, the Philippine economy benefits from the remittances sent by Filipino migrant workers. In a recent report by the Philippine Central Bank, the amount of cash sent home by Filipinos abroad was 2.48 billion dollars in January 2019 (Bangko Sentral ng Pilipinas, 2019). Due to the remittances that contribute to 10% of the country's gross domestic product, OFWs are applauded by the Philippine government as '*Bagong Bayani*', or modern-day heroes. Ultimately, the nationalist discourse and strategies deployed by the Philippine government indicate imaginaries of a bright future that position Filipino migrants as a 'partner' or even responsible for the nation's growth and future.

Here, I explore the key role of digital media use in assisting migrants to navigate a pathway towards achieving a 'plausible future' or a future that is more likely to happen based on current practices or trends (Amara, 1981). This articulation has been touched on tangentially across a cohort of studies on Philippine migration. First, the exchange of information in a polymedia environment allows the maintenance of intimate ties and connections (Madianou and Miller, 2012). This enables continuities despite family separation. Second, online channels such as Inq7.net and Philstar.com (Paragas, 2006, 2009) and YouTube (Bonini, 2011) are accessed by Filipino migrants to consume the latest information in national news and popular culture, paving the way for gaining knowledge and a sense of continued belonging. In some cases, websites and social media channels are accessed to keep track of developments in the Philippines, which enables migrants to integrate when they eventually return (Ong and Cabañes, 2011). Ultimately, digital media channels and their content contribute to the constant imagining and creation of the future. However, as the following sections will show, mobile practices and experiences expose the politics of imagined family futures especially when current practices operate as sites for reinforcing hierarchy and marginalization.

The envisioned 'gains' of cross-border mobility

The 12 migrants who I interviewed had a relatively common vision for themselves and their family members. For them, moving to and working in Australia is considered a great opportunity to provide the best possible future for themselves and their left-behind family members. Among the 12 migrants, 6 were single and 6 were married with children. For the single adult migrants, moving overseas was envisioned as affording professional growth and a well-paying job. This goal also included their hopes for left-behind family members. For example, Jeff, a 26-year-old registered nurse opted to work overseas because of the low pay for registered nurses in the Philippines. (He was earning 8,000 pesos (280 AUD) a month back home.) He also added that working in Australia would help him support his family members' needs. Although Jeff is not the breadwinner for his family, he regularly sends money to his family back home to fulfil his filial duty. In Philippine society, Jeff's practice of maintaining connections and sending money and even care packages is driven by the distinctly Filipino cultural value of *utang-na-loob* (debt of gratitude). Ultimately, having a well-paying job overseas allows Jeff to work on a stable future for himself and for his family members in the Philippines.

For participants who were married and with children, transnational migration was essentially deemed to be a practical means for addressing current needs and investing in the family's future. For instance, Roel, a 47-year-old panel beater in Melbourne, started working overseas in 1991 during the Gulf war. He then worked in Saudi Arabia and Kuwait before moving to Australia to work as a panel beater and welder. In my interview with him, he highlighted how his work allowed him to provide for his family as well as consider and plan for possible options for family migration, given Australia's family reunification scheme. In the interview, Roel also pointed out that it is best to work overseas because staying back home with his family members could be challenging. The decision to work overseas was also informed by the pressure to finance the medication for his youngest child, who has a heart condition. As he said, 'I really don't have a choice. What will I do back home? I can be physically co-present with my family, but we can be starving'. Nonetheless, working overseas is considered a viable option to address the needs of the family as well as contribute to mapping out a better future (Asis, 1994; Parreñas, 2001b).

Digital and familial continuities

To deal with family separation brought upon by transnational migration, the participants used a wide range of digital devices and online channels. They chose a particular online channel in an environment of communicative affordances (Madianou and Miller, 2012). These online platforms, as I have presented elsewhere, are crucial in enabling everyday intimate connections (Cabalquinto, 2018b) and care practices (Cabalquinto, 2018a) among transnational families. In this section, I highlight the different online platforms that the participants accessed to consume homeland information and therefore imagine their future settlement.

The findings revealed that all participants of this study accessed online news and local information through Facebook, selected websites and TFC (The Filipino Channel), a global subscription channel that hosts Filipino movies, news and so forth. Notably, Filipino migrants accessed information via Facebook pages or news articles that were shared by their online networks. For example, Efren, a 32-year-old chef in Melbourne, expressed his thoughts about the accessibility of homeland news through online channels. He said, 'Anytime, you can access news. You will get to access information with a smartphone'. This statement by Efren also resonated with Patrick, a 30-year-old registered nurse, who commented on the value of Facebook. For him, Facebook served as a space to scan or sometimes read news of home. He said, 'Through my feeds, people post the recent news about the Philippines on Facebook [...] I scan information. If it's interesting I read it, such as news about the typhoon...'. In my interview with Patrick, I discovered that he used Facebook, just like the majority of the participants, to get information about the conditions in the Philippines. This then allowed the participants to discuss matters through a phone conversation. Further, discussions on updates about the Philippines were enmeshed with other family-related matters, such as financial needs and household expenses. Nonetheless, the technological affordances of the mobile device and online platforms – ubiquitous and networked connectivity – provided a space of belonging (Appadurai, 2003).

On investing in the 'now' for the future

Online media channels were also used by several participants to access information to plan for the family's future. For example, Vic, a 45-year-old fridge mechanic, pointed out how he accessed information via online channels to plan and set up a family business. Currently, Vic has an apartment rental business, which his wife and another staff are managing. To augment the family savings, he considered setting up a food business. To generate ideas about his plan, he regularly watched an online show called *Kumikitang Kabuhayan* (Profit-Making Business) via TFC. In such an arrangement, homeland information is consumed to invest in a possible business and thus support a vision of a secure financial future for oneself and the family.

For some participants, accessing positive homeland information was crucial in justifying the importance of sending remittances to support the family and nation's future. A case in point is Reggie, a 34-year-old registered nurse, who regularly sent money to his mother in the Philippines. Although he was not obliged to send money, he still sent remittances as a way of giving back to his family in the Philippines. Notably, Reggie often accessed positive news about the Philippines through various online channels. As he said, 'Success stories motivate me to participate in [the] country's economic activities directly and indirectly'. Moreover, Reggie pointed out the importance of looking at what one should do to support one's family and the Philippine economy. He reiterated, 'I focus on things that I can do to help. Like for example my family, because of their purchasing power, that's a direct way to help the Philippines. Because they spend, they are paying tax'. Nonetheless, Reggie exemplified a Filipino migrant who imagined the security of one's family back home by focussing on positive news and sending remittances that would help the national economy.

Managing uncomfortable connectivity

As shown in the previous discussions, the participants embody what the Philippine government promotes as a good migrant – family-oriented and entrepreneurial. Indebtedness, strong family ties and community-oriented values also shape ways of sustaining ties and relationships beyond borders. Notably, the participants' expressions of care for their family members benefit the nation state in the form of remittances and investments. It is through this arrangement that the Philippine government aspires to an imagined progressive future, relying on Filipino migrants and their families who serve as 'nodes' in the circulation of money and goods (Francisco-Menchavez, 2018). This, I argue, characterizes the politics of imagined family futures as it reinforces existing hierarchical systems that exploit familial relations and homeland ties.

The affective experiences of mobile device use in sustaining homeland ties also indicate the politics of imagined family futures. In the first instance, the participants accessed essential information that was used to navigate a transnational terrain towards an eventual reunification and settlement. However, consuming homeland connections stirred ambivalent feelings. Here, Filipino migrants witnessed inequalities and social injustices, often reminding them of the privileges bestowed on those who are in power, such as government officials and celebrities, as they carry on with their personal and familial relationships and also bear the responsibility of 'fuelling' the nation's future.

For example, at the time of my interview with Efren, two main issues were making a headline in the Philippine media. The first was the Pork barrel scam, exposing how several members of Congress allegedly misused government funding. The second was the involvement of a Filipino celebrity in an alleged rape case. Efren, who read reports online regularly, was appalled and felt frustrated by the way cases were handled through the Philippine justice system. He was particularly referring to the slow process of addressing the cases. As he said, 'You see celebrity news and the politics too. Before I left the Philippines, those were the issues already. It's as if I am not able to escape such news from the Philippines!' He also added, 'It's as if nothing is changing in the Philippines'. Through this statement from Efren, it is clear that his frustrated feelings stem from witnessing the stagnant condition of the home country. There is a call for accountability especially among Filipino migrants who have been displaced from their homeland because of social inequalities and are then relied upon as providers for the nation's imaginaries of and journey towards advancement and stability. However, despite feeling frustrated, Efren revealed in the interview the importance of staying connected to the Philippines. For him, accessing homeland news was crucial in navigating the safety of his left-behind family members. As he noted, 'I need to know everything. Sometimes our place might be affected. So, I have to read the news'. In such a statement, sustaining ties and securing the family's future and safety entailed a constant tracking of homeland information.

Conclusion

This chapter has shown how the examination of various mobile practices of OFWs – transnational migration and digital connectivity – illuminates visions of their family's futures. Further, it has shown how imaginaries of a good and stable family life are constructed through homeland connections. However, these mobile practices are reflective of the politics of imagined family futures. First, Filipino migrants participate in the imaginaries of a stable future by the state by embodying a good, family-oriented and entrepreneurial subject. This arrangement primarily reinforces political structures and social hierarchy in Philippine society, enabling the Philippine government to rely on its migrant labour and the homeland connections that support the economy and contribute to a stable national future. Second, the ambivalent experiences of Filipino migrants in consuming homeland information reflect how the stagnation in homeland structures and systems has also paved the way for migrants' displaced conditions. The imaginaries of the future by the Philippine state for migrants and their left-behind family members reflect the promotion of overseas work, the enactment of family-oriented values through remittances and care packages and entrepreneurialism (Guevarra, 2010; Rodriguez, 2010). Notably, there is a gap in addressing the reunification of family members in the Philippines, which some scholars have already identified as a much-needed intervention via revised state-led initiatives on reintegration programs and national development planning (Asis, 2017). In such terrain, one is then prompted to rethink 'for whom' and 'where' such a better future can be realized. As for the majority of the participants in this study, family futures are imagined by working towards achieving family reunification in Australia.

In conclusion, this chapter highlights the existence of different futures, as imagined and constructed by different actors (Urry, 2016). Imaginaries circulate and shape worlds, lives and intimate relations. However, mobile practices and related 'ruptures' demonstrate how imagined futures are tied to broader social systems that perpetuate hierarchies and marginalization. Ultimately, exploring the influence of exploitative discourse and inadequate social systems on the practices and affective experiences of family futures provides a vantage point for problematizing the imaginaries of progress, inclusivity and a rewarding future in a digital and globalized world.

Note

1 The data presented here were drawn from in-depth interviews (Lindlof and Taylor, 2002) completed between December 2013 and June 2014. The interviews were conducted in Tagalog and Taglish (Tagalog-English), lasting for 45 minutes to an hour. Here, I use pseudonyms for the names of the participants.

Bibliography

Aksoy, A. and Robins, K. (2000). 'Thinking across spaces: Transnational television from Turkey', *European Journal of Cultural Studies*, 3, pp. 343–365.
Amara, R. (1981). 'The futures field: Searching for definitions and boundaries', *Futurist*, 15, p. 25.
Anderson, B. (1998). *The spectre of comparisons: Nationalism, Southeast Asia, and the world*. London: Verso.
Appadurai, A. (1996). *Modernity at large: Cultural dimensions of globalization*. Minneapolis: University of Minnesota Press.
Appadurai, A. (2003). 'Archive and aspiration'. In Brouwer, J. and Mulder, A. (eds.) *Information is alive: Art and theory on archiving and retrieving data*. Rotterdam: NAI Publishers, pp. 14–25.
Asis, M. (1994). 'Family ties in a world without borders', *Philippine Sociological Review*, 42, pp. 16–26.
Asis, M. (2005). 'Caring for the world: Filipino domestic workers gone global'. In Huang, S., Yeoh, B.S.A. and Rahman, N.A. (eds.) *Asian women as transnational domestic workers*. Singapore: Marshall Cavendish Academic, pp. 21–53.
Asis, M. (2017). 'The Philippines: Beyond labor migration, toward development and (possibly) return'. https://www.migrationpolicy.org/article/philippines-beyond-labor-migration-toward-development-and-possibly-return.
Australian Bureau Of Statistics. (2018). *2016 Census QuickStats Country of Birth - Philippines* [Online]. http://www.censusdata.abs.gov.au/census_services/getproduct/census/2016/quickstat/5204_036. [Accessed 15 January 2018].
Bangko Sentral Ng Pilipinas. (2019). *Overseas Filipinos' (OF) remittances* [Online]. http://www.bsp.gov.ph/statistics/keystat/ofw.htm. [Accessed 23 March 2019].
Bonini, T. (2011). 'The media as "home-making" tools: Life story of a Filipino migrant in Milan', *Media Culture Society*, 33, pp. 869–883.
Büscher, M. (2018). 'Social futures'. In Jensen, O., Kesselring, S. and Sheller, M. (eds.) *Mobilities and complexities*. London: Routledge, pp. 185–196.
Cabalquinto, E.C. (2018a). '"I have always thought of my family first": An analysis of transnational caregiving among Filipino migrant adult children in Melbourne, Australia', *International Journal of Communication*, 12, pp. 4011–4029.
Cabalquinto, E.C. (2018b). '"We're not only here but we're there in spirit": Asymmetrical mobile intimacy and the transnational Filipino family', *Mobile Media and Communication*, 6, pp. 1–16.
Cabalquinto, E.C. and Wood-Bradley, G. (2020). 'Migrant platformed subjectivity: Rethinking the mediation of transnational affective economies via digital connectivity services', *International Journal of Cultural Studies*, 23, pp. 737–802.
Cunningham, S. and Sinclair, J. (2001). *Floating lives: The media and Asian diasporas*. Lanham, MD Rowman and Littlefield Publishers.
Francisco-Menchavez, V. (2018). *The labor of care: Filipina migrants and transnational families in the digital age*. Oxford: Marston Book Services.
Gillespie, M. (1995). *Television, ethnicity, and cultural change*. London: Routledge.
Guevarra, A.R. (2010). *Marketing dreams, manufacturing heroes: The transnational labor brokering of Filipino workers*. New Brunswick: Rutgers University Press.
Karim, K.H. (2003). *The media of diaspora*. London: Routledge.
Larsen, G. (2013). *The subclass 457 visa: A quick guide* [Online]. http://www.aph.gov.au/About_Parliament/Parliamentary_Departments/Parliamentary_Library/pubs/rp/rp1314/QG/Subclass457Visa. [Accessed 20 June 2015].

Lindlof, T.R. and Taylor, B.C. (2002). *Qualitative communication research methods*. Thousand Oaks, CA: Sage Publications.
Madianou, M. (2005). *Mediating the nation: News, audiences and the politics of identity*. London: UCL Press.
Madianou, M. and Miller, D. (2012). *Migration and new media: Transnational families and polymedia*. Abingdon, Oxon: Routledge.
Mckay, D. (2007). '"Sending dollars shows feeling" - Emotions and economies in Filipino migration', *Mobilities*, 2, pp. 175–194.
Mckay, D. (2012). *Global Filipinos migrants' lives in the virtual village*. Bloomington: Indiana University Press.
Mckay, D. (2016). *An archipelago of care: Filipino migrants and global networks*. Bloomington: Indiana University Press.
Naficy, H. (1993). *The making of exile cultures: Iranian television in Los Angeles*. Minneapolis: University of Minnesota Press.
Naficy, H. (2003). 'Narrowcasting in diaspora: Middle Eastern television in Los Angeles'. In Karim, K.H. (ed.) *The media of diaspora*. London: Routledge, pp. 51–62.
Ong, J.C. and Cabañes, J. (2011). 'Engaged, but not immersed: Tracking the mediated public connection of Filipino elite migrants in London', *South East Asia Research*, 19, pp. 197–224.
Papademetriou, D. and Sumption, M. (2011). *Rethinking points systems and employer-selected immigration*. Washington, DC: Migration Policy Institute.
Paragas, F. (2006). *Eccentric networks: Patterns of interpersonal communication, organizational participation, and mass media use by Overseas Filipino Workers* [Online]. https://etd.ohiolink.edu/ap/10?0::NO:10:P10_ACCESSION_NUM:ohiou1147119861. [Accessed 21 August 2015].
Paragas, F. (2009). 'Migrant workers and mobile phones: Technological, temporal, and spatial simultaneity'. In Ling, R.S. and Campbell, S. (eds.) *The reconstruction of space and time: Mobile communication practices*. New Brunswick, NJ: Transaction, pp. 39–66.
Parreñas, R.S. (2001a). 'Mothering from a distance: Emotions, gender, and intergenerational relations in Filipino transnational families', *Feminist Studies*, 27, pp. 361–390.
Parreñas, R.S. (2001b). *Servants of globalization: Women, migration and domestic work*. Stanford, CA: Stanford University Press.
Parreñas, R.S. (2005). 'Long distance intimacy: Class, gender and intergenerational relations between mothers and children in Filipino transnational families', *Global Networks*, 5, pp. 317–336.
Parreñas, R.S. (2008). 'Transnational fathering: Gendered conflicts, distant disciplining and emotional gaps', *Journal of Ethnic and Migration Studies*, 34, pp. 1057–1072.
Poea. (2019). *Philippine overseas employment administration, 2015–2016 overseas employment statistics* [Online]. www.poea.gov.ph/ofwstat/compendium/2015-2016%20OES%201.pdf. [Accessed 21 July 2019].
Rodriguez, R.M. (2010). *Migrants for export: How the Philippine state brokers labor to the world*. Minneapolis: The University of Minnesota Press.
San Juan, E. (2000). 'Trajectories of the Filipino diaspora', *Ethnic Studies Report*, XVII, pp. 229–238.
San Juan, E. (2001). 'The Filipino diaspora', *Philippine Studies*, 49, pp. 255–264.
San Juan, E. (2011). 'Contemporary global capitalism and the challenge of the Filipino diaspora', *Global Society*, 25, pp. 7–27.
Tadiar, N.X.M. (2004). *Fantasy production: Sexual economies and other Philippine consequences for the new world order*. Hong Kong: Hong Kong University Press.
Urry, J. (2016). *What is the future?* Cambridge: Polity Press.

13
Higher education
The future university

Carl Gombrich and Ashley Jay Brockwell

Introduction

We are two academics engaged in founding a new university at the London Interdisciplinary School (LIS). Such a venture provides an opportunity to explore many of the underlying principles of a university, from its teaching, learning, assessment and research culture, to its admissions policy, to its role as an institution situated in the United Kingdom in the twenty-first century. And, indeed, the founders of LIS are committed to rethinking along all these dimensions; we recognize the high quality elsewhere throughout UK higher education and feel there is little value in starting something new in order to replicate existing ideas, norms and structures.

The call to discuss 'Social Futures' resonates with many of our institutional priorities and provides the broad canvas for this paper. However, in keeping with our name, the importance of *interdisciplinarity* in shaping the university (and in underpinning its social nature) is explored in detail and emerges as a central idea, uniting other themes. These themes include the level and type of commitment appropriate to furthering social and epistemic justice and the role of the spiritual in a contemporary university. Alongside these more normative topics about the curriculum, we describe two structural models – the Civic University and the Porous University – that may arise out of curricular commitments.

The main body of the paper is structured in the form of a conversation between the two co-authors – Professor Carl Gombrich, Academic Lead and Director of Teaching and Learning, and Dr Ashley Jay (Ash) Brockwell, a member of the founding faculty. We have chosen this structure over a traditional prose format for two interrelated reasons. First, our intent is to disrupt some of the tacit conventions of academic writing, thereby awakening the recognition that 'compliance with [conventions] cannot be taken for granted' (Burford, 2015, p. 5; Kagan, 2014, p. 409). This counter-conventional approach surfaces just a few of the many beliefs and habits that are widely regarded as 'common sense' and – in accordance with the subject matter – invites the reader to reflect on which of their other long-established assumptions and practices might ultimately be negotiable. Second, we feel that the conversational format preserves the distinctiveness of our separate visions of 'the future university' – allowing them to be contrasted, while also making their commonalities visible.

DOI: 10.4324/9780429440717-14

This approach means that we do not present one argument in the traditional way of an academic paper. Rather, we present a dialogue on shared interests but with divergent viewpoints and naturally occurring tensions, even contradictions. This reflects some of the best practices of interdisciplinary working itself – something we remark on towards the end of this chapter.

Background

Before our discussion, we describe some of the historical background against which the foundation of a university in the United Kingdom in the twenty-first century – and hence the material of our paper – is set. For brevity – and because this is the context of our university – this potted history is decidedly Eurocentric (or even Anglocentric). Nevertheless, remarks about the proportions of populations attending higher education and its historically elite nature apply broadly across many different cultures and civilizations.

In their long and complex histories, universities have not obviously always been about 'the social' – at least not if we understand the term as applying to some conception of wider society, a polity or a larger group of people bound by a shared culture, legal system or values. In Europe, the first universities of the medieval period educated a small elite to become lawyers, clerics and then medics (Ruegg and De Ridder Symoens, 2003). The Renaissance saw a widening of this mission to produce more worldly graduates, competent navigators of the new revolutions in knowledge (Brotton, 2006), and, especially in the nineteenth century, there were later intellectually significant shifts as new disciplines and new models of a university were established. However, such 'tertiary education' (as we now call it) applied to so few people that its relevance to wider society can only be considered through the lens of how such an education affected the world view of the ruling elite and how this then filtered down (if at all) to the lives of ordinary people. This elite nature of tertiary education in Europe lasted into the late twentieth century; in 1970, in the UK, only 8.4% of the population went to university (Bolton, 2012).

However, the explosion in higher education attendance (not just in the United Kingdom but throughout the world) in the late twentieth and twenty-first centuries (see e.g. Shofer and Meyer, 2005) has naturally wrought a conversation about the purpose of a university into a conversation more specifically about the role of the university *in society* (Sperlinger et al., 2018; Willetts, 2013).

If around 50% of a given society is undertaking some kind of tertiary education, then this is the concern of everyone in that society. Questions arise. If taxpayers' money is going to university, who benefits? Is it right that people who do not go to university should subsidize the education of those who do? What disciplines should be taught or prioritized? Should these disciplines be chosen according to the national interest (presumably defined by governments) or market demands, more driven by students (Jones and Cunliffe, 2020)? Or are 'disciplines' simply the wrong way to think about what is taught at a modern university? Can universities offer an education which is both liberal (in the sense of developing the mind of the individual) and neoliberal (in the sense of servicing the job market of a capitalist society)? Should universities be attempting to drive an agenda (political/social/cultural) – somewhat at odds with their historic purpose – or respond to some form of external needs, as they have formerly done? Or is there a 'third way' in which universities remain radically open to, informed by and integrated with wider society, while offering visions of and practical steps towards a better future?

It is these last two questions which our dialogue explores in more detail, with interdisciplinarity, one of the other subjects surfaced in the questions above, emerging as a point of focus.

Discussion

CARL: Ash, perhaps an obvious way in which a university can be 'social' is to concern itself with social justice. Could you first tell me more about the particular focus of eco-social justice and how you see this playing out in a university curriculum?

ASH: I'm using 'eco-social' here in the sense defined by Heather Boetto (2017),[1] in calling for a shift towards a transformative eco-social model. Whereas Boetto sets out this model within the context of social work as a profession, there are a lot of synergies with the ongoing conversations around education for sustainable futures, and it's in this latter context that I'm raising it here. In thinking about eco-social *justice* specifically, I'm highlighting the overlaps between Boetto's model and Miranda Fricker's ideas about epistemic justice (Fricker, 2009).

Boetto talks about an ontology of the eco-social as being consciously aware of our own interconnectedness with the natural world, at the level of identity – recognizing that our well-being depends on the collective well-being of others. Epistemologically, it draws on ideas like ecological literacy, eco-feminism, criticality, global citizenship, de-growth, sustainability and diverse Indigenous worldviews. Methodologically, it overlaps with ecotherapy at the individual level but also seeks ways to bring about transformative change at collective, community and political levels.

Boetto doesn't define eco-social justice as such, but discusses *ecological* justice from two different angles: First, in the sense of 'acknowledging justice as important for all living organisms' and, second, 'recognition of the disproportionate effect of the environmental crisis on the world's poorest citizens' (Boetto, 2017, p. 54). The latter is difficult to implement, but the concept itself is relatively straightforward. Justice for all living organisms is a much more challenging idea, though – opening debates about which organisms' rights should be upheld at the expense of which others. We can move beyond any impasse by using a lens of epistemic justice to link these ideas back to the ontology of interconnectedness.

Fricker (2009) distinguishes two types of epistemic injustice: *Testimonial injustice*, which refers to the impact of prejudice on individuals' credibility, and *hermeneutical injustice*, which is about how hegemony makes it difficult for marginalized people to communicate their insights because concepts that are central to their worldview don't exist in the dominant language. Thus, the beginning of what I'm calling eco-social justice' would involve creating space for Indigenous people to talk about embodied, spiritual and holistic aspects of human relationships with the natural world in their own terms and making those terms comprehensible to speakers of English and other dominant languages. This also overlaps with what Boaventura de Sousa Santos (2014) refers to as 'justice against epistemicide'.

CARL: I'd like to start from a different position regarding the social to explore how we might approach one another. Most universities are – as large, quasi-public institutions – embedded in societies. They are both, therefore, *of* that society and have an obligation *to* that society in the sense that they rely on the surrounding economic and societal norms for their existence. This leads us to the position espoused by Alan Wilson that we should look at immediate problems as they present themselves in other organizations, institutions and society outside universities and understand how we, as universities, can contribute to tackling these problems.

From what you have said of eco-social and epistemic justice, I would regard my position as more practical and less theoretical. This is not to deny that universities can move society in certain directions – and the importance of theory and conceptual work in this may be key – but it takes as a starting point a close listening to external partners embedded in society outside universities, rather than other theoreticians. This is what we mean by the Porous University, as first described by Michael Stewart (2015).

I am concerned that much modern academic work is, really, first and foremost of interest to other scholars and academics. It is twenty-first-century scholasticism. By this, I mean not just the content of the work, but a related cluster of things associated with current academia: Hyper-specialization – so that much research is unintelligible outside of small, initiated in-groups; the problem of the production of uncited and unread articles (Williams, 2014); elements of rent seeking and subtle forms of corruption in the peer review system (Fuller, 2016); and the problematic overheads of the current research funding system. This list of issues leads me to believe that large chunks of the current system cannot endure as they are essentially elitist and exclusive. Do you think this is a fair criticism?

ASH: I share your concerns about academic jargon making research inaccessible to those outside the respective hyper-specialized communities, but I'd question whether that's the norm. I've spent a large part of my academic career working in a post-1992 university – a former polytechnic – where a lot of effort was devoted to improving accessibility. Much of their research was conducted through practice in subjects such as nursing, social work or urban planning, often through long-term collaborations with charities and other civil society organizations. That led to a wide range of innovative research methodologies – participatory action research, transformative mixed method research, 'research through design' and so on.

Where I think we might agree is that there's a certain type of skill gap in higher education that very few of the established universities are effectively addressing. I'd say that's particularly true of transferable skills – such as how to collaborate effectively, how to distinguish information from misinformation and how to take a reflexive approach to everything you're doing – which often fall through the gaps between disciplines. The social sciences are strong on reflexivity, while the natural sciences are strong on weighing up evidence and assessing probabilities, but it's rare for someone to study both together – and, at least in the United Kingdom, higher education is still very individualistic. It's rare for students to be directly taught how to work with others or to be assessed on their teamwork skills. As such, I think an interdisciplinary approach is vital or something like Nicolescu's (2002) *Manifesto of Transdisciplinarity* to make space for the messy parts that don't mesh well with conventional understandings of academia.

CARL: Yes, I agree fully with your characterization of necessary skills across the traditional 'arts and sciences' divide, as well as your comments about the importance of collaboration. I am wary, however, about getting drawn into the somewhat tired philosophical debate about 'knowledge vs skills', 'knowledge that vs knowledge how'. Perhaps referring to 'research methods' as tools for knowledge production rather than 'skills' might steer us productively towards what university students should learn and be more appropriate for a conversation about tertiary education?

Be that as it may, what is interesting in this dialogue is that we agree that interdisciplinarity or transdisciplinarity is key, but for different reasons. Alan Wilson (2010) describes how interdisciplinarity arises through a systems science approach to tackling almost all real-world problems, and Steve Fuller (2012) builds on the well-known work of Gibbons et al. (1994) in defining transdisciplinarity as that intellectual work which specifically looks beyond the academy for its stimulation and evidence of importance. This more instrumental version of inter- or transdisciplinarity seems, if not at odds with, then orthogonal to Basarab Nicolescu's ideas. Would you agree with that?

ASH: I haven't seen much in Nicolescu's writings that specifically examine relationships between the academy and society. He hints at it in the Preface to *Transdisciplinarity and Sustainability*, though, where he critiques reductionistic and binary approaches to sustainable development – the tendency to reduce everything to 'society, economy and environment' and ignore what he describes as 'individual, spiritual and cosmic levels of Reality' (Nicolescu, 2012, p. VI).

Domingo Adame (2012) takes this further by citing Nicolescu's ideas in his reflections on moving from a disciplinary to a transdisciplinary university. Adame's core premise is that the nation and the university should be 'reinventing each other at the same time', in a circular process of social transformation. Do you think that's a realistic aspiration? Or should the role of universities centre on addressing problems as they're currently defined by corporate, state and community actors, rather than challenging those actors' ideas about what constitutes a problem?

CARL: It's hard to resist a warm, fuzzy feeling that universities are important enough to reinvent society, so I would go along with that! More seriously, Adame's idea is perhaps a good way to conceive of a university which is inherently more social, now that – as we noted – a significant proportion of many societies are directly involved in higher education. Whether or not we think sustainability is the key issue, I think it is attractive and democratic to think of this double causal loop between universities and parts of society 'outside' university. So long as universities really listen to 'outsiders' – even those they might not think of as their natural allies – then I would support this. Do you feel that the recent attempt to revive the concept of the Civic University in the United Kingdom makes any relevant contribution here?

ASH: I can see the concept of the double causal loop, as you call it, or 'mutual reinvention' in Adame's terms, resonating with the early history of the civic university movement in the United Kingdom. As Jones (2019) explains, the original mission of what later became known as 'redbrick universities' wasn't just to meet the needs of individuals, but also to serve their respective localities – building libraries and museums, offering public lectures, improving schools, training experts to improve and expand emergent industries and so on. In that respect, they both created and responded to demands within society

The recent interest in the concept – mainly led by John Goddard and the non-profit Universities Partnership Programme (UPP) Foundation, which set up a Civic University Commission in 2019 – does feel like a positive step towards reclaiming a sense of civic mission, which has arguably been neglected in recent decades. The Commission promotes a holistic view of active engagement with communities, rooted in an understanding of local needs and a focussed agenda, and calls on universities to serve as role models in areas like local and ethical procurement. It also encourages them to build partnerships with other 'anchor' institutions – local government, major businesses and non-profits and so on – to enhance the economic and social well-being of their communities (Brabner, 2019; UPP, 2019). But I feel it's too early to say how that's going to translate into practice.

CARL: I think this presents some interesting tensions around what we mean by the social and how universities should engage with it. On the one hand, I strongly agree that universities should be fully engaged with their local communities. And, as an aside, this gives me a chance to acknowledge your helpful corrective to my concerns about elitism and scholasticism above. In post-1992 universities, there may, as you say, be more of this sort of engagement anyway, but Russell Group universities also have strong public outreach and engagement programmes of different types. University College London, to take just one example, has been pioneering in its use of museums and collections for outreach and public engagement and, through programmes like Professor Helen Chatterjee's work in art, culture and health is now blending this with undergraduate and postgraduate courses that work directly with local community and health projects (Chatterjee and Noble, 2013). This should certainly be part of the thinking of all universities: Get students out of lecture halls and have them co-create projects and carry out research with local communities. And, again, I think this points (as with Chatterjee's work) to more interdisciplinary and mixed method programmes as you have outlined above.

However, to return to the nature of social engagement, for many graduates, work after university will be digital and thus, inherently, global – less local. There is little point in forcing a local connection to work and study if you are part of a user experience team or a digital health business with members based in Mumbai, Valparaiso and San Diego. In this tension, we see something like the dichotomy outlined by David Goodhart (2017), describing the 'somewheres' vs the 'anywheres' as categories helpful in understanding the growing polarization we see in politics – those loyal to tradition, local culture, local heritage and place vs those 'citizens of the world', committed to universal human values, to a shared sense of globalization and to cultural cosmopolitanism. In the recent votes for Brexit and throughout Europe and the United States, it is clear that universities are mostly populated by and aligned with the 'anywheres', but this puts them at odds with the small but significant majority of 'somewheres'. Universities ignore their local somewheres at their peril. So, in educating undergraduates, some blending of the local with an understanding of what a job in the global, digital economy looks like seems essential.

ASH: I agree with you there. I think there's a lot to be gained by recovering a sense of localism – of 'somewhereness', if you like – but that doesn't have to, and indeed shouldn't, come at the expense of an 'anywhere' (or even 'everywhere'?) mindset. It's important to bear in mind that a lot of the toughest problems we face are global rather than local in nature – climate change, pollution, COVID-19 and the enormous potential for spillover of new pandemic viruses from animals to humans and, of course, social issues like discrimination, the legacies of colonialism and enslavement and the widening gaps between rich and poor. John McMurtry (2002) talks about a global crisis of values resulting in the neglect of what he calls 'life capital', which encompasses all the things that we usually describe as ecosystem services – unpolluted fertile soil, breathable air, drinkable water and so on – but also includes community assets like literacy and shared knowledge.

These ideas bring me back to Domingo Adame, with his call for universities to reintroduce 'dimensions of life and, as far as possible, of love' into all domains of education. This feels like quite a controversial position – maybe less so in Mexico, where there's already a well-established movement of intercultural universities integrating Indigenous world views and spiritualities (see, for example, Burford et al., 2012), but in a British higher education context, it feels almost taboo to talk about love, sacredness or the soul outside theological colleges. Do these more intangible dimensions of human experience have any place in your vision of the future of universities, especially here in the United Kingdom?

CARL: I love this question! Alistair McIntyre (2009) makes the case that universities in the West have lost their way since they gave up a shared vision of God as their binding factor. Referencing Clark Kerr's earlier analysis of the modern university, he states, 'Universities have become, perhaps irremediably, fragmented and partitioned institutions, better renamed "multiuniversities"' and goes on to say that for both Aquinas and Newman, their conception of the university was 'informed by [their] conception of the universe' (MacIntyre, 2009, p. 174). I think there is a good case to be made that the fracturing of the disciplines in the twentieth-century West is connected to a lack of shared vision in universities: It is easier to create closed communities around academic disciplines and departments – with shared canons, methods, etc. – than it is to unite disciplines under one vision of 'God' or 'the universe' when what we mean by those things is increasingly contested.

However, MacIntyre's analysis highlights both the power and the danger of a 'shared vision' Whose vision? And who gets to share in it? I am sensitive to these dangers. Too often the intellectual classes have either been appropriated by a monolithic political or religious world view or propounded such a view themselves. This has happened in societies as divergent as the Third Reich, with Nazi Science and Saudi Arabia, with the Muslim Brotherhood – although, of course, both societies also had their notable (and brave) intellectual dissidents.

I would define myself as religious, so some kind of spiritual communion is important in my life. However, my squeamishness about totalitarian thought makes me reluctant to allow universities to bring in the explicitly spiritual or even 'holistic' – unless we can do that in a way that allows for the inherent diversity of humanity and multiple dissidents! This may be possible, and, indeed, perhaps we should try, but I think it is a great strength of a more classical liberal education that it allows students to work out such things for themselves.

ASH: I agree this is potentially perilous ground! As I understand Adame's position on spirituality, though, he's not talking about imposing a monolithic vision of religion or a political totalitarianism. Rather, he calls on universities to promote intercultural academic dialogues relating to 'the inner experience and culture of the soul', and to reflect on ways of meeting students' need for self-transformation. This may be easier said than done, and I understand your squeamishness here. Yet, I still feel that dimensions like love, inclusivity, equity, intercultural communication, individual and collective responsibility and explorations of the interdependence of human and non-human lifeworlds (which we might include under the umbrella of 'interconnectedness studies') are too important to humanity's future to be left out of the curriculum. I wonder if a focus on 'ethical values' might be a way of broaching these concerns, without alienating people by coming across as overly religious or esoteric? I'd argue that courses specializing in one or two disciplines often downplay the importance of ethical and moral questions, especially in engineering and the physical sciences – or perhaps it might be more accurate to say that they lack the tools to address them holistically.

CARL: Yes, I think I broadly agree with you and am supportive of your desire to open the possibility in academia for such things as love, inclusion and interconnectedness. I admire your attempt to be radical here – and I agree with the implication of what you are saying – that both ethics and interconnectedness are best served by an interdisciplinary curriculum.

Since many of the ideas we have so far discussed are, in our context, progressive ideas, I feel bound to say that they contrast with some of what we are seeing in the Social Justice activism-scholarship movement and related attempts to be radical. Many of the criticisms of Social Justice scholarship pertaining to its totalizing and illiberal attributes, such as recently described by Pluckrose and Lindsay (2020), are correct. It is illiberal to outlaw certain words, to privilege group identity over the individual or the universal, even – I would say – to deny science or dismiss the possibility of objectivity. None of these are well aligned with love, inclusion or a wider consciousness. This is not to say that social justice (in lower case) is not immensely important (how could it not be!), and perhaps the more extreme current elements of activism scholarship are playing a vital role in forcing us to look at uncomfortable truths which we have been avoiding, but in seeking positive change we should avoid jumping on this bandwagon as with any other.

ASH: That's a fair point. Identity is a difficult, murky and often painful area to grapple with, and the scholars of the future are going to need both creativity and empathy to solve this complex problem. Debates about the limits of free speech have been going on for centuries, but right now, people at both ends of the political spectrum seem to be escalating tensions rather than defusing them. On the one hand, as you point out, there's an emergent 'anti-scientism' and dismissal of expertise that is deeply worrying. On the other, terms like 'political correctness', 'cancel culture', 'social justice warriors' and so on are increasingly being weaponized against writers and speakers who – rightly, in my view – shine a light on what you describe as uncomfortable truths. I'd be inclined to put it more bluntly and talk about the real and lasting impacts of imperialism, slavery and genocide (e.g. Azoulay, 2020), as well as the effects of misogyny, homophobia and transphobia, on people's lived experiences and life chances. What position would you take on these imbalances of power and how they play out in society?

CARL: I think there is one obvious way that Social Justice scholarship has a narrow ontological (as well as epistemological) view: The privileging of 'power' as a lens through which all explanations must pass. This has all the hallmarks of a 'Theory of Everything' (ToE), such as one also finds in bad theoretical science.

ToEs over-simplify. It is easy (and misguided) to make a case that 'everything is a result of evolution' or 'everything is a result of the processes of entropy', just as it is easy and misguided to say 'everything is a result of power relations in human society'. All these explanations are simplifications, all are partial and none, to my mind, show sufficient epistemic humility or the possibility of radical emergence in knowledge and understanding.

So, to answer your question more directly: A discussion of social justice must take in more than just a discussion of the imbalances of power. It must include history, biology, psychology, philosophy. Interdisciplinarity again!

The concepts that can act as foundation stones for ToEs are a subset of 'superconcepts', a term coined by Alan Wilson (2010). He identified a range of concepts that emerge in disciplinary settings but go on to have explanatory power outside their original area of application. Such superconcepts give us powerful interdisciplinary tools for understanding the world – and students enjoy grappling with them. But they can be *too* beguiling! Spend two weeks immersed in the (super)concept of evolution, and you can come to believe that *everything* we experience and know – and thus our entire metaphysics and epistemology – is the result of evolutionary processes. This can also occur in many of the humanities and social science subjects where, to repeat, there is this tendency to say that *everything* is the result of power relations. On an interdisciplinary programme, perhaps this could be remedied by taking courses in other equally powerful, superconcepts.

Let us explore interdisciplinarity further, as we agree on its importance and share the belief that the future university must grapple with this idea. For me, interdisciplinarity often leads to *inherently emergent outcomes*. You literally cannot predict in advance what will emerge from many interdisciplinary collaborations. The same may of course be true of more creative monodisciplinary work, but it is a definitional claim of interdisciplinarity that it exists to provide outcomes 'which would not have been possible without two or more disciplinary perspectives' (Gombrich, 2020). So, the claim in the context of this discussion is that interdisciplinarity (and transdisciplinarity) are more radical and open-ended than any spiritual or politically motivated framework would allow. Such methodologies are inherently transformative and may, or may not, lead to more social justice, better environmental outcomes.

This may sound a little highfalutin: 'Let's just let all the disciplines mingle freely in a creative way and it's likely some great things will emerge'. And, in fact, I do believe that leaving some space for such an approach is important. When you note many of the great intellectual advances in history – from diverse societies – as recounted, for example in Waqas Ahmed's book on polymaths (Ahmed, 2018), you see that this sort of intellectual free play is essential to progress. However, we can also use the emergent properties of interdisciplinarity (or transdisciplinarity, with its properties of going beyond the binary) while focussing on concrete problems, things that matter to people outside the spheres that might usually be described as academic. It's in this latter approach that I think there is a big gap in UK education.

ASH: I agree with you that leaving space for free play and emergence in interdisciplinary education is crucially important, but the notion of focussing on 'concrete problems that matter to people outside academia' brings us back to the questions that you raised earlier – whose vision, and who gets to share in it? In this case, who gets to define what matters and what constitutes a concrete problem? From the perspective of a group of indigenous activists, the problem might be a fossil fuel company driving them off their ancestral land; but in the eyes of the CEO, it might be the activists that are the problem, in the sense that they're damaging the company's global brand and its profit margins.

An even greater concern for me is the unprecedented threat that global heating poses to our survival as a species. Can we, as interdisciplinary educators, afford to be blasé about whether or not our methodologies lead to better environmental outcomes? Most people ignore climate change scientists when they say things like 'we have 18 months left to fix this', or, worse, 'we should have fixed this 18 months ago', because it feels too frightening and too complex to think about. But if anyone's ever going to be equipped to persuade individuals, companies and governments to reduce their carbon emissions, it won't be single-discipline specialists. Precisely because it's enormously complex and challenging, this could be an arena where polymaths will have a real chance to shine.

CARL: Perhaps it won't be a surprise to either of us that we have reached a kind of 'meta'-point, often encountered in interdisciplinary working itself: In our differing positions, there are several areas of consensus – in which some kind of integration or synthesis takes place – but also elements of what I have characterized as dissensus (Gombrich, 2016). When dissensus occurs in interdisciplinary work, disciplinary positions are (at least temporarily) unable to integrate.

I would characterize our consensus as forming around the following:

- a desire to include a discussion of the 'social' in the role of the future university,
- an agreement on the importance of both the local and the global in any discussion of sociality,
- a recognition of the fact that it is essential to consider the theoretical and practical aspects of inter- and transdisciplinarity in such a discussion,
- an openness to hearing different views on how to progress this discussion,
- a willingness to include some talk of radical ideas, including spirituality and personal transformation.

However, we differ on several details as to where we think the drivers of social thinking should come from.

ASH: That's a fair summary of where we have arrived for now. I'd add that we share a recognition of the need to preserve space for free play and emergence within interdisciplinary encounters – even though there's a tension between this and my call for a focus on the climate emergency. More broadly, I'd say we differ on priorities, especially in relation to transdisciplinary work that centres epistemologies from the global South – which are often non-anthropocentric – and decolonial methodologies (e.g. de Sousa Santos, 2018).[2] I believe the urgency of this will become even more evident in the coming years, as the higher education sector grapples with the challenges of 'sustainability'. I agree with you, though, that this process of finding common ground – while holding space for diversity and dissensus in a positive and respectful way – mirrors the inter- or transdisciplinary process itself. It's been a very thought-provoking and interesting conversation.

CARL: Thank you, Ash. Perhaps here we might break the more traditional academic writing 'fourth wall' and say that we trust that, for our readers, this serves as a conclusion to our discussion of the nature of the 'social' in future universities and the centrality of interdisciplinarity in this discussion.

Notes

1 There have been other uses of the term in different contexts, notably in Nancy Krieger's eco-social theory of disease distribution (Krieger, 2001), which has some commonalities with this discussion but is beyond the scope of this paper to explore in detail.
2 'Epistemologies from the global South' are not used here as an exclusively geographical category; it includes, for example, the epistemologies of Black and Indigenous communities within the United States and Europe (see, for example, Meyerhoff, 2019).

Bibliography

Bolton, P. (2012). *Education: Historical statistics*. Available at: https://commonslibrary.parliament.uk/-research-briefings/sn04252/ (Accessed: 31 January 2021).

Brabner, R. (2019). 'Over 50 universities pledge commitment to local communities through Civic University Agreement - UPP Foundation (upp-foundation.org)'. https://upp-foundation.org/over-50-universities-pledge-commitment-to-local-communities-through-civic-university-agreement/ (Accessed 31 January 2021).

Brotton, J. (2006). *The Renaissance: A very short introduction*. New York: Oxford University Press.

Burford, G. (2015). 'Collaborative research for sustainability: An inside-out design manifesto'. Community Innovation and Social Innovation Centre (CASIC) Working Paper 1. Keele, UK: CASIC. http://www.doc.uments.com/s-collaborative-research-for-sustainability-an-inside-out-design.pdf (Accessed 31 January 2021).

Burford, G., Kissmann, S., Rosado-May, F.J., Alvarado Dzul, S.H. and Harder, M.K. (2012). 'Indigenous participation in intercultural education: Learning from Mexico and Tanzania', *Ecology and Society*, 17(4), p. 33. http://dx.doi.org/10.5751/ES-05250-170433

Chatterjee, H.J. and Noble, G. (2013). *Museums, health and well-being*. Farnham: Ashgate Publishing Ltd.

de Sousa Santos, B. (2014). *Epistemologies of the South: Justice against epistemicide*. London and New York: Routledge.

de Sousa Santos, B. (2018). *The end of the cognitive empire: The coming of age of epistemologies of the South*. Durham, NC: Duke University Press.

Fricker, M. (2009). *Epistemic injustice. Power and the ethics of knowing*. Oxford: Oxford University Press.

Fuller, S. (2012). *Steve Fuller (Warwick University) on interdisciplinarity, part 1*. Available at https://blogs.lse.ac.uk/impactofsocialsciences/2014/04/23/academic-papers-citation-rates-remler/ (Accessed: 31 January 2021).

Fuller, S. (2016). *The academic Caesar*. Thousand Oaks, CA: Sage Publications.

Gibbons, M., Limoges, C., Nowotny, H., Schwartzman, S., Scott, P. and Trow, M. (1994). *The new production of knowledge: The dynamics of science and research in contemporary societies*. London, Thousand Oaks, CA, and New Delhi: Sage.

Gombrich, C. (2016). 'What sort of interdisciplinary research can undergraduates do?', *Interdisciplinary Science Reviews*, 41(4), pp. 332–334.

Gombrich, C. (2020). *University evolution: interdisciplinary degree programmes*. Available at https://insights.ise.org.uk/policy/blog-university-evolution-interdisciplinary-degree-programmes/ (Accessed: 31 January 2021).

Goodhart, D. (2017). *The road to somewhere: The populist revolt and the future of politics*. New York: Oxford University Press.

Jones, D.R. (2019). *The origins of civic universities: Manchester, Leeds and Liverpool*. London: Routledge.

Jones, L. and Cunliffe, P. (2020). *Saving Britain's universities*. Available at https://www.cieo.org.uk/wp-content/uploads/2020/08/Saving-Britains-Universities-Cieo-1-1.pdf (Accessed: 31 January 20210).

Kagan, S. (2014). *Art and sustainability: Connecting patterns for a culture of complexity*. Columbia University Press.

Krieger, N. (2001). 'Theories for social epidemiology in the twenty-first century: An ecosocial perspective', *International Journal of Epidemiology*, 30(4), pp. 668–677.

MacIntyre, A. (2009). *God, philosophy and universities*. York: Continuum Books.

McMurtry, J. (2002). *Value wars: The global market versus the life economy*. Sterling, VA: Pluto Press.

Meyerhoff, E. (2019). *Beyond education: Radical studying for another world*. Minneapolis: University of Minnesota Press.

Nicolescu, B. (2002). *Manifesto of transdisciplinarity*. Albany: State University of New York Press.

Nicolescu, B. (2012). *Transdisciplinarity and sustainability*. Lubbock, TX: Atlas Publishing.

Pluckrose, H. and Lindsay, J. (2020). *Cynical theories*. Croydon: Swift Press.

Ruegg, W. and De Ridder-Symoens, H. (eds.) (2003) *A history of the university in Europe, Volume 1: Universities in the middle ages*. Cambridge: Cambridge University Press.

Schofer, E. and Meyer, J. (2005). 'The worldwide expansion of higher education in the twentieth century', *American Sociological Review*, 70(6), pp. 898–920.

Sperlinger, T., McLellan, J. and Pettigrew, R. (2018). *Who are universities for?: Remaking higher education*. Bristol: Bristol University Press.

Stewart, M. (2015). *The porous university*. Available at https://blogs.lse.ac.uk/impactofsocialsciences/2015/05/12/the-porous-university-michael-stewart/ (Accessed: 31 January 2021).

UPP Foundation (2019). *Truly civic: Strengthening the connection between universities and their places*. Final report of the Civic University Commission. www.upp-foundation.org (Accessed: 31 January 2021).

Willetts, D. (2013). *Robbins revisited: Bigger and better higher education.* Available at http://www.smf.co.uk/wp-content/uploads/2013/10/Publication-Robbins-Revisited-Bigger-and-Better-Higher-Education-David-Willetts.pdf (Accessed: 31 January 2021).

Williams, S. (2014). *Are 90% of academic papers really never cited.* Available at https://blogs.lse.ac.uk/impactofsocialsciences/2014/04/23/academic-papers-citation-rates-remler/ (Accessed: 31 January 2021).

Wilson, A. (2010). *Knowledge power. Interdisciplinary Education for a Complex World.* Abingdon, Oxon: Routledge.

14
Inquiries
Healthcare futures

Dawn Goodwin and Richard Tutton

Introduction: 'Learning the lessons' of healthcare failures – empiricism or imagination as a basis for anticipatory knowledge?

In the United Kingdom, independent inquiries have become a key tool in the government's response to high-profile organizational failures, disasters or flagrant abuses of professional standards. Their increasing frequency in the United Kingdom has led Jasanoff (2005, p. 218) to identify them as 'Britain's favoured mechanism for ascertaining the facts after any major breakdown or controversy', and, more recently, Norris and Shepheard (2017, p. 6) have claimed that inquiries in the United Kingdom 'are now a permanent fixture in public life'.

The NHS (National Health Service) is not exempt from such developments. Reflecting on a series of scandals at the turn of the century, the editor of the *British Medical Journal* noted: 'Inquiries into crimes and misdemeanours are becoming a way of life in Britain's NHS' (Smith, 2000). Inquiries into healthcare failures are primarily a method of investigation, generally expected to answer the questions: What happened, who is responsible and what can be learnt from the events (Norris and Shepheard, 2017). However, the increasing number of inquiries cannot be understood simply in terms of an increase in serious incidents (Burgess, 2011), rather it signals a shift in UK society as to how healthcare failures are investigated and redress achieved (Goodwin, 2018); inquiries are a more public form of investigation, with open hearings and interactive websites allowing for greater external scrutiny and more transparency for those affected by the events. As Greer and McLaughlin (2017, p. 16–17) observe, 'they are more explicitly victim-centred, incorporating victim input into their terms of reference and ensuring victim participation throughout proceedings' and, through their communication strategies, they can impact directly on public understanding of what went wrong.

The growing influence of inquiries in society, and their increasingly prominent role in the investigation and governance of healthcare, prompts questions about how they fulfil their remit to learn the lessons of the past and shape the future to avoid such disasters from recurring. In this respect, inquiries can be seen as a mechanism of governance involved in the construction and management of risk. This operates at two levels, First it is claimed the staging of an inquiry assists in managing the political situation by conveying a sense of decisive action in circumstances of public discontent (Smith, 2000; Walshe and Higgins, 2002; Greer and McLaughlin,

2017). If timely and conducted well, inquiries can provide reassurance and rebuild public confidence (Walshe, 2019) while distancing government from the scandal and positioning the state as part of the solution rather than part of the problem (Greer and McLaughlin, 2017).

Second, inquiries aim to intervene at a more operational level, specifying actions necessary to remediate organizational failings and intersecting with existing forms of regulation. Although not formally related to regulation, inquiries are linked to the expansion of regulation that often follows high-profile incidents. Burgess (2011) has called them 'instruments of micro-regulation' and warned that inquiries can 'reinforce the dangerous illusion that risk can be eliminated and that accidents are necessarily symptomatic of systematic negligence and likely to only grow worse without unlimited regulation'.

As a means of accountability, however, inquiries have been subject to much criticism. Boudes and Laroche (2009) question whether inquiry reports provide actionable recommendations, suggesting that history casts serious doubt in this regard. Many other commentators agree, pointing to the repetitive themes within inquiry recommendations (Dingwall, 1986; Williams and Kevern, 2016; Powell, 2019; Timmins, 2019). Dingwall (1986, p. 489) argues that 'this very recurrence suggests that these inquiries are actually failing to make any lasting impact on the everyday practice of the occupations and organizations under scrutiny'. Goodwin (2019) proposes an alternative explanation for the similarities: That inquiries adopt dominant paradigms of explanation in healthcare wherein individual transgressions are connected to systemic institutional failings. Accordingly, different failures of care are repeatedly framed in terms of concepts such as culture, leadership and teamwork and this is reflected in the kind of recommendations made.

It has also been suggested that Chairs of inquiries are not the best people to make recommendations. Given that they are rarely experienced policymakers, the practicality of the recommendations has been questioned, as has the appropriateness of the recommendations' target agents, their purpose (symbolic or practical) and their unintended consequences (Williams and Kevern, 2016; Powell, 2019; Timmins, 2019). Furthermore, there is no requirement for governments to act on the findings of an inquiry (Elliott and McGuinness, 2002) and no formal review mechanism even when they have accepted the recommendations (Timmins, 2019). Elliott and McGuinness (2002) suggest that without legal enforcement, organizations are unlikely to comply with the recommendations. Consequently, there are concerns about the growing number of recommendations made (Burgess, 2011; Timmins, 2019) and to whom the recommendations are aimed (Powell, 2019).

Inquiries are, therefore, orientated towards the past, the present and the future. For inquiries, the past serves as a disastrous potential future to be avoided and the present as a crisis to be managed in part by deferring public anger with the promise that the future will be different. How then should we analyse inquiries from the perspective of futures research? If the publicly stated and institutionally sanctioned aim of inquiries is to produce knowledge that ensures a disastrous past does not become an equally disastrous future, what forms of knowledge do they draw on and what ideas about the future do they express? In the context of healthcare, we examine how inquiries perform and seek to avoid specific future scenarios, paying particular attention to the extent to which futures are figured to be identifiable, controlled and averted.

Acting in advance of the future

We approach our discussion of inquiries from the perspective of work on anticipatory knowledge and action. Anticipation has become 'an integral, yet taken-for-granted, part of liberal-democratic life' (Anderson, 2010, p. 777) and 'pervades the ways we think about, feel and address our contemporary problems (Adams, Murphy and Clarke, 2009, p. 248; see also Groves in this volume). Anderson (2010, p. 780) frames the problem of the future in the following way: 'How to act in the here and now before the full occurrence of a threat and danger?' Each course of action is founded, as he elaborates, on certain assumptions about the relationship between the past, present and future – is the past a good guide to future events? To what extent is the future determined or 'locked-in' by past and present actions? To what degree is it open and indeterminate? Addressing forms of anticipatory action prompts concerns with epistemological difficulties of acting in advance of the future. How do we know which actions to take and whether they will produce the desired outcomes? In short, how can we know the future?

As Nelson, Geltzer and Hilgartner (2008, p. 546) observe, these epistemic difficulties result from how knowledge-making about the future involves a 'precarious mixture of fact, conjecture and fantasy' and 'is troubled by uncertainty and ignorance'. Nevertheless many institutions and organizations are committed to such knowledge-making because this helps with 'projecting the appearance of managerial competence when confronting a world of contingencies' (Nelson et al., 2008, p. 546) and without doubt many wish to act in the best way, to avoid potentially harmful futures and craft preferred alternatives. Therefore, 'acting in advance of the future' entails not only epistemological but also ethical concerns. These concerns animate the distinct modes in which 'acting in advance of the future' has been realized in practice: These include precaution, pre-emption and preparedness.

Precaution, a long-established mode of acting in advance of the future, derives in part from the German legal term *Vorsorgeprinzip* (translated into English as the 'precautionary principle') which, as de Goede and Randalls (2009, p. 865) relate, means to take 'care before acting'. The Declaration on Environment and Development, adopted by the United Nations Conference on Environment and Development in Rio de Janeiro in 1992, demonstrated the precautionary principle, stating that: 'Where there are threats of serious or irreversible damage, lack of full scientific certainty shall not be used as a reason for postponing cost-effective measures to prevent environmental degradation'. Precaution therefore is enacted in situations of uncertainty but on identified threats in advance of them becoming irreversible. As Anderson (2010) observes, precautionary action is separate from the process in which it intervenes and is predicated on the understanding that without doing so a potentially catastrophic outcome would otherwise materialize. Of course, if the negative future avoided is never experienced, one cannot know if that was because of actions taken or because the forecasts were wrong in the first place. Consequently, de Goede and Randalls (2009) argue that precaution therefore always involves a calculation about the current costs and putative future benefit of acting in advance of the future.

While NGOs and policymakers have adopted precaution as an appropriate mode of action in relation to processes such as climate change, the second mode of pre-emption we discuss here has been closely associated with threats of terrorism. Following the 2001 attacks in the United States, the Bush Administration adopted a strong policy of pre-emptive action against future threats that its architect, Secretary of State Donald Rumsfeld, described as 'the unknown, the uncertain, the unseen and the unexpected'. He went on: 'We must put aside comfortable ways of thinking and planning [..] so we can deter and defeat adversaries that have not yet emerged to challenge us' (Rumsfeld in Massumi, 2007). As President Bush himself remarked in 2002: 'If we wait for threats to fully materialize, we will have waited too long. We must take the battle to the enemy, disrupt his plans and confront the worst threats before they emerge' (Bush in Massumi, 2007). In short, pre-emption acts on threats which are still emergent, intervening before they take their final form and have irreversible consequences. Moreover, as Massumi (2007) argues, pre-emption is predicated on the assumption that the future is characterized not by 'a particular threat or sets of threats, but the potential for still more threats to emerge without warning'. According to Massumi, the future is 'threat-o-genic' and advance knowledge is impossible. Pre-emption therefore proposes that the condition in which states or other social actors find themselves is one defined by a radical and unavoidable lack of knowledge.

In contrast to pre-emption, preparedness as a mode of 'acting in advance of the future' does not aim to stop a future event from happening. Instead, the aim is to mitigate the deleterious effects of an event when it does occur, such as a disaster or terrorist attack, disrupting social and economic life. Considering the example of UK Civil Contingencies, Adey and Anderson (2012) explore preparedness in the form of collective exercises in which actors practise and act out particular scenarios, often drawing on previous emergencies that communities or organizations have experienced in the past. These types of exercises, Collier (2008, p. 225) proposes, produce a new form of knowledge, which he calls 'enactment-based knowledge generated by "acting out" uncertain future threats in order to understand their impact'. Enactment takes the form of simulations, war games or exercises that allow the participants to identify vulnerabilities that can be registered and catalogued.

Collier contrasts this form of anticipatory knowledge-making with the established system of 'archival-statistical knowledge' with which the insurance industry, for example, has long worked to assess future risks by analysing what they know about past events, their frequency and distribution in a population or place. However, as Adams et al. (2009) argue, our futures are characterized by an 'actuarial saturation', when this established method to calculate future risk from analysing an archive of past events is no longer sufficient. This is superseded, Adams et al. (2009, p. 255) argue, by a new mode of reasoning they call abduction in which

> Ideas about how to 'move forward' are generated by tacking back and forth between nitty-gritty specificities of available empirical information and more abstract ways of thinking about them. In anticipation, abduction also acquires a temporal form: The tacking back and forth between the past, present and future.

To find a way forward then, in deciding what to do and when to do it, actors navigate the uncertainties of their situation, the incompleteness of their knowledge, use existing 'archival-statistical' stores of knowledge but also more speculative methods to conjure up future events that are unprecedented or of such infrequent occurrence so as not to feature significantly in standard calculations of risk.

Given what this body of literature on anticipation shows, how should we then make sense of inquiries? If the general purpose of staging an inquiry is to produce a definitive account of what happened and to prevent the past from happening again, how well do inquiries offer a way to 'act in advance of the future'? To explore this, we selected a recent inquiry in the healthcare context, the Paterson Inquiry – an independent non-statutory inquiry, which investigated the malpractice of a surgeon who performed unnecessary operations and procedures. The inquiry found it was not just the rogue surgeon who was found wanting but that he had been inadequately supervised in both the NHS and the private sector; that regulators also failed patients by inadequate responses to complaints and compensation; and that, once the extent of harm was realized, recall procedures were haphazard and not patient-centred. As the inquiry comments, 'It is wishful thinking that this could not happen again' (James, 2020), we therefore examined how its recommendations anticipate and seek to shape the future. Our questions were:

1. What kind of threat is being conceptualized?
2. What kind of relationship does the past, present and future have in these recommendations?
3. What forms of knowledge and action are needed to shape the future?

What kind of threat?

In contrast to the abstract thinking evident in some of the above literature, throughout all of the recommendations, the kind of threat orientating the recommendations is a known, fully formed danger of the kind already witnessed by the inquiry, essentially replicas of what has gone before. There is a strong sense that these are conceptualized not as one-off events but recurring dangers.

For example, one issue that arose in the inquiry was non-compliance with existing guidance that every breast cancer patient should have their case discussed at a multidisciplinary team (MDT) meeting. This already forms part of the Care Quality Commission (CQC) inspection framework, therefore, the recommendation focusses on ensuring better observation and governance of existing practices:

> We recommend that CQC, as a matter of urgency, should assure itself that all hospital providers are complying effectively with up-to-date national guidance on MDT meetings, including in breast cancer care, and that patients are not at risk of harm due to non-compliance in this area. (James, 2020, p. 219)

This recommendation is less about the future and more about action to be taken in the present. Non-adherence to guidance is a well-defined danger, and the only projection forward is that by nature this danger will recur. Interestingly, the recommendation does not specify any different kind of activity from existing practice, rather it seeks to draw attention to the urgency and priority of this issue.

On the matter of complaints and a dissatisfactory response from the hospital, the inquiry found that patients were unaware of the appropriate routes through which they might escalate their complaint. And, in the case of private hospitals that do not subscribe to Independent Sector Complaints Adjudication Service, the patient has no access to independent investigation or adjudication of their complaint. Therefore, the inquiry recommended that

> information about the means to escalate a complaint to an independent body is communicated more effectively in both the NHS and independent sector. We recommend that all private patients should have the right to mandatory independent resolution of their complaint. (James, 2020, p. 219)

With this recommendation, the danger is of unspecified lapses in quality and safety, but it is clear that these will inevitably cause harm in the future. Here, acting in advance of the future takes the form of preparedness in terms of mitigating effects of future events – an issue we will return to below.

The inquiry also heard that the information Paterson gave about patients in general practitioners' (GPs[1]) letters was different to what he said to patients at their consultation. Such letters are routinely sent to GPs after consultation or treatment and copied to patients. Consequently, the inquiry recommended

> that it should be standard practice that consultants in both the NHS and the independent sector should write to patients, outlining their condition and treatment, in simple language, and copy this letter to the patient's GP, rather than writing to the GP and sending a copy to the patient. (James, 2020, p. 218)

The threat here comes from incomplete and esoteric knowledge, of the kind witnessed by the inquiry. The solution is a modification of existing practice. Both identified threats and responses indicated stay close to known practices and solutions.

Unlike modes of anticipation in other contexts, such as terrorism, an inquiry is not an imaginative exercise, rather the inquiry acts to archive knowledge of dangers and their consequences, and recommended actions are focussed closely on averting the documented dangers, presuming a future that looks very much like the present.

Relationship between the past, present and future

As indicated above, inquiries act on the past, present and future in various ways; they investigate and archive disasters and dangers, they manage the present and the public outrage caused by such events and they presume certain futures and aim to shape more desirable ones. In this section, we focus more closely on this relationship between past, present and future.

The inquiry found that recall of private patients harmed by Paterson was haphazard, with many receiving no communication about recall or attending an appointment. Here the inquiry acts as a bridge between past and future. It recommends that the private hospital involved

> should check that all patients of Paterson have been recalled, and to communicate with any who have not been seen, and that they should check that they have been given an ongoing treatment plan in the same way that has been provided for patients in the NHS. (James, 2020, p. 220)

This recommendation is focussed on acting now, in the present, to mitigate the effects of past events and their continued effect into the future. In doing so, it demonstrates key features of preparedness, where it differs is in its projections of the future. According to Collier (2008), preparedness involves simulations, war games or exercises to identify vulnerabilities and understand their impact. Inquiries, by contrast, demonstrate scenario planning only insofar as the assumption that past dangers will recur unless actively prevented.

For those patients who were recalled for follow-up, they reported that their experience was not patient-focussed, rather they were treated as a problem to be solved. Furthermore, the process lacked transparency and no national guidelines on recall exist. Consequently, the inquiry recommended

> that a national framework or protocol, with guidance, is developed about how recall of patients should be managed and communicated. This framework or protocol should specify that the process is centred around the patient's needs, provide advice on how recall decisions are made, and advise what resource is required and how this might be provided. This should apply to both the independent sector and the NHS. (James, 2020, p. 220)

Unlike the recommendations above, which focus largely on managing the present or mitigating effects of the past, this recommendation has a longer horizon of action; it proposes an evaluation of how things might be done differently in the future. Yet, it is not a distant future, and it is one that closely resembles the present. Unlike anticipatory regimes such as precaution and pre-emption, here there is no speculation about alternative futures and other potential threats.

On the issue of compensation for medical harms, ordinarily medical defence organizations cover the costs of claims and damages awarded to patients. However, given that Paterson's conduct was found to be criminal, the Medical Defence Union withdrew cover leaving patients uncompensated. In this case, the inquiry suggested that

> the Government should, as a matter of urgency, reform the current regulation of indemnity products for healthcare professionals, in light of the serious shortcomings identified by the Inquiry, and introduce a nationwide safety net to ensure patients are not disadvantaged. (James, 2020, p. 221)

Paterson is not the first doctor to be engaged in criminal activity, and this recommendation accepts that he will not be the last. The danger rogue doctors pose is thus positioned as unavoidable, and this recommendation aims to create a system that is better prepared to deal with the consequences. It demonstrates preparedness in not stopping but mitigating the harm this danger will cause in the future. Again, urgency is invoked, which as Anderson (2017) notes, gives a sense of future harms, not lying in wait, but racing towards the present.

In these recommendations, past harms are publicly addressed, actions are set out that are expected to avert recurrence of identified dangers or that ameliorate their consequences. Implicit in these recommendations is a perception of the future as predictable, known and, to a degree, malleable and controllable. There is little, if any, speculation of the different shape dangers might take and how different contexts produce different threats to safety.

Forms of knowledge and action

We have seen above that an inquiry serves to archive knowledge of threats to safety. Unlike the archival-statistical knowledge necessary for preparedness in a financial markets context, here the archive is largely descriptive, context-rich and qualitative. In this section, we explore what forms of knowledge and action are needed to shape futures of improved healthcare.

Regulatory systems are a key part of the existing armoury in preventing 'bad futures'. However, the inquiry observed that in spite of the scale of the UK regulatory system in healthcare, it does not effectively keep patients safe and is not accessible or understood by patients. Therefore,

> the Government should ensure that the current system of regulation and the collaboration of the regulators serves patient safety as the top priority, given the ineffectiveness of the system identified in this Inquiry. (James, 2020, p. 221)

While this seeks to improve prevention there is little specificity in the recommendation, handing over to the Government to identify a solution. It shows how inquiries rely on a range of actors to engage with their recommendations and that these cannot act alone. It does not, however, address its own finding that the regulatory system in healthcare is inaccessible and poorly understood by patients, giving some insight into the forms of knowledge the inquiry sees as integral (and dispensable) to shaping future regulation. Here might have been an opportunity to capitalize on the insights of lay knowledge but instead the work of thinking through how to improve governance is handed to those in government.

The inquiry heard that the knowledge available to patients about Paterson as a surgeon was unreliable, the result of hearsay and an inflated local reputation. Patients had no means of independently verifying the information they received and suggested to the inquiry that a single source of information relating to each consultant's practice would be welcome. This suggestion was endorsed by those who had a managerial or clinical responsibility for consultants. As a result, the inquiry recommended that

> there should be a single repository of the whole practice of consultants across England, setting out their practising privileges and other critical consultant performance data, for example, how many times a consultant has performed a particular procedure and how recently. This should be accessible and understandable to the public. It should be mandated for use by managers and healthcare professionals in both the NHS and independent sector. (James, 2020, p. 218)

This recommendation is based on the premise that statistical knowledge of past events serves as a good guide to the future, ideally permitting patients and their referring GPs to take decisions about procedures based on possible risks to them of things going wrong. This recommendation demonstrates aspects of preparedness in that it aims to create a resource for public and professional use. However, it is implicitly figured around *surgical* practice and competency of discrete procedures, which may be less relevant for other types of hospital consultants (for example, physicians, geriatricians, psychiatrists) so would not alert the public to rogue doctors in other specialties. Importantly, it presumes that statistical knowledge of this kind is enough to avert danger, but there are many other considerations that inform decision-making, lack of alternatives being a primary example. Moreover, local reputations will still circulate and obfuscate the statistics.

Service-providers' perceptions of risks to patient safety, and the regulatory mechanisms that manage these risks, also came under scrutiny by the inquiry as senior managers and healthcare professionals in both the NHS and the independent sector acknowledged that Paterson could and should have been suspended earlier than he was (concerns were first raised in the early 2000s). Factors that fed into this delay were the use of the Human Resource (HR) process to investigate, even though the concerns related to Paterson's clinical practice, and that concerns were not shared between the NHS and private hospitals. The inquiry subsequently recommended that

> when a hospital investigates a healthcare professional's behaviour, including the use of an HR process, any perceived risk to patient safety should result in the suspension of that healthcare professional. If the healthcare professional also works at another provider, any concerns about them should be communicated to that provider. (James, 2020, p. 221)

Again, in this recommendation future threats take the same shape as present threats. These are not seen as potential threats but actual dangers that will arise again. While there is a suggestion of scenario planning in this recommendation, the scenarios are based on the past not on possible futures. In these recommendations, the knowledge necessary to avert future dangers is empirical knowledge of the past, not speculations of alternative futures.

Discussion and conclusions

For reasons of space, we have only considered one inquiry's set of recommendations, and while the themes that we have identified here also resonate with other notable healthcare inquiries (e.g. the public inquiry into children's heart surgery at the Bristol Royal Infirmary, the Mid Staffordshire NHS Foundation Trust public inquiry and the Morecambe Bay investigation), it would be valuable to expand our analysis and examine more fully the way different forms of inquiry (e.g. statutory and non-statutory) might shape the scope and perspective of recommendations. With this caveat in mind, our analysis suggests the following conclusions can be drawn.

With forms of anticipatory action that scholars have discussed in the domains of climate change, terrorism or natural disasters, we argue that inquiries share only limited features. As opposed to acting ahead of a full occurrence of a threat or danger, inquiries deal only with those that have already occurred. Unlike preparedness exercises or pre-emptive strikes, inquiries do not as a rule engage with open and indeterminate futures; they do not participate in imaginative exercises and only draw on a very limited repertoire of scenario-making to consider how problems could be avoided in the future. They deal not in potentialities but in observed realities. Their mode is therefore empiricist rather than speculative.

This is not surprising, because, as other authors have observed, the purpose of staging inquiries is to produce a form of public accountability for past events and to inform public understanding of why the problem happened in the first place. Inquiries also aim to provide reassurance that the future can be managed and controlled by presuming that future dangers will be the same as present dangers and that their recurrence can be avoided through well-crafted recommended courses of action. As a political instrument, inquiries assist governments and professional bodies to project 'the appearance of managerial competence when confronting a world of contingencies' (Nelson et al 2008, p. 546) by narrowing down contingencies to known risks and dangers that resemble closely those they have already identified in the present or past.

Therein lies the limitations of inquiries as a mode of acting on the future: They only trade in known dangers, and, when making recommendations for change, they assume that future threats will be the same as past or present threats. However, the lack of imagination around potential harms and alternative futures works against 'learning the lessons' as, while future dangers might share some characteristics with past events, they are unlikely to be exact replicas.

As Goodwin (2019) argues, failures in healthcare tend to be explained from a systems perspective referring to features of institutional or organizational settings such as culture, leadership or teamwork, which can be utilized to account for why things went wrong and to frame recommendations for change. At a conceptual level, therefore, there may be similarities, but when the particularities of different institutional failures are examined, precisely what went wrong in each context varies widely. While inquiries painstakingly explore the relationship between events and the circumstances of their production, there is little consideration in the recommendations of the extent to which those precise circumstances might arise again elsewhere. This means that, at best, those who act on recommendations might prevent the same threat from recurring in the same set of circumstances the inquiry was set up to address, but to prevent the same threat from occurring in different circumstances requires more imagination around the different forms the threat might take.

One approach to recognizing and responding to this predicament is to adopt what Adams et al. (2009) call 'abductive reasoning' – to 'tack' between 'specificities of available empirical information' of the particular case in hand and more abstract ways of thinking about them. This might not be the task of one single inquiry but could be the responsibility of an Office of Inquiries, positioned with a degree of oversight, which would function to precisely tack between individual scandals or disasters and emergent, broader patterns that might be missed by the drafters of individual reports. This could provide the basis for a form of anticipatory governance that goes beyond seeing the future as replicating the present and presuming that future threats can be predicted from an archive of facts about the past. Already, governments have embraced innovative forms of anticipatory knowledge-making in other domains of social and political life, as we discussed above, so taking such an approach is not without precedent. We postulate that abductive reasoning could facilitate more imaginative, speculative and proactive engagements that redress past failings and bring more desirable futures into being.

Note

1 A GP (General Practitioner) is the British term for a doctor based in the community who treats patients with minor or chronic illnesses and refers those with serious conditions to a hospital.

Bibliography

Adams, V., Murphy, M. and Clarke, A.E. (2009). 'Anticipation: Technoscience, life, affect, temporality', *Subjectivity*. doi: 10.1057/sub.2009.18.
Adey, P. and Anderson, B. (2012). 'Anticipating emergencies: Technologies of preparedness and the matter of security', *Security Dialogue*. doi: 10.1177/0967010612438432.
Anderson, B. (2010). 'Preemption, precaution, preparedness: Anticipatory action and future geographies', *Progress in Human Geography*. doi: 10.1177/0309132510362600.
Anderson, B. (2017). 'Emergency futures: Exception, urgency, interval, hope', *Sociological Review*. doi: 10.1111/1467-954X.12447.
Boudes, T. and Laroche, H. (2009). 'Taking off the heat: Narrative sensemaking in post-crisis inquiry reports', *Organization Studies*, 30(4), pp. 377–396.
Burgess, A. (2011). 'The changing character of public inquiries in the (risk) regulatory state', *British Politics*, 6(1), pp. 3–29.
Collier, S. (2008). 'Enacting catastrophe: Preparedness, insurance, budgetary rationalization', *Economy and Society*. doi: 10.1080/03085140801933280.
Dingwall, R. (1986). 'The Jasmine Beckford affair', *The Modern Law Review*. doi: 10.1111/j.1468-2230.1986.tb01700.x.
Elliott, D. and McGuinness, M. (2002). 'Public Inquiry: Panacea or placebo?', *Journal of Contingencies and Crisis Management*, 10(1), pp. 14–25.
de Goede, M. and Randalls, S. (2009). 'Precaution, preemption: Arts and technologies of the actionable future', *Environment and Planning D: Society and Space*. doi: 10.1068/d2608.
Goodwin, D. (2018). 'Cultures of caring: Healthcare "scandals", inquiries, and the remaking of accountabilities', *Social Studies of Science*, 48(1), pp. 101–124.
Goodwin, D. (2019). 'NHS Inquiries and the problem of culture', *The Political Quarterly*, 90(2), pp. 202–209.
Greer, C. and McLaughlin, E. (2017). 'Theorizing institutional scandal and the regulatory state', *Theoretical Criminology*, 21(2), pp. 112–132.
James, G. (2020). *Report of the Independent Inquiry into the issues raised by Paterson*. Available at: https://assets.publishing.service.gov.uk/government/uploads/system/uploads/attachment_data/file/863211/issues-raised-by-paterson-independent-inquiry-report-web-accessible.pdf.
Jasanoff, S. (2005). 'Restoring reason: Causal narratives and political culture'. In Hutter, B.M. and Power, M. (eds.) *Organizational Encounters with Risk*. Cambridge: Cambridge University Press, pp. 209–232.
Massumi, B. (2007). 'Potential politics and the primacy of preemption', *Theory and Event*. doi: 10.1353/tae.2007.0066.
Nelson, N., Geltzer, A. and Hilgartner, S. (2008). 'Introduction: The anticipatory state: Making policy-relevant knowledge about the future', *Science and Public Policy*. doi: 10.3152/030234208X370648.
Norris, E. and Shepheard, M. (2017). 'How public inquiries can lead to change', *Institute for Government*. Available at: https://www.instituteforgovernment.org.uk/publications/how-public-inquiries-can-lead-change.

Powell, M. (2019). 'Learning from NHS Inquiries: Comparing the recommendations of the Ely, Bristol and Mid Staffordshire Inquiries', *Political Quarterly*, 90(2), pp. 229–237.

Smith, R. (2000). 'Inquiring into inquiries', *BMJ*, 321(7263), pp. 715–716. doi: 10.1136/bmj.321.7263.715.

Timmins, N. (2019). 'An elementary primer for politicians and potential chairs on public inquiries', *The Political Quarterly*, 90(2), pp. 238–244.

Walshe, K. (2019). 'Public inquiry methods, processes and outputs: An epistemological critique', *The Political Quarterly*, 90(2), pp. 210–215.

Walshe, K. and Higgins, J. (2002). 'The use and impact of inquiries in the NHS', *BMJ*, 325, pp. 895–900.

Williams, M. and Kevern, P. (2016). 'The role and impact of recommendations from NHS inquiries: A critical discourse analysis', *The Journal of New Writing in Health and Social Care*. 2(2), pp. 1–11.

15
Lines
Material cultures of future mobility

Nicola Spurling

Part 1: About lines

My starting point is Ingold's 'comparative anthropology of the line' (2007, 2015). It was Ingold's focus on different forms and classes of line across practices including walking, weaving, storytelling, drawing and writing that drew my attention to painted lines in the first place and raised a question for me 'how do painted lines do work in the world?'. Ingold provides some conceptual starting points with which to tackle this question.

For the purposes of this piece, I focus on a distinction of 'class' and 'kind', which is pertinent to the question in hand. He suggests that *threads* and *traces* form two major classes of line. Threads are defined as 'a filament of some kind, which may be entangled with other threads or suspended between points in three-dimensional space' (2016, p. 42). On the other hand, traces are 'any enduring mark left in or on a solid surface by a continuous movement' (2016, p. 44). This second class of line (the trace) can be further subdivided into two kinds: Additive and reductive. He explains

> A line drawn with charcoal on paper, or with chalk on a blackboard, is additive, since the material of the charcoal or chalk forms an extra layer that is superimposed upon the substrate. Lines that are scratched, scored or etched into a surface are reductive...
>
> *(2016, p. 44)*

From the conceptual definitions above, we can conclude that the class of painted lines is that of a *trace* and that in kind it is *additive*. It sounds rather rudimentary. But from this, some initial questions come to mind, which I expand on below: What are painted lines traces of? Or are painted lines acts of trac*ing*? In which case what is being traced, and who is doing it? As traces of the additive kind, painted lines have been created and added to the surface ('the substrate'). They are enduring marks left by the continuous movement of some painting implement or other (or more recently the laying down of some kind of plastic substance). They are the traces of practices of planners and transport engineers, and they are traces of practices of governance.

In the case of painted lines, roads and other tarmacked surfaces form the substrate. But roads themselves problematize Ingold's categories. These too are additive traces, in that they are lines set down by planners, transport engineers and so on. However, in some cases, they were originally reductive traces, becoming etched into the earth's surface by the movement of humans and their vehicles – the tracing and retracing of specific paths. In this instance, roads and the painted lines on them trace the etched paths of the generations before them. These initial reflections about painted lines are intriguing, but to say something more, to make an argument, I turn to the question of why I am interested in lines and the work that they do in the first place.

Decarbonized mobility practices, future transport and painted lines

My question 'what work do painted lines do in the world?' is located in substantive debates on future mobility practices to achieve low carbon travel (Marsden et al., 2018), specifically on how recent developments in practice theory can offer novel insights and thinking in this field.[1] Below, I outline two key ways that practice theory helps us understand materials – including painted lines – in everyday travel demand.

First, forms of mobility such as driving and cycling can be conceptualized as practices. Each involves requisite materials, meanings and skills (Shove et al., 2012) that are brought together in practice performance. For example, driving involves materials including the car, the road, traffic lights and satellite navigation devices or maps; it can involve meanings including convenience, comfort, masculinity and freedom; and it involves the skills, the know-how to bring such materials and meanings together in the performance of driving.

In this framing, painted lines might be materials of such practices (driving, cycling) which carry meanings (e.g. keep moving!, stop!), becoming semiotic devices which control and guide (Jensen, 2013, p. 120). In practice, these lines are combined in a variety of ways, with other materials, and require skilled performers to understand and interweave them in practice. The lines, therefore, do work in and through practice performance. We should also note that lines legitimize specific forms of mobility, they 'rule' some mobilities in and others out. In large part, lines paint cars into the world, though recent efforts to increase active travel (walking and cycling) have challenged this.

The second way in which practice theory contributes to understanding lines flips the focus. In this view, travel demand is an outcome of interconnected end use practices (Spurling and McMeekin, 2015). In transport planning, this is termed 'derived demand', in other words, movement is an outcome of the activities, such as shopping, commuting to work or taking children to school, that it is for.

In this sense, lines are drawn to provide space for certain interconnections between modes of travel and end use. Parking provision is an example of this, with algorithms developed over decades to ensure diverse end use practices such as sporting events, dog walking, shopping and working can all be done by car (Spurling, 2018). These spaces of interconnection are drawn onto the world with painted lines, and they reify relationships between specific modes of movement and specific forms of end use. We can also think of the sites and sizes of taxi ranks, drop off and pick up points (e.g. bus stops) and delivery bays as spaces defined and governed by painted lines, and which hold and normalize specific connections of mobility and end use activities in place. These ways of conceptualizing lines provide one answer to the question I began with, how do painted lines do work in the world?

In both the formulations above, the warp and weft threads of weaving can provide useful metaphors to further conceptualize the painted lines. Weaving is a kind of fabric production in which two distinct sets of yarns are interlaced to form a cloth. The warp yarns are held in place, fixed. The weft yarns are interlaced through these to create infinite patterns. Painted lines are like warp yarns through which the weft of everyday life weaves; such weaving requires skill and know-how. Actual lines of movement form the weft. Warp yarns presume a certain kind of weft. They make some patterns possible and others less so. To continue the metaphor, painted lines create legitimacy for certain patterns of everyday movement and everyday life – predominantly those that are car-centric – while rendering others less valid or less possible.

Painted lines thus contribute to the (re)production of forms and patterns of everyday mobility practices. From this point of view, new everyday movements require a changed warp and weft. In relation to the former by erasing it, or re-making it (e.g. through repainting or overlaying); in relation to the latter by disobeying, through bricolage, i.e. creatively piecing together the existing materials (including lines), meanings and skills in new ways, and by creating data that makes such alternative wefts visible. Such novel practices of line-making are significant for a decarbonized transport future, and it is to these practices that I turn in a moment. Before doing so, I briefly consider what further work would be needed to reveal and understand the work of current painted lines in everyday life.

To put in the groundwork, and evidence the significance of the preceding claims, we might undertake empirical work around the following questions:

1. Which forms of movement are normalized and legitimized by painted lines? How are painted lines therefore implicated in producing and perpetuating environmentally problematic forms and patterns of travel? (E.g. painted lines in general script what cars should do, thus inscribing the car into the urban environment).
2. What is the work of the painted line in holding specific mobility and end use practices together? (E.g. consider where it is possible to park a car, in contrast to parking a cargo bike).
3. Given cycling and walking cannot etch themselves in a built environment[2] how can the dominant warp and weft be challenged? How can less dominant or emerging mobilities be seen? (E.g. new forms of data from mobile apps have potential to reveal wefts that are otherwise invisible).

Part 2: How could novel line-making practices contribute to decarbonized mobility futures?

Now a more ambitious question: How could novel line-making practices contribute to decarbonized mobility futures? There are different ways in which this question can be tackled. For example, it would be possible to explore how practices of line-making currently shape mobility, or how car-based mobility and line-making practices co-evolved, each shaping the other in equal measure. This approach could reveal the evolution of practices of line-making, processes of standardization, their formalization in driving practice (e.g. through the Highway Code and driving test), their evolving status in law and associated fines. The analysis would predictably reveal that the current approach to line-making in large part presumes and reproduces a car-centric society. But then what? Could such an analysis enable novel line-making practices to develop – would it bring us closer to knowing what to do? It does not offer much in this regard. In the remainder of this chapter, I argue for a different approach that in my view holds more promise.

Let's take a moment to unpack the question so that we can see through to an approach that might help us answer it. The question assumes a link between lines and everyday mobility.

This link undoubtedly exists, lines provide an infrastructure of rules almost everywhere that we go. However, the manner or extent to which they shape practice is not straightforward. These are, after all, simply lines, and in practice they are not always obeyed – illegal parking, stopping, overtaking and so on. Second, they cannot be considered separately from the array of other materials which shape mobility practices – painted lines do not shape everyday mobility alone, but are part of a much wider set of materials, meanings and skills that are brought together in performance, and the attention paid to lines might vary by time of day or time of year. The question here then is what is the extent of the relative influence of lines within practice performances?

Even though we can likely identify a large degree of congruence between current infrastructure-in-use and the lines that govern it, this does not mean that a change in the lines would transform movement overnight. Practices and their rights and rules become ingrained; they take hold in a culture, in a country, in a city and can be incredibly difficult to shift. From this point of view, lines might be changed while everyday mobilities stay the same. Returning to the points above, taking a retrospective view, looking at how the present governance of lines came into being, does not reveal much about their power in practice or about their potential to instantiate change. To find this out, a different approach is needed. To quote Ingold, we need a way of 'feeling forwards rather than casting our eyes rearwards' (2013, p.2).

In his Introduction to 'Making', Ingold (2013, p. 3) hints at a potential foothold from which we might do this. He highlights that the aim of the anthropologist is not to seek out facts *about* the world, but to be taught by it. To start with the presumption that those living in the worlds or situations that we wish to understand have the most to tell us about it (Ingold, 2013, p. 2). In relation to the current chapter, this point might be translated into an approach that seeks to study practices of line-making that are already novel, to learn from those involved in bringing a new warp and weft into being and to explore the details of these examples.

It is necessary to distinguish such an approach from one that emphasizes the design, implementation and evaluation of pilot projects for 'what works?' with a view to 'scaling up and out'. A focus on 'what works' without exploring 'how things work' produces knowledge that guises as 'transferable' from one context to another. Exploring 'how things work' enables the relevance of interventions to be critically explored in relation to a range of specific situations (Cartwright, 2012).

In the final section, I draw on the earlier metaphor of warp and weft to identify some candidate cases of novel line-making practices that might form the basis of such a study. These candidate cases are, namely, line-making practices which change the warp: 'Erasing', 'overlaying' and 'repainting'; and line-making practices which change the weft: 'Disobeying', 'bricolage' and 'making data'. In the following sections, I indicate some instances of these practices already found in the world and return to Ingold's distinction between the additive and reductive trace to reflect on how painted lines are situated in these practices.

Changing the warp

Erasing

The first novel line-making practice that I suggest is erasing. Such practices would have the effect of erasing painted lines, creating an opening for alternative, non-dominant and new mobilities to thread through the world. An outcome of such practices would be that the warp that privileges some movements over others, and which 'rules' some mobilities in and others out, would no longer hold.

The mainstreaming of 'shared space' in the Department for Transport's (2007, 2010) 'Manual for Streets' means that, across the last decade, examples of 'erasing lines' have proliferated in the United Kingdom, and this reflects approaches to urban planning around the world. Shared space is an approach to the design of streets and public space that seeks to reduce dominance of motor vehicles, and prioritize 'place' rather than the fast movement of traffic (ibid.). It is often associated with a slowing down of motor traffic which negotiates its way through spaces in which all users have equal priority. Shared space design typically *removes all road markings*, alongside reducing excessive signage, and taking out controls such as traffic lights. As such it can be thought of a strategy of line erasure.

Shared space examples provide cases through which the potential of erasing lines to make new mobility futures can be studied. Key debates in this field actually focus on the different kinds of shared space, which can be ranked by the extent to which the warp is disrupted (Landscape Institute, 2019, Section 2.1), with analyses that reveal the positives and limitations of such schemes and their appropriateness in different settings.

Overlaying

Overlaying relates to the temporary creation of additive traces using a variety of materials, so as to impose a new warp through which movement must be woven. Examples of reallocation of road space throughout 2020 in response to the COVID crisis provide a pertinent current example of such overlaying.

In this example, the requirements of social distancing have resulted in government guidelines dissuading the use of public transport, while promoting alternatives other than the car. In an attempt to promote socially distanced cycling and walking in these circumstances, pop-up (temporary) infrastructure has been funded in towns and cities across the United Kingdom. This has emerged quickly and has taken a variety of forms, including the use of barricades, cones and bollards to create wider footways and cycle lanes; increased signage to indicate how various zones on urban streets should be used; and the use of barricades and temporary planting to close streets, creating outdoor eating and drinking places. These developments have already been the focus of critical discussion and debate vis-à-vis their impact on streets and mobility systems (e.g. The Street Improvement Collaboration, 2020), and a range of evaluative research projects on the implications of these interventions are in progress (e.g. Dunning, 2020; Parkes, 2020). In relation to the research question of this chapter, such sources might be analysed for the work that overlaid lines do and for the changed mobilities observed.

Repainting

As part of the tactical urbanism movement, artists, activists and more recently some city governments and local authorities have embraced an alternative use of paint on streets to reclaim city roadways from motor traffic (e.g. Bloomberg Associates, 2019, p. 7). These public art projects simultaneously transform city infrastructure by painting new lines and painting over old lines, to create public spaces and make space for new mobilities. This additive approach belongs to a broader family of initiatives that are collectively referred to as 'tactical urbanism' – low cost and temporary or seasonal interventions which disrupt the dominant script of the built environment, including the dominance of the private car. Examples include painting murals and new priorities onto intersections, such as at West Palm Beach in

Florida (Bloomberg Associates, 2019, p. 19) to slow down motorists. As public art projects, such initiatives also serve to bring communities together raising awareness of public space, its current use and possible alternatives. Such repainting projects provide a plethora of examples, which might help to answer the research question with which I began.

The wealth of initiatives focussed on active travel (e.g. DfT, 2020) could be analysed from a similar point of view. Of interest here is the recent shift of policy emphasis which explicitly states that painted lines are not enough and that more strongly scripted environments are needed: 'New cycle provision on busy roads which consist of painted markings or cycle symbols will no longer be funded. We want to see as many as possible of the existing painted lanes upgraded with physical separation' (DfT, 2020, p. 17).

Here is an opportunity to study the transformation of paint into a more scripted and obdurate material form. A chance to explore the circumstances and process through which the painted line has come to be viewed as 'not enough' and its instantiation in '3D' infrastructure justified.

Changing the weft

Disobeying

Thus far I have focussed on altering the warp threads – the painted lines through which movement weaves. However, transformed mobilities, and changes in practices of line making, might also result from changing the weft. I use the term weft to refer to the actual movements and mobilities occurring all around us. Everyday mobilities that must find ways to navigate and weave amidst the existing materiality of the warp, but which does so in a range of ways – sometimes obeying and following, sometimes by subverting the assumptions that underpin painted lines. Understanding and harnessing such patterns of alternative and new mobilities is significant for decarbonized mobility futures.

The standardization of painted lines which accompanied the development of automobility was in part a response to an ever-increasing demand for automobile infrastructure and a need to manage and control the moving and stationary materiality of car culture. Today, new urban mobilities are creating a new politics of urban space which challenges, crosses and disobeys these lines.

Aldred and Jungnickel (2013) note this in their paper on bicycles as matter out of place, where they highlight some of the cycle parking strategies of their study participants – all of which 'disobey' the script of built environments (e.g. locking to pedestrian railings on pavements, lamp-posts and benches). A 2017 report from the San Francisco County Transportation Authority on transport network companies such as Uber and Lyft highlights the new politics of the kerbside, as these services pause on double lines to drop off and pick up, or cut across painted cycle lanes. The recent use of micro-mobilities such as electric scooters and Segways pose new challenges to existing lines and the mobilities which they legitimize.

In an urban fabric comprised of hard surfaces, it is not always possible to see these alternative and new patterns of movement, movements that might well have left reductive traces in a less concrete world. This raises questions of how to make such patterns visible, which might reveal positive trajectories that could be harnessed. If such new demands could be more visible, their infrastructural needs highlighted, then the planning and drawing of lines would eventually need to catch up. The warp shifts to catch the weft.

Bricolage

An altered weft is not only about disobeying the lines, but might also involve creativity within the existing warp, generating new practices that harness the warp of painted lines in legitimate, albeit novel ways. The practice of 'hoteling' within last-mile delivery of freight provides such an example (Cherrett, 2016). Cherrett (2016) notes a range of trends that have resulted in last-mile delivery becoming increasingly challenging for delivery drivers over the last decade. These include a 50% growth in next day delivery (non-food) from 2012 to 2015; multi-tenanted buildings in cities, all with separate procurement processes generating freight activity; increased food delivery (e.g. deliveroo) adding to the number of small vehicle couriers; and a decrease in the stock space of high street retailers. Alongside this, kerbspace is increasingly in demand, for cycling and pedestrian infrastructure, mobility as a service and as public space. Delivery drivers therefore face the challenge of finding legitimate stopping space near to the consignee's address, without incurring fines and parking charges. In response to this, a practice of 'hoteling' has emerged, in which drivers identify legitimate bays within which to leave their vehicles – sometimes for up to six hours – and walking 77% of the delivery round, using the vehicle as an in situ warehouse for the goods (Cherrett, 2016).

Knowing the warp of a city well enough to engage in this new mobility practice is one way in which the weft changes. Yet, such practices – which might be viewed as significant for achieving low carbon mobility – can remain invisible to planners and so are not supported and developed to their full potential.

Making data

Just as lines co-developed alongside the emergence of automobility, so the mobilities made visible in transport planning data, take a car-centric view. Whether national-level data or at the city scale, much of the data available makes visible fossil-fuelled vehicles and existing mobility practices. Those concerned with engendering more sustainable ways of life, and of promoting less carbon-intensive movement, have emphasized the significance of creating data which make new movements visible. Crowdsourced geographic information from smartphone apps provides one such avenue (See et al., 2016; Sui et al., 2013). Mobile methods (Büscher et al., 2011) that trace specific journeys, as opposed to use of static sensor data from major roadways, provide another. Here, new practices of representation result in different data and the prospect of a new mathematics of mobility – one that is suited to low carbon transformation. Such data and maths open up our eyes to the new weft taking hold, challenging us to create a warp that supports these less carbon-intensive alternatives.

Conclusion

In this conceptual piece, I explore two questions: How do painted lines (on roads) do work in the world? And, how could novel line-making practices contribute to decarbonized mobility futures? In relation to the former, I suggest that lines have multiple forms of significance when it comes to the workings and conduct of everyday mobility. Painted lines connect and separate, and they insist on movement and on stopping. Lines tell us where to go and where not to go. Where to stop, pause and rest. Lines reflect and reify what is dominant, what has rights. Bound by guidelines and standards, and threaded through with governance, they shape, create and perpetuate the world as it is.

In response to the second question, I propose that much could be learned from studying novel line-making practices that have already intervened in warp or weft. I suggest a catalogue of such practices, namely Erasing, overlaying, repainting, disobeying, bricolage and making data. For each, I identify potential cases whose analysis might reveal how novel line-making practices contribute to the (re)production of problematic and transformed mobilities, always as part of a broader dynamic material environment.

In conclusion, the seemingly benign materiality of the line is significant for transformed future mobility. Looking beyond lines, the ideas in this chapter suggest that the creative rethinking of and intervention in other material cultures of mobility could have significant prefigurative qualities. This could include material cultures that are organized around traffic lights, direction signs, pavements and parking space, thus following things (Evans, 2018) as well as lines through novel practices that seek to shape the future and achieve zero carbon.

Notes

1 There are other more-than-human theories that might be brought to bear on the topic of lines. For a nuanced comparison of a range of such theories, including practice theory, see Maller, C. (2018) *Healthy Urban Environments: More than Human Theories*, Taylor and Francis Group, Part 1: Understanding More-than-Human Theories, pp. 21–89.
2 The statement draws on MacFarlane's observation

> Humans are animals and like all animals we leave tracks as we walk: Signs of passage made in snow, sand, mud, grass, dew, earth or moss... We easily forget that we are track-makers, though, because most of our journeys now occur on asphalt and concrete – and these are substances not easily impressed.
>
> (MacFarlane, 2012, p. 13)

Although such substances do eventually reveal the etches of such movements, this is over long timeframes, and so they do not reveal emergent mobility demands to planners – which is the concern in this chapter.

Bibliography

Aldred, R. and Jungnickel, K. (2013). 'Matter in or out of place? Bicycle parking strategies and their effects on people, practices and places', *Social and Cultural Geography*, 14(6), pp. 604–624.
Bloomberg Associates (2019). Asphalt art guide. Available online at http://tacticalurbanismguide.com/portfolio/asphalt-art-guide-2/. Accessed 23/10/2020.
Büscher, M., Urry, J. and Witchger, K. (2011). *Mobile methods*. London: Routledge.
Cartwright, N. (2012). 'Presidential address: Will this policy work for you? Predicting effectiveness better: How philosophy helps', *Philosophy of Science*, 79(5), pp. 973–989.
Cherrett, T. (2017). 'Trends in travel demand: Last-mile logistics', talk at the *Commission on Travel Demand*, Evidence Session 3, 13th June 2017, University of Leeds. Available online at http://www.demand.ac.uk/commission-on-travel-demand/events/evidence-session-3-changing-demand-part-2/. Accessed: 06/01/2021.
Department for Transport (2010). *Manual for streets 2: Designing and modifying non-trunk roads and busy streets*. Available online at https://www.gov.uk/government/publications/manual-for-streets-2. Accessed: 20/10/2020.
Department for Transport (2020). *Gear change: A bold vision for cycling and walking*, Available online at https://assets.publishing.service.gov.uk/government/uploads/system/uploads/attachment_data/file/904146/gear-change-a-bold-vision-for-cycling-and-walking.pdf. Accessed: 06/01/2021.
Department for Transport and Ministry for Housing, Communities and Local Government (2007). *Manual for streets: Designing and modifying residential streets*. Available online at https://www.gov.uk/government/publications/manual-for-streets. Accessed: 20/10/2020.

Dunning, R. (2020). *Liveable Liverpool City Region*, DecarboN8 seedcorn project. Available online at https://decarbon8.org.uk/decarbon8-research-projects/. Accessed: 06/01/2021.

Evans, D.M. (2018). 'Rethinking material cultures of sustainability: Commodity, consumption, cultural biographies and following the thing', *Transactions of the Institute of British Geographers*, 43, pp. 110–121.

Hui, A., Schatzki, T. and Shove, E. (2016). *The nexus of practices: Connections, constellations, practitioners*. London and New York: Routledge.

Ingold, T. (2007). *Lines: A brief history*. London and New York: Routledge Classics.

Ingold, T. (2013). *Making: Anthropology, archaeology, art and architecture*. London: Routledge.

Ingold, T. (2015). *The life of lines*. London and New York: Routledge.

Landscape Institute (2019). *Technical information note: Designing shared space*. 05/2019. Available online at https://landscapewpstorage01.blob.core.windows.net/www-landscapeinstitute-org/2019/07/18-5-Designing-Shared-Space.pdf. Accessed: 20/10/2020.

Jensen, O.B. (2013). *Staging mobilities*. Balkema: CRC Press.

MacFarlane, R. (2012). *The old ways: A journey on foot*. London: Penguin.

Maller, C. (2018). *Healthy urban environments: More than human theories*. London: Taylor and Francis Group.

Marsden, G., Dales, J., Jones, P., Seagriff, E. and Spurling, N. (2018). 'All change? The future of travel demand and the implications for policy and planning', *First Report of the Commission on Travel Demand*, ISBN:978-1-899650-83-5.

Parkes, S. (2020). *Room to move – Impacts of road-space reallocation*, DecarboN8 seedcorn project. Available online at https://decarbon8.org.uk/decarbon8-research-projects/. Accessed: 06/01/2021.

See, L., Mooney, P., Foody, G., Bastin, L., Comber, A., Estima, J., et al. (2016). 'Crowdsourcing, citizen science or volunteered geographic information?', *ISPRS International Journal of Geo-Information* 5, p. 55.

SFCTA (San Francisco County Transportation Authority) (2017). *TNCs today: A profile of San Francisco transportation network company activity*. Final Report, June 2017. Available at: https://www.sfcta.org/sites/default/files/content/Planning/TNCs/TNCs_Today_112917.pdf

Shove, E. and Trentmann, F. (2018). *Infrastructures in practice: The dynamics of demand in networked societies*. London and New York: Routledge.

Shove, E., Watson, M. and Spurling, N. (2015). 'Conceptualizing connections: Energy demand, infrastructures and social practices', *European Journal of Social Theory*, 18, pp. 274–287.

Spurling, N. (2018). 'Making space for the car at home: Planning, priorities, practices'. In Shove, E. and Trentmann, F. (eds.). *Infrastructures in practice: The dynamics of demand in networked societies*. London and New York: Routledge, pp. 128–140.

Spurling, N. (2019). 'Parking futures: The relationship between parking space, everyday life and travel demand', *Land Use Policy*, 91, pp. 1–8.

Spurling, N. and McMeekin, A. (2015). 'Interventions in practices: Sustainable mobility policies in England'. In Maller, C. and Strengers, Y. (eds.). *Social practices, intervention and sustainability*. London: Routledge, pp. 78–94.

Sui, D., Elwood, S. and Goodchild, M. (eds.) (2013). *Crowdsourcing geographic knowledge: Volunteered geographic information in theory and practice*. Dordrecht: Springer.

The Street Improvement Collaboration (2020). '*Street improvement manual*: Practical ideas for local councils tackling Climate Change and Decarbonizing Transport, Public Health, Obesity, COVID'. Available online: https://www.udg.org.uk/sites/default/files/events/files/Street%20Improvement%20Manual%20Part%201.pdf. Accessed: 20/10/2020.

Watson, M. (2012). 'How theories of practice can inform transition to a decarbonized transport system', *Journal of Transport Geography*, 24, pp. 488–496.

16
Literary futures
How fiction can help policy makers

Rebecca Braun

Introduction

This chapter sets out how literary texts both engage with methods that are central to futures studies – notably forecasting and back-casting – and are themselves a method for linking past, present and future in new, socially meaningful ways. Because narrative plots routinely upend any straightforward chronological understanding of causality, literature can itself be seen as a tool with practical application for work in social futures. Literary texts allow their readers to reposition themselves in relation to multiple possible worlds and sketch out distinct plans of action, for both themselves and others, that are informed by powerfully imagined lived experience. In so doing, they provide valuable insight into the different kinds of agency and resilience that are needed to sustain such future-forming activity and which other, more technocratic models of scenario planning tend to overlook.

Indeed, world literature (meant here in the simplest, canonical sense of well-known texts that have become significant points of reference in the institutional study of literature) can be mined as a repository for various conceptions of agency and resilience that have developed over the ages and spread from one cultural tradition to another. To date, literature's relationship to practice-focussed futures work, in as much as it has been explored at all, has been through the lens of science fiction. While not for a moment implying that science fiction is either not literature or not directly relevant to futures (indeed, see Liveley et al., 2021, as well as Urry, 2016), the focus of this chapter is elsewhere: On what we can learn from two very famous literary texts that do not explicitly reflect on possible future scenarios on the level of content. More broadly than the genre of science fiction, the novel and creative essay I invoke as representative here reflect on how we know about different worlds through the broad canon of world literature. They deal with the future in as much as all literature deals with the future, namely in the way they unfold alternative realities to those in which the reader is situated and make tangible what these realities demand from those who sustain them.

This general generative aspect of my two chosen texts points to a method inherent in all literature that can enhance the kind of futures thinking that is otherwise largely the domain of elite business schools, technology developers and scientific modelling (see Andrew Curry in this volume). If people involved in proactively shaping futures – I am presuming in the first instance policymakers – can get better at reckoning with the different kinds of reflexivity that are naturally found in literary texts, they are likely to produce models of alternative worlds that both are properly alive to the variable human elements within them and indicate what might be necessary to get there.

Agency and resilience

At this point, a word on the notions of agency and resilience is necessary. Bruno Latour sets out an inclusive understanding of agency in his actor–network theory, whereby anything that leaves a trace, whether human or non-human, within any network being studied is an actant in that network (Latour, 2005). The advantage of such a broad definition is that it encourages us to look widely when considering who – or what – can bring about traceable, significant change and where we might look for it. Latour's work plays to literary scholars' training in close textual analysis, while also reminding of the importance of tying this analysis back to the real-world contexts in which literary texts sit. Resilience, meanwhile, also benefits from the kind of critical perspective that has been advanced in recent work within the environmental humanities (Barry and Welstead, 2017). It is to be seen not just as a logistical operation– putting the right technocratic measures in place to deal with a potential threat (the conventional scientific understanding of the term) – but as one both requiring and unleashing significant emotional affect within the communities dealing with this uncertainty and thus developing a kind of broader 'social resilience' (Keck and Sakdapolrak, 2013). This notion of social resilience, which distinctly emphasizes individual physical and mental well-being within the broader survival of society, becomes most tangible when one looks at the kinds of stories these communities tell (O'Brien, 2017).

Forecasting

Traditionally, engaging with the future has entailed forecasting in the broadest sense, whether this has taken the form of divination, extrapolation or the subscription to a particular belief system regarding the fate of humanity. The basic approach is that we work with what is known or can be discerned around us and amplify the elements that appear most pertinent to make visible a future situation that has evolved from our current point in time. Whether this is reading tarot cards or weather maps, the underlying belief is that there is a pattern to life that can be read from what we already know and translated into a vision of how things will be (Woodhead, 2020). Compared with the ambitions of modern 'planning' (Heffernan, 2020), direct human agency on the part of the reader/observer of the pattern is often negligible. Human responsibility for climate change notwithstanding, for example, the scientist forecasting a rise in extreme weather events has no hand in making this world come about. Rather, they are making visible what appears to be a largely pre-ordained course in view of the current data available. There is of course also an element of systemic reflexivity in all this, as the scientist's predictions become part of a feedback loop that causes people to engage more or less with the trends described, and this in turn affects the future direction of those trends (Derbyshire, 2020). The significance of forecasting is however primarily to help people react – what is often described in scientific terms as increasing resilience and generally means dealing with something we discern on the horizon through a process of good anticipatory governance (Muiderman et al., 2020). We can prepare for flooding, just as the person who is told by the tarot cards that their life will be short may make adjustments to their priorities or reconsider a certain course of action in the hope that the fate can somehow be mitigated, if not averted. This latter is notably also a strong trope throughout the European folk tale tradition.[1]

Indeed, the model that something is going to happen, and you cannot personally do much about it, is the situation in which characters in a novel or a play routinely find themselves – we need to think only of Greek or Shakespearean tragedy here, for example. Each piece of literature, whether drawing on a hyper-realist or totally fantastical form of representation, has its own pattern of events and characters that will unfold over the course of the narrative. In this sense, the characters and events are subject to the pertinent patterns encapsulated in the literary text as it has been written by an author and perceived by a reader. The course their story will take, and the significance that is ascribed to it will be determined in advance, by others.

With regard to the modern literary canon, the most famous example of novels that build explicitly on extrapolatory models is the *Bildungsroman* (a genre particularly popular in the nineteenth and early twentieth centuries). Here, the hero illustrates a particular path through society that may help his readers think or do something differently in their life, but which is pre-ordained for him (and it almost always is a 'him' in these novels) by the overarching demands of the plot. His journey through life is the forecast to which the reader responds. This response, however, is also based on extrapolatory, forecasting behaviour on the part of the reader – first as they read and second as they apply their reading to their own life (on the intricacies of this, see Piper, 2009; Boes, 2012).

What I am describing, then, is a double kind of forecasting that is generally inherent in literary processes, but with a contrasting level of agency. At the cognitive level, anyone who engages with a literary text naturally extrapolates from what they know, in order, first, to make an educated guess as to what will happen as the narrative unfolds and, second, to place the alternative world of the text as they have perceived it by the end of the work into some kind of relationship with their lived reality. Age-old scholarly questions of literary quality and the emotional affect of texts in essence revolve around two simple tests: Does this text seem an accurate or a wild extrapolation from what I know about the world (including the language through which I know it)? And how does that make me feel? Even if any one piece of literature only makes an infinitesimally small change to what its reader thinks or feels about their own life, there is always the potential for this reader to revise their own behaviour as a result of it. Leaving to one side instances of meta-fiction to which I return below, the characters and events in a play or a novel, by contrast, have no agency to determine their own significance or aesthetic sensibilities to judge how they are portrayed: They are the content illustrating somebody else's forecast. Characters can learn nothing transformational from the alternative versions of reality unfolded in their stories; readers, a little.

Back-casting

Unlike projecting already known trends into an alternative world in order to ascertain how one should act in a certain situation, back-casting entails working backwards with a view to changing what we are actually doing in the present and then following an ongoing programme to sustain this change. Using this technique requires developing a vision of the future that we might like (or fear) to attain and then considering what the present needs to look like in order for this future (not) to come about. To continue with the climatic example above, many countries and corporations have set themselves the goal of being carbon neutral by a certain date in the future. This itself is a synecdoche for a cleaner, energy-efficient world that has found a good balance with nature – a preferred future that, after many decades of worrying about the forecasts implied by various trends, has achieved buy-in from major stakeholders around the globe. There is nothing in the data used for forecasting that implies we are on track to achieve it, nor in the prevalent actual behaviours of people across the globe. Rather, in order for this world to be brought about, policymakers work backwards from the vision of functional carbon neutrality in a more balanced world to ascertain what steps need to be taken from the present system to achieve this goal.

Looking backwards from the future not only encourages us to try out different paths leading from the present into better futures than those that historical trends analysis and forecasts from existing data imply will be the most important. Back-casting also places questions of agency and resilience centre stage where forecasting allows them to be more readily shirked or elided in reference to an unfolding chain of events that appears pre-ordained. It is not enough to see the trends and frame and react to them – back-casting demands we make new ones, working backwards from the data we want, rather than forwards from the data we have. If the vision of the future we thereby create is taken seriously, it demands different ways of thinking and acting to take hold *right now* and with a commitment to sustaining them until the vision has become reality. This is a different kind of resilience to the technocratic measures of responding and containing outlined above. It is a form of mental resilience that means key decision-makers – in the history of back-casting, this has particularly tended to be urban planners and their government sponsors – are not afraid to change course by breaking with empirical teleology and trusting in their own creative agency instead (Bibri, 2018; Saltelli et al., 2020).

Literary texts that seek to break with tradition routinely use back-casting techniques. This is not in any way new, even though back-casting as a futures technique only began to be articulated in the 1980s (Robinson, 1982). By contrast, one of the earliest examples of back-casting in literature comes from the founding of the modern novel, in the form of Miguel de Cervantes's (1547–1616) seminal work, *Don Quixote* (part I 1605, part II 1615). Specifically, *Don Quixote* illustrates how back-casting can be directly linked to resilience and agency, on the part of both the author and the characters. This is part of Cervantes's wider mission to re-align literature with a social commitment to guarding truth and knowledge as rare and valuable goods that can improve society – something which, in the era of fake news, seems once again relevant.

In line with the forecasting model described above, Cervantes grasps the world of literature as following its own internal rules: It presents a discrete platform for intellectual endeavour that exists alongside other occupations and institutions, a number of which he, as a serving military officer, royal purchaser and tax collector, had directly experienced, and all of which create trends that can be forecast into the future. He is, however, critical within the literary tradition of the predominance of chivalric romances across sixteenth-century Europe, which, by the turn of the seventeenth century, were considered to have had a generally stupefying effect on their many readers, with onward negative consequences for society. Although the heyday of the romance was already past, it still represented a normative trend that it was useful for him to position his work against. Unlike key proponents of the later *Bildungsroman* referred to above, however, he does not seek to counter these irresponsibly idealized narratives with a rather more plausible depiction of society. Rather, he makes logically impossible connections between real and fictional worlds into his starting point, working backwards from what his protagonist has been able to imagine as his own preferred future on the basis of his extensive reading. Don Quixote sees the world and his own legacy in it through the eyes of a knight errant, much to the merriment and occasionally to the dismay of all the other characters within the world of the novel. The account of his incredible deeds also comes to us at (at least) one remove from reality. The text, so we are told, has been reconstituted from an Arabic account of the original Spanish history, thereby introducing further slippages of translation and lost pages of manuscript into the fabric of this imagined literary world – itself a parody on similar conventions in the chivalric romance genre.

At a meta-level, then, the whole novel is about literary history and competing literary worlds: The text is designed to show how ludicrous the world of the chivalric romance is, not least because it is one dominated by linguistic hyperbole and extensive flights of fancy, which are objects of implied ridicule throughout and, frankly, make the people who engage with them look silly. This vision is indirectly countered by a team of author–editors who collectively document Don Quixote's ludicrous exploits, with the different authorial instances reflecting on one another's work as they go. This aside, for example, is taken from a little over mid-way through the text, which runs to nearly 1,000 pages in John Rutherford's English translation:

> At this point the author describes every detail of Don Diego's house – all the contents of any rich gentleman farmer's dwelling; but the translator of this history thought it better to pass in silence over these and other similar minutiae, because they aren't relevant to the principal purpose of the history, which derives its strength from its truthfulness rather than from dull digressions.
>
> *(Cervantes, 2003, pp. 600–601)*

Here and throughout, Cervantes's text, voiced through different implied author figures, reflects on literature's orientation towards the truth and being linguistically well-made. On this meta-level, the text can be read as itself an agent in trying to bring about a preferable literary future, first and foremost for itself, through action in the now. The vision of the world from which this text has been back-cast is one where responsible authorship thrives, taking care over how fact and fiction are marshalled, to the general betterment of mankind. The first step needed to move towards this is, according to the logic of this text, to undermine the existing prevalent genre of the chivalric romance. *Don Quixote* has accordingly been written to break decisively with the previous traditions of beguiling fantasy and establish a much more socially responsible form of literature that entails multiple checks and balances on the truth – without, of course, losing all the fun that makes people want to read a narrative romp in the first place.

In addition to this, back-casting is also the method driving the plot within the text. As a character, Don Quixote is created to back-cast from the imagined world of the chivalric romance how someone would have to behave if this literary code were actually to pertain in the real world – a vision of a social order that is clearly not very desirable in early modern Europe and is therefore parodied with impunity here. In this sense, Don Quixote sets about directly exerting agency in his own story. Quixote is making choices and living through them in the now in line with his vision of a literary world in a way that is ordinarily foreclosed to characters within a literary text, who are, as above, much more usually part of somebody else's forecast. Quixote is set apart – in simple terms, seen as deluded – precisely because his actions are driven by back-casting from a vision that no one else seriously shares, rather than building on the conventions and received norms that perpetuate known patterns of behaviour. Within the literary world, Quixote's peers learn from him the deleterious effects of believing naively in chivalric romances. In this sense, Quixote is linked to a double form of radically innovative agency. He creates his own narrative that breaks with all actual social norms, both of those around him and of his readers, by deciding to act out his own back-cast vision of himself as a character in a story he has set about creating. At the same time, he still serves his author's purpose of enlightening others on why the vision towards which he aspires is misguided, even as he himself does not see it.

In an unexpected twist of actual history, both levels – the meta-textual and the internal plot – come together in the actual circumstances under which the second part of *Don Quixote* was completed in late 1614, some ten years after the first. Cervantes directly experienced the arrival of a dystopian future of sorts for his literary character when an otherwise unknown author, Alonso Fernández de Avellaneda, published the continuation of his story with immediate popular appeal. This 'false' literary future is the result of a forecast: At the end of part I of Cervantes's text, parodying the chivalric tradition, the text indicates that Don Quixote goes to Saragossa and encourages others to take up the story. When Avellaneda did just this, he was creating a literary future in the entirely extrapolatory mode described earlier. Cervantes responded by having Don Quixote confronted with the fake sequel to his story in the (now hastily completed) official sequel. Quixote is as outraged as his author and takes action against the false narrative:

> They went on talking about the false book for much of the night. The two men tried to persuade Don Quixote to read it, but he refused. They then asked him where he was going next. He replied that he was going to Zaragoza to take part in the jousting tournament. Don Juan said that this was described in the new book, although in a dull and stupid way.
>
> 'In that case I shall not set foot in Zaragoza,' declared Don Quixote. 'That will show what a liar the author of the book is.'
>
> *(Jenkins and Riddell, 2010, p. 310)[2]*

Here and elsewhere he justifies all his subsequent actions as necessary in order to prevent the alternative future written for him by another becoming true. Within the fiction, then, he back-casts his actions as a character in a manner that increases his agency to that of author of his own story, not just in the eyes of his companions within the fiction, but in the eyes of Cervantes's actual readers as well. In so doing, he openly dislodges Avellaneda and also muddies the authority of Cervantes, who did, after all, encourage the forecast sequel in the first place. Further back-casting is of course also happening in the real life of Cervantes, as he is actively trying to ensure that his version of part II of Don Quixote trumps the 'fake' that is already in circulation and limits the damage that back-casting from this fake work might have on his oeuvre as a whole. Vexing as the fake sequel must have been for Cervantes, it also helped him strengthen the underlying point that motivated him to write *Don Quixote* in the first place. Using Quixote as a mouthpiece, he is able to hammer home again the difference between literature that opens up new knowledge and ways of seeing and false books that merely work within a normative paradigm of questionable wider social merit.

From literary futures to social futures

While the twists and turns outlined above may seem to be spiralling away from any usable futures model, in this closing section, I will set out how the kinds of agency and resilience deliberately highlighted in the character of Quixote, along with the confusion of temporality engendered by literary texts more broadly, are key to designing social futures that have the power to inspire real action in the present. The various kinds of back-casting that drive both Cervantes's text as a whole and Don Quixote's character in particular bring to the fore both the challenges and the benefits of daring to break with convention. First and foremost, we see the challenges: Within the text, Quixote himself suffers tremendous mental and physical strain from his endeavours. Hardly a young man when he sets out, he suffers repeat breakdowns in both his health and spirits. His determination to continue in spite of all this underscores the extreme resilience – meant now with reference to physical and mental health – that the enhanced agency of back-casting requires of those individuals who embrace it. This particular aspect of Quixote's character is in fact perhaps what he is best known for in popular memory: Somebody who carries on in spite of widespread derision and a seemingly impossible mission. It is a self-image with which futurists may well identify.

In a more recent take on this trope, the Argentinian writer Jorge Luis Borges (1899–1986) wrote a provocative piece, 'Pierre Menard, Author of the *Quixote*' (1939) that takes to a logical conclusion what it would mean for society if it were possible wholly to emulate Cervantes's work in a similar manner to the way Quixote turns himself into a knight errant. Presented as a corrective obituary, the narrator of Borges's piece tells the (fictive) tale of how a French scholar dedicated a great deal of his life to literally becoming the Cervantes who writes *Don Quixote*, but with the added complexity of never being able to disregard his own starting point in twentieth-century France. Accordingly, Borges underscores the extreme labour entailed for Menard to arrive at the exact same turns of phrase as Cervantes, but entirely of his own accord. Where for Cervantes certain ways of saying things in classical Spanish naturally seemed the best fit for his purposes, for Menard, the fact of opting for precisely these turns of phrase over all the other options meanwhile at his disposal as a French twentieth-century scholar not only becomes remarkable in itself, but also totally changes the meaning that any reader will perceive in those choices.

In line with the rules he set himself, it is out of the question for Menard to re-read the original text or to engage in any form of translation from it, nor is the aim of the game for him to pretend to dress and act as Cervantes; rather, from his current location, he must naturally arrive at the words of the text *as himself*. This massive effort of drafting everything from scratch towards a vision of a final product that is hazy (for Menard can hardly remember the order and detail of the plot, let alone all the words of Cervantes's original) underscores the effort required to work backwards from a vision, drawing solely on one's own agency, personal resilience and contemporary location. It also helpfully illustrates the difference between the back-casting undertaken by Menard, who must engage himself in a whole new way of thinking and being in the now, and Avellaneda's creation of literary futures through forecasting, where he openly extrapolated from Cervantes's established model.

Musing on the significance of Menard's undertaking – we are told that in the end he managed to write the 9th and 38th chapters, along with part of Chapter 22 – the narrator considers what his re-creative activity means more broadly for both literature and society. If it becomes possible for all literary texts to have been written exactly like the original but by different people in different times, then literature can mean radically different things to everyone, all the time, and any sense of chronologically determined tradition or causality vanishes from the book of human history. There is no reason to admire particular authors or follow in the normative forecasting their texts routinely provide. One can read this as a collapse of the cultural canon on the one hand, but also as the birth of actual resilience and agency with which individuals can author their own futures on the other. If any book can be read as if it had been written by anyone, at any time, then everyone has all the world's books potentially within them. The narrator draws his essay to a conclusion by quoting Menard's prophesy, 'Every man should be capable of all ideas, and I believe that in the future he shall be' (Borges, 2000, p. 42).

The point of this chapter has been to show how literature engages readers in thinking about alternative social worlds in ways that are not necessarily bound by conventional understandings of linear chronology. As such, it is naturally an ally of social futures work. The literary futures engendered by both forecasting and back-casting are significant not primarily because of how they place their authors, characters and readers in relation to time, but rather because of how they make tangible the degree of iterative agency and individual resilience on the part of all these individuals that such futures require. Authors, characters and readers each in their own way explore different social realities with differing levels of awareness of the existential challenges they are opening themselves up to. Those who are professionally tasked with bringing about better social futures – under current Western democratic systems, this means first and foremost government officials and policymakers – can gain practical, strategic advantage from intellectually engaging with this felt aspect of literary futures, because they can arrive at a more intuitive understanding of the complex, but distinctly human, societies they serve. The emancipatory message from *Don Quixote*, one of the founding texts of the modern novel, is consequently in itself far from Quixotic: When you use your experience of reading to act in line with desired futures, the physical and mental stakes for the individual become apparent, as do the potential broader repercussions for society at large. Literary futures explore the consequences, both technical and emotional, of everyone being capable of acting on all ideas at any time. It is in this radical sense that literature itself should be considered a core method for creating and acting upon social futures.

Notes

1 See Pullman 2012 for an accessible commented overview of the Grimm tales.
2 For brevity's sake, this is taken from the abridged and graphically illustrated version by Jenkins and Riddell. The equivalent longer passage in Rutherford's full English translation is in Cervantes, *Don Quixote*, p. 890.

Bibliography

Barry, P. and Welstead, W. (2017). *Extending ecocriticism: Crisis, collaboration and challenges in the environmental humanities.* Manchester: Manchester University Press.
Bibri, S.E. (2018). 'Backcasting in futures studies: A synthesized scholarly and planning approach to strategic smart sustainable city development', *European Journal of Futures Research*, 6(13), [n.p].
Boes, T. (2012). *Formative fictions: Nationalism, cosmopolitanism, and the Bildungsroman.* Ithaca, NY: Cornell University Press.
Borges, J.L. (2000). 'Pierre Menard: Author of the *Quixote*'. In Borges, J.L. (ed.) and Hurley, A. (Trans.). *Fictions.* London: Penguin. pp. 33–43.
de Cervantes, M. (2003). *Don Quixote.* Trans. Rutherford, R. London: Penguin.
Derbyshire, J. (2020). 'Answers to questions on uncertainty in geography: Old lessons and new scenario tools', *EPA: Economy and Space*, 52(4), pp. 710–727.
Heffernan, V. (2020). *Uncharted: How to map the future together.* London: Simon and Schuster.
Jenkins, M. and Riddell, C. (2010). *Don Quixote.* London: Walker.
Keck, M. and Sakdapolrak, P. (2013). 'What is social resilience? Lessons learned and ways forward', *Erdkunde*, 67, pp. 5–18.
Latour, B. (2005). *Re-assembling the social: An introduction to actor-network-theory.* Oxford: Oxford University Press.
Lively, G., Slocombe, W. and Spiers, E. (2020). 'Futures literacy through narrative', *Futures*, 125, pp. 1–9. https://doi.org/10.1016/j.futures.2020.102663
Muidermann, K., et al. (2020). 'Four approaches to anticipatory climate governance: Different conceptions of the future and implications for the present'. *WIREs Climate Change*, E673(Early View), 20pp.

O'Brien, S. (2017). 'Resilience stories: Narratives of adaptation, refusal, and compromise', *Resilience: A Journal of the Environmental Humanities*, 4(2/3), pp. 43–65.

Piper, A. (2009). *Dreaming in books: The making of the bibliographic imagination in the Romantic age*. Chicago, IL: Chicago University Press.

Pullman, P. (2012). *Grimm tales: For young and old*. London: Penguin.

Robinson, J.B. (1982). 'Energy backcasting: A proposed method of policy analysis', *Energy Policy*, 12, pp. 337–344.

Saltelli, A., et al. (2020). 'Pandemic politics highlight how predictions need to be transparent and humble to invite insight, not blame', *Nature*, 582, pp. 482–484.

Urry, J. (2016). *What is the future?* Oxford: Wiley.

Woodhead, L. (2020). 'Apocalyptic, world-repair, divination: Persistent modes of future-knowing'. In Kemp, S. and Andersson, J. (eds.) *Futures*. Oxford: Oxford University Press, pp. 213–25.

17
Mental health
What can social futures teach us?

Liz Brewster

Introduction

Interest in the future of mental health diagnoses and treatment often focusses on genetic explanations. The idea that psychobiological or neuroscientific advances may help to see the end of diagnosed mental health conditions is an enticing one; after all, few people wish to experience depression, anxiety or unwanted hallucinations, or to see friends and family members suffer. But there is increasing recognition, as this chapter will outline, that the future of mental health is not biological, it is social.

Social futures in mental health acknowledge the influence of powerful discourses around medicalization and stigma, but frame pathologies as socially produced, and engage in dialogues around prevention, not cure. By taking a social futures approach, it is possible to consider how mental health is experienced, not just the diagnosis or treatment of mental health problems. A social futures account allows for influences from diverse traditions and cultures to blend together to consider these experiences. As good physical health is often taken for granted until something goes wrong, so too is mental health ignored until a problem is experienced. This needs to change.

The science of mental health

Since the early twentieth century, mental health has been framed as part of the domain of medicine: Led by psychiatry and supported by neuroscience. Much research and effort has focussed on pathologies, or mental health problems, and categorizing then treating their symptoms. This has not always been the case, with pre-modern traditions taking a more holistic approach to understanding and managing madness (Scull, 2015). To present a brief gloss over the history of modern medicine, increasing knowledge led to changes in approach and advances in technique, and medicine took a clinical–pathological approach, diagnosing and treating in the presence of disease (for a more expanded explanation, see Bynum and Porter, 1993).

Medicine has colonized mental health, situating it as illness. This was in many ways a positive move, which left behind some deeply problematic constructions which place symptoms of mental health problems as moral failings (Foucault, 1967). The 'illness account' of mental health problems at least places the blame on the disease, but still presents an individualized account of mental health with the burden of recovery on the person experiencing symptoms, with obligations to be met (Williams, 2005).

Mental health has now, therefore, been positioned as only important when it is absent: A deficit model that has concentrated on seeking solutions for diseases. Little attention has been given to maintaining good mental health. Since colonization by medicine, symptoms of mental health pathologies have been treated with diverse physiological, psychopharmacological and psychotherapeutic interventions, from hypoglycaemic coma and electroconvulsive therapies, through antipsychotic and antidepressant medications towards talking therapies like cognitive behavioural therapy and acceptance and commitment therapy. The acceptability of different treatments rests firmly on the underpinning model of mental health used to understand what mental health problems *are*.

Over more recent times, as the economic, social and personal burden of mental health pathologies has increased, interest has shifted from thinking only about treatment to considering the aetiology of mental health. Recent efforts to understand the causes of mental ill health have, however, been focussed on one aspect: The genetics of mental health. As the UK research funder The Wellcome Trust (2019) recognized in their recent mental health programme strategy, 'the field is very focussed on debates seeking one ultimate cause'. The hope of a persuasive genetic explanation of mental illness has led to rapid growth in epigenetic research, but ultimately little impact on experiences of mental health. Caspi et al. (2003, p. 389) concluded that 'the expectation that direct paths will be found from gene to disease has not proven fruitful for complex psychiatric disorders'. More recently, neuroscientist Grisel's (2019) portrayal of the social and personal experiences of addiction (which can be considered a response to distress not just a physiological consequence of substance misuse) also reinforces how the dream of solving mental illness via genetic alteration is seductive, but unlikely to be realized any time soon.

Destabilizing categorization

A further concern about the illness account of mental health is around the question of labelling or categorization. Medical knowledge prides itself on being created in objective, neutral, test-and-retestable conditions. Stating whether a symptom, sign or behaviour is normal or not normal is crucial, and sorting these symptoms into diagnostic boxes is core medical work. Previous criticisms of this categorization project can be seen in the work of antipsychiatrists including R.D. Laing (1969) and Thomas Szasz (1974).

Diagnoses are essential to provide access to treatments and supportive services, but their existence comes with costs. The definition and diagnosis of post-traumatic stress disorder (PTSD) and its adoption into the American Psychiatric Association (APA)'s third *Diagnostic and Statistical Manual of Mental Disorders* (DSM-III), begun in 1974 and published in 1980, are often given as a classic example of the importance of framing. Military veterans returning from the Vietnam War were only able to access mental healthcare services when the traumatic nature of their experiences was acknowledged and codified into a pathology. Considering earlier reports of military personnel and mental health – the 'shell shock' of First World War and the 'war neuroses' of Second World War – emphasizes the importance of PTSD as a legitimization of the impact of the moral injury of warfare on veterans (Bourke, 2000).

Labelling theory engages with the idea that mental health problems 'qua concept [are] not neutral, value free or scientifically precise' (Scheff, 1967). Instead, what we decide is normal – or deviant – is based in sociocultural circumstances. As well as adding new 'diagnoses' including PTSD, the APA also removed other 'pathologies'. This decision, made by the APA in 1973 and formally encoded into the DSM-III in 1980, meant that, for the first time in the history of modern psychiatry, homosexuality was seen as a normal part of human behaviour rather than a pathological disorder. Depathologizing identities and practices around lesbian, gay, bisexual and transgender (LGBT) people as an illness was an important step, which then led to changes in law, rights and a move towards greater equalities (Drescher, 2015). While this was a positive first step, sexual and gender identities continue to be a contentious part of diagnostic manuals. Although the language around sexual and gender identities has shifted from talking about deviation, through disorder, to dysphoria (dissatisfaction, rather than disease), human behaviours continue to be pathologized in the DSM-V (Drescher, 2015). Thus, medical judgements and sociocultural ones sit uncomfortably next to each other, and what is agreed to be an illness is fundamentally socially produced.

The problem of existence

Another account of mental health problems steps away from biomedicine entirely. Mental distress can be seen as a normal, unavoidable, although not necessarily pleasant, part of human existence, and therefore, it is not the place of medicine to try to cure illness or mitigate the symptoms of distress. This account is more in line with, for example, Buddhist teachings on suffering and enlightenment. In this account, rather than seeing emotional reactions and behaviours as symptoms, there is recognition that such reactions are legitimate responses to distress, on a continuum of experience. The agreed appropriateness, or otherwise, of these symptoms is an artefact of what we find acceptable in society. In other words, boys don't cry.

Religion and philosophy have long engaged with concepts of human misery, suffering and making sense of life; perhaps these accounts of how to live well can add more to discussion around the future of mental health than can be gathered from biomedical accounts. Social futures' engagement with mental health could complete a reframing that removes any association with biomedicine. Paraphrasing Urry's (2016) conceptualization of futures thinking, is what we call 'mental health' 'too important to be left to states, corporations or technologists' – or clinicians?

This alternative 'existential' account might use terms like well-being, human flourishing and life satisfaction rather than mental health. The slippery, intangible and subjective nature of these terms sits in contrast with mental health diagnoses with defined symptoms that are easy to categorize and measure. Defining mental health as more than an absence of symptoms is a positive shift, aligning to the World Health Organization's 1948 definition of health (World Health Organization, 2020). It also encourages a focus on prevention, rather than treatment or seeking cure. However, accepting the argument that good mental health is more than the absence of these symptoms leaves questions around what makes life worthwhile, and who gets to say.

There are two key problems with this existential account. The first is that it still places the emphasis and responsibility for mental health (or being well) firmly with the individual. An individual emphasis ignores context; mental health problems (as physical health problems) disproportionately affect those of lower socioeconomic status, and social inequalities affect outcomes (Marmot, 2005). Males of African-Caribbean heritage in the United Kingdom have a higher incidence of schizophrenia and worse outcomes (Pinto, Ashworth and Jones, 2008). Medical professionals are less likely to refer people with a lower socioeconomic status to talking therapies (Shaw and Taplin, 2007, p. 366). Individuals cannot change their socioeconomic status, heritage or associated stereotypes that affect what treatments they are offered (see Littlewood, 1991; Van Ryn and Burke, 2000 for discussion of racism/'race thinking' in psychiatry).

The second problem with a demedicalized or existential account is that different philosophies and religions have particular standpoints that place value judgements on what a good life is. There is no agreement on how to live well, and adding in belief models and uncertainties about the fundamental nature of human existence further complicates questions that interplay with the social construction of mental health.

Living well – often framed as well-being – could nevertheless be a key concern for a social futures approach. Using terms like well-being might help to shift the conversation away from some of the constituent parts that pathologize within a medical approach to mental health; instead, well-being rests on ideas of 'feeling good and functioning well' (New Economics Foundation, 2008, p. 1). Again, this seems to position an argument that can take on prevention of mental health problems rather than just managing their symptoms.

Perhaps surprisingly, much of the current work in this area of mental health as wellbeing comes from economics, rather than drawing on previous holistic traditions that could inform thinking (see Wallis, this volume). The correlation between economic growth and self-reported life satisfaction has led to concerns about ensuring good well-being to support productivity. Neoliberal accounts of well-being, led by economist Richard Layard and organizations including the New Economics Foundation (NEF), are currently pervasive in the United Kingdom, with the 'Five Ways to Well-being' adopted by diverse organizations (Layard, 2005; New Economics Foundation, 2008).

The NEF Five Ways have become a dominant paradigm in the United Kingdom, but they are not a neutral account of well-being. They state that to have good well-being, we need to connect with others, be active, take notice, keep learning and give (usually interpreted as volunteering). On the surface, this list is a convincing one, but this economic construction of mental health has been co-opted into the illness model of mental health, where symptoms construct a diagnosis that requires biomedical intervention. It aligns well with an individual account of disease and prevention, but again places the responsibility for good well-being on the individual. Questioning the economic account of well-being highlights its close relationship with other forms of governmentality, focussed on increasing economic production. Its adoption into an illness account is biomedically incongruous. The economic account tries to reproduce existing constructions of knowledge by positioning itself as a set of 'evidence-based public mental health messages' that can be adopted and used within a medical context (New Economics Foundation, 2008). However, its knowledge claims are based on a construction of knowledge authority that would not be considered 'evidence-based' according to biomedical constructions of knowledge. While the notion of evidence-based medicine can be critiqued, the economic account tries to use this construction of evidence to reinforce its own agenda: That of economic transformation. Accounts that engage with ideas of mental health using this language of well-being are therefore inadequate for the purposes of a social futures approach.

Socially produced pathologies

If we move from an illness model to an existential or distress model, but refuse to accept the individual nature of mental health, where else can we look? Mental health problems could be seen as a reaction to legitimate social or personal concerns, in which distress is a reasonable or expected response. At one level, symptoms of mental health problems are emotional reactions and the behaviours that result from these emotional reactions. Concerns arise when these reactions or behaviours seriously affect the ability to function in society. When emotional reactions and behaviours are seen as inappropriate, diagnosis and pathology step in. To take an example, within Western society, grief is a legitimized response to a bereavement. Low mood, crying, depression, anxiety about the future, inability to cope with the world and sadness are all considered normal within the immediate context of a loss. The expectation, however, is that this response will change over time: There is a need to cope with loss, to mourn and to adapt. With this, the acceptability of emotions and behaviours changes over time.

Exploring experiences of bereavement in Western society also highlights the cultural construction of emotional reaction. If I were to tell you that I heard the voice of a friend after his death, you might worry that I was hallucinating or delusional, common symptoms of the psychiatric disorder schizophrenia. In contrast, for some indigenous communities in North America, it is considered normal to hear the voice of the deceased after a bereavement (Kleinman and Good, 1985). One argument is that it is the experience of hearing these voices that is more important; they could be intrusive or welcome, calming or inciting or entirely neutral (Woods et al., 2015). Palmer (2000) examined the delusions experienced by schizophrenics, concluding that whether hearing voices is considered a hallucination reflects power relationships in the situation; he cites the example of religious prophets to illustrate that 'whether a belief is seen as delusional or not is largely a matter of context' (Palmer, 2000, p. 665). These questions of context and power firmly locate mental health within a political framework: Who gets to say who is 'mad'? And what does this mean for those who experience mental health problems?

The politics of mental health

In *A Social History of Madness*, the historian Roy Porter explores the social contexts in which people have experienced, described and written about mental health problems, using memoirs to guide the reader through the complexities of the asylum age, through deinstitutionalization and towards psychotherapeutic interventions. By using memoirs, his aim was to explore how

> the writings of the mad challenge the discourse of the normal, challenge its right to be the objective mouthpiece of the times. The assumption that there exist definitive and unitary standards of truth and falsehood, reality and delusion, is put to the test.
> *(Porter, 1987, p. 3)*

Porter determinedly positions experiences of those with mental health problems at the centre to highlight the impact of power and context.

The idea that the stories of the mad are a challenge to dominant narratives is of particular interest given recent attempts to use these stories and experiences of mental health problems to 'break down the stigma' around such conditions. Current thinking states that much ill-founded prejudice is down to ignorance of what it means to have poor mental health, and that this will improve if there is more discussion about symptoms. Talking about mental health is equated to talking about physical illness: We would not feel ashamed of our broken leg, and so we should not be ashamed of our broken brain. Again, this depicts on an illness account of mental health that individualizes.

Tyler and Slater (2018) present a powerful critique of this position, using McWade's (2016) work, examining how stigma around mental health functions to tell people in mental distress how they should behave. By positioning mental health within a sphere of illness, rather than using it to question the 'cultural, political and economic… distribution of distress' (Davis, 2017, quoted in Tyler and Slater, 2018), the social is ignored and experience is individualized.

Stigma also functions to tell people what stories are acceptable and which are not. In this way, some stories of madness have become part of the dominant narrative rather than counter to it. These stories focus on recovery from distress, rather than cause – particularly if that cause is (uncomfortably) a social problem (McWade, 2016). Trauma, socioeconomic status and racism are not present in such recovery accounts.

Talking about experiences may also be positioned as a necessity to gain access to supportive services, triaging access to scarce resources (Woods, Hart and Spandler, 2019). Stories can also be commodified into a tool that is used to reinforce biomedical models of mental health (Costa et al., 2012). In particular, Costa et al.'s (2012) critique notes that the *obligation* to tell your story is particularly challenging. Should I have to tell you of my own experiences of madness to legitimize my right to write this chapter on mental health futures?

Interrogating mental health as a concept has demonstrated that there has been a shift from an illness model, in which removal of physical symptoms is the main legitimate outcome, to a more well-being focussed model, in which prevention and personal recovery are taken into account, but it is the responsibility of the individual to return to their previous role as a productive and acceptable member of society. Mental health activists argue that this personal recovery model has limits, highlighting concerns about how social factors are acknowledged in the neoliberal model (Woods et al., 2019). The service user collective 'Recovery in the Bin' argues for a 'social model of madness, distress and confusion' that prioritizes human rights (Recovery in the Bin, 2016).

The social futures approach to mental health can recognize and challenge the influence of these powerful discourses. Talking about mental health has become more acceptable, but only within a framing of it as illness, and the conversation has yet to take on pathologies as socially produced.

Beyond biomedicine

This chapter has predominantly focussed on the biomedical account of mental health, as this is the one that is most prevalent in current diagnosis and treatment models in the Western world. However, this has not always been the dominant model of mental health; pre-modern and non-Western traditions understand mental health in distinct and diverse ways, which also present useful alternative accounts. Pre-modern healthcare foregrounds the role of community. Acceptance of voice-hearing saints such as Joan of Arc demonstrates that hearing voices could empower unlikely candidates rather than disempowering them.

Other approaches, for example, Complementary and Alternative Medicine (CAM), emphasize a more holistic way of working across mental and physical health. In doing so, CAM highlights the way that taking an evidence-based medical approach to mental health is a 'pseudo-rational process' (Jackson and Scambler, 2007) that excludes several thousand years of more holistic care. Increasingly, alternative approaches such as meditation and mindfulness-based therapies are integrated into medical practice and can be seen as 'cultural practice bound up in new forms of bodily understanding and perception' (Barcan, 2011).

Feminist and other philosophies can be used to inform an ethic of care that acknowledges the intersubjective and relational nature of existence rather than a purely biomedical individualized one (Ahmed, 2004). However, these accounts mainly sit alongside medicine rather than being firmly embedded within it. A social futures approach could engage with these broader accounts in its construction, learning from the past and from different traditions rather than embracing a medical account.

Mental health, social futures

In *Our Psychiatric Future*, Rose (2018) argues for a position of neurobiologically informed psychiatry that places 'human organisms in their milieu' (Rose, 2018, p. 173). His account, which investigates how psychiatry has territorialized areas of life and therefore shapes understandings of mental health, focusses on the implications for understanding the causes, diagnosis, treatment and prevention of mental health problems. By framing a need for 'research-based' psychiatry, Rose acknowledges the need for a 'revolution' in psychiatry, but rejects more political antipsychiatry or rights-based accounts of mental health and illness, like that of Recovery in the Bin.

A social futures account of mental health, going beyond psychiatry, could usefully adopt some aspects of Rose's argument, though perhaps foregrounding some of the more relational aspects of a need for change. First, that diagnosis should be replaced with something more holistic, which Rose terms 'formulation' (2018, p. 187), but could also be regarded as a form of sense-making. Understanding the whole picture of experiences of mental health – from socioeconomic conditions to personally valued outcomes – not just symptoms is essential to the social futures approach explored in this chapter. Second, Rose maintains that psychiatric professionals still have a role to play in this formulation, helping to renormalize distress rather than diagnosing illness. Social futures scholars may find this second point more intractable, as it still places psychiatry in a gate-keeping role, arbiters of what is normal and what is not. Nevertheless, there is an implication that more is 'normal' than is currently seen as such. For example, many of us with a mobile phone will have experienced the feeling that it has vibrated to alert us to an incoming call or message, only to find on checking the screen that no such message has been received. We could be said to have hallucinated, but few of us would see this as a symptom of a disorder.

Rose's account is in many ways convincing; in particular, his call to consider what a 'mental health friendly city' (2018, p. 195) might look like, though the practices and affordances of such a city are not outlined in his book. Similarly, the World Health Organization (2018) focusses their strategy around creating an environment that supports good mental health. This more structural approach, acknowledging the wider cultural discourses, is persuasive. After all, current concerns acknowledge an epidemic of mental ill health among young people. Those same young people are currently most active in protests against the climate crisis, concerned about global heating and the future of the planet. Is it really surprising that they are experiencing anxiety?

A social futures account of mental health recognizes the interdependencies of the physical environment, socioeconomic conditions and structures and interpersonal relationships. It draws on previous accounts, with careful recognition of the limits of scientific rationalization. It prioritizes prevention over treatment, recognizing that much of what we regard as an individual mental health problem is influenced by what is happening in the world.

Bibliography

Ahmed, S. (2004). *The cultural politics of emotion*. New York: Routledge.
Barcan, R. (2011). *Complementary and alternative medicine: Bodies, therapies, senses*. London: Berg.
Bourke, J. (2000). 'Effeminacy, ethnicity and the end of trauma: The sufferings of "shell-shocked" men in Great Britain and Ireland 1914–39', *Journal of Contemporary History*, 35(1), pp. 57–69.
Bynum, W.F. and Porter, R. (1993). *Companion encyclopedia of the history of medicine*. London: Routledge.
Caspi, A. et al. (2003). 'Influence of life stress on depression: Moderation by a polymorphism in the 5-HTT gene', *Science*, 301(5631), pp. 386–389. doi: 10.1126/science.1083968.

Costa, L. et al. (2012). 'Recovering our stories: A small act of resistance', *Studies in Social Justice*, 6(1), pp. 85–101.
Drescher, J. (2015). 'Out of DSM: Depathologizing homosexuality', *Behavioral Sciences*, 5(4), pp. 565–575. doi: 10.3390/bs5040565.
Foucault, M. (1967). *Madness and civilization*. London: Random House.
Grisel, J. (2019). *Never enough: The neuroscience and experience of addiction*. London: Scribe Publications.
Jackson, S. and Scambler, G. (2007). 'Perceptions of evidence-based medicine: Traditional acupuncturists in the UK and resistance to biomedical modes of evaluation', *Sociology of Health & Illness*, 29(3), pp. 412–429. doi: 10.1111/j.1467-9566.2007.00494.x.
Kleinman, A. and Good, B. (1985). 'Culture and depression'. In Kleinman, A. and Good, B. (eds.) *Culture and depression: Studies in the anthropology and cross-cultural psychiatry of affect and disorder*. Berkeley: University of California Press, pp. 1–33.
Laing, R.D. (1999 [1969]). *Self and others*. London: Routledge.
Layard, R. (2005). *Happiness: Lessons from a new science*. London: Penguin.
Littlewood, R. (1991). 'Are British psychiatrists racist?', *British Journal of Psychiatry*, 158, p. 135. doi: 10.1192/bjp.158.1.135a.
Marmot, M. (2005). 'Social determinants of health inequalities', *The Lancet*, 365(9464), pp. 1099–1104.
McWade, B. (2016). 'Recovery-as-policy as a form of neoliberal state making', *Intersectionalities: A Global Journal of Social Work Analysis, Research, Polity, and Practice*, 5(3), pp. 62–81.
New Economics Foundation (2008). *Five ways to wellbeing: A report presented to the Foresight Project on communicating the evidence base for improving people's well-being*. Available at: https://neweconomics.org/uploads/files/8984c5089d5c2285ee_t4m6bhqq5.pdf.
Palmer, D. (2000). 'Identifying delusional discourse: Issues of rationality, reality and power', *Sociology of Health and Illness*, 22(5), pp. 661–678. doi: 10.1111/1467-9566.00225.
Pinto, R., Ashworth, M. and Jones, R. (2008). 'Schizophrenia in black Caribbeans living in the UK: An exploration of underlying causes of the high incidence rate', *British Journal of General Practice*, 58(551), pp. 429–434. doi: 10.3399/bjgp08X299254.
Porter, R. (1987). *A social history of madness: Stories of the insane*. London: Weidenfeld and Nicolson.
Recovery in the Bin (2016). *Recovery in the Bin*. Available at: https://recoveryinthebin.org/.
Rose, N.S. (2018). *Our psychiatric future: The politics of mental health*. Cambridge: Polity Press.
Scheff, T.J. (1967). *Mental illness and social processes*. New York: Harper and Row.
Scull, A. (2015). *Madness in civilization: A cultural history of insanity, from the Bible to Freud, from the madhouse to modern medicine*. Princeton, NJ and Oxford: Princeton University Press. doi:10.2307/j.ctvc77hvc.7.
Shaw, I. and Taplin, S. (2007). 'Happiness and mental health policy: A sociological critique', *Journal of Mental Health*, 16(3), pp. 359–373
Szasz, T.S. (1974). *The myth of mental illness: A theory of personal conduct*. New York: Harper and Row.
The Wellcome Trust (2019). *Mental health programme strategy*. Available at: https://wellcome.ac.uk/what-we-do/our-work/mental-health-transforming-research-and-treatments/strategy.
Tyler, I. and Slater, T. (2018). 'Rethinking the sociology of stigma', *Sociological Review*, 66(4), pp. 721–743. doi: 10.1177/0038026118777425.
Urry, J. (2016). *What is the future?* Cambridge: Polity Press.
Van Ryn, M. and Burke, J. (2000). 'The effect of patient race and socio-economic status on physicians' perceptions of patients', *Social Science and Medicine*, 50(6), pp. 813–828. doi: 10.1016/S0277-9536(99)00338-X.
Williams, S.J. (2005). 'Parsons revisited: From the sick role to…?', *Health: An Interdisciplinary Journal for the Social Study of Health, Illness and Medicine*, 9(2), pp. 123–144. doi: 10.1177/1363459305050582.
Woods, A. et al. (2015). 'Experiences of hearing voices: Analysis of a novel phenomenological survey', *The Lancet Psychiatry*, 2(4), pp. 323–331. doi: 10.1016/S2215-0366(15)00006-1.
Woods, A., Hart, A. and Spandler, H. (2019). 'The Recovery narrative: Politics and possibilities of a genre', *Culture, Medicine and Psychiatry*, pp. 9–15. doi: 10.1007/s11013-019-09623-y.
World Health Organization (2018). *Mental health: Strengthening our response*. Available at: https://www.who.int/news-room/fact-sheets/detail/mental-health-strengthening-our-response.
World Health Organization (2020). *Constitution*. Available at: https://www.who.int/about/who-we-are/constitution.

18
Mobility justice
Sustainable mobility futures

Mimi Sheller

Introduction

The worldwide disruption of all kinds of transportation and mobility during the COVID- 19 pandemic has demonstrated both the possibility of quickly reducing carbon emissions by changing the organization of social practices *and* the scale of radical transformations of everyday life that will be required to reduce emissions by the amounts suggested by climate science. While the economic slowdown and mobility disruption of the pandemic are projected to have reduced GHG emissions by 7–8% this year, the goal of keeping global temperature rise below two degree Celsius requires a similar (e.g. 7.6%) reduction in GHG emissions *every year* between 2020 and 2030 (UN Environment Programme, 2019). In the face of this momentous challenge, there is an urgent need for new approaches to planning, managing, designing, forecasting and back-casting possible mobility futures. How we get to different possible planetary futures is deeply premised upon how we transform complex systems for the mobilities of people, goods and information, a key theme within critical mobilities research over the last two decades.

Some prominent approaches to studying, planning and implementing alternative mobility futures include the multilevel perspective especially as applied to postautomobility transitions (Geels et al., 2011), transition management as developed within the Sustainability Transitions Research Network (Köhler et al., 2019), the growing use of scenarios in transport planning (Hickman and Banister, 2014) and critical scenario building and participatory experimentation within mobilities research (Urry, 2016). As sociologist and mobilities theorist John Urry argued, 'A new [mobility] regime involves reorganizing society over many decades, including its transportation system, population distribution and the nature of work and sociability' (Urry, 2014). But how does such social reorganization happen? What forces are shaping alternative mobility futures? Mainstream political agendas usually focus on new technological 'solutions' and policy 'innovations', imagined as having the capacity to reconfigure or 'disrupt' the current transportation mix; however, these disruptions are by no means inherently conducive to creating sustainable, liveable, socially equitable and fair communities, nor to creating mobility justice. This chapter seeks to show the contributions of critical mobilities studies to imagining more just social futures.

The search for 'Alternative Mobility Futures' sparked the first conference of the Centre for Mobilities Research, which I cofounded with John Urry at Lancaster University in

2003–2004, and led us towards articulating the idea of the 'new mobilities paradigm' and the launch of the journal *Mobilities* in 2006 (Sheller and Urry, 2006, 2016; Sheller, 2017). These initiatives fed directly into the founding of the Institute for Social Futures at Lancaster University. Around this time, Urry also became involved in the Liveable Cities project, (https://liveablecities.org.uk), a project funded by the Engineering and Physical Sciences Research Council in the United Kingdom that was involved in creating future scenarios. Against much influential policymaking, consultancy thinking and existing planning paradigms which focus on predicting the near-term effects of technological innovation or market trends, the social futures approach combines complexity theory, nonlinear processes, unintended consequences and questions of timing and competing actors to describe unstable adaptive systems that are fragile, uncertain and unpredictable. Mobilities research has also advocated for a strong emphasis on questions of uneven (im)mobilities and mobility justice, which I will emphasize in this chapter. The new mobilities paradigm offers a way to think about more complex problems of transformation of mobility regimes across many scales, and it especially emphasizes the power relations involved in any such transformations.

To transform entire mobility systems, energy cultures and infrastructure scapes will require not just technological innovation, market disruptions or policy adjustments, but will also demand deeper kinopolitical struggles that can challenge the social inequities that underpin the unsustainability of the current mobility system. A wide range of interdisciplinary and critical research has begun to theorize not only mobilities as a political question of the distribution of power, but also the political as mobile. The political, it could be said, is fundamentally mobile: Political boundaries and identities are formed by im/mobilities (i.e., who has the right to move). The concept of 'kinopolitics' – which combines *kinos* (or movement) with politics and was especially developed by Thomas Nail (2015, 2018, 2019), but has also been applied within mobilities research (e.g. Sheller, 2018) – recognizes mobilities as a foundational political relation and even as *constitutive of* all political relations. Not only does the power to control mobility inform all politics, but also political subjectivity, identities, borders and networks emerge from mobile processes and relations in the first place.

This chapter argues that we need to theorize mobility futures in ways that take into account kinopolitics, not simply rely on the 'transition' to new technologies such as electric vehicles and alternative fuels; shared mobilities such as bike-sharing, car-sharing and smart connected cars; or innovations such as automated cars and connected mobility services. These new mobility regimes, technologies and everyday practices will promote sustainability transitions only in a very limited sense if not coupled with wider analysis of kinopolitical power relations at many scales. I will first briefly introduce the limits of current approaches to imagining mobility innovation futures and then show how an approach highlighting kinopolitical questions of mobility justice opens new avenues for imagining social futures and provoking different kinds of mobility transitions.

The limits of 'innovation' futures

Everyday ways of life, habits and routine expectations around mobility, communication and convenience have come to generate massive amounts of greenhouse gases as well as many other forms of pollution such as mining waste, disrupted rivers and fluoride contamination. With estimates that by 2050, transportation will be responsible for 35% of all CO_2 emissions in the world, there is immense pressure to decarbonize the transport sector worldwide. Here I will focus especially on passenger transportation, although freight transportation and air travel must necessarily decarbonize as well. Despite a slight levelling off in the growth of automobility in industrialized countries between 2004 and 2014, the system of automobility continues to grow worldwide and continues to be one of the main problems facing those concerned with creating more sustainable human mobilities. How are societies meeting that challenge?

In order to address the many harms caused by the existing dominant system of automobility – air pollution, fossil-fuel-driven climate change, congestion, sprawl, social inequality, injuries and death due to crashes – many countries and cities are seeking to create not only a new transportation infrastructure of the future, but also a new mobility regime. That is to say there are shifts happening not only in the technologies and economic organization of the transportation sector itself, but also in the ways in which mobility more broadly speaking is regulated, governed and managed. The technological innovation approach can be understood as a variant of 'ecological modernization', a school of thought that emerged in the 1980s in Germany based on the premise that the economy will benefit from moves towards environmentalism (see Rickards, this volume). As a variant of 'transition theory', this approach posits that we can invent our way out of this crisis through improved governance and management and through a more 'reflexive modernization' along chosen pathways.

Within ecomodernization, technology and innovation are often understood as the drivers of changes in the dominant system of transportation, which currently centres on the system of private automobility (and ground freight transportation) which is deeply enmeshed in fossil fuel production and distribution. It is frequently noted that information and communication technologies are transforming mobility, with the advent of mobile, open data, big data, real-time data and route finding, interoperable systems and the desire for seamless multimodal travel information and fare systems. Shared use is also transforming mobility with the rise of collaborative consumption, fractional use services, ride hailing, mobility-on-demand and mobility-as-a-service models. New 'mobility enterprises' are emerging, driven by new strategic alliances between traditional transport manufacturing companies and digital economy companies, as well as mergers and acquisitions within both sectors, and experimentation with public/private partnerships and innovative financing mechanisms. Also on the horizon, many cities are actively preparing for the rollout of automated and driverless vehicles, with plans being made for new kinds of 'smart' or responsive infrastructure, regulation and insurance, cybersecurity and data collection.

In addition to these technological and economic changes, however, innovation is also driven by policy pressures instigated by climate change, linked to both adaptation (the need for more resilient systems) and mitigation (the need to shift away from fossil fuels). Here more reflexive transition theories come to the forefront, in which sensible governments will try to steer economies and technologies towards low-carbon transitions. Policy initiatives to reduce CO_2 emissions in the transport sector include a shift to electric vehicles and alternative fuels for ground transportation, but also reducing automobile dependence and shifting more people to mass transit and where possible active transport through better land-use planning, urban planning and street design. All of these developments are circulating through global policy networks and consultancy firms, with many advocating policies such as transit oriented development, bus rapid transit, complete streets, vision zero, travel demand management or costing the curb. As Nikolaeva et al. (2019) point out, however, even 'mobility austerity' policies and various measures to promote sustainable transportation have generally not challenged automobility itself or called for *reducing mobility*. Both the ecomodernization approach and the more reflexive strains of transitions management and the multilevel perspective have not directly dealt with the multiscalar challenges identified by mobilities theorists as problems of differential (im)mobility and kinopolitical power (Sheller, 2018).

While many European and Asian cities have already implemented sustainable mobility policies, the United States has been late to react and policymakers are bringing these ideas together for the first time in the proposals of the Green New Deal (GND). The GND is an ambitious congressional resolution put forth by new members of the House of Representatives calling for a ten-year mobilization towards an equitable transition to a 21st-century economy and clean energy revolution'. The GND proposes 'a broad and ambitious package of new policies and investments in communities, infrastructure and technology to help the United States achieve environmental sustainability and economic stability'. As part of a transition to 100% renewable energy by 2030, it calls for 100% zero emission passenger vehicles by 2030 and 100% fossil-free transportation by 2050. Specific policies envisioned to achieve this include scaling up electric charging infrastructure, consumer incentives for zero-emission vehicles and phasing out internal combustion engines after 2030 and, by 2050, scaling up research and development of biofuels and carbon-neutral fuels for aviation, heavy-duty vehicles and rail. The GND also calls for 'large investments… to increase access to safe pedestrian and bicycle travel, low-carbon bus rapid transit and electrified light rail' (https://www.dataforprogress.org/green-new-deal).

However, as a vision for a huge public investment in modernizing America's crumbling and fossil-fuel-intensive infrastructure, the GND misses the opportunity to rethink the connection between land use, transport, mobility and equity. Although it seeks to transform the American economy 'in a way that is environmentally just and distributes benefits equitably', the GND largely still relies on faith in ecomodernization (new technologies will come to the rescue) and existing policies of transition management (government can guide the transition). Will this be enough? While the GND proposes a buyback and phasing out of combustion engine vehicles, large investments in mass transit and the future transition of air travel to biofuels, the outline vision says nothing about *mobility justice* despite having a section on principles of justice. This is not simply a lost opportunity, in my view, but is a fatal flaw. To make any such large-scale social transition possible will require taking seriously mobility justice.

What is missing from the GND and from most other consultant-driven visions for future mobility transition policies? These policies say nothing about the uneven distribution of access to mobility (based on gender, race, age, disabilities, citizenship, etc.) and the ways in which power is exercised through control over differential mobilities; they say nothing about the indirect effects of infrastructure development, private automobiles and urban-centric 'placemaking' on land use, real estate investment, unaffordable housing and gentrification; and they do nothing to dislodge the high levels of mobility consumption by kinetic elites. The GND focusses its social equity arguments solely on job creation and giving workers access to healthcare, training and education. Yet it ignores the growing splintering of mobility systems into hypermobility and friction-free travel for the kinetic elite who impose their externalities on others, versus the slow and burdensome travel for the mobility poor and the majority subjected to mobility austerity despite adding little to harmful emissions (Sheller, 2018).

In the following section, I seek to highlight why mobility justice must be central to any comprehensive transition to sustainable mobility futures by sketching four future scenarios. These scenarios draw on John Urry's analysis in his book *What Is the Future?* and use the same names as found in some of his scenarios. However, by adding a more systematic contingency table approach with input from Hickman and Banister, I was able to highlight different axes of power (state versus market) and capital (real estate versus digital), which inform the four scenarios. This led me to delineate the four scenarios slightly differently; to identify the fourth scenario not as 'Fortress City' but as 'AI City' and to modify the narratives to highlight kinopolitical aspects of mobility justice through a systematic comparison of driving forces.

Mobility justice and low-carbon mobility transitions

We can develop four mobility future scenarios by drawing on trends that are already present in some ways and are influencing global urban trajectories of mobility transition. These can be formulated as a two-by-two contingency table on two axes: On one side, whether the drivers of the initiatives are place-based innovations (benefitting real estate investment) or predominantly digital technologies (benefitting digital capital); and on the other axis, whether the vision underlying it is predominantly market-led (and relatively deregulated) or state-regulated and government-led. This yields a typology of four types of future scenarios for mobility futures (see Figure 18.1), each of which will be described in turn:

1. Fast Mobility City: Place-based and free market-driven
2. Liveable City: Place-based but state-regulated
3. Digital 'Smart' City: Digital basis and free market-driven
4. AI City: Digital basis but state-controlled

The Fast Mobility City

This future rests on evermore speedy, extensive mobile lives for the kinetic elite; it is a city of growth, mobility, investment and ease and enticement for the wealthy. It looks something like Hudson Yards on the west side of Midtown Manhattan. This is the world of big engineering firms, star architects, high-paid consultants and luxury real estate developers. Here, real estate investment, jobs and urban population growth emerge as clusters of vertical towers, predicated on an ease of well-connected travel for the kinetic elite who will continue to make the city centre increasingly expensive. Tiered premium services will give the elite access to fast mobility, including high-speed rail, luxury car services, easy airport access and privately owned luxury automated vehicles. Cities will be increasingly vertical and orbited by many kinds of passenger and robotic aerial vehicles, including drone taxis and microdrones in swarms, on-demand delivery services by drone and automated robots. Space scrapers will emerge in core global cities, with increasing social inequality in the vertical high-mobility city (Graham, 2018), as elites benefit from premium access to escape the masses including growth in private jet air travel, multilocal work and residences and second and third homes.

Starting as a luxury item, driverless cars will become mobile meeting spaces for on-the-move work by the kinetic elite, and flexible on-demand workers will serve them in mobile work spaces blurring the distinction between office buildings, streets and transit. In contrast to the cheery projections of autonomous vehicle (AV)'s solving our congestion and pollution problems, AV usage could lead to more vehicle usage, more urban sprawl, declining transit use, privacy violations and increased inequity within "Mobility as a Service" (MaaS). However, so long as carbon capital remains in power, fossil fuel extraction will continue to power the Fast Mobility City, continuing global warming and undermining its own sustainability.

Many will be excluded from this high-cost vertical city, and life will be increasingly segregated into the protected groups with high-mobility capital and the precarious mobility poor who will most suffer the consequences of labour exploitation, displacement and climate change (Graham and Marvin, 2001). Huge income inequality, and premium real estate with fake civic spaces (private, policed, secured) will segregate the elite from working poor populations, who will be relegated to marginal spaces such as underground passageways, living under elevated highways or along polluted transport corridors and logistics zones. Critical infrastructure systems will be protected for the elite, but the poor will be increasingly exposed to extreme heat, flooding and food insecurity.

Mobility justice

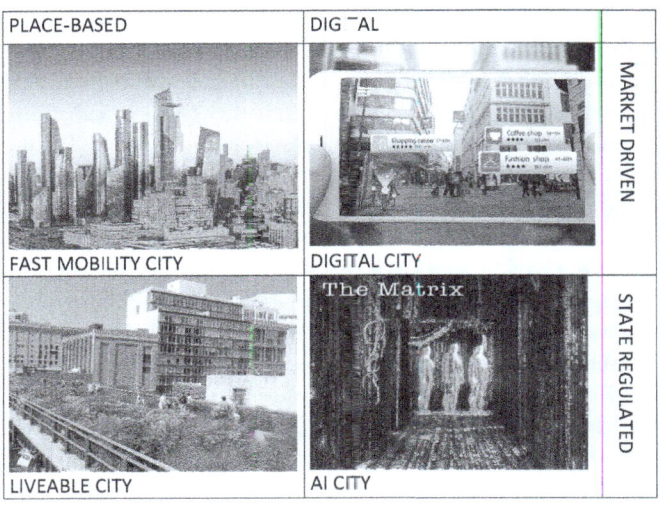

	PLACE-BASED	DIGITAL	
	FAST MOBILITY CITY: • Intense vertical real estate development; high prices • Splintered urbanism i.e., uneven access and spaces • MaaS exacerbates deep social inequalities	**DIGITAL CITY** • Tech company free-for-all • Labor exploitation within algorithmic gig economy • MaaS pulls people from public transit & walking & increases VMT/congestion	MARKET DRIVEN
	LIVEABLE CITY • Good place-making draws (white) knowledge workers & increases gentrification • Automobility restrictions price out lower income • Racial and ethnic disparities • Result is MaaS only for elite	**AI CITY** • Heavy state surveillance, data collection/ integration • MaaS becomes integrated into social control systems • AI social scoring used to restrict mobility options and punish "bad" citizens	STATE REGULATED

Figure 18.1 Contingency table of four future urban mobility scenarios.

The Digital 'Smart' City

A convergence of digital technologies such as the Internet of Things (IoT), big data, artificial intelligence, robotics and automation will replace many of the functions traditionally done by humans, providing what enthusiasts envision as exciting opportunities to change the nature of work, lifestyles, education, healthcare and how we get around. This is the city envisioned by digital capital – Apple, Alphabet, Microsoft, Sidewalk Labs and IBM Smart Cities (see also Raven and Dunn, this volume). It offers widespread substitution of physical movement of objects and people by many modes of digital communication and experience. Digital experiences will replace copresence; physical environments will become 'smart' and connected, the IoT sensing and adapting to people as they move through it and objects interacting independently through algorithms, smart controllers and artificial intelligence; people will move around virtually using digital doubles and interacting with intangible digital information using hand gestures.

When people do move physically, they will opt for shared, connected and increasingly automated cars enriched with virtual reality (VR) and augmented reality (AR) visualization capabilities. As Frauke Behrendt points out, current EU '[d]ebates around smart/intelligent/data mobilities and the IoT – including policy debates – tend to be dominated by motorized modes such as autonomous and networked cars' (Behrendt, 2019, p. 81). Pod-like connected vehicles will stream personalized navigation, music, media and Internet content, while also handling route selection, parking and payment automatically. Glenn Lyons (2015) describes such a scenario in terms of the emergence of 'multimobilities' in which people will use forms of physical and virtual mobility much more interchangeably. Distinctions between activity time and travel time will blur further, and individuals will move seamlessly between physical, AR and virtual encounters. Workers in the knowledge economy will have an increasingly weak link between where they live and who they work for and with. Car ownership will seem increasingly less important, and car use will seem increasingly banal. Shared use of mobility resources will be favoured. The car will be seen as a background technology serving a purely functional purpose, yet mobility will still be motorized and highly digitally mediated. For those who might still own cars, extensive 'costing the curb', congestion pricing and controlled parking will limit private vehicle access to the Digital City.

Streets and buildings will be permeated with ubiquitous computing and an IoT sea of sensors and activators. Fleets of shared electric automated vehicles of many different sizes and designs will begin to follow the pattern established by existing car-sharing and bike-sharing practices, repositioning themselves and being always ready on demand. AR and VR will take off, and automated cars will become mobile media devices and meeting spaces filled with screens and digital simulation; they will likely unlock through face recognition and biometric detection that will automatically set your personal preferences. Meanwhile, 3D printing and additive manufacturing will spawn new logistics systems with maker spaces and local warehouses linked to automated delivery systems.

As technology theorist Adam Greenfield trenchantly observes, such predictions of the future are ideologically driven, especially when coming from actors with deep investments in such futures. Automation, machine learning, algorithmic control and artificial intelligence are all interconnected developments that may be highly socially disruptive, but their direction depends on how they are enacted, regulated and made real. Their outcomes are not inevitable. We need to pay attention to the ways in which a company like Amazon, for example, is seeking to 'consolidate its investments in logistical innovation, deploying a mesh of autonomous trucking, mobile warehousing and drone-based delivery assets, knit together by network analysis and demand anticipation algorithms' (Greenfield, 2017, p. 278). This ongoing colonization of everyday life by information technologies leads to new forms of 'transmobility', argues Greenfield, in which there is risk of a loss of locality, loss of empathy, shallowing of experience, potential cascading effects of system disruptions and people who live nowhere in particular but become digital nomads, using small apartments-on-wheels, capsule hotels and shared spaces.

The Liveable City

This is the city of green entrepreneurs, bike advocates, place-makers, transit-oriented development and Europhiles and ecosocialists developing new practices to power down and reduce carbon intensity of cities. It is closest to the vision advocated in the GND. Cycling, walking and scootering will be more important along with small, light, connected, smart and potentially AV-sharing systems. Full build-out of bike infrastructure and pedestrian safety will be implemented, along with green buildings, green storm water management, more open green spaces and renewable energy plans; active transport and electric vehicle sharing, along with much improved public transit and investment in stations, will gradually replace all private cars, which will become obsolete. It would be an access economy with new mobility services. Cities will fragment into smaller-scale systems of neighbourhoods which would be more self-sufficient and less rigidly zoned. High-energy mobility machines would be less important in Liveable Cities, and centre-sprawl patterns would dissolve. As heavier fossil fuel-driven vehicles are phased out, there will be distributed electric vehicle microgrids that could rely on renewable energy to support a multiplicity of e-bikes, e-scooters, e-cargo and other small electric shared mobility systems, alongside simple nonmotorized cycling and walking.

The balance between roads for cars and pathways for cyclists and pedestrians would be fundamentally transformed, with far more space allocated to active forms of mobility, as is already starting to trend in parts of Madrid, Paris, Hamburg, Helsinki, Milan, Oslo and Copenhagen. Neighbourhoods will be of higher density in general and will function at smaller scales, with work, school, local production, consumption and repair all occurring nearby where people live, implying a systematic reduction in distances travelled by people, objects, goods and money. Each area will have its own resilient renewable energy microgrids, local manufacturing and production facilities, urban farming and sharing economies. Small-scale, tool-sharing FabLabs and organic farms will be collective and cooperative and have both digital and physical components. Innovation in local currencies, municipal bonds and new local financing mechanisms will be instituted using blockchain technology based not on energy-intensive Bitcoin, but on something more like Ethereum. The Liveable City relies on encouraging collaboration, using design as a transformative tool, involving the community in place-making, rejuvenating existing spaces, improving connectivity and creating new destinations (see liveablecity.org).

The possible downsides of this (from some perspectives) would be the imposition of mobility austerity and sharply reduced energy consumption. There would be strict limits on automobility achieved through congestion pricing, carbon pricing, personal carbon budgets, parking scarcity, road diets, delivery restrictions and other measures to reduce mobility. While many environmentalists see these as positive developments, many voters currently reject such policies and automobility continues to be massively expanding in the late-industrialized world. In some cases, people see road pricing and carbon pricing mechanisms as detrimental to the poor, who spend a greater proportion of their income on transportation. To be more socially just, it would at a minimum require guaranteed subsidies below certain thresholds of accessibility (Martens, 2016) and possibly a step further, support for Universal Basic Mobility through free public transit. Yet as seen in France, mobility austerity can trigger powerful backlash from automobile-dependent populist groups such as the Yellow Vest movement, and it is evident in the United States that many will not embrace the GND.

The AI City

The Artificial Intelligence (AI) City is similar to the Digital City, but it is far less egalitarian/horizontal and far more like Big Brother or The Matrix, with hidden control systems and user manipulation. In contrast to the free market vision of a liberating digital revolution, in this scenario, concentrated control over massive quantities of information, real-time responsive systems, big data analytical models and artificial intelligence tend instead to entrench a winner-takes-all economics due to network effects that concentrate power in very large organizations (businesses or states). While initially envisioned by John Urry as a walled 'Fortress City', it is more likely that the control systems in such a future city will be digital.

The rise of such systems will be linked to state securitization efforts in the face of growing social inequalities and divergent life chances. As climate change intensifies, this scenario is also associated with authoritarian state responses to growing refugee crises, food shortages, rising global inequality, social uprisings and terrorism.

This leads to an authoritarian digital city in which artificial intelligence has been incorporated into all kinds of algorithmic controls on citizen behaviour: Algorithmic predictive policing (PredPol), automated vehicle control systems that can override the passenger's wishes, responsive infrastructure and buildings embedded with sensors, personal tracking and total surveillance via cellphone tracking of comprehensive digital interactions and personal scoring systems like those currently being used in China where there are plans to rank all its citizens based on their 'social credit' score (see also Lupton, this volume). People can be rewarded or punished according to their scores. The AI City has a high degree of tracking and data collection – bringing personalized experience and locational marketing as well as surveillance and digital policing. Drone surveillance, video surveillance and facial recognition technology combined with massive biometric databases screen people at borders, stations and other checkpoints. The rise of COVID-19 tracking apps could instigate the requirement for people to enrol in such systems around the world, normalizing the trade-off of locational privacy to mitigate health risks.

The introduction of AI and algorithmic management in the mobility services workforce will also have profound impacts on work. Workers will face impersonal algorithmic control in the gig economy and long hours due to a kind of self-exploitation that arises through manipulation of surge pricing. Workers displaced from the city centre will also have challenging commutes just to get to work, tending towards workers simply waiting in their vehicles and engaging in a kind of continuous state of being at-the-ready and on-the-move. Of course, it is already being predicted that AVs will rapidly displace such workers, removing an entire workforce from urban centres and further exacerbating social inequalities in terms of who has access to the city. Mobility injustice in such a scenario will reinforce existing racial and ethnic hierarchies, in which 'racialized' subgroups are excluded from the right to the city or the right to mobility.

Discussion: Moving towards just mobility futures

Each of these mobility future scenarios has woven into it various aspects of mobility injustice. Insofar as we leave mobility transitions either to market-driven forces or to state regulation, we are missing the elements of social mobilization and kinopolitical struggle that might shape these outcomes differently. Likewise, we need to pay greater attention to the injustice of digital systems and the ways in which the concentration of digital power is in tension with democratic determination of mobility transitions. The concept of mobility justice suggests that we must open a space for civic engagement, between the state and the market, to empower more just transitions. To transform entire mobility systems and infrastructure scapes will require kinopolitical struggles for mobility justice that also span hybrid physical and digital spaces.

Transitions of mobility systems cannot be driven by either market-based technological innovation and concentrations of digital capital, on the one hand, or the authoritarian imposition of low-carbon policies and state regulation, on the other, because when left to work alone, these forces will continue to reproduce mobility injustices and exacerbate inequitable social futures. Responses to climate change and to environmental injustice should entail not only a reduction in energy demand or a shift to noncarbon fuels (the main current policy measures), but also a critical stance involving more socially just forms of life and ultimately new material assemblages of mobilities and mobilization of publics – and what I have called mobile commoning – for determining distributions of infrastructure and energy (Sheller, 2018). To do this, we need to pay attention to the different kinds of social forces driving current transitions, that is, whether pushed by kinetic elites, digital capital, green gentrification or concentration of power and state securitization, and compare them against processes of mobile commoning (see also Nikolaeva et al., 2019).

For some time, I have argued for the need for a dual transition towards environmentally sustainable mobility *and greater mobility justice* to ensure that future urban mobility transitions will not entrench ever greater social inequities, exclusions and externalization of harms (Sheller, 2011, 2018). The transformations of mobility wrought by the COVID-19 pandemic, and the deep inequities in who was most exposed to infection and who could protect themselves, have made this even more imperative. We need regional and urban planning processes that reject technological determinism and claims of market inevitability and instead seek to ensure deliberative and procedural justice, facilitate communication across communities and social strata and purposefully build more equitable mobility futures. This demands social movements and social mobilization through commoning mobilities.

Bibliography

Behrendt, F. (2019). 'Mobility and data: Cycling the utopian internet of things', *Mobilities*, 15(1), pp. 81–105.
Geels, F., Kemp, R., Dudley, G. and Lyons, G. (eds.) (2011). *Automobility in transition? A sociotechnical analysis of sustainable transport*. London: Routledge.
Graham, S. (2016). *Vertical*. London: Verso.
Graham, S. and Marvin, S. (2001). *Splintering urbanism: Networked infrastructures, technological mobilities and the urban condition*. London: Routledge.
Greenfield, A. (2017). *Radical technologies*. London and New York: Verso.
Hickman, R. and Banister, D. (2014). *Transport, climate change and the city*. Abingdon and New York: Routledge.
Köhler, J. et al. (2019). 'An agenda for sustainability transitions research: State of the art and future directions', *Environmental Innovation and Societal Transitions*, 31, pp. 1–32.
Lyons, G. (2015). 'Transport's digital age transition', *The Journal of Transport and Land Use*, 8 (2), pp. 1–19.
Martens, K. (2016). *Transport justice: Designing fair transportation systems*. London and New York: Routledge.
Nail, T. (2015). *The figure of the migrant*. Stanford: Stanford University Press.
Nail, T. (2018). 'Kinopolitics: Borders in motion'. In Braidotti, R. and Bignall, S. (eds.) *Posthuman ecologies: Complexity and process after Deleuze*. New York: Rowman and Littlefield, pp. 183–204.
Nail, T. (2019). 'Migrant climate in the Kinocene', *Mobilities*, 14(3), pp. 375–380.
Nikolaeva, A. Adey, P., Cresswell, T., Lee, J.Y., Novoa, A. and Temenos, C. (2019). 'Commoning mobility: Towards a new politics of mobility transitions', *Transactions of the Institute of British Geographers*, 44, pp. 346–360.
Sheller, M. (2011). 'Creating sustainable mobility and mobility justice'. In *Mobile/Immobile: Quels choix, quels droits pour 2030?*. Paris: Forum des Vies Mobiles, pp. 113–123.
Sheller, M. (2017). 'From spatial turn to mobilities turn', *Current Sociology*, 65(4), pp. 623–639.
Sheller, M. (2018). *Mobility justice: The politics of movement in an age of extremes*. London and New York: Verso.
Sheller, M. and Urry, J. (2006). 'The new mobilities paradigm', *Environment and Planning A*, 38, pp. 207–226.
Sheller, M. and Urry, J. (2016). 'Mobilising the new mobilities paradigm', *Applied Mobilities*, 1(1), pp. 10–25.
United Nations Environment Programme (2019). *Emissions Gap Report 2019 Global progress report on climate action*, https://www.unenvironment.org/interactive/emissions-gap-report/2019/
Urry, J. (2014). 'The problem of energy', *Theory, Culture and Society*, 31(5), pp. 3–20.
Urry, J. (2016). *What is the future?* Cambridge: Polity Press.

19
Multi-planetary worlds
Mobilities of the space age

Katarina Damjanov

Introduction

Our futures steadily gather momentum in outer space. As advances in techno-science propel a range of objects and ideas, data and images and affects and capital beyond the globe, their proliferation progressively entangles human societies with their planetary outside. The proceedings of the space age extend and magnify the prospective reach of our futures in the making. They propagate into Earth's exterior, into an inhuman environment that is nevertheless conceived as a shared domain of the 'global commons', whose exploration would transform its expanses into 'a province of humankind' (United Nation, 1967). The many hands-on attempts to render it a part of human worlds span diverse governmental and commercial enterprises – from the growing constellation of earth orbiting satellites and an increasing population of Mars rovers, across developments in space tourism and preparations to mine moons and asteroids to elaborate plans to terraform planets. As our ways of life exhaust resources on Earth, the need to sustain them directs their productive, reproductive and destructive forces into the commons of space. To overcome our terrestrial limitations, space entrepreneur Elon Musk, for instance, advocates colonizing Mars – a move that would cast humans as a 'space bearing civilization and a multi-planetary species' (2017, p. 46). Opening up opportunities for multi-planetary projections of the species, space advances protract the horizon of our common world, fuelling all desires and anxieties surrounding the unfolding of its futures on and off the globe.

Our space affairs lie at the forefront of the ways in which terrestrial societies strive to advance onwards and upwards into the future. Born out of a long history of daring imaginaries, ground-breaking technological innovations, visionary scientific discovers and risky entrepreneurial ventures, they are evidence of substantial creative, financial, logistical and epistemological investments in the design of human futures. Their evolving courses are also a platform from which the species envisions its future at large, opening up avenues through which we can seek its countless prospects across great distances and scales of time. The conquest of space gathers governments, markets and communities around the endeavour of progress into the shared planetary exterior, advancing myriad political, economic, technoscientific, social and cultural processes outside their terrestrial confines. Uprooting all the movements and moorings that undergird the species' drive to be more, to know more and to have more, its many routes set the very makings and directions of our futures on the move. The space age resituates the transformative potential of the 'mobile' disposition of the species into a 'more than' planetary arena, at once accelerating and distilling the ongoing processes of making and remaking the human world.

Complex provisions towards making ourselves at home in space are already very much part of our many worlds. As new spacefaring states emerge and more private companies invest in various space enterprises, its expanses mature as a promising site in which to test and contest the multiple visions of our futures-in-the-making. Yet the transformation of outer space into a species' province not only involves an extension of our exploits from a planetary to a 'more-than' planetary scale, but also engenders the multiplication of the possible worlds that we can find or that can be found out there and the accompanying multitude of their political–economic and socio-environmental purviews. Assembling human societies around the bounty of space perpetuates and augments patterns of uneven access and unequal participation in shared resources, displacing familiar issues surrounding the creation and destruction of commons into a range of novel settings and situations. Alongside the technological advances, myriad direct and remote exchanges between *down here* and *out there* continue to problematize the species' affinity towards mobility, spanning from issues such as the increasing accumulations of orbital debris and circulations of mediated space experiences to a race to 'return to the Moon' and groundworks for occupation of Mars. Engaging with the breadth of mobilities involved in configurations of human collectivities in the space age, this chapter outlines their key directions, exploring the established and emerging ways in which they inflect the material and relational ambits of our shared world. I suggest that the push to progress them outside the home planet is not only integral to the strategic positioning of socio-technical processes around the malleable domain of the human future, but also pivotal for the development of their capacities to affect it at scale. The species' endeavour to hasten the courses of 'life as we know it' towards their multi-planetary prospects itself already looms large as a common matter of concern.

Planetary mobilities in their space age

All our lively motions are but a minute episode within the dynamic life of the universe. Brimming with all the comotion of organic, inanimate and technological matter that constitutes the continuum of our 'planetary mobilities' (Szerszynski, 2016), the Earth joins the swing and sway of other celestial bodies, pulsations of remote stars and tremors of galaxies far away. Moving together with the rest of the cosmos, we are approaching a future which, as science informs us, is quite certain to include the death of the Sun and, consequently, the end of life on the planet. But even such a terminal outlook might not forestall earthly movements altogether. As they exceed their terrestrial confines, our earth-born mobilities assume their 'extraplanetary' modes, heralding methods and means for assembling a human abode beyond the globe (Damjanov and Crouch, 2018). Sixty years since Sputnik, our activities disperse beyond the planet in many directions – all the way out to Voyager doggedly traversing the interstellar regions or space telescopes capturing light travelling from distant stars that once existed deep in the past of the universe. Human envoys too have taken steps outwards, astronauts have travelled to the Moon and back and space tourists have begun to accompany them aboard the International Space Station (ISS). A range of nonhumans have also joined our forays in space – dogs, monkeys and mice, bees and trees, seeds and microorganisms and various other fellow earthlings. The varied mobilities of the space age facilitate lively transactions between Earth and its exterior, repositioning the planetary moorings of life and its biological, social and technological forces within their boundless cosmic environment.

The ongoing 'conquest' of space spurs a variety of terrestrial activities and movements, mobilizing a flow of financial investments, vectors of technological innovations, grids of elaborate logistics, networks of collaboration and arenas of competition that engage a range of governments, industries and organizations. Their current manoeuvres register the accelerating activities of states to secure their space interests. In 2018, US president Donald Trump announced a space policy directive for the creation of a Space Force, suggesting that America's 'destiny, beyond the Earth', is essentially 'a matter of national security' (The White House, 2018). At the same time, efforts to set forth into space also draw in the increasing involvement of private businesses, as tech entrepreneurs such as Elon Musk, Jeff Bezos and Richard Branson commence their various space enterprises. SpaceX, for example, has been developing reusable rockets and shuttles for low-cost launches, developing a fast-speed global satellite Internet and selling tickets for prospective tours to the Moon (TechRadar, 2019). Outer space has become a promising site in which to assure the prospects of capitalism and its drive towards expansion into new domains of life (Dickens and Ormrod, 2007; Parker, 2009; Valentine, 2012). As military–industrial complexes gradually array the twin forces of exploration and exploitation around vital resources, the shared commons of space become increasingly central for the securities of terrestrial societies and their pursuits of power, knowledge and wealth.

These aspirations undergird both our movements in space and our hold upon it. Carrying and being carried by technologies, they diffuse across and beyond our solar system, where they are conditioned by their alien surroundings. The Curiosity rover, for instance, slowly roves the rocky terrain of Gale Crater, occasionally getting stuck in its rusty soil; coated in dust and taking selfies, with the outlandish environment wearing away at its wheels, it lives its Martian life on our behalf. And it is not just inquisitive technologies that breathe our ways of life into outer space, but it is *in situ* 'domestications' that are also engendered by all those living humans and nonhumans that leave the Earth, travel into orbit and to the Moon or reside aboard space stations. The complex socio-technical systems involved in the choreographies of sustaining our presence out there consolidate the mobile disposition of the species, extending but also altering their 'space-bearing' configurations. They introduce us to entirely new environments and entangle us into novel sets of encounters and interactions. As such, they sit at the crux of new ecologies of mobilities evolving on and beyond the planet. Poised at the edge of encounters between new arenas of movement and new struggles to secure them, they exert their own effects upon the unfolding of our cosmic futures.

The transformative impetus of space mobilities also disperses back to the Earth through multiple trajectories continuing to galvanize all manner of movement across the planet. A wealth of data, images and maps collected by space technologies such as GPS satellites, the Curiosity rover or New Horizons are subsequently fed into a range of military, commercial and scientific projects and services – from where this content is further spread into the varied mores of life on Earth. The impressions of astronauts and tourists who have returned from space excursions are also widely shared, and sample materials that are retrieved such as Moon rocks and various items of space equipment and memorabilia are curated and exhibited. Everything and anything that comes in contact with space – whether humans or nonhumans, beings or objects – accrues a particular public status. Contemporary media cultures in particular facilitate the ever-widening outreach of space mobilities, allowing their distribution to global audiences through the broadcast of launches and landings, the real-time and remote tracking of spacecraft, live camera feeds from the ISS, interactive maps and immersive virtual reality (VR) experiences, while becoming integral to attempts to transform portions of outer space into 'places' (Messeri, 2015). These mediations draw the earth-bound masses to join in and participate in space mobilities, igniting a gamut of social activity around assertions of our cosmic abode (Damjanov and Crouch, 2018). While our *in situ* space mobilities might always remain the province of a selected few states and companies, people and technologies, the participatory activity they generate on Earth is wide-reaching and influences our space enterprises and wider cultural life.

Dispersing across multiple scales, the mobilities of the space age stretch from far to near, the elite to the masses, the organic to the inanimate and the material to the nonmaterial indexes of life. On Earth, their already tangled roots and routes continue to draw humans and nonhumans, technologies and environments together into different patterns of relations, entwining them into new lively assemblages (Hannam, Sheller and Urry, 2006). Projected into the commons of space, these arrangements and relativities are not only perpetuated and extended, but also resituated and given room to evolve.

Common futures and their cosmic bearings

The mobilities of the space age configure the human domain, enhancing our capacity to reassert its precincts outside their planetary confines. However, while the project of making ourselves at home out there evokes a vision of 'common' endeavour, it nonetheless replicates and precipitates the systems of demarcation and separation that structure our tenancy down here on Earth. It is directed by particular states and private parties and undergirded by specific ideas about which 'earthly' ways of life should be sent forth, towards which destination and to what effects. The multi-planetary prospects of human futures further problematize our interference with the world in which we live, protracting a host of political–economic and socio-ethical issues surrounding the species' relations with their spaces. Their forays are thus far limited to a small pool of governmental and industry players, reproducing familiar patterns and concentration of power over access to shared resources. In outer space, a multitude of geostrategic conjectures surrounding our 'uneven mobilities futures' (Sheller, 2016) are extended but also further upended. Their collisions with the cosmic commons rearrange the species' collectivities within the malleable boundaries of a shared world and amidst the competing visions of their multi-planetary futures.

Our space exploits are still tentative, but nevertheless already leave notable effects. Their imprints are most striking closest to home, at the very fringes of the planet, in orbital space, which has since Sputnik's pioneering visit developed into a busy techno-industrial zone, becoming a kind of overcrowded exurbia occupied by ever-more satellites. Adding to this congestion is a simultaneous accumulation of technological waste that has built up in their wake and now revolves around the planet – and which has its own alternate mobilities that largely lie outside our control. Space debris has also been left across the orbits and the surfaces of other celestial bodies – much of it on the Moon, where tons litter its surface, including objects discarded and erected, derelict personal items and even an artwork. Inaugurating space futures, we are already embracing their dark side. The commons of space are becoming another province for the same exploitative processes that have long structured our occupation of Earth, recasting their perennial problems of the accumulation of waste, depletion of resources and environmental destruction. Transposing our occupational patterns upon alien space places the material impact of technological progress into sharp relief, indicating its widening reach and a growing capacity to leave a lasting impression.

One direction in the accelerations of these transformative processes can be observed in renewed interest in the Moon, as the lunar stage is redressed for a new set of future impositions. A number of missions have been recently dispatched – with some crashing, such as Beresheet, the first privately funded lunar probe launched by SpaceIL and Israel Aerospace Industries (Wall, 2019) – and a few successful ones, such as the visit of the China National Space Administration's Chang'e-4 spacecraft to the Moon's 'dark side' (Devlin and Lyons, 2019). Another race to the Earth's only natural satellite advances our lunar claims, yet this time around, they concern a very different set of human futures – the next giant leap that is to be made on the Moon is apparently geared towards the mining of its minerals (Klinger, 2017). High-tech initiatives and competitions have already been organized to expedite our return, such as the completed Google Lunar X Prize, aka Moon 2.0, which sought to find ways of efficiently landing and operating a new generation of robotic lunar vehicles. New approaches to the Moon register the changing arrangements and shifting imperatives of species' mobilities and the rescaling of the problems associated with securing the resources needed to sustain them. Participation in common resources often precipitates 'tragedy' (Hardin, 1968), and one such calamity may be suggested by the looming prospects of lunar extraction. Barely half a century into the space age, and our impositions already demand solutions – from dealing with orbital debris (Damjanov, 2017), sustainable space tourism (Spector, Higham and Doering, 2017), the ethics surrounding space mining (Kearnes and van Dooren, 2017), terraforming (Schwartz, 2013) and settlement (Fogg, 2000).

And extracting lunar futures it seems would not be nearly enough to satisfy the species' voracious appetites. Musk (2017) suggests that the Moon is only one small step, a jumping-off point for a much larger journey, a longer set of movements towards a more vital target site – that of our Martian futures. Mars is already a popular destination, with many missions having been sent over the decades and much public interest generated around the image of the red planet as a possible human abode. The number of probes into its capacity to harbour life is set to increase – with scheduled missions such as NASA's Mars 2020 and ExoMars 2020, a joint venture of the European Space Agency (ESA) and Russian Roscosmos readied for departure. These increasingly sophisticated technologies and their mobilities might assist in asserting us as a 'multi-planetary' species, yet important in this equation is the presence of humans themselves. Preparations for a Martian 'giant leap' have already begun; research on the requirements of a human round-trip is being carried out, such as the Mars-500 isolation experiment by ESA and the Russian Institute for Biomedical Problems (ESA, 2012), which trialled a long and confining journey to Mars in laboratory conditions. The technological moorings that would support a prospective human future on Mars are already being designed – as one example, NASA's '3D-Printed Mars Habitat Challenge' encouraged the construction of technology for 'sustainable housing solutions' (NASA, 2019). At the same time, plans are being made to make Mars itself liveable within elaborate schemes to 'terraform' it into an earthlike environment – and such aspirations often surpass the capacities of science and technologies, pushing the development of imaginative solutions. Such experimentations are part of our evolving 'multi-planetary imaginaries' and their pursuit of an inventiveness that heralds a future making and remaking of socio-technical relations (Tutton, 2018). However, as experimental modes of inhabiting and habituating Mars are proposed and composed, we already begin to live our Martian futures.

The incorporation of outer space into human mores demands a host of strategies for negotiating their alien environments not only *in situ* but also from afar. Our remote encounters are distilled through minute studies of planets and moons and macro-cartographies of stellar and galactic formations, from tours simulating explorations of Mars rovers to spectacular

Hubble images. The ongoing multi-scalar capturing and dissemination of distant cosmic worlds opens them up, and makes them closer, more accessible and inspectable, but at the same time reframes their features. Hubble images that are shared with the public, for example, are produced from the raw data that the telescope collects, and which is then extensively enhanced and altered to resemble familiar landscapes (Kessler, 2012). Making distant cosmic settings and locations known and visible through the apparatus and logics of technology and science, national agendas and creative industries might make them appear more 'homely', but at the same time, the outward gaze of the species remains calculative and evaluative, passed through the filters of the space powers that shape its perspectives and make them possible. While the avenues leading to myriad space futures keep widening, our capacity to take them in remains restrained. Dictated by pre-arranged itineraries, controlled encounters and prescribed modes of access, they embody and reflect the technological underpinnings of the political and economic order that conditions our social relations, shapes forms and bodies of knowledge and predetermines all outward routes and engagements.

And it is not only our technologies and political economies that place restrictions on our movements; space itself demands that we adjust how we move and remain mobile. The vast size, alien nature and unknown assets of outer space require us to establish connections, but also to negotiate and overcome many forms of barrier, disjunction and disruption. In outer space, any carefully planned passage can easily get out of control; spacecraft often crash suddenly, microorganisms stow away and take a ride on spacecraft and satellite links regularly break down. Largely out of our hands, such prospects demand an adjustment of life as we know it, but also an invitation to rethink its multiple worlds; to reimagine their making; and to reconceive their organization, networks of relation and their social effects. Perhaps there is some indication of this in the Martian future imagined by Kim Stanley Robinson (2015) – whereby, after being colonized by states and multi-national corporations and gradually terraformed, the planet is not merely transformed into an outpost of Earth, but provides a setting for the emergence of an organic Martian society with its own dispositions and aspirations. Multi-planetary worlds present a chance to renegotiate our political, economic, scientific and social practices and approaches and redevise their rationalities and strategies. And in this sense, our multi-planetary bearings involve more than just a 'duplication' of planets; they also concern the 'habituation' of unfamiliar mobilities and relations, and their inscriptions into our shared worlds on and beyond the globe.

Conclusion

While the terrestrial life of the species already encompasses many multi-planetary futures, our social and material progress towards realizing these prospects is not exclusively human. On Earth, we have become increasingly aware and attuned to the 'more-than-human' composition of our worlds (Whatmore, 2006), and this alertness and attentiveness involves robust politico-ethical approaches to the ways in which we relate, partake and take care. In inhuman outer space, such developments are stark and even more pronounced as they also become 'more-than-planetary'. Entangling various humans, nonhumans and environments, these still-evolving capacities to relate require new kinds of regard and solicitude, which are not always earth-centred, or necessarily even human-centric. And all the while, these more-than-planetary and more-than-human futures contend with larger cosmic movements, the imposition of their unstoppable forces, unfamiliar gravities, gyrations and implosions. In the end, 'moving on' might be all that is left – onwards and outwards towards new distant cosmic riches and provisional resting places. The future destruction of our home planet perhaps only highlights the fragile ecologies sustaining the species' place in the universe. While outer space might offer somewhere to reproduce and duplicate our early ways of life, it also demands that we uproot its routes, keep its courses uncertain and its futures always on the move.

Bibliography

Damjanov, K. (2017). 'Of defunct satellites and other space debris: Media waste in the orbital commons', *Science, Technology, & Human Values*, 42(1), pp. 166–185.

Damjanov, K. and Crouch, D. (2018). 'Extra-planetary mobilities and the media prospects of virtual space tourism', *Mobilities*, 13(1), pp. 1–13.

Devlin, H. and Lyons, K. (2019). 'Far side of the Moon: China's Chang'e 4 probe makes historic touchdown', *The Guardian*, 3 January; https://www.theguardian.com/science/2019/jan/03/china-probe-change-4-land-far-side-moon-basin-crater

Dickens, P. and Ormrod, J. (2007). *Cosmic society: Towards a sociology of the universe*. London and New York: Routledge.

ESA. (2012). 'Mars 500: Study overview'; http://www.esa.int/Our_Activities/Human_and_Robotic_Exploration/Mars500/Mars500_study_overview

Fogg, M.J. (2000). 'The ethical dimensions of space settlement', *Space Policy*, 16(3), pp. 205–211.

Google Lunar X Prize. (2019). https://lunar.xprize.org/prizes/google-lunar

Hannam, K., Sheller, M., and Urry, J. (2006). 'Editorial: Mobilities, immobilities and moorings', *Mobilities*, 1(1), pp. 1–22.

Hardin, G. (1968). 'The tragedy of the commons', *Science*, 162(3859), pp. 1243–1248.

Kearnes, M. and van Dooren, T. (2017). 'Rethinking the final frontier: Cosmo-logics and an ethic of interstellar flourishing', *GeoHumanities*, 3(1), pp. 178–197

Kessler, E.A. (2012). *Picturing the cosmos: Hubble space telescope images and the astronomical sublime*. Minneapolis: University of Minnesota Press.

Klinger, J.M. (2017). *Rare earth frontiers: From terrestrial subsoils to lunar landscapes*. Ithaca, NY: Cornell University Press.

Messeri, L. (2016). *Placing outer space: An earthly ethnography of other worlds*. Durham, NC: Duke University Press.

Musk, E. (2017). 'Making humans a multi-planetary species', *New Space*, 5(2); https://doi.org/10.1089/space.2017.29009.emu.

NASA. (2019). 'NASA's centennial challenges: 3D-printed habitat challenge'; https://www.nasa.gov/directorates/spacetech/centennial_challenges/3DPHab/about.html

Parker, M. (2009). 'Capitalists in space', *Sociological Review*, 57, pp. 83–97.

Robinson, K. (2015). *The complete Mars trilogy: Red Mars, green Mars, blue Mars*. London: Harper Collins.

Schwartz, J. (2013). 'On the moral permissibility of terraforming', *Ethics and the Environment*, 18(2), pp. 1–31.

Sheller, M. (2016). 'Uneven mobility futures: A Foucauldian approach', *Mobilities*, 11(1), pp. 15–31.

Spector, S., Higham, J.E.S., and Doering, A. (2017). 'Beyond the biosphere: Tourism, outer space, and sustainability', *Tourism Recreation Research*, 42(3), pp. 273–283.

Szerszynski, B. (2016). 'Planetary mobilities: Movement, memory and emergence in the body of the Earth', *Mobilities*, 11(4), pp. 614–628.

TechRadar. (2019). 'SpaceX: Everything you need to know', April 23; https://www.techradar.com/news/spacex-everything-you-need-to-know

The White House. (2018). 'Remarks by President Trump at a meeting with the National Space Council and signing of Space Policy Directive', 3 June; https://www.whitehouse.gov/briefings-statements/remarks-president-trump-meeting-national-space-council-signing-space-policy-directive-3/

Tutton, R. (2018). 'Multiplanetary imaginaries and utopia: The case of Mars One', *Science, Technology, and Human Values*, 43(3), pp. 518–539.

United Nations. (1967). *Treaty on principles governing the activities of states in the exploration and use of outer space, including the Moon and other celestial bodies*; http://www.oosa.unvienna.org/oosa/SpaceLaw/gares/html/gares_21_2222.html#a5

Valentine, D. (2012). 'Exit strategy: Profit, cosmology, and the future of humans in space', *Anthropological Quarterly*, 85(4), pp. 1045–1067.

Wall, M. (2019). 'Israel's Beresheet spacecraft crashes into Moon during landing attempt', *Space.com*, April 11; https://www.space.com/israeli-beresheet-moon-landing-attempt-fails.html

Whatmore, S. (2006). 'Materialist returns: Practising cultural geography in and for a more-than-human world', *Cultural Geographies*, 13(4), pp. 600–609.

20
Narrative
Telling social futures

Genevieve Liveley

> Narratology has made it clear that, while narrative can have any number of functions (entertaining, informing, persuading, diverting attention, etc.), there are some functions that it excels at or is unique in fulfilling. Narrative always reports one or more changes of state but, as etymology suggests (the term narrative is related to the Latin gnarus – 'knowing,' 'expert,' 'acquainted with'…), narrative is also a particular mode of knowledge. It does not merely reflect what happens; it discovers and invents what can happen.
>
> *Prince (1990, p. 1)*

Forecasting (sometimes super). Foresight (sometimes strategic). Prediction. Prognostics. Trendspotting. Futurism. Anticipation. Prospection. There are many descriptors for the discipline of futures thinking. And despite the image of prophecy and 'fortune-telling' that some of these terms evoke, they each claim credibility through appeals to a common grounding in predictive-empirical-analytical approaches and methods. Their future visions and scenarios are typically informed by scientific or quasi-scientific methodologies: Statistical and mathematical data modelling and simulation, geo-political and sociotechnical analyses and trend and pattern recognition (increasingly made possible by artificial-intelligence (AI)-supported analysis of complex data sets).[1] But the discipline of futures thinking is not (only) a science, it is (also) an art. At some level, as this chapter sets out to explore, all such future-focussed analyses and forecasts make use of *narrative*.[2]

There are almost as many variant definitions of 'narrative' in popular circulation as there are labels for futures research – although none quite captures the richness of Jim Phelan's 'rhetorical' definition. For Phelan, narrative is simply: 'Somebody telling somebody else on some occasion and for some purpose(s) that something happened' (Phelan, 2007, p. 203). This definition places emphasis on narrative as an action that seeks to accomplish some purposeful goal or *telos* and is the broad definition of narrative adopted in this chapter – albeit with one important modification. As Phelan's definition suggests, most narratives look to the past, telling somebody in the present about something that has already happened. Yet any narrative can give signals (weak or strong) both about the present and about the future, about possible things that may or will yet happen (in the near, medium or long term). And if the narrator's intention is to accomplish some future purpose or action, then any narrative can also have a future focus – whether or not the story makes use of future-tensed language or aspects. To modify Phelan's definition to serve the present purposes of this narrator and this audience, then, we might define narrative in the context of social futures as: *Somebody telling somebody else on some occasion and for some purposes that something has happened, is happening and will or may yet happen.*

To supplement the heuristics of this broad working definition of narrative, we might also usefully add Marie-Laure Ryan's fuzzy-set description (2007, p. 24) which identifies the following set of narrative's core characteristics, in order to remind us that[3]:

- Narrative is about problem-solving.
- Narrative is about conflict.
- Narrative is about interpersonal relations.
- Narrative is about human experience.
- Narrative is about the temporality of existence.

Characterized thus, it is no surprise to find that social futures research (and associated activism) is, in turn, about narrative. Social futures thinking is explicitly concerned with these narrative elements: Temporality (past, present and future); experientiality (neatly defined by Monica Fludernik (1996, p. 12) as 'the quasi-mimetic evocation of real-life experience'); relationships (social, political, local, global, no less than personal); conflicts (potential and actual, arising from conditions of volatility, uncertainty, complexity and ambiguity) and problem-solving (particularly in societal, technological, economic, environmental and political contexts).

Work in the social futures research space upon utopian thinking and counterfactual visioning, or speculative and science fiction futures, is perhaps the area most obviously and creatively engaged with narrative and stories. However, narrative as a vehicle for futures thinking is prevalent across more scientifically focussed predictive-empirical-analytical approaches and methodologies too. For example, trend analysis may appear to be a predominantly quantitative, data-driven exercise, but its focus upon key temporal-causal events and their mapping – or, in narrative terms, their 'emplotment' – clearly characterizes this as a qualitative narrative practice. Trend analysis precisely involves *telling somebody else on some occasion and for some purposes that something has happened, is happening and will or may yet happen.* Back-casting, which identifies a desired future *telos* and then extrapolates backwards to identify the chain of actions and events necessary to realize a temporal-causal sequence of events that will link that desired future to the present, is similarly shaped and driven by narrative.[4] This process too is a storytelling exercise in which narrative emplotment is key. Similarly, the futures scenario method, developed in the 1940s and still the dramatic centrepiece of much futures research, draws explicitly from the world of storytelling in its foundational appeal to the film scenario – the preliminary narrative script and storyboard of a cinematic text.[5] Indeed, it is in this light that Peter Schwartz in his ground-breaking study *The Art of the Long View* characterizes futures scenarios as 'stories that give meaning to events', as 'myths of the future' (Schwartz, 2007, p. 39). For, as Wendell Bell explains (1997, p. 319):

> The scenario […] is the preeminent method of futures research and it is involved to some degree in all the other methods. Stories are the most characteristic products of futures research, stories about what the future can be or could be, about what it is likely to be,

about what it ought (or ought not) to be, or about what we ought to do to create a desirable future or prevent an undesirable future. Futurists tell stories.

Indeed, futurists tell stories for a variety of reasons.[6] Bell aptly emphasizes the fact that stories – such as those used in scenarios – are typically used for communicating the outputs of futures thinking (that is, narrative as futures *form*). However, narrative also offers a potent medium for collecting futures-focussed data and ideas (narrative as futures *content*). And narrative is also a powerful sense-making tool in its own right (narrative as futures *process*). In the context of social futures, therefore, narrative is not only a 'social product' but also a 'social process or performance in action' and a social 'structure of knowledge' – at once 'text, shared discourse and emergent cognitive and communicative process' (Paschen and Ison, 2014, p. 1084).

There are, then, three key functions of narrative (and narratives) in social futures research: The *rhetorical* function, by which stories are employed in various forms to communicate ideas and plans for diverse futures (possible, plausible, probable and preferred) to different audiences; the *investigative* function, by which stories about the past, present and future (and, crucially, the temporal-causal connections and discontinuities between them) are elicited from a broad spectrum of futures stakeholders; and the *epistemic* function, by which stories are used as devices to help understand and make sense of the changing world – past, present and future. In practice, however, these discrete narrative functions intertwine. It is, after all, precisely because narrative is a powerful sense-making tool that it is simultaneously such a powerful means of eliciting and communicating ideas about the future. As Wittmayer et al. remind us (2019, p. 3):

> Narrative is one of the key modes of knowing for human beings, who have been recognized as *homo narrans* [...] and who, in and through stories, learn about, make sense of and act in and on the world. It is through narrative structures, that human beings think, perceive, imagine and make moral choices.

There are, inevitably, some problems with this narrative foundation to social futures thinking. Neil MacDonald (2012) identifies a set of limited narrative 'archetypes' that shape the plots and storylines of futures scenarios (Progress, Catastrophe, Reversion and Transformation). He questions whether the prevalence of these archetypes in futures research suggests that they may be '"hard-wired" into our narrative imagination' (2012, p. 290).[7] This reminds us that the four classic futures scenario plots described by Dator (2009) – 'Continued Growth', 'Collapse', 'Discipline' and 'Transformation' – reflect formal restrictions upon the narratives that we are able not only to *tell* but to *think* about our social futures. For, as Gerald Prince observes (1990, p. 1): 'Narrative [...] does not merely reflect what happens; it discovers and invents what can happen'. Futurists tell stories, it seems, but prefer only a handful of different plot types. And, just as historians tend to emplot their narratives according to familiar plot types or genres (tragedy, comedy, satire and romance), so futurists appear to emplot their stories about the future according to similar formal types. This emplotment may be 'hard-wired' into futures storytelling – much as storytelling itself is 'hard-wired' into futures thinking *homo narrans* – but we should recognize that this does not render its typologies natural, intrinsic or inevitable. As Haydn White writes of narrative historiography, but with direct applicability to futures narratives too (1990, p. 44):

> any given set of real events [past or future] can be emplotted in a number of ways, can bear the weight of being told as any number of different kinds of stories. Since no given

set or sequence of real events is intrinsically tragic, comic, farcical and so on, but can be constructed as such only by the imposition of the structure of a given story or type on the events, it is the choice of story type and its imposition upon the events that endow them with meaning.

Indeed, if we apply Ryan's fuzzy set to this problem, we see that, if narrative is about (among other things) conflict, interpersonal relations and human experience, then whether the events narrated as part of a given scenario are read as progress or catastrophe (say) will depend upon the audience's point of view. For example, for some societies and groups, Dator's 'discipline' future might well equate to catastrophic 'collapse' if it entailed the loss or compromise of liberal values and freedoms.

There are other risks involved in applying narrative models to real-life social futures scenarios (Morson, 1994, p. 20):

> Lives include all sorts of extraneous details leading nowhere, but good stories do not. Narratives are more successful if they display a structure, which it is hard to find in life [...] If we forget this and treat our lives as if they possessed the shape of narratives, we may run into trouble. Such confusion is of course a time-honored theme of novels themselves, from *Don Quixote* to *War and Peace* ... [But] politicians, especially those with a utopian or other ahistorical end in mind, typically try to persuade us to overlook the differences between our lives and our stories (to treat them as isomorphic). It is easiest to impose a [future] myth on those who are already inclined to think history has a mythic structure.

As Morson suggests, one of the risks of employing narrative models to shape futures thinking is that stories tend to be goal-oriented towards a predetermined *telos* or end point. Narratives have more or less clearly structured beginnings, middles and ends. Real life and real-life events do not. In the opening chapters of a story, the future is open and the forking paths leading into it offer multiple possibilities. As the story develops and particular paths are chosen, however, those possibilities are reduced and the openness of the future is gradually narrowed until the final chapters are reached, and the reader is left with only one path leading to one goal and a single point of closure – the end. The ongoing and repeating bifurcation of paths and the opening up of new possibilities that inform the best social futures research and thinking fit poorly with this traditional teleological narrative structure. In sum, the imposition of any narrative structure (whether mythic archetype or otherwise) upon possible futures scenarios will unavoidably tidy up and thus obscure the future's inherent messiness – its uncertainty, complexity and ambiguity. This, in turn, may smooth over and thus obscure the surprising plot point, the improbable yet probable event, the unexpected nodal point and the unanticipated tipping point.

Perhaps one of the greatest risks posed by the narrative dynamics involved in social futures thinking, however, lies in the narrative pull of the future back towards the present and past. Phelan's definition of narrative as 'somebody telling somebody else on some occasion and for some purposes that something *happened*' (Phelan, 2007, p. 203 – emphasis added) aptly stresses the past or preterite aspect to this present telling. Indeed, the tendency for narrative to 'presentify the past' in this way is well understood.[8] What is less recognized is the particular tendency of narrative to presentify the *future*. The presentifying (and, indeed, historicizing) aspects of futures methodologies and concepts themselves are already widely acknowledged. Gidley's *Short history of the future* (Gidley, 2017, p. 80), for example, offers an overview of the evolution of futures studies, variously describing: Husserl's concept of 'protention' as the future-orientated present; the concept of De Jouvenel's 'transferred presents' as 'structural features of the present, which our thought automatically carries forward into the future'; and Gebser's concepts of 'futures latency' and 'presentiation' as the 'demonstrable presence of the future' in the present. Yet, the particular role of narrative in shaping this retrospective mode of futures thinking is often overlooked – despite the fact that as early as the fourth century, Augustine noticed that narrative and reading both depend upon a complex synergy between *memory* (of what has passed – both inside and outside of the story), *attention* (to the present moment) and *anticipation* (of the future that is to come). Thus, (Augustine, *Confessions*, 11.xxvii, 1942, p. 37)[9]:

> The mind anticipates (*expectat*), attends (*attendit*), and remembers (*meminit*). What it anticipates crosses over into what it pays attention to and so into what it remembers. Who would deny that future things do not yet exist? But yet already, in the mind, there exists the anticipation of future things that are going to be.

Paul Ricouer (1984) famously developed Augustine's tripartite temporal model in his own theory of time and narrative, with memory and anticipation overlapping in a kind of feedback loop mutually informing the interconnected phases he identified as narrative 'prefiguration' and 'refiguration' (or Mimesis 1 and 3). For, as Ricouer explains (*pace* Augustine), any narrative anticipation of the future is coloured by our (necessarily selective) memory of past events and our (necessarily particular) focus of attention in the present moment.

Ricoeur identified three discrete but interdependent temporal components to narrative, corresponding to Augustine's tripartite paradigm of memory, attention and anticipation[10]:

- *Prefiguration* describes the narrative competence that allows us to process a narrative in the first place (whether as the teller or the told), the pre-existing expectations and experiences of the real world *and* of other narratives that shape our preunderstanding of how narrative works, based on our past experiences of life and of other stories.
- *Configuration* describes the relation of incidents and events into a coherent series of cause and event through emplotment. There is a key teleological dimension to Ricouer's concept of emplotment in this phase, concerning (to borrow Frank Kermode's phrase) the 'sense of an ending' in which meaning is made as a story progresses towards an end point, and is only fully understood retrospectively from that end point, when and where the narrative can be seen as a whole.
- *Refiguration* describes the understanding and interpretation of a narrative following its conclusion, a phase of transformation as the story enters the 'real world' of action and lived experience, as it teaches its readers about human experience and shapes their future narrative competence.

Ricouer's theory of narrative offers important insights, then, into the 'presentification' of our social futures as they are imagined, communicated and created in story form. In particular, it reminds us that there are limitations to what we are able to think about our possible futures, but it also draws our attention to the fact that future – and, indeed, *futures* – narrative competence involves a skill set that can be refined and honed by the iterative act of telling, reading and thinking about stories.

It seems wholly appropriate, therefore, that United Nations Educational, Scientific and Cultural Organization defines 'the skill that allows people to better understand the role that the future plays in what they see and do' as futures *literacy*.[11] For Riel Miller (2006, p. 27), one of the pioneers of this approach to futures thinking and research, futures literacy (or FL) represents the skill set that enables people 'to identify and distinguish different forms of the "potential of the present", to use the future in the same way that an accomplished reader can distinguish and invent (co-create) many meanings from a given text'. As Miller explains (2006, p. 27):

> FL [futures literacy] uses 'rigorous imagining' to develop and question the theories and models that define the variables and relationships, metrics and definitions being used to make sense of the present (note: Pattern recognition/data mining is insufficient). The point of FL is to become more adept at inventing imaginary futures: To use these futures to discern system boundaries, relationships and emergence; to invent and detect changes in the conditions of change; to rethink the assumptions we use to understand the present.

Narrative competence is a fundamental part of such literacy and speaks especially to the dynamics of 'rigorous imagining', of 'inventing imaginary futures' and of 'invent[ing] (co-creat[ing]) many meanings' in both the telling and the reading of social futures. Miller's model of FL also serves to remind us that in the domain of social futures thinking we are never dealing with concrete certainties (even when we have quantitative data to play with) but are always with 'present *imaginaries* of future situations' – that is, with social future scenarios and strategies which are narrative fictions (Beckert, 2013, p. 325 – emphasis added).

As we've seen, one of the chief limitations of narrative in social futures thinking is its pull towards the past and present (through memory and attention), resulting in blind spots that obscure possible and probable differences between past, present and future(s). As Bode and Dietrich complain (2013, p. 100) 'Being able to think about the future [...] is perpetually spoilt by our present incapacity to be sufficiently imaginative, to think the unexpected, to factor in surprise, discontinuities, reversals, tipping points, etc.' Through reading and telling stories, however, it seems that we have an opportunity to expand this capacity, to develop our social futures literacy through developing our narrative competence.

Recent narratological research into the phenomenology of reading and narrative sense-making reveals that Ricouer (and Augustine before him) was right to see an interplay between memory, attention and anticipation at work in the dynamics of processing a story. Studies in the 1970s and 1980s had already found that the cognitive processes – the narrative competencies – involved in reading narrative fiction differed significantly from those involved in reading non-narrative and non-fictional texts. In the non-fiction category of texts, readers tended to seek fixed meanings and definite consequences, to focus narrowly on concrete ideas; whereas in processing texts in the fictional category, readers tended instead to find multiple meanings and possibilities, to focus on ambiguity and openness.[12] What is more, readers of essays typically built up a mental model of the information contained in the text in a linear fashion, connecting each new element to something preceding it. Readers of stories, on the other hand, were found to be building models of the narrative storyworld in non-linear ways, speculating, forwarding and revising hypotheses; anticipating second-, third- and fourth-order consequences; and constantly 'looking ahead, trying to anticipate where the story is going' (Miall, 1995, p. 279).[13] In the light of these findings, Miall (1995, p. 279) accordingly characterized the reading of non-narrative and non-fiction as a predominantly 'retrospective' process and the reading of narrative fiction as a characteristically 'prospective' process. These anticipatory skills appear to translate well from the reading of fictional storyworlds to the reading of real-life future storyworlds too: As Mark Currie explains (2007, p. 6), 'the reading of fictional narratives is a kind of preparation for and repetition of the continuous anticipation that takes place in non-fictional life'.

Indeed, there is now, as Caracciolo and others have identified, 'extensive psycholinguistic evidence that readers [...] construct mental models of the scenarios represented by narrative' and that these models are typically 'volatile, *ad hoc* constructs that readers update as they process a narrative', constantly anticipating – looking ahead for new information which will change what they think they know about the storyworld and its latent futures – and revising their mental models as they gather this new information (Caracciolo, 2019, p. 127). That is, in the process of narrative configuration (to revisit Ricouer's terminology), readers are particularly attuned to any signals (weak and strong, true and false) that may be indicators of future surprises, reversals or tipping points. They are, in other words, constantly primed to expect the unexpected. Perhaps, then, we ourselves should not be surprised to find that these narrative experiences for readers of fiction – these narrative competencies – equate to a particular kind of FL. If being futures literate entails the ability to 'use the future in the same way that an accomplished reader can distinguish and invent (co-create) many meanings from a given text' (Miller, 2006, p. 27), then reading narrative fiction may offer an ideal platform for FL practice and thus for developing new proficiency in reading and telling social futures.[14]

Notes

1 On the naming and associated 'scientific' foundations of futures research, see Gidley (2017, pp. 1–10) and Jarva (2014).
2 For narrative approaches to futures thinking, see especially Milojevic and Inayatullah (2015) and Jarva (2014).
3 Ryan defines 'fuzzy set' in this non-mathematical context (where the theory originates) as a 'set allowing variable degrees of membership, but centred on prototypical cases that everybody recognizes' (2007, p. 28). In narratology, a fuzzy set avoids the need to define something in binary terms as either a 'story' or 'not a story' depending upon its possession or otherwise of a 'crisp set' of characteristics (a plot, a temporal sequence of events, etc.). Instead, it allows for an appreciation of 'storiness' or narrativity along a spectrum.
4 On the narrative dynamics of back-casting, see Dreborg (1996).
5 On the indebtedness of the scenarios method to narrative, see Raven and Elahi (2015), for whom: 'Storytelling lies at the heart of scenario and design practices' (p. 49). See also Curry in this volume.
6 See Wittmayer et al. (2019), for an overview of the recent burgeoning interest in the potential of narrative approaches particularly for social futures research and social innovation initiatives – including the power of storytelling in futures practice as a transformative social practice. See also Hofvenschioeld and Khodadadi (2020) for a literature review and comprehensive bibliography detailing the appearance of 'narrative', 'story' and 'storytelling' in futures literature – highlighting a continuing trend linking narrative and futures communication (outputs), alongside an increasing trend for narrative to be used as a tool in participatory futures research and practice (process).
7 On this human 'hard-wiring' for story, see also Kermode ([1967], 2000, p. 52):

> it is our insatiable interest in the future (towards which we are biologically oriented) that makes it necessary for us to relate to the past, and to the moment in the middle, by plots: by which I mean not only concordant imaginary incidents, but all the other, perhaps subtler, concords that can be arranged in a narrative.

8 See especially Currie (2007, 2010) and Liveley (2017).
9 All translations are my own.
10 See Kermode ([1967], 2000). For a Ricouerian take on the implications of this model for social futures thinking, see Uprichard (2011, pp. 107–110):

> Just as our understanding of the present conditions our narratives about the past, so do our narratives of the present help us to contemplate the future, which in turn recursively impacts

on how we consider the present [...] [therefore] narratives of the future are but re-constructed possibilities, relative to our re-interpretations of the past and the present as conditioning the parameters of the range of possible futures.

11 This definition of FL comes from UNESCO's dedicated web page: https://en.unesco.org/themes/futures-literacy#:~:text=Futures%20Literacy%20is%20a%20capability,present%20(Miller%2C%202015).
12 For a summary of this research and its findings, see Miall (1995).
13 Miall's findings nicely confirm Augustine's intuitions (Miall, 1995, p. 280):

> The reader of a literary text must at one and the same moment recall, respond, discriminate, and anticipate. Literary reading must frequently cope with surprise or contradiction, both on the local level [...] and more globally; it must deal with narrative switches, shifts of scene, and uncertainties of various kinds.

14 Thanks to fellow members of Futures Literacy through Narrative (FLiNT) – Emily Spiers and Will Slocombe – for helping me to refine some of the ideas presented in this chapter.

Bibliography

Augustine, and Sheed, F.J. (1942). *Confessions of St. Augustine, Books I-X*. New York: Sheed and Ward.
Beckert, J. (2013). 'Capitalism as a system of expectations: Toward a sociological microfoundation of political economy', *Politics and Society*, 41(3), pp. 323–350.
Bell, W. (1997). *Foundations of futures studies*, vol. 1. New Brunswick, NJ: Transactions Publishers.
Bode, C., and Dietrich, R. (2013). *Future narratives*. Berlin: W. de Gruyter.
Caracciolo, M. (2019). 'Ungrounding fictional worlds: An enactivist perspective on the "worldlikeness" of fiction'. In Bell, A., and Ryan, M.-L. (eds.). *Possible worlds theory and contemporary narratology*. Lincoln: University of Nebraska Press, pp. 113–131.
Currie, M. (2007). *About time*. Edinburgh: Edinburgh University Press.
Dator, J. (2009). 'Alternative futures at the Manoa school', *Journal of Futures Studies*, 14(2), pp. 1–18.
Dreborg, K.H. (1996). 'Essence of backcasting', *Futures*, 28(9), pp. 813–828.
Fludernik, M. (1996). *Towards a natural narratology*. London and New York: Routledge.
Gidley, J.M. (2017). *The future: A very short introduction*. Oxford: Oxford University Press.
Hofvenschioeld, E., and Khodadadi, M. (2020). 'Communication in futures studies: A discursive analysis of the literature', *Futures*, 115, p. 102493.
Jarva, V. (2014). 'Introduction to narrative for futures studies', *Journal of Futures Studies*, 18(3), pp. 5–26.
Kermode, F. (2000 [1967]). *The sense of an ending*. Oxford and New York: Oxford University Press.
Liveley, G. (2017). 'Anticipation and narratology'. In Poli, R. (ed.). *Handbook of Anticipation*. New York: Springer Publishing, pp. 1–20.
MacDonald, N. (2012). 'Futures and culture', *Futures*, 44(4), pp. 277–291.
Miall, D. (1995). 'Anticipation and feeling in literary response: A neuropsychological perspective', *Poetics*, 23(4), pp. 275–298.
Miller, R. (2006). 'From trends to futures literacy. Reclaiming the future', *Centre for Strategic Education. Seminar Series Paper* (No. 160). Victoria: CSE Publications.
Milojević, I., and Inayatullah, S. (2015). 'Narrative foresight', *Futures*, 73, pp. 151–162.
Morson, G. (1994). *Narrative and freedom*. New Haven, CT: Yale University Press.
Paschen, J.A., and Ison, R. (2014). 'Narrative research in climate change adaptation—Exploring a complementary paradigm for research and governance', *Research Policy*, 43(6), pp. 1083–1092.
Phelan, J. (2007). 'Rhetoric/ethics'. In Herman, D. (ed.). *The Cambridge companion to narrative*. Cambridge: Cambridge University Press, pp. 203–216.
Prince, G. (1990). 'On narratology (past, present, future)', *French Literature Series*, 17, pp. 1–14.
Raven, P.G., and Elahi, S. (2015). 'The new narrative: Applying narratology to the shaping of futures outputs', *Futures*, 74, pp. 49–61.
Ricœur, P. (1984). *Time and narrative*. Chicago, IL: University of Chicago Press.
Ryan, M.-L. (2007). 'Toward a definition of narrative'. In Herman, D. (ed.). *The Cambridge companion to narrative*. Cambridge: Cambridge University Press, pp. 22–35.
Schwartz, P. (2007). *The art of the long view: Planning for the future in an uncertain world*. New York: Wiley.

Uprichard, E. (2011). 'Narratives of the future: Complexity, time and temporality'. In Vogt, W.P., and Williams, M. (eds.). *Sage handbook of innovation in social research methods*. London: Sage, pp. 103–109.

White, H. (1990). *The content of the form: Narrative discourse and historical representation*. Baltimore, MD and London: Johns Hopkins University Press.

Wittmayer, J.M., Backhaus, J., Avelino, F., Pel, B., Strasser, T., Kunze, I. and Zuijderwijk, L. (2019). 'Narratives of change: How social innovation initiatives construct societal transformation', *Futures, 112*, p. 102433.

21
Postcolonial futures
Urban eventualities

AbdouMaliq Simone

What is the urban that works?

Any consideration of social futures would inevitably think through the work that contemporary urbanization processes do and could do. This is often confused for work on the urban itself, work oriented towards fixing problems, making the urban work better, as if it was some kind of integrated machine and some kind of coherent entity. Long accustomed to the by now banal citation that the world is thoroughly 'urbanized', it is too easy to assume some unitary toolbox of production modes, spatial fixes, or social logics that simply extend themselves across the globe, extracting from and colonizing the non-urban, as if the latter were also some definitive domain.

Urbanization has proven trickier. For even if it reflects a continuous rescaling of extractive, logistical, industrial and financial operations, and the continuous refiguring of territorial integrations (Brenner, 2019), specific instantiations of urbanization operate as a nebulous intercalation into the interlinkages of space and populations (Zeiderman et al., 2015). In other words, the extension of urbanization across the world, far from being the viral spread of a stabilized entity, reflects rather the volatility of the ways in which things are articulated, gathered up, and momentarily cohered within specific territorial parameters (Lefebvre, 2003). The nebulous aspects of the urban are found in the inherently unstable intersections of centrifugal and centripetal forces, whereby the urban draws in and carves out relationships through the gravitational forces it exerts but also propels outwards implications and dispositions that cannot be held, framed or governed within specific spatial forms (Soederberg and Walks, 2017).

What is clear is that the urban no longer, if ever, is synonymous with the city (Keil, 2018) and that it is an ongoing 'project' of constituting and shaping territory, not as a set series of interoperable articulations, but an always conflictual, generative assemblage of land, labour, language, materials, bodies, buildings and metabolisms capable of producing both planned and unplanned effects. Whose productive capacities both feed forward and feed back in ways that are capable of providing integrating forces but also those that exert implications beyond their own recognized and always tenuous borders (Adams, 2018).

DOI: 10.4324/9780429440717-22

So an important aspect, then, of the work that the urban does goes beyond colonization or expropriation and goes beyond the revitalization and recalibration of capitalist operations, to produce a surfeit of ways of living (and lives worth living) that exceed anything we know, that cannot be readily framed, where the proportions of what constitutes them are not figured out.

But we must always keep in mind, while assessing these excesses and potentialities, that they intersect with what might be viewed as a temporality of the provisional. Here, the majority of residents are dispossessed of their certainties, of their confident strivings to attain more viable livelihoods and a sense of stability in place. So this surfeit of the urban is not only the potentiality of the urbanization process but also a byproduct of the way in which the prospects of viable inhabitation are continuously repositioned, where certainty and security become assets to be accumulated and extracted from. Urban 'surplus' is thus a 'both-and', that is a continuous and contested reworking of the interactions between potential and vulnerability, of generative and debilitating uncertainty. The ways in which these tensions are proportioned become critical instruments of spatial planning and control. They set up the importance of eventualities, that is the prospects that *eventually* something will work out, be attained or be reshaped, as a means of leveraging different temporalities as guarantees against failure, against the risks residents face about losing everything, and for sustaining the promise that urban life offers something resourceful and redemptive for all, regardless of the empirical evidence.

A future (present) of eventualities

If at one level of analysis the notion of global urbanization would seem to connote an unyielding homogenization of space, the rollout of a uniform built environment and the conversion of built environment in general as financial assets, there is another future here that suspends such predictability and rather is articulated as *eventualities*. Here, eventualities are important not only in the guarantee that something will happen, something at least alluded to or produced by present conditions, but also in the plural, posit a multiplicity of possible futures that already exist within the present. While it is not evident what will eventually happen, the eventuality itself becomes something that is staked on, becomes an object of investment, as well as a way of inhabiting urban space. In what follows, I discuss two of these eventualities in the specific context of Tanah Tinggi in Jakarta, Indonesia.

Eventuality 1: Generative encounters

The sense of eventuality also points to the ways in which certain residents believe their actions are carried forward in a range of interactions beyond their immediate control. For Tanah Tinggi, situated within the urban core of Jakarta, eventuality operates as a concrete abstraction of the agglomerated transactions of residents scraping by in intensely dense conditions. Tanah Tinggi is what might be considered an emblematic 'majority' district – an amalgam of working poor, working class and barely middle-class residents. Its density is not only one of population numbers and physical proximity, but also of the proliferation of different economic 'games', of discrepant aesthetic styles of dwelling and the physical surfaces of buildings and of the ways to exert local authority and influence, alongside more conventional diversities such as ethnic background. Residents not only have to navigate the circulations and emplacement of a large number of bodies in crowded conditions, but the heterogeneity of ways of doing things, of all the tricks of the trade that are used to exercise limited advantages, eke out cooperation and complicity and manipulate people into doing things they otherwise would be reluctant to do. Old-fashioned solidarities and reciprocities exist of course, and places like Tanah Tinggi could not exist without them. But the prevalent sensibility is that securing life and livelihood rests not so much in the predictable rhythms of neighbourly cooperation but in the unspecified outcomes of all of these densities colliding and acting on each other, producing eventualities of all sorts. Not readily or even always clearly discernible as virtuous or destructive, these eventualities become the things that will alter lives, lift household beyond mere survival and become that which is actually lived for.

Such eventualities are a collective product of the district, as important as the combined labour of the street seller, the deliverer, the repairer, the construction worker, the child minder, the cook, the cleaner, the metalworker, transporter and so forth. Of course, most livelihoods did not change much. But even as this was the case, residents of Tanah Tinggi would be quick to point out that they knew others in their neighbourhood for whom things did change, despite being hard-pressed to cite specific examples. That eventually their own lives would change in unexpected and welcomed ways, because these eventualities were indeed the results of the very density of things taking place in the district.

The work the urban does in Tanah Tinggi can also be seen as that of institutions honed over long periods of time. These institutions are not so much instruments of governance, but of figuring, recalibrating and experimenting – institutions such as shrines, burial societies, ethnic associations and guilds. In addition, more ephemeral forms of collective life also play a role in circulating personal experiences and perspectives through an array of networks and neighbours without fixing residents to particular positions and responsibilities (Bayat, 2013). This circuitry of movement and exchange drives a continuous process of incremental adjustments and sometime inexplicable leaps in the compositions of space.

At the same time, districts like Tanah Tinggi are under great pressure, in part by the rush to build. There is a concerted push in many cities, Cairo, Jakarta, Karachi, Delhi and Lagos, to name a few, to exactly excise the possibilities of the eventualities produced by the heterogeneities of urban core popular neighbourhoods.

In many urban areas, a fabric of small sutures and proximities of discrepant ways of life constituting a tremulous solidarity are subjected to 'counterinsurgencies', assaults against the population through targeting the very intimacies of everyday life and its promiscuous socialities (Warburg and Jensen, 2018). Not content to simply suppress forms of popular political participation that question sclerotic and authoritarian practices of rule, politicians, police and bureaucrats increasingly instigate an atmosphere of constant anxiety and suspicion in the conduct of everyday relations. They selectively distribute privileges of both licit and illicit accumulation, which stokes and rewards internecine conflict – all of which exponentially maximizes the effort needed in order to maintain networks of local cooperation (Tadiar, 2016).

This is a matter of settlement. Popular majority districts like Tanah Tinggi remain 'unsettled', at least within the convictions of residents, which inform their practices and orientations. Even if conditions do not change much, the predominant sense of residents of Tanah Tinggi is that matters remain unsettled. This unsettling, manifested in the highly sensuous, rough-and-tumble, improvised styles of people dealing with each other, is the very thing that eventually will generate a different kind of a life for them, as well as their belief, that as long as this is their orientation, the life they experience now in the present is 'not that bad'. This conviction of sufficiency in the present and that 'real development' will occur through the agglomerated messiness of everyday encounters mean that these populations remain 'unsettled'. While getting an education, playing by the rules and in general 'doing the right thing' are self-professed values.

But everyone knows that, really, these acts of self-discipline are not going to get one anywhere. No matter how well a young person does at school, the sheer fact that they come from Tanah Tinggi, on an ID card that can only be altered at a great price, means that employers will never hire them. There are stories, of course, about how certain youth did 'make it', and they do assume pride of place. Still, residents have little conviction in any linear progression towards a better future, and instead put their faith in the rambunctious and unsteady mechanisms of bluffing, coaxing, luring and blustering their way into work, money, resources and opportunities.

Governments often demonstrate little interest and provide limited resources to sustainably settle majority populations. Maintaining these populations as transient, minimally capable of making any needed adjustments on their own, becomes a key instrument of governance for regions that have to demonstrate their creditworthiness and increase their investments in the logistical infrastructures that capitalize on interconnections of land and productive capacity at regional and global levels – that is, transport hubs and networks, storage and port facilities, export processing zones, administrative districts, high-end zones of elite and internationalized consumption. Implicit social compacts across cities such as Jakarta, Delhi and Lagos were based on allowing majority populations to fend for themselves in ways that depended upon the circumvention of legalities and the ambiguities of regulatory systems. Incivility has been allowed as long as these populations do not become an existential political threat. This tacit compact is being dissolved, through overt evictions, but more frequently through accumulation of numerous pressures. These include escalating property valuation, increased tensions in the competing uses of districts for residential and commercial activities, the overcrowding of small trade and service sectors, still bulging youth populations unable to find work and decaying infrastructure beyond repair.

Eventuality 2: Fugitivity

Increased numbers of residents are being forced to the peripheries of urban regions, largely to secure more affordable housing or decongested conditions, but also often in the interest of trying to assess prospective futures and how best to address them. A growing majority of residents of Tanah Tinggi I have got to know over the years complain that the everyday life was becoming too labour intensive, and the amount of work required to maintain basic relationships with neighbours increasingly is tedious. Where once the informal levies imposed by a host of local authorities as the price of doing business, small though it might be, where directly traceable to the need to ward off the police and other prying bureaucrats, these extractions were becoming excessive and punitive, disrupting an ethos of egalitarianism that needed to be a major part of the operating procedure of street-level transactions. Ethnicity, that primarily functioned as a punctuation in those transactions – as different groups had different specialization and networks that were intersected for the well-being of all – increasingly has been manipulated as a means to 'divide and rule'.

As a result, larger numbers of residents have been heading out towards the outskirts of the city. While they retained pride in what Tanah Tinggi was able to accomplish in terms of livelihood and collective intelligence given its general impoverishment, overcrowded conditions and reputation for 'bad behaviour', they no longer saw this way of living as best suited for 'what was coming'. They did not exactly know what these future conditions would be, and the destinations they now chose were viewed as mostly only temporary, but they saw this shift as the means through which they could better access these eventualities. As long as they stayed in Tanah Tinggi, no matter how sufficient they viewed their lives there, it would be out of synch with what they perceived was required of them in order to be most adept in adapting to the conditions to come. Again, they did not seem to know what those requirements were exactly. They did not have a specific imagination of what they would end up being in the long run. But they knew that they could not find this out if they stood still.

Here the priority then was on investing in circulation, spending the time, effort and resources in getting to know the wider urban region better. To test out different employment opportunities, hustles or ways of accessing opportunities to earn money or get access to other resources, they needed to 'park' themselves and their households somewhere that did not exhaust their earnings or savings. Some would hold, if they could, to their former abodes, rent them out and take cheaper quarters somewhere else. They had to balance access to more affordable housing with the costs of transportation, as many would work their same jobs, now much farther away than before. Households would often split up, spreading out across cheap boarding house rooms across the city in order to have a foothold in many different locations at the same time.

It is possible to see the structural corollary to this provisionality as the generalization of dispossession. Futures in general are increasingly a matter of speculation, as in line with the predominant machines of value creation (Abourahme, 2018). The capacity of urban residents across much of the South to effectively and confidently narrate a coherent trajectory of movement forward is consistently undermined. The question of 'what will happen to me if I take this specific step, pursue this specific trajectory?' becomes increasingly difficult to answer. This uncertainty instigates a more extensive process of jockeying for advantage, of gambling on faint possibilities and opportunistic orientations of all kinds. Such dispossession of anchorage, of coherent stories and of positionality is compensated by other forms of dispossession, reflected in more tentative commitments on the part of residences to particular ways of emplacing themselves in and navigating through urban space (Arese, 2018; Thieme, 2018).

Incessant circulation has long been a critical modus operandi for those who could not afford to fully instantiate themselves in the city, and who depend upon moving back and forth between the urban and the rural. The importance of circulation is now widely generalized, even as it takes on different modalities for different kinds of residents (Caldeira, 2017; Sopranzetti, 2017). Institutionalized restlessness and dissatisfaction characterize the very being of urban inhabitation with its concomitant emphasis on provisionality and risk.

Eventuality becomes something that is the product of circulation, of opportunistic moving around and of being at the right place at the right time. The density of transactions among many different things and bodies in place becomes the density of itineraries across diverse places. To inhabit means to increasingly move. If the advantage of density was the intensive circulation of things, affects, bodies and games in place, circulation now increasingly takes place across larger circuits as economic processes become more dispersed and urbanization more extended. Yet, many residents remain stuck in place, consigned to narrow territories of manoeuvre. Additionally, the aspiration for the stability of 'home' has in most cases not disappeared. After all, many of those former Tanah Tinggi residents in motion say that their present circumstances are only provisional, that eventually they will settle somewhere. But the discovery, the actualization of such eventuality, appears contingent upon these provisional inhabitations.

So the work that the urban does, beyond the familiar generation of surplus values, agglomerated economies, rescaled articulations among rural areas that have become factory floors and central cities that have become recreational jungles, is this production of eventualities, registered and experienced in various forms and degrees. In each of the instances I have described, the operations of eventualities are very much embedded in the present and become organizing principles for the distribution and use of urban space. Eventuality is a multivariant temporality, an objective, a destination and an accomplishment. While this is not all the urban does, for the global South, such a breadth of eventualities is particularly salient. Its resonance is rooted in its variegated histories and ongoing anticipation of a postcolonial future that has only partially arrived.

A generic South?

How do these notions of eventuality play out on a broader canvass of Southern urbanism? Does it mean that eventually the global South completely disappears as any kind of useful category, and that eventually urban space is completely remade in terms of imported modernist imaginaries not clearly demarcated in terms of North or South, as in the valourization of Singapore, Dubai or China? As I have indicated earlier, massive mobilizations of real-estate capital have altered significant portions of Southern landscapes in ways that often self-consciously aim at erasing historical distinction or fulfilling historical destinies, albeit in forms that tend to match the concretized imaginaries of the West. Whatever eventualities are considered, it remains necessary to consider why and how lands of Central and South America, Africa and Asia were turned into the 'South' in the first place, as various acts of othering that either deemed those lands empty or populated by people so devalued that cheap extractions of resources could be legitimated and external modalities of rule imposed (Mingolo, 2000; Santos, 2001; Rehbeinn, 2010).

While most Southern regions possessed long legacies of urban life of markedly different longevities, by the late nineteenth century, most existent cities were simply treated as logistical hubs, centres of administration for resource-laden hinterlands and their populations not capable of being sufficiently urban. They were the locus through which space was racialized and exemplified in the widespread designation of different parts of the city being either 'white' or 'black' (Kipfer, 2007; Kooy and Bakker, 2008; Prakash, 2010; Linke, 2014).

Urbanization would come to provide an important impetus and infrastructure for the anticolonial struggles of the twentieth century even as nascent governments would inherit an amalgam of spatial designs, institutional operations and densely populated landscapes that would be difficult to alter or sustain (Burton, 2007; Aljunied, 2013). Such a disjointed process has continued in the massive expansions of established primate cities, the proliferation of towns and secondary cities and the enfolding of surface rural areas into vast 'factory floors'. The promises of urban modernity centred on coherent production systems, decent livelihoods for residents and the materialization of national confidence and pride have dispersed into highly erratic provisioning systems, disjointed landscapes and vast social inequities, which in their aggregate signal widespread dysfunction, but not only that. It is this remainder that is a future promising something else yet to be fully fleshed out, some unknown incipience in the very long list of problems that contemporary urbanization seems to have generated. What might be the outlines, traces or 'smoke signals' of such an incipience? Where is it worth looking for these unsettled promises?

Perhaps ironically, one place to start may be in seemingly mundane environments, the faceless homogeneity of 'affordable' housing blocks and the 'terroir vague' of eroded industrial and commercial zones that offer an almost systematic array of social and entrepreneurial experiments under the radar (Boano and Leclair-Paquet, 2014; Nielsen and Simone, 2016).

Given the expropriation of wayward and vanguard socialities as premises for gentrification or restructuring, the intensities of violence directed towards the expanding volume of those deemed marginal and the almost compulsory inclination of residents to talk about who they are and what they do, the mundane proves to be a potentially generative working atmosphere in contrast to its usual connotations. Instead of signalling the end of imaginative urban futures, the expanse of the generic provides a mode of visibility capable of compressing many different agendas, actors and resources. They operate as platforms facilitative of extensions across urban regions and beyond, a means of 'parking safely' the practicalities of everyday stability so that risks can be assumed elsewhere. For denizens and residents of such housing developments, recessed commercial zones and barely functional districts of retail, servicing and repair, the agenda is not so much to cultivate the semblance of a dynamic interior or local collective life but to amplify the sense of anonymity and ordinariness these urban fabrics convey in order to craft itineraries of movement, exchange and investment elsewhere.

The objective of residents in these contexts of mass housing is to deflect scrutiny as much as possible and yet be at least indirectly exposed to a wide range of livelihood pursuits, transactional networks and household arrangements that also try to couch themselves within various forms of neutrality or genericity. It is also ironic then that these forms of dissimulation and opacity also aim for maximum exposure to the larger urban region and beyond. So as residents attempt to deflect being paid attention to, of having their lifestyles and practices of accumulation scrutinized by other residents and agencies, they seem to adopt living situations where there is not that much to actually pay attention to. They may limit the length of stay in any particular location; they may decline to acquire goods or statuses. They do this so as to maximize their ability to operate in a larger world with fewer possessions and agendas to defend.

This sense of maximum exposure valourizes a profusion of details whose framings and genealogies are to be deferred, for the time being. This apparent withdrawal from civic or neighbourhood engagement and reclusiveness within the interior of highly individualized projects may seem like the collapse of solidarities. Indeed, while the publicization of activisms, local developmental initiatives and NGO activities may be more extensive, residents have tended to curtail involvement in discernible associations. But this withdrawal may simply be a means of crafting ways for residents to be together without seemingly being together (Smith and McQuarrie, 2012; Kelty, 2017; Swerts, 2017).

In urban regions where the future is preempted as a mechanism to justify vast expenditures on commercial and residential buildings, new spatial development, with little concern for their viability in the present and everything staked on their 'eventualities', residents' orientations to the future become increasingly provisional. Whereas residents may have once had clear destinations in mind, now for some the incessant travel across repeated circuits in order to stay afloat for themselves and for others, the restless search for the 'new' renders destinations as objects of either fear, tedium or deception.

Settling the future for now: Political settlements

The second place to look for heretofore unsettled eventualities of viable urban futures also, ironically, might rest with provisional political settlements in the present. These are ways for creating opportunistic spaces for now and ways of governing urban processes that do not attempt to settle key questions once and for all. For, despite larger numbers of residents living with and through displacement, territories, no matter how constituted, have to be governed, ruled or controlled. No matter how temporary or incidental, residents have to be identified with and through an address, as that address becomes a prerequisite for many of the trappings of citizenship. Here, postcolonial cities exhibit a wide range of systems and political settlements. Some manage tightly composed institutions capable of exerting their authority across the city or region, with clear sectoral divisions and managerial competencies. But most must continuously negotiate a patchwork of arrangements in order to have real traction in specific domains, operating through various clienteles or local 'authorities' (Benjamin, 2008; Menocal, 2017; Franz, 2018; Goodfellow, 2018).

Not only have many municipal services and responsibilities been subcontracted to private companies but even where the appearance of a univocal metropolitan government is maintained, real governmental operations must also often be distributed across many different accords and working relationships among formal and informal political actors. While planning and methodical interventions are still valuable tools, the bulk of the refiguring of the future will happen in the midst of messy, problematic socialities, down and dirty politics.

Rather than integration being a process of subsuming different tendencies and ways of life to a consensual or imposed set of standards, integration here is a means of recalibrating ways of doing things and different degrees of authority through negotiated settlements that are rarely contractual. This may include highly differentiated governance frameworks for markets, special industrial zones, gated communities, illegal settlements or intensely conflictual districts. Various modalities of political settlement can waver between productive integrative mechanisms, and those of expropriation and subjugation. In their more productive instantiations, these processes proceed as a matter of different actors 'feeling each other out', testing their respective strengths and vulnerabilities and manipulating opportunities but never aiming to disable other protagonists.

Conclusion

What then might this range of eventualities considered here be? What proportion of speculation, endurance, collective aspiration or extraction might characterize the shaping of multiple eventualities as they unfold in places like Tanah Tinggi? These are matters of continuously refiguring the relationships among authorities, residents, planners and developers. It is not a matter of implementing consensually determined distributions of work and authority, but a process of different actors moving simultaneously against and with each other. The subsequent dispositions are more questions of 'give and take', and this exchange then is the integrative force. There are many moments when such a process is cumbersome, seemingly in no one's interest, and the frictions among different ways of seeing things, different political pressures and expectations would seem to protract an endless game of compensations and small adjustments. Yet, in complex and volatile urban environments, these continuous negotiations, subject to intense confrontations and acquiescence, are perhaps the only means through which divergent eventualities can be attuned to each other.

Bibliography

Abourahme, N. (2018). 'Of monsters and boomerangs: Colonial returns in the late liberal city', *City*, 22, pp. 106–115.

Adams, R.E. (2018). *Circulation and urbanization*. London: Sage.

Aljunied, S.M.K. (2013). 'Against multiple hegemonies: Radical Malay women in colonial Malaya', *Journal of Social History*, 47, pp. 153–175.

Arese, N.S. (2018). 'Seeing like a city-state: Behavioural planning and governance in Egypt's first affordable gated community', *International Journal of Urban and Regional Research*, 42, pp. 461–482.

Benjamin, S. (2008). 'Occupancy urbanism: Radicalising politics and economy beyond policy and programs', *International Journal of Urban and Regional Research*, 32, pp. 719–729.

Boano, C. and Leclair-Paquet, B. (2014). 'Potential, freedom and space: Reflections on Agamben's potentialities in the West Bank', *Space and Polity*, 18, pp. 17–38.

Brenner, N. (2019). *New urban spaces: Urban theory and the scale question*. New York: Oxford University Press.
Burton, A. (2007). 'The haven of peace purged: Tackling the undesirable and unproductive poor in Dar es Salaam, ca.1950s-1980s', *The International Journal of African Historical Studies*, 40, pp. 119–151.
Caldeira, T.P. (2017). 'Peripheral urbanization: Autoconstruction, transversal logics, and politics in cities of the global south', *Environment and Planning D: Society and Space*, 35, pp. 3–20.
Franz, T. (2018). 'Power balances, transnational elites, and local economic governance: The political economy of development in Medellín', *Local Economy*, 33, pp. 85–109.
Goodfellow, T. (2017). 'Urban fortunes and skeleton cityscapes: Real estate and late urbanization in Kigali and Addis Ababa', *International Journal of Urban and Regional Research*, 41, pp. 786–803.
———. (2018). 'Seeing political settlements through the city: A framework for comparative analysis of urban transformation', *Development and Change*, 49, pp. 199–222.
Keil, R. (2018). 'The empty shell of the planetary: Re-rooting the urban in the experience of the urbanites', *Urban Geography*, 39, pp. 1589–1602.
Kelty, C.M. (2017). 'Too much democracy in all the wrong places. Toward a grammar of participation', *Current Anthropology*, 58 (Supplement 15), pp. S77–S90.
Kipfer, S. (2007). 'Fanon and space: Colonization, urbanization, and liberation from the colonial to the global city', *Environment and Planning D: Society and Space*, 25, pp. 701–726.
Kooy, M. and Bakker, K. (2008). 'Technologies of government: Constituting subjectivities, spaces, and infrastructures in colonial and contemporary Jakarta', *International Journal of Urban and Regional Research*, 32, pp. 375–391.
Lefebvre, H. (2003) [1970]. *The urban revolution*. Minneapolis: University of Minnesota Press.
Linke, U. (2014). 'Racializing cities, naturalizing space: The seductive appeal of iconicities of dispossession', *Antipode*, 46, pp. 1222–1239.
Mignolo, W. (2000). *Local histories/global designs*. Princeton, NJ: Princeton University Press.
Prakash, G. (2010). *Mumbai fables: Tales of an enchanted city*. Princeton, NJ: Princeton University Press.
Rehbeinn, B. (2010). *Critical theory after the rise of the global South: Kaleidoscopic dialectic*. London and New York: Routledge.
Rocha, M.A. (2017). 'Political settlements and the politics of transformation: Where do "inclusive institutions" come from?', *Journal of International Development*, 29, pp. 559–575.
Santos, B. de Sousa (2001). 'Nuestra America: Reinventing a subaltern paradigm of recognition and redistribution', *Theory, Culture and Society*, 18, pp. 185–218.
Smith, M.P. and McQuarrie, M. (eds.) (2012). *Remaking urban citizenship. Organizations, institutions and the right to the city*. New Brunswick, NJ and London: Transaction Publishers.
Soederberg, S. and Walks, A. (2017). 'Producing and governing inequalities under planetary urbanization: From urban age to urban revolution?' *Geoforum*, 89, pp. 107–113.
Sopranzetti, C. (2017). *Owners of the map: motorcycle taxi drivers, mobility, and politics in Bangkok*. Berkeley and Los Angeles: University of California Press.
Swerts, T. (2017). 'Creating space for citizenship: The liminal politics of undocumented activism', *International Journal of Urban and Regional Research*, 41, pp. 379–395.
Tadiar, N.X.M. (2016). 'City everywhere', *Theory, Culture & Society* 33, pp. 57–83.
Thieme, T. (2018). 'The hustle economy: Rethinking geographies of informality and getting by', *Progress in Human Geography*, 42, pp. 529–548.
Warburg, A.B. and Jensen, S. (2018). 'Policing the war on drugs and the transformation of urban space in Manila', *Environment and Planning D: Society and Space*. https://doi.org/10.1177/0263775818817299
Zeiderman, A., Kaker, S.A., Silver, J. and Wood, A. (2015). 'Uncertainty and urban life', *Public Culture*, 27, pp. 281–304.

22
Prospection
Producing social futures

Barbara Bok and Ted Fuller

Introduction

Statements about the future contain predictions, in a general sense. In that sense, this Handbook contains predictions of social futures. Such predictions are visions conveying facts of what might be, and they can be used in shaping what will be. When you study these statements about the future, is it the facts, as such, that hold your attention? Do you ponder the activities of an 'enterprise' that make the statements what they are? Do you reflect on something else, perhaps individuals' skills to produce the statements? For this chapter, we are not focussing on the facts related to prediction or individuals' skills. Rather, we focus on the enterprise of prediction-performing activities and making claims about the knowledge status of the statements. In justifying their claims, prediction enterprises often go beyond the truth claims about the facts to claims about the realities they enact (e.g. about epistemology and ontology). Two realities are of interest: One regarding the phenomena being predicted and the other relating to the prospection enterprise itself. The 'standing of knowledge' (about the future) and how it is achieved is a methodological (and performative) issue.

Methodological contributions to the possibility of prediction and of predicting are well established in foresight and futures studies literature. These contributions reflect wider efforts to develop a more sophisticated understanding of predictions and prediction, such as super forecasting. They often examine predictions as prophetic statements of facts. However, Batty and Torrens (2005) argue that the complexities of open social systems pose limits to 'accurate' prediction. Errors in the use of prediction include category errors such as evaluating historical statements about the future in terms of their accuracy, even when made for non-predictive purposes, and, significantly, not factoring in 'predictions' elaborated to inspire avoidance of undesired possible futures that could, in their own sense, be successful. Bell and Olick (1989) argue that attempting to know the future when the future cannot be known raises fundamental problems for acceptable justification of predictions. Aligica (2003) argues that prediction and explanation are not identical and hence that prediction should, at least, be based 'on a theory of evidentiary argumentation' (p. 1040). The prophetic meaning of 'prediction' is thus narrow and exemplifies why it tends not to be used in the more exploratory domain of futures studies.

In this chapter, we examine categories of methodologies that lead to statements about the future. In doing so, we wondered how best to label a methodological concern for prediction. We recognize that social futures as empirical 'cultural facts' (Appadurai, 2013) are not primarily a prophetic enterprise. Nevertheless, we do accept Rosen's (1991) assertion that anticipation is a characteristic of 'life itself' and, as a result, being social involves anticipation. Anticipation is a predictive mode, but we endorse a more sophisticated understanding of prediction. We thus accept that different methodologies can be selected to engender social futures. We therefore decided to encapsulate methodological issues in terms of prospection. Prospection can be understood as the metabolization of the 'past and present into projected futures' (Seligman et al., 2016, p. x). Hence, in this chapter, we consider examples of current social science methodologies from a prospective stance, attempting to illuminate their methodological engendering of social futures.

Introducing three social science methodologies

Three parallel and overlapping agendas in social science are developing new approaches to addressing the loss of confidence in the reliability of tradition and history to provide effective guides to the future. This is especially the case when the forward view is increasingly an issue in contemporary social and scientific debates. We chose these three because, methodologically, they reflect the standing of and engendering of knowledge about social futures.

Postnormal science (PNS)

Jerome Ravetz and Silvio Funtowicz conceived of PNS in the late 1980s. The 'ideal' image of 'normal science' (hereafter NS, described by Kuhn (2012)) is curiosity-driven research aiming to discover unquestionable value-free facts (Funtowicz and Ravetz, 1993). However, 'science' refers to work done with an extended community of 'peers' with a plurality of value-loaded knowledge cultures in contexts unrelated to NS, for example issues-driven policy development (Ravetz and Funtowicz, 1999, 2015).

As a result, the claims for PNS methodology centre on the complexity of the scientific problem-solving system, linking epistemological issues with governance. Different methodological styles suit problem situations according to the severity of stakes and level of system uncertainties. NS methodology with risk-probability calculations is sufficient for solving technical problems (e.g. engine efficiency). In contrast, PNS methodology is required when stakes and system uncertainty are high (e.g. climate change, biotechnology and epidemiology) (Ravetz, 2011). According to the contributors to Ravetz and Funtowicz (1999), PNS scientists involve themselves in the full contexts of natural systems and social values to maintain and improve the quality of knowledge-producing processes. PNS practice differentiates risk from uncertainty, ignorance and indeterminacy to improve quality. For PNS, 'what-if?' questions are essential additions to 'what/how?' and 'how/why?' questions for open inquiry with all who desire to participate.

Anticipation studies (AS)

The contributions to the *Handbook of anticipation* (Poli, 2018b, chapter numbers in parentheses) provide a window onto AS methodology that reveals a wide diversity of anticipatory phenomena assuming a plurality of metaphysics (e.g. indigenous (20), process (16), autocatalysis (17) and critical realism (5)). Anticipatory processes have two components: A future orientation component for forming 'ideas' that indicate future possibilities and an action component to bring about change based on the ideas. For example, a foraging animal, upon noticing a predator, chooses between its options to continue grazing or to flee (12). AS describe and study anticipatory phenomena, theorize about them and investigate the implications of anticipation in complex situations (e.g. computing (70–71), risk (73–74) and global governance (54, 72)).

AS argue that anticipation cannot be adequately examined with mechanistic accounts (Newtonian methodologies) because they exclude the Aristotelian final cause (13–15, 49). This is not the only problem. Built-in dualism, reductionism, performative effects and predicativity (see Poli, 2018b, pp. 1–14) contribute to erasing mutual causal relations (18, 53), excluding the relations of the full complexity of convoluted wholes (10, 52, 68), producing self-fulfilling or self-denying effects (28, 69), disallowing self-reference and assuming maximal models that encompass others (1, 2, 6). AS consider futures literacy (FL) to be a critical reflexive capability for anticipation (4, 64).

Science and technology studies (STS)

STS, an interdisciplinary field, emerged between the 1960s and 1980s from the interests in (respectively) science and technology (SandT) of scholars, such as Thomas Kuhn, from the humanities and social sciences (e.g. the history and philosophy of SandT and the sociology of scientific knowledge and sociology of technology, see Felt et al. (2017), Fuller (2007) and Shapin (1995)). STS have expanded into diverse areas investigating how people 'construct and perform' SandT and how they thereby 'make and remake themselves' and their worlds (p. 1). Thus, 'STS may be understood as the study of method in practice' where method is broadly conceived (Law, 2017, p. 31).

STS repurpose numerous theories, methods and approaches of their and other (sub)disciplines to examine 'how webs assemble themselves to stage effects' (effects such as dualisms), how such webs are performative and/or format a multiplicity of realities (Felt et al., 2017, pp. 39–44). For example, STS have investigated how futures and expectations are involved in shaping society and innovation (e.g. research into sociotechnical imaginaries (Jasanoff and Kim, 2015) and the sociology of expectations (Brown and Michael, 2003) have highlighted the performative aspects of futures and foresight methods). STS approaches, such as actor–network theory (ANT) and diffraction (Barad, 2007), have gained recognition as discourses of relational thinking (DoR), which attempt to understand the constitutive processes and relations of complex phenomena (Walsh, Böhme and Wamsler, 2021). DoR offer new language and growing repositories of examples for STS enquiry (Blok, Farias and Roberts, 2020).

Futures studies/foresight inspired by three social science methodologies

Futures studies and foresight literature evidence that these three social science methodologies are inspiring methodological innovations in futures studies. We examine the literature for signs of this influence on futures studies methodologies with a focus on the activities and claims of the prospection enterprises.

PNS inspiring prospection methodology

Postnormal times (PNT) theory extends the PNS proposition from science to the cultural period subsequent to recent classic, modern and postmodern periods. Sardar (2016) explains that PNT are not a prediction of the next period to come, but a description of an in-between state already happening. This postnormal present is characterized by complexity, plurality and the emergence of postnormal phenomena (Sardar, 2010). Like the claims of PNS methodology, PNT's claims centre on a time wherein systems develop complexity due to the interconnectedness of diverse communities, plurality of perspectives and values, all in a context of uncertainty and ignorance. Some systems in this time are already postnormal (e.g. 'science'). Not all systems are equally affected and may become postnormal in different ways. PNT theory also makes a claim about knowledge of the future: While some trends or phenomena may (already) be predicted for the extended present, it is assumed that 'perfect knowledge of what might be ahead remains impossible' (Sardar, 2016, p. 117).

The Three Tomorrows (3Ts) framework is a multilayered approach complementary to other futures methods to, with imagination and creativity, enact governing in (and through) PNT (Sardar and Sweeney, 2016). Sardar (2015) appeals to futurists to 'give serious attention to how we are going to *navigate* the postnormal condition' (p. 37, emphasis added). Users of 3Ts must 'navigate' three time horizons and examine whether systems could become postnormal. They then find ways to prevent that from happening by 'simplification as well as complexification' (Sardar, 2016, p. 129). Simplification could be achieved by removing (unnecessary) systems interconnections. Complexification could be achieved by blocking positive feedback or dealing with contradictions and complex interactions by making systems interventions. Interventions could be policy changes, protests or power shifts. 3Ts can also be used as a tool of critique of already-created futures statements.

AS inspiring prospection methodology

AS's self-description includes reference to the entire futures studies/foresight field. AS are inspiring futures studies in two main ways: Developing the FL capability of people and adapting futures methods with AS. People are engaging in FL programmes to develop their capacities to 'use-the-future' in a wide range of contexts (Miller, 2018). Being futures literate means people are capable of remaining conscious of their 'fictions about the later-than-now and the frames they use to invent these imaginary futures' (Miller, 2018, p. 2). FL means people make choices about how and why to use the future before actually engaging in prospection. FL entails being able to describe the specific framing assumptions of anticipatory activities (i.e. the nature of the anticipatory systems, the purposes for using the future, the kinds of futures being used and the methods chosen) (Miller and Sandford, 2019).

AS scholars have been adapting futures and foresight methods, as well as developing new methods, according to studies in Poli (2018b, chapter numbers in parentheses). We compiled four types of activity: First, to stimulate re-perception of the present by updating a theory of social cycles with reflexive foresight in the latest cycle (34); second, updating futures methods by fully acknowledging the role and presence of the observer or decision-maker in the use of the method (50) and analysing vision-making processes for extremely complex dynamic environments to make suggestions for improvement (60); third, identifying AS concepts already in methods by exploring how games and simulations already use the future (63) and identifying the necessary qualities of narratives that 'story' the future, while avoiding merely extending present possibilities (43); and finally, directing attention to how different sets of assumptions or frameworks of reality (e.g. levels or layers) change the futures produced through developing contrasting futures (22) and examining futures studies for its historical development and different approaches to knowledge development (77).

STS inspiring prospection methodology

Futures studies scholars have been inspired by STS in three distinct areas: Technoscientific (TS), human social (HS) and the DoR. In TS, futures studies using forecasting, technology foresight and technology assessment methods have worked with leading STS scholars since the early 1980s to improve futures methods. They have, for example, involved wider and more diversified participation in prospection exercises (e.g. Miles, 2010). In HS, futures studies have been referring, since the late 1980s, to STS scholars critical of the presumed ideology-free nature of scientific knowledge (e.g. Clark, 1987). Since then, HS studies, like the PNT developments, have richly benefited from theories derived from STS insights (e.g. sociotechnical futures (Konrad and Böhle, 2019)) integrated with and modifying futures methods. They have identified the constructivist epistemological perspective of STS scholars' work at the roots of futures methodological developments (e.g. Fuller and Loogma, 2009). They have also reacted against TS studies by developing critical futures (e.g. Slaughter, 1998; Inayatullah, 2005).

The DoR are inspiring a growing list of futures studies investigating futures-making 'methods in practice' or using insights from DoR to diagnose difficulties found in futures activities (e.g. Compagna and Kohlbacher, 2015; see also Newmarch in this volume). Studies based on assemblage DoR show the mediating effects (to exclude citizens) of discourses in futures exercises (Engelbert, van Zoonen and Hirzalla, 2019), demonstrate how the entanglement of presents and imagined futures is involved in the futures-making process (Schneider and Lösch, 2019) and also examine the roles of 'how the future is anticipated' and 'ontological commitments' in power relations (Groves, 2017, p. 36; Van Hemert, 2017). Inspired by DoR, Davis and Groves (2019) show how the political significance of master planning can be understood. Inspired by post-ANT, Rowland and Spaniol (2015) show how the entanglement of the singular 'future' and the plural 'futures' (multiplicity) helps scenario planners to manage the complexity of multiple futures.

Sketching distinctive qualities of prospection methodologies

What can we imagine for *prospection methodology* if we creatively sketch connections between the methodologies described above? We describe four interrelated qualities at work in the enactment of prospection. Each quality has an indicator of the choices made for staging prospection methodology. We imagine that qualities like these could matter as much to prospection methodology as the explanatory and truth qualities of producing knowledge. The four qualities are thickness of relational complexes, degrees of sensitivity to how prospection is performed, openness of ecologies of practice and the extent of distributed engendering of social futures. Much of what is discussed next is already known or assumed implicitly and practised *ad hoc* in prospection activities. Nonetheless, many challenges arise for what these qualities mean for rigorous prospection practice.

Thickness of relational complexes

Complex social systems are replete with interconnections and interdependencies. Such relations can be acknowledged, ignored, denied, faked or deleted (and more) by social actors. Prospection enterprises reflecting complex social systems tend to identify relations that have a role in prospection activity (e.g. relations between model variables) explicitly. Explicitly acknowledging relations does not mean other relations disappear from the enterprises' activities; rather, those relations are also 'dealt with', often implicitly.

We identify two opposing impulses in making choices about relations in prospection methodology. One aims for parsimony: Eliminating relations that do not contribute to explaining the predicted phenomenon (e.g. prediction according to positivist *covering law* theory). The other aims to make 'thick' accounts: Recognizing all the relations that affect prospection activity. Eliminating relations (e.g. making objective accounts) is not necessarily easier to do rigorously than making thick accounts.

The methodologies reviewed in this chapter demonstrate the second impulse. PNS/PNT recognize that the relations of the full contexts of natural and social systems influence the quality of futures knowledge. PNS/PNT reconfigure the relations between future knowledge and its qualifications as risk, uncertainty, ignorance and indeterminacy. Time relations too are recognized. Poli (2017) conceptualizes 'thick presents' as relating different human experiences of time (e.g. cyclical) with different dimensions of time (e.g. order and location). 3Ts connect different future horizons with different levels of cultural complexity. DoR also recognize that relations do not remain constant or unaffected, bringing into focus relations of change, including emergence, discontinuity and surprise.

Simpler relational complexes help simplify methodology and prospection performances but enact various effects (such as contradictions and reductionism) that have real-world consequences. Enacting rich relational complexes aims to overcome the reductionist problems but complicates prospection. It also hinders people from noticing whether and how prospection methodology produces such problems.

Degrees of sensitivity to how prospection is performed

Action is necessary for prospection, and prospection performances are expected to produce responsible action (Fuller and Loogma, 2009). Models, broadly conceived, are salient in prospection methodology. Allow, if you would, that the models incorporated in complex anticipatory systems (CAS) are like the black boxes of STS (Latour, 1987; Louie and Poli, 2017). Models, like black boxes, are a means of enclosing and concealing relational complexes and actions (including the work that was needed to settle controversies) on the assumption that the contents are no longer disputable.

Prospection methodologies often have opportunities for creating models of to-be-predicted phenomena, but fewer opportunities to examine and unpack those models. Such opportunities are indications of sensitivity to how prospection is performed. We identify two opposing impulses. One is to restrict opportunities, thus reducing sensitivity. The other is to encourage opportunities, thus increasing sensitivity.

The methodologies reviewed in this chapter demonstrate the second impulse. Relations and actions concealed in models produce structuring, conditioning, constraining and performative effects that often limit actors' freedom to produce alternative futures. The models of CAS that are in closed loops can become constrained and conditioned by others' actions to realize mutual adjustment (Louie and Poli, 2017). Foregoing sensitivity to such model effects means mutual adjustment may lead to being stuck in self-reinforcing cycles of conditioning and constraining. With sensitivity, models could be changed to produce different predictions allowing the CAS to alter their behaviour.

Prospection methodology could encourage sensitivity by establishing open-feedback environments, wherein social actors can experience transgression of their own and others' self-limiting behaviour and boundaries. Such staging could motivate some social futurists to see that it is in their interest to reveal their implicit 'contracts' or 'terms of engagement'. Sensitivity to models' effects could help them ask new questions, recognize novelty, notice subtle effects and be ready to act on what is 'constantly emerging' (Miller and Sandford, 2018, p. 78). A prospection enterprise that understands action to be 'a source of uncertainty' (Latour, 2005, pp. 44–45) could recognize that it cannot be certain what the right methodological choices are, except to know that 'we can only experiment' (Miller and Sandford, 2018, p. 78).

Openness of ecologies of practices

Social futurists are primarily interested in recognizing, explaining and enacting difference germane to multiple divergent, open and complex social realities (Fuller and Loogma, 2009). Nevertheless, methods 'not only describe but also help to produce the reality that they understand' (Law, 2004, p. 5). This makes them 'badly adapted to the study of the ephemeral, the indefinite and the irregular' (p. 4), something that the study of difference requires.

We identify two opposing impulses in making choices about methods and practices for prospection methodology. One is to handle difference according to the principles of a single methodology. The methodology wields the authority to encompass all other methodologies; it enacts a common, transcendent reality. The other exposes the chosen methodology to differences between multiple realities enacted by different methodologies; the chosen methodology transforms freely towards the unknown multiple methodologies it will be (Stengers, 2005). Here, there is no maximal methodology that encompasses, but also no enclosing methodology in the space *between* methodologies (Poli, 2018a). The methodologies reviewed in this chapter demonstrate the second impulse.

To handle difference, prospection methodology must, at least sometimes, enact practices that foreground difference. This can be achieved by focussing on *opening* and *closing* activities (Poli, 2018a) or exploring difference across boundaries (e.g. with 'polylogues', see Sardar, 2016, p. 15). Another practice observed in prospection performances is controlled equivocation, like the planners whose practices use the ambiguity between singular 'future' and plural 'futures' to, with ease, blend and switch between three methodologies to produce distinct futures (Rowland and Spaniol, 2015).

The benefit of a closed ecology of practice is that with repetition of the same practice comes speed. However, no matter how 'good' the intentions of the enterprise, the common ground that encompasses all is that of the enterprise's choosing. The benefits of an open ecology of practice are that it can expand and evolve with the reality it enacts. It expands by adding more methods and practices. It evolves in cascades of qualitatively different transitions from preceding ecologies. To evolve, not solely expand without transformation, requires inviting active participation of all those whose practices engage with the prospection activity, a slowing down so those who agreed to participate can explain themselves without demanding their compliance or disqualification (Stengers, 2005).

Extent of distributed engendering of social futures

Prospection requires participation in a wide sense, but more significant than inclusion is *the way in which* methodology enacts participation (Fuller and Loogma, 2009). In that sense, we identify two opposing approaches to participation in the methodology. For the first approach, prospection is an activity performed by core groups of experts, at organized events, giving others marginal roles as 'data input' providers. Such an approach views prospection methodology as enacting a system of production that works on principles of freedom, the central role of humans and mechanistic movements (Latour, 2018). For the second approach, participation is an activity of all those who engage in multiple modes on multiple occasions (sometimes organized) in prospection. Such an approach views prospection methodology as enacting a 'system of engendering', a development that works on principles of dependency, a distributed role for humans and responsibility for genesis (Latour, 2018).

The methodologies reviewed in this chapter provide insights into the second impulse. PNS/PNT advocate active participation of scientists – the experts – with the extended (human) peer community. However, practices and methods for determining participation have effects that complicate determining who or what participates. Some methodologies, by looking at something through abstraction, exclude from participation the one that 'sees' (Rosen, 2012, p. 400). In addition, the same breath that names participants for certain methods also names the non-participants and excludes most others (Law, 2004).

This leads us to consider the question of participation in relation to engendering. The participants who engender social futures are greater in number, more varied (human, non-human), more active and more connected to times and places than ordinarily assumed. For ANT, the participant is not simply the person, but rather 'a vast array of entities swarming toward it' (Latour, 2005, p. 46). For Poli (2018b), the 'causal sequences which can occur in nature' outstrip the impoverished entailment of purely syntactical models attempting to mirror it (p. 11).

The smaller and more homogeneous the participation, the greater the control over specific prospection activity. Wider participation recognizes the heterogeneous actors desiring and demanding to be active in social futures. Nonetheless, the responsibility for the genesis and engendering of social futures with such participation in methodology is complicated.

Conclusions: The methodological implications of three categories of prospection methodology

In this chapter, we considered three current social science methodologies that are inspiring developments in prospection methodology in futures studies/the foresight field of practice: PNS, AS and STS. We illuminated their claims about the explanation and validity concerning social futures, and we examined the conceptions and constitutions of realities they enact. We considered their specific methodological arrangements that play a role in their claims and enacted realities. Then we presented four qualities of prospection methodology creatively synthesized from the methodological developments described: The thickness of relational complexes, the openness of ecologies of practice, the degrees of sensitivity to how prospection is performed and the extent of distributed engendering of social futures. While we could also have examined other methodologies such as gaming, design methods, probabilistic methods, ecological economics or non-Western methods, we nevertheless propose that sets of *qualities* such as these will rise in importance given the changes sweeping through science.

The story we told is about a growing interest in new prospection methodological arrangements that are in step with the complexities of the contemporary social world. We have staged prospection methodology as enacting two realities: One relating to the phenomena being explored and the other relating to the characteristics of the prospection enterprise itself. This separation is not clear-cut in practice. The hope is that, with this distinction, those who produce social futures in practice will awaken to the gap between the methods they design for producing social futures and their understanding of the world's futures-making methods.

Bibliography

Aligica, P.D. (2003). 'Prediction, explanation and the epistemology of future studies', *Futures*, 35(10), pp. 1027–1040.

Appadurai, A. (2013). *The future as cultural fact: Essays on the global condition*. London: Verso.
Barad, K. (2007). *Meeting the universe halfway: Quantum physics and the entanglement of matter and meaning*. Durham, NC: Duke University Press.
Batty, M. and Torrens, P.M. (2005). 'Modelling and prediction in a complex world', *Futures*, 37(7), pp. 745–766.
Bell, W. and Olick, J.K. (1989). 'An epistemology for the futures field: Problems and possibilities of prediction', *Futures*, 21(2), pp. 115–135.
Blok, A, Farias, I. and Roberts, C. (eds) (2020). *The Routledge companion to actor-network theory*. London and New York: Taylor and Francis Group.
Brown, N. and Michael, M. (2003). 'A sociology of expectations: Retrospecting prospects and prospecting retrospects', *Technology Analysis and Strategic Management*, 15(1), pp. 3–18.
Clark, N. (1987). 'Similarities and differences between scientific and technological paradigms', *Futures*, 19(1), pp. 26–42.
Compagna, D. and Kohlbacher, F. (2015). 'The limits of participatory technology development: The case of service robots in care facilities for older people', *Technological Forecasting and Social Change*, 93, pp. 19–31.
Davis, J. and Groves, C. (2019). 'City/future in the making: Masterplanning London's Olympic legacy as anticipatory assemblage', *Futures*, 109, pp. 13–23.
Engelbert, J., van Zoonen, L. and Hirzalla, F. (2019). 'Excluding citizens from the European smart city: The discourse practices of pursuing and granting smartness', *Technological Forecasting and Social Change*, 142, pp. 347–353.
Felt, U., Beck, S., Fouché, R., Miller, C.A. and Smith-Doerr, L. (2017). *The handbook of science and technology studies*. 4th edn. Cambridge, MA and London: The MIT Press.
Fuller, S. (2007). *New frontiers in science and technology studies*. Cambridge: Polity Press.
Fuller, T. and Loogma, K. (2009). 'Constructing futures: A social constructionist perspective on foresight methodology', *Futures*, 41(2), pp. 71–79.
Funtowicz, S.O. and Ravetz, J.R. (1993). 'Science for the post-normal age', *Futures*, 25(7), pp. 739–755.
Groves, C. (2017). 'Emptying the future: On the environmental politics of anticipation', *Futures*, 92, pp. 29–38.
Inayatullah, S. (2005). 'Causal layered analysis: Post-structuralism as method'. In R. Slaughter, S. Inayatullah and J. Ramos (eds). *Knowledge base of futures studies, CD-ROM*, Professional edn, vol. 3. Brisbane: Foresight International.
Jasanoff, S. and Kim, S.H. (eds) (2015). *Dreamscapes of modernity sociotechnical imaginaries and the fabrication of power*. Chicago, IL and London: The University of Chicago Press.
Konrad, K. and Böhle, K. (2019). 'Socio-technical futures and the governance of innovation processes: An introduction to the special issue', *Futures*, 109, pp. 101–107.
Kuhn, T.S. (2012). *The structure of scientific revolutions*. 4th edn. Chicago, IL: University of Chicago Press.
Latour, B. (1987). *Science in action: How to follow scientists and engineers through society*. Cambridge, MA: Harvard University Press.
Latour, B. (2005). *Reassembling the social: An introduction to actor-network-theory*. Oxford: Oxford University Press.
Latour, B. (2018). *Down to earth: Politics in the new climatic regime*. Medford, MA and Cambridge: Polity.
Law, J. (2004). *After method: Mess in social science research*. 1st edn. London: Taylor and Francis e-Library.
Law, J. (2017). 'STS as method'. In U. Felt, S. Beck, R. Fouché, C.A. Miller and L. Smith-Doerr (eds). *The handbook of science and technology studies*. 4th ed. Cambridge, MA and London: The MIT Press, pp. 31–58.
Louie, A.H. and Poli, R. (2017). 'Complex systems'. In R. Poli (ed). *Handbook of anticipation*. Cham: Springer, pp. 1–19.
Miles, I. (2010). 'The development of technology foresight: A review', *Technological Forecasting and Social Change*, 77(9), pp. 1448–1456.
Miller, R. (ed) (2018). *Transforming the future: Anticipation in the 21st century*. Paris: United Nations Educational, Scientific and Cultural Organisation (UNESCO).
Miller, R. and Sandford, R. (2018). 'Futures literacy: The capacity to diversify conscious human anticipation'. In R. Poli (ed). *Handbook of anticipation*. Cham: Springer, pp. 73–91.
Poli, R. (2017). 'Social time as a multidimensional category', *World Futures Review*, 9(1), pp. 19–25.

Poli, R. (2018a). 'Something about science: Mulling over impredicative systems', *Ecological Complexity*, 35, pp. 6–12.

Poli, R. (ed) (2018b). *Handbook of anticipation*. Cham: Springer.

Ravetz, J. and Funtowicz, S. (1999). 'Post-Normal Science—an insight now maturing', *Futures*, 31(7), pp. 641–646.

Ravetz, J.R. (2011). 'Postnormal science and the maturing of the structural contradictions of modern European science', *Futures*, 43(2), pp. 142–148.

Ravetz, J.R. and Funtowicz, S.O. (2015). 'Science, new forms of'. In J.D. Wright (ed). *International encyclopedia of the social and behavioral sciences*. 2nd edn. Oxford: Elsevier, pp. 248–254.

Rosen, R. (1991). *Life itself: A comprehensive inquiry into the nature, origin, and fabrication of life*. New York: Columbia University Press.

Rosen, R. (2012). *Anticipatory systems: Philosophical, mathematical, and methodological foundations*. 2nd edn. New York: Springer.

Rowland, N.J. and Spaniol, M.J. (2015). 'The future multiple', *Foresight*, 17(6), pp. 556–573.

Sardar, Z. (2010). 'Welcome to postnormal times', *Futures*, 42(5), pp. 435–444.

Sardar, Z. (2015). 'Postnormal times revisited', *Futures*, 67, pp. 26–39.

Sardar, Z. (ed) (2016). *The post normal times reader*. London: Centre for Postnormal Policy and Futures Studies.

Sardar, Z. and Sweeney, J.A. (2016). 'The three tomorrows of postnormal times', *Futures*, 75, pp. 1–13.

Schneider, C. and Lösch, A. (2019). 'Visions in assemblages: Future-making and governance in FabLabs', *Futures*, 109, pp. 203–212.

Seligman, M.E.P., Railton, P., Baumeister, R.F. and Sripada, C. (2016). *Homo prospectus*. Oxford: Oxford University Press.

Shapin, S. (1995). 'Here and everywhere: Sociology of scientific knowledge', *Annual Review of Sociology*, 21(1), pp. 289–321.

Slaughter, R.A. (1998). 'Transcending flatland: Implications of Ken Wilber's meta-narrative for futures studies', *Futures*, 30(6), pp. 519–533.

Stengers, I. (2005). 'The cosmopolitical proposal'. In P. Weibel and B. Latour (eds). *Making things public: Atmospheres of democracy*. Cambridge, MA: MIT Press, pp. 994–1003.

Van Hemert, M. (2017). 'Speculative promise as a driver in climate engineering research: The case of Paul Crutzen's back-of-the-envelope calculation on solar dimming with sulfate aerosols', *Futures*, 92, pp. 80–89.

Walsh, Z., Böhme, J. and Wamsler, C. (2021). 'Towards a relational paradigm in sustainability research, practice, and education', *AMBIO*, 50(1), pp. 74–84.

23
Publics
Infrastructuring proto-futures

Georgia Newmarch

Who builds the future?

Future-making is embedded into our everyday lives. Prior to any direct engagement with the future, individuals, publics, organizations and governing bodies are already on the path to it, working on and designing what is needed, considering the interventions that are required for these to become fully realized ways of living. In order to have 'better' futures, the views and actions of publics need to be more involved in shaping the pathways towards those futures. Thinking about social futures requires using the models of publics during moments of disruption, incorporating their actions, while also increasing their 'futures literacy'. Futures literacy, defined here as 'the capacity to think about the future', involves developing particular expertise in thinking about the future using 'future-based information [and] acting in the present' (Poli, 2017, p. 260; cf. also Miller, 2006, 2015). This is vital. Apocalyptic claims about the risks and dangers that lie ahead as resources run out, as populations grow and as expectations escalate are dispelled through education (Urry, 2013). Those who are living through an event begin to reassess their perceptions of the present, depictions of the past and aspirations for the future (Miller, 2018; Sent, 2002). By beginning to acquire futures literacy, publics become better at placing their futures in their own history and contexts. Official accounts of the future are yet fully to utilize these visions in their strategic foresight practices.

Publics are co-produced with issues (Marres, 2005); the nature of membership is reconfigured by the ongoing inclusion and exclusion that infrastructures, technologies and practices generate; and anyone who subscribes to a particular issue is involved within a public. Moments of disruption, those that break away from the status quo, when things do not function 'normally', highlight how life, technology and infrastructure can be seen in ways that are rarely possible when such systems are functioning normally (Graham, 2010). They highlight a pause in the perceived trajectory of time, which is not always a complete revolution of current practice, but rather a period that creates a prototype of what the future – what comes next – could be. Prototyping the future (henceforth referred to as 'proto-futures'), whether intentional or not, is a process whose complexity becomes particularly apparent when things break down.

This chapter argues that moments of disruption highlight new ways of living; how resilience shapes future publics; how cases of disruption constitute proto-futures, space-times in which hopeful practice emerges and where dysfunctional dynamics become visible. Proto-futures integrate the experimental space of fleeting potentials. In this chapter, I therefore shift the focus from looking *at* the future to looking *into* the future. Moving away from the ideas of what we can and cannot know about futures, from anticipation to action, is one of the ways in which design, among other disciplines, aids futures practices. 'From Wicked Problems to Infrastructuring' gives an overview of the ideas of 'wicked problems' and infrastructuring, namely the ongoing processes embedded in the structures and the socio-technical mechanisms for constituting and supporting particular publics. 'Infrastructuring the Future', in turn, discusses the infrastructuring that publics use to aid resilience. 'Building on a Proto-Future' discusses how the blackout that occurred in Lancaster, in the United Kingdom, in December 2015 is an example of a proto-future that created new ways of understanding and approaching the future for the communities who experienced disruption.

The COVID-19 pandemic is one such experiment in living in a 'future' once considered a fictional potential of the present. It is a moment that for the average person – those who are not epidemiologists – did not seem to fit into the perceived trajectory of the future prior to disruption occurring. Publics have sought to work with the issues at play and create new ways of getting by, rather than trying to work around the obstacles they face. COVID-19 has encouraged new ways of thinking about how things can be different, how working patterns and spaces can be altered. There is a need for publics to incorporate the threat of disruption into their daily lives and to reassess how things need (or need not) change. With change, there is not always a deliberate 'before' and 'after', rather the future is an adaptation enveloped in the past and present. Publics need to be equipped with the right tools, practical ways of working through disruption. Proto-futures aid the development of community futures and allow for a mouldable approach for considering what comes next. This chapter will address the ways in which proto-futures do so.

Proto-futures

Visions of the world are not value-neutral and have no singular starting point, 'many of us are in very different "places" and with very different sets of futures' (Tonkinwise, 2014). Such world views are presented as feeding into a bigger global picture: localized flooding being due to climate change; the decline of small towns a symptom of the shift towards metropolitan areas and greater funding for cities. Proto-futures are the beginnings of new ways of living. As with prototypes in design, they are a minimal viable product, a way of thinking through what does and does not work while providing physicality to concepts that may need multiple iterations to reach a desired goal.

Here, I take a micro-moment of disruption, an electrical blackout caused by Storm Desmond that affected Lancaster, over the period of a week in December 2015, to highlight how important small shifts in perceived futures are vital to understanding how publics deal with disruption on a wider scale. Place is important, as local studies can illuminate new methodological tools for dealing with complexity. On 5 December 2015, at 10.30pm, the whole of Lancaster lost power and electricity was not fully restored for a week. This was the most widespread loss of power in North-West England since the Carlisle floods of 2003. The storm had knocked out the electrical power supply for 60,000 homes and consequently disrupted communication and transport infrastructures. Moments of disruption, such as the Lancaster blackout, appear to shift ways of thinking, seeing and doing. The future of the communities that become forged in such moments of disruption is constructed in the present, alongside new attitudes that develop with and as a result of the disruption.

'Normality' renders certain flows, behaviours, routines and practices invisible. What appears to work on the surface is a compacted view of a complex web of actions, legislation and infrastructures. Even though things appear to be working, they might not be. The lights may be kept on; however, the systems supporting their functionality may not represent the state of affairs that is wanted. This multiplicity of actions and states is complexity; the intricacies of moments need to be understood and approached in such a way that does not flatten the network, as this is where the tension between what the future *is* and what the future could *be* come into play. Electrical blackouts are a fitting focus through which to view complexity and the issues of the future, as they demonstrate shifting ways of thinking and multiple courses of action (Newmarch, 2020). This is because increased levels of social complexity, communication and capacities have been inseparable from rising levels of fossil fuel energy (Urry, 2015). When something is physically taken away (the light, the electricity), infrastructures are viewed in different ways and proto-futures become visible.

Moments of disruption become individualized when members of publics have key agendas that they wish to serve. For example, having to travel on the bus to work in the morning because the train drivers are on strike affects your immediate future – you spend two hours travelling, you arrive to work late, you miss a meeting. Why is this happening? Do the train drivers know how much of an inconvenience their actions are on others? On the other hand, when things work, there appears to be no problem. However, there may be very real problems underpinning 'normality'. Hidden practices, meanings and patterns that demonstrate the complexities of everyday life are always around us. The train may turn up on time every day at 7:23, but it is over capacity, the guards cannot do their jobs properly due to the congestion, more trains are put on to deal with this and more effort is required from the train operators.

Ignoring the intricate relationships between behaviours and systems fails to acknowledge and address all the issues that are at play in situations like the one described above. The notion of 'wicked futures' is one way of avoiding this. Rittel and Webber (1974) define wicked futures as an issue difficult to solve because of changing requirements, what suits one group will not please another. Peters (2017), in turn, sees wicked problems as those where there is 'no magic bullet to solve the problems and viewing issues in this way can only help to facilitate what may be only limited answers' (p. 385). My goal in this chapter differs in that I seek to unpack a publics approach to complexity and their modes of infrastructuring. This approach allows us to consider the 'known unknowns' (Snowden and Boone, 2007) by acknowledging the small moments of co-creation that occur.

From wicked problems to infrastructuring

Members of a public, communities and neighbourhoods are co-produced around certain issues as they seek to create and reorganize the infrastructures around them. Bruno Latour re-centred the debate on the concept of power and publics, viewing power as an outcome achieved via the successful assemblage of networks, rather than via the capacity of actors (Latour, 2005). The production of knowledge is shaped by the role of both human and non-human actors; objects are vessels through which social futures can become 'visible'. Infrastructuring, attending to activities of organizing and knowing relations (Ehn, 2008; Karasti and Syrjänen, 2004), also allows us to move away from the 'wicked problems' paradigm that renders issues 'unsolvable'. In many ways, considering wicked problems to demonstrate complexity could be useful; the concept applies when there is a lack of definitive formulation and no one clear definition (Horst and Rittel, 1974). 'Clumsy solutions' demonstrate how previous policy solutions have failed, generating uncertainty which leads to opportunities for social innovation (Verweij, 2006). The activism related to, for example, climate change creates a new part of the network that does not serve to provide solutions, but rather alternatives to current issues.

Those who experience issues first-hand during disruption, regardless of their role or status within a network, seek a greater understanding of what is going on, as they are present in the moment, living through an event. This can only come through action because it is being witnessed first-hand. This is where infrastructuring the future begins and new publics are formed. What is needed are people-focussed perspectives that are small, localized images of the 'problems in situ', as without these, the ways in which the future will be 'known' will only serve those who create it for their own means. By the time problems of any social consequence (e.g. deciding a public health policy or instigating a more democratic society) are identified, conjectured and defined, they are already deemed as 'solved' according to the frame of the professional, politician or activist. Problem framing is a contingent, fraught and contested process for which there is no authoritative set of rules, criteria or methods.

So how then do publics use the future to become more resilient? Moments of disruption serve as 'systemic innovation labs' (Zivkovic, 2018). Le Dantec and DiSalvo highlight that failing to connect to actual practices and contexts sees futures projects become spectacles 'to arrest us and pique our interest' (2013), explicitly referring to speculative design projects. A narrow mindset of what shapes the future does not address alternative models of how our cultural, moral and even religious values might change (Prado and Oliveira, 2016). Dominant industry methods and concepts used in future-making – such as scenario planning (see Curry in this volume), modelling and technology 'roadmaps' – methods that present images of the future that appear highly probable, are grounded in economic foresight and planning. This strengthens their sense of apparent robustness; however, these forecasts often turn out to be wrong. Greater 'bottom-up' futures literacy, where publics approach the future equipped with ways of working through issues, can add greater validity to scenarios, using what publics know alongside their infrastructuring practices, which brings us closer to better pathways to multiple futures. Social futures as a mode of study can be used to highlight this temporal choreography of participation, and how we can imagine futures that involve publics in a different way. This approach brings together past, present and future as well as the global, local and national. The following section explores how, by focussing on the Lancaster blackout of 2015.

Infrastructuring the future

During the Lancaster blackout in 2015, the community learnt to understand infrastructure through its disruption, through technologies that were considered to be old-fashioned, such as the radio. The blackout brought people together and as a result created new publics who could cope with the absence of daily practices, including the use of mobile communications. These publics shared responsibility with those in charge of the network, later taking it into their own hands with emergency plans to reverse the impact of future disruption. However, throughout the event, there was a sense that this was like previous moments of disruption – in this instance, the rolling blackouts of 1974 that took place in the United Kingdom due to industrial action. Even the national newspaper *The Guardian* highlighted this sense of familiarity through a past event as a coping mechanism (Martin, 2015).

By positioning the narrative of the past event as central to the situation being experienced in the present, the problems of the moment are hidden by a need to believe that a recent moment of disruption is less severe than one previously, despite the causes and consequences being different. For example, the effects and rate of climate change today are different to those in 1974. The journalist of *The Guardian* piece continues by commenting that communication technologies of today are the problem: 'What's different now is our shocked disbelief at the disappearance of the internet' (Martin, 2015). This version of the 'Blitz Spirit' myth – that communities have a historic ability to endure suffering by 'keeping calm and carrying on' – is damaging to use when looking ahead to the future as it prevents a recognition of previous failures, current problems and subsequent events (Gilroy, 2004). It overlooks the technologies and practices in place in the present, suggesting that those who experienced the 1970s are the individuals who can be resilient during further disruption and that both the nature and management of disruption were the same in 2015 as it was in 1974. This was not the case. As 2015 demonstrated, not everyone who lost power had experienced previous blackouts, yet the community was still able to cope through the disruption. This false belief highlights how not only the present is inherently connected to the past, but additionally how futures and change are dependent on what has gone before. Memories and path dependency (Magnusson and Ottosson, 2009) matter because they set into place actions and attitudes that remain for more than one generation, and memories are shared between generations – as are policy decisions. The public sought to be resilient to the threat of further disruption and cope with what was happening by coming together. However, their actions were not about creating innovative ways of coping with the threat and change. Instead, actions and affect during the blackout were about utilizing the current systems of power while considering how to adapt rather than radically overhaul and change them. Here, the key tool used by the public in Lancaster that enabled them to deal with this event was a practical assessment of what needed to remain and what needed to change.

This blackout spirit observed in Lancaster illustrates the perceived emotions of community that prevent possible new futures from emerging – by viewing the situation as a temporary event that will be solved by mechanisms of the past, a temporary stabilization of a temporary event. Mediation through a 'blackout spirit' acted as a 'process of relation that involved translation and change' (Anderson, 2014). Power systems, the network and government during 2015 were different in their structures and standards to those in 1974. Similarly, the electrical grid and methods of management were different in 1974 to those in the 1940s and the Second World War. How people in the present respond to the past and act on the future are meshed together in a way that needs to be understood by those living with the systems that are affected by disruption. The proximity of the cultural experience of hardship and pulling together in the war made a difference in 1974 at a national level, as it was a time when publics had been formed to cope with disruption to everyday practices, with national importance. In the case of the 2015 blackout, this was not lost but rather adapted to the local level – those who had lived through 1974 became the ones who referred back to previous cultural experience.

Building on a proto-future

After the blackout, the community in Lancaster set about putting structures in place to build on the shared resources, ideas and tools that had emerged during disruption. The disjuncture between expectations of the future with the practical predictions it had created caused those who experienced the mismatch of ideas and who held responsibility first-hand during the Lancaster blackout to take responsibility for their own communities. Neither Electricity North West, the organizing body for electricity in the city, nor the council coordinated action in a way that took full responsibility for all of those affected in Lancaster. As a result, residents felt the need to create their own mechanisms of resilience and create further iterations of the infrastructures that had been created during disruption. Since the storm, 11 community emergency plans have been devised because of the increased understanding of risk in the area. The plans are available online and accessible to all. They 'make use' of the blackout, citing the effects of Storm Desmond on and in the community as a key reason for the development of the plans: 'There is no statutory duty to participate but the community saw it as a positive step to take in improving their resilience after the recent flooding and electricity failure'.[1] The voluntary work involved with the plans was not viewed as a transfer of the labour and work required by the council, but as a way of continuing to create a community, 'a positive step' in improving resilience for the future. Anticipating an event in such a way allows communities to test their own interpretations, which arise during disruption, of how the future is created.

By considering the complexity of an event, the material parts are put in direct conversation with the publics who interact with them. These publics can be viewed as 'designers', who find methods and ways of creating, adapting and changing their futures and their power relationships. Infrastructure both supports and constrains the scope of design action; it separates what might be considered reasonable – for example, adding something new to a home – from something that might not be considered at all – redesigning the electrical grid. The Lancaster blackout highlights how big-state solutions to disruption are not always the answer. Change occurred through how the publics affected moved on from an event, rather than being a top-down assessment of what needs to happen. A proto-future is not only a form of anticipation, looking forward to moments that are yet to come. Instead, anticipation itself is a form of co-creation, supporting publics to cope if disruption occurs again. This is true not only for physical infrastructure and for systems, such as the electric grid, but additionally the publics that are formed, prior, during and after the moment of disruption. Power structures remain the same, yet, through prototyping how they might live, communities can have an influence on the infrastructures of which they are part. Through the influence of a 'blackout spirit', imaginaries are held back by conforming to the ideas of what has happened in the past.

In this way, disruption becomes a tool to create preferable futures, testing ideas for future moments, combining past and present with what is yet to come. In the case of Lancaster, through publics becoming aware of the 'systemness' of energy at community and local levels, private energy companies communicated the importance of workers in the system. At the same time, publics were able to create maintenance plans that highlighted potential actions that would be taken when further disruption occurred. Throwing light on the visibility of systems revealed the ways in which publics processed immediate futures after an event and how institutional response changed from one that was heavily involved in shaping response to one that provided help only when disruption occurred. Establishing communication between 'ordinary people' is vital to aiding futures literacy, as they are more prepared for what is yet to come. A citizen-set agenda creates a space for a myriad of concerns, articulating their needs and desires. What is required after prototypes of the future have come to light are open spaces where publics that own issues can come to the fore. These spaces may both create and be created in the unusual atmospheres of disruption where the sharing of practices across timescales can then aid future action.

Phrases such as 'lessons learned' suggest that there are things that states, publics and individuals need to be taught from the past, yet this rhetoric is insufficient in prompting action in the present (see also Goodwin and Tutton in this volume). Short-lived events have an impact on the actions of those who experience disruptions, not only through small acts of maintenance in the home, but also through the restructuring of the modes of governance during moments that communities perceive themselves to be in crisis. There is a demonstrable shift from 'governing through resilience' to governing through testing futures-in-action, asserting power through the need to maintain the systems in place when disruption is not occurring, rather than when breakdown happens (Sircar et al., 2013). Whereas publics are perceived to be slower than those making policy decisions through the top-down structures of communication, in reality communities take the future into their own hands – at their own pace and mould the future into one they wish to see.

Conclusion

Proto-futures are essential to social futures, as the subject requires an understanding of presents that engage with the complexities of time, old and new social spaces and objects, as well as how ordinary people work through ideas. These new understandings of the world might lead to change and new eventualities, engaging publics with the hope of change rather than the explicit intention of change. Instead of asserting grand narratives of change into infrastructures, learning to cope with complexity in the present is as important as thinking about solutions for the future. Understanding this issue requires an analysis of past and present cases where disruption has occurred; 'people must live in the here and now' in order to anticipate what is yet to come (Nye, 1999). Action exists within a political economy, yet the cultural political economy at play (Jessop, 2016) – the *meanings* of these acts – has influenced social practices. Through repeated actions, performance and re-enactments, these meanings become embodied. If issues can be highlighted early through a sharing of practice, policy decisions based on creating targets and shaping different futures may be met with less friction, thus creating less disruption.

The lens of this chapter has focussed on a small-scale approach to making futures, the Lancaster blackout. Only when moments of disruption develop can more futures be seen and incorporated into a proto-future. Everyday resilience, an act of emotional co-creation, made or honed by crises, equips people with ways of reviving memories and imaginations of living in another way and creates material coping mechanisms, such as resilience groups and community practices. Co-creation cannot be undertaken by simply looking at what publics do, as this will only reinforce top-down structures of expertise. Ordinary people have to be involved in the process of making futures and test ideas as and when they arise. Through forming community groups and 'emergency' services to deal with disruption, the public in Lancaster developed new systems that required prototyping over new 'innovatory' models. The future is a gradual process. Attention to situated detail in one small-scale scenario can help us unpack a world of complex and sometimes global issues. Pathways in policy have often been developed to meet specific needs; methods for understanding systems are something that is often left out of policy, where decision-makers want to focus on other factors, such as those that are purely economic or political, before considering the needs of individuals and how to address them. This is why proto-futures and looking at more localized, small examples, such as Lancaster, are vital because somewhere our futures might already be being played out, explored and experimented with.

Note

1 See the online register here: http://www.lancashire.gov.uk/media/224827/Community-Risk-Register.pdf

Bibliography

Anderson, B. (2014). *Encountering affect: Capacities, apparatuses, conditions*. Ashgate Publishing, Ltd.
Dantec, C.A.L. and DiSalvo, C. (2013). 'Infrastructuring and the formation of publics in participatory design', *Social Studies of Science*, 43(2), pp. 241–264.
Ehn, P. (2008). October. 'Participation in design things'. *Proceedings of the tenth anniversary conference on participatory design 2008* (pp. 92–101). Indiana University.
Gilroy, P. (2004). *After Empire: Multiculture or postcolonial melancholia*. Routledge.
Jessop, B. (2016). 'State theory'. In Ansell, C. and Torfing, J. (eds). *Handbook on Theories of Governance*. University of California Press.
Karasti, H. and Syrjänen, A.L. (2004). July. 'Artful infrastructuring in two cases of community PD'. In Clement, A., et al. (eds). *Proceedings of the eighth conference on Participatory design: Artful integration: Interweaving media, materials and practices-Volume 1*, pp. 20–30.
Latour, B. (2005). *Reassembling the social: An introduction to actor-network theory*. Oxford University Press.
Magnusson, L. and Ottosson, J. (eds.) (2009). *The evolution of path dependence*. Edward Elgar Publishing.
Marres, N.S. (2005). *No issue, no public: Democratic deficits after the displacement of politics*, PhD Thesis, University of Amsterdam.
Martin, I. (2015). '"Hammering, grim, brainless" – how Storm Desmond hit Lancaster', *The Guardian*, 9 December 2015, https://www.theguardian.com/uk- news/2015/dec/09/storm-desmond-lancaster-floods-chaos-power-neighbourliness-ian-martin.
Miller, R. (2006). 'From trends to futures literacy. Reclaiming the future', *Centre for Strategic Education. Seminar Series Paper* (No. 160). CSE Publications.
Miller, R. (2015). 'Learning, the future, and complexity. An essay on the emergence of futures literacy'. *European Journal of Education*, 50(4), pp. 513–23.
Miller, R. (2018). *Transforming the future: anticipation in the 21st century*. UNESCO Publishing.
Mirowski, P. and Sent, E.M. (eds.) (2002). *Science bought and sold: Essays in the economics of science*. University of Chicago Press.
Newmarch, G. (2020). *Publics, complexity and social futures: Blackouts, infrastructuring and maintenance*, PhD Thesis, Lancaster University.
Nye, D.E. (1999). *Consuming power: A social history of American energies*. MIT Press.
Peters, B.G. (2017). 'What is so wicked about wicked problems? A conceptual analysis and a research program', *Policy and Society*, 36(3), pp. 385–396.
Poli, R. (2017). *Introduction to anticipation studies* (Vol. 1). Routledge.
Prado, L. and Oliveira, P. (2016). 'Design in times of crisis (2014–2016)'. Available at http://a-pare.de/2014/brasil-july-2038.
Rittel, H.W. and Webber, M.M. (1974). 'Wicked problems', *Man-made Futures*, 26(1), pp. 272–280.
Sircar, I., Sage, D., Goodier, C., Fussey, P. and Dainty, A. (2013). 'Constructing resilient futures: Integrating UK multi-stakeholder transport and energy resilience for 2050', *Futures*, 49, pp. 49–63.
Snowden, D.J. and Boone, M.E. (2007). 'A leader's framework for decision making', *Harvard Business Review*, 85(11), p. 68.
Tonkinwise, C. (2014). 'Design studies—What is it good for?', *Design and Culture*, 6(1), pp. 5–43.
Urry, J. (2013). *Societies beyond oil: Oil dregs and social futures*. Zed Books Ltd.
Urry, J. (2015). 'Climate change and society'. In Michie, J. and Cooper, C. (eds). *Why the social sciences matter*. Palgrave Macmillan, pp. 45–59.
Verweij, M., Douglas, M., Ellis, R., Engel, C., Hendriks, F., Lohmann, S., Ney, S., Rayner, S. and Thompson, M. (2006). 'Clumsy solutions for a complex world: The case of climate change', *Public Administration*, 84(4), pp. 817–843.
Zivkovic, S. (2018). 'Systemic innovation labs: A lab for wicked problems', *Social Enterprise Journal*, 14(3), pp. 348–366.

24
Queering
Liberation futures with Afrofuturism

*Lonny J Avi Brooks, Jason Tester,
Eli Kosminsky and Anthony D. Weeks*

Introduction

We develop Queer Futures as an alternative lens to recreate and reframe current future visions that usually project racial, segregated and elite future landscapes. The demographics of forecasting expertise have been traditionally dominated by Eurocentric and patriarchal perspectives, which requires us to question who forecasts the future and towards what ends. Creating a language for Queering the Future involves retelling and critiquing forecasts as they are made and deployed. We augment visions of anticipatory democracy as a vital social network for the purposes of social justice and diversity in bringing forth Queer Futures with Afrofuture frames and tactics.

Black[1] people have always been futurists. We had to be. Afrofuturism aims to reclaim and transform the trauma of the forced voyage of enslaved Africans across the Atlantic and subsequent past atrocities against African peoples, Black and Afro-Queer Diaspora. Think of the Middle Passage as a science fiction horror story where Black people were forcibly transported from western Africa, the home planet of the Black Diaspora, during which previously unseen technologies of transportation and bondage were used to dislocate and kidnap large numbers of people to a new world. Arriving in this new world, they were killed if they spoke their own languages or practised their own rituals. They had to adopt a new religion and infuse it under the radar with their own rituals. In this world, they had to innovate, adapt, capitulate, succumb and rebuild their former lives and traditions. Spirituals became a form of sonic utopias, articulating Black visions of a future of uncolonized minds and bodies.[2] This is a form of futurism.

Afrofuturism delivers a wider aperture on the future. Indeed, Africological theories see the African philosophy of *ntu* as universal life rhythms that encompass human beings within a holistic realm and 'treat human behaviors as manifestations of the spirit/forces behind and between words, images, illusions and other signs' (Woodyard, 2003, p. 21). It is intersectional and rejects binaries. An Afrocentric perspective innately sees the interconnectedness of all things and the world as more fluid than binary categories and posits the rhetorical question: Now, tell me that doesn't describe the future as you're feeling it right now, where multiple crises from pandemic to systemic racism and climate change are occurring simultaneously.

Rather than trying to see the future through a straw, one can grasp a wider radius of multiple cultural imaginations happening in front of you and on the street. The signals of the future start popping up more readily.

Moreover, forecasting is stronger, not weaker, when it includes the fullness of the forecaster, stronger as *advocate* than as *agnostic*, as 'canonical' foresight research had been taught for decades to successive generations of our forecasting leaders. Four hundred years of enslavement, Jim Crow style segregation and the resulting legacies of inequity have challenged the Black Diaspora to bring into being new resilient forms of defiant culture. These legacies have similarly haunted and emboldened Queer liberation visions. We start defining Queer Futures in sharing our Queer Futures toolkit, which includes theoretical approaches to reframing time and its episodic quests. We have arrived back from the past and future to recover an Afro-Queer past; to interrogate how cruelty has shaped Black and Queer spaces; to outline a pathway for Queer liberation that emerged from Black legacies; and to design a game to create Afro-Queer imaginary future worlds to heal trauma as a teaching tool for a National LGBTQ Task Force conference, Creating Change, and for the launch of a Community Futures School.

We rethink how forecasting works to imagine our futures while simultaneously visualizing *Black Fantastics* (Iton, 2010) of radically empowering and queer diversity. Tracing the *Black Fantastic* identifies the '[m]inor-key sensibilities generated from the experiences of the underground…' (Iton, 2010). Tracing the *Black Fantastic* means to recover past counter-futures, sprouting them into the present while reading their *radically hopeful possibilities* into a future *augmented with progressive values* **infused with more Black soul.** Queer in this instance means to 'queer the Infrastructure […] To queer: To challenge the basis on which categories are constructed' (Star, 2002). In the spirit of José Esteban Muñoz (2009), we queer the categories of futures studies and foresight as they are practised and relate to the social. C.L.R. James notes '[t]he fundamental task is to recognize the socialist [and in our case Afro-Queer utopian] society and record the facts of its existence' where these scenes are read as 'outposts of a new society' (Muñoz, 2009).

In the most recent past, the Queer liberation movement launched in the aftermath of the Stonewall rebellion in 1968 unleashed moments of mobilization to create celebrations of Queerdom for liberation in the first Pride parade in New York City, 1969. We expand Queering Futures by proposing a Queer Futures taxonomy based on a history of social justice activism that owes its voice to over 400 years of Black liberation spaces defining Afro-Queer imagination as 'a disposition and pattern of thinking cultivated' by Black and Queer folx to 'see hidden resources, alternative systems, and radical solutions—basically: New futures. Transformational thinking to smash the patriarchy, reinvent capitalism and avert the apocalypse' (Brooks and Tester, 2019). As documentary film-maker Leo Herrera reminds us, transformative Queer spaces emerged out of the early drag shows of the Harlem Renaissance, Black labour organizations holding the first Mardi Gras parades, Black civil rights leaders creating the first blueprints for LGBTQIA protests, Black Panthers voicing support for gay liberation, Sylvester's disco hits and androgyny, Black Lesbian AIDS activism and Voguing (Herrera, 2020). At its core, Queer liberation is suffused with Black ancestral power.

Coming out from cruelty to queering futures

Any conversation about or exploration of Queer Futures requires an address of cruelty. As queer people, we know cruelty: Expulsion, homelessness, violence, unemployment and everyday acts of humiliation. The degree to which we endure cruelty often becomes our badge of identity as well as our cri de coeur, often at the expense of expression of self as sexual, sensual and sentient beings. We define ourselves 'in resistance to' and 'in survival mode' rather than 'in an embrace of'. Our being queer and our relationship to dominant cultures hostile to queer identities necessarily mean that we know cruelty in intimate and personal ways. The imagining of Queer Futures is as much about liberating ourselves from cruelty as it is about finding ways to collaborate with and innovate even within its maddening embrace (Brooks, 2018; Schalk, 2018).

If we are to reclaim our lives from cruelty, how shall we proceed? Is it a taking by force? Is it a negotiation? Is it an education? Is it an act of introspection and self-discovery? Are we beholden to the whims of sociopaths whose benevolence and kindness we may never enjoy because our liberation does not serve them? Will we be in conversation with our bullies and nemeses, whose actions are guided not as much by pathological disregard but from a fragile ignorance easily punctured and dissected by a shrewd campaign of empathy and education? With sociopaths and psychopaths – people who are inured to our suffering and may even enjoy it, if it brings them personal gain and satisfaction – our imagining of Queer Futures involves outwitting them, outmaneuvering them and creating spaces in which we neutralize and transcend their impact on our lives. With our ignorant bullies, even if they don't see themselves as such, we have a different opportunity: To engage with them around radical empathy, to appeal to senses of justice they may not have even realized and to transform everyday acts of mundane cruelty into meaningful infusions of consciousness about how they – and we – would like to live together in the world (Brach, 2004; TEDx Talks, 2015).

For those of us who live in marginal worlds, we rehearse cruelty all the time, if only to thicken our skins and hone our abilities to withstand offenses, big and small, that have become a familiar cadence in our lives. Whether we 'play the dozens' – the long-standing tradition of banter among African-American men, often involving barbs regarding 'your mama' – 'throw shade', best illustrated by the balls exemplified in the documentary 'Paris Is Burning' or the TV series 'Pose' (Livingston, Swimar and Livingston, 1991; Murphy, Falchuk and Canals, 2018; Percelay, Ivey and Dweck, 1994; Wald, 2012), or engage in BDSM (bondage-discipline-sadomasochism), our rehearsal of cruelty reminds of the presence of cruelty in our lives, as well as our hope for navigating it, neutralizing it and even reclaiming and transforming it for ourselves.

In the contemplation of Queer Futures, how do we make allowances for safety when the going gets too hard? One might argue that pushing the boundaries and creating discomfort, through scenarios and games, is of value. Radical empathy and visions of justice often reside in a place of discomfort and vulnerability. Still, envisioning Queer Futures does not mean ADVOCATING for violence or the deliberate and wanton infliction of pain and suffering. Queer Futures ask us to contemplate the presence of cruelty in our lives – and how we learn from it, how we live with it, what we want from it and what we need from it. We need to know *what we do not want* in order to move more authentically towards that which we do.

Claiming cruelty for ourselves. Would we want that? Many would offer that the most aspirational and desirable futures are the ones that are guided by love, kindness and mutual regard. Perhaps, we find cruelty more empowering if we recast it as our ability to act with 'ferocity' and 'fierceness'. Put another way, the ability to entertain cruelty is the ability to love myself so deeply that I will inflict pain and suffering in order to ensure my right to live. Imagine this: I am riding my bike on a wooded path. Suddenly, out of nowhere, a mountain lion pounces upon me, knocks me off my bike and sinks its teeth into my flesh. This is a beautiful creature – muscular, powerful and instinctual. What do I do, for my survival? Do I rely on this creature to love me enough to liberate me – or do I fight with everything I have in order to liberate myself? What does cruelty endow me to do? My ability to act with ferocity is the key to my survival (Weeks, 2019).

Undoubtedly, claiming cruelty for ourselves and creating environments and stories where we envision Queer Futures that do not benefit or even include non-queer people will lead to allegations of exclusion and discrimination. 'We have become the enemy!'…has become the newest rallying cry as conservative ideologies face significant losses over LGBT protections and rights. No, we are not the enemy. Queer Futures thinking does not always require us to be inclusive. We are within our rights to imagine futures without our oppressors. It <u>does</u> require us to act with safety – along with incisive conversation about what 'safe' means and for whom. Who is holding the whip – and what feeling does that inspire within us? Ultimately, our reimagining of cruelty produces valuable insight into power structures and our relationship with them. We have often been the victims of cruelty. By queering the future and the cruelty therein, we become the experts at understanding cruelty, how to adapt it and transform it and how to imbue it with new meaning (Brooks, 2018a; Califia, 2002; Jennex, 2013; van Veen and Anderson, 2019).

Building a global initiative of Queer liberation foresight

Queer foresight research is as important for the future well-being and even survival of straight, cisgender people as is it for LGBTQ individuals alive today and those who will be born in the next century. This counter-intuitive argument will become clearer to the reader as a case is presented of the urgent need for a better understanding of how major future forces will disproportionately disrupt the lives of sexual and gender minorities around the world. This urgent need to begin a global queer foresight initiative with both professional and grassroot components is also nested within a proposed framework that, at a minimum, ensures an equal level of caution and resilience for LGBTQ people in the face of the future as for the majority straight and cisgender people on the planet. However, at its highest potential, this framework proposes to harness the neurodiverse cognitive and creative skills of many LGBTQ minds. Their imagination – born of cruelty, adaptation, code-switching, influence, trendsetting and most of all resilience – will be essential to imagine and implement unique cultural, economic and technological systems and adaptions that can help the entire human species thrive and survive the interlocking wicked problems and grave existential threats of the next century. This is a story of progress in which homosexuality and gender nonconformity begin to evolve from the frameworks of widespread taboo, clinical malady and fatally illegal condition through the majority of human existence and could be reframed rapidly within this century as the 'queer imagination'. This constitutes a potentially fruitful, venerated and unparalleled foundry not just of cultural and artistic innovations but also apocalypse- and/or misery-averting transformative solutions.

A proposed framework of equal > equitable > liberation futures work

Many of the theoretical underpinnings of social justice activism and advocacy involve a distinction between achieving, as end-states and ideal goals, equality or achieving equity or achieving liberation. This distinction can be found in the core ideas and ideals of racial justice work, gender equality, reproductive rights, economic inequality, disability advocacy and indeed in LGBTQ advocacy. There are many sources for a deeper understanding of the origins and elaborations of the framework itself and the three distinct goals as scenarios where a pervasive injustice will be considered to be righted. What follows will be a synopsis description of each goal that is generic to many forms of injustice-correcting theory and programs, accompanied with an example from past, present and future work and aims of the LGBTQ movement.

- **equality** is typically defined as the same legal right to pursue a course of action as others
- **equity** is largely seen as a foundation level of equality but with more interventions and assistance for persons of lower privilege in the dominant cultural, societal and economic systems
- **liberation** as it relates to social justice theory and activism is the least shared concept of these three but one consensus may be an entire revolution or reordering of the dominant systems such that no one group is prioritized (i.e., monetarily, in terms of health outcomes, power) over others for their contributions, inherent value and, most fundamentally, their existence.

To illustrate each of these archetypes, we will consider the specific fight for LGBTQ people to be able to hold full-time gainful employment legally while being known by colleagues and supervisors to be LGBTQ at their place and culture of work – to be 'out'. To bind the example, and because there are enough vastly different present and future states as to provide sufficient rich terrain, we will only consider LGBTQ employment in the United States:

A queer **equal future** would be one in which no person employed in the United States can be denied employment, or subsequently fired, because they openly identify as LGBTQ. At the time of this writing, 31 US states offer such protections and some larger cities in the remaining 19 states have passed employment nondiscrimination protections that cover municipal government jobs and private or public companies operating in those cities (LGBT People in the United States Not Protected by State Nondiscrimination Statutes. [March 2019] The Williams Institute, UCLA, Los Angeles, CA). For the remaining states and areas of the United States, at the time of writing, it is perfectly legal to not hire an LGBTQ person applying for employment or to fire an LGBTQ person currently employed, solely citing their identity as LGBTQ as a cause. To achieve an equitable future, the LGBTQ movement continues to focus its efforts on the 19 states without gender orientation or sexual identity protections – a process that may take well into mid-century to achieve for all 50 US states, while at the same time working to passing the EQUALITY Act in Congress which would offer these protections to every US worker immediately but also require Democrat party control of both chambers of Congress and likely a Democrat-identifying president to sign such legislation into law. LGBTQ activists are hopeful that this equal future scenario can happen by 2030.

A queer **equity future** for LGBTQ employment is complementary to an equal future, and many would consider it essential to strive towards both before legal protections are in place and after, since LGBTQ people can work (or try or strive to work) without needing to outwardly openly identify their sexuality or gender-nonconforming identity – to 'stay in the closet'. An equity future will consider the disparities between the lived experiences of LGBTQ and straight, cisgender persons – where the former tend to have more lingering effects of childhood and adolescent trauma and ostracization; more health problems as adults (American Psychological Association, 2016; Ryan, 2010); and higher levels of depression, anxiety and substance misuse (Kates et al., 2018) – and account for these disparities and their disproportionately negative impact on nearly every aspect of training for, locating, maintaining and succeeding at employment. One example of an early signal from an equity future is the Trans(gender) Employment Program run by the San Francisco LGBT Community

Center that assists transgender individuals in all of these employment prerequisites and requirements while also understanding that even larger economic and cultural systems can have enormous impacts on holding down a job. As part of their work towards equitable trans employment, the Trans Employment Program holistically considers elements from stable housing and transportation credits (since stable sleeping and affordable commuting are essential to anyone's relationship with work) to transgender sensitivity training at companies participating in their #Hiretrans job placement initiative.

Before moving on to exemplifying a queer liberation future, it may be worth noting that these two archetypes of future justice – and a future likely measured in decades where justice permeates our world as a norm – may land with something of a shock for straight, cisgender readers of this chapter. It is both sad and true that when LGBTQ futurists, activists and individuals speak about future states for our communities, we are indeed speaking about such radical developments and innovations as 'not being fired for talking about your spouse to a coworker' or trans young adults learning how to get and keep a job because their gender identity shut them out from family and academic assistance', yet such is the current state of many LGBTQ people even in the United States that even relatively small interventions, deployed everywhere an LGBTQ person in need lives, can make for radically more equal and equitable Queer Futures.

A queer **liberation future** would understand universal equality and privileged-linked equity as foundational values in this new paradigm, not subjects for even well-meaning debate. Just like the idealized versions of queer equal futures and queer equity futures may seem hopelessly limited because queer lives are still so marginalized, readers from outside the United States may feel pity that one minimum example of a liberation future would be universal healthcare, and again with no debate for full and robust LGBQ and transgender mental health services and LGBQ and transgender health, and gender-realigning physical health services, including eradication of and cure for AIDS. Higher education would be liberated from out-of-reach costs for all young people, including LGBTQ people-of-colour for whom rising tuition fees have even more often been a privilege-stacked barrier. In a queer liberation future, the planet would stop warming well below 2°C with most carbon and lifestyle sacrifices coming from developed societies, along with climate mitigation resources from wealthy nations to poorer areas most affected by climate-catalysed limitations, extreme weather and sea-level rise, including the tens of millions of LGBTQ people living in these areas who may otherwise be deprioritized for limited resources and shelters. Ultimately, it may be that capitalism cannot be retooled to achieve liberation and a new more liberation-compliant economic system rises in place. Liberation will most likely include some form of universal basic income or universal basic assets like housing, education and transportation. Since LGBTQ people have had near-universal levels of job insecurity in the modern movement, we can speculate that many would welcome a world where one's worth is not derived from jobs, including increasingly automated work.

We propose that queer foresight research adopt this framework as a tool for generating speculative outcomes and implications, both threats and opportunities, of important future drivers as they relate to LGBTQ people, and as a scaffolding to share and disseminate research. The authors would hope that presenters and facilitators of Queer Futures research share the explicit and biased instruction that equality futures are a bare minimum for LGBTQ survival in the twenty-first century and also no guarantee. Equity futures at least add in an accounting for the trauma, the often intersecting marginalized identities of LGBTQ people and the enduring cultural stigma that will conservatively take centuries to root out of every country and society on the planet As the United States becomes less white, due to a growing number of intersecting identities, social justice movements are increasingly focussing on intersections with other issues and movements not just as opportunities but priorities. Fully developing scenarios for LGBTQ equity futures, along with their implications and opportunities, can therefore be powerful tools for finding common ground with other movements – if not developed from the beginning with abundant intersections of identities, stakeholders, funders and, when applicable, on-the-ground service providers such as LGBTQ community centres.

Nevertheless, LGBTQ liberation futures are where the case for this section's reverse-power thesis – queer minds saving straight (and all) societies – can most persuasively be made. Put simply: If achieving liberation is a transformation of the dominant systems and structures that cause injustices to people and the planet, then the LGBT/Queer movement fuelled by the queer imagination might just strike upon, or influentially adopt and inspire, the new systems, structures and major adaptions that will halt or shrink the growing threats to peace, prosperity and existence faced by everyone this century. While there may not be distinct cognitive patterns or processes unique to LGBTQ brains yet studied, there may be a queer imagination rising from our inherent lives navigating spaces – in society, culture, academia, politics and industry – in different ways. On the question of queer people in the spaces, companies and contexts of innovation, the futurist MJ Petroni comments:

> [LGBTQ people] have existed in lots of different worlds, and in walking back and forth between these spaces and never being fully at home, they learn a lot about the unspoken rules, assumptions, codes, and values that exist. At the same time, because they become at home in traversing all of those things, they develop a native skill set in connecting the dots and translating their own identities or questions in response to radically changing circumstances.
>
> *(Powers, 2019)*

The framework in practice

Our coauthor Jason Tester serves on the Board of the National LGBTQ Task Force, a prominent activist organization in the struggle to secure rights for Queer people in the United States, and has helped to secure important legislative victories for Queer communities nationwide. In January 2019, the Task Force held its annual conference, Creating Change, in Detroit. This conference offers adults and especially young adults the opportunity to experience and practise Queer liberation during a day-long conference initiated by the Racial Justice Institute. Detroit holds a special place of significance as a nexus of Black, Indigenous Queer pathways as the historical site for Native American and Black civil rights, the sonic utopian sounds of Motown and the promise of auto-manufacturing jobs securing some measure of upward mobility. In the aftermath of the city's bankruptcy, Detroit has experienced a renaissance of Black and Indigenous ingenuity full of Do-It-Yourself visions of new technical fixes for Internet accessibility, experiments in cryptocurrency and new creative artistic expression.

As a designer, Jason Tester specializes in transforming present landscapes into near futures immersive experiences as seen in Figure 24.1, where he challenges Creating Change attendees to use their Queer imaginations to think about the future of Creating Change, both as a conference and as a real implementable metaphor for manifesting Queer liberation in the every day and in the coming decades. Tester created a booth for the Queer community at Creating Change to don space suit costumes and have Tester take a professional style self-portrait photograph of individuals or groups as they imagined themselves setting foot on Mars with Pride flags in hand.

Figure 24.1 Jason Tester's Mars Booth at Creating Change (2019)

The other coauthor Lonny Avi Brooks brought a new game, *United Queerdom*,[3] to Creating Change as a workshop celebrating Queer Futures and its core, the inherited Black legacy of radical creativity at the margins. We played the game with a predominantly Black audience of young Queer activists, social workers and social scientists. Imagine a game and map of the fictitious land of *United Queerdom* (UQ), where various queer tribes live, celebrate and imagine their cultural futures. The quest? To journey through, observe and partake in these shared imaginations, to create a shared memory of the future by creating pathways, quests and visions of a collective queer future by 2054 in an imagined transformative space such as the UQ. The initial origins of the game were generated by rethinking the forecasting game *Thing from the Future* created by Stuart Candy and Jeff Watson.

We also wanted to build upon the insights from the only other Queer forecasting game that had been created, *My2024*, co-led by the Institute for the Future and the Arcus Foundation in 2014. *My2024* was the largest online foresight game to ask thousands of LGBTQ adults and students about the 'hopes for their lives' and 'fears for the LGBTQ movement' set in 2024. Participants submitted hundreds of 'idea cards', speculative videos set in the future and illustrated postcards of artefacts-from-the-future where Queerness was widely accepted by society writ large, and, sometimes, a yet-to-be future artefact of acceptance (*My2024*, 2014).

In 2017, we asked students from marginalized working-class communities to reimagine their social, media and digital spaces into 2054 – the imagined year for the film *Minority Report*, highlighting the minority reports of future visions too often ignored. The UQ aims to create spaces built on other foundations than the master's tools, house and land.

Further development on *United Queerdom* and its sister game *Afro-Rithms from the Future* began when in late 2018 Dr. Lonny Brooks met Eli Kosminsky at a mixed reality computer lab in Oakland called *Dynamicland*. The film, *Black Panther*, had excited imaginations worldwide and galvanized regional Bay Area pride from Oakland to San Francisco where the real Black Panther Party and its legacies of care and Black Power took place. Brooks, along with other scholars, noticed how much the film inspired them while simultaneously commenting on its strong heteronormative themes and barely signalling the romance of two fiercely proud women warriors set within the film. In this context, Brooks reimagined the Queer community as if it were its own prideful nation called United Queerdom teeming with vibrant tribes from Bears to the Leather community to the Transgender village.

2019 marked the Task Force's first public apology for its role in historically ignoring the pivotal role played by the Trans community in the Queer liberation struggle and diminishing its voice. At the same time, Brooks and Eli Kosminsky, as a game designer and staunch ally, collaborated to bring Afrofuturist storytelling into a new, communal medium with the intention of helping everyone share their visions of the future, especially those who are not traditionally advantaged by technology. Several game jams and physical prototypes later, *United Queerdom* and *Afro-Rithms from the Future,* were born. Gaming, as Brooks and Pollock (2018) note, can serve as a pathway to grasp and reflect processes of traditionally marginalized imaginations, including the queer imagination. Gaming as part of experiential futures, as Candy (2014), Dunagan (2004, 2010), and Rosa and Sweeney (2019) have evidenced, can provide the opportunity to both imagine and think about the neuroscience of memory and future-making (Dunagan et al., 2019). This research inspired the game quest in search of queer liberation as an experiential future quest to create new memories of the future nurtured by ancestral gender-fluid modes of being.

Conclusion

The *United Queerdom* game ultimately aims to centre the margins of Queer existence and resistance, embrace and negotiate the nuances of diverse Queer communities and reject binary thinking (Tester, 2020). The UQ aspires to embrace the pleasure and joy of being Queer by adapting the tools of what Adrienne Maree Brown calls pleasure activism. Queer sex is not beside the point. We must reclaim and acknowledge our own desires before we can remake the world! Ancestral Queer pleasure wisdom resonates in our bodies. As Ni'ja Whitson (2020) proclaims

> I am a Black Queer Trans Nonbinary Artist, "flowing fluently like the memory of my" superfluid slipping ancestors and transcestors. As my elder Iya Fakayode often reminds me "If *we* are then someone else in our line was. We are not the first".

United Queerdom offers glimpses into multiple universes of Queer Futures where we can rework time itself as *Queertime*, a moment where our liberation reaches into our past and reimagines our future to change the present with pleasurable and mindful freedom.

Notes

1 We intentionally use terms in this chapter to celebrate and represent the active and performative use of language as an affirmation of identity, relationship and transformation. Our work will capitalize the term Black with a capital B when referring to peoples of the Black Diaspora or when describing people and cultures of African origin. See Coleman (2020) for the *New York Times* discussion of 'Why We're Capitalizing Black'. The term 'folx' makes visible marginalized communities as a common and familial form of address that constitutes Black, Indigenous and People of Colour as the people to whom we hold ourselves accountable, as well as the organizations and institutions that represent them. The word fragment '-Rithms', in reference to, for example, the forecasting imagination game *Afro-Rithms from the Future*, adapts the term 'rhythms'. Replacing the 'hy' with an 'i' gestures towards the ubiquity of algorithms in our digital society, and it urges us to become aware of how the algorithms invented by our major technology companies are created by predominantly white, male engineers within a white, male-dominated patriarchal culture. Therefore, 'Afro-Rithms' intentionally allows and asserts the necessity of offering algorithms from other,

traditionally marginalized, cultural perspectives within our digital society. *Afro-Rithms from the Future* aims to shift our digital lens, which often reinforces and perpetuates dominant inequities, and aspires to expand our range of possible and more equitable, liberating multiverses.
2 For more information about African-American spirituals, see *African American Spirituals*. Web. Retrieved from the Library of Congress, www.loc.gov/item/ihas.200197495/.
3 See Appendix for instructions on how to play the game.

Bibliography

American Psychological Association (2016). 'Stress in America: The impact of discrimination'. Retrieved from: https://www.apa.org/news/press/releases/stress/2015/impact-of-discrimination.pdf

Brach, T. (2004). *Radical acceptance: Embracing your life with the heart of a Buddha*. New York: Bantam.

Brooks, L. (2018a). 'Cruelty and Afrofuturism', *Critical/Cultural Journal of Communication*, 15(1), pp. 101–107. https://doi.org/10.1080/14791420.2018.1435078

Brooks, L. (2018b). 'Afrofutures with Lonny Brooks'. Plenary lecture at the Institute for the Future as part of the Ten Year Forecast Program, *Looking Back, Moving Forward*. September 26, 2018, Computer History Museum, Mountain View, CA.

Brooks, L. and Kosminsky, E. (2019). National LGBTQ Task Force, *Creating Change* Conference. LGBTQ Resilient Futures Game panel and workshop on debuting the game: 'United Queerdom: Imagining Queer futures with an Afrocentric perspective', Detroit, January 2019.

Brooks, L. and Tester, J. (2019). Primer 19, 'Imagining Queer futures with Afrofuturism'. June 14, 2019, New Parsons School of Design, New York City. Retrieved from: https://vimeo.com/348102990

Brown, A.M. (2019). *Pleasure activism: The politics of feeling good*. Stirling: AK Press.

Califia, P. (2002). *Speaking sex to power: The politics of queer sex*. Jersey City, NJ: Cleis Press.

Califia-Rice, P. (1988). *The lesbian s/m safety manual: Basic health and safety for woman-to-woman s/m*. Denver: Lace.

Candy, S. (2014). 'Experiential futures: Stepping into OCADU's time machine', *The Futurist*, 48(5), p. 34.

Coleman, N. (2020). 'Why we're capitalizing Black', *New York Times*, July 5. https://www.nytimes.com/2020/07/05/insider/capitalized-black.html

Dator, J. (2019). 'Alternative futures at the Manoa school'. In Dator, J. (ed.). *Jim Dator: A noticer in time*. Cham: Springer. pp. 37–54.

Dunagan, J.F. (2004). 'Neuro-futures: The brain, politics and power', *Journal of Futures Studies*, 9(2), pp. 1–18.

Dunagan, J.F. (2010). 'Politics for the neurocentric age', *Journal of Futures Studies*, 15(2), pp. 51–70.

Dunagan, J., Draudt, A., Hadley, J.J., Hogan, R., Murray, L., Stock, G. and West, J.R. (2019). 'Strategic foresight studio: A first-hand account of an experiential futures course', *Journal of Futures Studies*, 23(3), pp. 57–73.

Eshun, K. (2003). 'Further considerations on Afrofuturism', *CR: The New Centennial Review*, 3(2), pp. 287–302.

Gamson, J. (2006). *The fabulous Sylvester: The legend, the music, the seventies in San Francisco*. London: Palgrave Macmillan.

Guthrie, R.D. (2005). *The nature of Paleolithic art*. Chicago, IL: University of Chicago Press.

Herrera, L. (2018). 'The Father's Project', a web series out of San Francisco, imagines a world in which people who died of AIDS never died, to create an image of queer utopia. Retrieved from: https://www.iftheylived.org/

Herrera, L. [@herreraimages] (2020, July 7). 'The drag shows of the Harlem Renaissance'. [Photograph]. Instagram. https://www.instagram.com/p/CITpe61hry7/

Iton, R. (2010). *In search of the black fantastic: Politics and popular culture in the post-civil rights era*. Oxford: Oxford University Press.

Jennex, C. (2013). 'Diva worship and the sonic search for queer utopia', *Popular Music and Society*, 36(3), pp. 343–359.

Kates, J. et al. (2018). 'Health and access to care and coverage for lesbian, gay, bisexual, and transgender (LGBT) individuals in the U.S'. Kaiser Family Foundation Report. Available at: https://www.kff.org/report-section/health-and-access-to-care-and-coverage-lgbt-individuals-in-the-us-health-challenges/

Livingston, J., Swimar, B. (Producers), and Livingston, J. (Director). (1991). *Paris is burning*. Janus Films.

Muñoz, J.E. (2009). *Cruising utopia: The then and there of queer futurity*. New York: NYU Press.

Murphy, R., Falchuk, B. and Canals, S. (Program Creators). (2018). *Pose*. New York: Fox 21Television Studios.

My2024: Imagining new futures for LGBTQ people in the United States: Report of a nationwide conversation October 7–16, 2014. Convened by the Institute for the Future for Arcus Foundation. Retrieved from: https://www.arcusfoundation.org/wp-content/uploads/2015/03/My2024-Final-Report1.pdf

Percelay, J., Ivey, M. and Dweck, S. (1994). *Snaps: the African American art of verbal warfare*. New York: Morrow.

Powers, D. (2019). *On trend: The business of forecasting the future*. Champaign: University of Illinois Press.

Rosa, A. and Sweeney, J.A. (2019). 'Your move: Lessons learned at the interstices of design, gaming, and futures', *Journal of Futures Studies*, 23(4), pp. 137–42.

Ryan, C. (2010). 'Engaging families to support lesbian, gay, bisexual, and transgender youth: The family acceptance project', *Prevention Researcher*, 17(4), pp. 11–13.

Schalk, S. (2018). *Bodyminds reimagined: (Dis)ability, race, and gender in black women's speculative fiction*. Durham, NC: Duke University Press.

Star, S.L. (2002). 'Infrastructure and ethnographic practice: Working on the fringes', *Scandinavian Journal of Information Systems*, 14(2), p. 6.

TEDx Talks. (2015, November 11). *Radical Empathy | Peter Laughter | TEDxFultonStreet*. Retrieved from: https://www.youtube.com/watch?v=qkEG4sw5qn0

Tester, J. (Nov. 20, 2020). IFTF Foresight Talk: 'Queering the future to save the future', A presentation delivered for the Institute for the Future Foresight Talks series. Palo Alto. https://www.youtube.com/watch?v=j5fg5h3K7NA

Tinsley, O.E.N. (2008). 'Black Atlantic, queer Atlantic: Queer imaginings of the middle passage', *GLQ: A Journal of Lesbian and Gay Studies*, 14(2–3), pp. 191–215.

van Veen, T.C. and Anderson, R. (2019). 'Fabulous camps of the Black Fantastic: Sylvester James, Queer Afrofuturism, and Black vernacular becomings'. In Anderson, R. and Jones, C.E. (eds.). *The Black speculative arts movement: Black futurity, art + design*. New York: Lexington Books, pp. 217–230.

Wald, E. (2012). *The Dozens: A history of rap's mama*. Oxford: Oxford University Press.

Weeks, A. (2019). 'Albino Squirrels'. Queer Solo Performance Festival, June 2019. San Francisco.

Whitson, N. (2020). 'Super fluid/super Black: A sacred physics read on trans erasures'. In Butler, P. (ed.). *Critical black futures: Speculative theories and explorations*. London: Palgrave Macmillan, pp. 165–180.

Woodyard, J.L. (2003). 'Africological theory and criticism: Reconceptualizing communication constructs'. In Jackson, II, R.L. and Richardson, E. (eds.). *Understanding African American rhetoric: Classical origins to contemporary innovations*. New York: Routledge, pp. 133–154.

Appendix

Imagining Queer futures as a gaming quest

Welcome to United Queerdom

Queer Futures: United Queerdom 2054 is a new game to generate objects and paper prototypes of participants' individual and collective imaginations and aspirations for a Queer Future (see Figure 24.2). Participants chose one of four possible future scenarios (see Dator, 2019, pp. 37–54) as part of their quest: Growth (status quo), Constraint (carefully managed future), Collapse (life falls apart) and Transformation (change occurs).

Imagine a game and map of the United Queerdom (UQ), where various queer tribes co-exist. Using the artefacts and stories that drive them, elders of each region develop visions of the future and exchange them with nearby lands. Those tales inspire the production of new technologies and ideas that spread throughout the Queerdom, weaving a web of interconnected futures (see Figure 24.3).

Our goal in designing *Queer Futures* was to give players an approachable and lighthearted way to engage in the act of collaborative storytelling. The game mechanics encourage players to reflect on their own queer identity and learn from the identities, values and tensions of others.

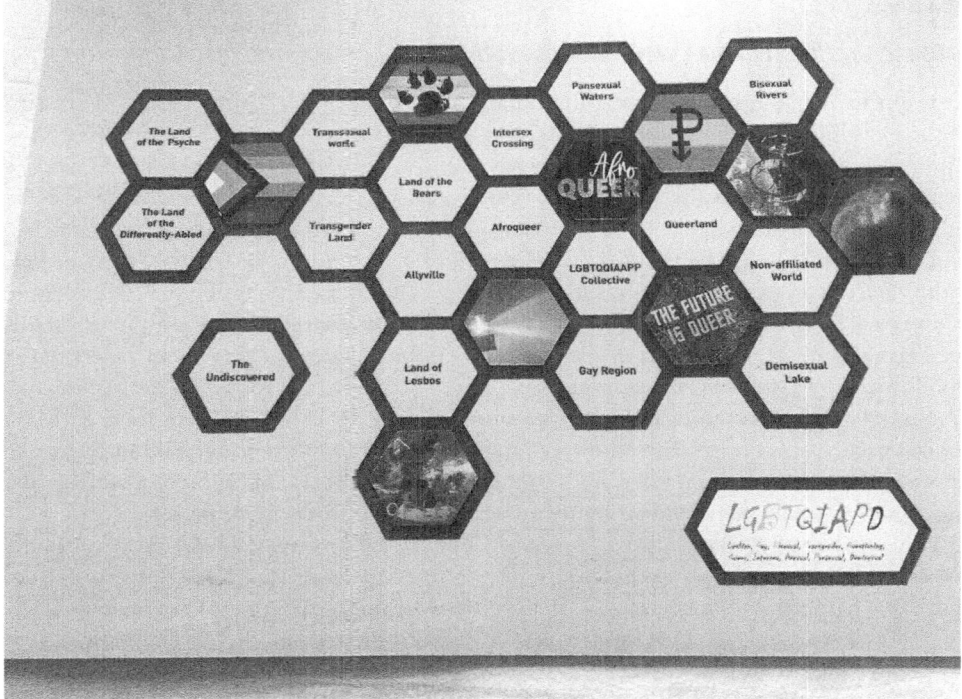

Figure 24.2 The *United Queerdom* Game Board

Figure 24.3 Envisioning a Queer California with its Pride flag at Creating Change (2019)

Phase 1: creating tribes

The game begins with the formation of groups around Queer identities, ranging from the Pansexual Rivers to the Afro-Queer Plains. Within these groups, players record characteristics of futures and artefacts they would like to form.

Phase 2: world building Queer futures with tension, object and inspiration cards

To begin their quest, players have to build an initial world. As a group, players select two Tension cards to form their Queer multiverse (see Figure 24.4). Tension cards identify a significant issue or trend to explore speculatively. Tensions cards like 'Less or More LGBTQ+ Representation' or 'More/Less white Terrorism'? ask: what does a world look like framed by these issues? In 2030, what happens in a world with more LGBTQ+ representation and less white terrorism? Once the tensions of our future world are created, we populate this universe with Object and Inspiration cards. Object cards (see Figure 24.5) describe the basic form of an everyday object and imagine how it may look and change in the future. Inspiration cards (see Figure 24.6) are usually cultural prompts that inspire change in movements, methods or moods from the Queer musical refrains from Janelle Monáe to the rhythmic sway of Beyoncé's Black Panther Party inflected song *Formation*. In a later version of this game held with 150 players, participants creatively transformed the object card of 'Buttons' into a transformative device that would assist us in 'dialling' through our Queer liberation in order to engage the full expressive spectrum of our sexuality and reflect on our biases as we do so.

This portion of *Queer Futures* is developed intentionally to scaffold the process of self-expression. The cards given to the groups help set the tone and are drawn from a variety of LGBTQ+ passions and concerns. Their purpose is to make the game more approachable, especially for participants who are new to forecasting activities. However, players will have a range of interests that extend beyond what they can find in randomly drawn cards. Tools must be created to give players the agency to focus on what matters to them – we have found worlds based on personal experience to be much more compelling.

Queering

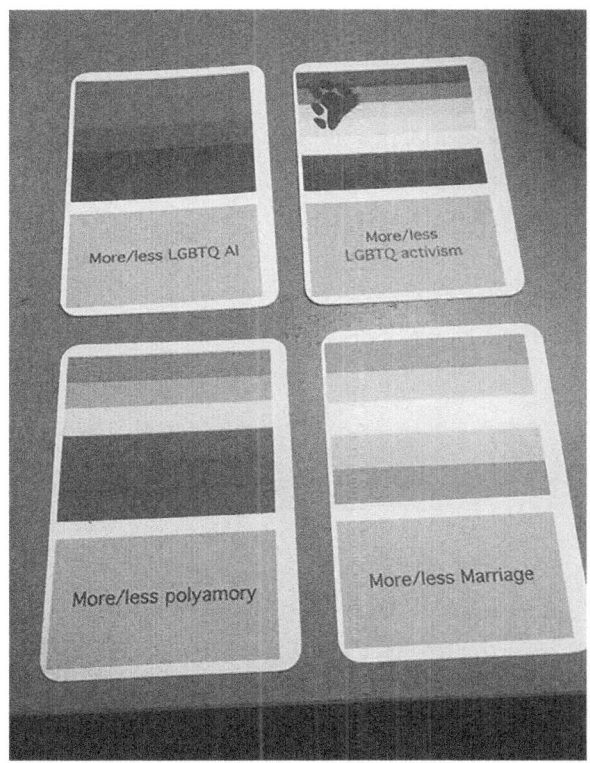

Figure 24.4 UQ Tension cards ©2019

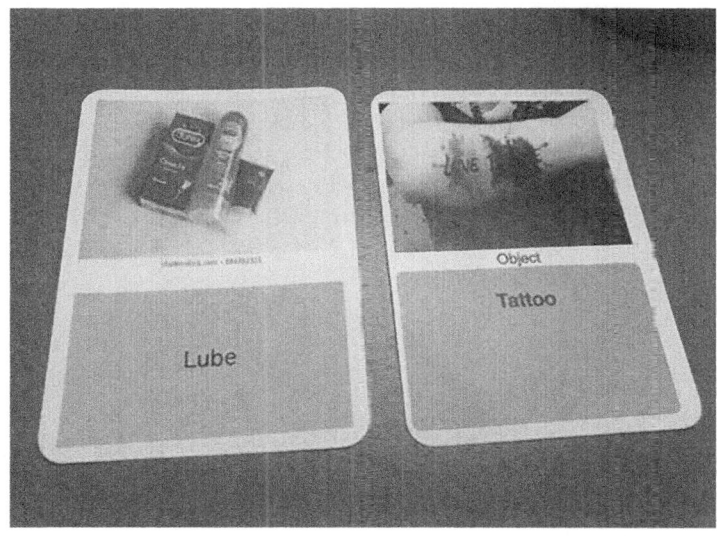

Figure 24.5 UQ Object cards ©2019

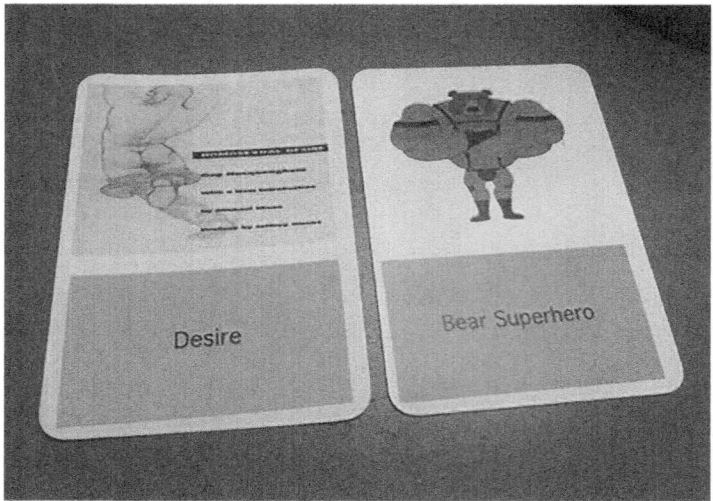

Figure 24.6 UQ Inspiration cards ©2019

The Tension cards accomplish two main goals. first, it encourages participants to develop utopias, dystopias and the worlds in between. This forces them to consider a variety of possible outcomes, some of which inspire hope and others of which acknowledge the hardships of our ancestors and ourselves. The second goal is to foster creative thoughts about unusual worlds.

Phase 3: exchanging objects from the future as currency in the game

The final phase of *Queer Futures* involves summits between the elders of neighbouring tribes. Players present their futures to other groups, who in turn use elements from phase 1 to develop objects from those futures. These are shared back with the tribe that originated the world where the objects belong and who can decide whether or not to incorporate those objects into their world. If a neighbouring tribe accepts the other tribe's imagined objects from the future, the contributing tribe increases its influence and sway in the game. Again, this phase serves two purposes. first, it encourages players with different sexual and personal identities to collaborate and consider one another's perspectives. Second, it adds depth to the worlds created in phase 2 and creates new opportunities for creative expressions, such as drawing or sculpting new artefacts or role-playing scenes centred on them.

25
Smart cities
Policy without polity

Paul Graham Raven

Introduction

A good essay should begin by providing a concise definition of its topic of focus. In the case of the 'smart city', however, this is an insuperable challenge – not because of an absence of definitions, but rather their sheer profligacy. In any case, I am not interested in defining the 'smart city' so much as in investigating its persistent resistance to definition and exploring alternatives to its problematic framing of technologically mediated urban futurity. I will argue (1) that the 'smart city' can be treated as a generic utopian narrative, a form of science fiction; (2) that the 'smart city' further represents a stalling of the urban future imaginary in a discredited and predatory modality of technological utopia; and (3) that we may turn to the critical utopian mode of science fiction as a guide for developing new narratives of urban futurity which move beyond the empty signifier of the 'smart city' and its corporate storytellers. Note that the term 'smart city' will remain in quotation throughout, as befits a term which I will show to be an entirely fictional construct.

Part 1: Urban fantasy: The 'smart city' as a science fiction subgenre

Narrating perfection: The story of 'smart'

To claim that the 'smart city' is a story is not to underestimate the concept – on the contrary, its durability as a narrative template or vehicle is remarkable, retaining a momentum in policy and commercial arenas which activists would likely love to replicate. This durability is due in part to its vagueness, which leaves plenty of space for ambiguity, and allows each storyteller who takes it up to twist it into the shape which best accommodates their preferred policies. Indeed, the precision with which the 'smart city' might be rigorously defined has decreased in proportion to the quantity of publications which deploy it as a keyword or within a title, and those definitions which are offered are often contradictory (Cavada et al., 2014; Grossi and Pianezzi, 2017)

Furthermore, any given technology/policy combination only acquires its 'smart city' associations through being included in the 'smart city' narrative, which acts 'as both a container for innovation and a yardstick for evaluating innovation' (Sadowski and Bendor, 2019, p. 541) whose political function is that of 'an anticipatory vision [...] a set of orienting assumptions and operationalizable propositions about urban planning and development' (p. 542). As such, the 'smart city' is rooted in 'computational thinking', a 'belief that any given problem can be solved by the application of computation [... which] internalizes solutionism to the degree that it is impossible to think or articulate the world in terms that are not computable' (Bridle, 2018, p. 4). But how did this story emerge?

The formation of the 'smart city' as a generic form can be traced to the *ur-text* of IBM's 'smarter cities' marketing campaign, beginning around 2008, through which IBM problematized the urban as an engineering challenge (a data-engineering challenge in particular) and positioned themselves as an 'obligatory passage point' in the process of finding a 'solution' to the problem(s) so identified (Söderström et al., 2014). As such, IBM itself is the author of the narrative, as well as being one of the principle actors or characters, the other of which is 'the municipality' – the governing body of a city, rather than the city itself. The generic 'smart city' plot is based on 'an Enlightenment rhetoric' whereby systems-theoretical approaches and the analysis of vast data sets enable the municipality to transcend the emotionally inflected subjectivities of the actual city as an organic and qualitative entity, to arrive instead at a rational and objective knowledge (Söderström et al., 2014, p. 312). Actual cities – their haecceities, if you like – serve only as set-dressing for re-stagings of the generic plot, in which IBM (or their equivalent) and a municipality take up the arsenal of quantification in order to do battle with 'disorder' and 'inefficiency' and end their threat to 'growth'. Meanwhile, citizens are reduced to data points in an agent-based model based on behaviourist principles: Economically rational robots and/or sources of the sort of disruption that doesn't deliver shareholder value.

The generic nature of the 'smart city' is not (merely) an issue of literary aesthetics, however. Genres form around tacit assumptions, and those of the 'smart city' rely upon an implicit homogenization of the urban with a strong bias towards conditions in the global North. But the resulting template is often no more suitable to a global-Northern city than to any other: 'Cities are no longer made of different – and to a large extent incommensurable – sociotechnical worlds', but are instead constituted 'as data within systemic processes'; the discourse of smartness thus 'tends to reduce the analysis of the city to a machinic vision' (Söderström et al., 2014, p. 314).

Since IBM's establishing of the subgenre, it has been reproduced by a number of other technology firms (e.g. Cisco and, more recently, Google, operating in Toronto under the *nom de guerre* of Sidewalk Labs). Its success in attracting flows of investment is indicated by the hordes of futurists, consultants and other such camp followers, reiterating the narrative like door-to-door salesmen who are paid on commission (which is, of course, exactly what they are). In these cases, IBM's role in the story is replaced by whoever stands to make a profit from peddling the possibility of 'solutions', and the plot is loose enough that the most prevalent or 'sexy' local issues might be folded in as required for the available audience. Whether it's flooding, gang violence or traffic jams, when The Corporation and The Municipality join forces, there's no problem that can't be quantified and optimized away!

The 'smart city' is a narrative of inevitability, positioned as a response to a crisis concocted as an explanation for the seeming intractability of the messy and chaotic urban assemblage to rational, quantified planning: 'For those in the business of providing solutions, solvable problems are essential. The crises are tailored to justify the solutions, and the latter come in different forms and guises' (Sadowski and Bendor, 2019, pp. 552–553). It has also been shown that the 'smart city' is exemplary of the neoliberal paradigm (Grossi and Pianezzi, 2017); the 'there is no alternative' subtext to the story pegs it as endemic to what Mark Fisher presciently identified as *capitalist realism* (Fisher, 2009). It is also a manifestation of Keller Easterling's concept of 'the zone', a form of 'software for making urban space' which 'typically provides premium utilities and a set of incentives—tax exemptions, foreign ownership of property, streamlined customs, cheap labour and deregulation of labour or environmental laws—to entice business' (Easterling, 2014, p. 15).

This, then, is the sense in which the 'smart city' is a story: As a call-to-action for mobilizing state, corporate and academic actors towards a constructively ambiguous notion of civic justice to be delivered through quantification and data analysis – a battleflag for rallying technological, financial and policy elites. But one category of character is conspicuously absent from this story-type, at least in terms of agency: The citizen of the 'smart city' is a cypher, a digit, mere data. Thus my contention that the 'smart city' is *policy without polity*.

Rewiring the future city: Science fiction and the urban sociotechnical imaginary

Sadowski and Bendor (2019) identify the 'smart city' as a *sociotechnical imaginary*. According to Jasanoff and Kim (2009), sociotechnical imaginaries are collective representations of how novel technologies might (or indeed might not) be woven into future sociotechnical practices and systems; however, they also inform us as to how lives which incorporate those technologies and systems 'ought, or ought not, to be lived' (Jasanoff, 2015, p. 4). As such, sociotechnical imaginaries are perhaps closer to science fiction than most other *narratives of futurity* (see Raven and Elahi, 2015). Furthermore, it has been suggested that the relationship between science fiction and technological innovation is duplex, with ideas, concepts and even designs and form factors moving easily from one 'side' to the other (Bassett et al., 2013).

This easy flow of memes and tropes between the imagined futures of the sociotechnical imaginary and of science fiction suggests that all such imagined futures operate on a similar set of narratological principles. It follows, then, that we might productively apply analytical and (de)constructive tools developed to deal with one type of imagined future (namely science fiction literature) to other types with which it shares such commonalities (Raven, 2017b). In that spirit, I will demonstrate that we can not only position the 'smart city' story-type in the lineage of utopian modes in science fiction, but further that we might use that same lineage of utopian modes to guide the critique and (re)development of new narratives of urban futurity which move beyond the empty capitalist–realist signifiers of the 'smart city'.

Part 2: Three types of non-place: The evolution of urban utopian fictions

From political to critical: A swift history of the utopian genre

Drawing on the work of Tom Moylan (to which we will return), Edward James (2003) sets out a schema for the science fiction utopia which has three distinct modes: The *classic*, the *technological* and the *critical* utopia. Thomas More's *Utopia* established what James (p. 219) labels as the classic utopia, and which I will instead refer to as the political utopia: Its dominant thematic is the presentation of an idealized society, whose perfection has been achieved through legislative and constitutional changes, and/or what we would now think of as 'policy interventions'. This is not to say that the political utopia is necessarily devoid of technological innovations, but to emphasize that the project of improvement is seen as being first and foremost a constitutional one.[1]

The technological utopia, by contrast, is defined not only by the dominance of technological solutions to social problems, but also by the ideological assumption that the advent of technologies with the potential to reconfigure societal arrangements renders political means of reconfiguration irrelevant, if not inherently suspect and retrograde. While it has some clear antecedents, James ties the hegemony of the technological utopian mode to John W. Campbell's stint as editor of the pulp science fiction magazine *Astounding* from 1937 through to the early 1960s, during which he installed a supposedly pragmatic and rationalist scientism at the ideological and aesthetic heart of the genre. Note per James (2003, p. 222) that the mode of science fiction which Campbell championed was intended to depict a *better* world, as distinct from the *ideal* world of the political utopia: Indeed, the very possibility of the ideal was seen as suspect, and political action was positioned as an obstacle to radical change, rather than a crucial component thereof. The notion of iterative and quantifiable improvement, on the other hand, was seen as achievable, necessary and inevitable: The polity is reimagined as an engineering problem, and solutions proposed accordingly.

The critical utopian mode emerged in the late 1970s. Writers identified with the New Wave movement were working within (and responding to) the failed utopias of the 1960s, and as such were wary of quick-fix utopian projects – but they also recognized the possibility and desirability of a better world, even as they distrusted those who promised that it might be delivered easily through technological means. As such, they wrote in new ways in order 'to criticize not only the society in which they wrote, but also the possible utopian alternatives' (James, 2003, p. 225). These literary strategies were later identified by Moylan (1980) as *critical* utopias: Critical of the supposedly apolitical solutionism of the technological utopias which preceded them, but inheriting from the same source a suspicion of the very possibility of the ideal or perfected society. To put it another way, as shall be shown below: *The critical utopia is concerned with the depiction of a utopian project in the process of undergoing its inevitable failure, even as it sustains the critique of the status quo implied by all utopian modes.*

Arrested development: The stalled evolution of the science fiction city

To reiterate: The 'smart city' is a utopian form 'depicting a model of a perfectly functioning urban society' which 'in contrast with classical utopianism [...] is governed by code rather than spatial form' (Söderström et al., 2014, p. 315). It is thus a technological utopia and is characterized by a *restlessness* in contrast to the political modality: 'Optimization needs to be constantly renewed: Novel technologies need to be constantly introduced for that purpose and codes constantly rewritten. If IBM's storytelling rests on a utopian rhetoric it constantly makes sure that the future it promotes is a realistic one' (Söderström et al., 2014, p. 316) – a capitalist-realistic one, we might go so far as to say.

The ideological similarities between the 'smart city' generic form and the technological utopia run deeper still. It relies on 'the systems metaphor' as a technological update to and continuation of the organicist approach of the utopian town planning tradition: Where the latter deployed the body as its governing metaphor for the city, the former makes use of the computer (Söderström et al., 2014, pp. 312–313). This lends the 'smart city' genre 'a sense of travelling back to the heroic times of post-war cybernetics' (p. 313) – a period during which the technological utopian modality of science fiction was at its perigee of power and influence. (It is perhaps not surprising that, in seeking to resurrect its flagging fortunes in the early twenty-first century, IBM might return to ideas which prevailed during its own 'golden age'.)

It also bears noting that when it comes to the city as a theme or subject (as opposed to merely a backdrop), science fiction has only recently transcended a knee-jerk phobia of the urban that reflected a broader cultural revulsion prevalent throughout the Anglophone culture of the 1970s and 1980s. As Abbott (2016) has shown, the arc of science fiction's in-house urbanisms has bent slowly in a more progressive direction, but while it may have transcended visions of future cities as either perfectible 'machines for living' and/or seething fleshpots of tech-augmented vice, violence and decline, it has yet to advance much beyond a conception of the city as a largely undifferentiated technological substrate for economic and social exchange.

Thus, I contend that the critical utopian mode represents the necessary next step in the evolution of narratives of urban futurity: That we can raid the critical utopias of science fiction for the tools, tropes and approaches which will enable us to critique and transcend the techno-utopian policy-without-polity of the 'smart city', and thus build imaginaries of urban futurity in which technology exists to support a diverse and dynamic pool of human agency and opportunity, rather than to corral and control it.

Part 3: Plasti-city: Towards critical urban utopia-as-method

Opposition imagination: The craft of the critical utopia

Moylan (1980) argues that the critical utopias of the 1970s illustrated 'a possible shift in the imaginative direction of United States culture [...] from simple negation to a negation with alternatives [...] the critical utopia is both an artifact of contemporary capitalism and an artistic action against it' (pp. 236–238). It is exactly the 'negation with alternatives' that Moylan describes which is required in the case of late-neoliberal narratives such as the 'smart city'.

Moylan's objects of analysis in this paper are seminal novels by the late Ursula K Le Guin (*The Dispossessed*) and Samuel Delany (*Triton*). Per Moylan, *The Dispossessed* revitalized the utopia form by balancing it against a more traditionally science-fictional extrapolation narrative in which 'aspects of present-day society are extrapolated, and the resulting social vision provides a critical perspective on the present historical situation' (1980, p. 242).

By contrast, through drawing (albeit somewhat loosely) on Foucault's notion of the heterotopia, Delany created in *Triton* a 'utopia of the streets' in which 'the gap between utopian and non-utopian is less evident, the borders less defined' than in *The Dispossessed* (Moylan, 1980, p. 243). As parsed by Moylan, *Triton*'s broader conceptual approach seems almost proleptic regarding the needs of new narratives for our networked age:

> Utopia affords consolation, but the heterotopia is disturbing and challenging [...] *Triton* does not express utopia directly as in the traditional works or negatively as in the dystopia; rather *it expresses the utopia in the interconnections within the social system from which it is developed and with which it is still in conflict.*
>
> (p. 244; emphasis mine)

Or, more succinctly: *Triton*'s criticality is a function of the tension between the status quo and the heterotopian alternative, but also of its explicit acknowledgement that even 'utopia' isn't perfect, but rather flawed, contested, incomplete. This stands in stark contrast to the bland homogeneity of the 'smart city', which promises the idealized perfection of the political utopia to be delivered through the computational means of the technological utopia: A failed synthesis, the worst of both worlds.

Utopia is not merely a literary genre, however – as Levitas (2013) has argued, it can be a progressive political and sociological strategy:

> The core of utopia is the desire for being otherwise, individually and collectively, subjectively and objectively. Its expressions explore and bring to debate the potential contents and contexts of human flourishing. It is thus better understood as a method than a goal...
>
> *(p. xi)*

Levitas's operationalization of utopianism 'requires a holistic approach fundamental to the distinctive character of sociology' (p. xv) and

> allows ... an element of ethical and institutional separation from the present [... the] utopian method involves both making explicit the kinds of society implied in existing political programmes and constructing alternatives. It entails also considering the kinds of people we want to become and that different forms of society will promote or inhibit.
>
> *(p. xviii)*

Critical utopian narratives, then, provide us the tools with which to perform a sort of *speculative* urban sociology – not just for entertainment, nor for persuasion *per se* (which Dobraszczyk, 2019, identifies as being a major role of utopian architectural visioning processes; p. 10), but for generating potentially normative imaginaries.

The critical utopian paradigm can be seen as a precursor to Haraway's more recent philosophical and methodological injunction for us to 'stay with the trouble' (Haraway, 2017). Acknowledging the influence (pp. 117–125) of Le Guin's 'Carrier Bag Theory of Fiction' (1996), Haraway insists that we reject solutionist technofutures and disaster-dystopias alike in favour of futurities (urban or otherwise) in which issues remain in contention, and where the sympoietic work of making connections and constructing networks ('making kin', as Haraway would have it) is an ongoing and unending process of composting – a warm, moist and messily organic business (Haraway, 2017, pp. 4–5) that stands in sharp distinction from the cold and bloodless managerial protocols that inform the 'smart city'.

Utopia as method: Stories against teleology, not technology

To argue against the technological utopia of the 'smart city' is not to argue against the integration of technology into the urban fabric. For one thing, that horse has long since bolted: 'The urban' might perhaps be better thought of as the situated mutual integration of human collectives with their increasingly complex infrastructures of transportation and transformation (Raven, 2017a), in a *fait accompli* that's arguably as old as the grain-based state itself (Scott, 2017). Indeed, a vital objection to the 'smart city' is that it promises nothing that the urban has not always promised to provide. After all, we can identify claims of 'smartness' in 'the urban genome [...] all the way back to ancient Rome, Uruk and Çatalhöyük', claims Shannon Mattern (2017, p. xi). She continues:

> That intelligence is simultaneously epistemological, technological and physical: It's codified into our cities' laws and civic knowledges and institutions, hard wired into their cables and protocols, framed in their architectures and patterns of development.
>
> *(p. xii)*

Mattern's discipline of media archaeology can provide the raw materials from which our critical utopian urbanisms might be built: As Moylan indicated, critical utopian narratives are necessarily extrapolative, building on the *status quo* of the present, which is in turn built upon the sedimentary layers of countless *statuses quo ante*, on those earliest urbanisms with which Mattern is fascinated.

Mattern (2017) has another important point to make, which speaks not only to the 'smart city' but to other such empty signifiers of technological transition: A city (or region, or nation, or organization) does not suddenly change from one thing to another; change is perpetual, incremental, ongoing, incomplete and – to reclaim a much-misused line, originally stolen from William Gibson – unevenly distributed (p. xxiii). Perhaps the greatest flaw of the 'smart city' and its cousins is this assumption that they represent some teleological halting state at which perfection will have been attained in fulfilment – or perhaps I should say 'delivery'? – of the blueprint's promise.

What the 'smart city' refuses to concede is that utopia is not a destination or a product, but rather a process, an orientation, a direction of travel to be debated afresh each morning. Hence, this essay's refusal to provide a ready-made alternative to the 'smart city' – because the seductive notion of the ready-made 'solution' is exactly the problem.

Conclusion: The hacienda must be (perpetually re-)built

In terms of urban futures, my concluding argument is that the 'smart city' is in fact a paleofuture: A future first imagined in the past (and, crucially, never subsequently realized) which persists through various modes of cultural and commercial reproduction, thus providing a recognizable (and comfortingly aspirational) template or shorthand for 'change for the better'. Despite its trendy veneer of digital renderings, the 'smart city' rehashes a generic narrative of tech-enhanced urban futurity whose essence has changed little (if at all) since its earliest iterations, such as the famed Futurama exhibit at the 1939 World's Fair – and which not only represents a nostalgic return on the part of its progenitor IBM to the theories which prevailed during its post-war heyday (see 'Narrating perfection' above), but furthermore reiterates aspirations of urban intelligence that can be traced back as far as urban civilization itself (see 'Utopia as method' above).

The persistent prevalence of the 'smart city' memeplex might be ascribed to a number of factors, not least the connection of the technological utopian modality (of which it is a paradigmatic non-literary exemplar) to capitalist technoscience during its period of greatest hegemony, but also to the second wind of positivist cybernetics ushered in by the triumph of the 'Californian ideology' (Barbrook and Cameron, 1996) over the imaginaries of the global North. (The parrotings of click-bait media coverage and consultancy boosterism are surely also complicit, but that's another story.) The 'smart city' is therefore certainly not 'the new utopia'; on the contrary, it's the *same old* utopia, a discredited dream of infallible surveillance and control, wrapped up in fresh new fonts and the 'dark patterns' (Gray et al., 2018) of manipulative user-experience design.

In the current context of capitalism's interlocked metacrises – with climate change, the dogma of perpetual growth and the neoliberal evisceration of the social sphere all combining in such a way as to foreclose on the ability to imagine alternatives – the need for fresh imaginaries has never been greater. These new urban futures must of course be social – but this is not necessarily to reject the potential benefits of cybernetic systems in the urban context. It is not the constituent content of the 'smart city' vision which we must reject, but rather its status as *policy without polity*: The managerial-behaviourist and 'machinic vision' of its generic form, which – as has been shown – is a city of (and for) cyphers, a rigid and over-quantified simulacrum, a hyperreal dystopia for all but those sat safely within its 'nerve centres' and control rooms.

Critique aside, we might be set on the path to the construction of more contested and critical urban utopias by the suggestions of Francesca Bria, chief technical and digital innovation officer of the citizen-municipalist mayoral administration of Barcelona. She suggests that municipalities must, on the one hand, acknowledge that data-centric technologies can help devolve the addressing (as well as the identification) of urban challenges to citizens, and, on the other hand, acknowledge that the platforms and infrastructures in question 'cannot be run using business models based on the manipulation of collective behaviours'; rather, '[t]hey must be in public hands and controlled by citizens themselves' (Bria, 2020). This fairly moderate vision dares to mix the collectivity of grassroots urban democratic processes with the latest technological tools. It's a good place to start from – though the ultimate direction of travel must be decided by not even the most well-meaning bureaucrats or technologists. The imagining, critique and perpetual (re)construction of new urban futurities can only be the work of those who are always already their citizens.

As such, the utility of fictions – of science fictions, certainly, but also of narratives of futurity (Raven and Elahi, 2015) more generally – as a tool for social futures, urban or otherwise, lies in their accessibility. While the production of stories has become something of a specialist role in contemporary society, I would argue that we may nonetheless see narrative as a form of literacy which precedes literacy: To put it crudely, even a person who cannot read or write can appreciate a story, and tell their own. Furthermore, to borrow a phrase with considerable currency in the arts, *people are experts in their own lives*: No researcher or consultant can ever match the situated understanding of place held by those who live in and identify with a particular location, nor fully appreciate the panoply of practices and lifeways that exist to either side of the central bulge of the statistical bell-curve. Thus, stories – plural and co-produced, conflicting and contradictory – offer a way of (re)mapping urban futures, and indeed all futures, in which citizens can participate… and perhaps even take control.

Note

1 While James (2003) pegs Thomas More's *Utopia* as exemplary of the 'classic' mode, and Moylan files it as the pioneering work of 'rationalist bourgeois utopia' (1980, p. 237), it bears noting that while Book II of More's text contains a 'totalizing, self-contained, systematic vision' of an alternative society (López-Galviz et al., 2020, p. 5), Book I – actually written some time subsequently – delivered a description of Tudor England which provided a social critique and context for that vision. This is to say that while James's typology, which is foundational to the argument of this chapter, places More's utopia outside of its 'critical' category, this is not to say that there is not some element of critique inherent to it or other utopias in the same lineage. James builds specifically upon Moylan's definition of the critical utopia, which – as shall be shown – centres on an (auto)critique of not only the *status quo* context in which the utopia has been written, but also of the utopian impulse and genre itself. This autocritical aspect of the critical utopian mode is, I argue, particularly important as opposition, critique and corrective to the technological utopian mode, of which the 'smart city' is only one example among many.

Bibliography

Abbott, C. (2016). *Imagining urban futures: Cities in science fiction and what we might learn from them*. Middletown, CT: Wesleyan University Press.

Barbrook, R. and Cameron, A. (1996). 'The Californian ideology', *Science as Culture*, 6(1), pp. 44–72.

Bassett, C., Steinmueller, E. and Voss, G. (2013). 'Better made up: The mutual influence of science fiction and innovation'. *NESTA working paper No. 13/07*. Retrieved on May 15, 2019, from http://www.nesta.org.uk/publications/better-made-mutual-influence-science-fiction-and-innovation

Bria, F. (2019). 'You're thinking about smart cities in completely the wrong way'. *Wired*.co.uk. Retrieved April 20, 2020, from https://www.wired.co.uk/article/reboot-britain-francesca-bria

Bridle, J. (2018). *New dark age: Technology and the end of the future*. London: Verso Books.

Cavada, M., Hunt, D.V. and Rogers, C.D. (2014). 'Smart cities: Contradicting definitions and unclear measures'. In *Proceedings of the 4th World Sustainability Forum*, Vienna, Austria (pp. 1–12).

Dobraszczyk, P. (2019). *Future cities: Architecture and the imagination*. London: Reaktion Books.

Easterling, K. (2014). *Extrastatecraft: The power of infrastructure space*. London: Verso Books.

Fisher, M. (2009). *Capitalist realism: Is there no alternative?*. Alresford: Zero Books

Gray, C.M., Kou, Y., Battles, B., Hoggatt, J. and Toombs, A.L. (2018). 'The dark (patterns) side of UX design'. In *Proceedings of the 2018 CHI Conference on Human Factors in Computing Systems* (pp. 1–14).

Grossi, G., and Pianezzi, D. (2017). 'Smart cities: Utopia or neoliberal ideology?', *Cities*, 69, pp. 79–85.

Haraway, D.J. (2016). *Staying with the trouble: Making kin in the Chthulucene*. Durham, NC: Duke University Press.

James, E. (2003). 'Utopias and anti-utopias'. In Edward James and Farah Mendlesohn (eds.), *The Cambridge companion to science fiction* (pp. 219–229). Cambridge: Cambridge University Press.

Jasanoff, S. (2015). 'Future imperfect: Science, technology, and the imaginations of modernity'. In Shiela Jasanoff and Sang-Hyun Kim (eds.), *Dreamscapes of modernity: Sociotechnical imaginaries and the fabrication of power* (pp. 1–33). Chicago, IL: University of Chicago Press.

Jasanoff, S. and Kim, S.H. (2009). 'Containing the atom: Sociotechnical imaginaries and nuclear power in the United States and South Korea', *Minerva*, 47(2), p. 119

Le Guin, U.K. (1996). 'The carrier bag theory of fiction'. In Glotfelty, C. and Fromm, H. (eds.), *The Ecocriticism reader: Landmarks in literary ecology* (pp. 149–154). Athens: University of Georgia Press.

Levitas, R. (2013). *Utopia as method: The imaginary reconstitution of society*. New York: Springer.

López-Galviz, C., Büscher, M. and Freudendal-Pedersen, M. (2020). 'Mobilities and utopias: A critical reorientation', *Mobilities*, 15(1), pp. 1–10.

Mattern, S. (2017). *Code and clay, data and dirt: Five thousand years of urban media*. Minneapolis: University of Minnesota Press.

Moylan, T. (1980). 'Beyond negation: The critical utopias of Ursula K. Le Guin and Samuel R. Delany', *Extrapolation*, 21(3), pp. 236–253.

Raven, P.G. (2017a). '(Re) narrating the societal cyborg: A definition of infrastructure, an interrogation of integration', *People, Place and Policy Online*, 11(1), pp. 51–64.

Raven, P.G. (2017b). 'Telling tomorrows: Science fiction as an energy futures research tool', *Energy Research and Social Science*, 31, pp. 164–169.

Raven, P.G. and Elahi, S. (2015). 'The new narrative: Applying narratology to the shaping of futures outputs', *Futures*, 74, pp. 49–61.

Sadowski, J. and Bendor, R. (2019). 'Selling smartness: Corporate narratives and the smart city as a sociotechnical imaginary', *Science, Technology, and Human Values*, 44(3), pp. 540–563.

Scott, J.C. (2017). *Against the grain: A deep history of the earliest states*. New Haven, CT: Yale University Press.

Söderström, O., Paasche, T. and Klauser, F. (2014). 'Smart cities as corporate storytelling', *City*, 18(3), pp. 307–320.

26
Urbanism
Creating urban futures

Cecilia Dinardi

Introduction

In 1951 the journal *The Town Planning Review* published an article entitled 'Creative Urbanism' where Christopher Tunnard, Director of City Planning at Yale University, described the lack of art in the urban environment as one of the more serious social problems of the time. The crucial question was, in his view, how to build 'to satisfy the eye' at the same time as satisfying existing social demands. Creative urbanism was presented as a city planning approach, a creative form of urban design and a solution to the problem of urban ugliness, which had resulted from rapid industrial development and post-war destruction. As such, the figure of an imaginative creative designer was invoked, who would be equally adept in the fields of architecture, the arts and visual planning. 'If we include the art approach as part of our daily thinking then our practical solutions may change in character and become a better fusion of form and function, of the practical and aesthetic' (Tunnard, 1951, p. 229).

Echoing the American 'city beautiful' movement of the late nineteenth century with its emphasis on design, aesthetics and landscape architecture, the challenge ahead was how to incorporate imagination into planning and, fundamentally, how to take the past into account when planning the cities of the future as works of art. Past and future are deeply intertwined with the present (Urry, 2016, p. 71). In this sense, visions of the past have shaped different understandings of urban planning in the present. London, Vienna and Paris have all been seen as monuments, places of dwelling, playgrounds or artistic creations for visual delight (Olsen, 1986) and have informed different creative urban practices, as demonstrated by López Galviz's (2019) cultural and urban history of the past futures of nineteenth-century cities.

In recent years, the term creative urbanism has acquired a different meaning beyond the notion of urban beauty. Since the 2000s, it has commonly been associated with the spatialization of the new post-Fordist economy, involving processes of urban transformation that adopt cultural activities and creative strategies or involve the work of artists to satisfy more than just a visual need. The emergence of the (new) creative economy, comprising a range of cultural and creative industries that are differently defined across contexts, has given rise to both new urban and social formations as well as city branding labels such as the creative city (Landry and Bianchini, 1995; Landry, 2000), the creative class (Florida, 2002), creative place-making (Markusen and Gadwa, 2010), creative clusters (Montgomery, 2003; Evans, 2004), creative hubs (Evans and Hutton, 2009; Gill, Pratt and Virani, 2019) and creative enterprise zones (i.e. in the work of the Greater London Authority), to name just a few.

In its original conception, the creative city is a toolkit for urban innovators, a new approach to urban planning and a new way of thinking about cities that challenges habitual practices, organizational structures and power configurations and overcomes deeply entrenched obstacles (Landry, 2000, p. xlix). The term, now used by developers, policymakers and scholars, implies at a basic level the existence of non-creative urban planning or city-making, referring to cities that exist solely for trade and commerce. Creative urbanism ultimately refers to how culture and the arts relate to, make and transform the city in creative ways. From a temporal dimension, it can be both ephemeral, as in the case of pop-up festivals and events, and enduring, through more permanent capital projects for culture or the physical demarcation of specific areas as 'creative zones'.

This chapter offers a conceptualization of the term creative urbanism and the contested social futures that lie ahead. The first section traces the origin of the unfolding of creative urbanism in relation to the rise of the so-called symbolic economy of cities. The second section discusses scholarship that has sought to move the 'creative city' debate forward by formulating critiques of Richard Florida's controversial proposition of the 'creative class'. The final section concludes by considering the social futures of creative urbanism in the light of its contemporary neoliberal uses and potential for alternative applications.

The foundations of creative urbanism

Although cities have always been spaces of creation and vernacular creativity, the development of creative urbanism, as we know it today, can be linked to the rise of the creative economy in post-Fordist, knowledge-based societies, which are marked by flexible specialization, high-technology industry and specialized locational clusters (Scott, 2006). The creative economy is comprised of the economic activities of the creative industries – defined differently depending on the context, but originally conceived in the United Kingdom as those industries based on individual creativity, skill and talent, with the potential to generate wealth and jobs through the exploitation of intellectual property (DCMS, 1998). This definition, which has economic value and individual entrepreneurship at its centre, initially identified the 13 (now seven) sectors that would become the objects of creative economy policy. These range from advertising, architecture, crafts, arts and antiques, to design, designer fashion, film and video, TV and radio, as well as interactive leisure software, software and computer services, music, performing arts and publishing. However, new versions – with reduced or expanded sector scope and formations – have been developed over time and across space. Despite the plurality of definitions, existing confusion and multiple approaches to measuring the economic value of culture and creativity, the 'creative economy' is still the prevailing term used in the academic, policy and industry literature.

The invention of the creative economy as a global orthodoxy with the production and dissemination of certain political discourses (Schlesinger, 2016) has had resonance all over the world, promoting a competitive, and at times collaborative, landscape of urban creativity. This global trend is epitomised by UNESCO's launch of the Creative Cities Network in 2004; UNCTAD's publication of the Creative Economy reports in 2008, 2010, 2013 and 2018; and EU's support programmes for creative cities and networks of creative business, incubation and digital innovation. Beyond Europe, in Asia, Africa and the Americas, we can also find a rapidly emerging institutional infrastructure of urban creativity that sees the United Kingdom as the 'pioneering model' and finds in the UN conferences, publications and recommendations a framework to develop new cultural infrastructures, secure international funding and host international cultural events. The publication of the Orange Economy manual by the Inter-American Development Bank in 2013 was meant to act as a 'wake-up call' for policymakers in Latin America and the Caribbean about the enormous 'development opportunities' that the creative economy holds for the region, particularly in social and economic terms. This transnational mobility of Western creative economy discourses, technologies, finance and images (Kong, 2014), in places as dissimilar as Chinese, Japanese, Indonesian and Australian cities, shows the complexity, heterogeneity and widespread presence of creative urbanism. In Africa, the launch of the Arterial Network of African Creative Cities and the publication of research, for instance, on the South African and Senegalese experiences of cultural policy and the creative industries (i.e. Oyekunle, 2017; Mbaye and Dinardi, 2019) presented renewed interest in the use of creativity for urban development and city branding. This research highlighted the key role that local civil society actors play, especially with their (sometimes hidden) informal urban interventions, in a context where, while the importance of creativity is acknowledged by policymakers, insufficient public support is offered. It is interesting to note how these global perspectives of urban creativity reinforce the constitution of creative urbanism as a global urban policy field, interweaving top–down discourses and practices with bottom–up grassroots initiatives.

To put it another way, creative urbanism can be defined as the urbanism of creative cities (Borja, 2009), and creative cities, as we have seen, constitute an example of the new urban forms and styles of urbanizations that have been unleashed by the structures of the new informational economy (Scott, 2006). But creative urbanism can also exist outside such labels, for the very definition of cities as 'creative' takes us into an arena where the very meaning of creativity is contested. If creative cities are, as some believe, a mere city branding or urban marketing strategy, then creative urbanism would encompass much more than the promotion of a brand. Cities such as Barcelona, Medellin or Glasgow are good examples of so-called creative urbanism. Despite their very different histories and urban regeneration trajectories, these cities have transformed themselves and been rebranded through culture, innovation and the arts, not without social contradictions. In the first, through a new cultural infrastructure related to mega-sport events; the second, through fighting drug-related urban violence with cultural planning and social urbanism; and in the third, through regenerating its port legacy and becoming a European 'Capital of Culture'.

If we consider urbanism as 'a way of life', in the classical sense of the term defined by Louis Wirth in 1938, what would be the distinctive social characteristics of living in cities under creativity? Examples of creative urban life abound. There are citizen-led solutions to meet basic needs in informal settlements where the state had left a void. There are also, for example, innovative modes of transport, food production and clothing alternatives that focus on reducing their environmental impact. This sense of creative urbanism as the development of *creative solutions* to social and urban problems was already contained in the early notion of the 'creative city' as originally conceived by Landry and Bianchini (1995). However, the more prevalent idea of creative urbanism, as promoted by policy discourses, nowadays gets materialized in strategies that develop or promote the city's new economy: The use of public art in urban spaces and iconic cultural infrastructure; the recycling of abandoned, industrial infrastructure; the organization of pop-up festivals and arts events; the launch of incubation programmes for small creative companies; the creation of museum quarters or creative districts; and the use of creative city branding campaigns, among others.

These initiatives – many of which are inspired by the work of international organizations – testify to the existence of a paradigmatic global model of urban creativity. Its contested politics, however, suggest both a present of exclusions and a future of uncertainty. This manifests in the myriad examples of local resistance to regeneration projects which dispute the cultural representations and uses of urban spaces and the creation of expensive, flagship infrastructure by 'starchitects'.

If the creative city is in the past, what is in store for the future of creative urbanism?

In the present, global trends have shown both the allure and dismissal of the creative city promise. The disillusionment with the creative city narrative resulted from two key factors – the strong criticism that Richard Florida's notion of the 'creative class' received (for being reductionist, elitist and individualistic) and the compelling evidence demonstrating how discourses of urban creativity have been used to pave the way for gentrification, real-estate speculation, social displacement and the privatization of public space. Creative strategies, thus, can 'extend and recodify entrenched tendencies in neoliberal urban politics, seductively repackaging them in the soft-focus terms of cultural policy' (Peck, 2005, p. 740). In this way, creative urbanism can hardly escape the broader policies of neoliberal urbanism, marked by institutional restructuring programmes, the deregulation of market forces and the privatization of state-owned services and facilities. The links between creative industry policy frameworks and a neoliberal paradigm that praises an open market ideology and advocates the dismantling of the welfare state show the existing contradictions with the more progressive elements of the creative economy (Newsinger, 2014). That is, creative urbanism can, potentially, either be put at the service of social inclusion or generate social exclusion and perpetuate urban inequalities.

Further critique of the concepts of the creative economy and the creative city pointed to their underlying misrepresentation and commodification of race and ethnicity (Saha, 2017) and the displacement of poorer racialized communities with their neoliberal ideologies (Cantugal and Leslie, 2009). Furthermore, the reductionist views on the urban development processes upon which they, in turn, are based have also been challenged (Chatterton, 2010). The need has been expressed for evidence-based, situated approaches that question the universal place-marketing scripts of urban competition and acknowledge the contradictions of the creative class and the creative city (Peck, 2005; Pratt, 2011). If there is anything that the creative city as a global trend has achieved, apart from generating public interest and investment, it is the need to think creativity in place and embedded in particular local contexts which are intersected by competing and complex place narratives (Waitt and Gilbson, 2009). Critiques have also been made in relation to how market-oriented arts interventions 'entangle women artists in the cultivation of spaces of depoliticized feminism, homonormativity and white privilege' (McLean, 2016, p. 38), showing the links between neoliberal 'creativity' and intersectional exclusions.

Asking ourselves questions such as 'what is possible?', 'what is likely?' and 'what is desirable?' can shed light on the social futures of creative urbanism – its present future, its past future and its future present (Ramos Torre, 2017). In turn, distinguishing between 'the probable, the possible, and the preferable' (Urry, 2016, p. 13, citing Bell, 1971) also demarcates different types of futures. These can be defined, following Ramos Torre's analysis of the sociology of time scholarship, as: The present future, signalling the ideas or images that we have in the present about the future horizon; the past future, referring to those conceptions we had about the future in the past that helped ease uncertainty about the future at the time; and finally, the future present, indicating what will actually happen when the future becomes present (p. 5). We can then argue that the present future of creative urbanism is one that in many policy and industry circles of the global South appears full of promises, seeing the creative economy as part of the city's future, a vision of the desired future. In the global North, the substantial academic literature instead warns and gives evidence of the exclusionary nature of so-called creative cities and argues that the creative economy presents a dystopian present future of anxiety, informality, precarization, unpaid jobs and self-exploitation for those working[1] in the creative sector. There, the past future was defined by the (now unfulfilled) promise of freedom and equal opportunities that the creative economy was believed to offer in its early days. In terms of the future present, it is of course harder to ascertain what will happen as each region poses specific challenges and offers different opportunities.

The notion of 'social futures' (Urry, 2016) brings to the fore the contention over different social interests, views and conflicts permeating (uncertain) visions of the future. Past visions are important, as they affect people's lives in the present, and future visions have powerful implications. Therefore, our understanding of 'futures must be embedded within analyses of multiple social institutions, practices and movements' as a certain future is not inevitable and outcomes are not always determined (Urry, 2016, p. 188). Following Urry we may ask: Who has the power to make the future of creative urbanism? How can such a future be democratized?

The context of public austerity, social discontent and economic crises, instead of dissolving the future of creative urbanism, might create new visions of what it is to come. The extent to which communities are directly involved in the conception, implementation and evaluation of creative urban projects, events and initiatives will probably shape the extent to which there are more inclusive social futures. How can the arts contribute here? As a political force in the city, arts interventions have been used in activism and protest movements disputing the future of cities. Concepts such as social urbanism, participatory planning and tactical urbanism have attempted to put people back at the centre of the making and remaking of cities, and in this sense, creative urbanism has underscored the importance of culture, creativity and the arts for place-making, urban revitalization and social cohesion. Mould (2014) warns, however, of an existing risk showing how tactical urbanism needs new tactics if it is not to continue becoming part of a mainstream strategy of creative urban development that follows neoliberal agendas to serve the market. In a similar vein, urban regeneration and gentrification may become further intertwined, especially when 'state-led gentrification is being promoted today in the name of community regeneration' (Lees and Ley, 2008, p. 2381).

If the future is a perspective in the present about something that will happen, or in Luhmann's words, 'a temporal horizon of the present' that cannot begin or be approached (1976, pp. 139–141), we can foresee a future present of creative urbanism as apocalyptically defined by a fatal diagnosis. This refers to the planetary destruction and mass extinction of species already caused by the existing model of market-oriented economic growth. Future trends, such as climate change with rising temperatures, natural disasters and the extinction of life on the planet, have been largely ignored by creative urban visions. The ways in which urban cultural and creative policy can contribute to (not) damaging the planet have only recently begun to be examined. In the United Kingdom, the work of London-based charity Julie's Bicycle has been paramount in bringing together cultural policy thinking with urban sustainability and environmental justice. In the last decade, there has been rising awareness about the need to move away from oil industry sponsorship for culture and the arts (see, for example, the campaigns by the Art Not Oil Coalition and Culture Unstained, and research by Mahony, 2017 and Evans, 2015). In this regard, the political economy that sustains creative urbanism needs to be carefully scrutinized if we are to shed light on the power dynamics that sustain the creative economy of cities.

Conclusion

We can trace three main pathways that can demarcate the social futures of creative urbanism, particularly its present future and its future present. As Luhmann stated, differentiating between the present future and the future present allows for the existence of an open future as a 'present future which has room for several mutually exclusive future presents' (1976, p. 140). First, arts, cultural and creative interventions will need to be citizen-led (or, if not, at least show considerable involvement from local communities throughout the conception and implementation processes) if they are to avoid resulting in gentrification. Second, they will need to be sustainable, if they are to protect, rather than further deteriorate, the environment they are in, without harming future generations; to put it simply, they should not have a large carbon footprint. 'It is time that cultural policy becomes environmental policy and not just a side-lined player in the global movement for sustainable development' (Maxwell and Miller, 2017, p. 182). Third, they need to be socially inclusive if they are to bring benefits to people, rather than markets, either through arts and skills training, audience development or a wider and just cultural funding distribution.

Although creative urbanism policy agendas imagine a future full of promises, many will probably not be fulfilled in the light of the present circumstances. It is also worth asking whose futures these city visions reflect and which publics they represent (López Galviz, 2019). At stake seem to be the cultural representations of urban spaces; the contentious uses of public space; the distribution of public funds for culture and the arts; the improvement (or worsening) of labour conditions in the creative sector; and the benefits from creative clustering in the form of districts, hubs or quarters. A comprehensive view of creative urbanism must challenge the logic that equates (or reduces) urban creativity to (only) the commercial activity of the cultural and the creative industries, leaving out the informal creative economy.

The development of creative urbanism in austere, intolerant and conservative contexts faces threats to its democratic and public nature. The connections and the interactions between (market-driven) urban transformations, in our case through 'creativity', and ongoing, uneven and contradictory processes of neoliberalization (Peck, Theodore and Brenner, 2009) cannot be ignored. Challenging prevalent neoliberal ideologies that sustain some of the present manifestations of creative urbanism demands collective action and organization – with regard to how gentrification can be resisted, how artists can engage with the local areas they are now based in and how policy can better support grassroots creative projects. As Cremin (2012, p. 69) puts it:

> A sociology of social futures must engage with the dialectical totality, to diagnose the situation and propose alternatives to it. More dystopian than economic collapse is the prospect that capitalism and the apparatuses that sustain it will somehow muddle through this crisis intact with the consequences of even greater hardships, atrocities and catastrophes to come.

If history is open-ended (Hall, 2016), so is the future with its alternative scenarios. Yet can the future of creative urbanism be constructed in an inclusive way in capitalist, entrepreneurial societies marked by a context of crisis and in a world facing environmental emergency? Can it distance itself from the intricacies of neoliberal urbanism? That remains to be seen.

Note

1 The vast scholarship on the issues affecting creative labour at present is not reviewed here due to space limitations.

Bibliography

Borja, J. (2009). 'El urbanismo de las ciudades creativas: entre el azar y la necesidad', *Ciudades Creativas*, 1, pp. 19–24.
Catungal, J.P. and Leslie, D. (2009). 'Contesting the creative city: Race, nation, multiculturalism, *Geoforum*, 40(5), pp. 701–704.
Chatterton, P. (2010). 'Will the real Creative City please stand up?', *City*, 4(3), pp. 390–397.
Cremin, C. (2012). 'Towards a sociology of social futures', *New Zealand Sociology*, 27(1), pp. 60–70.
DCMS (1998). *Creative industries mapping document.* London: Department for Culture, Media and Sport.
Evans, G.L. (2004). 'Cultural industry quarters: From pre-industrial to post-industrial production'. In Bell, D. and Jayne, M. (eds), *City of quarters: Urban villages in the contemporary city*, pp. 71–92. Aldershot: Ashgate.
Evans, M. (2015). *Artwash: Big oil and the arts.* London: Pluto Press.
Evans, G. and Hutton, T.A. (2009). 'Creative cities, creative spaces and urban policy', *Urban Studies*, 46(5–6), pp. 1003–1040.
Florida, R. (2002). *The rise of the creative class.* New York: Basic Books.
Gill, R., Pratt, A.C. and Virani, T.E. (2019). *Creative hubs in question: Place, space and work in the creative economy.* Cham: Palgrave Macmillan.
Hall, J. (2016). 'Social futures of global climate change: A structural phenomenology', *American Journal of Cultural Sociology*, 4(1), pp. 1–45.
Kong, L. (2014). 'Transnational mobilities and the making of creative cities', *Theory, Culture and Society*, 31(7–8), pp. 273–289.
Landry, C. (2000). *The creative city: A toolkit for urban innovators.* London: Earthscan.
Landry, C. and Bianchini, F. (1995). *The creative city.* London: Demos.
Lees, L. and Ley, D. (2008). 'Introduction to special issue on gentrification and public policy', *Urban Studies*, 45(12), pp. 2379–2384.
López Galviz, C. (2019). *Cities, railways, modernities. London, Paris and the nineteenth century.* London: Routledge.
Luhmann, N. (1976). 'The future cannot begin: Temporal structures of modern society', *Social Research*, 43(1), pp. 130–152.
Mahony, E. (2017). 'Opening spaces of resistance in the corporatized cultural institution: Liberate Tate and the Art Not Oil Coalition', *Museum and Society*, 15(2), pp. 126–41.
Markusen, A. and Gadwa, A. (2010). *Creative placemaking.* Washington, DC: National Endowment for the Arts.
Mbaye, J. and Dinardi, C. (2019). 'Ins and outs of the cultural polis: Informality, culture and governance in the global South', *Urban Studies*, 56(3), pp. 578–593.
McLean, H. (2017). 'Hos in the garden: Staging and resisting neoliberal creativity', *Environment and Planning D: Society and Space*, 35(1), pp. 38–56.
Montgomery, J. (2003). *Cultural quarters as mechanisms for urban regeneration: A review.* Adelaide: Planning Institute of Australia National Congress.
Mould, O. (2014). 'Tactical urbanism: The new vernacular of the creative city', *Geography Compass*, 8(8), pp. 529–539.
Newsinger, J. (2015). 'A cultural shock doctrine? Austerity, the neoliberal state and the creative industries discourse', *Media, Culture and Society*, 37(2), pp. 302–313.
Olsen, D. (1986). *The city as a work of art.* New Haven, CT and London: Yale University Press.

Oyekunle, O.A. (2017). 'The contribution of creative industries to sustainable urban development in South Africa', *African Journal of Science, Technology, Innovation and Development*, 9(5), pp. 607–616.

Peck, J. (2005). 'Struggling with the creative class', *International Journal of Urban and Regional Research*, 29(4), pp. 740–770.

Peck, J., Theodore, N. and Brenner, N. (2009). 'Neoliberal urbanism: Models, moments, mutations', *SAIS Review of International Affairs*, 29(1), pp. 49–66.

Pratt, A. (2011). 'The cultural contradictions of the creative city', *City, Culture and Society*, 2(3), pp. 123–130.

Ramos Torre, R. (2017). 'Futuros sociales en tiempos de crisis', *Arbor: Ciencia, Pensamiento y Cultura*, 193(784), pp. 1–14.

Saha, A. (2017). *Race and the cultural industries*. Cambridge: Polity Press.

Schlesinger, P. (2016). 'The creative economy: Invention of a global orthodoxy', *Enjeux de l'Information et de la Communication*, 17(2), pp. 187–205.

Scott, A. (2006). 'Creative cities: Conceptual issues and policy questions', *Journal of Urban Affairs*, 28(1), pp. 1–17.

Tunnard, C. (1951). 'Creative Urbanism', *The Town Planning Review*, 22(3), pp. 216–236.

Urry, J. (2016). *What is the future?*, Cambridge: Polity.

Waitt, G. and Gibson, C. (2009). 'Creative small cities: Rethinking the creative economy in place', *Urban Studies*, 46(5–6), pp. 1223–1246.

27
Utopia
Futurity, realism and the social

Lisa Garforth

Introduction

The concept of utopia is an old one and a capacious one. It was named when Thomas More launched the literary genre in 1516. But utopia as a mode of thinking predates and far exceeds More's book and his island. Utopia – the good place that does not exist – cannot be limited to descriptions of a perfect imaginary place or detailed blueprints for a better society. In contemporary approaches, the term indicates a range of ways of imagining and desiring better worlds and suggests they are at work across culture and society. Their distinctive feature is a tension between the social arrangements we have and those we want. Utopia speaks to desires, impulses and expressions, individual and collective, that reach beyond what is towards a better alternative. Utopia is at work not despite but because of the conditions that make different social forms and collective ways of living seem impossible. Utopias are products of specific historical, social and political circumstances, consequences of what is absent, lost or wrong in the present. Pressing contemporary concerns – rising economic precarity and social inequality, environmental injustice, the entrenchment of neoliberal capitalism, climate crisis – generate imaginary resolutions that keep open spaces for exploring the good and for potential transformation.

Utopias really matter when we think about social future-making. They matter not as attempted solutions to real problems, but because they capture something about the ordinary ways in which hopes and desires for alternatives are always in play in society. Utopia reminds us that when social scientists turn towards the future we need not restrict our attention to what is predictable, possible or probable. We can and should explore also what is desirable. In both social life and critical thinking, wanting and hoping are as important as extrapolating, anticipating and projecting. Utopia foregrounds the ways in which the future is about fantasy, fiction and imagination as well as calculation, pragmatism and rationality. But utopia has not always been welcome in the social sciences. Political philosophy was dominated by anti-utopian critiques for much of the post-war period (Sargisson, 2007; Ingram, 2017). Ruth Levitas (2013) has traced the history of sociology's disavowal of utopia in the early twentieth century to maintain a stance of scientific certainty, and later how later critical theories have been antipathetic towards explicit descriptions of better societies (see also Urry, 2016, pp. 2–5).

Recently, however, we have seen a reorientation towards utopia as hermeneutic and method in sociology, political theory and cultural geography (Wright, 2010; Jacobsen and Tester, 2012; Levitas, 2013; Thompson and Zizek, 2013; Gardiner, 2014; Dawson, 2016; Urry, 2016; Bauman, 2017; Chrostowska and Ingram, 2017; Davies, 2018; Martell, 2018; Storey, 2019). This shift has taken place alongside but not always in dialogue with the wider turn towards social futures to which this collection attests. The key idea of this turn is that, as Urry has argued, the future 'should be reclaimed for social science' and for citizens and social actors. It is too important to be left to states, capital and technologists (2016, p. 5) which tend to evacuate questions of collective practice, everyday life, social inequalities and political injustice from future planning and visions. Analysing the future as social means examining where, how and by who the future is being made in the present, critiquing the power relationships that shape emergent trajectories and the discourses through which we talk and think about what we collectively expect and want. Seen from the perspective of contemporary futures studies, utopia might be one method of future-making – alongside, for example, extrapolation, scenario-building and dystopias (Urry, 2016, pp. 86–98). It is distinctive insofar as it figures desires rather than expectations, and because it expands the realm of the possible rather than assuming that the future will follow predictably from the present. Utopia insists on 'the necessity of envisioning alternative futures from a place enabled by hope, rather than risk, crisis and fear' (López Galviz et al., 2020, p. 2). Seen from the point of view of utopian studies, however, as we will see, the future is only one aspect of the utopian mode. So the relationship between utopia and social futures is one of overlap and sometimes tension, not a neat parallel.

These tensions and differences can be productive as the field of social future studies is expanded and enriched. In this chapter, I aim to bring resources from utopian studies, offering a multifaceted idea of utopia to contemporary work on social futures and hoping to promote and extend the effective conversations between the fields that are already underway (see, for example, Urry, 2016; López Galviz et al., 2020). In what follows I sketch a brief history of recent work on the concept of utopia, foregrounding the ideas of Ruth Levitas and Ernst Bloch. I then explore two paradoxes that I argue are constitutive of utopia and its generative power and potentially important to the study of social futures. The first explicitly concerns utopia and the future. At first glance, utopia seems to be self-evidently about the future and a better world to come. Certainly the progressive rationalities of modernity shaped a forward-looking, goal-oriented mode of utopianism. But that historical moment has passed – and contemporary theory often situates utopia in the present. I suggest that utopia's complex relationship with futurity is not a problem but a resource for resisting and complicating instrumentality, prediction and banal optimism. My second paradox concerns utopia and the real. In recent years, we have seen attempts to (re-)imbricate utopia with realist political projects (Wright, 2010; Bregman, 2018) and arguments for the use of utopia as a method for working on the real (Levitas, 2013). While celebrating these moves, I want to insist also that the point of utopia is not to be realistic or to be put to work. Its job is to demand the impossible, and its value is irreducibly linked to desire, to fantasy and to play. With these tensions in mind, I ask what utopia can do with and for us in the name of both making better social futures and nourishing hope in the present.

Concepts

Contemporary utopian studies is a wide-ranging interdisciplinary endeavour. Within its inclusive aegis, utopia can be many things. There are a couple of things, however, that most theorists insist it is not. It is not a blueprint – a rigid, detailed plan of a better society to be imposed, by force if necessary. Utopian scholars today tend to agree that utopia is a kind of process, consisting of gestures towards rather than exhaustive descriptions of alternative ways of organizing collective life. And utopia is not esoteric or obscure. Contemporary theories of utopia treat it as ubiquitous, widely present within and across cultures and even in individual psyches. These features are reflected in influential attempts to define utopia. Levitas, in her comprehensive survey of the concept (2010, originally published 1990), defines it as 'the expression of the desire for a better way of living and being' (2010, p. 9). For Sargent, utopias are the 'dreams and nightmares that concern the ways in which groups of people arrange their lives and which usually envision a radically different society from the one in which the dreamers live' (1994, p. 1). Utopia then is not (only) the object or the goal. It is the dreaming and desire, the capacity to imagine and want something different, the willingness to share a vision of a better society.

Jameson (2005) helps to elaborate on this tension between process and object. In his approach, utopianism or utopian desire is a way of thinking and feeling, an open-ended impulse oriented towards something better. By contrast, a utopia or utopian programme is a specifically instantiated idea/l of a better society, the image of a transformed state. Utopianism is widely present in cultural texts and social and political movements. It is emancipatory and creative, but always subject to co-optation by the dominant economic system and ideology. A utopia is more committed to radical transformation, expresses a more systematic critique of the way things are. But its power and therefore its danger come from a totalizing vision which implies the violence needed to impose it and which tends towards the static, rigid and oppressive. The utopian impulse registers that something is wrong with our social world. The literary utopia or political form elaborates a vision of a social alternative. For Jameson, both are in some sense exercises in the impossibility of imagining something fundamentally other than what ideology makes thinkable. The value of the literary utopia in particular is not so much the substantive content of its envisioned society but rather the capacity of the form to interrogate and expose the limits of what is imaginable.

Here both utopianism and utopia are primarily modes of critique, and indeed in contemporary approaches utopia is often understood as a way of making critical sense of the social worlds we inhabit by expressing a desire for a different way of being. It is closely associated with the literary form that More initiated, but not reducible to it. Utopian fiction continues to flourish,[1] but the form has become less didactic and static (Ferns, 1999), more reflexive, open and 'critical' (Moylan, 1986; Wagner-Lawlor, 2013). The utopian impulse is vividly present in texts that are formally dystopian, or anti-utopian (see Moylan, 2000; Moylan and Baccolini, 2003; Viera, 2013; Stock, 2018), or more broadly speculative, fantastical and magical realist (see Edwards, 2019).[2] Utopia is inseparable from the content of radical political visions – Marx and Engels' communist and Haraway's cyborg-feminist manifestoes (Weeks, 2013); green blueprints for the end of growth (Garforth, 2017) and post-capitalist visions of automation and a universal basic income (Srnicek and Williams, 2015). But utopia cannot, as Levitas shows (2010, p. 5), satisfactorily be defined by its content. Theorists have also located a utopian impulse (albeit a conservative one) in the technocratic third way politics of the 1990s; in contemporary populism and in the supposedly anti-utopian hegemony of neoliberalism itself (see Zizek, 2009, p. 79; Bell, 2017, p. 23; Bregman, 2017, p. 244).

As form and content have become less central to definitions of utopia and it becomes harder to pin down what utopia *is*, debates have centred increasingly around questions what utopia *does*. Levitas (2010) traces the idea of approaching utopia in terms of its function or effect to Marx and Engels' rejection of utopian socialism on the grounds that detailed visions of a better society compensate for or distract from real struggles and historical transformation.

More recent traditions in utopian studies focus on the capacity of utopian images and impulses to challenge or unsettle the way things are (Bammer, 1991; Jameson, 2005; Sargisson, 2012). Utopia here is about the refusal of the status quo in the name of something better. It is linked on the one hand to cognition, alienation and critique – as in Suvin's classic formulation of (utopian) science fiction (2016 [1979]), in which representations of other, better societies estrange us from common sense reality. It is linked on the other hand to affect, hope and transformation (Bloch, 1986; Dyer, 2000; Dolan, 2001; Anderson, 2002, 2006; Garforth, 2009), the possibility of what Abensour calls the 'education of desire' – teaching 'desire to desire, to desire better, to desire more, and above all to desire in a different way' (Abensour *Les Forme de l'Utopie* cited in Thompson 1977, p. 330).

The work of Ernst Bloch has been a vital resource in contemporary utopian theory, especially in relation to the idea of utopia as ubiquitous, the move away from the blueprint and the focus on desire and function. Bloch's historical and intellectual position in mid-century German philosophy is eccentric. He was mentor and teacher to many of the scholars of the Frankfurt School but not fully of it, both Marxist-materialist and extravagantly Romantic-spiritual in his political and philosophical commitments (see Geoghegan, 1996). His reception in Anglophone traditions of critical social and cultural theory has been 'strange and uneven' (Muñoz, 2009, p. 13). But contemporary utopian theory draws heavily on his legacy (Geoghegan, 1996; Daniel and Moylan, 1997; Muñoz, 2009; Levitas, 2010; Thompson, 2012), not least his survey and theory of utopia *The Principle of Hope* (1986).[3] In this book, Bloch traces manifestations of utopia from the intimate, personal, fleeting daydreams of everyday experience; through 'wishful images in the mirror', the utopian figures and tropes that permeate so much of contemporary culture; to elaborate utopian fictions and visions; to spiritual and aesthetic moments of transcendence (see Geoghegan, 2008 for an excellent summary). Bloch offers a 'vastly expanded idea of the utopian' (Muñoz, 2009, pp. 2–3) which encompasses 'everything from games to patent medicine, from myths to mass entertainment, from iconography to technology, from architecture to Eros, from tourism to jokes and the unconscious' (Jameson, 2005, p. 2).

For Bloch, all these forms of utopia are rooted in a future-oriented utopian impulse that speaks to the feeling of being fully at home (*Heimat*) or unalienated (Levitas, 2010, pp. 113, 115) in a transfigured world. He argues that this most defining of human desires is a necessary element of everyday life in conditions constrained by capitalist relations where collectivity, creativity and freedom are absent. Utopia in this sense is always a product of social limits and lacks (Levitas, 2010, pp. 210–211). But Bloch's approach is not simply descriptive; it is materialist, politically committed, even teleological. His work opens the door definitionally to a vast range of what he calls abstract utopias. In order for these utopian impulses – imaginative and hopeful but vague and co-optable – to matter, they must be linked to collective struggles for social transformation and become the concrete utopias of material projects: Oppositional, emancipatory and transformative (Bloch, 1986, vol 2, p. 580; vol 1, p. 146). Bloch insists on a broad and inclusive sense of the utopian forces at work around us in the social. He also sets up the idea of utopia as a method rather than an object that is now central to utopian studies and has become familiar in the study of social futures (Levitas, 2013; Urry, 2016) – a method that always works on the present through anticipation and critique, and that sometimes becomes part of material and hopeful change.

Forgoing the future?

Bloch's work also helps us to think about the puzzle of temporality at the heart of utopias and utopian thought. For Bloch, utopianism emerges from what is unfulfilled in the present moment and what reaches towards what might become, that is, from the *noch nicht*, which Levitas translates as both 'not yet' and 'still not' (2010, p. 102). It has two modes. The not-yet-conscious is a feature of the human psyche, a forward-looking and hopeful orientation distinctive to humans. The not-yet-become is the material or social counterpart of the utopian un/conscious and speaks to the always unfinished, unfolding, incomplete nature of collective life. For Bloch, utopia is an anticipatory – future-oriented – force. But he insists that what might be, via the individual capacity to anticipate and the emergent nature of social life, is part of the existing situation. In Bloch's philosophy, the present moment is replete with 'still unrealized potentialities' from the past which remain 'latent in the present', and with 'signs and foreshadowings that indicate the tendency of the direction of movement of the present into the future' (Kellner, 1987, p. 81). Dreaming forward is in the now, in the messy phenomenology of the everyday (Levitas, 2010, p. 104).

Utopianism's relationship with the future then is complex. It is also historically contingent. Utopia becomes strongly associated with the future as modernity becomes dominant and progressive. Earlier modern utopias were linked to spatial metaphors and 'spatial play' (Marin, 1984). The no/good place of utopia, and *Utopia,* emerged from so-called voyages of discovery and worked through their potentially destabilizing contradictions with European societies.[4] In other times and places, the desire for a better way of living and being might be expressed not as a claim on the future or in relation to mappable spaces, but through myth, Cockagygne fantasies and floating worlds, religious afterlives, paradises and Arcadias. Utopia becomes about the future specifically in relation to the European Enlightenment: Its assertion of the perfectibility of the human mind and the reimagining of society as a human artefact amenable to rational improvement. From the late eighteenth century to the mid-twentieth, utopia in the West was caught up and reimagined in the terms of a progressive futurism. Kumar calls the nineteenth 'the most utopian century of modern times' (1986), alive with the sense of a dynamic history moving towards ever-expanding freedom, prosperity and equality. For some this would come through education and incremental reform; for others through revolutionary transformation and emancipation. Formal manifestations – political manifestoes, communal experiments,[5] a reinvented utopian novel[6] – reflected, it is argued, a wider intellectual culture of optimistic futurity (Jacoby, 1999; Kumar, 2010; Urry, 2016).

Confident futurism however has not been a viable mode for utopia for some time. A mood of 'new catastrophism', Urry suggests, has dominated Western cultures and social theory since the turn of the twenty-first century (2016, p. 33). But more than that, the very idea of a collective history and future seems to have been lost in the era of what Bauman calls 'liquid' modernity (Bauman, 2000, 2003). Our period is marked by the lack of history except as conservative nostalgia or 'retrotopia' (Bauman, 2017). The prospect of a better future together has dissipated into individualistic life-projects in an extended present of consumer gratification, personal self-transformation and keeping options open. Utopia shrinks into desires wholly shaped by neoliberal rhetorics of choice, markets and individualism. Lauren Berlant has argued that in this way the state and economic institutions of late capitalism offer a kind of 'cruel optimism' (2011): The promise of a better future within the terms of the economic system keeps people trapped in the very conditions of inequality, injustice and precarity that are the most damaging. Here the 'bright-sidedness' (Ehrehnreich, 2009) of the positive thinking industry, the change-the-world altruism of Silicon Valley optimists (Giridharadas, 2018) and blandly positive figures of hope in contemporary politics (Halberstam, 2013) become antithetical to critical politics and the prospect of a fundamentally transformed future. Instead, we are left with 'post-politics' (Wilson and Swyngedouw, 2014) and relentless reinscriptions, state and cultural, of a 'capitalist realism' insisting that 'there is no alternative'

(Fisher, 2010). This is the 'privatization of hope' (Thompson, 2013), the depoliticization of the future and the naturalization of neoliberalism.

It is unsurprising under these circumstances that many political philosophers, as Bell explains citing Berardi's *After the Future*, ask us to 'abandon the illusion of the future' (2017, p. 61). Utopian theory too, Bell suggests, should be rethought in terms of a 'prefigurative politics that operates within and against – rather than beyond – that which exists' (2017, p. 61; on prefiguration see also Kinna, 2017). Over the last 20 or more years, utopian studies have come to suggest that utopia should be understood not in terms of prediction or projection but instead in relation to 'what it does to the present' (Sargisson, 1996, p. 41). This partly reflects a shift away from narrow associations between utopian theory and totalizing and historicizing Marxist critique. By the end of the twentieth century, the concept of utopia was being reworked under the signs of post-structuralism and feminism in approaches that emphasized deconstruction, process and desire (Bammer, 1991; Siebers, 1994; Sargisson, 1996). By the early twenty-first century, utopian studies also encompassed strongly spatial approaches offered by cultural and social geographers (Hetherington, 1994; Pinder, 2001; Anderson, 2006a, 2006b), often drawing on Foucault's (1986) introduction of the spatial/discursive idea of the heterotopia as a direct alternative to the historical/future-making idea of utopia. Utopia became less about describing the better future and instead about tracing the utopian affects, practices and spaces through which the present is unsettled, enacted and imagined otherwise (Garforth and Kraftl, 2009). Utopia becomes defined processually: As a method of intervening in linear and instrumental futurities, breaking with the future as endpoint or goal, enacting provocations and experiments against the continuation of business as usual.

And yet, utopia cannot be separated from the future so easily if it is to remain concrete (in Bloch's terms), to remain connected – even if sometimes tenuously – with the desires and hopes of groups struggling for change against a present that is not good enough. Muñoz persuasively sets out this position in his account of utopianism as 'queer futurity' (2009). He suggests that the hegemonic here and now of a 'reproductive majoritarian heterosexuality' is 'impoverished and toxic for queers' and other non-normative subjects (2009, pp. 22, 27). Utopia is what promises a different 'there and then', anticipates a 'restructured sociality' (2009, p. 7). Futurity here is primarily understood, after Bloch, in terms of 'anticipatory illumination' whereby emancipatory possibilities intrude into the present to disrupt its settled norms, often mobilizing and reinventing the promises of failed past revolutionary moments (Muñoz, 2009, pp. 7, 16). This is not a utopianism of telos, endpoints or blueprints. But Muñoz makes a powerful argument that utopianism must operate on and with futurity as the point at which both political demands and the fulfilled identities of those oppressed in the present can be met.[7] A similarly powerful sense of the need for different futures runs through contemporary Afrofuturist thought. Black politics needs collective 'countermemories' to contest racialized histories and the colonial archive (Eshun, 2003). But it is only transfigurative when the 'imaginary restitut[ion] of the catastrophe of modernity as slavery' is projected into the future – as in Gilroy's assertion that utopia is the 'postmodern-yet-to-come' of the Black Atlantic (1993, p. 36).

It is precisely utopia's ambiguous relationship with the future that makes it so valuable to social projects or analyses of future-making. Utopia exists between the present and the future. It pulls forward in anticipation and pulls back in reflexivity and critique. Utopia can be historically constructive, but it is also temporally disruptive. Its futurity is tentative, emergent and revisable (Levitas, 2013) It invites us to restitch connections between past, present and future. In contemporary utopian studies, utopia's futurity is not about ultimum or *telos* but about tendency, approach and emergence. Bell characterizes it as a flight towards something new unfolding from practices and ideas in the present (2017, p. 123). As such, utopia works to foreground desire and possibility and to limit or counter prediction and prescription. Utopia is about undoing as well as building. It is invaluable in social contexts that celebrate only the present, restrict futurity to prediction and extrapolation or project existing values to colonize the future.

Remaking reality

If utopia is constituted in the tension between the present and the future, what can we say about its relationship to the real? Conventionally utopia has been negatively situated in relation to reality and realism in two ways. First, utopia is frequently dismissed in common-sense rhetoric as unrealistic – fanciful, dreamy and impractical. Materialists have likewise associated utopia with escapism and compensation rather than active resistance to social injustice. Second, utopia has become widely associated with a kind of violence against the real, as in political critiques of totalitarian blueprints in which one person's vision is imposed on a victimized mass. Bregman describes this as the 'subordina[tion] of real people to fervent dreams' (2017, p. 20). In conventional opinion, then, the problem is that utopia is detached from or opposed to the real. In utopian studies, this is precisely its value! Utopia matters because it refuses a realist assessment of the status quo. It depends on a cognitive or affective negation of what exists in order to insist that things can change. Utopia demands the impossible. It starts with what is desired, what is needed and what is missing – what is absent from the real (Levitas, 2010, p. 9).

This leaves utopia in a complex relationship with politics and attempts to remake reality. Although utopia is in some ways always political (Bell, 2017; Sargisson, 2007), it is not about the *realization* of an imagined better society.[8] Utopia is 'a normative "might" that can, in principle, never be reduced to the empirical "is"' (Alexander, 2001, p. 580). There are therefore fundamental problems with attempts to theorize how utopia might be made more real or more productive. Utopia cannot easily be put to work as part of political projects or social movements. Wright's 'real utopias' project (2010) is an example of the promises and problems of such an approach. Utopia is defined in the tension between powerful but fantastical designs for a better world, on the one hand, and 'practical realities', that is, 'hard-nosed proposals for pragmatically improving institutions', on the other (2010, pp. 5–6). Wright's arguments suggest that an 'emancipatory social science' is needed to clean up utopian desires, assess the viability and achievability of specific visions and make a practical political contribution to social change (2010, pp. 10, 21). In Urry's work too utopias are valuable, but problematic insofar as they lack specific plans for moving from the present to a desired future (2016, p. 93). In his model of social future-making, utopias are celebrated but ultimately subordinated to the more practical, productive and instrumental technique of scenario-building.

Along with other recent calls for 'real' or 'realistic' utopias (Mason, 2016; Bregman, 2017; Kennedy, 2018), Wright's arguments make clear that radical left proposals to overcome economic injustice – for example, a universal basic income, radical reductions of the working week, a green new deal – are currently ruled out not because they are irrational or undesirable, but because they are unthinkable within the hegemonic terms of 'capitalist realism' (Fisher, 2009). Wright makes a rich empirical contribution describing instances of noncapitalist practice,[9] and a theoretical contribution in exploring the complexity of paths to social change in pluralist societies. But he reduces utopianism by valuing only those strands that can be put to work in relation to pragmatic anti-capitalist politics – i.e. by privileging realization. Wright's account suggests that utopias must be made useful by helping to plot an orderly move from the existing present to the better future (2010, p. 26). This resonates with the main idea in Bregman's *Utopia for Realists*, in which (after Wilde's oft-cited and rarely examined quote) 'progress is the realisation of utopias' (cited Bregman, 2017, p. 249).[10] Urry similarly seeks to put utopias to work for a progressive social science project of social future-making. But I have argued here that utopia operates alongside, in-between and even before theoretical accounts of social injustice and analytical future-making. Utopianism is not only ideas to be tested and put to work in political theory. It is also affects and practices at play around us in the social. If utopianism is not solely an idea it cannot logically be a linear precursor to realization. If utopia is a social response to loss, lack and absence then it emphatically cannot be solely the province of social theory, policy proposals or political programmes.

A very different way of understanding change and the value of utopia emerges if we start by situating utopias as part of the real, as forces at play in the everyday where they 'animate[s] the nooks and crannies, the spheres and subsystems of the social order'. Here, the 'reality' of utopia does not depend on its 'realization' but rather on the recognition that resistance to the way things are 'permeates the entire world in which we live' (Alexander, 2001, pp. 580–581). Gardiner's (2014) approach to utopia as immanent and everyday is instructive here. Drawing on critical theorists including Mikhail Bakhtin, Michel de Certeau and Henri Lefebvre (Gardiner, 2000), Gardiner's utopianism is linked to 'forces, tendencies and possibilities' at work in 'the pragmatic activities of daily existence' (2014, p. 20). Utopia 'lies semi-dormant' within ordinary life, promising, 'under the right conditions. [to] emerge with explosive force to rupture the smooth surface of dominant beliefs and ideologies' (Gardiner, 2014, p. 18). This is not a utopia of abstractions or political proposals but of moments and practices – affective, experiential and cultural – that gesture beyond the banalized present and the fragmentation of capitalist life.

Sometimes those practices can be understood as intentional. Cooper's (2013) work focusses on utopia as an ethos or set of felt values attuned to 'the possibility of enacting and performing the tissue of everyday life differently' (2013, p. 3). Her 'everyday utopias' are 'hot spots of innovative practice' which contribute to remaking reality by 'building and forging new ways of experiencing social and political life' rather than through campaigning, advocacy and policy proposals. Far from blueprints, totalizing critique or pragmatic planning, Cooper links utopia with small-scale experiments that are 'under the radar', inward-looking and immersive. The value of everyday utopias is not that they are places where prior visions are put into practice, but that they are 'promising spaces' for thinking differently *through* alternative everyday practices (Cooper, 2013, pp. 2, 9, 11). Similarly, López Galviz et al. suggest that utopian mobilities practices might shake up and open out 'path dependent and locked in processes' (2020, p. 8). Cooper's examples include Speaker's Corner and LETS (Local Exchange and Trading Schemes), public nudism and a women's and trans bathhouse. In each case, she locates degrees of intention to transform everyday practice. But if we accept that utopia is about the desire for something different and better then we cannot limit it to examples that explicitly promise to change the real. The concept of utopia as I have developed it here must include the creative, the unrealistic, the ephemeral, the open-ended and the fantastical. It does not have to be intentional (Kraftl and Garforth, 2009). If we take away the dreaming, fictional, playful side of utopia, we risk losing the value of its nowhereness.

The notion of utopia as method that can be put to work for political change by social scientists is a powerful one. But reducing utopia to practical uses and realistic purposes is impossible and, I argue, unwelcome. Muñoz reminds us that the desire at the heart of utopianism cannot be neatly divided into political, cognitive abstractions (such as a better world or freedom) on the one hand, and immediate, sensuous, playful, fictive and affective elements on the other (2009, p. 30). Both are about the disruption and interruption, the opening up and out of the status quo (2009, p. 32). For Muñoz, utopian dreaming links queer politics, erotics and aesthetics. For me, the fictional, irrational, speculative dimensions of green utopianism are intricately interwoven with ecopolitical philosophy and projects (Garforth, 2017). For Womack, Afrofuturism's utopias are constituted in 'imagination, technology, culture and innovation' – together (2013, p. 16). Its 'critical theory' is inseparable from its otherworldly and excessive 'artistic aesthetic' (p. 9). In the current push to put utopia to work in political projects, it is vital that we keep hold of the paradoxes that define the concept, finding ways to register the social value of the unrealistic and the fantastical, utopia's ineradicable association with uncommitted pleasure and play.

What can utopia do for us?

I have laid out in this chapter an approach to utopia that stresses its ubiquity and its processual temporality. I have suggested that utopia is vital for projects of social future-making – but that this vitality depends to a great extent on utopia's function as provocation and critique, rather than in relation to confident projections, plans or blueprints. I have suggested that it is useful to think about utopian desires as part of everyday reality, as playful and fantastical, and that this matters as much as the capacity of utopia to perform as an ingredient in realistic political and social scientific projects. With this in mind, I want to suggest that rather than asking what we can do with utopia, as in my title, it is more generative to wonder what it can do to and for us. Reversing the logic of the question can help us think more fruitfully about the relationship between utopia and social practices of future-making. A utopia that is emergent in the present is not contingent on realization for its value. A utopianism that is always – already, excessively – emerging in and through everyday social life cannot be fully tamed as a method for expert social scientists. A utopia that need not – cannot, perhaps – be realistic offers creative ways of interrogating the very idea of planning, prediction and pragmatic policymaking. It suggests instead the need to identify and enhance already-existing spaces of dreaming differently.

Notes

1 Since the 1970s this has largely been within genre science-fiction – from Ursula K Le Guin's *The Dispossessed* to more recent examples including Kim Stanley Robinson's *New York 2140* (2017); Cory Doctorow's (2017) *Walkaway*; and within subgenre movements like Solarpunk which deploys the speculative powers of science fiction to reflect on positive prospects for planetary survival and socio-environmental justice (in the face of the climate crisis see for example eds. Wagner and Wieland (2017) *Sunvault*).
2 Dystopias which express a utopian sensibility in recent science fiction include Octavia Butler's *Parable of the Sower*; Ursula K Le Guin's *The Telling*; Marge Piercy's *He, She and It/Body of Glass* and Margaret Atwood's Maddaddam trilogy for example. We can also see the utopian impulse at work in speculative fantasy including N K Jemisins's Broken Earth trilogy; Charlie Jane Anders' *All the Birds in the Sky*; in the so-called New Weird e.g. China Mieville's *The City and the City*; and as Edwards (2019) explores in genre-crossing contemporary fiction which feeds on science fictional tropes – for example in the work of David Mitchell, Maggie Gee or Jim Crace.
3 Originally written between 1938 and 1947 in German; revised and published in successive volumes in 1954, 1955 and 1959; first translated and published in three volumes in English in 1986.
4 The early modern spatial utopia was both a product of European voyages of exploration in the sixteenth and seventeenth centuries and a critical component of the modern colonial imagination with its fantasies and violent realities of occupying and remaking global spaces. See for example Hardy (2012), Balasopoulos (2004). Balasopoulos notes how More's *Utopia* anticipates the discourses of civilization of unoccupied land that justified colonial settlement: The identification of 'native' occupants and the land itself as primitive, underdeveloped, backwards.

5 Most famously Robert Owen's experiments at New Lanark in Scotland and New Harmony in the United States; see Kumar (1987) on Owen and others.
6 Notably Edward Bellamy's *Looking Backward 2000–1887*, first published in 1888, and William Morris's *News from Nowhere*, published in 1890. See Ferns (1999).
7 Muñoz's work presents a sympathetic critique of Lee Edelman's *No Future* and related moves in queer theory to refuse the future insofar as it has functioned hegemonically as a space only of heterosexual biological and social reproduction in mainstream Western culture. See Muñoz (2009, pp. 91–95).
8 The basic position that utopia is about desire and not its realization also undermines the critique of utopias as totalitarian. As Levitas argues: It is totalitarianism that is totalitarian, not utopia (2010). Utopia as it is currently understood in utopian studies is not even programmatic, let alone totalitarian.
9 See Wright (2010, pp. 2–5) for an overview of participatory city budgeting in Porto Alegre Brazil, Wikipedia and Mondragon worker-owned cooperatives.
10 'If we want to change the world, we need to be unrealistic, unreasonable and impossible. Remember those who called for the abolition of slavery, for suffrage for women and for same-sex marriage were also once branded lunatics. Until history proved them right' (pp. 264–265). What I resist in Bregman's argument is not that utopia is about demanding the impossible, or his partially worked-through claims that what counts as real is socially constructed (pp. 254–255, 263–264). It is the teleological assertion that the *only* valuable utopianism is ideas that ultimately come to be 'proved right' and the progressive and linear construction of history that frames this assertion.

Bibliography

Alexander, J. (2001). 'Robust utopias and civil repairs', *International Sociology*, 16(4), pp. 579–591.
Anderson, B. (2002). 'A principle of hope: Recorded music, listening practices and the immanence of utopia', *Geografiska Annaler*, 84B(3–4), pp. 211–227.
Anderson, B. (2006a). '"Transcending without transcendence": Utopianism and an ethos of hope', *Antipode*, 38(4), pp. 691–710.
Anderson, B. (2006b). 'Becoming and being hopeful: Towards a theory of affect', *Environment and Planning D: Society and Space*, 24, pp. 733–752.
Baccolini, R. and Moylan, T. (eds.) (2003). *Dark horizons: Science fiction and the dystopian imagination*. New York: Routledge.
Balasopoulos, A. (2004). 'Unworldly worldliness: America and the trajectories of utopian expansionism', *Utopian Studies*, 15(2), pp. 3–35.
Bammer, A. (1991). *Partial visions: Feminism and utopianism in the 1970s*. London: Routledge.
Bauman, Z. (2000). *Liquid modernity*. Cambridge: Cambridge University Press.
Bauman, Z. (2006). 'Living in utopia', *Soundings*, 33, pp. 13–23.
Bauman, Z. (2017). *Retrotopia*. Cambridge: Polity.
Bell, D. (2017). *Rethinking utopia: Place, power, affect*. London: Routledge.
Bregman, R. (2017). *Utopia for realists, and how we can get there*. London: Bloomsbury. Transl. Elizabeth Maston.
Chrostowska, S.D. and Ingram, J.D. (2017). *Political uses of utopia: New Marxist, anarchist, and radical democratic perspectives*. New York: Columbia University Press.
Cooper, D. (2013). *Everyday utopias: The conceptual life of promising spaces*. Durham, NC: Duke University Press.
Daniel, J.O. and Moylan, T. (1997). *Not yet: Reconsidering Ernst Bloch*. London: Verso.
Davies, W. (ed.) (2018). *Economic science fictions*. London: Goldsmiths Press.
Dawson, M. (2016). *Social theory for alternative societies*. New York: Palgrave Macmillan.
Dolan, J. (2001). 'Performance, utopia, and the "utopian performative"', *Theatre Journal*, 53(3), pp. 455–479.
Dyer, R. (2002 [1992]). 'Entertainment and utopia'. In *Only entertainment*. London: Routledge.
Edwards, C. (2019). *Utopia and the contemporary British novel*. Cambridge: Cambridge University Press.
Ehrenreich, B. (2009). *Bright-sided: How the relentless promotion of positive thinking has undermined America*. New York: Metropolitan Books.
Eshun, K. (2003). 'Further considerations on Afrofuturism', *CR: The New Centennial Review*, 3(2), pp. 287–302.

Ferns, C. (1999). *Narrating utopia: Ideology, gender, form in utopian literature*. Liverpool: Liverpool University Press.
Foucault, M. (1986). 'Of other spaces,' *Diacritics*, 16, pp. 22–27. http://www.jstor.org/stable/10.2307/464648
Gardiner, M.E. (2014). *Weak Messianism: Essays in everyday utopianism*. Oxford: Peter Lang.
Garforth, L. and Kraftl, P. (2009). 'Introduction: Utopia and the problem of intention', *Journal for Cultural Research*, 13(1), pp. 1–4.
Geoghegan, V. (1996). *Ernst Bloch*. London: Routledge.
Gilroy, P. (1993). *The Black Atlantic: Modernity and double consciousness*. London: Verso.
Giridharadas, A. (2018). *Winners take all: The elite charade of changing the world*. New York: Knopf.
Hardy, K. (2012). 'Unsettling hope: Contemporary indigenous politics, settler-colonisation, and utopianism', *Spaces of Utopia, An Online Journal*, 2(1), pp. 123–136.
Hayden, P. and el-Ojeili, C. (2009). *Globalization and utopia: Critical essays*. New York: Palgrave Macmillan.
Hetherington, K. (1997). *Badlands of modernity: Heterotopia and social ordering*. London: Routledge.
Ingram, J. (2017). 'Introduction: Utopia and politics'. In Chrostowska, S.D. and Ingram, J. (eds.). *Political uses of utopia: New Marxist, anarchist, and radical democratic perspectives*. New York: Columbia University Press, pp. ix-xxxiv.
Jacobsen, M.H. and Tester, K. (2012). *Utopia: Social theory and the future*. Aldershot: Ashgate.
Jacoby, R. (1999). *The end of utopia: Politics and culture in an age of apathy*. New York: Basic Books.
Jameson, F. (2005). *Archaeologies of the future: The desire called utopia and other science fictions*. London: Verso.
Kellner, D. and O'Hara, H. (1976). 'Utopia and Marxism in Ernst Bloch', *New German Critique*, 9, pp. 11–34.
Kinna, R. (2017). 'Utopianism and prefiguration'. In Chrostowska, S.D. and Ingram, J.D. (eds.). *Political uses of utopia: New Marxist, anarchist, and radical democratic perspectives*. New York: Columbia University Press, pp. 198-215.
Kumar, K. (1987). *Utopia and anti-utopia in modern times*. Oxford: Blackwell.
Kumar, K. (2010). 'The ends of utopia', *New Literary History*, 41, pp. 549–569.
Levitas, R. (2010 [1990]). *The concept of utopia*. Oxford: Peter Lang.
Levitas, R. (2013). *Utopia as method: The imaginary reconstitution of society*. London: Palgrave Macmillan.
López Galviz, C., Buscher, M. and Freudendal-Pederson, M. (2020). 'Mobilities and utopia: A critical reorientation', *Mobilities*, 15(1), pp. 1–10.
Marin, L. (1984). *Utopics: Spatial play*. London: Palgrave Macmillan.
Martell, L. (2018). 'Utopianism and social change: Materialism, conflict and pluralism', *Capitalism and Class*, 42(3), pp. 435–452.
Marx, K. and Engels, F. (1969 [1848]). *The manifesto of the Communist Party*. Version taken from *Marx/Engels selected works*, Vol. 1. Moscow: Progress Publishers, pp. 98–137, translated: Samuel Moore in cooperation with Frederick Engels, 1888. Online at Marxists Internet Archive: https://www.marxists.org/archive/marx/works/download/pdf/Manifesto.pdf. Accessed 24 July 2019.
Moylan, T. (1986). *Demand the impossible: Science fiction and the utopian imagination*. London: Methuen.
Moylan, T. (2000). *Scraps of the untainted sky: Science fiction, utopia, dystopia*. Boulder, CO: Westview.
Muñoz, J.E. (2009). *Cruising utopia: The there and then of queer futurity*. New York: New York University Press.
Pinder, D. (2001). *Visions of the city*. Edinburgh: Edinburgh University Press.
Sargent, L.T. (1994). 'The three faces of utopianism revisited', *Utopian Studies*, 5(1), pp. 1–37.
Sargisson, L. (1996). *Contemporary feminist utopianism*. London: Routledge.
Sargisson, L. (2007). 'The curious relationship between politics and utopia'. In Moylan, T. and Baccolini, R. (eds.). *Utopia method vision: The use value of social dreaming*. Bern: Peter Lang, pp. 25–46.
Sargisson, L. (2012). *Fool's gold: Utopianism in the 21st century*. London: Palgrave Macmillan.
Siebers, T. (1994). *Heterotopia: Postmodern utopia and the body politic*. Ann Arbor: University of Michigan Press.
Srnicek, N. and Williams, A. (2015). *Inventing the future: Postcapitalism and a world without work*. London: Verso.
Stock, A. (2018). *Dystopian fiction and political thought: Narratives of world politics*. London: Routledge.
Storey, J. (2019). *Radical utopianism and cultural studies: On refusing to be realistic*. London: Routledge.

Suvin, D. (2016 [1979]). *Metamorphoses of science fiction: On the poetics and history of a literary genre.* Bern: Peter Lang.
Thompson, E.P. (1977). *William Morris: From Romantic to revolutionary.* London: Pantheon Books.
Thompson, P. (2012). 'What is concrete about Ernst Bloch's concrete utopia?' In Jacobsen, M.H. and Tester, K. (eds.). *Utopia: Social theory and the future.* Aldershot: Ashgate, pp. 33–46.
Thompson, P. and Zizek, S. (2013). *The privatization of hope.* Durham, NC: Duke University Press.
Vieira, F. (ed.) (2013). *Dystopia(n) matters.* Newcastle upon Tyne: Cambridge Scholars Press.
Wagner-Lawlor, J. (2013). *Postmodern utopias and feminist fictions.* Cambridge: Cambridge University Press.
Wilson, J. and Swyngedouw, E. (2014). 'Seeds of dystopia: Post-politics and the return of the political'. In Wilson, J. and Swyngedouw, E. (eds.). *The post-political and its discontents: Spaces of depoliticisation, spectres of radical politics.* Edinburgh: Edinburgh University Press, pp. 1–30.
Womack, Y.L. (2013). *Afrofuturism: The world of black sci-fi and fantasy culture.* Chicago, IL: Lawrence Hill Books.
Wright, E.O. (2010). *Envisioning real utopias.* London: Verso.

28
Visible cities
Envisioning social futures

Nick Dunn

The failure of the future?

What do we think of when we think of the future? Many of us might envisage space travel, off-earth communities, sleek architecture, airborne personal transportation or, perhaps, a bleaker version involving environmental degradation, inhospitable places and societal collapse. Critically, when we consider the future, it is usually situated, i.e., it is a time and place we can imagine, even if that location is very different from our present one. It is through *place* that we are able to assemble different elements to compose an image of our future, not an ambiguous space. Unsurprisingly, when we think about the future, we are drawn to visions for them. Indeed, it is precisely through the act of locating oneself in the future that orientation towards it becomes tangible. This is the power of creativity and imagination in supporting the 'futures literacy' needed to 'introduce the non-existent future into the present' (Miller, 2018, p. 15). It is integral to iterative and exploratory methods that form one of the four-stage methodological approach for thinking about the future developed by Richard Slaughter (1997). Iterative and exploratory methods include back-casting, scenarios and visioning. All require activism on behalf of the individual or group of participants involved. Joseph Voros (2003) has described these methods as aligning to prospective methods that seek to produce future images. This is why futurists, including designers, apply visioning as a method not only to forecast but also to stimulate potential futures into being. Through creating multiple futures, visioning presents us with the ability to discover and explore different options and thereby begin to negotiate values and preferences. The primary benefit of iterative and exploratory methods is their capacity to reveal new ideas and challenge existing assumptions about the future. Visualization can play a critical role within the visioning process enabling those exploring potential futures to capture their ideas and share them. As Kwartler and Longo (2008) have shown, these methods have particular applications and implications in the context of future placemaking. So, where does this position us at this moment in time?

In a visualization for a future city, there is an intentionality that the ideas, values and hopes it seeks to depict become visible, though this is not always the case. This leads us to consider the power and agency of the images themselves, which, when coupled with the process of futuring, can be highly effective in promoting or discrediting particular agendas.

Visualizations for future cities carry and project the concepts and ideologies behind them. They are clearly not neutral since what they omit can be as important as what they depict. In most cases, visions for alternative ways of living are bound up in ideologies and agendas, especially when they strive to illustrate a radical departure from prevailing conditions. This reminds us of the plurality of futures and the transition from an empiricist approach to *the* future towards a diversity of approaches to multiple futures. Thus, as Law and Urry (2004) observe, there is a plurality of both pasts and futures that are individually constructed to assemble an individual reality. This is especially relevant to future cities where manifold possibilities for how urban life could be have been produced.

Yet, despite this general shift in how we think of futures plus the plethora of tools and techniques available to help us create visions for places, futures remain dominated by technological aspirations and determinism over other possibilities (Urry, 2016; Sand, 2019). Why does this matter? Well, put bluntly, it is the world that is at stake. Societies shape themselves partly through the images of the future they construct (Polak, 1973). Different ways of thinking about cities and their futures are vital if we are to avoid path dependency and identify alternatives to business-as-usual scenarios (Albrechts, 2015). This situation is increasingly urgent given our collective responsibility in mitigating planetary consequences and providing a safe, sustainable world for future generations (Swilling, 2020). A lack of imagination hinders our capacity for change as Hajer and Versteeg (2019) emphasize in their discussion of post-fossil futures, since it seriously limits our ability to conceive of coherent visions for alternatives. The next section, therefore, examines the current status of visions for future cities to contextualize the position of this chapter.

Utopic bubbles and echo chambers

In 2014, I was commissioned by the UK Government's Office for Science as part of its wider Foresight Future of Cities project to write a report on the subject of how we have envisioned future cities throughout history (Dunn et al., 2014). In our research, we examined nearly 1,000 different future cities. These were drawn from a variety of sources including mainstream visualizations created by architects, town planners and urban designers; avant-garde works from architects, artists and designers; and examples from popular culture such as film, graphic novels and video games. Given the sheer volume and diversity of material available, it soon became evident that we needed to find a method of analysing these visions. This led to a number of attempts to understand how they could be classified and related to one another so that we could make sense of what we were studying and provide insights. The scope of the report meant the period under scrutiny spanned from 1900 to 2014 when it was produced. To best illustrate the various concepts and themes identified across the material, we chose 94 visions that were prominent types to provide an overview as comprehensive as possible to the reader. We classified the materials to ascertain primary elements within each image and then recorded these. This was a dual process. We organized the visualizations by association to categories and the technique by which they had been produced. Parallel to this, we also analysed the thematic content of these images to identify dominant elements of urban life, or their alternatives, they conveyed. Upon collating this information, we then sought to establish clusters and groupings of visualizations to understand patterns and trends within the visions. Our attempt to visualize the relationships between these examples, what type of media and techniques were used to generate them and what themes they communicated, was complex to say the least (see Figure 28.1).

Nick Dunn

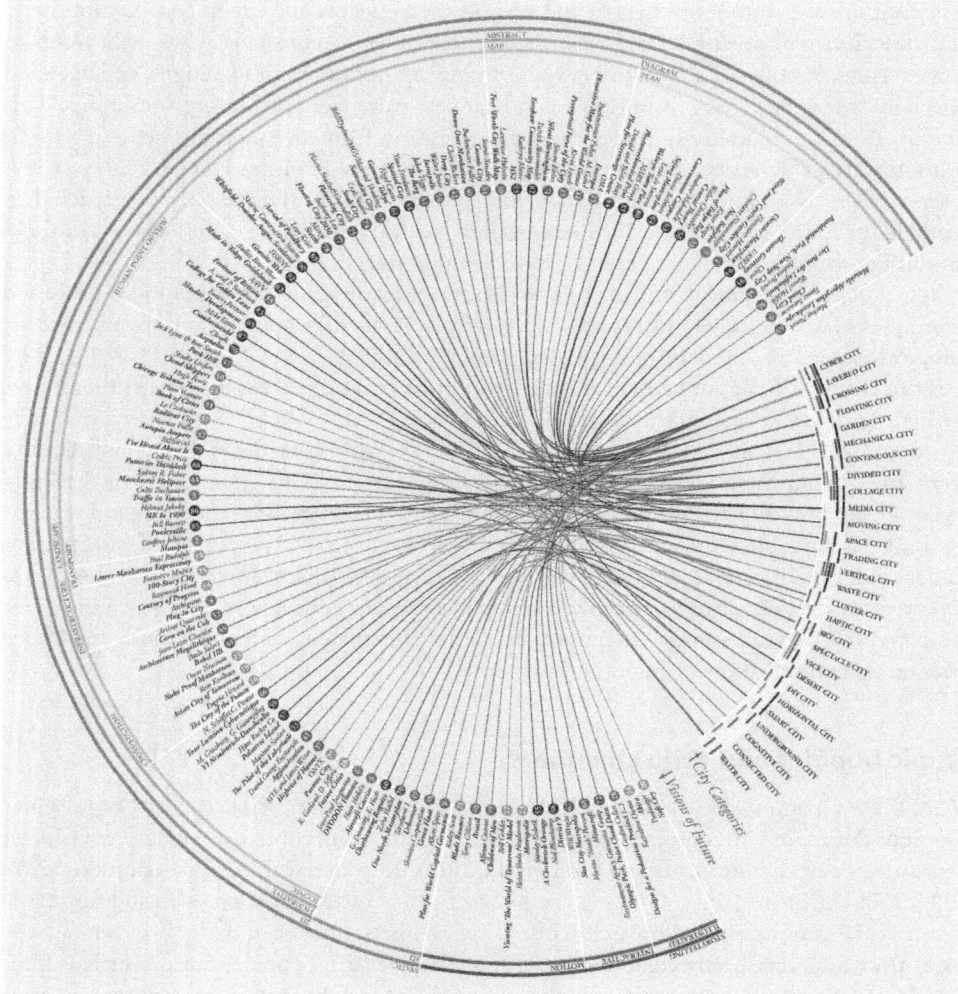

Figure 28.1 Taxonomy for visualization of future cities 2014. Nick Dunn, Paul Cureton and Serena Pollastri

This process enabled us to draw out overarching narratives and thematic patterns for how future cities have been envisaged. We established a set of 28 categories that fit within 6 dominant paradigms as follows:

> *Regulated Cities* - urban visions that integrate aspects of rural/country/green living.
> *Layered Cities* – portrayals that have explicit multiple but fixed levels typically associated with different mobilities.
> *Flexible Cities* - urban depictions that allow for plug-in components and changes but still fixed in some manner to context.
> *Informal Cities* – present visions that suggest much more itinerant and temporary situations and include walking, nomadic and non-permanent cities.

Visible cities

Ecological Cities - illustrations of cities that demonstrate explicit ecological concerns, renewable energies and low or zero carbon ambitions.

Hybrid Cities - urban visions that deliberately explore the blurring between physical place and digital space, including augmented reality and 'smart' cities.

When arranged in a timeline, these different paradigms can be appreciated from a historical perspective, illustrating connectivity and recurrence over time (see Figure 28.2). The aim of this work was to provide a useful resource and method for the analysis of visions for future places. It facilitated trends and patterns to become legible, e.g. the apparent re-emergence of more socially engaged ideas for collective life. Yet, it is important to be cautious when attempting to draw tidy conclusions from this kind of visual survey. For example, the growth

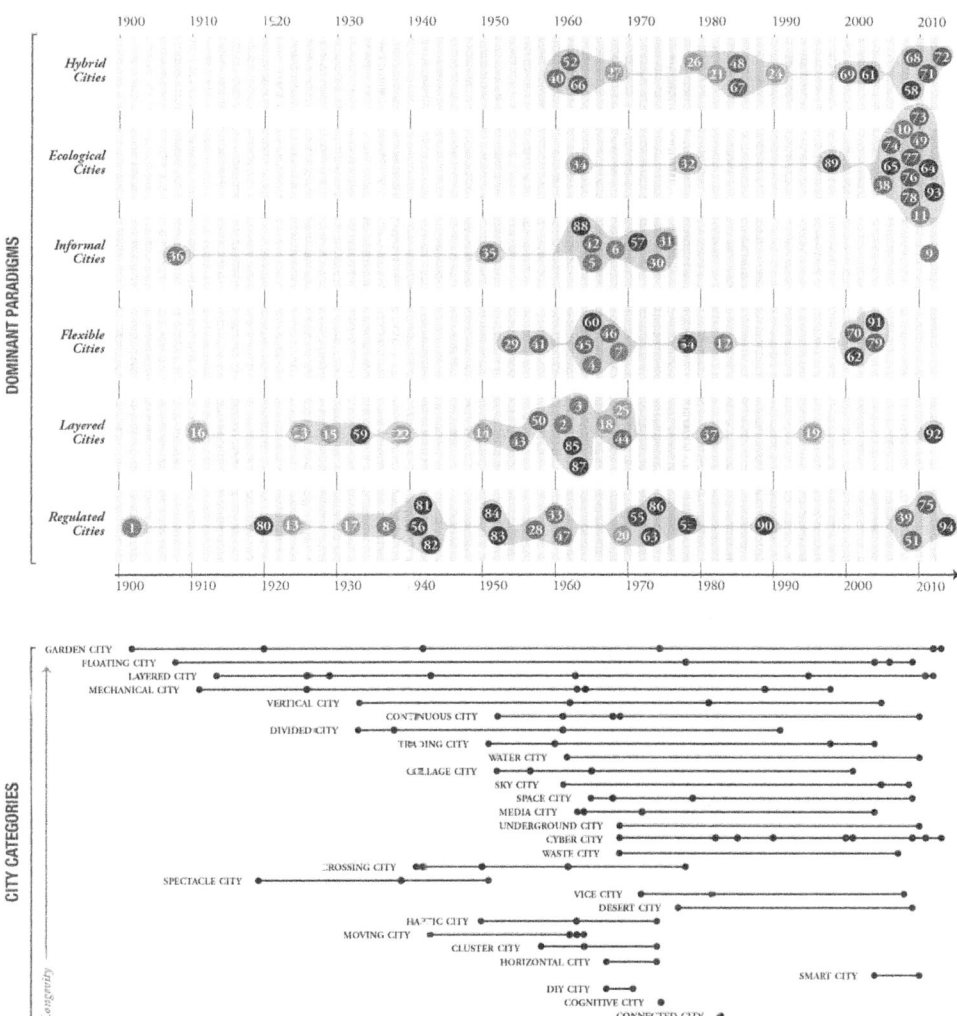

Figure 28.2 Timeline of the 6 principal paradigms and 28 future city categories between 1900 and 2014. Nick Dunn, Paul Cureton and Serena Pollastri

307

in socially engaged visions may reflect greater societal and global ambitions for sustainability. However, an alternative reading might indicate a deliberate branding of contemporary visions to align with political agendas. Within this apparent movement of socially driven visions, therefore, is the full gamut of possibilities from legitimate strategies to deliver low or zero carbon urban development to proposals that have been subject to 'greenwashing' to improve their reception. This demonstrates the agency and plasticity of visualizations for prospective futures. It also raises complex issues with regard to the communication and interpretation of such images.

This study also illustrates that the more radical alternatives to traditional development principles for cities, i.e., Informal Cities and Flexible Cities, have to date been 'utopic bubbles', bound in time and reflective of short periods where there was considerable optimism for different futures away from business-as-usual pathways. It is interesting to note that Informal Cities that were stimulated by counter-cultural conditions in wider society became conceptually exhausted by the mid-1970s. This is no coincidence given the peak oil crisis and the general rise of conservatism in the latter half of the 1970s onwards. Concomitant with this shift was the upsurge in digital technologies, notably in the growth and widespread use of new forms of representation, to generate images including visualizations, and the production of new environments, within which to explore spatial possibilities that did not have to contend with the limits of reality such as gravity. This retreat into digital space enabled designers to explore the more fantastical side of their ideas, accounting for the re-emergence of Flexible Cities as part of broader anticipation and anxiety at the turn of the new millennium. These latter visions were highly influential within the subfields of digital architecture and computational design, further spurring new ideas, theories and practices. Aside from a few seminal projects, however, they were essentially operating as echo chambers for novel visualization techniques, emblematic of the increasing delamination of these forms of architectural and urban design from those that directly impacted upon the physically built environment.

Technological potential and environmental concern signify the two most prominent paradigms in the visual materials studied. This situation, in the intervening years since the report was published, has continued to increase their influence as Ecological Cities and Hybrid Cities. Of relevance to our discussion is how these two types are often coupled in a compelling vision, the Smart City. As an umbrella term that encompasses a significant variety of different futures for place, the Smart City is a powerful imaginary, flexible and capable of assimilating many other forms of technologically driven visions for future cities. The ambiguity and intangibility of what a Smart City is have led to it becoming pervasive in the first two decades of the twenty-first century given its predication on technological impulses, which can be seductive in their own right, and its capacity to absorb other possible futures into its rhetoric. This, as I have discussed in detail elsewhere (Dunn, 2018), has led to convergence of futures, the consequence of which occludes viable alternatives. How might we counter this confluence of futures and explore different ones? I next examine this phenomenon further before considering a number of ways that may support the production of alternative visions for collective life.

Tensioning frictionless futures

For a long time, visions for future cities have typically been the product of a singular, seemingly heroic designer who has sought to bring order and control to the messiness of urban life. As the complexity of issues in cities has increased, so too has the size of teams needed to design strategies for addressing them. Of particular significance has been the steady rise in major corporations developing visions for future places through the implementation of information and communication technology to provide management and operation of cities (Söderström et al., 2014; Rose, 2018). This shift is reflective of a wider development, the ongoing abstraction of place towards space that has resulted in a false yet alluring dematerialization and deterritorialization of cities. It is crucial to recognize that this transition has been catastrophic since it has allowed humans to ignore the impacts of climate change, finding ourselves as we do on a specific planet with a specific biosphere where place, not space, has emerged in all its non-human dimension (Morton, 2016). Through this detachment, Smart Cities are portrayed as complex entities, but this refers to the challenges of handling Big Data rather than the enmeshed intricacies of urban life (see also Raven in this volume). An important aspect of these futures has been the emphasis on short-term dynamics that, rather than reinforcing time horizons as end-states that are far away, has brought the temporal dimension of cities onto the agenda by focussing on the now and next (Batty, 2018). Furthermore, with their origins in management software, the premise of a solution-oriented approach and borrowed language of systems, processes, outputs, etc., implies that existing places can become more efficient through a flattening of layered realities that can be reproduced elsewhere. Not surprisingly, the visions constructed to convey Smart Cities are characterized by technology that supports apparently frictionless and seamless movement, accompanied by green and blue infrastructures, gleaming and shimmering architecture, all coming together under a bright blue sky where the future city is conspicuously free from debris, dirt and pollution. The significance of these features and colour palette is notable for the way they support an untainted view of the world, where trees and park spaces are always verdant and canal and rivers are azure. In both these cases, they are unrealistically manicured and shown without detritus, seasonal change or inclement weather. Such clear, glitch-free worlds are utopian 'frictionless futures in which the city is easily disassembled and reassembled into a coherent whole for operational optimization without question' (Dunn and Cureton, 2019, p. 19). In promoting these futures, other possibilities are hidden or even discredited. So how can we explore alternatives to those futures that are principally driven by technology and that currently dominate our purview?

This leads us to consider what or who makes cities. Despite the inclination to assume we make cities in terms of human attributes such as reason and other ways of acting that give us a sense of control over such matters, the gap between intention and realization remains (Williams, 2019). It is clear we need a more expansive view of visions for future places that can accommodate a greater degree of plurality and diversity. More recently, my work has sought to redress this balance and demonstrate that alongside Technological Futures, there are also visions that embody what might be understood as Social Futures and Global Futures. To aid clarity of these terms within the context of visions for urban futures, they are defined as follows (Dunn and Cureton, 2020)

> *Social Futures* investigates the experimental and experiential visions for future cities led by an impulse to provide for a new society or create novel urban situations.
> *Global Futures* takes account of those visions produced in response to the significant challenges of climate change and how we might enable collective life to be sustained.
> *Technological Futures* examines the optimism of those visions driven by technology and their dialogue with their expressions within science fiction.

In doing so, the aim is to provide new critical lenses through which visions for future places are generated and communicated; this enables us to better understand how such images are interpreted, i.e., who is using them to push an agenda, why they are doing so and when. By explicitly positioning the social and global alongside the technological, our intention is to stimulate new debate about how futures are categorized. The original study was primarily focussed on examples based in or relevant to the UK context, whereas this second study was deliberately more global in its scope and included a larger number, 165, of visions for future cities to be accounted for. Again, these examples were drawn from a much larger collection of work, in this case comprising nearly 2,000 images assembled from many archives and other sources. To provide as comprehensive survey as possible, these visions included an array of mainstream visualizations created by architects and city planners, avant-garde works and examples from popular culture. Revisiting the timeline of principal paradigms six years after the original study, four key findings are evident (see Figure 28.3). First is what seems to be a re-emergence of Hybrid Cities, Ecological Cities and Layered Cities during the last 10 to 15 years. Given the ubiquity of Smart Cities, environmental concerns and renewed interest in addressing the complexity of soft and hard infrastructures that support urban life, this perhaps is unsurprising. Second is a notable growth in Informal Cities, Flexible Cities and Regulated Cities in the same period. This may be reflective of the considerable uncertainty of the present and our tendency to look to the past for the ideological seeds of our futures. It may also be indicative of the increasingly manifold and rapidly shifting dynamics of contemporary cities. Third, the findings illustrate that when visions are intentionally viewed through different critical lenses, the various registers of information, the respective themes and features, within the visualizations come to the fore in different ways. To expand on this point, by actively identifying visions that represent Social Futures and Global Futures parallel to Technological Futures, it becomes possible to have a broader conversation on what

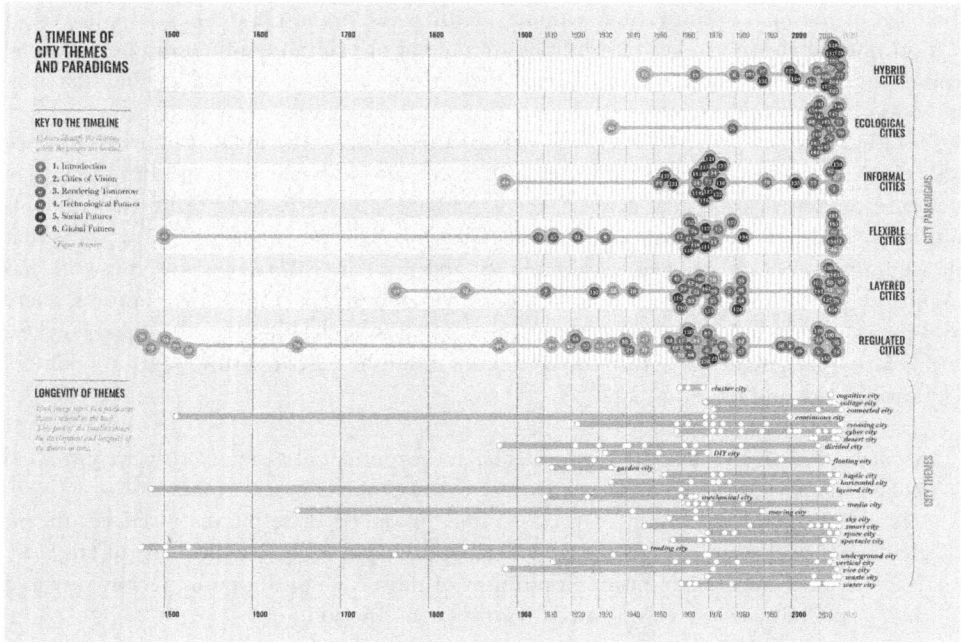

Figure 28.3 Timeline of principal paradigms 2020. Nick Dunn, Paul Cureton and Serena Pollastri

is preferable and how this is framed. Fourth, this research found that such classification of visions remains flexible and open to challenge as it did in the original study. Although this suggests this approach is useful as a method of analysis, it reinforces the need for a greater inquiry into these categories through further application of them to develop more nuanced definitions and subcategories as appropriate. It is essential to acknowledge the nascent quality of this work and its attempt to offer a foundation from which subsequent research into the diversity and plurality of visions for future cities may evolve.

Making futures visible

Returning to the premise of this chapter, it has been shown how the use of visual methods can open up alternative visions for collective life that have their basis in social and environmental issues rather than solely being driven by technological innovation. What has not been determined is how we can leverage these different futures into being. This is no small task. Recent work in speculative non-fiction has been compelling in its warning of the radical changes we need to make to slow down the impacts of climate change, either through articulation of how catastrophic the future could become (Orsekes and Conway, 2014) or potential steps to reduce its worst effects (Porritt, 2013). Visualization and visioning need to be taken seriously given their fecund potential for the 'midwifing of futures' (Ache, 2017).

It is beyond the scope of this chapter to be able to define such a process in detail; yet, it is possible to sketch out a framework for envisioning social futures towards which this work constitutes the first stage. By setting out a new agenda within futures studies for how visions for place are analysed, I have aimed to illustrate the role of the novel visual analysis method applied in two studies as a means of propagating alternative futures that lie outside of the dominant technological view. The purpose of this work is to increase the acceptability and adoption of a wider array of ideas, values and hopes that may influence the production of new visions for future places. The second stage will be to develop appropriate methods of involving people in the co-design of these visions (Pollastri et al., 2018) empowered with the knowledge that there are radical alternatives to business-as-usual scenarios for their future. Key here is the 'who' in such processes, which is inherently political since it concerns, 'what is seen and what can be said about it, around who has the ability to see and the talent to speak, around the properties of spaces and the possibilities of time' (Rancière, 2009 [2000], p. 13). The third stage will be to formulate potential delivery mechanisms that can connect on the ground (Campbell, 2018; Rogers, 2018) to reduce the gap between intention and realization. This is essential if we are to find viable ways through the mirage of 'frictionless futures' detached from the realities of cities. The latter has been brought into sharp focus following the global outbreak of COVID-19, wherein the specificity of place and its impact upon how we live have been profoundly significant. The fourth stage will be to recognize the amount of time, action and commitment that the prior three stages represent by establishing a multidisciplinary field of research to scrutinize this framework, to continue to challenge assumptions and to bring in a more diverse assemblage of actors to the ongoing inquiry of such work.

Making futures visible requires us to examine the history of the future, question its dominant voices and better understand those that have been marginalized, underrepresented, silenced or unable to speak (Sand, 2019). Such processes will need to become further nuanced if we are to take account for the many non-human actors that need representation in visions for future places (Haraway, 2016). Likewise, we will need to be vigilant when technological developments enhance our human capacities within post-human futures to ensure we are equipped to care for more than human worlds (Puig de la Bellacasa, 2017). The framework set out here proposes tentative steps. Through it, we can form the foundations of valuable counter-positions and identify new connections woven through time and place that suggest new and vital alternatives, rendering cities and the polyphony of voices and narratives that co-constitute them to be visible. By opening up the processes and dialogue of futuring through visions to a wider set of stakeholders, we will be better positioned to rethink the global transitions required to safeguard our health, that of other species and the environment we share.

Bibliography

Ache, P. (2017). 'Vision making in large urban settings: Unleashing anticipation?'. In Poli, R. (ed.). *Handbook of anticipation: Theoretical and applied aspects of the use of future in decision making*. Cham: Springer, pp. 1–21.

Albrechts, L. (2015). 'Ingredients for a more radical strategic spatial planning', *Environment and Planning B: Urban Analytics and City Science*, 42(3), pp. 510–525.

Batty, M. (2018). *Inventing future cities*. Cambridge, MA: The MIT Press.

Campbell, K. (2018). *Making massive small change: Building the urban society we want*. White River Junction, VT: Chelsea Green Publishing.

Dunn, N. (2018). 'Urban imaginaries: Palimpsest of the future'. In Linder, C. and Meissner, M. (eds.). *The Routledge companion to urban imaginaries*. London: Routledge, pp. 375–386.

Dunn, N. and Cureton, P. (2019). 'Frictionless futures: The vision of smartness and the occlusion of alternatives'. In Figueiredo, S.M., Krishnamurthy, S. and Schröder, T. (eds.). *Architecture and the smart city*. London: Routledge, pp. 17–28.

Dunn, N. and Cureton, P. (2020). *Future cities: A visual guide*. London: Bloomsbury.

Dunn, N., Cureton, P. and Pollastri, S. (2014). *A visual history of the future*. London: Foresight Government Office for Science, Department of Business Innovation and Skills, HMSO.

Hajer, M. and Versteeg, W. (2019). 'Imagining the post-fossil city: Why is it so difficult to think of new possible worlds?', *Territory, Politics, Governance*, 7(2), pp. 122–134. https://doi.org/10.1080/21622671.2018.1510339

Haraway, D. (2016). *Staying with the trouble: Making kin in the Chthulucene*. Durham, NC: Duke University Press.

Kwartler, M. and Longo, G. (2008). *Visioning and visualization: People, pixels, and plans*. Cambridge, MA: Lincoln Institute of Land Policy.

Law, J. and Urry, J. (2004). 'Enacting the social', *Economy and Society*, 33(3), pp. 390–410.

Miller, R. (2018). 'Sensing and making-sense of Futures Literacy. Towards a Futures Literacy Framework'. In Miller, R. (ed.) *Transforming the Future: Anticipation in the 21st Century*. London: Routledge, pp. 15–50.

Morton, T. (2016). *Dark ecology: The logic of future coexistence*. New York: Columbia University Press.

Oreskes, N. and Conway, E.M. (2014). *The collapse of western civilization: A view from the future*. New York: Columbia University Press.

Polak, F. (1973). *The image of the future*. Trans. E. Boulding. Amsterdam: Elsevier Scientific Publishing Company.

Pollastri, S., Dunn, N., Rogers, C., Bokyo, C., Cooper, R. and Tyler, N. (2018). 'Envisioning urban futures as conversations to inform design and research', *Proceedings of the Institution of Civil Engineers – Urban Design and Planning*, 171(4), pp. 146–156.

Porritt, J. (2013). *The world we made*. London: Phaidon.

Puig de la Bellacasa, M. (2017). *Matters of care: Speculative ethics in more than human worlds*. Posthumanities. Minnesota, MN: University of Minnesota Press.

Rancière, J. (2009 [2000]). *The politics of aesthetics*. Trans. G. Rockhill. New York: Continuum.

Rogers, C. (2018). 'Engineering future liveable, resilient, sustainable cities using foresight', *Proceedings of the Institution of Civil Engineers – Civil Engineering*, 171(6), pp. 3–9.

Rose, G. (2018). 'Look Inside™: Corporate visions of the smart city'. In Fast, K., Jansson, A., Lindell, J., Ryan Bengtsson, L. and Tesfahuney, M. (eds.). *Geomedia Studies: Spaces and Mobilities in Mediatized Worlds*. New York: Routledge, pp. 97–113.

Sand, M. (2019). 'On "not having a future"', *Futures*, 107, pp. 98–106. https://doi.org/10.1016/j.futures.2019.01.002

Slaughter, R.A. (1997). 'Developing and applying strategic foresight', *ABN Report*, 5(10), pp. 13–27.
Söderström, O., Paasche, T. and Klauser, F. (2014). 'Smart cities as corporate storytelling', *City*, 18(3), pp. 307–320.
Swilling, M. (2020). *The age of sustainability: Just transitions in a complex world*. Routledge Studies in Sustainable Development. Oxon: Routledge.
Urry, J. (2016). *What is the future?* Cambridge: Polity.
Voros, J. (2003). 'A generic foresight process framework', *Foresight*, 5(3), pp. 10–21.
Williams, R.J. (2019). *Why cities look the way they do*. Cambridge: Polity.

29
Walking futures
Following in the footsteps of mobility pioneers

Farzaneh Bahrami

Introduction

We as a species have been used to walking far greater distances than we currently walk on an average basis in contemporary cities. Humans are genetically adapted to profoundly different patterns of daily physical activities with considerably higher energy expenditure. The recent shift to an indoor and largely inactive lifestyle has been abrupt in terms of an evolutionary timescale (Christie, 2018). Our hunter-gatherer genetic legacy has shaped our body poorly for sitting, only a little better for standing, but unrivalled for walking. However, the current spatial organization of our lives in cities largely undermines the capacities of the healthy human being as a 'walking animal' and therefore diminishes the potential benefits for both cities and their inhabitants.

The dominantly inactive urban lifestyle of the twenty-first century is at odds with our Palaeolithic genome (O'Keefe and Cordain, 2004). Insufficient physical activity, according to the World Health Organization, is currently the fourth highest risk factor for mortality rates across the world and acts as a considerable driving force behind the rising trend of obesity, coronary heart disease, stroke, several types of cancer, diabetes mellitus, gallbladder disease, gout and several pulmonary diseases worldwide (WHO, 2011). Yet, to reduce radically and significantly many of the above-mentioned health risks one does not need to be a professional athlete or even a particularly sporty individual. The health gain per unit of energy expenditure is far greater for sedentary people than for those who are already very physically active (Kyu et al., 2016). This implies that by introducing modest levels of physical activity into the routines of the inactive population, like daily walks, a huge gain can be made in terms of global public health. With this assumption, targeting inactive or insufficiently active populations, academic research and policy efforts aimed at encouraging physical activity have often focussed on promoting walking and cycling for short trips (Pooley et al., 2013).

Nevertheless, walking is not spread equally across countries, nor is it within societies. Some people walk long distances, but little is known about this potentially significant niche practice. In Switzerland, for example, the average person walks around 1.8–1.9 kilometre per day. Yet, this average conceals surprising discrepancies: While over one-third of all the inhabitants do not walk at all in public space as a daily routine, around 13% of the population walk at least 5 kilometre every day (Christie, 2018, p. 89). In the United Kingdom, people walk 16 minutes per day on average according to the National Travel Survey (2019). However, the results of the Active Lives Surveys – that are based on respondents remembering how many days they have walked in the last 28 days and for how long – open another perspective. While more than 20% of the respondents have not walked at all on most days, another 20% of the surveyed population have usually walked more than two hours on a regular day (Department for Transport, 2020).[1]

Who are long-distance walkers? Why and where do they walk? What motivates their walks? How have they developed such a habit, and how do they fit walking into their daily schedules? Scattered academic work has attempted answering these questions. In a qualitative approach, Christie (2018) focussed on 'individuals who walk for an hour or more in public space on most days of the week' in the Geneva-Lausanne area of Switzerland, concluding that concern with personal health, pleasure and well-being are key motivators for long-distance walking. An earlier study by America Walks looked into the attitudes and behaviours of 'Frequent Walkers' – defined as individuals who reported walking at least 3–4 days a week. The survey suggested that 10% of their studied sample ($n = 7,019$) walk for more than one full hour each day, and health benefits appeared to be the main motivation for this group of walkers even when walking was their means of transportation (Reilly, 2011).

Positive attitudes towards walking can be interpreted in the frame of the increasing value of physical effort and its integration in daily routines (Bahrami and Rigal, 2017; Cook, 2020), and within the larger context of the 'emergence of new cultures of mobility' characterized by increasing rates of walking and cycling in cities (Sheller, 2011). This coincides with an increase in the use of digital self-tracking devices and mobile health technologies for routinizing health habits and tracking personal objectives (Presset et al., 2020). A distinction has to be made between voluntary and involuntary pedestrians, between having the opportunity to choose to walk for health motivations and walking due to poverty or lack of transport options. The weak association between the quality of the built environment and walking rates in neighbourhoods with lower socio-economic status (Steinmetz-Wood and Kestens, 2015) can suggest where walking may not be a choice.

The social meanings and functional roles of walking have been redefined constantly throughout its long history. This chapter examines the hypothesis that the share of walking could radically increase in future cities and voluntary long-distance walking could become a wider practice. In what follows, I will first offer a reminder of the changing status of walking, its rise and decline in Europe and suggest that a shift is possible and timely. Further, I present three snapshots of the daily experiences of long-distance walking pioneers in different geographic contexts, for whom walking is not a profession, nor are they highly skilled athletes or walking activists. Walking is rather their mode of transportation. Presenting these instances is an attempt to depict a possible future, hoping that 'the possible can give the real a sense of direction, an orientation, a path to the horizon' (Lefebvre, 2003, p. 45).

Walking: Changing status

The extent, intensity and function of walking, as well as its social meanings, have constantly changed throughout its long history, from our hunter-gatherer ancestors' long walks to its practice in contemporary cities. Although an essentially practical, and often overlooked, means of locomotion, walking has been invested with different symbolic meanings, and has been praised or despised at different times.

A pedestrian is someone who travels on foot. Historically, however, the term has conveyed pejorative metaphorical senses such as 'lacking inspiration; dull'. To be pedestrian was to be unimaginative or commonplace, 'as if plodding along on foot rather than speeding on horseback or by coach' (Merriam Webster). Until the late eighteenth century, walking along the public roads often signified that one was either a pauper or a footpad (Solnit, 2001). The peons, pawns and پیاده [2] had been at the bottom of a hierarchical system, and had long dreamt of escaping the humiliation of having to use their own body to move in space (Lévy, 2008). The perception of walking changed with the transport revolution and the advent of trains, as travel in general became easier and more affordable. Since the common person did not need to travel by walking, walking came across as a voluntary and pleasurable experience, rather than an economic necessity. 'As walking became a matter of choice, it became a possible positive choice' (Wallace, 1994, p. 62).

In his book *Romantic Writing and Pedestrian Travel*, Jarvis (1997) suggests that, besides changes in transport infrastructure, deliberate social nonconformity and oppositionality constituted the early expeditions of pedestrians, as in the writings and walks of English poets Dorothy and William Wordsworth in the northern English countryside, which established walking as an aesthetic practice (Jarvis, p. 27). In France and Switzerland, likewise, people walked and climbed mountains. The summit of Mont Blanc was reached in 1786. The Genevan philosopher, Jean Jacques Rousseau, wrote extensively about his walks and mind-body-place relations. While in the early Romantic period, cross-country walking emerged as a literary motif, cities also transformed to accommodate new urban walking by the deployment of sidewalks, promenades, plantations and park systems (Forestier, 1906; Loir et al., 2011).

Failing to compete with the comfort and speed of the car, pedestrians were looked down upon again during the first half of the twentieth century. Two parallel processes started to converge around walking from the 1950s: On the one hand, the increasing awareness and the emerging body of research on the health benefits of physical activity (e.g. Morris et al., 1953), and, on the other hand, the critiques of car urbanism by advocates of public space, such as Jane Jacobs. These processes started independently but converged down the road to shape new interdisciplinary fields. The notion of active mobility, that is travel based on metabolic energy as opposed to motorized means, advocated and created an alliance between transportation, public health and public space.

The revival of walking, which planned for a transition from 'all-car', underestimated the need for and the capacity of the healthy human body to walk. The considerations for human scale in cities in this period acknowledged 'the right of the individual over the tyranny of mechanical tools' (CIAM, 1952) but concentrated specifically on the 'heart of the city', namely, the limited perimeters of city centres as civic landscapes to be protected from car traffic.[3] Hence, the earlier (pre-car) plans for promenades and park systems with continuous pedestrian (and bicycle) networks connecting the city and the country were abandoned in favour of pedestrian precincts, traffic-free shopping cores (Buchanan, 1963; Gruen, 1964) and pedestrian pockets (Calthrope, 1993).

Mobility pioneers

Is it possible to reimagine the role and place of walking in contemporary cities? How can we stimulate a shift in walking scales and lengths towards a future where walking longer distances becomes a common practice and a healthy routine for many? For some, this is already the case. During the last few years of research on sustainability transitions and futures of mobility, I have encountered several 'mobility pioneers', individuals who already live in post-car worlds, who constantly innovate in their daily patterns of mobility and, with a socially and environmentally desirable practice, pioneer change. Presenting instances of the lives of three long-distance walkers, I propose to reconsider walking as a wild card of social mobility futures, suggesting that a radical advancement in walking is possible and it can become as much of a breakthrough for future cities as technological measures such as autonomous driving and delivery drones. Rather than focussing on one single research project, I take the subjects from different geographic contexts in order to outline a more general global perspective. These projects were defined by different scopes and varied in their data collection methods. Nevertheless, they all employed qualitative interviews with local residents probing their mobility practices and aspirations.

The first interview was conducted as a part of an ongoing study that aims at providing an understanding of frequent walkers in the Greater London area through semi-structured qualitative interviews. The ultimate objective is to bring the research outcomes to a wider audience through a medium-length documentary film.[4] The second interview was conducted as part of background research for a documentary film that explored the relation between mobility infrastructures and mobility behaviour in the context of the recent urban transformations in the city of Tehran, Iran. The film, *Blue Barrier* (2018), was supported by the *Post-Car World,* a Swiss National Science Foundation project,[5] and was screened at the *Art and Experience* cinemas in Iran between May and October 2019. The third interview is derived from the *Post-Car World* project itself (2013–2017), an interdisciplinary research project that explored the future of mobility through the role of the car in Switzerland.[6] The three snapshots open up windows onto the daily practices and motivations of Sophie, Sadeq and Jacques who live in London, Tehran and Lausanne, respectively.

London

Acceptable and preferred walking distances vary by destination and in relation to the purpose of the walk, but also within different spatial contexts and cultures of mobility. In London, the average walking distance for people without mobility impairment in 2019 was estimated to be about 1 kilometre, less than one-ninth of most journeys recorded over a century ago (Self, 2012; Transport for London 2019). In 1851, London was already extended over 51.8 square kilometres, and public transport was not always an option.[7] Even before the First World War, there are reports of long commutes of workers, for example, living in Kennington and walking to and from Finsbury Park every day (Armstrong, 2000). Regarding walking inequalities and privileges, Gilbert and Southall (2000) argue that in the early nineteenth century walking longer distances was the privilege of those who could afford to separate their locations of work and home. In Dickens' London, for example, it was possible for the clerk in *Great Expectations* to work in the city and walk home to the then-greenery of Walworth every day (about 7 kilometre round trip).[8]

The subsequent decline of walking towards the end of the twentieth century is now being reversed slowly and unspectacularly. The substantial growth in the amount of travel in London since early 2000 – corresponding to population growth – has been together with a consistent shift in mode share away from the private car towards walking, cycling and public transport, broadly reflecting investment in these modes. The current target is set to increase the share of active and efficient modes from 63% in 2019 to 80% by 2041 with strong expected growth in walking and cycling (Transport for London, 2019).

Sophie (Accountant, 33) has lived in London since 2008 and has walked to work on most days ever since. She has changed residence and office locations a few times but her journeys (round trip) have remained constant at about 10 kilometre or more. She has contributed to the growth of travel in London but also to the recent trend towards active and efficient transport. She walks from home close to Tower Bridge to her office in Marble Arch for a round trip of more than 12 kilometre, most days of the week. On Mondays and Thursdays, she extends her walk in the afternoon to Highbury and Islington for Pilates sessions, adding another 6 kilometre to her total daily journey on foot. Walking was not an abrupt decision or a new discovery for Sophie. 'We always walked a lot with my father, always had dogs and used to take long walks together'. However, it was not until moving to London that walking became her main way of getting around in the big city. 'There I started to realize you can get almost anywhere if you walk'. The initial concern was turning up at work in trainers. 'For a long time, I used to change my shoes at work. Now I know it's not a problem. Nobody cares about my shoes'.

Walking is a reliable way to get around London, not just pleasant but very practical as well. 'When you leave on time, you know you arrive on time'. It requires easy scheduling. 'You have very good visibility on how long your journey takes'. Sophie compares this punctuality with car trips in and around London, which depend on unforeseeable or uncontrollable variables. Unlike many other frequent walkers in London, she does not use tracking applications or measure the daily calories burnt off from walking. 'I know I walk a lot! And I do not need to motivate myself'. She walks throughout all seasons. 'I cannot let the weather plan for me, plus on a rainy day, to be honest, I'd rather walk than being in the humid public transport'.

Sophie describes a highly active travel time, besides the physical activity in itself: Radio 4 in the mornings, reflections and preparation for the day, audiobooks and phone calls.

> I even used to read fiction books while walking, properly carrying a book! I never bumped into anyone, never had an accident, or stepped on dog poo. But for some reason I could only do this with fiction, plus carrying the heavy book was not very practical. Then I discovered *audible* and that is what I do now.

She explains her plan to start an MBA degree next year. Initially, it did not seem very feasible to her as she was about 200 hours short of the expected study time. Until she learnt that over 80% of the course material was going to be available to listen to as online lectures. 'That gives me back 200 hours easy! I have that time when I walk'. She explains why this is not an option on a bike or while driving. 'I think you should not be distracted while you drive. You should not even be wearing headphones on a bike I would say'. The cognitive effort of walking safely in coordination with the environment is not comparable to other modes. 'Walking is like being on autopilot'. She values the continuity in a walking journey and hence the concentration that comes with it, as opposed to various stages of a journey on public transport.

When walking relatively longer distances – like a recent 12 miles walk to a friend's place in the Borough of Bromley – she does not meander and takes Google's suggestions for the shortest route, unless that is along a major traffic road. She wishes to have a route-finding mobile application to avoid air pollution. Normally, she tries to walk through parks and green spaces as much as possible, as she worries the exposure to pollution might outweigh the health benefits of walking. She finds London quite generous in that regard. London, indeed, is rich in terms of natural and green capital. The metropolis hosts nearly as many trees as inhabitants (Wood, 2019), and it is recognized by the UK Forestry Commission as the world's largest urban forest.

Tehran

Tehran, like London, has above eight million inhabitants, and both cities struggle with environmental challenges like air pollution. While London has sought a transition from car dominance especially in central boroughs, Tehran, over the past few decades, has constructed 500 kilometre of highways and about 350 grade intersections and overpasses through a programme known as the 'Highway Construction Movement'. From a walking city at the end of the nineteenth century, Tehran expanded rapidly beyond its walls. Establishing its first traffic regulation document for horse carriages in 1938, in the 1960s it was already radically transforming to accommodate the proliferating cars. In this period, highways and monumental roundabouts began to replace the old urban fabric. While at the same time, boulevards and high streets emerged to host urban strollers, providing space for this new urban pastime. Walking, being a fundamental component of public space, was neglected in post-revolution plans where public life and public appearance were not a priority. During the last few decades, Tehran has disproportionately invested in car infrastructures, and pedestrianizing projects have been sporadic and have created isolated destinations rather than a vision for the walkable city. Nevertheless, recently, walking as a way of urban life, reclaiming public space, is gaining interest and investment from independent initiatives and walking communities in Tehran such as the NGO Bahamestan (https://bahamestan.net/), which has campaigned for pedestrian rights, spaces, accessibility and safety, within the broader scope of the right to the city since 2012.

Sadeq (Taxi driver, 52) walks across the city of Tehran through what is often a hostile car-dominant environment. He is an airport taxi driver, driving from the airport, 50 kilometres south of the city through its most congested areas. Nevertheless, Sadeq walks everywhere when he is off work. He walks from his home in the centre-north (Sohrevardi area) to visit his daughter close to the railway station area in the south (Rah-Ahan). Part of this 10-km journey is a pleasant walk through the old fabric of the city. He walks straight down *Vali-asr,* the longest street in the Middle East that stretches from the northernmost part of the city at the foot of the mountains to the railway station in the south, with large and generous sidewalks lined with sycamore trees. Sadeq contrasts this pleasant bit of his journey to the times he walks along the green shoulder of highways or on the narrow platforms inside tunnels. 'To reach my in-laws, for example, I need to cross a highway, I have to make a long detour to take a pedestrian overpass, or simply walk along with cars inside the tunnel'. Sadeq knows different tunnels of the city by their characteristics of walkability, their length, level of pollution and the efficiency of their ventilation system. He explains 'you can walk through some of them, but others are death tunnels. You won't exit alive from the other side'. Despite the challenging environment, he finds walking relaxing and finds a balance with his intensive driving hours as a taxi driver. 'In walking I find refuge from the traffic that we create ourselves'.

Walking is efficient and practical. 'It is not necessarily slower than driving if you travel during the rush hour'. In one of his walks along a congested highway, he started a conversation with a driver whose speed was low enough to engage in a conversation.

> He offered me to hop on, I thanked him and said I preferred to walk. We overpassed each other a few times during the next half an hour or so. At the end, he said he wished he was walking too.

Sadeq associates walking with a sense of freedom, in stark contrast to the moments he spends in his taxi. When asked about gadgets, applications or specific instruments for his walks,

Sadeq underlines the importance of shoes. 'You have no idea how far a good pair of shoes can take you', he says. 'It is not about what you need, but everything that you do not need to carry with you'. Emphasizing on the essential lightness of the traveller, he underlines the psychological benefits of walking for him.

Sadeq was hesitant to reveal that he started his long-distance walks in Tehran after the second time he had been to Karbala for pilgrimage. The Arbaeen pilgrimage, or Arbaeen walk, is a religious ritual for the commemoration of the 40th day of the martyrdom of a Shia Imam. It is known as the world's largest annual pilgrimage as millions of Shia Muslims make their journey to the city of Karbala in Iraq on foot. Walking from different distances and origins, most people cover the 80 kilometre between Najaf and Karbala in four to five days. Sadeq, however, walks from an Iran-Iraq border terminal for about 300 kilometre over many days. Sadeq describes this physically demanding journey, across rough terrain and sometimes during very hot summer days, as a rewarding experience. 'Those 30 days per year were my only time off work. I used to work hard to earn those days. It was the time for myself, to reflect and to improve, to enjoy my solitude'. Sadeq describes the pilgrimage as a transformative and pleasant experience, which triggered his long-distance walks in Tehran.

Lausanne

Leisure walks along iconic trails is the Swiss people's most preferred outdoor and sport activity. Protected by the Swiss constitution and a federal law, a network of 66,000 walking trails with unified signalization characterizes the Swiss countryside and mountains, starting from 1934 when the *Fédération suisse de tourisme pédestre* (now *SwissRando*) was founded. Positioned within this context, the city of Lausanne hosts about 350 hectares of parks, gardens and promenades within its urban area, making it proportionally one of the greenest cities in the world and a great place for walking. According to the federal mobility survey,[9] the share of walking as a transport mode in Canton Vaud, where Lausanne is the capital city, has been increasing in a consistent but modest trend during the last two decades. In the city centres of Lausanne and Geneva, families are increasingly abandoning cars; four out of ten families move around without a private car and nearly 50% of all trips are carried out by walking. However, as we move further from the centres, the number of carless families drops to less than one household per ten. Despite the persisting prevalence of car ownership in lower-density areas, the share of walking is increasing.

Jacques (Journalist, 64) lives in the city centre of Lausanne in Switzerland. He combines long walks and train journeys to reach every corner of the country. His mobility patterns reflect the specific territorial organization of the country, characterized by connectivity within extended and layered conditions of inhabitability. In 1990, André Corboz already conceptualized Switzerland as a metropolis, describing it as a 'Großstadt in formation from St Gallen to Geneva' (Vigano et al., 2015). In terms of population, the country compares to metropolises like London and Tehran and is marked by its strong commuting patterns, where over 70% of employed population commute to another commune from the one in which they live every day.

Jacques stopped driving 35 years ago. The decision was triggered by a car accident but was formed gradually by an aversion to what Jacques describes as an expanding consumerist culture at the time. 'So, I told myself, let's make something positive come out of this accident'. From that moment, he has comfortably relied on the combination of public transport and his long walks, while conducting a very mobile lifestyle as a journalist. He explains that he has been on day trips to Zurich, Neuchatel and Vevey this week. 'I won't walk to Neuchatel obviously, but Vevey? Maybe'. Vevey is a small city, 18 kilometre east of Lausanne by the lake. A few days earlier Jacques went there for a work meeting. He has walked the first 6 kilometre along the lake before taking the train and did the same on his way back. He emphasizes that it makes about 12 kilometre walk along an exceptionally scenic landscape, while saving 1.8 Swiss francs twice on the train ticket.

Jacques credits the long mountain hikes with his family as a kid for his passion for walking today. 'Sometimes I found it a bit hard, but still I had a certain pleasure'. He considers himself privileged for having access to such outstanding natural capital. In Lausanne, Jacques walks everywhere. The distances covered are relatively short for his standards but the city's topographic features pose a challenge, which makes it worthwhile. In recent years, walking has also been a substitute sport for him and the physical effort is a rewarding experience. 'An uphill road is not an obstacle, but rather an achievement. Even on the ski slopes, he sometimes climbs with his ski gear instead of taking the ski lift Jacques reminds that he saves 2.40 Swiss francs every time he walks in the city instead of taking public transport. 'Of course, it wears out the soles of my shoes, but I spend on shoes voluntarily'. Jacques underlines the importance of shoes, the only consumer product that he does not mind spending on.

Discussion: Walking as a wild card of mobility futures

Sophie, Sadeq and Jacques walk in very different spatial conditions, and their walks are differently motivated. Sadeq walks as an act of dissidence. Questioning the existing order, he refuses to take part in 'the perpetuating traffic that is ourselves', transcending the limits set by the spatial configuration of his city. Sophie's search for originality is combined with a pragmatism that underlies her highly productive commutes, while for Jacques walking is a politically and economically driven lifestyle. A common ground across the three stories is the sensory and embodied experience of walking in their past. Before adopting walking as their means of transport, they had a 'formative trip' either in its archetypal form as a pilgrimage or in other stages of their lives. A formative trip – transforming the traveller – offers initiation experiences that can open up possibilities and lead to a learning process (Rigal, 2019). Our mobility potentials are also determined by our competences and skills (Kaufmann et al., 2004). While walking is the most common way of getting around, practising long-distance walking and integrating it into daily schedules is a competence that can be acquired, trained and put into 'practice' (Sloterdijk, 2014).

Besides the personal pleasure of walking, the emphasis on the stimulus to mind-body relations and the fundamental health factor, the protagonists of the three snapshots briefly surveyed in this chapter qualify walking as a reliable and resilient means of transport. Walking does not come across necessarily as a slow mode; it is not praised for its slowness. On the contrary, it is put against the relative low efficiency of the alternatives, which in highly urban contexts (Tehran and London) are also likely to save unremarkable amounts of time. This is especially in the range of distances that can be covered on foot, a radius reaching to about an hour, which corresponds to a general constant travel time-budget as proposed by Zahavi (1974). While the limited range of walking is considered as its main disadvantage in the literature (van Soest et al., 2019), re-evaluating walkability potentials by putting into perspective distances that healthy adults can cover, how it compares to the alternatives and what it means from a public health standpoint can constitute both a research agenda and a public policy pathway. Long-distance walking has to be recognized and empowered in order to be able to contribute to the processes of transition towards more sustainable and healthy modes of travel. Research agendas for better understanding avid walkers can potentially bring such niche practice to a broader discourse, seeking to encourage it through supporting infrastructures and policies and facilitate greater changes in travel behaviours by focussing on social norms and altering the 'perceptions of normality' (Pooley et al., 2013).

Increasing walking is a deceptively simple instrument capable of addressing unremitting health challenges in cities, while simultaneously reshaping them towards more environmentally and socially sustainable futures. The surge in walking during the 2020 pandemic, as a part of a general increase in outdoor physical activities[10], can potentially serve as an initiation experience, sustain and develop into new mobility habits. A radical increase in the length and duration of urban walking could potentially displace the standards that currently guide transport planning and could bring about a paradigm shift with considerable impact on public transport systems whose running times, frequencies and network configuration are defined by assumptions on 'acceptable walking distances' for their users. Projecting such futures entails the democratization of walking, the rediscovery of the pedestrian as the transcalar, fundamental element of mobility and walking as an essential 'preventive medicine' (Tudor-Locke, 2012).

Notes

1. The declared time in this case is 'the total time the respondents most regularly or frequently walked on each day. It is not the average time they spent on walking on those days'.
2. پیاده: *Piâdeh* in Persian means pedestrian, on foot, as opposed to riding a horse or a carriage, from *Pâi–* or *Pâ* for foot (Dehkhoda Encyclopedic Dictionary).
3. CIAM VIII (Congrès internationaux d'architecture moderne), 1951, *The Heart of the City: towards the humanization of urban life,* Hoddesdon, England.
4. 'Learning from Frequent Walkers: motivations, practices, and spaces' (2020–2021) in collaboration with Active Travel Academy, University of Westminster http://blog.westminster.ac.uk/ata/visiting-fellows-2020/farzaneh/
5. *Blue Barrier* (2018) was screened, among other public screenings, at *AlternatiYve Festival, Voyages et Transports Ecologiques* in Yverdon, Switzerland 2018. https://vimeo.com/280947137
6. The interviews were conducted in collaboration with the research team of the 'Post-Car World' project (2013–2017) in French and in German and have been translated here to English. https://archiveweb.epfl.ch/postcarworld.epfl.ch/
7. As late as 1897, a questionnaire of 160,000 trade unionists resident in south London disclosed that well over three-quarters used no public transport for journeys to and from work.
8. Gilbert and Southall explain what prevented such a separation for the poor, and kept them penned into crowded slums, was not lack of transport but poverty and insecurity: a family that must often depend on the generosity of others cannot afford to live among strangers. Highly localized contact networks were crucial to survival (Gilbert and Southall, 2008, p. 626); moreover, long working hours expected of them left no time to spare on regular journeys (Armstrong, 2000).
9. Office fédéral de la statistique suisse, ARE – Microrecensement mobilité et transports – MRMT (2015).
10. See for example: A YouGov survey on impact of Covid-19 on transportation with an increase in walking from 11% to 17% https://docs.cdn.yougov.com/x4waef2cdw/ECF_TransportSurvey_October2020_w1.pdf, and released Strava data showing an increase in outdoor exercise in 2020 where it was allowed https://www.strava.com/yis-community-2020.

Bibliography

Armstrong, J. (2000). 'From Shillibeer to Buchanan: Transport and the urban environment'. In Daunton, M. (ed.). *Cambridge urban history of Britain*, vol. 3, 1840–1950 (pp. 229–257). Cambridge: Cambridge University Press.

Bahrami, F. and Rigal, A. (2017). 'Spaces of effort, exploration of an experience of mobility', *Applied Mobilities*, 2(1), pp. 85–99.

Buchanan, C. (1963). 'Traffic in towns: A study of the long-term problems of traffic in urban areas', reports of the Steering Group and Working Group appointed by the Minister of Transport. HM Stationery Office.

Calthorpe, P. (1993). *The next American metropolis: Ecology, community, and the American dream*. New York: Princeton Architectural Press.

Christie, D.P. (2018). *Frequent walkers: From healthy individual behaviours to sustainable mobility futures* (No. 8506 THESIS). EPFL.

Cook, S. (2020). *Run-commuting in the UK: The emergence, production and potential of a mobile practice* (Doctoral dissertation, Royal Holloway, University of London).

Department for Transport (2016). CW0304: Usual time spent per day walking or cycling, by purpose and time interval: England (with chart). Retrieved from https://www.gov.uk/government/-statistical-data-sets/walking-and-cycling-statistics-cw#walking-and-cycling-table-index

Forestier, J.C. (1906). *Grandes villes et systèmes de parcs*. Paris: Institut Français d'Architecture (IFA).

Gilbert, D. and Southall, H. (2000). 'The urban labour market'. In Daunton, M. (ed.). *Cambridge urban history of Britain*, vol. 3, 1840–1950 (pp. 593–628). Cambridge: Cambridge University Press.

Gruen, V. (1964). *The heart of our cities. The urban crisis, diagnosis and cure* (1st edition). New York: Simon and Schuster.

International Congress of Modern Architecture (CIAM). Rogers, E.N., Sert, J.L. and Tyrwhitt, J. (1952). *The heart of the city: Towards the humanisation of urban life*. Edited by J. Tyrwhitt, J.L. Sert, E.N. Rogers. [With Illustrations.]. London: Lund Humphries.

Jarvis, R. (1997). *Romantic writing and pedestrian travel*. Cham: Springer.

Kaufmann, V., Bergman, M.M. and Joye, D. (2004). 'Motility: Mobility as capital', *International Journal of Urban and Regional Research*, 28(4), pp. 745–756.

Kesselring, S. (2006). 'Pioneering mobilities: New patterns of movement and motility in a mobile world', *Environment and Planning A*, 38(2), pp. 269–279.

Kyu, H.H., Bachman, V.F., Alexander, L.T., Mumford, J.E., Afshin, A., Estep, K., Veerman, J.L., Delwiche, K., Iannarone, M.L., Moyer, M.L. and Cercy, K. (2016). 'Physical activity and risk of breast cancer, colon cancer, diabetes, ischemic heart disease, and ischemic stroke events', systematic review and dose-response meta-analysis for the Global Burden of Disease Study 2013', bmj, 354, p. i3857.

Lefebvre, H. (2003). *The urban revolution*. Minneapolis: University of Minnesota Press.

Lévy, J. (2008). 'Ville pédestre, ville rapide', *Urbanisme*, 359, pp. 57–59.

Loir, C., Turcot, L., Brault, Y., Lelarge, A., Coquery, N., Borsay, P., Bernard, B., Vanhulst, H., Preyat, F., Dubois, S. and Rommelaere, C. (2011). *La promenade au tournant des XVIIIe et XIXe siècles (Belgique–France–Angleterre)*. Bruxelles: Editions de l'Université de Bruxelles.

Morris, J.N., Heady, J.A., Raffle, P.A.B., Roberts, C.G. and Parks, J.W. (1953). 'Coronary heart-disease and physical activity of work', *The Lancet*, 262(6796), pp. 1111–1120.

O'Keefe Jr., J.H. and Cordain, L. (2004) 'January. Cardiovascular disease resulting from a diet and lifestyle at odds with our Paleolithic genome: How to become a twenty-first-century hunter-gatherer'. In *Mayo Clinic Proceedings*, 79(1), pp. 101–108. Elsevier.

Pooley, C.G., Horton, D., Scheldeman, G., Mullen, C., Jones, T., Tight, M., Jopson, A. and Chisholm, A. (2013). 'Policies for promoting walking and cycling in England: A view from the street', *Transport Policy*, 27, pp. 66–72.

Presset, B., Kramer, J.N., Kowatsch, T. and Ohl, F. (2020). 'The social meaning of steps: User reception of a mobile health intervention on physical activity', *Critical Public Health*, pp. 1–12. https://www.tandfonline.com/doi/epub/10.1080/09581596.2020.1725445?needAccess=true

Reilly, M., Bricker, S., Tuckel, P. and Milczarski, W. (2011). National walking survey. Retrieved from https://www.changelabsolutions.org/sites/default/files/documents/National_Walking_Survey.Sept_.2011.pdf

Rigal, A. (2019). 'Formative trip, mobile lives forum'. Accessed on 15 Oct. 2020. Retrieved from https://en.forumviesmobiles.org/marks/formative-trip-12955

Self, W. (2012). 'Walking is political', *The Guardian*, Accessed 10 Dec. 2020. Retrieved from https://www.theguardian.com/books/2012/mar/30/will-self-walking-cities-foot

Sheller, M. (2011). 'The emergence of new cultures of mobility: Stability, opening and prospects'. In Geels, F.W., Kemp, R., Dudley G. and Lyons, G. (eds.). *Automobility in transition?: A socio-technical analysis of sustainable transport* (pp. 180–202). New York: Routledge.

Sloterdijk, P. (2014). *You must change your life*. Hoboken, NJ: John Wiley & Sons.
Solnit, R. (2001). *Wanderlust: A history of walking*. New York: Penguin.
Steinmetz-Wood, M. and Kestens, Y. (2015). 'Does the effect of walkable built environments vary by neighborhood socioeconomic status?', *Preventive Medicine*, 81, pp. 262–267.
Sussman, A. and Goode, R. (1980). *The magic of walking*. New York: Fireside.
Transport for London. (2019). 'Travel in London', Report 12. Retrieved from http://content.tfl.gov.uk/travel-in-london-report-12.pdf
Tudor-Locke, C. (2012). 'Walk more (frequently, farther, faster): The perfect preventive medicine', *Preventive Medicine*, 55(6), p. 540.
van Soest, D., Tight, M.R. and Rogers, C.D. (2019). 'Exploring the distances people walk to access public transport', *Transport Reviews*, 40(2), pp. 160–182.
Viganò, P., Cavalieri, C., Barcelloni Corte, M., Arnsperger, C. and Lanza, E.C. (2017). 'Rethinking urban form: Switzerland as a "horizontal metropolis"', *Urban Planning*, 2(1), pp. 88–99.
Wallace, A.D. (1994). *Walking, literature, and English culture: The origins and uses of peripatetic in the nineteenth century*. Oxford: Oxford University Press.
WHO World Health Organization (2011). World health report.
Wood, P. (2019). *London is a forest*. South Yarra: Hardie Grant Publishing.
Zahavi, Y. (1974). *Traveltime budgets and mobility in urban areas*. Topeka, KS: Federal Highway Administration.

Index

Note: *Italic* page numbers refer to figures and page numbers followed by "n" denote endnotes.

Abbott, C. 279
abductive reasoning 172, 177–178
Abensour, Miguel-Hervé 295
academic discourse 15n1; *see also* higher education; interdisciplinary approach
accountability 57n8, 101, 154, 170, 177
activism: on climate change 71, 255; eco-dystopian 69; environmental 132; liberation futures work 263–268; pleasure activism 268; scholarship on 164; for social justice 112, 164, 263
actor-network theory (ANT) 190, 244, 249
Adam, Barbara 5, 28, 34n16, 41
Adame, Domingo 161, 163
Adams, V. 172, 177
adaptation: climate change and 93–101; coping 94–95; defined 93–94; development and 94; ecology and 128, 130; incremental 94–95, 98; transformational 95–101
Adey, P. 172
affect: care and 112; futures literacy and 41–43, 48–49; literature and 191; migration and family connections 149–150, 153–154; personal data and 118–119, 123–124; resilience and 190; utopia and 295, 297–299; *see also* emotions
Afghanistan 14
Afrofuturism 10, 260–274, 297, 300
Afro-Queer identity 260–261, 267, 272
Afro-Rithms from the Future (game) 267–268, 268n1
ageing 72
agency 8; anticipation and 39, 66; back-casting and 192–194; concept of 38; of culture 114; desirable futures and 25; futures literacy and 38–49; literature and 189–196; money and 44; multiple futures and 46–49; narrative-driven creativity and 3, 40–43; of nature 131; power and 40, 44; scenarios and 20, 41–42; of visualizations 304–305, 308

agriculture 93, 96–99
Ahmed, Waqas 165
AI (artificial intelligence) 9, 52–57, 120
AI City *211*, 213–214
Aldred, R. 185
algorithms 56, 57n12, 120, 124, 181, 212, 214, 268n1
Aligica, P.D. 242
Allen, William 141
Alliance for Sustainability and Prosperity 138
alterity 7
alternative futures 6, 23–24; agency and 40–41; collaborative future-making and 104–105; literature and 194; stability and 64–65; visual analysis and 301; *see also* multiple futures
Amara, Roy 21
American Psychiatric Association (APA) 199–200
American Walks 315
Anders, Charlie Jane 300n2
Anderson, B. 150, 171–172, 175
Andersson, J. 7
Anscombe, G E.M. 57n9
Ansoff, H. 22
Anthropocene 129, 133, 136
anticipation 6, 59–67; agency and 39, 66; climate change and 177; community and 66–67; inquiries and 170–173, 176–178; living systems and 64–65; loss of 59–60, 66–67; as metacapability 8, 60, 63–67; narrative and 228; prospection and 243; social inequalities and 59–60; socio-environmental conditions and 66; utopia and 296–297
Anticipations (1902) 74
anticipation studies 24, 32, 63–64, 243–245, 249
anticipatory assumptions 42, 47–49
anticipatory knowledge-making 171–172
apocalypse 252, 261, 288
Appadurai, Arjun 59–60, 62–63, 65, 150
Aradau, C. 131
Arcus Foundation 257

325

Index

art: arts-based research 82–90, 119; in urban environment 284–290; *see also* creativity
Arterial Network of African Creative Cities 286
artificial intelligence *see* AI
Art Not Oil Coalition 289
Art of the Long View ([1991]/1996) 23
aspiration: agency and 39–40; capacity for 59–60, 63, 65–66; foregrounded 5; as metacapability 62; migration and 149
Asubpeeschoseewagong Ojibwa 59–60, 66
asylum-seekers 89; *see also* refugees
Atwood, Margaret 300n2
Augé, Marc 5
augmented reality (AR) 212
Augustine 228–229, 231n13
Australia 120, 124, 144–145, 286; Filipino migrants in 9, 148–154
automobiles 14, 180–187, 207–208, 210, 212–213, 316–321
autonomous vehicles (AV) 14, 210, 212–214
autonomy 44–46
autopoiesis 34n15
Avellaneda, Alonso Fernández de 194

back-casting 2, 189, 191–196, 225, 304
Bahamestan 319
Bahrami, Farzaneh 13–14
Bakhtin, Mikhail 299
Balasopoulos, A. 300n4
Bangkok 6
Bangladesh 10–11, 93–101
Bangladesh Climate Change Strategy and Action Plan (BCCSAP) 97
Bangladesh Climate Change Trust Fund (BCCTF) 97
Bangladesh Delta Plan 2100 (BDP2100) 11, 100
Banister, D. 209
Barcelona 282, 286
Batty, M. 242
Bauman, Z. 296
Bayesian techniques 54
Beckert, Jens 3–4, 30
Beer, Stafford 33n3
Behrendt, Frauke 212
Bell, Wendell 3, 20, 29, 225–226, 242, 297–298
Bendor, R. 277
Berardi, Franco 297
Beresheet (lunar probe) 220
Berger, Gaston 21, 24
Berger, P. 33n8
Berlant, Lauren 296
Bezos, Jeff 218
Bianchini, F. 286
bicycles *see* cycling
Big Brother 121
Big Data 309
Big Futures 119

Big History 15n4
Bildungsroman 191–192
biodiversity 128, 136–137
BioFutures 10, 69–77
Biological Time Bomb, The (1968) 73
biomedicine 203
biotechnology 71–74
Bishop, P. 20, 27
Black Atlantic 297
Black Diaspora 260–261; *see also* Afrofuturism
Black Fantastic 261
Black Panther (film) 267
Bloch, Ernst 69, 293, 295–297
Blue Barrier (2018) 317
Boas, Franz 74
Bode, C. 229
Boetto, Heather 159
Bok, Barbara 8
Bookchin, Murray 132
borders 79–90, 207
Borges, Jorge Luis 195
Boudes, T. 170
Boulding, Elise 21, 24
Brand, Stewart 130
Branson, Richard 218
Braun, Rebecca 8
Brave New World (1932) 74
Bregman, R. 298–299, 301n10
Brewster, Liz 10
Bria, Francesca 282
bricolage 182–183, 186–187
Brockwell, Ashley Jay 9
Broderick, Damien 72
Brooks, Lonny Avi 10, 267–268
Brown, Adrienne Maree 268
Bruun, H. 27–28
Burgess, A. 170
Büscher, M. 14, 149
buses 79–90, 181, 208–209, 254
Bush, George W. 171
Bus Stop Nickelsdorf (graphic novel) 79, 86–88, *87*, 90
Butler, Octavia 133n1, 300n2

Cabalquinto, Earvin Charles 9
Caidin, Martin 72
Cairo 235
calculation 54–55
Cambridge Analytica 117
Campbell, John W. 278
cancel culture 164
Candy, Stuart 267–268
capabilities 60–63; relational 66; *see also* metacapabilities
capitalism 130, 137, 281, 296–298; *see also* entrepreneurialism
Caracciolo, M. 230

326

carbon emissions: carbon neutrality 191–192; creative urbanism and 289; transportation-related 14, 180–187, 206–215
Care Quality Commission (CQC) 173
Caribbean region 286
cars *see* automobiles
Carson, Rachel 71
Caspi, A. 199
catastrophe 11, 71, 136, 138, 171, 226–227, 289, 296–297, 309, 311
Cato 141
causal inferences 26
causality 189, 195
Causal Layered Analysis (CLA) 24, 29, 31–32
CAVs (connected autonomous vehicles) 14; *see also* autonomous vehicles
Centre International de la Prospective 21
Certeau, Michel de 299
Cervantes, Miguel de 192–196
change: drivers of 41–42, 47; emotions and 256; possibility of 44–46; practices of 104; *see also* climate change; system change
Chang'e-4 spacecraft 220
Chatterjee, Helen 162
Chermack, Thomas 20, 26, 33n6, 34n11
Cherrett, T. 186
Chesterton, G.K. 74–76
children 41–49
China 124, 214, 220, 238
chivalric romance genre 192–193
choice 14, 54–55, 74, 126, 193, 245–248, 296, 315–316
Chouliaraki, L. 88
Christie, D.P. 315
circulation 237
Cisco 14, 276
cities 11–14; in global South 238–239, 238; mobility systems 14, 314–322; politics and 239–240; taxonomy for visualization of 306; timeline of principle paradigms 307, 310; urban poor and climate change 97; visualization of 12, 304–312; walking and health 314–322; *see also* smart cities; urbanization; urban planning
Civic University Commission 161–162
Civic University model 157
climate change 2, 10–11; activism 71, 255; adaptation and 93–101; anticipation and 177; back-casting and 191–192; Bangladesh and 96–101; biotechnology and 73; creative urbanism and 288; ecology and 129; economics and 136; forecasting and 190; impacts of 5–6, 96–101, 309, 311; poverty and 97, 101; precaution and 171; preparedness and 172; queer liberation future and 265; women and 99–100; *see also* activism; carbon emissions; environmental crises; global warming

Coates, Joseph 23
Cold War 80, 83
collaborative engagement 106–114
collaborative future-making (CFM) 9, 104–114
Collier, S. 172, 174
Collins, T. 20, 27
Collyns, Napier 23
colonization: of outer space 11; in Philippines 150; utopias and 300n4; *see also* extractive industries; First Nations; indigenous peoples
communication technologies 255–256; migrant families and 148–155; smartphones 119, 152, 186; transportation and 208, 212; *see also* data, personal
community: anticipation and 66–67; emergency plans 257; Filipino migrants 153; universities and 161–162
Community Futures School 261
Complementary and Alternative Medicine (CAM) 203
complex anticipatory systems (CAS) 247
composting 109, 280
computers 52, 54, 56, 57n12, 69, 72, 278, 285; *see also* AI (artificial intelligence); data, personal; digital technologies; Turing Machine
Comte, Auguste 28
configuration 228
connectedness 128; *see also* interconnectedness
connection 140, 145
consciousness 54–55, 57n7, 72
conservation 2, 12, 128, 130, 132–133
constraint 44–46, 61, 74, 271
consumption 5, 112, 129, 208–209, 213, 236
contingency 131, 209–210, *211*
Cook, Julia 41
Cooper, D. 299
Copenhagen 213
coping adaptation 94–95
co-production 2, 252, 254, 282
Corboz, André 320
coronavirus *see* COVID-19 pandemic
corporate futures 1; rationality and 32; scenario planning and 22–30
Costa, L. 203
counterfactual visioning 225
COVID-19 pandemic: economic system and 137; mental health and 49; mobility and 14, 90, 184, 214–215, 322; place and 311; publics and 253
Coyle, Geoff 33n7
Crace, Jim 300n2
Craftivist Collective 112
Creating Change conference 261, 266–268
Creative Cities Network 285
creative class 12, 285, 287
creative destruction 130

327

creative economy 285
creative urbanism 284–290
creativity: material cultures of mobility and 186–187; meanings of 286; visioning and 304; *see also* imagination; visionary futures
Cremin, C. 289
Crews, C. 25
critical and epistemological futures studies 24
critical imagination 9, 104–114; *see also* imagination
critical utopia 278–281, 282n1
cross-impact analysis 26
cruelty 261–263; 'cruel optimism' 296
Crumb, Robert 126–133, *127*
cryonics 72
culture: cities and 284–290; modern 59–60; shared practices and ideals 65; social futures and 15
Culture Unstained 289
Currie, Mark 229–230
Curry, Andrew 8, 16n5, 26, 50n2, 189
Cyborg (1972) 72
cycling 181–182, 184–186, 207, 209, 212–213, 314–317
cyclones 97–98

Damjanov, Katarina 11
Dark Ecology 133
Darwin, Charles 69–72, 75, 128
data, personal 9, 117–124; agency and 44; authoritarian digital cities and 213–214; cities and 309; smart cities and 12, 276–277; transport planning 186
datafication 9, 117–124
Data Personas project 118–124
dataveillance 117–124
Dator, James 24, 39, 226–227
Davies, Russell T. 72
Davis, J. 246
Dawkins, Richard 75
Declaration on Environment and Development (UN) 171
decolonial methodologies 165
Deep Ecology 132–133
deep time 6
deficit model 40, 199
defuturing 6
de Goede, M. 171
de Grey, Aubrey 69, 72, 76
de Jouvenel, Bertrand 5, 13, 16n5, 21, 228
Delany, Samuel 279
Deleuze, Gilles 82
Delhi 235–236
democracy 107–108
Dennett, D. 57n9
Descartes, René 132
design and experiential futures 32

desirable futures 25, 119, 292–293; *see also* utopias
de Sousa Santos, Boaventura 159
development 11–12; adaptation and 94; climate change and 97; collaboration and 107–108; creative economy and 286
Dewey, John 90n1
Dhaka 6
Diagnostic and Statistical Manual of Mental Disorders (DSM-III) 199
diagnostic inferences 26
Dialectic of Sex, The (1970) 74
Dickens, Charles 317
Dietrich, R. 229
diffraction 244
digital technologies: migrant families and 148–155; visual cities and 308–309; *see also* communication technologies; computers; data, personal
dignity 10, 52, 61–63, 139, 145
Dinardi, Cecilia 12
Dingwall, R. 170
disabilities 61, 209, 263
DiSalvo, C. 255
disempowerment 43–44
displacement 239, 287; forced 14, 90; *see also* refugees
Dispossessed, The (Le Guin) 279, 300n1
dispossession 13, 234, 237
disruption 253–258
Disturbance Ecology 130–131
diversity 128–130, 142, 163, 166, 260–261, 305, 309, 311; *see also* biodiversity
divination 6, 190
Doctorow, Cory 300n1
Don Quixote (Cervantes) 192–196
DoR (discourses of relational thinking) 244, 246–247
Douglas Aircraft Corporation 21
drawings 82–88
Dubai 238
Dunagan, J.F. 268
Dunn, Nick 12–13
dystopias 11; biology and 69–74; Cervantes and 194; creative urbanism and 288; eco-dystopianism 71; in fiction 46, 294, 300n2; personal data and 119; smart cities as 12; *see also* utopias

Easterling, Keller 277
eco-dystopianism 71
eco-feminism 132
Ecological Cities *307*, 307–308, 310
ecological citizenship 110–112
Ecological Disaster 126–131, 133
ecology 2, 10–11, 126–133; climate change impacts on 96–98 (*see also* climate change);

environment and 128–129; sustainable ecological capacity (SEC) 62–63, 66; see also environmental crises
ecomodernization 208–209
economic inequality 136–137; see also poverty; social inequalities; wealth
economy 1; borders and 80; ecology and 130; forecasting and 3–5; human needs and *139*; large-scale system change 136–146; social futures and 15; well-being and 4, 136–146, 201; see also development; financial crises; political economy
eco-social model 159–160
Ecotopian Solution 126, 131–133
Edelman, Lee 301n7
Edelman Trust Barometer Report 137
education see higher education
Edwards, C. 300n2
eight thresholds theory 15n4
Einstein, Albert 28
Eklund, E. 27
elites 141, 158; kinetic 209–210, 215
Elliott, D. 170
emergencies 90; community plans for 257; publics and 253–258
emotions: change and 256; mental health and 201–202; regulation of 64–65; see also affect
empirical futures 25
employment 97, 120, 141, 237, 264–265; see also unemployment
Ending Aging (2007) 69, 72
Engels, Friedrich 294
Enlightenment 132, 296
entrepreneurialism 107, 151, 153–154, 212, 216, 218, 238, 285, 290; see also capitalism
environmental crises: precautionary principle and 171; scenario planning and 22; see also climate change; global warming; pollution
environmentalism 132; see also activism
Environment of Evolutionary Adaptation (EEA) 75–76
epistemic injustice 159–160
epistemology 9, 20, 24–25, 48, 107, 159, 164–166, 171, 216, 242–243, 246; see also knowledge
equality 2; see also social inequalities; social justice
EQUALITY Act (U.S.) 264
Erikson, Kai 59–60, 63, 66
escapism 11, 298
ethnicity see race and ethnicity
eugenics 74–75
Eugenics and Other Evils (Chesterton, 1922) 74
Eurodac 88
Europe: border crossings 80–81 (see also borders); creative cities 285–286; universities 158 (see also universities); see also specific countries and cities in Europe
European Commission 3
European Environment Agency 27
European Food Safety Authority (EFSA) 73
European Space Agency (ESA) 220
eventualities, urban 233–240
evolution 70–71, 75–76, 128, 130, 165
evolutionary psychologists (EP) 75–76
exclusion 10, 15, 59, 149, 215, 252, 263, 287–288
experientiality 32, 225, 268, 299, 309
extinction 71, 77, 288
Extinction Rebellion 69
extractive industries 12, 31, 128, 136, 238
extrapolatory models 191, 194

Facebook 117, 152
facial recognition systems 214
fairness 2, 140, 145
family 73–75; Filipino migrants and 148–155
FAR (field anomaly relaxation) 33n7
Farrington, T. 25
fear 48, 65
feminist studies 1, 297
fiction 189–196; see also literature; narrative; science fiction; speculative fiction
Filipino migrants 9, 148–155
financial crises: economic system and 137–138; prediction of 3–4; see also economy
Firestone, Shulamith 74, 76
First Nations 59–60, 140; see also Indigenous peoples
Fisher, Mark 276–277
Fisher, R.A. 75–76
Flechtheim, Ossip 16n5, 24
Flexible Cities 306, *307*, 308, 310
Florida, Richard 12, 285, 287
Fludernik, Monica 225
FM-2030 (Fereidoun M. Esfandiary) 72
food security 99–100
forecasting 2–4, 6, 189–192; Afrofuturism and 260–261; critiques of 16n5; genius forecasting 23; literature and 189, 191, 194–196; scenarios and 21
foreshadowing 63, 65–66
foresight 6; anticipation and 63, 65–66; approaches to 28; scenarios practice and 20; social science methodologies and 244–249
Foresight Future of Cities (UK) 305
Foucault, Michel 279, 297
fragility 14, 72, 95, 112–113, 207, 222, 262
France 316
Frankenstein (1818) 72–74
Frankenstein (1977) 73
Fricker, Miranda 159
'frictionless futures' 308–309, 311
fugitivity 236–238

Fukuyama, Francis 73, 76
Fuller, Buckminster 33n3
Fuller, Steve 161
Fuller, Ted 8, 25
Fullilove, Mindy 67
functionings 60–62
Fun Future 126, 130–131
Funk, McKenzie 31
Funtowicz, Silvio 243
Futurama exhibit (1939 World's Fair) 281
Future, The (2013) 73
Future Generations Act 142
future present 41, 49, 288–289; *see also* past, present, and future, relationship between
future-proofing 1
Future Search conferences 33
Future Shock (1970) 73–74
futures literacy (FL) 6; affect and 41–43, 48–49; agency and 38–49; anticipation studies and 245; concept of 38–39; creativity and 304; narrative and 229–230; publics and 252, 255, 257
futures studies 1–3, 20; social science methodologies and 244–249
futures thinking 1–3; contemporary era 8; intelligence and 52–53; mid-twentieth century 8, 20; narrative impulse in 3, 224–230; three-part framework 126
Futuribles 21
futuring 6

Galtung, Johan 16n5, 22, 24–25, 75
games 52–57, 267–268, 271–274
game theory 21
Gardiner, M.E. 299
Garforth, Lisa 11
Gatherer, Derek 10
GBM delta (Ganges-Brahmaputra-Meghna) 96
Gebser, Jean 228
Gee, Maggie 300n2
Geltzer, A. 171
gender identities 200, 263; *see also* Queer Futures
gender inequality 99–100
gender studies 1
General Electric 22–23, 33n5
Generation Z 38–49
genetically modified organisms (GMOs) 73
Genetical Theory of Natural Selection, The (Fisher, 1999) 75
genius forecasting 23
gentrification 287
geology 5–6
Georgiou, M. 88
Gerards, Pien 144
German Democratic Republic (GDR) 83, 89
Gessner, Linda 144

Ghosh, Amitav 6
Gibbons, M. 161
Gibson, William 281
Giddens, Anthony 73, 76
Gidley, J. 22, 227–228
Gilbert, D. 317, 322n8
Gilroy, P. 297
Glasgow 286
Glenn, J. 26
Global Business Network (GBN) 19, 23–24, 26, 28, 33n6
Global Futures 309–310
global North 276, 281, 288
global South 13, 165, 238–239, 288
global warming 6; extractive industries and 31, 34n18; impacts of 93; interdisciplinary approach to 165; *see also* climate change; environmental crises
Go (game) 52, 54
Goddard, John 161
Gombrich, Carl 9
Gonzales, Glo 144
Goodhart, David 162
Goodwin, Dawn 9, 170, 177
Google 14, 276; Lunar X Prize (Moon 2.0) 220
Gordon, T. 26
Gore, Al 73, 76
governments: collaboration and 107–108; economics and 142; literary texts and 189–196; personal data and 124; scenario planning 33; *see also* economy; legislation; political economy; politics; regulations; urban planning
Graeber, David 105, 112
Great Acceleration 6
Great Depression 141
Greenfield, Adam 212
Green New Deal 14, 140, 209, 212–213
Green politics 132
Greer, C. 169
Grisel, J. 199
Groves, Christopher 5, 8, 28, 34n16, 39–41, 47, 67, 246
Gruber, H.K. 73
Guattari, Felix 82
Guevarra, A.R. 151
Guyer, J.I. 15

habits 64, 120, 122, 138, 157, 207, 315, 322
Hadidimoud, Sahar 33
Hajer, M. 305
Hamburg 213
Hamel, Gary P. 30
Haque, Shababa 10
Haraway, D.J. 112, 114, 280, 294
Harper, Richard 9

Harvard Economic Society 3
Hawai'i school 24–25
health: biopsychosocial model of 10; in cities 314–322; *see also* mental health
health services 137; inquiries into failures 9, 169, 172–178; LGBTQ people and 265; *see also* medicine
Hegyeshalom, Hungary 80, 84
Heidegger, Martin 28
Heinlein, Robert A. 133n1
Helsinki 213
Henson, K. 25
Heritage 141
Herman, J. 34n12
Herrera, Leo 261
heterotopia 279, 297
Hickman, R. 209
hierarchy 151, 153–154
Hieslmair, Michael 13–14, *83–84, 86–87*
higher education 9, 157–166, 265
Hilgartner, S. 171
Hillgren, Per-Anders 9
Hines, A. 20, 27
Hirsch, Werner 75
Holland, Breena 62–63, 66
Holocene 129
homo economicus (fictive character) 4
Hong Kong 12
hope 29, 39, *42*, 49, 60, 62–63, 65–66, 112, 132, 262, 274, 292–297; *see also* optimism; utopias
horizon scanning 6
Hossain, Riadadh 10
housing 12, 85, 120, 139, 209, 220, 236–239, 265
Hubble telescope 221
Hudson Institute 23–24
Hukkinen, J. 27
Human/Nature dualism 132–133
human needs *139*, 139–140
human/non-human distinction 132
Hungarian Revolution (1956) 83, 89
Hungary 89
Huq, Saleemul 10
Husserl, Edmund 228
Huxley, Aldous 74, 76
Hybrid Cities *307*, 307–308, 310
hydroponic farming 99

IBM 14, 276, 278, 281
Iceland 142
identities 1; agency and 40; AI and 52; mobility and 207; universities and 164
imagination: agency and 40–49; critical 9, 104–114; images of the future 24, 304–305; migration and 149, 154; *see also* creativity; sociotechnical imaginaries; visionary futures

Inayatullah, Sohail 24–25, 29, 31, 34n17
inclusivity 2, 15, 90, 105–106, 114, 149, 155, 163–164, 252, 263, 287–290, 295
incremental adaptation 94–95, 98
Independent Sector Complaints Adjudication Service 173
indigenous peoples 128, 159, 163, 165, 202, 266; *see also* First Nations
individuality 106–107
inequality *see* social inequalities
Informal Cities 12–13, 306, *307*, 308, 310
information technologies 212–214; *see also* computers
infrastructure: border crossings 79–90; climate change adaptation 97–98; creative urbanism and 286; ecomodernization of 208–209; lines and decarbonized mobility futures 14, 180–187; proto-futures and 252–258; publics and 79, 88, 90n1; urban 210, 236 (*see also* urban planning); *see also* mobility
Ingold, Tim 14, 65, 82, 180, 183
innovation 5; adaptation to climate change and 101; creative cities and 285–286; ecology and 129; in mobility systems 207–209; techno-innovation 130; urbanization and 12
Inq7.net 151
inquiries: anticipatory action and 170–173, 176–178; into healthcare failures in UK 9, 169–178; risk management and 169–170; scenario planning and 174, 176–177
Institute for Social Futures (ISF) 2–3, 41, 207
Institute for the Future 267
Institute of Economic Affairs 141
integral futures 24, 29
Intel 14
intelligence 9, 52–57; *see also* AI (artificial intelligence)
Inter-American Development Bank 286
interconnectedness 90n1, 95, 128, 132–133, 149, 159, 163–164, 181, 212, 228, 236, 245–246, 260, 271, 279
interdisciplinary approach 3, 15, 160–161, 164–166, 207
interest aggregation 107–108
Intergovernmental Panel on Climate Change (IPCC) 93–94, 126, 133
International Labour Organization 137
International Monetary Fund 3
International Space Station (ISS) 217, 219
Internet of Things (IoT) 211–212
intersectionality 265, 287
intuitive logics 19, 24, 26–28, 30, 33; 2x2 scenario matrix 19, 33n2, 33n6, 34n10; *see also* scenario planning
Iraq 14

Iron Curtain 80, 84, 89
Israel Aerospace Industries 220

Jacobs, Jane 316
Jakarta, Indonesia 6; Tanah Tinggi 13, 234–237, 240
James, C.L.R. 261
James, Edward 277–278, 282n1
Jameson, Fredric 11, 105, 294
Jasanoff, S. 118–119, 169, 277
Jemisins, N K 300n2
Jimenez, J. 33
Jonas, Hans 64–65
Jones, D.R. 161
Jones, R. 57n9
Jönsson, Li 9
Julie's Bicycle 288
Jungermann, Helmut 26
Jungk, Robert 16n5, 22, 24–25, 33n4, 43, 75
Jungnickel, K. 185
justice 2; capabilities approach to 60–63; *see also* mobility justice; social inequalities; social justice

Kahane, Adam 26
Kahn, Herman 6, 21, 23, 26–27
Kant, Immanuel 57n8
Karachi 235
Karbala 320
Kelvin, Lord (William Thomson) 5
Kemp, S. 7
Kermode, Frank 228, 230n7
Kerr, Clark 163
Keynesian economics 141
Khakee, Abdul 20
Kim, S.H. 277
kinopolitics 207–209, 214
Kleiner, A. 32
knowledge 6–7; anticipatory knowledge-making 171–172; claims to 8–9; healthcare futures and 175–176; mental health and 201; production of 254; prospection and 242–247; *see also* epistemic injustice; epistemology
Kolbert, Elizabeth 71
Kolkata 6
Koselleck, Reinhart 41
Kosminsky, Eli 267–268
Krieger, Nancy 165n1
Kuhn, Thomas 244
Kull, Kalevi 64
Kumar, K. 296
Kupers, R. 28, 33n6
Kurzweil, Ray 69, 72, 76
Kwartler, M. 304

labor migration 9, 148–155
Lagos 235–236

Laing, R.D. 199
Lancaster, UK 2, 253–258
Landry, C. 286
Laroche, H. 170
Latin America 286
Latour, Bruno 82, 190, 254
Lausanne, Switzerland 14, 315, 317, 320–321
Law, J. 305
Layard, Richard 201
Layered Cities 306, *307*, 310
Leading for Wellbeing 138
Leakey, Louis 69, 71, 76
learning 9; *see also* higher education; knowledge
Le Dantec, C.A.L. 255
Lees, L. 12
Lefebvre, Henri 299
legislation 14, 142, 254, 264; *see also* regulations
Le Guin, Ursula K 279–280, 300n1–2
Leopold, Aldo 129
Levitas, Ruth 279–280, 292–294, 296, 301n8
Lewin, Roger 69, 71
LGBTQ (lesbian, gay, bisexual, transgender, and queer) people 200, 264; *see also* Queer Futures
Li, Z. 30
liberation futures work 263–268
Light, Ann 9, 105, 113
Limbeck, Hans-Paul 83, 89–90
Lindsay, J. 164
Lindström, Kristina 9, 112
Lines (2007) 82
lines, decarbonized mobility futures and 14, 180–187
List, D. 28
literature: affect and 191; agency and 189–191; back-casting and 189, 191–196; forecasting and 189, 191, 194–196; policy makers and 189–196; resilience and 8, 189–190; *see also* narrative; science fiction; speculative fiction
Little Futures 119
Liveable Cities project 207
Lively, Genevieve 7–8
localism 162
Locke, John 25
'Logistic Worlds' (2014) 82
London 12, 14, 284, 317–318, 321, 322n7
London Interdisciplinary School (LIS) 157
Longo, G. 304
Loogma, Krista 25
López Galviz, C. 284, 299
Luckman, T. 33n8
Luhmann, Niklas 41, 60, 288–289
Lupton, Deborah 9
Lynch, Kevin 86
Lyons, Glenn 212

MacDonald, Neil 226
MacFarlane, R. 187n2

macro-historical models 15n4
Madrid 213
Malmö University 104
Malthus, Thomas Robert 69–71, 73, 75–77
Mandel, Thomas 26
Mankind 2000 22–24, 33n4, 75
Manoa School 39; Manoa method 6, 24
maps and mapping 79, 81, 82; Nickelsdorf border checkpoint 84, 86
marginalization 10, 151, 154, 210, 262
Marland, Linda 42, 49
Marris, Peter 67
Mars 216–218, 220–221, 256
Marx, Karl 294, 297
Masini, Elenora 25
Maslow, Abraham 15n3
Mason, Colin 72
Mason, D. 34n12
Massumi, B. 171–172
material futures 9–10; see also Afrofuturism; BioFutures; mental health; proto-futures; Queer Futures
Mattern, Shannon 280–281
Maturana, Humberto 34n15
Mayerhofer, Wolfgang 85
McDaniel, Jeffrey 44
McGuinness, M. 170
McHale, John 22
McIntyre, Alistair 163
McLaughlin, E. 169
McMurtry, John 162
McNay, Lois 39–40
McWade, B. 202
meaning-making 39, 60, 65
Medellin 286
media 9, 73, 85, 105, 117, 119, 144, 150–154, 212, 218, 305
Medical Defence Union 175
medicine: evidence-based 201, 203; mental health and 198–199; see also health services; mental health
memory 79, 256; narrative and 228; refugee crises and 89–90
Mental Deficiency Act (1913) 74
mental health 10, 198–204; alternative approaches 203; categorization of 199–200; children and young adults 49; politics of 202–203; problem of existence and 200–201; science of 198–199; social futures and 204; socially produced pathologies 201–202
metacapabilities 8, 61–67
methods 8–9; predictive-empirical-analytical approaches 224–225; see also agency; anticipation; collaborative engagement; narrative; prospection; scenario planning
Miall, D. 229, 231n13
Michael, M. 119

Middle Passage 260
Mieville, China 300n2
migration 13–14; border crossings 79–90; climate-induced 97–98; family separation and digital communication technologies 148–155
Milan 213
military scenario planning 21–22, 33
Miller, Riel 7, 38–41, 49, 229
Millett, S. 28, 30, 33n5
Minority Report (film) 267
Mitchell, David 300n2
mobile communication *see* communication technologies
mobility 14; border crossings and 79–90; innovation futures 207–209; line-making practices and decarbonized mobility futures 14, 180–187; of space age 216–222; *see also* automobiles; cycling; infrastructure; migration; transportation; walking
mobility justice 206–215; AI City 211, 213–214; carbon emissions and 206–215; Digital City 211, 211–212; Fast Mobility City 210, 211; Liveable City 211, 212–213; typology of future urban mobility scenarios 210, 211
modernity: cultural 59–60; ecology and 129; utopia and 293, 296
Modern Utopia, A (1903) 74
Moon 216–220
Moore's Law 72
More, Thomas 70, 74, 76, 277, 282n1, 292, 294, 300n4
Morson, G. 227
Morton, Timothy 133
Mould, O. 283
movement 13–14; *see also* migration; mobility
Moylan, Tom 277–280, 282n1
multi-planetary futures 216–222
multiple futures 22, 31, 33n3; agency and 46–49; scenario planning and 246; urban eventualities and 234; visualization of 304–305
Muñoz, José Esteban 261, 297, 299–300, 301n7
Musk, Elon 216, 218, 220
My2024 (foresight game) 267

Naess, Arne 132
Nail, Thomas 207
narrative 7–8, 224–230; agency and 3, 40–43; definitions of 224–225; epistemic function 226; forecasting in 191; investigative function 226; literacy and 282; rhetorical function 226; scenarios and 21, 225–226; smart cities as 275–277, 282; *see also* storytelling
NASA 220
National Health Service (UK) 9, 169, 172–177
National LGBTQ Task Force 261, 266–268
natural history 128

Index

natural resources 128–129
natural selection 70, 128
nature: conservation of 128; economy and 140, 145; threats to 127–129, 131; *see also* climate change; ecology; global warming
Neilson, Brett 82
Nelson, N. 171
neoliberalism 130–131, 136, 141, *142*, 150, 201; creative urbanism and 285, 287–290; mental health and 203; smart cities and 276–277, 281; utopia and 297
networks 80–81, 207, 322n8
New Ecology 130–131
New Economics Foundation (NEF) 140, *142*, 143; 'Five Ways to Well-being' 201
New Economy and Social Innovation Forum 138
Newlands, Ted 23
Newmarch, Georgia 10
New Wave movement 278
New York 12
New Zealand 142
NGOs 89, 97, 100, 106–107, 143, 171, 239, 319
Nickelsdorf, Austria 13–14, 79–90
Nicolescu, Basarab 160–161
Nikolaeva, A. 208
1984 (Orwell) 121
noch nicht (not-yet) 69, 296
nomadic lifestyles 13, 306
Norris, E. 169
Nuremberg trials 74–75
Nussbaum, Martha C. 38, 60–63, 65

Occupy Movement 2
Ogilvy, Jay 23, 25
Ohmae, Kenichi 32
oil crisis (1973) 23
Olick, J.K. 242
ontology 242
optimism 48, 112; cruel 296; personal data and 124
Orange Economy manual 286
Organisation for Economic Co-operation and Development 3
organizations: purpose and practice 29–30; as systems 32; *see also* corporate futures
Origin of Species (Darwin) 70–71, 75
Osborn, Fairfield 71, 129
Oslo 213
Our Plundered Planet (1948) 71, 129
outer space: extraction of resources 11, 216, 218–220; as global commons 11, 216; mobilities of space age 216–222
Owen, Robert 76, 301n5
Oxfam 138
Oxford scenario planning 32

Palmer, D. 202
palm-reading 6
Paris 12, 213, 284
Parliamentary Committee on International Trade (UK) 107
participation 140, 145
participatory design 104, 106, 114
past, present, and future, relationship between 3–5; inquiries and 174–177; literature and 189; narrative and 227–228; resilience and 256
past future 288
Paterson Inquiry 172–176
path dependency 110, 256, 299, 305
pathologies 198–203
pedestrians 316; *see also* walking
performative futures 74
personal data 9, 117–124
PESTLE 42
Peters, B.G. 254
Petroni, MJ 266
Phelan, Jim 224–225, 227
Philippine Overseas Employment Agency (POEA) 150
Philippines 9, 149–151, 154; *see also* Filipino migrants
Philstar.com 151
Piercy, Marge 300n2
'Pierre Menard, Author of the *Quixote*' (Borges) 195
place 65, 67; abstraction of 309; visions for 304–311
plastics 109
pleasure activism 268
Pluckrose, H. 164
plural futures *see* multiple futures
Polak, Fred 21, 24, 39–40
Poli, Roberto 29, 63–64, 245, 247
political economy 136, 146n1, 219, 221, 258, 289; *see also* economy
politics: agency and 44; collaboration and 114; democratic 107–108; mobility and 207; political utopia 277–279; social futures and 15; in urban areas 235, 239–240; utopias and 298–300, 301n10; *see also* governments
Pollock, Ian 268
pollution 34n18, 63, 66, 114, 162, 207–208, 210, 309, 318–319
Polynesia 5–6
pop futurism 24
population 12, 69–70, 73–75, 129, 137, 210, 317
Porous University model 157
Porter, Michael 30
Porter, Roy 202
positivism 8, 21, 28, 31, 42
possible futures 21, 23, 25
Post-Car World project 317

postcolonial futures 233–240
postcolonial studies 114
post-normal futures 24, 32
Postnormal science (PNS) 243–245, 247, 249
Postnormal times (PNT) theory 244–245, 247, 249
post-structuralism 39, 82, 297
poverty 137; climate change and 97, 101; migration and 150; mobility and 322n8; urban 210
power: agency and 40, 44 creative urbanism and 289; economic change and 141; mapping and 82; migration and 149; mobility systems and 207; publics and 254, 257; scenarios and 31, 33; space and 219; universities and 164–165
Prahalad, C.K. 30
precarity 13–14, 292, 296
precautionary principle 171
predictions 6; as guesses 8; prospection and 242–243, 245, 247
pre-emptive action 171–172, 177
preferable futures 21; literature and 191–193; *see also* utopias
prefiguration 228
preparedness 172, 177
present: BioFutures and 71; thick 112; *see also* past, present, and future, relationship between
present future 41, 49, 288–289
Prince, Gerald 226
privacy 121–124
privatization 287
privilege 124
probabilistic techniques 3–4, 16n5, 21; AI use of 54–55; trends analysis 21, 24, 26, 225
probable futures 25
problem-oriented futures 24
progress 4–5, 59, 117, 136–137, 165, 216–217, 227, 263, 299
prospection 6, 8, 242–249
PROTIC programme (OXFAM) 99–100
proto-futures 10, 252–258
psychiatry 204; *see also* mental health
publics: infrastructure and 79, 88, 90n1; mobility and 215; proto-futures 252–258; sociotechnical imaginaries and 118–119

Queer Futures 10, 260–274; Afro-Queer identity 260–261, 272; cruelty and 261–263; equality future 264; equity future 264–265; liberation future 264–265 Queer liberation foresight research 263–268; *see also* LGBTQ (lesbian, gay, bisexual, transgender, and queer) people
Queer Futures: United Queerdom 2054 (game) 267–268, 271–274

queer theory 301n7
'Quiet World, The' (McDaniel) 44

race and ethnicity 10, 214, 287
Rae, Michael 69, 72
RAND (Research and Development) 21, 24
Randalls, S. 171
rationality 28, 32, 292
Raven, Paul Graham 12
Ravetz, Jerome 243
Raworth, Kate 4
Reagan, Ronald 141
refiguration 228
refugees 79–90, 90n10
Regulated Cities 306, *307*, 310
regulations 14, 170, 175–176, 208, 214; *see also* legislation
relational complexes 246–247
religion 62, 140, 163, 200–202, 255, 260, 296, 320
reproduction 73–75
Reset Report 140
resilience 10; affect and 190; back-casting and 192; ecology and 130–131; literature and 8, 189–196; publics and 253, 256–258
resource distribution 11; capabilities and 60–61; *see also* economic inequality; social inequalities
Rickards, Lauren 11
Ricouer, Paul 228–229
risk management 131, 169–178
Ritchey, Tom 33n7
Rittel, H.W. 254
Robeyns, I. 61, 66
Robinson, Kim Stanley 221, 300n1
Rodriguez, R.M. 151
Rome 12
Rosa, A. 268
Rose, N.S. 204
Rosen, R. 243
Rosenzweig, P. 22
Rossiter, Ned 82
Rousseau, Jean Jacques 316
Rowland, N.J. 20, 32, 246
Rumsfeld, Donald 171
Runaway World (1999) 73
rural spaces 8, 13, 97, 237–238, 306
Russell Group universities 162
Russian Institute for Biomedical Problems 220
Russian Roscosmos 220
Rutherford, John 193
Ryan, Marie-Laure 225, 227, 230n3

Sadowski, J. 277
Sand, Martin 39, 43
San Juan, E. 150

Index

Sardar, Z. 244–245
Sargent, L.T. 294
Sassen, Saskia 12
scenario planning 2, 6, 19–33; 2x2 matrix 19, 33n2, 33n6, 34n10, 41–42; Bangladesh Delta Plan 2100 and 100; deductive method 25–28, 33n6; ecology and 131; embodied futures 28–29; incremental change 27–28; inductive method 25–26; inquiries and 174, 176–177; intuitive logics 19, 24, 26–28, 30, 33; lens of practice 29–30; Mankind 2000 22–24, 33n4, 75; methodology 304; mobilities research and 206–207; multiple futures and 246; narrative and 21, 225–226; positivist approach 28, 31; power relations and purpose 31, 33; publics and 255; relativist approach 28, 31; social construction and 30–31; typologies 24–27
Schengen Agreement 80–81, 89
Schneider, Bridgit 126
Schnelle, Helene 144
Schoemaker, P. 27, 30
Schon, Donald 28, 32
School of International Futures (SOIF) 50n2
Schultz, W. 24–27
Schumpeter, Joseph 130
Schwartz, Peter 23, 25, 32, 33n6, 225
science 129, 243
science and technology studies (STS) 244, 246, 249
science fiction 133n1, 189, 225, 260, 275–282, 300n1
Scotland 142
scrying 6
Sears, Paul 129
Seeds of Hope 32
Seefried, E. 22
seeing 6
self-development 2
Sen, Amartya 38, 43, 60–62
Shanghai 6
Shell 22–24, 26–28, 30–32, 33n5–6, 34n13, 34n18
Sheller, Mimi 13–14
Shelley, Mary 72–74, 76
Shepheard, M. 169
Short History of America, A (Crumb) 126–133, *127*
Sidewalk Labs 276
Silent Spring (1965) 71
Silicon Valley 23
Simone, AbdouMaliq 12–13
Singapore 238
singularity 55, 57n7, 72
Singularity Is Near, The (2005) 69, 72
Sistema B 142
Sixth Extinction, The (1996) 69, 71
Slater, T. 202
Slaughter, Richard 24–25, 27, 29, 304

slavery 260–261
smart cities 12, 211–212, 275–282, 308–310
smartphones 119, 152, 186; *see also* communication technologies
Smith, J.M. 119
Snijder, Esther 144
Snowden, Edward 117
social constructionism 25, 33n8
social credit 214
Social Credit System (China) 124
social displacement *see* displacement
Social Ecology 132
social futures, overview of 1–15
social inequalities 2, 10; anticipation and 59–60; creative urbanism and 12, 287–288; economic inequality and 136–137; migration and 153–154; mobility and 14, 210, 214–215; outer space and 217; sociology and 293; urbanization and 238; wealth and 4
social justice: activism 112, 164, 263; universities and 159–164; utopias and 298–300, 301n10; *see also* activism; mobility justice
social science methodologies 243–249
socio-environmental conditions: anticipation and 66; capabilities and 61; shared practices and ideals 65
sociotechnical imaginaries 118–124, 277
Solarpunk 300n1
Sousanis, Nick 82
Southall, H. 317, 322n8
space age *see* outer space
Space Force (US) 218
SpaceIL 220
SpaceX 218
Spaniol, M.J. 20, 32, 246
speciation 77
species 128
speculative fiction (SF) 7, 42, 225
Spelda, P. 56
Spiers, Emily 8
Spinoza, Baruch 65
spirituality 163; *see also* religion
Spurling, Nicola 13–14
SRI 21, 23–24, 26–28
Ståhl, Åsa 108, 112
Stanford Research Institute 21, 23
Stanford University 57n2
sterilization 75
Stewart, Michael 160
stigma 202–203
Stopes, Marie 75
storyknowing 7–8
storytelling 6–7, 88; *see also* narrative
Strange, Michael 9
strategic planning 32
Stritecky, V. 56
Sturgeon, Nicola 138–139
subjectivity 39, 47

surveillance 117, 213–214; *see also* dataveillance
sustainability 12, 132, 209
Sustainability Transitions Research Network 206
sustainable ecological capacity (SEC) 62–63, 66
Suvin, D. 295
Swedish International Development Agency (SIDA) 32
Sweeney, J.A. 268
Switzerland 14, 314–317, 320–321
Syria 14
system change: economic 136–146; strategies for *143*
systems, living 34n15, 64–65
Systems Ecology 131
Szasz, Thomas 199

tactical urbanism 184, 288
Tadiar, Neferti 150–151
Tanah Tinggi 13, 234–237, 240
TAPESTRY project 98–99
Tarak, Pedro 142
tarot 6
Tatzgern, Gerald 85
Taylor, Gordon Rattray 73
Technical Rationality 28 32
techno-innovation 130
Technological Futures 309–310
technological utopia 277–278, 282n1
technology 1; biotechnology 71; cities and 308–310; forecasting and 4; space exploration and 218; transportation and 208–209; *see also* AI (artificial intelligence); communication technologies; data; smart cities
techno-utopianism 71–72
Tehran, Iran 14, 317, 319–321
Teilhardian theology 72
teleology 192, 227–228, 280–281, 295, 301n10
Ternate Essay, The (Wallace, 1858) 70, 77
terrorism 171–172, 177, 214
tertiary education *see* higher education
Tester, Jason 266
TFC (The Filipino Channel) 152–153
Thaler, Mathias 133n1
Thatcher, Margaret 141
Theory of Everything (TcE) 164–165
thickening of futures 112–114
thin futures 112
Thing from the Future (game) 267
think-tanks 141, 143
Third Wave, The (1981) 73
Thompson, Judith Jarvis 62
Thomson, William (Lord Kelvin) 5
Three Horizons 32
Three Tomorrows (3Ts) 245, 247
Tibbs, Hardin 29–30
Tidwel, A.S.D. 119

time: rhythms of 65; scenarios and 28; sociology of 288; timescales 3, 5–6, 10, 30; *see also* past, present, and future, relationship between
Time Machine, The (1895) 77
TINA ('there is no alternative') 71
Tipler, Frank 72
Tippmann, Mara 144
Toffler, Alvin 73–74, 76
Tokyo 12
Torre, Ramos 287–288
Torrens, P.M. 242
traces 180–181, 184–185, 190, 238
trade policy 107–108
transdisciplinarity 160–161, 165–166
transformational adaptation 95–101
Trans(gender) Employment Program, San Francisco LGBT Community Center 264–265
transhumanism 72, 76
transition theory 208
transportation: revolution in 316; scenarios and 206–207; technologies 14, 180–186; *see also* automobiles; buses; cycling; infrastructure; mobility; walking
trends analysis 21, 24, 26, 225
Triton (Delany) 279
Trump, Donald 218
Tunnard, Christopher 284
Turing Machine 56, 57n12; Turing test 54
Turner, Fred 23
Tutton, Richard 9
Tuvalu 5–6
Tyler, I. 202

Uexküll, Jakob von 64
uncertainty: climate change impacts and 96; creative cities and 287; ecology and 133; eventualities and 234; mitigating against 6, 8; movement and 13–14; multiple futures and 47; narrative and 227; vulnerability to 64
UNCTAD 285
unemployment 52, 137, 150, 261; *see also* employment
'Unflattering' (2015) 82
UN-Habitat III 11–12
United Kingdom (UK): Civil Contingencies 172; economics 140; walking, rates of 315; *see also* National Health Service
United Nations: Educational, Scientific and Cultural Organization (UNESCO) 228, 285; Refugee Agency 14; Sustainable Development Goals 12
United States: Federal Reserve 3; Green New Deal 14; LGBTQ liberation futures 264–266; personal data and 124; sustainable mobility policies 209; wartime operational planning 20–21

337

universities 9, 157–166; interdisciplinarity 160–161, 164–166; social justice and 159–164; spirituality and 163
Universities Partnership Programme (UPP) Foundation 161
University College London 162
University of Canberra, Human Research Ethics Committee 120
University of Oxford 32
University of Pretoria 138
un/making 108–109, 114
unpredictability 8, 14, 32, 64, 95, 207
Uprichard, E. 230n10
urbanization 11–12, 97, 286; postcolonial urban eventualities 233–240; *see also* cities; smart cities
urban planning 14, 67, 160, 184, 308–309; creative urbanism and 284–290; mobility and 210–215, *211*; *see also* infrastructure
Urry, John 2, 28, 34n14, 149, 200, 206–207, 209, 213, 288, 293, 296, 298–299, 305
Utopia (More, 1516) 70, 74, 277, 282n1, 292, 300n4
utopias 11, 25, 292–300; BioFutures and 69–71; biology and 76; cities as 308; concept of 293–295, 301n8; critical utopia 278–281, 282n1; ecology and 132; futurity of 295–298; narrative and 225; political utopia 277–279; reality and 293, 298–300; smart cities as utopian fictions 277–279; social justice and 298–300, 301n10; sociology and 292–293; technological utopia 277–278, 282n1; three-part framework 126; *see also* dystopias

values 2; agency and 38–39, 47, 49
van der Heijden, K. 30, 32
van Notten, P. 20
Varela, Francisco 34n15, 64
Venkatapuram, Sridhar 62
Versteeg, W. 305
Vienna *81*, 284
virtual reality (VR) 212, 219
visionary futures 6, 24–25
visualization of cities 12, 304–312
Vogt, William 129
voice 3, 8; agency and 44
Voros, Joseph 304

Wack, Pierre 23, 30–31
Wales 142
Walker, Jeremy 130
walking 14, 180–187, 212–213; long-distance, in cities 314–322
Wallace, Alfred Russel 70, 77
Wallerstein, Immanuel 71
Wallis, Stewart 4
Wanalo, Robert 145
warnings 22, 76, 94, 127–129, 133, 172, 288, 311

Watson, Jeff 267
We (1924) 74
wealth 2, 4–5, 21, 44, 63, 101, 136–137, 140, 210, 218, 265, 285; *see also* elites; poverty; social inequalities
Webber, M.M. 254
Weissman, David 38–39
well-being: agency and 38; economy and 4, 136–146, 201; mental health and 201
Wellbeing Economy Alliance (WEAll) 4, 136, 138–146
Wellbeing Economy Governments (WEGo) 142, 145–146
Wellbeing Economy (WE) Portal 145
Wellcome Trust 199
Wellesley-Wesley, James 33n4
Wells, H.G. 74–77
White, Gilbert 128
White, Haydn 226
Whitson, Ni'ja 268
Whole Earth Discipline (2009) 130
wicked problems 254–255
Wilkinson, A. 30, 33n6
Wilson, Alan 159, 161, 164
Wilson, Ian 23, 26
Wirth, Louis 286
Wittgenstein, L. 57n10–11
Wittmayer, J.M. 226
Womack, Y.L. 300
women: climate change adaptation 99–100; in Philippines 151
Wood, Denis 82
Woodhead, Linda 2
Wordsworth, Dorothy and William 316
World Bank 97
world-building 42, 272
World Futures Studies Federation (WFSF) 25
World Health Organization 200, 204, 314
world literature 189–196
Worlds workshops *110–111*, 110–112
worldviews 114; collaborative engagements and 106–107
World War II 8, 20
Wright, Alex 27, 30
Wright, E.O. 298–299

Years and Years (2019) 72
Yew, Lee Kuan 75
young adults 41–49
YouTube 151
Yugoslavia 13
Yugoslav wars 90n10

Zahavi, Y. 321
Zamyatin, Yevgeny 74
Zapfl, Gerhard 83–85, *86*
Zinganel, Michael 13–14, *83–84*, *86–87*